SIXTH EDITION

 # Writing
in the
Disciplines

*A Reader for Writers*

**Mary Lynch Kennedy**
*SUNY Cortland*

**William J. Kennedy**
*Cornell University*

**PEARSON**
Prentice
Hall

Upper Saddle River, NJ 07458

Library of Congress Cataloging-in-Publication Data

Kennedy, Mary Lynch
   Writing in the disciplines: a reader for writers/Mary Lynch Kennedy, William J. Kennedy—6th ed.
      p. cm.
   ISBN–13: 978-0-13-231999-7
   ISBN–10: 0-13-231999-3
   1. College readers. 2. Interdisciplinary approach in education—Problems, exercises, etc. 3. English language—Rhetoric—Problems, exercises etc. 4. Academic writing—Problems, exercises, etc. I. Kennedy, William J. (William John), II. Title.
   PE1417K45 2008
   808'.0427—dc22                                                            2007014503

**Editorial Director:** Leah Jewell
**Senior Acquisitions Editor:** Brad Potthoff
**Editorial Assistant:** Megan Dubrowski
**Production Liaison:** Joanne Hakim
**Director of Marketing:** Brandy Dawson
**Senior Marketing Manager:** Windley Morley
**Marketing Assistant:** Kimberly Caldwell
**Assistant Manufacturing Manager:** Mary Ann Gloriande
**Cover Art Director:** Jayne Conte
**Cover Design:** Bruce Kenselaar
**Cover Image:** Hannibal Hanschke/Reuters/Corbis
**Manager, Cover Visual Research & Permissions:** Karen Sanatar
**Director, Image Resource Center:** Melinda Patelli
**Manager, Rights and Permissions:** Zina Arabia
**Manager, Visual Research:** Beth Brenzel
**Photo Coordinator:** Ang'john Ferreri
**Photo Researcher:** Kathy Ringrose
**Full-Service Project Management:** Kathy O'Connor/TexTech Inc.
**Composition:** TexTech International
**Printer/Binder:** The Courier Companies
**Cover Printer:** Phoenix Color Corp.

Credits and acknowledgments borrowed from other sources and reproduced, with permission, in this textbook appear on appropriate page within text.

Pearson Education LTD., London
Pearson Education Singapore, Pte. Ltd
Pearson Education, Canada, Ltd
Pearson Education–Japan
Pearson Education Australia PTY, Limited

Pearson Education North Asia Ltd
Pearson Educación de Mexico, S.A. de C.V.
Pearson Education Malaysia, Pte. Ltd
Pearson Education, Upper Saddle River, New Jersey

PEARSON
Prentice
Hall

10 9 8 7 6 5 4 3 2 1

ISBN 13: 978-0-13-231999-7
ISBN 10:    0-13-231999-3

# Brief Contents

## *Humanities* 536

# Contents

MOTHERHOOD IDEOLOGIES AND MOTHERHOOD MYTHS
• Deirdre D. Johnston and Debra H. Swanson    76
*Literature review of research on popular images of working mothers.*

THE LEAST WORST CHOICE: WHY MOTHERS "OPT" OUT
OF THE WORKFORCE • Judith Stadtman Tucker    81
*Synthesis: Source-based argument of economic and cultural factors that affect*
*women's choices.*

MANY WOMEN AT ELITE COLLEGES SET CAREER PATH
TO MOTHERHOOD • Louise Story    91
*Newspaper feature about women from elite colleges who prefer stay-at-home*
*motherhood to balancing careers and motherhood.*

WEASEL-WORDS RIP MY FLESH! • Jack Shafer    96
*Rhetorical analysis of Louise Story's verbal compromises that weaken her argument.*

CRITIQUE OF "MANY WOMEN AT ELITE COLLEGES SET CAREER PATH
TO MOTHERHOOD" • Tracey Meares    100
*Critical analysis of Louise Story's failure to take race and class into account*
*for her report on elite women.*

DESPERATE HOUSEWIVES OF THE IVY LEAGUE? • Katha Pollitt    101
*Critical analysis of Louise Story's misrepresentation of Yale women and the larger*
*problems of working mothers.*

HOMEWARD BOUND • Linda R. Hirshman    104
*Argument that women from elite colleges with privileged backgrounds should*
*ve as role models for women with less privileged backgrounds.*

## 5   Rhetorical, Comparative, Literary, Process, and Causal Analysis, and the Classic Comparison and Contrast Essay   183

## 6   Visual Analysis   216

## PART II
## An Anthology of Readings   333

### Natural Sciences and Technology   335

## 10  Cloning   339

# 7 Synthesis   235

# 8 Argument   256

# 11  Human/Machine Interaction    371

# 12  Crime-Fighting Technology: Balancing Public Safety and Privacy    411

# Preface

## TO OUR READERS IN APPRECIATION

In the sixth edition of *Writing in the Disciplines: A Reader for Writers*, we incorporate the suggestions of students and instructors who have used the fifth edition, as well as the recommendations of other reviewers. We continue to emphasize scholarly, source-based academic writing, and in this edition we provide a solid body of academic readings that serve as touchstone texts for the essays we teach students to write.

We retain over half of the reading selections from the fifth and earlier editions and add twenty-six new selections for a total of fifty-four readings. We keep the chapter topics of Cloning, Human/Machine Interaction, Crime-Fighting Technology, The Changing American Family, and Social Class and Inequality, and, as reviewers requested, we reinstate the topic of Rock Music and Cultural Values from the fourth edition. We have renamed the literature chapter "Stories of Ethnic Difference" and have added a new social science chapter on the "Mommy Wars."

## ORGANIZATION AND APPROACH

*Writing in the Disciplines: A Reader for Writers* teaches students how to use reading sources as idea banks for college papers. It offers extensive coverage of critical reading and the fundamental writing strategies of planning, organizing, drafting, revising, and editing. In addition to covering paraphrasing and quoting, it offers guidelines for writing a wide range of classroom genres. We cover genres that play a major role in writing courses and are frequently assigned in courses in various disciplines: response to a text, summary, abstract, précis, critical analysis, rhetorical analysis, comparative analysis, literary analysis, process analysis, causal analysis, comparison and contrast, critique of visual argument, explanatory synthesis, literature review, thesis-driven synthesis, argument synthesis, and research paper. Knowledge of these genres is indispensable for students to become skilled critical readers and proficient academic writers.

*Writing in the Disciplines* also provides an anthology of readings in the humanities, the natural sciences and technology, and the social sciences, with articles representing various rhetorical approaches across academic disciplines. These articles, along with the accompanying instructional apparatus, help develop students' abilities to think critically and reason cogently as they read, compose, and revise. The activities and questions that accompany each reading encourage students to **approach academic writing as a process**: to preview the source, set reading goals, and ponder the general topic before reading; to annotate the text and think critically while reading; and to reflect on the source and identify content, genre, organization, stylistic features, and rhetorical context after reading. We also show students how to draw on annotations, notes, and preliminary writing to produce first drafts of academic essays and how to revise essays at the drafting stage as well as later in the writing process. Additional activities help students to use ideas from different sources to produce synthesis essays and research papers.

Chapter 2 focuses on personal responses to texts: paraphrases; summaries, including the abstract and the précis; and quotations. Throughout the sixth edition, we refer to source-based writing as an **academic conversation**. In Chapter 3, we provide a source-book of thirteen readings that represent an academic conversation on the debate of whether women should stay at home as full-time mothers or resume their careers after childbirth. Chapter 3 also functions as a **compendium of touchstone texts** that we use as examples of the various forms of academic writing we cover in the book. Chapter 4 focuses on critical analysis. It also provides a detailed demonstration of the reading-writing process, from prereading to editing. It examines essay structures, from the introduction and thesis statement through the body of the essay to its conclusion, and teaches students how to revise for content, organization, style, grammar, and mechanics. Chapter 5 deals with some particular kinds of analytical writing that address readings of specific texts. The kinds of analysis include rhetorical, comparative, literary, process, and causal. The chapter also covers the classic comparison and contrast essay. Chapter 6, Visual Analysis, explains how to analyze visual images and guides students through the process of writing an essay analyzing a visual argument. Chapter 7 guides students through the process of writing three forms of synthesis essays: explanatory synthesis, review of the literature, and thesis-driven synthesis. Chapter 8 provides detailed explanations of how to write source-based argument essays, and Chapter 9 covers library research strategies and writing research papers.

In Chapters 10 through 17 we provide an anthology of forty-one reading selections. We have organized the anthology by dividing the academic curriculum into three major fields: the natural sciences and technology, the social sciences, and the humanities. Each chapter of readings deals with a topic that is widely studied in the field. For example, the social sciences section has chapters on redefining the American family and on social class and inequality. These chapters complement the social science selections on "The Mommy Wars" in Chapter 3. Such reading assignments help students view each topic from a range of perspectives, and they provide diverse views from experts within the discipline and from journalists and specialists in other academic fields.

The anthology chapters and Chapter 3 contain scholarly documented readings as well as articles written for nonspecialized readers. We believe articles derived from popular as well as scholarly sources represent the types of readings professors assign in introductory and lower-level courses. Psychology professors, for instance, know that first-year students cannot interpret most psychological research reports until they acquire a basic knowledge of the discipline and learn its principles of experimental methodology and statistical analysis. However, first-year students can read summaries and analyses of psychological research written for nonspecialists. Many of the selections in *Writing in the Disciplines* are readings that might appear on a reserve list as supplements to an introductory-level textbook. We make no assumptions about students' prior knowledge. Our intent is to model first-year-level reading assignments, not to exemplify professional standards within the disciplines.

In the introduction to each section, we characterize the field of study with a discussion of its subdisciplines, methodology, logic, and vocabulary. We then describe writing within the field by examining authors' perspectives, goals, organizational patterns, literary devices, and rhetorical styles. We recognize that there is no absolute standard for categorizing intellectual activities. For example, although we have classified technology as a discipline within the sciences, we could as well have placed it within the social sciences, depending on the methodology the researchers use. Throughout the book, we point out overlaps among disciplines and also capitalize on them in synthesis assignments at the end of each chapter. Despite the imprecision of these categories, we believe that important differences in approaches to scholarship and writing do exist among the three main academic areas. Students who understand these differences will read more critically and write more persuasively.

# IMPROVEMENTS IN THE SIXTH EDITION

## Part I: Rhetoric

The language that is privileged and rewarded by the academic community is vastly different from our students' way of talking and writing. It is wishful thinking to assume that students will learn this language through assimilation and gradual socialization. Even engaged, committed students find the standards and conventions of scholarly writing abstract. We are increasingly convinced that we need to make explicit the role students play as participants in academic conversations and make transparent the language they are expected to write and speak. For that reason, the sixth edition explicitly addresses the conventions of a wide range of genres of academic writing, analyzes published texts that represent these genres, and guides students through the process of mastering the genres and reproducing them in academic papers.

We differentiate between journalistic styles of writing that draw on other texts but do not involve parenthetical citation, lists of references, and footnotes, and scholarly academic writing that employs these conventions. A sizable number of our anthology selections are written in the scholarly style of academic writing that we are asking students to practice in the essays they write for this book. Ironically, many composition anthologies rely solely on selections from popular discourse but expect students to write about the readings using the language and conventions of academic discourse. Our text asks students to join the conversation of academic discourse by reading and writing in its conventions from the start.

In the sixth edition, we place a stronger emphasis on the habits of mind that favor academic reading and writing, especially the habit of asking questions. Throughout the book we stress the importance of developing a questioning frame of mind. Every chapter contains guidelines for posing and answering questions about texts. For example, in Chapter 1 we have Questions for Analyzing the Literal Content of Texts, Questions for Analyzing the Genre of Texts, Questions for Analyzing Stylistic Features of Texts, Questions for Analyzing the Rhetorical Context of Texts, and Questions for Analyzing Writing Assignments.

Also in Chapter 1, we introduce the concept or intertextuality, and across the book we carry the motif of academic writing as a conversation among the voices in a text. In Chapter 3, we provide a concrete example of such a conversation. The constellation of readings in this chapter focus on "The Mommy Wars," the controversy over stay-at-home versus working mothers. Chapter 3 shows students what a debate entails and how it is played out by academics, journalists, and writers in the popular press. Students whose exposure to public debate is restricted to *Good Morning America* or afternoon talk shows have a very limited view of argument and think of it as shallow and angry. The set of readings in Chapter 3 illustrates the give-and-take of a current debate that is being waged in both public and academic settings. Chapter 3 is lengthier than the chapters in the anthology section of the book. We provide thirteen reading selections in order to give students an opportunity to analyze a complex social issue in depth. The readings also show students the various ways participants in academic conversations view and write about a debatable issue. In subsequent chapters, we draw upon these thirteen selections and use them as touchstone texts for various genre conventions and principles of academic writing.

We would like to mention other changes to Part I. We introduce a new chapter on visual analysis and visual argument that teaches students analytical skills for viewing visual representations and writing about them with expression and conviction. We also provide expanded, in-depth coverage of:

- Analysis and evaluation (eight forms of analysis)
- Synthesis (four forms of synthesis)
- Source-based argument, including discussion of using different types of arguments for different purposes
- Research paper (three forms) and updated advice for using online databases, subject directories, search engines, and other electronic tools

Part I of the sixth edition reflects a major change in our approach. Before asking students to write papers in a particular genre, we introduce them to the genre by having them read and analyze a representative touchstone text. Then we guide them through the reading-writing process by tracing the path of a student writer.

## ■ Part II: Anthology

In Part II of *Writing in the Disciplines*, we have retained our readers' favorite selections, and, at their request, we have reinstated some selections from earlier editions. The three anthology chapters on natural science and technology include four new readings that focus on recent developments in those fields and Carl Sagan's "In Defense of Robots" from the third edition. The two social science chapters in Part II contain three new readings, and Chapter 3, the social science chapter in Part I, contains thirteen new selections. In the humanities section, at the request of our reviewers, we have reintroduced Rock Music and Cultural Values and included four readings from the fourth edition as well as three new selections. Chapter 16 contains three selections from previous editions and three new short stories. In the sixth edition, we introduce Chapter 17, Three Visual Portfolios, which contains sets of images on three of the topics covered elsewhere in the book: families, inequality, and ethnic diversity. Finally, we have refined the guide to documentation and the comparison of the MLA (Modern Language Association) and APA styles in the appendix.

## ■ COLLABORATIVE LEARNING ACTIVITIES

Some of the exercises in *Writing in the Disciplines* are collaborative learning activities that require students to work together in groups to clarify and extend their understanding of material presented in Chapters 1 through 9. Occasionally, we construct pairs of individual and collaborative exercises, so instructors may assign out-of-class work and follow with in-class collaborative activities. Some instructors may use the collaborative exercises to emphasize points they or their students deem particularly important or problematic.

It is important to prepare students for group work by teaching them the collaborative skills they need in order to work together—requisite social skills, group dynamics, methods of interaction, and strategies for learning from each other as well as from the teacher. Some instructors pair off students at first. Then, when they move the students into groups, they give them time to become acquainted. Another technique is to redefine the groups frequently until everyone in the class has gotten to know each other.

Each collaborative exercise in this textbook requires students to divide into work groups. Experiment with different ways of grouping students together. You might allow them to choose their groups, or you might assign them to groups on the basis of working style, personality types, or role. We have found Kenneth Bruffee's methods for conducting collaborative learning groups particularly useful (28–51). The following procedure, which draws heavily on Bruffee's *Collaborative Learning: Higher Education, Interdependence, and the Authority of Knowledge*, is applicable to all the collaborative exercises in this textbook.

---

### WORKING IN COLLABORATIVE LEARNING GROUPS

1. Students form groups of five or six by counting off. (Bruffee maintains that groups of five are particularly effective for collaborative activities.)

2. Each group selects a recorder who will write down the results of the group's deliberation and will eventually report to the entire class.

3. Each group selects a reader who then reads the collaborative task from the textbook.

4. Group members attempt to achieve a consensus on the question or issue posed by the collaborative task. All viewpoints should be heard and considered. Bruffee recommends that instructors refrain from taking part in or monitoring collaborative learning groups. He believes that teacher interference in groups "inevitably destroys peer relations among students and encourages the tendency of well-schooled students to focus on the teacher's authority and interests" (29).

5. When a consensus is reached, the recorders read their notes back to the groups, and the notes are revised to make sure they reflect the groups' decisions. Differences of opinion are also included in the notes.

6. When all groups have completed the assignment, recorders read their notes to the entire class. The instructor may choose to summarize each group's report on the chalkboard. A discussion involving the entire class may follow.

---

Other methods of forming and conducting collaborative learning groups will also work with the exercises in Chapters 1 through 9. Although we have had success with Bruffee's technique, we encourage instructors to pick the methods that work best for them and their students. The following resources will be helpful:

Angelo, T. A., and K. P. Cross. *Classroom Assessment Techniques: A Handbook for College Teachers.* San Francisco: Jossey-Bass, 1993.

Goodsell, Anne, Michelle Maher, and Vincent Tinto. *Collaborative Learning: A Sourcebook for Higher Education.* University Park, PA: NCTLA, 1992.

Johnson, David W., Roger T. Johnson, Karl A. Smith, and E. Holubec. *Circles of Learning: Cooperation in the Classroom.* Edina, MN: Interaction, 1993.

## ◼ ACKNOWLEDGMENTS

Once again, in the sixth edition we have relied on the work of many researchers and scholars in composition and reading. We are particularly grateful to Ann Brown, Kenneth Bruffee, Linda Flower, Christina Haas, John Hayes, and Bonnie Meyer. We used pilot versions of *Writing in the Disciplines* in first-year-level writing courses at Cornell University, Ithaca College, and SUNY at Cortland, and we are indebted to our students for their comments and suggestions. We appreciate the generous assistance we received from Brad Potthoff, Senior Editor, English Composition, who supervised our project with consumate skill and professionalism. We also appreciate the assistance we received from Editorial Director, Leah Jewell, and Editorial Assistant Megan Dubrowski, as well as from Editor-in-Chief for English, Craig Campanella; Marketing Manager for English Composition, Windley Morley; and Director of Marketing for Humanities, Brandy Dawson. We give special thanks to our meticulous copyeditor, Simone Payment, and to our infinitely resourceful production editor and full-service manager at Stratford/TexTech Inc., Kathy O'Connor. We are also indebted to our reviewers for their helpful ideas and suggestions: Timothy McGinn, NW Arkansas Community College; Andrea Van Vorhis, Owens Community College; Anita Guynn, UNC Pembroke; Karen Clark, University of Arkansas; Karen Radell, Central Michigan University; James Laughton, NW Arkansas Community College; Laima Sruoginis, University of Southern Maine; Jette Morache, College of Southern Idaho; Carole Lane, University of Arkansas; Joyce Pihlaja, Lake Superior College; Monika Brown, UNC Pembroke; and Kimberly Gunter, UNC Pembroke.

Finally, we are grateful to Hadley M. Smith, Ithaca College, for his constant generosity, support, good humor, and sound advice. He joined us in editing the first five editions of this book and contributed to that project the lion's share of work on chapters dealing with science, technology, research, and library materials, as well as infinite computer-related expertise and technological savvy. His collaboration is still evident on every page of this edition, except where we have floundered in the absence of his counsel.

*Mary Lynch Kennedy*
*William J. Kennedy*

### WORK CITED

Bruffee, Kenneth. *Collaborative Learning: Higher Education, Interdependence, and the Authority of Knowledge.* Baltimore: Johns Hopkins UP, 1993.

# Reading and Writing in the Academic Disciplines

# One

# Active Critical Reading:
## *Prereading and Close Reading*

## ■ ACADEMIC READING-WRITING PROCESS

In college, you will encounter English that is more formal and specialized than the spoken and written language you know. We refer to this language as *academic* reading and writing. Eventually, you will become comfortable with it, but first you must learn its conventions and practice using them to communicate with your professors and fellow students. This textbook will help you to do so.

Most of the writing assignments you receive in college will require you to write about material you have read in books, articles, or other sources. Reading and writing go hand in hand. For that reason, you should familiarize yourself with a process that combines the two activities. We describe that process in the box below. It begins with critical reading and progresses to writing as you plan, draft, and revise your work.

---

### OVERVIEW OF THE ACADEMIC READING-WRITING PROCESS

**Active Critical Reading**

*Prereading.*   Preview the text, set your goals, and freewrite.

*Close reading.*   Mark, annotate, elaborate on, and pose questions about the text. Questions address three areas: (1) content; (2) genre, organization, and stylistic features; and (3) rhetorical context.

*Postreading.*   Write a personal response; compose paraphrases and summaries; and record quotations.

(continued on the next page)

---

### Planning

*Formulating a thesis.*    Arrive at a preliminary understanding of the point you wish to make in your paper.

*Organizing.*    Decide how you will use the textual sources in your paper and how you will develop your argument.

### Drafting

*Drafting.*    Weave the source material (usually in the form of quotations, paraphrases, and summaries) with your own ideas to create paragraphs and, ultimately, a complete paper, typically with an introduction, a body, and a conclusion.

### Reworking

*Revising.*    Lengthen, shorten, or reorder your paper; change your prose to make it more understandable to your reader; make sentence-level, phrase-level, and word-level stylistic changes; or, in some cases, make major conceptual or organizational alterations to incorporate what you learned during the process of drafting.

*Editing.*    Proofread your paper for errors in sentence structure, usage, punctuation, spelling, and mechanics, and check for proper manuscript form.

**You don't have to follow the stages of this process in lockstep fashion, beginning with prereading and ending with editing.** Your movement may be **recursive** and the phases may be intermixed. You may find yourself revising *as* you are drafting as well as after you have completed a draft of your paper. You will read the texts before you write, but you will probably reread portions of them during and after the drafting phase. Writing occurs at any point in the process. You will jot down ideas before you read the texts, annotate the texts as you read, or rewrite parts of the initial draft of your paper.

## ◼ CONVERSATION WITH THE TEXTS

You will be having a **conversation with your texts** throughout the entire process of reading and writing. Both reading and writing constitute forms of conversation. When you read, you converse with an author. When you write, you converse with your readers. The more you think of the reading-writing process as an extended form of conversation, the easier it will be for you to develop your academic skills in both reading and writing.

> Recursive: a conversation as you go back and forth
> from reading to writing to rereading to rewriting.

We devote the first two chapters of this book to describing and illustrating the academic reading-writing process as a form of conversation. For convenience, we begin with reading and proceed through the phases in the order outlined in the preceding overview. Keep in mind that academic writers may not apply the process sequentially.

## ■■ ACTIVE CRITICAL READING

Effective reading is essential because academic writing is frequently based on reading sources. College writers rarely have the luxury of composing essays based entirely on their own ideas and personal experiences. Typically, professors specify a topic and expect students to formulate a thesis or position and support it by drawing on published sources — textbooks, scholarly books, journal articles, Web sites, newspapers, and magazines — along with lecture notes, interviews, and other forms of information. When you use sources in your papers, you need to practice effective paraphrasing, summarizing, and quoting. The key to becoming an accomplished academic writer is to become a skilled reader.

> Academic writing depends on paraphrasing, summarizing, and quoting from sources.

Critical readers are *active readers*. They relate the text to texts they have read before, they tap into prior knowledge, and they engage personal experiences. These activities enable them to self-regulate their reading comprehension. Usually when we have difficulty understanding texts, it is because we lack the appropriate background and cannot make connections.

To become an active reader, try out the strategies listed in the box below.

---

### ACTIVE CRITICAL READING STRATEGIES

**Prereading**

- Preview the text and derive questions that will help you set goals for close reading.
- Recall your prior knowledge and express your feelings about the reading topic. Freewrite and brainstorm.

**Close Reading**

- Mark, annotate, and elaborate on the text.
- Take notes.
- Pose and answer questions about three aspects of the text: (1) content; (2) genre, organization, and stylistic features; and (3) rhetorical context.

**Postreading**

- Review the text and your notes.
- Write a personal response.
- Record paraphrases, summaries, and quotations for future reference.

---

## ■ Keeping a Writer's Notebook

As you can see from the strategies listed in the box above, critical reading is accompanied by various types of writing: freewriting and brainstorming, taking notes, posing and answering questions, responding from personal experience, paraphrasing, summarizing, and quoting. Readers need a place to record all this writing. We suggest that you use a writer's notebook. You can purchase a notebook or create one online.

You will fill your writer's notebook with informal writing, some of which will emerge in the formal writing you do at a later date. Writer's notebooks are places to collect material for future writing. They are different from journals in this respect. Journal writing can be an end in itself. You can keep a journal to record and reflect on what happens each day or you can use a journal for more specific purposes, for example, to respond to teachers' questions. A writer's notebook is not an end in itself. The entries are recorded with an eye toward later writing. They may become the basis for an essay, provide evidence for an argument, or serve as repositories of apt quotations. Consider your writer's notebook a record of your conversations with texts, as well as a storehouse for collecting material you can draw on when writing.

> Active reading requires active, responsive writing.

## ■ PREREADING

Prereading lays the groundwork for comprehension. Just as you wouldn't plunge into an athletic activity "cold," you wouldn't set out to read a difficult text without preparation. The more challenging the reading, the more important the prereading activities become. The prereading strategies you select depend on the text's character and level of difficulty. Two useful techniques are (1) **previewing** and asking questions that will help you set goals for close reading, and (2) **freewriting** or **brainstorming** to recall your prior knowledge or feelings about the topic.

### ■ Preview the Text and Ask Questions That Will Help You Set Goals for Close Reading

Before you do a close reading, give the text a quick inspection. This overview will give you a general idea of the content and organization. You will improve your comprehension if you ask yourself the questions in the box below.

---

### PREREADING QUESTIONS

- What does the title indicate the text will be about?
- How do the subtitles and headings function? Do they reveal the organizational format (for example, introduction, body, conclusion)?
- Is there biographical information about the author? What does it tell me about the text?
- Do any topic sentences of paragraphs seem especially important?

- Are there other salient features of the text, such as enumeration, italics, boldface print, indention, diagrams, visual aids, or footnotes? What do these features reveal about the text?
- Does the text end with a summary? What does the summary reveal about the text?
- What type of background knowledge do I need to make sense of this text?
- Why am I reading this text?

An especially useful previewing technique mentioned above is to turn the title and the subheadings into questions and try to answer them before reading. Consider how one of our students used this technique to preview Charles Krauthammer's article, "Crossing Lines: A Secular Argument Against Research Cloning" (Chapter 10). Converting the title into a question, she asked, *"What is the secular argument against cloning? How does it differ from a religious argument?"* Then she converted the subheadings—"The Problem," "The Promise," "Objection I: Intrinsic Worth," "Objection II: The Brave New World Factor"—into questions.

## STUDENT'S CONVERSION OF SUBHEADINGS INTO QUESTIONS

Subheadings: "The Problem" and "The Promise"
Student's question: Will Krauthammer first describe the problem with cloning and then talk about the promise it holds?

Subheading: "Objection I: Intrinsic Worth"
Student's question: Does the first objection refer to the intrinsic worth of each individual?

Subheading: "Objection II: the Brave New World Factor"
Student's question: Does the second objection refer to science fiction?

Student's Answer to Questions: We are probably going to get the argument that research cloning will lead to a brave new world with genetically engineered inhabitants like "Star Wars Attack of the Clones."

## EXERCISE 1.1

Continue where our student left off. Turn to pages 355–58 and convert the subheadings into questions. Answer them as best you can.

Your response to the previous Prereading Questions will give you a sense of what the text is about. Based on that information, you will respond to "Why am I reading this text?" by setting an appropriate **purpose** for your close reading. You may be used to your high-school teachers setting a purpose for reading assignments. For example, "Read this chapter to find three factors that influence global warming" or "When you have finished the story, write your reaction to Sammy's decision to quit his job at the A&P."

> Prereading: Ask questions about
>
> Title
> Subtitle and headings
> Author's biography
> Topic sentences
> Printed format
> Summary

In college, you will often set your own purpose for reading, and the purpose you select will depend on your overall goal. This textbook focuses on the overall **goal of reading** for the purpose of writing. If your immediate goal is to search for a fact or relevant bit of information to put in your essay, you may scan looking for key words. Or you may read for other reasons: to locate an opposing position, to obtain background information, to determine how other writers have approached your topic. What is important to remember is that after you have sized up the text, you need to decide why you are reading it.

> Goals for reading:
> - information
> - opposing position
> - additional background

## ◼ Use Freewriting and Brainstorming to Recall Your Prior Knowledge and Express Your Feelings about the Reading Topic

The background knowledge, experiences, and biases you bring to bear on a text affect your understanding. As you read, you construct new knowledge by relating the text to what you already know. Prior knowledge paves the way for understanding. For example, before reading about alternatives to the traditional nuclear family in Pauline Irit Erera's "What Is a Family?" (pp. 462–74), think about the kinds of families you already know: two-parent families, single-parent families, families including stepparents, families with stepsiblings, and so forth. Your prior knowledge will help you to process Erera's argument. Or, before reading Simon Frith's "Toward an Aesthetic of Popular Music" (see p. 543), reflect on your tastes in music.

Two ways to trigger prior knowledge and experiences are freewriting and brainstorming. By **freewriting**, we mean *jotting down anything that comes to mind about a topic*. Write nonstop for five or ten minutes without worrying about usage or spelling. Put down whatever you want. **Brainstorming** uses a *process of free association*. Start the process by skimming the reading source and listing key words or phrases. Then run down the list and record associations that come to mind when you think about these target concepts. Don't bother to write complete sentences; just write down words and phrases. Give your imagination free rein.

> Freewriting triggers prior knowledge.

> Brainstorming builds upon a preview of key words.

For an example, look at the freewriting and brainstorming of our student as she continues to read Charles Krauthammer's "Crossing Lines: A Secular Argument Against Research Cloning" (pp. 352–58).

### *EXCERPT FROM STUDENT'S FREEWRITING:*

I know when people talk about using cloning for research or medical purposes, they are referring to stem-cell research. I'm not sure what the scientific procedure involves, but I've heard that the stem cells can be used to cure Parkinson's disease and other diseases.

### *EXCERPT FROM STUDENT'S BRAINSTORMING LIST:*

1. How cloning works: I'm confused about this. People talk about cloning as reproducing carbon copies. I'm not sure how cloning is used for curing diseases.

2. When does life begin? For many people, this is an unanswerable question. Some believe life begins at the moment of conception. Others think an embryo or fetus is not yet a human being.

3. Brave New World Factor: This refers to science fiction and the fear that cloning will result in new life forms and Frankenstein monsters.

4. Using embryos from IVF clinics: My older sister had fertility treatments. She had four eggs implanted, and she gave birth to twins. They froze some of her fertilized eggs. I still don't understand how embryos from IVF clinics would be used for cloning.

When you use freewriting or brainstorming to tap into what you already know about a topic, you will better understand the text and read more objectively. You will be more conscious of your opinions and biases and less likely to confuse them inadvertently with those of the author. You may also find that freewriting and brainstorming help break ground for the paper that you will eventually write. They enable you to generate ideas for comparison, contrast, reinforcement, or contestation in your paper. As an argumentative "other" voice that helps to test the claims of your reading, freewriting can show the direction that your further reading and rewriting might take.

## ■ CLOSE READING

When you read, you actively construct meaning. You are not a passive decoder who transfers graphic symbols from the written page to your mind. Think of the process **as a two-way conversation between the reader and the text**. Articulate what you are thinking, and ask questions when you need more information or have difficulty understanding. To keep the interaction between the reader and the text dynamic, read with pencil in hand, annotating and marking the text, taking separate notes, and posing and answering questions.

> Close reading is a two-way conversation between reader and text.

## ■ Mark, Annotate, and Elaborate on the Text

**Mark** the text by underlining, highlighting, circling, drawing arrows, boxing, and bracketing important ideas. **Annotate** by making marginal notes and recording brief responses. **Elaborate** by amplifying or supplementing the text by adding comments. Draw on your knowledge and experiences to extend, illustrate, or evaluate. You can apply the text to situations the author does not envision, or you can provide analogies, examples, or counterexamples.

> Mark texts
> Make notes
> Supplement text

We provide a complete set of strategies for elaborating on texts in the box below.

---

### STRATEGIES FOR ELABORATING ON TEXTS

Expand Text.

- Agree or disagree with a statement in the text, giving reasons for your agreement or disagreement.
- Compare or contrast your reactions to the topic (for example, "At first I thought . . ., but now I think . . .").
- Extend one of the points. Think of an example and see how far you can take it.
- Discover an idea implied by the text, but not stated.
- Provide additional details by fleshing out a point in the text.
- Illustrate the text with an example, an incident, a scenario, or an anecdote.
- Embellish the text with a vivid image, a metaphor, or an example.
- Draw comparisons between the text and books, articles, films, or other media.
- Validate one of the points with an example.
- Make a judgment about the relevance of one of the statements in the text.
- Impose a condition on a statement in the text. (For example, "If . . ., then. . . .")
- Qualify an idea in the text. Take a single paragraph and speculate on extensions of or exceptions to its claims.
- Extend an idea with a personal recollection or reflection. Personalize one of the statements. Try to imagine how you would behave in the same situation.
- Speculate about one of the points by:

  Asking questions about the direct consequences of an idea

  Predicting consequences

  Drawing implications from an idea

  Applying the idea to a hypothetical situation

  Giving a concrete instance of a point made in the text

## Question Text

- Draw attention to what the text has neglected to say about the topic.
- Test one of the claims. Ask whether the claim really holds up.
- Assess one of the points in light of your own prior knowledge of the topic or with your own or others' experiences.
- Question one of the points.
- Criticize a point in the text. Take a single paragraph and question every claim in it.
- Assess the usefulness and applicability of an idea.

## Diagram Text

- Classify items in the text under a superordinate category.
- Look for unstated text relations. Skim through the text once more to see whether statements at the end connect with those at the beginning and middle. Draw arrows to display the connections.
- Outline hierarchies of importance among ideas in the text.

Here is how one of our students marked, annotated, and elaborated on a passage from Charles Krauthammer's "Crossing Lines: A Secular Argument Against Research Cloning" (pp. 356–57). In the paragraph preceding the one printed below, Krauthammer summarizes the arguments against research cloning and points out that the same arguments can be used against stem-cell research.

**Passage from Krauthammer**

*Student Annotations*

These arguments are serious—serious enough to banish the insouciance of the scientists who consider anyone questioning their work to be a Luddite—yet, in my view, insufficient to justify a legal ban on stem-cell research (as with stem cells from discarded embryos in fertility clinics). I happen not to believe that either personhood or ensoulment occurs at conception. I think we need to be apprehensive about what evil might arise from the power of stem-cell research, but that apprehension alone, while justifying vigilance and regulation, does not justify a ban on the practice. And I believe that given the good that might flow from stem-cell research, we should first test the power of law and custom to enforce the seven-day blastocyst line for embryonic exploitation before assuming that such a line could never hold. This is why I support stem-cell research (using leftover embryos from fertility clinics) and might support research cloning were it not for one other aspect that is unique to it. In research cloning, the embryo is created with the explicit intention of its eventual destruction. That is a given because not to destroy the embryo would be to produce a cloned child. If you are not permitted to grow the embryo into a child, you are obliged at some point to destroy it.

*Insouciance?*

*Someone who opposes technology?*

*He explained blastocyst earlier.*

*He emphasizes using leftover embryos. Is this the only way he will support stem-cell research?*

Notice how the student marks the text. She does very little underlining and high-lighting. Do not overuse highlighting markers. It is hard to decide what is important when you read through a text for the first time. Every sentence may seem significant. But if you highlight a large percentage of the text, you will have a lot to reread when you study for an exam or look for material to put in a paper. Highlighting is a mechanical process that does not actively engage you with the text. It merely gives the illusion that you are reading effectively. **Instead of highlighting, write out summary statements and reactions**. Writing will help you to process the information.

In addition to her judicious underlining, our student circles unfamiliar vocabulary ("insouciance," "Luddite," "blastocyst"), boxes key transitions ("yet" and "but"), and draws arrows to indicate where Krauthammer repeats himself to provide emphasis. You might prefer stars or asterisks to circles and boxes. **Feel free to develop your own symbol system for marking texts**, but be sure to use it consistently.

> Instead of highlighting, write summaries and mark text with symbols.

After marking and annotating the passage, our student adds her own ideas.

### ELABORATION OF KRAUTHAMMER'S ARGUMENT

*I support stem-cell research because it puts leftover embryos to good use. Otherwise, they will be discarded. But this raises a question about Krauthammer's argument. In IVF clinics, they create many embryos they will not need. My sister had seven fertilized eggs, but only three were implanted. The rest were frozen. But both the doctor and my sister knew that when she got pregnant, the four frozen eggs would be destroyed.*

The student's response is an example of assertive reading. Instead of accepting Krautham-mer's position on IVF as undisputed fact, she challenges it. As she continues to question and rebut the author, she will begin to formulate her own position on the controversy.

**Record your elaborations in your writer's notebook**. This record will be useful if you intend to write a paper that gives your view on the ideas in the text. It will certainly help your critical analysis of the reading material by pointing to passages that raised questions, offered insights, and provoked your responses the first time you read them. The ultimate goal of marking, annotating, and elaborating is to involve you intellectually with the text and to give you access to it without rereading. Writing out marginal or separate notes is the best way to accomplish this.

> Record in writer's notebook.

### EXERCISE 1.2

Read Louise Story's "Many Women at Elite Colleges Set Career Path to Motherhood" (pp. 92–95). Use the critical reading strategies we have described so far and practice the process approach to reading. First, preview the text and derive questions. Then recall your prior knowledge and express your feelings by freewriting and brainstorming. Finally, mark, annotate, and elaborate on the text.

## ■ Take Effective Notes

When you encounter difficult texts, you may want to take more extensive notes to supplement your annotations and elaborations. These supplementary notes can be in the form of outlines, summaries, or paraphrases of key passages, lists of significant pages or paragraphs, or any combination of these elements. Regard them as a record of your conversation with the texts. When you take notes, pay special attention to thesis statements and topic sentences. The **thesis** is the focal point of the entire piece: the major point, position, or objective the author demonstrates or proves. A **topic sentence** is the main idea of a paragraph or another subdivision of the text.

Thesis statements express major idea of essay.

Both the thesis and the topic statement may require more than one sentence, so do not assume that you should always search for a single sentence. Nor should you make assumptions about their location. The thesis statement is typically in the introductory paragraph, but it can also appear elsewhere. Topic sentences are often at the beginnings of paragraphs, but not always; they can appear in the middle or at the end as well. Some paragraphs do not contain explicit topic sentences; the main idea is implied through an accumulation of details, facts, or examples.

Topic sentences express major idea of each paragraph or subdivision.

If the text is easy to read and has straightforward content, you can streamline notetaking and annotating procedures to capture only the most basic ideas. But remember that it is natural to forget much of what you have read; even relatively simple ideas can slip from your memory unless you record them in notes or annotations. And, of course, when you are working with library sources, note-taking is indispensable.

## ■ Pose and Answer Questions about the Text

A useful method for note-taking is to pose questions about the text and answer them as you read. If you are reading a textbook chapter, first look at the reader aids: the preview outline at the beginning, the introductory or concluding sections, and the review questions at the end. Also check out chapter or section headings for the concepts or issues that the chapter covers. Using these reader aids, generate questions about what the chapter will be about and answer them as you read. Formulate questions based on section headings and visual layout. This strategy works best if you record your answers as you locate the relevant material. Write your answers in your writer's notebook so that you can return to them later and find the important ideas you took away from the reading. Too often, students spend hours reading only to find several days later that they remember virtually nothing and must reread all the material. Although it takes extra time to pose and answer questions, it can reduce time spent rereading texts.

A powerful strategy that will increase your reading comprehension is to ask questions about three specific aspects of the text: (1) content; (2) genre, organization, and stylistic features; and (3) rhetorical context. When you ask these questions, you will be reading in three different but not necessarily separate ways. Critical readers use all three strategies simultaneously and harmoniously, but for convenience sake we will discuss them one by one.

> Determine:
> - content
> - genre, organization, and stylistic features
> - rhetorical context

## Reading for Content

When you read for content, you read to determine the literal meaning of the text. Begin with the big picture—the overall topic—and then delve deeper to determine the main idea and the support for the main point. Ask yourself the questions in the box below:

---

### QUESTIONS FOR ANALYZING THE LITERAL CONTENT OF TEXTS

- What is the topic or focal point of the text?
- What is the main idea, major point, or central claim?
- What other ideas are important?
- How does the text support, qualify, and develop the claim or position?
- What inferences, judgments, or conclusions are drawn?

---

Let's reread Krauthammer's argument asking these questions.

### PASSAGE FROM KRAUTHAMMER

These arguments are serious—serious enough to banish the insouciance of the scientists who consider anyone questioning their work to be a Luddite—yet, in my view, insufficient to justify a legal ban on stem-cell research (as with stem cells from discarded embryos in fertility clinics). I happen not to believe that either personhood or ensoulment occurs at conception. I think we need to be apprehensive about what evil might arise from the power of stem-cell research, but that apprehension alone, while justifying vigilance and regulation, does not justify a ban on the practice. And I believe that given the good that might flow from stem-cell research, we should first test the power of law and custom to enforce the seven-day blastocyst line for embryonic exploitation before assuming that such a line could never hold.

    This is why I support stem-cell research (using leftover embryos from fertility clinics) and might support research cloning were it not for one other aspect that is unique to it. In research cloning, the embryo is created with the explicit intention of its eventual destruction. That is a given because not to destroy the embryo would be to produce a cloned child. If you are not permitted to grow the embryo into a child, you are obliged at some point to destroy it.

- What is the topic or focal point of the text? *The topic is stem-cell research, but in the second paragraph Krauthammer also discusses research cloning.*

- What is the main idea, major point, or central claim? *In the first paragraph, Krauthammer asserts that he opposes a legal ban on stem-cell research that uses embryos left over from fertility clinics. In the second paragraph, he reiterates this position and he expresses reservations about research cloning.*

- What other ideas are important? *Toward the beginning of the passage, he comments that arguments against stem-cell research should be taken seriously; however, they are insufficient to prohibit the practice. Another important idea is Krauthammer's position that an embryo is not yet a person.*

- How does the text support, qualify, and develop the claim or position? *Krauthammer qualifies his position by cautioning scientists to proceed with stem-cell research with vigilance and with the expectation that researchers will hold to the seven-day limit for using embryos. In the second paragraph, he explains that he opposes research cloning because the embryo is created for the sole purpose of extracting the stem cells and eventually being destroyed.*

- What inferences, judgments, or conclusions are drawn? *We can conclude that Krauthammer cautiously supports stem-cell research so long as the stem cells are obtained early on from embryos that have already been developed in fertility clinics. He is opposed to research that creates embryos for the sole purpose of using the stem cells.*

Asking pointed questions about content enables you to read with an active purpose rather than merely trying to get through all the words on the page. In addition to being able to restate and interpret the meaning of the text, it is important to be able to describe its characteristics and structure.

## Reading for Genre, Organization, and Stylistic Features

### Genre

You may recall your English teacher using the word *genre* to characterize different types of literature, for example, novel, short story, poem. *Genre* is a French word meaning "kind," "sort," or "style." Traditionally, in English class, the word is used to refer to different categories of writing that are marked by distinctive content, form, and style. Recently, *genre* has acquired a broader meaning. This new perspective views genres in terms of their social situation and purpose. For example, letters enable us to communicate with others in writing.

> Genre, a specific kind of writing ——➤ social situation and purpose

Particular genres of letter writing allow us to express amorous feelings (love letter), seek a job (letter of application), sympathize with a loved one (letter of condolence), or criticize the manufacturer of our new microwave (letter of complaint). These letters share attributes, yet they differ according to the writer's purpose. You would not open your business letter with the salutation, "My Dear Personnel Director." Nor would you add the postscript, "P.S. I forgot to mention that I am an expert typist." In order to achieve the goal of presenting yourself as an intelligent job applicant, you would be much more formal and concise.

At the end of her watershed essay "Genre as Social Action," Carolyn Miller writes, "For the student, genres serve as keys to understanding how to participate in the actions of a community" (165). By the time you arrive at college, you know how letter writing and other genres in the public realm function in the wider community, and you are probably very knowledgeable about more specialized genres in areas that interest you. Those who enjoy rock music will know the characteristics of heavy metal, punk rock, glam rock, and grunge, and enthusiasts of electronic music will be able to differentiate among techno, trance, industrial music, house music, and electro hip-hop.

## EXERCISE 1.3

As a class, come up with a list of television genres. Then break into small groups. Each group will select a genre, explain its purpose, describe its features and conventions, and answer the following questions:

- What purpose does the genre serve?
- To what audience is it directed?
- How are the features and conventions adapted to the purpose and audience?

A representative from each group will report to the class.

Some of you may know more about genres of the music you listen to and the genres of the shows you watch on television than genres you see in print. To test your knowledge of written genres, complete the exercise presented below.

## EXERCISE 1.4

Break into small groups. Assign each of the numbered passages to a different group. Read the passage and answer the following questions:

- What purpose does the text serve?
- Who is the audience for the text?
- Are assumptions made about class, age, gender, ethnicity, and class?
- What knowledge is the reader assumed to have?
- Would you characterize the style as literary or scientific?
- Can you describe other characteristics and textual properties?
- What is the genre?

*Passage 1*

"TOM!"

No answer.

"TOM!"

No answer.

"What's gone with that boy, I wonder? You TOM!"

No answer.

The old lady pulled her spectacles down and looked over them about the room; then she put them up and looked out under them. She seldom or never looked THROUGH them for so small a thing as a boy; they were her state pair, the pride of her heart, and were built for "style," not service—she could have seen through a pair of stove-lids just as well. She looked perplexed for a moment, and then said, not fiercely, but still loud enough for the furniture to hear:

"Well, I lay if I get hold of you I'll—."[1]

*Passage 2*

Two roads diverged in a yellow wood,

And sorry I could not travel both

And be one traveler, long I stood

And looked down one as far as I could

To where it bent in the undergrowth.[2]

*Passage 3*

More recently, a study of 8000 male Harvard graduates showed that chocaholics lived longer than abstainers. Their longevity may be explained by the high polyphenol levels in chocolate. Polyphenols reduce the oxidation of low-density lipoproteins and thereby protect against heart disease. Such theories are still speculative.

Coincidentally or otherwise, many of the world's oldest supercentenarians, e.g. Jeanne Calment (1875–1997) and Sarah Knauss (1880–1999), were passionately fond of chocolate. Jeanne Calment habitually ate two pounds of chocolate per week until her physician induced her to give up sweets at the age of 119—three years before her death aged 122. Life-extensionists are best advised to eat dark chocolate rather than the kinds of calorie-rich confectionery popular in America.[3]

*Passage 4*

[Enter the Ghost, and Prince Hamlet following]

Hamlet: Whither wilt thou lead me? Speak. I'll go no further.

Ghost: Mark me.

Hamlet: I will.

Ghost: My hour is almost come

When I to sulph'rous and tormenting flames

Must render up myself.

Hamlet: Alas, poor ghost![4]

*Passage 5*

HOUSE THINKING

A Room-By-Room Look at How We Live

By Winifred Gallagher

329 pp. HarperCollins Publishers $24.95

I spend my days examining, room by room, how we live—"house thinking," as Winifred Gallagher would have it. Mine is a job that some intellectuals might disdain. No matter: most people (including some of the smartest) spend a great deal of time thinking about houses, whether professionally or out of sheer love. So I welcome any book that takes seriously a subject as old as recorded history and as deeply felt as anything else in our lives.[5]

*Passage 6*

Respondents were administered the *Celebrity Attitude Scale* (CAS: McCutcheon et al., 2002). Originally termed the Celebrity Worship Scale, this instrument is a 34-item scale in which respondents are asked to indicate their attitude towards a favourite celebrity (that they themselves have named) using a number of items that use a response format of "strongly agree" equal to 5 and "strongly disagree" equal to 1. Please refer to Table 1 for all the items of this scale.[6]

Most likely, the above exercise demonstrated that you are already familiar with literary genres such as novels, plays, and poems, and nonliterary genres such as book reviews and scientific articles. If knowledge of genre is a key "to understanding how to participate in the actions of a community" (Miller 165), in order to succeed in college, you need to learn additional genres of academic writing.

***Genres in Academic Writing and in Writing Classes***    As you become more familiar with academic writing, you will be able to identify specialized genres such as scientific research articles, engineering reports, case histories, and legal briefs. In this book, we concentrate on the classroom genres that play a major role in writing courses and are frequently assigned in courses in various disciplines: response to a text, summary, abstract, précis, critical analysis, rhetorical analysis, comparative analysis, literary analysis, process analysis, causal analysis, comparison and contrast, critique of visual argument, explanatory synthesis, literature review, thesis-driven synthesis, argument-synthesis, and research paper. Knowledge of these genres is indispensable if you want to become a skilled critical reader and a proficient academic writer. See Table 1–1 for an overview of each genre.

***Role of Genre in Reading and Writing***    Knowledge of the genre of a text aids reading comprehension because it prepares you to approach the text with a set of expectations and make intelligent predictions. When reading a newspaper article, you look for a headline and a byline, and you expect answers to five questions—who? what? where? when? and how?—to be placed early in the article. If you are familiar with the genre of the scientific research article, you anticipate four major subdivisions: Introduction, Methods, Results, and Discussion.

> Genre sets up expectations about content.

When reading an argument essay, you expect the writer to lay out both sides of the controversy, make concessions to parties holding opposing views and then refute their claims by marshalling evidence to support his or her thesis. Genre knowledge is a shorthand for making sense of the text.

You should be aware that the form of writing called "argument" is found in many genres besides the classic academic essay. The major forms of writing—argument, exposition,

TABLE 1–1    Classroom Genres of Academic Writing

| Genre | Characteristics | Writer's Rhetorical Purpose |
|---|---|---|
| Response to a text | An essay in which the writer relates his or her own ideas to those in the text and, in so doing, presents an *informed* outlook. The essay balances personal expression and textual content. | Share reaction to the text with other readers. |
| Summary | A condensed version of an original text that shortens the original without changing its meaning. | Give readers a condensed version of the original text. |
| Abstract | A brief summary, usually only a paragraph or two. It usually appears after the title of a paper and before the longer text itself, though sometimes it is presented on a separate page. | Give readers descriptive summary information that will help them decide if it is worth their time to read the entire article. |
| Précis | A summary that strictly follows the order of the original text. It is usually no longer than one-quarter of the original. | Give readers a miniature version of the original text. |
| Critical analysis | An analysis that examines the text's argument by looking closely at the author's line of reasoning. | Share interpretation with readers, and, ideally, convince them of an enlightened reading of the text that warrants their attention and should be taken seriously. A more focused purpose is to evaluate the author's argument in terms of its strengths and weaknesses. |
| Rhetorical analysis | An examination of *how a text is written*. It pays attention to what the text talks about, but its main focus is the strategies and devices the author uses to convey the meaning. | Share interpretation with readers, and, ideally, convince them of an enlightened reading of the text that warrants their attention and should be taken seriously. A more *focused purpose* is to evaluate the author's rhetorical context and strategies. |
| Comparative analysis | An analysis of a focal text through the lens of a text that is comparable. | Show how one text corroborates or debates the other. |
| Literary analysis | An analysis of a story, novel, poem, play, or other literary text to interpret and evaluate its meaning and cultural significance. | Prompt readers to uncover similar layers of meaning and significance when they read such text. |
| Process analysis | An outline and explanation of the steps in an operation. | Explain and comment on the sequence of particular steps in a process, emphasize important points, provide supplementary information, and include caveats about what can go wrong. |
| Causal analysis | An identification and explanation of the reasons why something happens. | Examine why a phenomenon or event is occurring, investigate possible causes of a problem, or examine effects. |
| Comparison and contrast essay | An analysis of texts that shows what the similarities and differences represent, reveal, or demonstrate. | Analyze texts to show what the similarities and differences represent, reveal, or demonstrate. |
| Critique of visual argument | An analysis of a photograph, film, video, or other visual text to interpret and evaluate its meaning and cultural significance. | Prompt viewers to find similar layers of meaning and significance when they view visuals. |

*(Continued)*

**TABLE 1–1    continued**

| Genre | Characteristics | Writer's Rhetorical Purpose |
| --- | --- | --- |
| Explanatory synthesis essay | An analysis of two or more texts that share a topic or interest. It identifies grounds for grouping the textual components and organizes this textual material under a controlling theme. The writer presents informative results in a straightforward manner. Such a synthesis often tries to define a topic or issue in an expository style that emphasizes the coverage of data rather than any further questioning or interpretation of the data. | Unfold or unravel a topic or question to make it clearer to readers. The synthesis might crack open a concept, place an issue in historical context, or clarify sides in a controversy. The synthesis is objective and nonjudgmental. |
| Literature review | An analysis of two or more texts that share a topic or interest. It identifies grounds for grouping the textual components, and organizes the textual material under a controlling theme. | Provide background and explain a topic, problem, or issue to readers by examining a wide array of published research studies. |
| Thesis-driven synthesis | A synthesis of two or more texts that share a topic or interest. It identifies grounds for grouping the textual components and organizes the textual material under a controlling theme. | Communicate thesis and point of view. The writer takes a position on the topic or issue. The writer's position is explicit in a direct statement of judgment or opinion on the matter at hand. The thesis is supported by reasons that are based on evidence. |
| Argument synthesis | A synthesis of two or more texts that share a topic or interest. It identifies grounds for grouping the textual components and organizes the textual material under a controlling theme. | Persuade readers that position is reasonable and worthy of support. The synthesis focuses on an issue or question that is debatable. The writer anticipates, acknowledges, and addresses alternative views. |
| Research paper | A paper that starts with a question or problem that requires collecting facts, opinions, and perspectives from books, journal articles, Web sites, newspapers, and other sources. The writer analyzes the texts, identifies grounds for grouping the textual components, and organizes this textual material under a controlling theme. A research paper may include the genres listed above. | Unfold or unravel a topic or question to make it clearer to the readers or take a position on the topic or issue or persuade readers that writer's position is reasonable and worthy of support. |

description, and narration—are sometimes referred to as genres. They are really the building blocks with which various genres are written, and they can play important roles in many genres. For example, narration can be used in fictional genres, such as novels and short stories, as well as in nonfictional genres such as travel writing and historical accounts. A genre such as source-based synthesis may incorporate narration, description, exposition, and argument.

As you move from one genre to another, you will soon learn each genre's conventions and stylistic techniques. You will recognize that genres written in a literary style have personal pronouns and active verbs, and genres written in a scientific style contain passive voice, a large amount of information packed into sentences, lengthy subjects composed of many words, restricted use of "I," heavy nominalization, and abstraction. You will learn that writing related to technology (for example, Web documents) has relatively short paragraphs, topic sentences for each paragraph, conciseness, summaries, inverted pyramid style, and use of hypertext links.

Just as genres provide frameworks for readers, they act as structuring devices for writers as well. A knowledgeable writer knows that her book review will differ from her book report. For both genres, she will begin by giving her readers general information about the text (title, author, publisher, copyright date, number of pages, genre). She will discuss setting, characters, plot; and she will offer a personal opinion.

> Awareness of genre helps readers and writers.

However, the knowledgeable writer knows that the two genres differ in purpose. The purpose of the book report is to summarize the main characteristics of the book and to offer a brief personal opinion. The object of the book review is to evaluate the book. The writer does this by assessing whether or not the author has accomplished his or her purpose and by comparing the text to other books in the genre or to other books written by the same author. The writer knows her readers will expect her to devote a good portion of the review to evaluation.

Readers of book reviews assume that they will receive a synopsis of the book, but more important, they expect to read the writer's evaluation. Their purpose for reading the review is to see whether the book is worth reading. If the writer breaches the contract by offering too much summary and too little evaluation, readers will be dissatisfied. As you familiarize yourself with the genres of academic writing, you will acquire clear expectations about the purpose of texts, their conventions and organization, and their stylistic features.

---

### QUESTIONS FOR IDENTIFYING THE GENRE OF TEXTS

- Does the text demonstrate an identifiable genre?
- Can I describe the form or components of this genre?
- How is the text organized?
- How do the different parts function in relation to the whole?
- Can I identify distinctive conventions of the genre?

---

To identify the genre, ask questions about how the text functions. The questions are presented in the box below.

## Organization

As you know, texts have recognizable parts, such as introductions, conclusions, theses or main-idea statements, topic sentences, and paragraphs. As you read, ask yourself such questions as:

- Where does this introduction end?
- What point is the author making in this paragraph?
- How does this paragraph relate to the one that comes before and after it?
- How does the paragraph contribute to the main idea?

**TABLE 1–2    Patterns for Developing and Organizing Texts**

| Pattern | Writer's Purpose |
| --- | --- |
| Time order, narration, process | To present ideas or events in a chronological sequence, to tell what happened (narration), or to describe a sequence of actions (process) |
| Antecedent and consequence | To present causes (antecedents) or examine effects or cause-and-effect outcomes (consequences); to reveal the causes of a particular outcome or phenomenon or to explain its consequences, usually by explaining the relationship between the causes and effects |
| Description | To present the physical attributes, parts, or setting of the topic, often in order to give a personal impression of the person, place, or thing being described |
| Statement and response | To present a statement and give a reaction, often in a question-and-answer, problem-and-solution, or remark-and-reply format |
| Comparison and contrast | To present the similarities or differences between objects, approaches, or viewpoints |
| Example | To present illustrations or instances that support an idea |
| Analysis and classification | To divide the topic into parts (analyze) or to group parts or facets of the topic according to some principle or characteristic (classify) |
| Definition | To explain a word, concept, or principle |
| Analogy | To show the similarity between things that otherwise bear little or no resemblance, to explain something by comparing it point by point with something similar |

Texts are also arranged in identifiable patterns. In your own essays, you have used organizational patterns such as cause and effect and comparison and contrast. Table 1–2 identifies the most common patterns and gives a brief description of each.

Occasionally, writers tell readers how they are organizing the text. In the introductory paragraph to "Academic Dishonesty: What Is It and Why Do Students Engage in It?" Bernard E. Whitley, Jr. and Patricia Keith-Spiegel inform their readers that they will explore four features of the topic:

> In this chapter we discuss the nature of academic dishonesty and its definitions, reasons students give for cheating, institutional and student characteristics associated with cheating, and the extent to which cheating actually leads to higher grades. (16)

When writers explain what they are doing and direct you to read in a certain way, you know what to expect. When they don't supply this information, you have to determine the pattern of development yourself.

A key to unlocking the meaning of a text is to identify the pattern of organization. **Texts may display a single organizational pattern, but more likely they have overlapping patterns**. An initial, quick read will give you a sense of the text's major organizational pattern. Keep this pattern in mind during your close reading. At that time, annotate the passages that display other patterns of development. Consider how our student annotated the following passages from Joshua Foer's article, "The Kiss of Life."

## Joshua Foer, "The Kiss of Life"[1]

Since it's Valentine's Day, let's dwell for a moment on the profoundly bizarre activity of kissing. Is there a more expressive gesture in the human repertoire?

**Comparison and contrast**

When parents kiss their children it means one thing, but when they kiss each other it means something entirely different. People will greet a total stranger with a kiss on the cheek, and then use an identical gesture to express their most intimate feelings to a lover.

**Example**

The mob kingpin gives the kiss of death, Catholics give the "kiss of peace," Jews kiss the Torah, nervous flyers kiss the ground, and the enraged sometimes demand that a kiss be applied to their hindquarters. Judas kissed Jesus, Madonna kissed Britney, a gambler kisses the dice for luck. Someone once even kissed a car for 54 hours straight.

**Time order**

Taxonomists of the kiss have long labored to make sense of its many meanings. The Romans distinguished among the friendly oscula, the loving basia and the passionate suavia. The 17th-century polymath Martin von Kempe wrote a thousand-page encyclopedia of kissing that recognized 20 different varieties, including "the kiss bestowed by superiors on inferiors" and "the hypocritical kiss."

— Analysis

**Analysis**

The German language has words for 30 different kinds of kisses, including nachkussen, which is defined as a kiss "making up for kisses that have been omitted." (The Germans are also said to have coined the inexplicable phrase "a kiss without a beard is like an egg without salt.") How did a single act become a medium for so many messages?

— Definition

Statement and response
Question-and-answer format

[1] Joshua Foer, "The Kiss of Life." *The New York Times*, February 14, 2006, section 1, Op Ed page. Copyright 2006 *The New York Times* Company.

The general plan for this article is **Statement and Response**. The opening paragraph asks about kissing, "Is there a more expressive gesture in the human repertoire?" and the article answers this question. Within this overall pattern of question-and-answer, we see paragraphs organized to present comparisons and contrast (see paragraph 2, "When . . ., but when . . ."), examples (paragraph 3), and time order (paragraph 4). And in a paragraph organized with time order, we see sentences that display analysis.

> **EXERCISE 1.5**
>
> Choose from among the nine patterns of organization in Table 1–2 to identify the patterns in the following passages:
>
> - Pages 347–49, paragraphs 2–9, John J. Conley, "Narcissus Cloned"
> - Pages 383–84, paragraphs 19–23, Sherry Turkle, "Loving Technology"
> - Pages 456–57, paragraph 5, Robert L. Barret and Bryan E. Robinson, "Children of Gay Fathers"
>
> Remember that in some instances patterns of development will overlap.

## Stylistic Features

In addition to identifying genre and organizational patterns, critical readers pay attention to stylistic features of texts. They examine sentence structure and vocabulary. They observe that scholarly writers often draw extensively on evidence from published sources or original research that they carefully document. They expect academic texts to be written in a formal voice, in sentences with a number of coordinated and parallel elements. They notice when academic texts adopt a more conversational tone and informal style and deviate from accepted conventions.

As you become familiar with a range of academic texts, you will anticipate certain textual features. For example, when you read texts dealing with technological innovation, the subject of the first three chapters in our anthology, you will take note of specialized terminology. You will do this because you recognize that technical vocabulary changes constantly, so that mastering the current buzzwords is crucial. Like other critical readers of technical literature, you will seek out experimental verification of any new, startling conclusions or look for references to other work in the field.

> Style: sentence structure, choice of diction and specialized terminology, formal or informal voice, coordinated and parallel elements.

To give you a clearer understanding of stylistic features, we will examine two texts. Read the following passages by Barbara Ehrenreich and Pauline Irit Erera before you read our comparison of the two texts. In the first passage, drawn from "Serving in Florida" (p. 515), Ehrenreich is describing Jerry's, a restaurant where she has taken a job as a server.

*Ehrenreich (paragraph 11):*    Picture a fat person's hell, and I don't mean a place with no food. In there is everything you might eat if eating had no bodily consequences—the cheese fries, the chicken-fried steaks, the fudge-laden desserts—only here every bite must be paid for, one way or another, in human discomfort. The kitchen is a cavern, a stomach leading to the lower intestine that is the garbage and dishwashing area, from which issue bizarre smells combining the edible and the offal: creamy carrion, pizza barf, and that unique and enigmatic Jerry's scent, citrus fart. The floor is slick with spills, forcing us to walk through the kitchen with tiny steps, like Susan McDougal in leg irons. Sinks everywhere are clogged with scraps of lettuce, decomposing lemon wedges, water-logged toast crusts. Put your hand down on any counter and you risk being stuck to it by the film of ancient syrup spills, and this is unfortunate because hands are utensils here, used for scooping up lettuce onto the salad plates, lifting out pie slices, and even moving hash browns from one plate to another.

In the second passage, drawn from "What Is a Family?" (p. 463), Erera distinguishes among institutional, ideological, and actual-practice definitions of "family":

***Erera (paragraph 4):***    The family is not simply a social institution. It is an ideological construct laden with symbolism and with a history and politics of its own. As Jagger and Wright (1999) put it, "The groupings that are called families are socially constructed rather than naturally or biologically given" (p. 3). In studying families, we need to keep clear the distinctions between the institutionalized family, the ideology of the family, and the lives of actual families. Although social and economic forces shape family life, our understanding of family is shaped by the evolving patterns of the actual families around us. Furthermore, conceptions of what constitutes a family are necessarily rooted in time and place. White, Western, two-parent families have generally been regarded, explicitly or implicitly, as the model or template against which we compare all families, regardless of culture, ethnicity, race, or class. This parochial view distorts our understanding of diverse families by considering them deviations from the norm (Smith, 1995; Thorne, 1982).

## Comparison of the Stylistic Features of the Texts

| *Ehrenreich* | |
| --- | --- |
| **Point of view** | Addresses readers directly prompting them to action: "Picture a fat person's hell. . ."; "Put your hand down on any counter . . ."; and uses informal second-person, "you," as well as first-person, "I" point of view. |
| **Voice** | Uses active voice and assertive is/are verbs that register the writer's personal observation: "This is unfortunate"; "The kitchen *is* a cavern"; "The floor is slick." |
| **Language and tone** | Uses informal language, including contractions—"don't"—and colorful colloquial language: "pizza barf," "citrus fart"—and creates an informal tone. Also uses figurative language: compares the kitchen to a stomach and the garbage and dishwashing areas to the lower intestine; makes a humorous simile comparing the servers, walking in small steps, to "Susan McDougal in leg irons." Susan McDougal, a former business partner of President Clinton, was convicted of fraud and of refusing to testify against the president. Newspaper photos pictured her being led off to jail, shackled in ankle chains and handcuffs. |
| **Sentence structure** | Uses complex sentence structure, but lengthy phrases and clauses seem clear to readers because their movement is sequential. |
| **Textual sources** | Does not include parenthetical citations, a list of references, or endnotes. |

| *Erera* | |
| --- | --- |
| **Point of view** | Uses more formal third-person point of view. |
| **Voice** | Employs passive voice: "our understanding of family is shaped"; "two-parent families have generally been regarded." |
| **Language and tone** | Uses formal language and tone: "we need to keep clear the distinctions"; "regarded, explicitly or implicitly, as the model or template." |
| **Sentence structure** | Uses complex sentence structure, and lengthy phrases and clauses require readers to connect their parts to larger wholes in order to understand their meaning. |
| **Textual sources** | Includes parenthetical citations in the text and a list of references at the end of the article. The parenthetical citations indicate where Erera found the information she has quoted, summarized, or paraphrased; for example: (Smith, 1995; Thorne, 1982). |

Our analysis is based on point of view, voice, language, tone, choice of sentence structures, and reliance on other textual sources. **Point of view** establishes *whether a text is written in the first-person (I, we), second-person (you), or third-person (it, they) form* and **voice** refers to *whether the verb is cast in an active mode (e.g., "I made a mistake") or a passive mode (e.g., "A mistake was made")*. Both are important stylistic features of academic writing. Use of the first-person form is frowned upon in many fields of academic writing. If writers use it at all, they use it sparingly. First-person is appropriate for Ehrenreich, however, because she is writing about her own experiences doing investigative fieldwork. Ehrenreich's use of the first person "I" and her direct references to the reader, "you," lend force and vigor to her prose and enable her to write in a strong active voice. Erera on the other hand uses the third-person point of view and the passive voice, exemplifying a typical fashion of academic writing. For example, "Although social and economic forces shape family life, our understanding of family is shaped by the evolving patterns of the actual families around us."

As our analysis shows, Ehrenreich's word choice and tone are less scholarly and more down-to-earth than Erera's. Ehrenreich uses witty, everyday language; humor; and vivid detail. Erera's vocabulary is straightforward. She doesn't use specialized terminology or jargon, but her language is much more formal than Ehrenreich's. Both writers use complex sentences, some of which are packed with a good deal of information.

The stylistic feature that clearly distinguishes Erera's style from Ehrenreich's and marks Erera as a classic academic writer is her citing of textual sources. Ehrenreich draws on published sources elsewhere in *Nickel and Dimed*, the book from which we excerpted the passage, but not to the extent we see in the Erera text. The practice of relating one's own text to other published texts by citing, quoting, paraphrasing, and summarizing them is called **intertextuality**. We will discuss this hallmark of academic writing below.

Our analysis of the two passages leads us to conclude that Erera writes in a formal style characteristic of many genres of academic writing. She uses a certain amount of passive voice, scholarly tone, and references to prior publications. In contrast, Ehrenreich has a relaxed, conversational style that we associate with informal writing. We have provided a detailed analysis of the two passages in order to show you the roles stylistic features play in writing. We don't expect you to perform an exhaustive stylistic analysis each time you read a text. However, knowledge of stylistic features such as point of view, voice, language, tone, choice of sentence structures, and reliance on other textual sources will better enable you to read critically and appreciate how the writer's style contributes to the text. On the occasions when you wish to delve deeper to analyze style, ask yourself the questions in the box below.

In your own writing, you will learn to master styles that are appropriate to particular fields. The lab reports you write for science courses will be formal, with concise sentences

---

### QUESTIONS FOR ANALYZING THE STYLISTIC FEATURES OF TEXTS

- Is the text written in first person (I, we), second person (you), or third person (it, they)? What does the point of view contribute to the style?
- Are the verbs in active voice or passive voice?
- Does the text contain straightforward language or is the vocabulary specialized?
- What can I say about sentence length and complexity? Are the sentences simple and unpretentious or complex, remote, and scholarly?
- How do the point of view, language, and sentence structure contribute to the tone?

> • How extensive are the references to other texts? Are there parenthetical citations, lists of references, footnotes, or endnotes?
>
> • What do my answers to the preceding questions indicate about the stylistic features of the text?

describing procedural matters. The personal essays you compose for English courses will be less formal, with free-flowing sentences rich in descriptive detail. The stylistic feature that will be most important to master is the practice of drawing on other texts.

*Intertextuality*    **Intertextuality** is *a conversation that a text records with other texts*. It refers to the way writers relate the findings of other texts to their own texts, often by incorporating them in the form of direct quotations, paraphrases, summaries, or other types of references such as footnotes or endnotes, and always citing the source of the information. Footnotes and parenthetical references provide classic examples of intertextuality. Look back to the passage by Pauline Erera on page 25. Erera quotes from G. Jager and C. Wright's book, *Changing Family Values*, and she summarizes information from two scholarly articles, one by T. E. Smith and the other by B. Thorne. She fully identifies these sources in the list of references at the end of her article.

The convention of drawing on other texts is not confined to academic writing. Newspapers and magazines contain articles that incorporate information from other texts. But frequently the journalistic style of writing does not involve parenthetical citation, lists of references, footnotes, or endnotes. On page 23, we provided excerpts from Joshua Foer's *The New York Times* article "The Kiss of Life." Consider an additional paragraph from the article:

> Even though all of this might suggest that kissing is in our genes, not all human cultures do it. Charles Darwin was one of the first to point this out. In his book "The Expression of the Emotions in Man and Animals," he noted that kissing "is replaced in various parts of the world by the rubbing of noses." Early explorers of the Arctic dubbed this the Eskimo kiss. (Actually, it turns out the Inuit were not merely rubbing noses, they were smelling each other's cheeks.)

Foer quotes from Charles Darwin's book, *The Expression of the Emotions in Man and Animals*, but nowhere does he provide citations to pages or give bibliographical information about publisher and date of publication. The convention of meticulously citing and documenting sources is not always followed outside of the academic community. Sometimes magazine writers even cite facts without explaining where they came from, and depending on their editorial policies, some newspapers publish stories based on statements of unnamed sources. In Chapter 9 and in the Appendix, we explain how you, as an academic writer, should follow the conventions for citing sources.

## EXERCISE 1.6

For this exercise, use the Questions for Analyzing the Stylistic Features of Texts (pages 26–27) to analyze the stylistic features of passages from three reading selections:

• Raymond Kurzweil, "Live Forever," paragraphs 44–45, page 390.

• Lori Andrews and Dorothy Nelkin, "The Business of Bodies," paragraphs 11–12, page 362.

• Ronald Takaki, "A Different Mirror," paragraph 9, page 601.

## Reading for Rhetorical Context

Critical readers have a keen interest in the rhetorical context of the text. When we speak of *rhetoric*, we mean the author's use of language for an intended effect. An important word here is *intended*. Both writing and reading are intentional. They are deliberate actions, guided by a purpose.

> Rhetorical context: author's purpose, author's intended audience, circumstances of production, author's position toward other texts, the larger conversation.

When you do a close reading of the text focusing on its content, genre, organization, and stylistic features, you perform a **textual analysis**. Another type of analysis is also important: **rhetorical analysis**. Rhetorical analysis examines *the author's purpose and motivation for writing the text, the intended audience, the circumstances surrounding the text's production, the author's position toward other writers and other texts, and the larger conversation of which the text is a part.* It also explores *how the author's choice of genre, organizational structure, and stylistic features advance his or her purpose.* To perform a rhetorical analysis, ask yourself the questions in the box below.

---

### QUESTIONS FOR ANALYZING THE RHETORICAL CONTEXT OF TEXTS

- What is the author's purpose? What do I perceive as the effect the author intends to have on the audience? What role does the author assume in relation to the audience?
- What do I know about the author's background and credibility?
- How does the choice of genre, organizational structure, and stylistic features advance the author's purpose?
- For whom is the author writing? In what type of publication—scholarly journal, popular magazine, local or national newspaper—was the text first published? Who reads this publication?
- In what year was the text published? What was on people's minds? Is the text current or dated?
- What feeling, event, phenomenon, circumstance, or social practice prompted the author to write the text?
- How is the author drawing on other writers and other texts? How does he or she view what others have said about the topic?

---

You can answer some of these questions by drawing inferences from the text itself. Other questions require you to undertake research.

Equally important as the environment in which the author writes the text is the environment in which the reader receives it. You also need to consider the rhetorical context of the **act of reading**—*the reader's purpose and the circumstances surrounding the reading.* In this section, we explain how to analyze both contexts as a means of improving comprehension.

## *Rhetorical Context of the Text*

We have depicted the rhetorical context of the text in the diagram in Figure 1–1.

Our diagram is based on the classic communication triangle. There are three points of the triangle: the writer, the reader, and the circumstances surrounding the text's production. Each point influences the other, and all directly inform how the reader responds to the text. To illustrate the process of analyzing the rhetorical context of a text, we will use Wade F. Horn's "Promoting Marriage as a Means for Promoting Fatherhood," pages 479–85, as an example. Study the diagram, read Horn's article, and then read the sections devoted to the various questions.

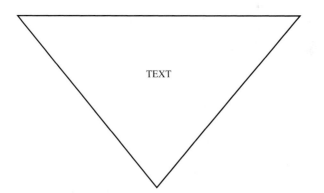

### RHETORICAL CONTEXT OF A TEXT

**AUTHOR/WRITER**

- What is the author's purpose?
- What do I perceive as the effect the author intends to have on the audience?
- What do I know about the author's background and credibility?
- How does the author's choice of genre, organizational structure, and stylistic features advance his or her purpose?

**AUDIENCE/READER**

- For whom is the author writing?
- Where was the text first published?
- Who reads this publication?

TEXT

**CIRCUMSTANCES SURROUNDING TEXT'S PRODUCTION/ LARGER CONVERSATION OF WHICH THE TEXT IS A PART**

- In what year was the text published? What was on people's minds?
- What prompted the author to write the text? Can I identify a circumstance, event, or social practice?
- How is the author drawing on other writers and other texts? How does he or she view what others have said about the topic?

**Figure 1–1**

- *What is the author's purpose? What do I perceive as the effect the author intends to have on the audience? What role does the author assume in relation to the audience?* From Horn's title, "Promoting Marriage as a Means for Promoting Fatherhood," we can infer that the author sees a need for promoting fatherhood. He hopes to convince his readers that marriage is the best means of strengthening the father–child relationship. The writer's purpose may not be obvious, but if you ask the right questions, you will discover the imperative—the feeling, view, incident, or phenomenon—that inspired the author to write. You'll be entering the author's conversation in a meaningful way.

- *What do I know about the author's background and credibility?* Horn's biography suggests that he has a professional commitment to preserving families and fatherhood. He has served as Assistant Secretary for Children and Families for the U.S. Department of Health and Human Services during the Bush II administration; he is cofounder and former president of the National Fatherhood Initiative; and he has served as Commissioner for Children, Youth, and Families. It seems reasonable to infer that his goal as a writer is to promote the preservation of traditional mother–father families. This does not mean that Horn is distorting the truth in any way. But if we were to contrast Horn's article with one that is less enthusiastic about maintaining nuclear families, it would be useful to take into consideration each writer's rhetorical goals.

- *How does the choice of genre, organizational structure, and stylistic features advance the author's purpose?* In order to answer this question, you need to step back to ask how the author uses various rhetorical strategies to achieve a particular effect. As we discovered earlier, Horn wants to convince his readers that marriage is the best means of preserving fatherhood. He grabs their attention and makes them aware of the seriousness of the problem by opening the article with alarming statistics about the number of children living in "father-absent homes" and the deleterious effects of this social trend. Then, he develops his argument by acknowledging that others, his readers included, have proposed three ways of dealing with the problem: child-support enforcement, enhanced visitation rights for absent fathers, and cohabitation outside of wedlock. He builds his case by systematically refuting each proposal, enumerating reasons why it is a less satisfactory solution to the problem than his proposition of using marriage to strengthen father–child relationships.

    A closer look at the stylistic features of the article reveals that Horn uses straightforward language that will appeal to a general audience. And he draws extensively from the empirical literature to demonstrate his command of the material.

- *For whom is the author writing? In what type of publication—scholarly journal, popular magazine, local or national newspaper—was the text first published? Who reads this publication?* The Horn selection originally appeared in *Revitalizing the Institution of Marriage for the Twenty-First Century*, a collection of essays edited by Alan H. Hawkins and published by Greenwood Press, a publisher that specializes in reference books for academic audiences. From the title of Horn's book, we can infer that the writers of the essays advocate the strengthening of marriage.

    Proficient writers tailor their texts to their readers. If you can identify the audience, you're well on your way to determining what the author is trying to accomplish. An important factor is where the text was published. Academic writers address the university community whereas staff writers for magazines such as *Newsweek* or *Time* write for general audiences. Writers may address readers of a particular political persuasion. For example, writers for *The National Review* anticipate a readership that is conservative whereas writers for *The Nation* expect their readers to be liberal.

■ *In what year was the text published? What was on people's minds? Is the text current or dated?* The collection of essays, *Revitalizing the Institution of Marriage for the Twenty-First Century*, was published in 2002. Marriage has been a hot topic in the United States, especially since 1996, when President Clinton signed into law the Federal Defense of Marriage Act, which defines marriage as the union between a man and a woman and does not recognize legal marriages between same-sex partners. President George W. Bush proposed a number of initiatives to strengthen marriage, including a Federal Marriage Amendment to the Constitution.

■ *What feeling, event, phenomenon, circumstance, or social practice prompted the author to write the text?* The first sentence of the essay identifies the social practice that impelled Horn to write:

> The most disturbing and consequential social trend of our time is the dramatic increase over the past four decades in the number of children living in father-absent households.

At the end of his introduction, he says, "The question is no longer whether father-lessness matters. The new question is what can be done about it?" Horn's intentions are clear. He wants to persuade his readers that the solution to the problem of father-absent households is marriage.

■ *How is the author drawing on other writers and other texts? How does he or she view what others have said about the topic?* Many academic texts are multivocal because they represent the voices of many different writers. As we noted earlier, academic writers often draw on the words and utterances of other writers. Sometimes the author simply mentions another writer or text. Other times, the text is quoted, paraphrased, or summarized. Writers draw on other texts to acknowledge what other individuals have written about the topic, to provide the reader with background information, to support their position, and to develop their argument.

We can categorize the ways authors use sources to build arguments according to the following scheme. A writer constructs a one-dimensional argument by presenting a thesis and supporting it with texts that argue a similar viewpoint. A writer creates a two-dimensional argument by drawing on sources for direct support and also for counterarguments. Such a two-dimensional argument anticipates and deals with views that are contrary to those of the writer. Horn relies heavily on secondary sources. His eight-page article contains thirty-eight footnotes. His argument is two-dimensional. As he makes his case that marriage is the best means for dealing with the crisis of fatherlessness, he draws on other texts to present and refute other proposals; for example, child-support enforcement, enhanced visitation rights for fathers, and cohabitation.

## EXERCISE 1.7

As a homework assignment, your professor will assign one of the selections in the anthology section of this book. In class, form collaborative learning groups and assign one of the Questions for Analyzing the Rhetorical Context of Texts, p. 28, to each group.

Reconvene the entire class. On the chalkboard, construct a triangle similar to the diagram we presented on page 29. As each group representative reads the group's answers to the rhetorical reading question, have someone record the answers on the diagram. After all have been heard from, the entire class can discuss any points on which students disagree.

## Rhetorical Context of Your Own Reading

As a critical reader, you should be just as aware of the circumstances surrounding your own reading and writing process as you are of the circumstances surrounding the production of text(s) you are reading. Take the book you are reading right now. We wrote Part I with you in mind. We address the text directly to students in a college writing class. We selected the readings in Part II with you in mind, but the authors of these selections wrote them for other audiences in response to other rhetorical situations. All were originally published elsewhere. For example, in "Narcissus Cloned" (pp. 347–49) John J. Conley addresses readers of the magazine *America*. This publication describes itself as an "online weekly Catholic magazine of news, opinion, book reviews and articles for the thinking Catholic and those who want to know what the Catholic people are thinking" (http://www.americamagazine.org/). Herbert J. Gans addresses readers of *Dissent* in "The War Against the Poor Instead of Programs to End Poverty." *Dissent* is a quarterly magazine of politics and culture. It is important to acknowledge that the audience a writer has in mind is not the only audience that ends up reading the text.

When you read texts, enunciate clear-cut rhetorical goals. In college writing courses, you will be expected to write about reading sources. If your assignment is to summarize the text, read with the goal of extracting and rewording main ideas. If your assignment is to write a critical analysis of a text, read to examine its various elements and judge them according to a set of established criteria.

Assignments:
- detailed and directive
- loosely structured and open-ended

## *Analyze Writing Assignments*

The first step is to be sure you understand the writing assignment. In college, you will receive writing assignments that include detailed direction and explicit criteria and writing assignments that are more loosely structured and open-ended. Read the assignment two or three times, underline key words that are crucial to your aim and purpose, and ask yourself the questions in the box below.

These questions will help you develop a mind-set for the assignment and define a rhetorical purpose that will direct your work. If you are unable to answer them, ask your professor for additional information.

---

### QUESTIONS FOR ANALYZING WRITING ASSIGNMENTS

- What is the topic or issue I will be writing about? Has the professor specified the topic and supplied all the readings? Do I have to select the readings and define and limit the topic myself?
- What task do I have to perform? What words serve as clues to the nature of this task? The list that follows includes typical directives for assignments. As you read each directive, speculate about what you would have to do.

**Directives for Academic Assignments**

abstract, agree (or disagree), analyze, appraise, argue, assess, classify, compare/contrast, convince, criticize, critique, defend, define, delineate, demonstrate, describe, differentiate, discuss, distinguish, establish cause-effect, estimate, evaluate, exemplify, explain, explore, expound on, furnish evidence, give examples, identify, illustrate, judge, list, make a case for or against, paraphrase, picture, predict, present, prove, recount, refute, relate, report, respond to, restate, review, show, solve, state, suggest, summarize, support, survey, trace

- Does the assignment require me to adopt a particular perspective on the issue, a recognizable genre, or a particular plan of development?
- Do I already hold a position on the issue that I intend to develop or defend?
- For whom am I writing—for the professor, classmates, or some other audience? What are the audience's expectations? How much knowledge does my audience have about the topic? Is the audience familiar with the reading source? Will I have to supply background information?
- What reading sources will I use? Will the professor allow me to include personal reactions, experiences, and subjective interpretations? Does the professor expect me to demonstrate knowledge I have acquired from lectures, discussions, or experiments as well as from readings? Am I limited in the number and kind of reference materials I can use?
- How shall I document and list my sources? Which style sheet shall I use?
- What is the approximate length of the paper?
- Does the professor expect me to submit preliminary drafts as well as the final copy?

---

### EXERCISE 1.8

Examine the assignments presented below by writing out answers to the Questions for Examining Writing Assignments. Make note of the questions you are unable to answer. When you have finished, exchange your work with a peer and discuss any of your answers that differ.

*Assignments*

- When you were growing up, were you ever involved in class wars? When did you first become conscious of social class, social stratification, and economic inequality? Write a narrative essay recounting your experiences.

- Write a critical analysis of Benazir Bhutto's argument about the difference between reactionary Islam and progressive Islam with particular attention to her interpretation of Islamic teaching about women's equality with men and their mutual capacity for public action and political leadership. Address your essay to a student who might have a different assessment of Islamic teaching.
- Drawing on Isabel Allende's "The Proper Respect" and Bharati Mukherjee's "Jasmine," write a five- to six-page essay in which you evaluate the two authors' narrative representations of outsiders' efforts to succeed as insiders in multicultural societies. Address your essay to members of the academic community at large as a critical review in your college newspaper.

## ENDNOTES

1. Twain, Mark. *Tom Sawyer.* Retrieved 6 June 2006 from http://www.pagebypagebooks.com/Mark_Twain/Tom_Sawyer/CHAPTER_1_p1.html.
2. Frost, Robert. "The Road Not Taken." In *Complete Poems.* New York: Henry Holt, 1949.
3. Chocolate. Retrieved 18 March 2006 from http://www.chocolate.org.
4. Shakespeare, William. *Hamlet.* Retrieved 6 June 2006 from http://net.gurus.com/netscape101/hamlet.htm.
5. Browning, Dominique. "House Thinking." *The New York Times Book Review,* 26 March 2006.
6. Maltby, John, Liza Day, Lynn E. McCutcheon, James Houran, and Diane Ashe. "Extreme Celebrity Worship, Fantasy Proneness and Dissociation: Developing the Measurement and Understanding of Celebrity Worship within a Clinical Personality Context." *Personality and Individual Differences* 40.2 (2006): 273–283.

**WORKS CITED**

Miller, Carolyn, "Genre as Social Action." *Quarterly Journal of Speech* 70 (1984): 151–67.

Whitley, Bernard E., Jr., and Patricia Keith-Spiegel. *Academic Dishonesty, An Educator's Guide.* Mahwah, NJ: Erlbaum, 2002.

*Two*

# Active Critical Reading:
*Postreading*

In Chapter 1, you learned the importance of *prereading*—previewing the text, freewriting, and setting your goals—and *close reading*—marking, annotating, elaborating on, and posing questions about (1) content; (2) genre, organization, and stylistic features; and (3) rhetorical context. After your close reading of the text, you enter a phase we call *postreading*.

## ■■ PERSONALLY EXPERIENCE THE TEXT

**Postreading** is *the period in which you revisit, reread, and reexamine the text*. It is also the time for transforming yourself from a reader to a writer. We recommend that before you make this transition, you take time to reflect on the text you have just comprehended. Focus on your experience of reading the text for your own enjoyment. Express your personal thoughts about it, and connect it to your real-life experiences. This mode of response will make you more aware of what you bring to the text as a reader. Your personal experiences may cause you to react in certain ways, and they may draw you to certain compelling words, phrases, and sentences that record your conversation with the text.

### ■ Write an Informal Response

Open your writer's notebook and draft a page or two, writing freely in response to self-directed prompts or respond to the questions in the box below. The purpose of this exercise is to write from a personal point of view. Bring emotion, personal association, and narrative to bear on the text, and react from your own interpretive framework.

---

**PROMPTS FOR PERSONAL RESPONSE TO THE TEXT**

- How do the ideas in the text connect with my own life? What associations can I make?
- What experiences do I recall?
- What images does the text create in my mind?
- Am I drawn to particular words, phrases, or sentences?
- Is there anything in the text that I agree with, reject, or wonder about?
- Does the text contain ideas that lead me to speculate, reflect, or make predictions?
- What else in the text do I relate to?

---

## EXERCISE 2.1

Read the article by Ronna Vanderslice, "When I Was Young, an A Was an A: Grade Inflation in Higher Education," on pages 36–37. The author is a professor of education at Southwestern Oklahoma State University, and her article was published in 2004 in *Phi Kappa Phi Forum*. This publication is the quarterly magazine of Phi Kappa Phi, an honor society for faculty and students in colleges and universities.

After you've read the article, analyze it by using the critical reading strategies you learned in Chapter 1. Ask and answer questions about its content (p. 14); genre, organization, and stylistic features (p. 21, pp. 26–27); and rhetorical context (p. 28).

### *RONNA VANDERSLICE*

### WHEN I WAS YOUNG, AN A WAS AN A: GRADE INFLATION IN HIGHER EDUCATION[1]

People often criticize elementary and secondary schools for their low standards and elevated grades. Political candidates use higher standards in education as a platform for their campaigns; yet institutions of higher education cannot deny the statistics: only 10 to 20 percent of all college students receive grades lower than a B−. This figure means that between 80 and 90 percent of all college students receive grades of either A or B (Farley, cited in Sonner). In 1969, 7 percent of all students received grades of A− or higher. By 1993, this proportion had risen to 26 percent. In contrast, grades of C or less moved from 25 percent in 1969 to 9 percent in 1993. The pattern, which continues today, reveals an issue that concerns academicians and the general public alike.

One may wonder why this is a problem. For one, employers seem very concerned that good grades on transcripts have very little meaning. It is extremely difficult to differentiate between competent students and incompetent ones by viewing a transcript from most

---

[1] Ronna Vanderslice, "When I Was Young, an A Was an A: Grade Inflation in Higher Education." Reprinted from *Phi Kappa Phi Forum*, Vol. 84, no. 4 (Fall, 2004). Copyright by Ronna Vanderslice, By permission of the publisher.

institutions of higher education today. Also, students may be left with an incorrect picture of their own competence. Most importantly, how grades relate to student learning and understanding is not clear. Variety in grading practices across disciplines and between institutions further complicates the question of what exactly an A means.

Universities must initiate reforms that increase standards instead of decreasing them. Even though some educators clearly see the wrong in grade inflation, for others it has become such a routine that universities must be explicit in their plan of remedy for this situation. A head–on approach that has been used lately is to include on student transcripts not only the grade for the class, but also the average grade for all students enrolled in the class. Indiana University, Eastern Kentucky University, and Dartmouth College are institutions that have used some type of indexing system. Harvey Mansfield, a longtime critic of grade inflation, uses a similar approach within his own classroom at Harvard University, giving each student two grades: one for the registrar and the public record, and the other in private. The private grades give students a realistic, useful assessment of how well they did and where they stand in relation to others.

Indiana University also proposed a three-year moratorium on the use of student evaluations in personnel decisions as a method to curb the problem of too many high grades. The university believes that removing concerns over student complaints about receiving lower grades might motivate all instructors to reset their standards, free from the pressures to give A's in exchange for high evaluations (McSpirit). Felton recommends that universities rethink the validity of student-opinion surveys as a measure of teaching effectiveness.

Other institutional practices include requiring schools and departments to review grading practices with the goal of bringing rigor to their programs. An emphasis in student recruitment on what is expected of students in terms of academic preparation also may be worthwhile (Wilson). In addition, faculty should take an active approach in insisting that academic standards are an essential part of the academic ethic and that by rewarding mediocrity, we discourage excellence (Wilson). Simply recognizing that grade inflation devalues your content to students is a necessary step in the right direction. Wilson points out that grade inflation reveals a loss of faculty morale. It signifies that professors care less about their teaching. Anyone who cares a lot about something is very critical in making judgments about it. Far from the opposite of caring, being critical is the very consequence of caring.

# REFERENCES

Felton, J. et al. "Web-based Student Evaluations of Professors: The Relations between Perceived Quality, Easiness, and Sexiness." *Assessment and Evaluation in Higher Education*, 29.1 (2004): 91–109.

Mansfield, H. C. "Grade Inflation: It's Time to Face the Facts." *Chronicle of Higher Education*, 47.30 (2001): B24.

McSpirit, S. "Faculty Opinion on Grade Inflation: College and University." *The Journal of the American Association of Collegiate Registrars*, 75.3 (2000): 19–26.

Sonner, B. A. "A Is for 'Adjunct': Examining Grade Inflation in Higher Education." *Journal of Education for Business*, 76.1 (2000): 5–9.

Wilson, B. P. "The Phenomenon of Grade Inflation in Higher Education." *National Forum*, 79.4 (1999): 38–41.

**EXERCISE 2.2**

When you have completed your close reading of the text, use the prompts we have provided to write a personal response of at least 100 words.

After you have written your response, break into groups of three. Each student will read his or her response to the rest of the group. Then, as a group, read the sample student response below. Compare it to the responses you shared in your groups.

### STUDENT'S PERSONAL RESPONSE

*I question whether grade inflation is as widespread as Vanderslice claims. My writing teacher told the class not to expect high grades because the average grade for all sixty sections of the composition courses is between a B− and a C+. At my college 80 and 90 percent of students aren't getting As and Bs.*

*The solutions aren't very appealing to students. I'm already hyper about grades. I don't need two grades instead of one. I don't care if my B− in English is below the class average of B+. I do my best. I'm not trying to be better than everyone else. I feel the same about public grades and private grades. They focus on competition. Ever since kindergarten, I've been compared to my peers. I want to reduce the emphasis on grades. If we must have them, one is enough. I think the proposal to get rid of student evaluations is self-serving on the teachers' part. If they're going to do that, they should also get rid of professors' evaluations of students.*

## ■ Convert Informal Response to Response Essay

Occasionally, professors ask students to write formal essays in response to designated texts. Your informal postreading response can serve as the basis for this type of formal response essay. Consider the following assignment:

Write a brief essay in response to one of the reserve readings on grade inflation.

The assignment does not ask you to draw exclusively on personal experience. Nor does it require you to draw exclusively on the reading source. It asks you to relate your own ideas to those in the text—and in so doing to present an *informed* outlook. Using the student response to Ronna Vanderslice's "When I Was Young, an A Was an A: Grade Inflation in Higher Education," we will show you how to write an essay that balances personal expression and textual content.

## Compose a Thesis

Your first move is to compose a thesis. A **thesis** is *the central idea you intend to develop in your essay*. In a response essay, the thesis expresses the writer's overall reaction to the text; for example, agreement and disagreement, criticism and speculation, qualifications and extensions.

Thesis: the central idea in the essay, the motor of the essay.

Reread the student response on page 38 and characterize the student's reaction to the text. In her opening sentence, the student says she thinks Vanderslice is exaggerating the problem of grade inflation. Later she questions Vanderslice's solutions for dealing with the problem. Thus, her overall response is to question and disagree with the text. This goal is central to her response essay. For the present, her preliminary or working thesis is "Vanderslice has exaggerated the problem of grade inflation and offered unsatisfactory solutions."

## Move from Writer-Based Prose to Reader-Based Prose

As you transform your informal personal response into a formal response essay, you should be aware of two important concepts: writer-based prose and reader-based prose. **Writer-based prose** is *writing for self* whereas **reader-based prose** is *writing for others*. Writer-based prose is egocentric. The ideas make sense to the writer but the writer makes minimal if any effort to communicate the ideas to someone else. You can compare writer-based prose to a set of personal notes in which the writer puts down information that is meaningful personally but may not make sense to a larger audience. In contrast, reader-based prose clearly conveys ideas to other people. The writer does not assume that the reader will understand automatically but, rather, provides information that will facilitate the reader's comprehension. It is easy to forget about the audience amid all the complications in producing the first draft of an academic essay. That's why first drafts are quite often writer-based. An important function of revising is to convert this writer-based prose to something the reader can readily understand.

> Writer-based prose: writing for yourself
> Reader-based prose: writing for others to read

To convert an informal, writer-based personal response to a formal, reader-based response essay, follow the procedure in the box below.

---

**CONVERTING AN INFORMAL PERSONAL RESPONSE TO A FORMAL RESPONSE ESSAY**

- Reread your personal response and formulate a thesis.
- Convert writer-based prose to reader-based prose by:

  identifying the text and author
  summarizing the text
  making explicit connections between your personal reactions and the target text
  changing casual language to more formal prose
  adding a title
  citing and documenting the source

---

### EXERCISE 2.3

This exercise is divided into two parts: a homework assignment and an in-class collaborative writing assignment.

*Homework assignment:* Reread Ronna Vanderslice's "When I Was Young, an A Was an A: Grade Inflation in Higher Education" on pages 36–38 and the student personal response on page 38. Use the procedure in the box above to convert the personal response to a response essay. Make two copies of your essay and bring it to the next class.

*In-class assignment:* Divide the class into groups of three. Each student should distribute the copies of his or her essay to the other students in the group and then read his or her essay to the group. When everyone has had a turn, compose a group essay by drawing on the positive features of each student's essay. Then read the sample response essay printed below. Compare your group essay to the sample and make revisions as necessary.

## SAMPLE RESPONSE ESSAY

CENTER TITLE          AUTHOR'S LAST NAME     PAGE NUMBER

1/2"
Sarver 1

1"

Julian Sarver

English 12

September 23, 2006

Perspectives on Grade Inflation

Is grade inflation so serious a problem that professors should change the way they grade their students? Ronna Vanderslice, a professor of education at Southwestern Oklahoma State University, thinks grade inflation is a major issue that colleges and universities need to address. According to Vanderslice, forty years ago very few students received high grades. Now most receive As and Bs. In "When I Was Young, an A Was an A: Grade Inflation in Higher Education," Vanderslice suggests a number of reforms that will curb grade inflation and raise standards. I question whether grade inflation is as widespread as Vanderslice claims, and I have grave reservations about the solutions she proposes.

Vanderslice writes that "grades of C or less moved from 25 percent in 1969 to 9 percent in 1993," and today they continue to spiral upward. My writing teacher told our class not to expect high grades because the average grade for all sixty sections of the composition courses is between a B– and a C+. This leads me to question Vanderslice's claim that "between 80 and 90 percent of all college students receive grades of A or B" (24). That is not happening at my college.

Even if grade inflation is getting out of hand, the solutions Vanderslice proposes are not very appealing to students. One suggestion

1"

1"

1"

USE 8½" BY 11" PAPER FOR EACH PAGE. USE DOUBLE SPACES BETWEEN ALL LINES. LEFT JUSTIFY ALL LINES IN THE TEXT OF THE PAPER. DO NOT RIGHT JUSTIFY, EVEN IF YOUR WORD PROCESSOR PROVIDES THIS FEATURE.

INDENT
FIVE SPACES                                                          AUTHOR'S LAST NAME        PAGE NUMBER

1"                                                                                    1/2"
                                                                                     Sarver 2

is "to include on student transcripts not only the grade for the class,
but also the average grade for all students enrolled in the class" (000).
I am already overly anxious about grades. I do not need two grades
instead of one. I have no desire to know that my B— in English is below
the class average of B+. I do my best. I am not trying to be better
than everyone else.

    A second suggestion is to give students public grades and private
grades. Vanderslice explains, "The private grades give students a
realistic, useful assessment of how well they did and where they stand in
relation to others" (000). Again, the focus is on competition. Ever since
1" kindergarten, I have been compared to my peers. I propose that we reduce    1"
the emphasis on grades. If we must have them, one is enough.

    A third recommendation is to abolish students' evaluation of courses
so that professors would be "free from the pressures to give A's in
exchange for high evaluations" (000). I think this proposal is self-
serving on the teachers' part. Colleges should eliminate professors'
evaluations of students as well as students' evaluations of professors.
This would lead to a healthier, less competitive atmosphere.

1"

---

1"                                                                                   1/2"
                                                                                     Sarver 3
                              Work Cited

1" Vanderslice, Ronna. "When I Was Young, an A Was an A: Grade Inflation in    1"
     Higher Education," *Phi Kappa Phi Forum* 84 (2004): 24-25.

1"

AFTER THE FIRST LINE OF              INCLUDE IN THE LIST OF WORKS CITED *ONLY* SOURCES THAT ARE        DOUBLE SPACE
EACH ENTRY, INDENT FIVE SPACES.            REFERRED TO DIRECTLY IN THE TEXT OF THE PAPER.

## EXERCISE 2.4

Compare the student personal response on page 38 and the sample response essay on
pages 40–41. On the response essay, mark and annotate the following elements:

Thesis

Identification of text and author

Summary of text

Explicit connections between the personal reactions and the target text

Places where casual language has been changed to more formal prose

Title

Citation and documentation of the text.

Share your work with a peer and discuss any differences in your markings and annotations.

## ■▀ COMPOSE PARAPHRASES AND SUMMARIES AND RECORD QUOTATIONS THAT MAY BE USEFUL AT A LATER DATE

As we mentioned earlier, in the postreading phase of the reading-writing process, you will shift perspectives and transform yourself from a critical reader to an academic writer. Whenever you intend to draw on reading sources in your future writing, take some time immediately after reading to paraphrase, summarize, or quote passages that may be particularly useful as a record of your conversation with the text. You will continue to paraphrase, summarize, and quote as you compose and revise your essay, but you are best prepared to do this while the reading is still fresh in your mind. Remember that one of the chief goals of active reading is to eliminate the need for rereading the source when you sit down to draft your essay.

> Paraphrase, summarize, and quote as a record of conversation with the text.

### ■ Paraphrasing

When you **paraphrase** a sentence, paragraph, or other segment of a text, you *translate it into your own words*. Paraphrasing is a powerful operation for academic writing. Too often, beginning academic writers use direct quotations instead of paraphrases. Quotations are necessary only when you need the precise wording of the original. We will discuss reasons for quoting later in this chapter. Because paraphrasing is an active process that forces you to grapple with the text, it promotes comprehension. It is no wonder that professors ask students to paraphrase rather than quote. They know that if students can paraphrase a text, then they understand it.

> Paraphrase: an active effort to grasp all the meaning in a passage.

A paraphrase differs from a summary. *A paraphrase includes all the information in the original, whereas a summary contains only the most important ideas.* When you want to record the fully detailed meaning of a passage, paraphrase it. If you are only interested in the gist, write a summary. In general, relatively small sections of the original—often a sentence or two—are paraphrased, and larger chunks of text are summarized.

Paraphrasing requires you to make substantial changes to the vocabulary and sentence structure of the text. It is not enough to substitute a few synonyms and keep the same sentence structure and order of ideas. The following examples, based on an excerpt from Michael Heim's "From Interface to Cyberspace" (see Works Cited, p. 68), show adequate and inadequate paraphrases.

*Original sentence:* Virtual-reality systems can use cyberspace to represent physical space, even to the point that we feel telepresent in a transmitted scene, whether Mars or the deep ocean.

*Inadequate paraphrase:* Virtual-reality systems can represent physical space by using cyberspace, even to the extent that people feel telepresent in a scene that is transmitted, perhaps Mars or the deep ocean (Heim 80).

*Adequate paraphrase:* We can achieve the illusion of being present in remote locations, for example the planet Mars or deep parts of the ocean, by using virtual-reality equipment that creates a cyberspace representation of real-world space (Heim 80).

The writer of the inadequate paraphrase reshuffled the words in the original sentence but retained the vocabulary, sentence structure, and order of ideas. If you do not intend to make major changes to the passage, then quote it word for word.

## Simplified Paraphrasing Procedures

You can sometimes paraphrase by using simple paraphrasing procedures. We will describe two of them: (1) look away from the text and restate the ideas, and (2) rewrite the original passage for a new audience.

### *Look Away from the Text and Restate the Ideas*

We will illustrate this strategy with a passage from John J. Conley's "Narcissus Cloned." Read the passage twice. Then ask yourself, "What is the main idea, and what are the details that support this idea?" Look away from the text and restate the main idea and details in your own words. Then look back at the text to check the accuracy of your paraphrase.

> *Text:* The task of developing a moral response to the advent of human cloning is rendered all the more problematic by the superficial debate our society is currently conducting on the issue. Whether on the editorial page of *The New York Times* or on Phil and Oprah's television screen, the discussion tends to obscure the key moral problems raised by this practice. (Conley 349)

The text asserts that it is difficult to formulate a moral response to the practice of human cloning because the public debate about it is so shallow. The text supports this assertion by pointing out that neither newspaper editorials nor talk shows give in-depth treatment of the topic. Looking away from the text, we come up with the following paraphrase:

> *Paraphrase:* Public debates about human cloning, especially what we read in newspaper editorials and see on talk shows, gloss over serious issues and are so shallow and superficial that it is difficult to develop a serious moral response to this new practice (Conley 349).

Next, we reread the original to check the accuracy of our paraphrase, and then we weave the paraphrase into our essay. We have summarized the procedure in the box below.

---

### SIMPLIFIED PARAPHRASING PROCEDURE

- Read the passage two or three times.
- Ask yourself, "What is the main idea, and what are the details that support that idea?"
- Look away from the text and restate the main idea and details in your own words.
- Reread the original to check the accuracy of your paraphrase.
- Weave the paraphrase into your essay.
- Provide documentation.

---

## *Rewrite the Original Passage for a New Audience*

Another simple procedure for paraphrasing is to rewrite the text for a new audience. To illustrate, look at the following sentence from "Being and Believing: Ethics of Virtual Reality," an editorial from a medical journal (see Works Cited, p. 67). The sentence describes a computer-based system (virtual reality) designed to simulate a real-world situation:

> The overall effect was that the observer experienced a computer-generated artificial or virtual reality (VR) whose credibility depended largely on the agreement between the simulated imagery and the familiar sensible world. (283)

Let's say your objective is to paraphrase the sentence for an audience of high-school students. You don't want to talk over the students' heads, so you put the sentence into simpler language:

> The effectiveness of a virtual reality system depends upon the extent to which it can create an environment of computer images that appear lifelike ("Being and Believing" 283).

Notice that the parenthetical documentation gives an abbreviated article title rather than an author's name. That is because the article was written by the medical journal's editorial staff and was not attributed to a specific author. To learn more about documentation conventions, see the Appendix.

### EXERCISE 2.5

Break into pairs. Both students in the pair will use simplified procedures to paraphrase the same passage from Clifford Stoll, "Isolated by the Internet" (p. 394). One student will look away from the text and restate the ideas and the other will rewrite the text for a new audience. When you have finished, compare your paraphrases and decide which is more accurate.

> Psychologists point out that the best predictor of psychological troubles is a lack of close social contacts. There's a surprisingly close correlation between social isolation and such problems as schizophrenia and depression. Long hours spent online undercut our local social support networks; this isolation promotes psychological troubles. (Stoll 394)

## Systematic Paraphrasing Procedure

Paraphrasing often requires you to express abstract ideas in a more concrete form. When a passage includes difficult concepts and complex language, it may be hard to reword it and still preserve the original meaning. You will need a systematic paraphrasing procedure, such as the one in the following box.

---

### SYSTEMATIC PARAPHRASING PROCEDURE

- Read the passage two or three times.
- Identify the major ideas.
- Change the order of major ideas, maintaining the logical connections among them.
- Substitute synonyms for words in the original, making sure the language in your paraphrase is appropriate for your audience.
- Combine or divide sentences as necessary.
- Compare the paraphrase with the original to make sure that the rewording is sufficient and the meaning has been preserved.
- Weave the paraphrase into your essay in accordance with your rhetorical purpose.
- Document the paraphrase.

---

Paraphrasing is not a lockstep process that always follows the same sequence. You may use fewer than all eight strategies or vary the order in which you apply them. For illustration, follow along as we paraphrase a sentence from Carl Sagan's article "In Defense of Robots" (p. 379), using all the strategies in approximately the order listed. We are addressing an audience of first-year college students.

> There is nothing inhuman about an intelligent machine; it is indeed an expression of those superb intellectual capabilities that only human beings, of all the creatures on our planet, now possess. (Sagan 379)

### Identify the Major Ideas

First, read the text two or three times to determine the major ideas.

Major ideas

There are two central points: (1) an assertion about intelligent machines: they are not inhuman, and (2) an argument to back up the assertion: that these machines demonstrate humans' unique intelligence.

1. There is nothing inhuman about an intelligent machine;
2. It is indeed an expression of those superb intellectual capabilities that only human beings, of all the creatures on our planet, now possess.

### Change the Order of Ideas, Maintaining the Logical Connections among Them

Next, change the order of the sentence, placing the second point before the first. To accommodate this switch, substitute the noun phrase *an intelligent machine* for *it* so the subject is clear at the outset of the sentence. Then add *which demonstrates that* to indicate the logical relationship between the two units.

1. An intelligent machine is indeed an expression of those superb intellectual capabilities that only human beings, of all the creatures on our planet, now possess;
2. which demonstrates that there is nothing inhuman about an intelligent machine.

Reorder and connect.

## Substitute Synonyms for Words in the Original

At this juncture, it is important to think about your audience. Sagan's language is easy to understand. If the words in the original text are too formal or sophisticated, choose vocabulary more accessible to your readers. Begin your search for synonyms *without* consulting a dictionary or a thesaurus. Many students rush to reference books and copy synonyms without considering how they fit into the general sense of the sentence. Paraphrases filled with synonyms taken indiscriminately from a dictionary or a thesaurus can be awkward and confusing.

Search for synonyms.

As a rule of thumb, try not to repeat more than three consecutive words from the original. Occasionally, you may need to repeat a phrase, but whenever possible, substitute synonyms. You don't have to substitute a synonym for every word in the text. Repeat words that are central to the meaning or have no appropriate synonyms, such as the word "inhuman" in our example.

Returning to the example, by substituting synonyms, doing a little more rearranging, and providing context where necessary, you will arrive at the following paraphrase:

Since artificial intelligence results from humans beings' unique intellectual talents, the technology should not be regarded as inhuman (Sagan 379).

## Combine or Divide Sentences as Necessary

There is no particular need to divide the paraphrase, but for illustration split it into two short sentences:

Artificial intelligence results from humans beings' unique intellectual talents. Thus, the technology should not be regarded as inhuman (Sagan 379).

Tighten or break down: Combine or divide sentences.

## Compare the Paraphrase with the Original

Compare the paraphrase with the original sentence to see if you have reworded sufficiently yet have retained the meaning of the original.

Size up the texts.

*Original:* There is nothing inhuman about an intelligent machine; it is indeed an expression of those superb intellectual capabilities that only human beings, of all the creatures on our planet, now possess.

*Paraphrase:* Since artificial intelligence results from humans beings' unique intellectual talents, the technology should not be regarded as inhuman (Sagan 379).

In this case, the paraphrase seems adequate. In other cases, you might need to revise the paraphrase, possibly by reapplying one of the strategies we have already discussed.

## Weave the Paraphrase into Your Essay

Weave the paraphrase into your essay in a way that helps further your rhetorical purpose.

Blend into your own text.

Consider the following example:

*Excerpt from essay:* Even though we live in a technologically advanced society, many Americans still feel uncomfortable with the idea of machine intelligence. Science fiction abounds with stories of computers whose "inhuman" logic poses a threat to human values. But as Sagan points out, since artificial intelligence results from humans beings' unique intellectual talents, the technology should not be regarded as inhuman (379). These thinking machines are an extension of our own abilities rather than a challenge to our humanity.

Notice that we did not plop the paraphrase into the paragraph. Instead, we tried to show the role it plays in our conversation with the original text. Since Sagan's view contrasts with the point expressed in the preceding sentence, we began with the word "but." Then, we attributed the material to Sagan by writing "as Sagan points out." At the end of the sentence, we provided the page number in parentheses. A paraphrase is successful only to the extent that it fits smoothly into the essay for which it was intended.

## Document Your Paraphrase

Failing to document a paraphrase is considered plagiarism, an offense that can have serious consequences. Always cite the author of the text, enclose the page numbers in parentheses, and provide an entry on the works cited page. Notice how we documented the paraphrase in the preceding example.

- Cite your source
- Document your citation

## EXERCISE 2.6

Apply the steps in the Systematic Paraphrasing Procedure (p. 45) to the following passage taken from Raymond Kurzweil's "Live Forever" (pages 386–91). Work through the steps in the process one by one and record the results of each step, just as we did on pages 45–47 with the sentence from Carl Sagan's article. Write your paraphrase for an audience of first-year college students who have not read the article.

> The issue of consciousness will become even more contentious in the twenty-first century because nonbiological entities—read: machines—will be able to convince most of us that they are conscious. They will master all the subtle cues that we now use to determine that humans are conscious. And they will get mad if we refute their claims. (Kurzweil 389)

Revise your paraphrase. Submit with the final paraphrase all the preliminary work you produce at each stage of the paraphrasing process.

## EXERCISE 2.7

Form collaborative learning groups of three students each. Have each group member take responsibility for one of the following passages from Pauline Erit Erera's "What Is a Family?" (pages 462–74).

a. The decline in the number of babies placed for adoption precipitated an increased interest in international adoptions as an alternative. Because these adoptions often involved children who were racially and/or ethnically different from their adoptive parents, the adoption could not be kept secret as had been the practice in the past. The growing acceptance of adoptive families, in turn, facilitated a greater acceptance of step-families and other families not related by blood. (466)

b. With the increasing numbers and visibility of single-parent, step-, and adoptive families, the gay liberation movement opened the way for the emergence of gay and lesbian families. Some gay men and lesbians were divorced and had custody of the children, becoming in the process single-parent families. Others chose to give birth to a child within the lesbian/gay relationship. (466)

c. Another factor contributing to family diversity since the 1970s, and especially to foster families and grandmother-headed families, has been a dramatic increase in the imprisonment of women and mothers, a legacy of the war on drugs with its harsh sentencing policies. Most of the women in prison are there for drug-related offenses, often because of the activities of a male partner. (466)

- Use the Systematic Paraphrasing Procedure (page 45) to paraphrase your passage. Write your paraphrase for an audience of first-year college students who have not read Erera's article.
- When all group members have finished their paraphrases, pass the sheet with your paraphrase to the person on your left and receive the paraphrase of the person on your right. On a new sheet of paper, paraphrase the passage you received from the person on your right. Do not refer to the original text.
- When all group members have finished their paraphrases, pass sheets once more to the left and again paraphrase the passage you receive.
- Your group should now have serial paraphrases that have gone through three versions for each of the passages from Erera. Working together, compare the original of each passage with the final version of the paraphrase. Does the paraphrase preserve the meaning of the original? If not, where did the meaning get lost? Which steps in the paraphrasing process

worked well, and which were problematic? Make sure your group recorder notes the conclusions the group comes to.

- When the class reconvenes, have the recorders explain the conclusions groups reached about the paraphrasing process.

## ■ Summarizing

Whether you are writing a standard summary, a brief abstract of a journal article, or a formal précis of an extended argument, your fundamental task is to capture the overall gist of the text, to shorten the original without changing its meaning.

> Summarize in broad strokes.

The following strategies will serve you well.

---

### SUMMARIZING STRATEGIES

- Preview the text and recall your prior knowledge of the topic.
- Read the text using critical reading strategies (marking, annotating, elaborating, taking content notes, and posing and answering questions).
- Identify the most important ideas and the significant connections among those ideas.
- Delete unimportant detail, irrelevant examples, and redundancy.
- Identify and imitate the organizational pattern of the text.
- Construct a graphic overview.
- Identify and incorporate the rhetorical context and purpose.
- Combine ideas in sentences and paragraphs.
- Document your summary.

You need not apply these strategies in order. Nor do you have to use all nine of them. Choose ones that are appropriate for the source with which you are working. You can write a standard summary simply by explaining the rhetorical context and purpose. Lengthy, complex summaries may require the full range of strategies.

---

## Standard Summary

You can construct a standard summary by using strategies that you will find useful for all summaries.

### Apply Summarizing Strategies

Strategies for summarizing include:

**Preview the Text, Recall Your Prior Knowledge of the Topic, and Use Critical Reading Strategies**    The first two summarizing strategies recap the active reading techniques that we covered earlier in this chapter. Assertive reading is imperative for summarizing. Marking and annotating main ideas, taking notes, and identifying the organization plan and rhetorical purpose and context are helpful preparation.

> Preview.

***Identify the Most Important Ideas and the Significant Connections among These Ideas***
Your annotations and notes should direct you to the most important ideas in the text. Write out the main ideas and explain how they are related to each other. A summary is more than a retelling of main ideas; it should indicate relationships among the ideas and tie them together in coherent paragraphs.

> Identify main ideas.

***Delete Unimportant Detail, Irrelevant Examples, and Redundancy***    Cross out or label as nonessential any material that is repetitive, excessively detailed, or unrelated to the main idea. Academic sources are often highly redundant because authors repeat or illustrate complex concepts in order to give the reader more than one chance to understand them.

> Eliminate details.

***Identify and Imitate the Organizational Pattern of the Source***    On page 22, we identified nine organizational plans for academic writing: (1) time order, narration, process; (2) antecedent-consequent, cause-effect; (3) description; (4) statement-response; (5) comparison/contrast; (6) example; (7) analysis/classification; (8) definition; (9) analogy. Rarely do authors restrict themselves to a single plan; they usually use these plans in combination. When you identify the organizational pattern, you can follow it as the skeleton for your summary. Organization conveys meaning, so you will be helping your reader to follow the train of thought.

> Determine organizational pattern.

### Construct a Graphic Overview

A useful technique for identifying the principal ideas and determining how they tie together is to create a visual display. You may choose from among many different types of displays, including flow charts, spider maps, Venn diagrams, cluster diagrams, fishbone diagrams, sequence charts, column charts, and ladders. We will focus on the graphic overview. A **graphic overview** is *a diagram that represents the central ideas in a reading source, shows how they are related, and indicates the author's overall purpose.* It is a blueprint charting the text's main ideas.

> Visual display: graphic overview.

We will walk through the process of constructing a graphic overview. First, review your underlining, notes, and annotations, and select key words and concepts. Determine the overall organizational structure of the text and identify subsidiary organizational patterns. Then, depict the relationships among the ideas by drawing boxes or circles connected by lines or arrows. Label the boxes to show how the various points are interrelated. Be creative!

The graphic overview shown in Figure 2–1 was constructed by one of our students to represent the principal content of Ronna Vanderslice's "When I Was Young, an A Was an A: Grade Inflation in Higher Education," which appears on pages 36–38. Reread the article before you study the student's graphic overview. Keep in mind that creating a graphic overview is a highly individual process. A single, definitive graphic overview does not exist for each text. Countless variations are possible.

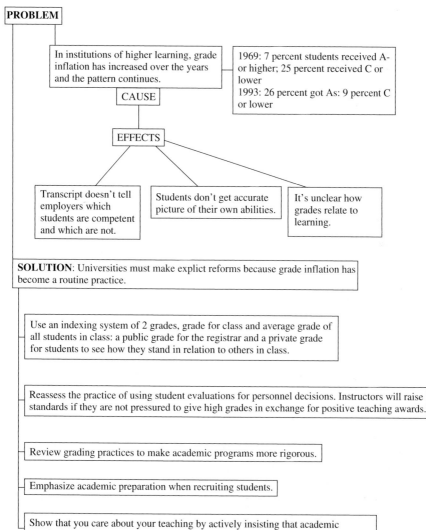

**Figure 2–1    Sample Graphic Overview**

The graphic overview forces you to think about the big picture. You have to manipulate chunks of information like pieces in a puzzle and determine how they best fit together. The graphic overview allows you to visualize relationships among main ideas and perceive the text's web of meaning. Notice that the overview of Vanderslice's article highlights the central organizational pattern of problem-solution as well as the secondary pattern of cause-effect. You should find it easy to summarize this source after you have seen its main ideas diagrammed on a single page.

You can make a graphic overview of a text of any length—a single paragraph, sequence of paragraphs, or complete article—but the strategy works best if you fit the diagram on a single page so that you can see it all at once. This limits the amount of detail in the graphic overview, but if you cram in lots of details, you will soon lose sight of the big picture. The graphic overview works best for recording the general outlines of an argument. When you are working with lengthy texts and want more than a broad outline, you may find the one-page format too restrictive.

You may wish to work with computer-generated graphic overviews. We provide directions for creating a simple graphic overview with Microsoft Word. If you are working with other word-processing software, consult the software's Help directory and search for "diagrams."

---

### DIRECTIONS FOR CREATING A GRAPHIC OVERVIEW WITH MICROSOFT WORD

1. Open a blank Word document.
2. Go up to the main menu bar and click **Insert**.
3. Select **Text Box** from the Insert menu. A box will be displayed. Select the box by clicking on it.
4. Click on the corner of the box and drag your mouse to make the box the size you want it. Then click outside the box to deselect it.
5. Click inside the box and type in words and sentences.
6. Create additional boxes by repeating steps 3, 4, and 5.
7. Move boxes around by selecting them (click on the edge). With your cursor on the edge, drag the box around the page.
8. Connect the boxes with the following procedure:

   - Go up to the Main menu and click on **View**. Scroll down to Toolbars.
   - From the Toolbar menu, select **Drawing**. The Drawing toolbar contains a button with a line on it. Click on this button to highlight it.
   - Bring your cursor to the edge of one box and drag it to the edge of a second box. A line will appear. Each time you wish to draw a line, go back to the line button and highlight it.
   - To delete boxes and lines, click on the edge of the box or on the line to highlight it. Then press **Delete**.

---

Before we show you how to convert a graphic overview to a written summary, we need to remind you about the importance of the rhetorical context of the text.

## *Identify and Incorporate the Rhetorical Context and Purpose*

Your summary needs to include information about the rhetorical context of the text. This is particularly true if it is a stand-alone summary rather than one that will become part of a longer essay.

> Rhetorical context and rhetorical purpose

To determine the rhetorical context, ask yourself the Questions for Analyzing the Rhetorical Context of Texts on page 28. Rhetorical purpose refers to how the author tries to affect or influence the audience. Sometimes the purpose is easily identified because it emerges as a controlling feature of the piece, such as in an argumentative text or a highly opinionated editorial. At other times the purpose may not be self-evident.

As the following summary of Ronna Vanderslice's "When I Was Young, an A Was an A: Grade Inflation in Higher Education" (see pages 36–38) illustrates, once you have identified the rhetorical context and purpose, you have launched a concise summary.

### SAMPLE BRIEF SUMMARY OF RONNA VANDERSLICE'S "WHEN I WAS YOUNG, AN A WAS AN A: GRADE INFLATION IN HIGHER EDUCATION"

In her article "When I Was Young, an A Was an A: Grade Inflation in Higher Education," Ronna Vanderslice, a professor of education at Southwestern Oklahoma State University, asserts that grade inflation is an increasingly serious problem that universities must counteract. She develops her position by pointing out that college transcripts no longer give accurate information to students or to their potential employers. Writing in *Phi Kappa Phi Forum*, she urges university faculty to reform their grading practices and offers various suggestions for doing so.

## *Combine Ideas in Sentences and Paragraphs*

For your summary to flow clearly, you need to take the key ideas you have depicted in your graphic overview, make elements parallel, or add logical connectors. You may also compress several words or phrases into fewer words and reduce items in the same class to a single category.

> Combine and reduce.

## *Document Your Summary*

Even when you have summarized a text in your own words, you must acknowledge the title and the author. As with paraphrasing, summarizing a source without proper documentation is considered plagiarism. Always cite the text at the point where you use it in your writing and include a complete reference in the works cited list at the end of your paper. We explain how to set up a works cited list in the Appendix.

> Document your citation
> Cite your sources

Now we will draw on several of the strategies described above to illustrate the process of writing a summary. Let's assume that you are preparing to write an essay on grade inflation. You locate the Vanderslice article on pages 36–38. You read the article using the active strategies we described earlier—carefully previewing, annotating, taking notes, and posing and answering questions as you read. After identifying the main ideas and significant connections among them, you delete unimportant details and examples. Then, using the text's organizational pattern as your cue, you construct a graphic overview. (See Figure 2–1, p. 51.) You identify the rhetorical context of Vanderslice's article. Lastly, using the graphic overview as your guide, you combine ideas in sentences and paragraphs and compose the summary.

### *SAMPLE SUMMARY*

### SUMMARY OF RONNA VANDERSLICE'S "WHEN I WAS YOUNG, AN A WAS AN A: GRADE INFLATION IN HIGHER EDUCATION"

In her article "When I Was Young, an A Was an A: Grade Inflation in Higher Education," Ronna Vanderslice, a professor of education at Southwestern Oklahoma State University, asserts that we should be concerned about increasing incidents of grade inflation in colleges and universities. As a result of this lowering of standards, college transcripts do not tell employers which students are competent and which are not. Students themselves are not getting accurate pictures of their abilities. Most important, there is no clear standard of how grades relate to learning.

Vanderslice asserts that universities must make explicit reforms to halt this routine practice. She offers a number of concrete suggestions for raising standards. One recommendation is to use an indexing system of two grades, the grade for the class and the average grade of all the students in the class: a public grade for the registrar and a private grade for students to see how they stand in relation to their peers.

Another suggestion is to reassess the practice of using student evaluations for personnel decisions. Instructors will raise their standards if they are not pressed to give high grades in exchange for positive teaching evaluations. Other recommendations are for professors to review their grading practices to make academic programs more rigorous, for college recruiters to make students aware of the academic preparation they will need, and for professors to show they care about their teaching by actively insisting that academic standards are of paramount importance and by rewarding excellence instead of mediocrity.

### WORK CITED

Vanderslice, Ronna. "When I Was Young, an A Was an A: Grade Inflation in Higher Education." *Phi Kappa Phi Forum* 84 (2004): 24–25.

### EXERCISE 2.8

Read a selection from Chapter 3 or from Part II of this book. Use the summarizing strategies we have discussed to produce a 250-word summary of the text. Write for an audience of first-year college students who have not read the article. Submit your graphic overview as well as the final summary.

## EXERCISE 2.9

First-Day Activities:

- Form collaborative learning groups of five students each.
- Assign to each group one of the reading selections from Part II of this book. Each group should work with a different text. Group members should read their articles outside class.

Second-Day Activities:

- Divide into collaborative groups.
- Working as a group and following the steps outlined in this chapter, produce a graphic overview and a 250-word summary of your article. You may want to work through each step in the process together, with the recorder noting the results of your discussion. Write for an audience of first-year college students who have not read the article.
- Reconvene the entire class. Each group recorder should read the group's summary and describe any problems the group encountered.

## The Abstract

An **abstract** is *a brief summary*, often only a paragraph or two. It usually appears after the title of a paper and before the longer text itself, though sometimes it is presented on a separate page. Abstracts often accompany lab reports, journal articles, grant proposals, and conference presentations. They can also be published as stand-alone documents. When you conduct research, you will use databases of abstracts, for example, *Periodical Abstracts, Social Science Abstracts*, or *Education Abstracts*.

> The abstract: a very brief, descriptive key tool

The purpose of an abstract is to give readers a descriptive summary of information that will help them decide if it is worth their time to read the entire article. Chapter 13 in Part II of this book contains articles on the changing American family. Let's say you have read these articles and are conducting further research on children in single-parent families. In the database *Social Science Abstracts*, you locate a reference to "Family Structure Effects on Parenting Stress and Practices in the African American Family," an article by Daphne S. Cain and Terri Combs-Orme published in June 2005 in the *Journal of Sociology and Social Welfare*:

### FAMILY STRUCTURE EFFECTS ON PARENTING STRESS AND PRACTICES IN THE AFRICAN AMERICAN FAMILY

#### CAIN, DAPHNE S.; COMBS-ORME, TERRI

Journal of Sociology and Social Welfare v. 32 no. 2 (June 2005) pp. 19–40

**Abstract**: The predominant approach to African-American parenting research focuses on disadvantages associated with single parenthood to the exclusion of other issues. The current research suggests that this does not represent the diversity in family structure configurations among African-American families, nor does it give voice to the parenting resilience of single mothers. We argue that rather than marital status or family configuration, more attention needs to be given to the inadequacy of resources for this population. In the current study, we examined the parenting of infants by African-American mothers and found that mothers' marital status and family configuration did not affect parenting stress or practices. This suggests, then, that single mothers parent as well as their married, partnered, and multigenerational counterparts. It seems that the economic status and parenting perceptions of mothers contributed more to parenting stress than did marital status or family structure. Our study, then, challenges the accepted wisdom in our political and popular culture that has insisted upon the centrality of the nuclear family to all aspects of familial and even national health. Instead, we have shown that a true commitment to strong families and healthy children begins with a focus on the debilitating effects of poverty in the African-American community.

After reading the abstract, you decide whether it will be worth your while to read the twenty-one-page article.

## Components of an Abstract

An examination of the sample abstract reveals the following components:

- Title and Author Information

    "Family Structure Effects on Parenting Stress and Practices in the African American Family"
    Cain, Daphne S.; Combs-Orme, Terri
    Journal of Sociology and Social Welfare v. 32 no. 2 (June 2005) pp. 19–40

- Objective, purpose, question, or problem—what the author is researching or demonstrating

    "We argue that rather than marital status or family configuration, more attention needs to be given to the inadequacy of resources for this population."

- Why the research is important?

    "The predominant approach to African-American parenting research focuses on disadvantages associated with single parenthood to the exclusion of other issues. The current research suggests that this does not represent the diversity in family structure configurations among African-American families, nor does it give voice to the parenting resilience of single mothers."

- Methods or design—how the topic was studied or how the study was implemented

    "In the current study, we examined the parenting of infants by African-American mothers."

- Results or outcomes—what the researcher discovered

    ". . . and found that mothers' marital status and family configuration did not affect parenting stress or practices. This suggests, then, that single mothers parent as well as their married, partnered, and multigenerational counterparts. It seems that the economic status and parenting perceptions of mothers contributed more to parenting stress than did marital status or family structure."

■ Conclusions, implications, or further questions

"Our study, then, challenges the accepted wisdom in our political and popular culture that has insisted upon the centrality of the nuclear family to all aspects of familial and even national health. Instead, we have shown that a true commitment to strong families and healthy children begins with a focus on the debilitating effects of poverty in the African-American community."

The abstract follows the sequence of the original text, and it is written in a style that is clear, concise, and direct.

## Writing an Abstract of Your Own Work

If you receive an assignment to write an abstract of a published journal article or of an essay, project, or study you have undertaken, keep in mind that your goal is to give readers a mini version of the text so that they can decide if it is worthwhile to read the entire document. Include the essential components.

---

### COMPONENTS OF AN ABSTRACT

• Title and author information
• Objective, purpose, question, or problem—what researcher has researched or demonstrated
• Why the research is important
• Methods or design—how the study was implemented. In certain fields—for example, the sciences and social sciences—you need to explain the particular research method, the setting, the population, and the instruments used.
• Results or outcomes—what was discovered
• Conclusions, implications, or further questions

---

When writing an abstract of a published article, pay special attention to the introduction and summary, for they will contain key points, and make note of the headings and subheadings.

### EXERCISE 2.10

Read the following abstract and write a paragraph explaining the extent to which the abstract contains the components listed above.

*JAMA, The Journal of the American Medical Association,* Sept 22, 1989 v262 n12 p1659(5) Adolescents and their music: insights into the health of adolescents. *Elizabeth F. Brown; William R. Hendee.*

**Abstract**: During adolescence teenagers are expected to progress toward more adult-like behavior despite the fact that these years are normally marked by rebellious and alienating expressions toward adults and authority figures. The music that adolescents choose to listen to is an important element in their lives, considering that they usually listen to over 10,000 hours of music between the seventh and twelfth grades. The sexual and violent lyrics of rock music and a considerable body of existing research on the interplay between adolescent development and music is examined. Selection of music may reflect the teenager's inner struggles and serve as a medium for socialization. Several studies indicated that students with poor academic performance were more involved in rock music than their successful peers; a researcher suggested that this immersion may reflect their alienation from school. Adolescents often incorrectly interpreted the explicit messages of current rock music; they may respond more to general themes of rebellion than to specific lyrics. Immediately after watching violent and sexual videos teenagers indicated a change in their opinions about acceptable sexual behaviors. Whether their behavior changed and whether some teens are more vulnerable than others is unknown. Physicians are advised to be familiar with the music preferences of adolescents in attending to their general mood, health and well-being.

## EXERCISE 2.11

Your college is holding an undergraduate conference and you have decided to submit a paper. Select an essay you have written for this or another college class and write an abstract of no more than one hundred words. Give your abstract to a peer and ask the student to explain what your paper is about. If your classmate is unable to describe your paper, you need to revise the abstract and resubmit it.

## The Précis

Another type of summary is called the **précis** (pronounced *pray-see*). The word *précis* is sometimes used interchangeably with *summary* but a précis is different from a summary in that it does not include the title, author, or information about the rhetorical context and rhetorical purpose of the text. It also omits references to the author, such as "Vanderslice asserts." *A précis strictly follows the order of the original text, and it is usually no longer than one-quarter of the original.*

> Précis: a neutral summary that parallels the order of the original.

Reread the summary of Ronna Vanderslice's article, "When I Was Young, an A Was an A: Grade Inflation in Higher Education" on page 54 and compare it to the following précis.

### SAMPLE PRÉCIS

### PRÉCIS OF RONNA VANDERSLICE'S, "WHEN I WAS YOUNG, AN A WAS AN A: GRADE INFLATION IN HIGHER EDUCATION"

*Statistics show that grade inflation continues to be a problem in higher education. College transcripts do not tell employers which students are competent and which are not. Students do not get accurate pictures of their abilities, and there is no clear relationship between grades and student learning. Universities must raise standards. One reform is to use an indexing system of two grades, a public grade for the record and a private grade for students to see how they stand in relation to their peers. Colleges should also reassess the practice of using student evaluations for personnel decisions because instructors will raise standards if they are not pressed to give high grades in exchange for positive teaching evaluations. Professors should review grading practices and make academic programs more rigorous, and college recruiters should stress the importance of academic preparation. Professors should actively insist on high academic standards and reward excellence instead of mediocrity. (Vanderslice 36)*

Notice that the précis eliminates attribution to the author; for example, "Vanderslice asserts" and "she offers," and it pares down the 252-word summary to 149 words, which is one-fourth of the original text.

## Procedures for Writing a Précis

We have outlined the procedure for writing a précis in the box below.

---

### PROCEDURE FOR WRITING A PRÉCIS

- Read the text using critical reading strategies (marking, annotating, elaborating, taking content notes, and posing and answering questions).
- Identify the most important ideas and the significant connections among these ideas.
- Delete unimportant detail, irrelevant examples, and redundancy.
- Combine ideas in sentences and paragraphs, following the same sequence as the original text.
- Continue to pare down the précis until it is roughly one-fourth of the original.
- Document your précis.

---

### EXERCISE 2.12

Divide the class into groups of three. Your professor will assign a reading selection to each group, or you may choose a selection from Chapter 3 or from Part II of this book. One student will write a summary of the article, another an abstract, and the third a précis. When you have finished, exchange papers and critique each other's work.

## ■ Quoting

When you compose essays based on sources, make an effort to use summaries or paraphrases rather than quotations. As a general rule, repeat passages word for word only if they are exceptionally well expressed or contain special forms of writing, such as definitions, key concepts, clever sayings, testimonials, or poetic language. When you take notes, paraphrase the original text instead of quoting it, unless its wording is particularly striking.

For convenience, in this section we will explain how to incorporate quotations in drafts of your essay, as well as how to select quotations for inclusion in your postreading notes.

## Reasons for Quoting

When is it advisable to use a direct quotation instead of a paraphrase? We have provided tips in the box below.

---

### WHEN TO USE DIRECT QUOTATIONS

- To retain the meaning and authenticity of the original text
- To lend support to an analysis or evaluation
- To capture exactly language that supports your point
- To employ a stylistic device
- To capture language that is unusual, well crafted, striking, or memorable

---

A typical reason for quoting is *to retain the meaning or authenticity of the original text*. Assume you have read the selections on Crime-Fighting Technology: Balancing Public Safety and Privacy in Chapter 12, and have received an assignment to write an essay on civil liberties and individuals' constitutional rights. You decide to quote directly from relevant parts of the United States Constitution. It would not be wise to paraphrase the Constitution, since the exact wording is crucial to its interpretation. When precise wording affects your argument, you need to quote.

Another purpose for quoting is *to lend support to an analysis or evaluation*. When you analyze and evaluate texts, you need to identify specific passages that support your interpretation. We discuss analysis and evaluation of essays in Chapter 5. For now, we illustrate with a passage from an essay by Valerie Babb, "'The Joyous Circle': the Vernacular Presence in Frederick Douglass's Narratives" (see Works Cited, page 67).

> In the *Narrative* Douglass recalls slavery's intent to foster fragmentation:
>> My mother and I were separated when I was but an infant—before I knew her as my mother. It is a common custom, in the part of Maryland from which I ran away, to part children from their mothers at a very early age. [. . .] For what this separation is done, I do not know, unless it be to hinder the development of the child's affection toward its mother, and to blunt and destroy the natural affection of the mother for the child. This is the inevitable result. (48)
>
> Douglass's detailing of lost domesticity is especially moving, designed to elicit empathy from all but the most resistant reader. (368)

A third purpose for quoting is *to capture exactly language that supports your point*. In "A Different Mirror" (pages 599–608), Ronald Takaki quotes two immigrants as he explains that the stories of immigrants deserve space in our history books:

> They also re-vision history. "It is very natural that the history written by the victim," said a Mexican in 1874, "does not altogether chime with the story of the victor." Sometimes they

are hesitant to speak, thinking they are only "little people." "I don't know why anybody wants to hear my history," an Irish maid said apologetically in 1900. "Nothing ever happened to me worth the tellin'." (601)

These quotations lend a sense of reality to Takaki's discussion. The exact language tells the reader much more than a paraphrase would reveal.

Another reason to use a direct quotation is *to employ it as a stylistic device*—for example, to open or close an essay. Peter Elbow opens his essay, "Closing My Eyes as I Speak, An Argument for Ignoring Audience" (see Works Cited, page 68), with an apt quotation:

> Very often people don't listen when you speak to them. It's only when you talk to yourself that they prick up their ears. When I am talking to a person or a group and struggling to find words or thoughts, I often find myself involuntarily closing my eyes as I speak. (50)
>
> John Ashberry

A final reason for quoting is *to capture language that is unusual, well crafted, striking, or memorable*. Notice how our student Karla Allen employs Charles Dickens's memorable lines:

> In Charles Dickens's words, "It was the best of times, it was the worst of times" (3). While big corporations were reaping larger profits than ever before, many smaller companies and individuals found themselves out of work.

## Altering Quotations

It is permissible to alter direct quotations, either by deleting some of the author's words or by inserting your own words, as long as you follow conventions that alert your audience to what you are doing. The sentence below, taken from an editorial in *The Lancet* entitled "Being and Believing: Ethics of Virtual Reality" (see Works Cited, p. 67), was quoted in a student paper. The student used an *ellipsis*, a set of three spaced periods, to show where words were left out.

### ORIGINAL

Although the motives behind clinical VR experimentation may be praiseworthy—e.g., it may replace the prescription of harmful psychotropics—the fact that experimentation may be well intended does not preclude early examination of ethical issues.

### STUDENT'S QUOTATION

Using virtual reality to help disabled people extend their physical capabilities seems attractive, but it is not without pitfalls. As the editors of the medical journal The Lancet state, "Although the motives behind clinical VR experimentation may be praiseworthy. . . the fact that experimentation may be well intended does not preclude early examination of ethical issues" (283).

To show an omission at the end of quoted material, use three spaced periods followed by a normal period. Do not use ellipsis to indicate that words have been omitted from the beginning of a quotation. You may have noticed the bracketed ellipsis [. . .] in the example from Valerie Babb's article (page 60). The brackets indicate that Babb omitted words from the quotation by Douglass. The Modern Language Association (MLA) requires writers to bracket the ellipsis when the ellipsis shows that part of the original has been eliminated.

When you insert your own words into a quotation, signal your insertion by placing the words within brackets. Notice how our student uses this convention, as well as ellipses, when she quotes from Mary Ann Rishel's short story "Steel Fires" (see Works Cited, page 68):

### ORIGINAL

They had a hand in it. Helped make the steel. Forged. Pressed. Rolled. Cast. Hammered steel. But they didn't invent steel. They didn't design a bridge. They didn't think up new uses for steel. They weren't idea men.

### STUDENT'S QUOTATION

Rishel explains, "They [laborers] had a hand in it. . . . But they didn't invent steel. . . . They weren't idea men" (13).

By inserting the bracketed word *laborers*, the student clarifies the meaning of the pronoun *they*.

## Documenting Quotations

If the quotation occupies no more than four typed lines on a page, enclose it in double quotation marks. If it is longer, set the entire quotation apart from your text by indenting it ten spaces (see Fig. 2–2).

Notice that in the long, set-off quotation in Figure 2–2, the parenthetical citation goes outside the final punctuation. For short quotations, place the parenthetical citation between the final quotation marks and the closing punctuation. The following example draws on Warren Robinett's article "Electronic Expansion of Human Perception," published in *Whole Earth Review* (see Works Cited, p. 68).

> Robinett observes, "Though it [virtual reality] sounds like science fiction today, tomorrow it will seem as common as talking on the telephone" (21).

The phrase "Robinett observes" leads into the quotation and acknowledges the author. It is important to introduce quotations rather than dropping them into your paper without providing a context. Later in this chapter, we provide tips for weaving quotations into your essay.

At the end of his article Stephens reminds us of both the promise and threat of high-tech crime fighting.

> Once privacy is gone it will be difficult to restore. Once mind control is accomplished it will be difficult to reestablish free thought. But with proper safeguards the superior investigative techniques and more effective treatment of offenders that the new technology offers promise a safer saner society for us all. (25)

Unfortunately, Stephens overlooks important advantages of crime fighting technology and the. . . .

**Figure 2–2**

## Quoting a Direct Quotation

When you quote a quotation, you must acknowledge the author of the quotation as well as the author of the text in which the quotation appears. Consider the following example from Melissa Ianetta's article (see Works Cited, page 68) about the Scottish scholar, Hugh Blair:

> In order to make his ideas available both for schoolroom study and for the private learner, Blair revised and expanded the lectures he gave at Edinburgh University between 1762 and 1782. Evidently, his pedagogical purpose answered a widely felt need: the Rhetoric was, as William Charvat observes, a book "which half the educated English-speaking world studied" (qtd. in Schmitz 96). As Stephen Carr has recently calculated, from the time of its publication to 1911, there were "283 versions of Lectures on Rhetoric and Belles Lettres [. . .] including 112 complete Lectures, 110 abridgements, and 61 translations" (78). As this range of publication might indicate then, Blair's text was widely popular, if such an appellation should be applied to a work commonly used as a textbook. (406)

Ianetta includes a quotation from William Charvat which she found in a book by Schmitz. She informs the reader by placing "(qtd. in Schmitz 96)" immediately after the quotation. On her Works Cited page, she gives an entry for Schmitz's book; she does not list William Charvat. "Qtd. in" is the standard MLA abbreviation for "quoted in." Whenever you present a quotation, you must link both the original author's name (in this case, Charvat) and the quoting author's name (in this case, Schmitz) to the quotation in order for the documentation to be complete.

## Weaving Quotations into Your Essay

You can weave a quotation into your writing in several ways. You can refer to the author by citing the name before the quotation, within the quotation, or after it. Another option is to acknowledge the author in a complete sentence followed by a colon, as in option d in the box below. Option e is permissible, but it should be used sparingly. Whenever possible, use an **attributive verb or phrase** to integrate quotations into your essays. These verbs signal your conversation with the text that you are quoting. Consider examples from a student paper; the page numbers refer to the journal in which the article originally appeared. We have italicized the attributive verbs or phrases.

---

### WEAVING QUOTATIONS INTO YOUR ESSAY

Here are five options:

*Option a*—Acknowledgment of author before the quotation:

*Robinett writes*, "Virtual reality, as its name suggests, is an unreal, alternate reality in which anything could happen" (17).

*Option b*—Acknowledgment of author within a quotation:

"Virtual reality, as its name suggests," *states Robinett*, "is an unreal, alternate reality in which anything could happen" (17).

*Option c*—Acknowledgment of author after a quotation:

"Virtual reality, as its name suggests, is an unreal, alternate reality in which anything could happen," *observes Robinett* (17).

*Option d*—Acknowledgment of author in complete sentence followed by a colon:

*Robinett provides us with a concise definition of this new technology:* "Virtual reality, as its name suggests, is an unreal, alternate reality in which anything could happen" (17).

*Option e*—Quotation followed by author's name:

"Virtual reality, as its name suggests, is an unreal, alternate reality in which anything could happen" (**Robinett** 17).

---

Note that all five options require you to cite the page numbers in parentheses. If you are using Modern Language Association (MLA) style, the foregoing method of documentation will suffice. The style of the American Psychological Association (APA) is slightly different in that the publication date follows the author's name, and the abbreviation for page is always included. For options a, b, c, and d, you would write (1991, p. 17). For option e, you would write (Robinett, 1991, p. 17). When you use option e, don't forget to provide transitions between your own ideas and those of the text. Inexperienced writers sprinkle their papers with direct quotations that have little connection with the rest of the text. You can avoid this problem by leading into quotations with the verbs listed in the following box.

| VERBS AND PHRASES FOR INTRODUCING QUOTATIONS | | |
|---|---|---|

**Verbs**

| | | |
|---|---|---|
| accuses | acknowledges | admits |
| adds | advocates | agrees |
| ascertains | asks | analyzes |
| assents | assesses | argues |
| agrees (disagrees) | addresses | answers |
| begins | believes | categorizes |
| challenges | claims | comments |
| compares | complains | concedes |
| contends | contrasts | critiques |
| considers | concurs | concludes |
| continues | cites | declares |
| defines | delineates | describes |
| determines | demonstrates | differentiates |
| discovers | distinguishes | emphasizes |
| envisions | evaluates | examines |
| explores | expounds on | finds |
| furnishes | grants | implies |
| investigates | inquires | identifies |
| interjects | lists | maintains |
| makes the case | measures | notes |
| objects | observes | offers |
| points out | posits | postulates |
| presents | proposes | proves |
| questions | rationalizes | reasserts |
| remarks | replies | refers to |
| reports | reviews | says |
| shows | states | stipulates |
| stresses | suggests | summarizes |
| surveys | synthesizes | traces |
| views | warns | winds up |
| writes | | |

(continued on the next page)

**Phrases**

| | |
|---|---|
| According to X | In her recent essay, X notes |
| As X argues | In his article, X claims |
| As X explains it | Scholars such as X argue |
| As X has shown | To cite X |
| As X puts it | X calls attention to the problem that |
| As X reminds us | X provides the evidence that |
| As X sees it | X pursues the claim that |
| In X's view | X puts the point well that |
| In X's words | X seems to suggest that |

You can use these verbs and phrases as lead-ins to summaries and paraphrases as well as to quotations.

## Practices to Avoid

Two practices to avoid are **floating quotations** and **quotations strung together** without adequate connecting sentences. A floating quotation is plopped into the paper without any connecting ideas or transitional phrases.

> *Floating quotation:* Today single-parent families, especially those headed by mothers, are subjected to increasingly demanding schedules and levels of stress. "Despite the number of women who take on both parental and economic roles, not all women can do so; few can parent totally alone" (Goldschneider and Waite 202). The viability of single-parent families became a major issue in the presidential campaign.

> *Revision:* Today single-parent families, especially those headed by mothers, are subjected to increasingly demanding schedules and levels of stress. Sociologists Francis K. Goldschneider and Linda Waite explain, "Despite the number of women who take on both parental and economic roles, not all women can do so; few can parent totally alone" (202). Goldschneider and Waite emphasize that women today need more help than ever when raising families.

The revised paragraph provides a framework for the quotation. The quoted text is introduced ("Sociologists Francis K. Goldschneider and Linda Waite explain") and then commented upon ("Goldschneider and Waite emphasize that women today need more help than ever when raising families"). Valerie Babb uses a similar sequence in the example on page 60. She leads the reader into the quotation with the author, title, and an introduction, and she follows it with a comment.

A good rule-of-thumb, especially if you are writing for an English or other Humanities course that requires MLA documentation, is to use the following convention in your writing:

- Introduce the quotation with an attributive verb or phrase
- Give the quotation
- Follow it with a comment or explanation.

The other practice to avoid is stringing quotations together without connections. Never string a sequence of quotations together without communicating the significance of the quoted material to your reader. If you use nothing more than transitions to link the quotations, your text will resemble a patchwork quilt. Always introduce the quotations and integrate them with your own thoughts on the topic.

> *Quotations strung together:* On the subject of crime in the inner cities, Magnet does not think that "society has so oppressed people as to bend them out of their true nature" (48). "Examine the contents of their minds and hearts and what you will find is free-floating aggression, weak consciences, anarchic beliefs, detachment from the community and its highest values," he states (48). This condition is a "predictable result of unimaginably weak families, headed by immature irresponsible girls, who are at the margin of the community, pathological in their own behavior . . ." (Magnet 48).

> *Revision:* On the subject of crime in the inner cities, Magnet does not think that "society has so oppressed people as to bend them out of their true nature" (48). Magnet maintains that criminals lack conscience and internal inhibitions. He exhorts us: "Examine the contents of their minds and hearts and what you will find is free-floating aggression, weak consciences, anarchic beliefs, detachment from the community and its highest values" (48). Magnet attributes this condition to inadequate socialization. He argues that it is the "predictable result of unimaginably weak families, headed by immature irresponsible girls, who are at the margin of the community, pathological in their own behavior . . ." (48). To put it another way, lawlessness is a consequence of inadequate parenting.

## EXERCISE 2.13

Scan Pauline Irit Erera's "What Is a Family?" (pages 462–74) for places where the author has quoted directly. Can you make any generalizations about how Erera uses direct quotations to build her argument?

## EXERCISE 2.14

- Form collaborative learning groups of five students each, as described in the Preface, or fashion groups according to your own method. Assume that your group is preparing to write a collaborative essay about rock music. (You will not actually write the essay.)

- Choose one group member to read aloud the first five paragraphs of Venise Berry's "Redeeming the Rap Experience" (pages 572–85). After each paragraph, decide which sentences, if any, contain information that you might use in your essay. Which of these sentences would you paraphrase, and which would you quote? Explain your decisions.

- At the end of the small-group session, the recorder should have a list of sentences and, for each sentence, an indication of whether it would be quoted or paraphrased and why. Reconvene the entire class. Have each group recorder read the list of sentences and explanations. Discuss points of agreement and difference.

## WORKS CITED

Babb, Valerie. "'The Joyous Circle': the Vernacular Presence in Frederick Douglass's Narratives." *College English* 67 (2005): 365–77.

"Being and Believing: Ethics of Virtual Reality." Editorial. *The Lancet* 338 (1991): 283–84.

Brown, Elizabeth F., and William R. Hendee. "Adolescents and Their Music: Insights into the Health of Adolescents." *The Journal of the American Medical Association* 262 (1989): 1659. InfoTrac OneFile Plus. SUNY Cortland Memorial Library, Cortland, New York. 28 Mar. 2006, A8110115 <http://intrac/galegroup.com>.

Cain, Daphne S., and Terri Combs-Orme. "Family Structure Effects on Parenting Stress and Practices in the African American Family." *Journal of Sociology and Social Welfare* 32 (2005): 19–40. Abstract, p. 19. In: Social Science Abstracts. Online. H. W. Wilson. SUNY Cortland Memorial Library, Cortland, New York. 28 Mar. 2006 <http://vnweb.hwwilsonweb.com>.

Dickens, Charles. *A Tale of Two Cities*. New York: Pocket Library, 1957.

Elbow, Peter. "Closing My Eyes as I Speak, An Argument for Ignoring Audience." *College English* 49.1 (1987): 50–69.

Goldschneider, Frances K., and Linda J. Waite. *New Families, No Families? Demographic Change and the Transformation of the American Home*. Berkeley, CA: U of California P, 1991.

Heim, Michael. "From Interface to Cyberspace." *The Metaphysics of Virtual Reality*. New York: Oxford UP, 1993. 72–81.

Ianetta, Melissa. "'To Elevate I Must First Soften': Rhetoric, Aesthetic, and the Sublime Traditions." *College English* 67 (2005): 400–420.

Magnet, Myron. *The Dream and the Nightmare: The Sixties' Legacy to the Underclass*. New York: William Morrow, 1993.

Rishel, Mary Ann. "Steel Fires." Unpublished short story, 1985.

Robinett, Warren. "Electronic Expansion of Human Perception." *Whole Earth Review* Fall 1991: 17–21.

Sagan, Carl. "In Defense of Robots." *Broca's Brain*. New York: Ballantine, 1980.

# *Three*

# Sourcebook of Readings:

## *An Academic Conversation about the "Mommy Wars"*

This chapter offers a preview of the anthology format that you will find in Part II of our textbook. It presents thirteen reading selections illustrating scholarly academic writing, journalistic writing, popular magazine writing, and personal writing, as well as the various genres to be discussed in the following chapters. These genres include:

- Critical analysis and evaluation
- Rhetorical analysis
- Comparative analysis
- Causal analysis
- Explanatory synthesis
- Thesis-driven synthesis
- Review of the scholarly academic literature
- Argument synthesis
- Critique of an argument

Sometimes a particular selection combines two or more of these genres: few genres exemplify a pure, unmixed, idealized form, and the readings that follow are no exception to the rule.

As you will see, each article begins with a brief biographical sketch of its author to provide a context for its style and argument. Then we propose a **prereading** exercise to orient you to the article topic. After each selection, we suggest several exercises to hone your skills in:

- **Reading for content** (or isolating the dominant ideas in the selection)
- **Reading for genre, organization, and stylistic features** (or identifying the selection in terms of its family resemblance to other writing in the same mode, its structural composition, and its style)

- **Reading for rhetorical context** (or examining how the selection tries to persuade the reader of its argument)

All of the articles in this chapter focus on a common topic that exemplifies a current intellectual debate. In this case, the debate concerns the so-called "Mommy Wars." The term refers to the conflicts that women feel when they evaluate choices available (or not available) to them as working mothers or stay-at-home mothers. It is a topic that will affect most of you directly, whether men or women, as prospective—or perhaps current—life-partners and parents, and that affects all of you indirectly—now and in the future—as members of a family, a community, a workplace, a marketplace, and an ever-changing society.

## ■▟ TERMS OF THE ARGUMENT

We have selected these articles and arranged them to show you how the issues of this debate raise several problems, what they entail, how they play out, how they impinge or do not impinge upon one another, how their exponents clarify or complicate them, and how the points of view that they express relate or fail to relate to one another. The selection amounts to a sourcebook of readings for you to draw upon in your own writing assignments (if your instructor advises you to do so). Because the remaining chapters in Part I will provide an in-depth treatment of how to use these readings when you write, this selection will be longer than those in the rest of our textbook. We want to display a variety of possibilities available to you in a textbook of this sort.

Like all conversations or debates, the one about "Mommy Wars" has a history that shapes its rhetorical context. The term "Mommy Wars" appeared prominently in a newspaper article by Tracy Thompson, "A War Inside Your Head," in the *Washington Post*, Sunday, February 15, 1998. Here the author used it to evoke "the cultural and emotional battle zone we land in the minute we become mothers" (p. 12).

A few years later, the term took on a different profile when Lisa Belkin published her article on "The Opt-Out Revolution," in *The New York Times*, Sunday, October 26, 2003. Here, as the author delineates differences between working mothers (especially from elite backgrounds) and those who stay at home, a set of conflicting values comes to distinguish the two sets of parents. A rhetorical "war" soon broke out between those who uphold divergent opinions on these values.

## ■ Genres

We do not include Thompson's or Belkin's articles in the selections that follow, but we instead begin with a review of the literature on ideologies of motherhood and myths about working mothers by Dierdre D. Johnston and Debra H. Swanson. Then we examine an argument that questions why the media focus on the career choices of well-to-do college graduates instead of the economic and cultural factors that affect all women: Judith Stadtman Tucker's "The Least Worst Choice: Why Mothers 'Opt' Out of the Workforce." Our next selection, Louise Story's *New York Times Magazine* article on career plans held by current undergraduate women at Yale University, reignited the "Mommy Wars." In "Many Women at Elite Colleges Set Career Path to Motherhood," Story wrote that many such women planned to work for a few years after graduation but then to retire more or less permanently as full-time mothers after their first child arrives. Story's article drew a predictable volley of criticism from men and women who objected to its simplistic rhetoric, its narrow sociological frame, and its limited argument. Jack Shafer examines Story's rhetoric in his "Weasel-Words Rip My Flesh!" Tracey Meares focuses upon her sociological base in "Critique of 'Many Women at Elite Colleges Set Career Path to Motherhood.'" And Katha Pollitt interrogates Story's misrepresentation of Yale peers in "Desperate Housewives of the Ivy League?"

---

### TERMS OF THE ARGUMENT

Deirdre D. Johnston and Debra H. Swanson, "Motherhood Ideologies and Motherhood Myths"—Synthesis: Literature review of research on ideological myths about working mothers

Judith Stadtman Tucker, "The Least Worst Choice"—Synthesis: Source-based argument about "Mommy Wars"

Linda Story, "Many Women at Elite Colleges Set Career Path to Motherhood"—News story that well-educated women are choosing to be stay-at-home mothers

Jack Shafer, "Weasel-Words Rip My Flesh!"—Rhetorical analysis of Story's argument

Tracey Meares, "Critique of 'Many Women at Elite Colleges Set Career Path to Motherhood'"—Critical analysis of Story's article

Katha Pollitt, "Desperate Housewives of the Ivy League?"—Critical analysis of Story's article

---

A longer article by the feminist advocate Linda R. Hirshman goes yet further in its critique of Story's article and soon drew heated responses to its own claims. This author's "Homeward Bound" mounts a blistering attack on highly educated women from privileged backgrounds who abandon their professional talents and skills for a life of one-dimensional motherhood instead of providing role models for working women in less privileged environments. The conservative commentator David Brooks responds in his "The Year of Domesticity" that women exercise more power in the kitchen than in the workplace. Cathy Young replies in "The Return of the Mommy Wars" that Hirshman is too harsh in questioning how women exercise choices open to them. Don Feder argues in his "Feminists to Women: Shut Up and Do as You're Told" that, by disparaging stay-at-home mothers, Hirshman becomes more of an antifeminist than a feminist for coercing women to conform to a single standard.

---

### PROGRESSIVE FEMINISTS VS. CONSERVATIVE CRITICS

Linda R. Hirshman, "Homeward Bound"—Argument synthesis and critique of educated women who abandon their professional talents instead of providing role models for working women

David Brooks, "The Year of Domesticity"—Critical analysis and conservative comment that women exercise more power in the kitchen than in the workplace

(continued on the next page)

Cathy Young, "The Return of the Mommy Wars"—Critical analysis of Hirshman, arguing that she is too harsh in questioning how women exercise choices open to them

Don Feder, "Feminists to Women: Shut Up and Do as You're Told"—Critical analysis commenting that Hirshman is an antifeminist for coercing women to conform to a single standard

These selections end with efforts to coordinate the arguments. In "Paradise Lost," Terry Martin Hekker urges—on personal experience as an older, divorced mother—that young mothers should cultivate their career skills to protect their own futures. In "At Home with David Brooks," Rebecca Traister tells David Brooks that he should read Terry Martin Hekker to learn about the problems of real-life stay-at-home moms. In "Mother Yale," Frances Rosenbluth brings forth social-science data to show that the status of working mothers is changing, but that improvements are slow in taking shape.

## COORDINATING ARTICLES

Terry Martin Hekker, "Paradise Lost"—Personal experience that young mothers should cultivate their career skills

Rebecca Traister, "At Home with David Brooks"—Comparative analysis, tells David Brooks he should read Terry Martin Hekker to learn about real-life stay-at-home moms

Frances Rosenbluth, "Mother Yale"—Causal analysis of how the status of working mothers is slowly changing

## ■ Participants in the Conversation

Our account of these articles barely conveys the conversation that they carry on among themselves. The participants in this conversation include professors whose writings convey academic research (such as Deirdre D. Johnston and Debra H. Swanson, Judith Stadtman Tucker, Tracey Meares, Linda R. Hirshman, and Frances Rosenbluth), distinguished journalists and editorial writers (such as Katha Pollitt, David Brooks, Cathy Young, and Rebecca Traister), and popular newspaper and magazine writers (such as Louise Story, Jack Shafer, Don Feder, and Terry Martin Hekker). These participants explicitly refer to one another, as well as to other writers on the same topic. They implicitly evoke responses from their predecessors as well as stimulate replies from their readers. They jostle, prod, tease, enrage, endorse, affirm, appease, echo, and size up one another, and then they draw into the discussion others who agree or disagree with their terms. In short, they conduct a living conversation just as you and I would if we were addressing this topic in a shared space. In later exercises, we're going to suggest how you might extend this conversation in the classroom with other students. Here we want to make sure that you hear the conversation rattling around in the printed articles that you will be reading.

# ■ Questions to Ask about Academic Conversation in Print

In an academic conversation, context means a great deal—and often it provides the best entry for your understanding of the stakes. (Imagine joining an Internet chat group without knowing the players or the causes they champion or whether they're intent on destroying one other, or are instead joking with and perhaps trying to help one another to reach some common goal.) Much depends upon the who, why, what, when, and where that determined the conversation, as the questions in the following box will show.

---

**QUESTIONS TO ASK ABOUT ACADEMIC CONVERSATIONS IN PRINT**

**The Writing Participants**

- Who are the participants and where do they come from?
- Are these participants observers-at-large or contributors with particular skills and appropriate experiences?
- Have these participants just joined the debate or do they have a record of engaging in it?
- Have these participants held consistent views on the topic or have they changed their positions over time?
- Who are on which side? Who switch sides? Who belong to no side?

**The Reading Audience**

- What might we assume about the readers whom they specifically address?
- What might we assume about other readers who confront these writings?
- Have the dynamics of the original situation changed since these articles were published?
- Have recent circumstances modified, challenged, rejected, or upheld their claims?
- Has our thinking advanced beyond their positions, or is it still worthwhile to return to them to deepen and extend their claims?

**Rhetorical Context**

- Why do the participants engage in this conversation? What interests are they furthering or protecting?
- When did these writings appear in print?
- Where did these writings appear in print? Do they derive from largely popular newspaper or magazine articles? Or from predominantly specialized publications for experts in a particular field? Or from some hybrid of the two? Or from some free-wheeling Internet blogosphere?

---

It's not always easy for newcomers to answer these questions. But with some exposure to the sources of dialogue, the venues of exchange, and the backgrounds of the engaged parties, anyone can begin to map out the investments. (Think of how you first began to make sense of baseball stats or the styles of rap stars or rock artists.) In academic conversations, it pays to know the perceived reputation of the source's appearance:

- Scholarly sources such as academic or professional journals, university press publications, or academic textbooks
- Substantial news or general interest sources, such as national newspapers, documented periodicals, specialized journals
- Popular press sources, such as local newspapers, general-circulation magazines, mass-market publications
- Sensationalized sources such as tabloid newspapers or magazines

It also pays to know where the authors have been and what they have previously published:

- Have they had professional experience in the field?
- Is it their primary field of expertise?
- Have they received funding for their work, and from where has it come?
- What else have they written, and who refereed it in reviews and public airing?
- What criticism, approval, or disapproval has their work received, and from whom?

Some of these identifications can be or become pretty esoteric. (One wag declared that professors are people who talk or write in someone else's sleep.) But with a few clues and a little practice, any student in an academic community can draw some picture of the various camps. We aim to provide some clues.

## ■ Situating the Conversation

We begin with a table of contents for our selections on the "Mommy Wars." We specify the general content and the particular genre for each. In Figure 3–1, we provide a visual

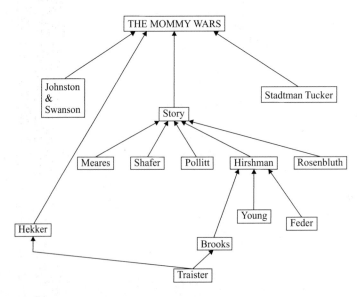

**Figure 3–1   The "Mommy Wars": Participants in the Academic Conversation**

display of the participants in this academic conversation. The arrows indicate who is talking to whom. Then, in **Prereading** exercises for specific articles, we offer a biographical statement about the author and a few notes to orient readers into the article's conversation. Finally, in exercises after each article, we direct the reader's attention to matters of content, organization, style, and rhetorical argument that affect the drift of conversation:

> In **Reading for Content** exercises after each article, we point to crucial passages that signal the direction and the major outcome of the discussion and its line of reasoning.

> In **Reading for Genre, Organization, and Stylistic Features** exercises, we point to characteristics that signal the type of discourse maintained in the article, the means of its development, and its major expressive traits.

> In **Reading for Rhetorical Context** exercises, we point to the situation of its argument, the membership of its intended audience, and the efforts that it makes to persuade its audience.

## ■ TABLE OF CONTENTS

(9) THE RETURN OF THE MOMMY WARS * Cathy Young
Analysis of Hirshman's argument, concluding that it is too harsh in questioning how women might exercise choices open to them.

(10) FEMINISTS TO WOMEN: SHUT UP AND DO AS YOU'RE TOLD * Don Feder
Critical analysis of Hirshman's argument which asserts that, by disparaging stay-at-home mothers, Hirshman becomes more of an antifeminist than a feminist for coercing women to conform to a single standard.

(11) PARADISE LOST * Terry Martin Hekker
Personal change of viewpoint recounting how her divorce left her unprepared for the modern workplace.

(12) AT HOME WITH DAVID BROOKS * Rebecca Traister
Comparative analysis that argues why Brooks should read Terry Martin Hekker's personal story.

(13) MOTHER YALE * Frances Rosenbluth
Causal analysis of why, among working mothers, change happens but is slow in coming.

■ ■ ■ ■ ■ ■ ■ ■ ■ ■ ■

# Motherhood Ideologies and Motherhood Myths

## *Deirdre D. Johnston and Debra H. Swanson*

*Deirdre D. Johnston is a Professor of Communication Studies at Hope College. She is the author of* The Art and Science of Persuasion *(1993). Debra H. Swanson is an Associate Professor of Sociology at Hope College. Both Johnston and Swanson have published several research studies on contemporary motherhood. They are currently collaborating on a book based on interviews with 100 mothers,* To Work or Not to Work: What Every Mother Needs to Know before She Decides to Work, Work Part-Time, or Stay at Home.

## PREREADING

Since the genre of the following article is a review of the literature and synthesis of research on the topic of working mothers, you will want to know how the authors narrow this vast topic for the purposes of their review. Skim through the article and jot down key terms that appear often throughout the review. Compare your list of terms with those of classmates. The terms "ideologies" and "myths" appear in the title, so are clearly important. Other terms such as "culture," "patriarchy," "class," "employed mothers," and "at-home mothers" also seem important. Speculate about how the authors have narrowed their topic and what the focus of their review of the literature will be.

From: "Invisible Mothers: A Content Analysis of Motherhood Ideologies and Myths in Magazines," *Sex Roles*, vol. 49, nos. 1/2, July 2003. pp. 21–23

# Motherhood Ideologies

To explore ideologies of motherhood, it is useful to recognize that motherhood is not biologically determined or socially ascribed. Motherhood is a social and historical construction (Bassin, Honey, & Kaplan, 1994; Glenn, 1992; Risman, 1998). Coontz (1992) argued that the "traditional family" with a wage-earner father and a stay-at-home mother is an historical and cultural aberration. Culture tells us what it means to be a mother, what behaviors and attitudes are appropriate for mothers, and how motherhood should shape relationships and self-identity.

Jayne Buxton (1998) described the adversarial climate of competing ideologies as the "mother war." She documented how stereotypical characterizations of the Superwoman (who efficiently manages her household and children with the same cold-hearted equanimity she employs in the business world) are pitted against the Earth Mother (who, barefoot and wearing kaftans, feeds her children home-grown organic foods with an everpresent beatific smile). Each motherhood camp justifies its own ideology by co-opting the values of the other: "I am a better mother if I work"; "I am resisting the dominant culture and exercising my free choice and power as a woman to stay at home with my children."

A dominant ideology supports the cultural hegemony by creating social expectations for a social group. For example, a patriarchial ideology of mothering denies women identities and selfhood outside of motherhood (Glenn, 1994). Feminist scholars have explored how current motherhood ideologies sustain patriarchy (Rothman, 1994), perpetuate the economic dependency of middle-class women and the economic exploitation of working-class and migrant women (Chang, 1994), and project White, middle-class mothers' experiences as universal and ideal (Collins, 1994). Culture defines and rewards "good mothers," and it sanctions "bad mothers."

There are many mothers who fall outside the club of "good motherhood" as defined by dominant motherhood ideologies. A number of scholars have noted the relegation of teenage mothers (Bailey, Brown, & Wilson, 2002), older mothers, single mothers, and lesbian mothers (Lewin, 1994) to the bottom rungs of the hierarchy of motherhood (DiLapi, 1989). A number of researchers have addressed both the historical and contemporary exclusion of African, Asian, and Latina American mothers from the cult of domesticity that defines American motherhood (Collins, 1994; Dill, 1988; Glenn, 1992).

There are clearly racial and class biases in the social construction of good and bad mothers. Solinger (1994) found that whereas Black single mothers are labeled deviant by the dominant culture, White single mothers are considered "troubled" but "redeemable." Although the conventional motherhood ideology maintains that mothers should not work outside the home, economically or financially privileged mothers continue to hire working-class women, and Women of Color, who are often mothers themselves, to perform the more arduous childcare work (Blair-Loy, 2001; Chang, 1994). Thus, the construction of motherhood, particularly in the form of dominant ideologies, may have little correspondence to the lived social realities of mothers.

# Motherhood Myths

The building blocks of ideologies are myths. Barthes (1972) defined a myth as an uncontested and unconscious assumption that is so widely accepted that its historical and cultural origins are forgotten. As such, myths of motherhood are presented as "natural," "instinctual," and "intuitive" as opposed to "cultural," "economic," "political," and "historical" (Hrdy, 2000). Ideologies are born when myths are combined into coherent philosophies and politically sanctioned by the culture.

Myths of employed and at-home mothers abound in the culture. A cursory glance   7
at the motherhood section of a bookstore is revealing. Employed mothers are tired, busy, and guilty (e.g., *The Third Shift*, Bolton, 2000; *Motherguilt*, Eyer, 1996). At-home mothers live in a state of bliss (e.g., *Home by Choice: Raising Emotionally Secure Children in an Insecure World*, Hunter, 2000; *Mitten Strings for God*, Kenison, 2000). On the negative side, at-home mothers suffer from "mommy mush brain" due to lack of intellectual stimulation (e.g., "I told one man, 'I'm a mother at home,' and was greeted with the sight of his back as he wandered off to find someone more important to talk to"—from the book jacket of *Staying Home: From Full-Time Professional to Full-Time Parent*, Sanders & Bullen, 1992). Employed mothers neglect their children, or at the very least have difficulty meeting children's basic needs of adequate food, clothing, protection, supervision, and security (e.g., *Parent by Proxy: Don't Have Them If You Won't Raise Them*, Schlessinger, 2000). Employed mothers put their family relationships at risk and jeopardize mother-infant bonding (cf. *Bad Mothers*, Ladd-Tayler & Umansky, 1998; and *Mother-Infant Bonding: A Scientific Fiction*, Eyer 1992, that challenge the veracity of these myths). In contrast, at-home mothers are bonded and attached to their children, to the point of being overinvolved, controlling, and enmeshed (e.g., *When Mothers Work: Loving Our Children Without Sacrificing Our Selves*, Peters, 1997). On the positive side, at-home mothers are ever present and therefore competent in protecting and supervising their children (e.g., *Children First*, Leach, 1995).

Scholars have sought to identify the underlying causes of maternal myths   8
(Chodorow, 1978; Hays, 1996; Maushart, 1999; McMahon, 1995; Rich, 1976; Ruddick, 1983, 1989; Thurer, 1995; Trebilcot, 1983). These scholars agree that the primary cause of maternal myths is the perpetuation of patriarchy. The maternal bliss myth—that motherhood is the joyful fruition of every woman's aspirations—perpetuates systems of patriarchy by attributing any maternal unhappiness and dissatisfaction to failure of the mother. A good mother is a happy mother; an unhappy mother is a failed mother. This myth attributes responsibility for the conditions of motherhood to the individual, not the system.

# References

Bailey, N., Brown, G., & Wilson, C. (2002). 'The baby brigade': Teenage mothers and sexuality. *Journal of the Association for Research on Mothering*, 4(1), 101–110.

Barthes, R. (1972). *Mythologies*. New York: Hill & Wang. (Original work published 1957)

Bassin, D., Honey, M., & Kaplan, M. (1994). *Representations of motherhood*. New Haven, CT: Yale University Press.

Blair-Loy, M. (2001). Cultural constructions of family schemas: The case of women finance executives. *Gender and Society*, 15, 687–709.

Bolton, M. (2000). *The third shift: Managing hard choices in our careers, homes, and lives as women*. San Francisco: Jossey-Bass.

Buxton, J. (1998). *Ending the mother war: Starting the workplace revolution*. London: Macmillan.

Chang, G. (1994). Undocumented Latinas: The new 'employable mother'. In E. N. Glenn, G. Chang, & L. N. Forcey (Eds.), *Mothering: Ideology, experience, and agency* (pp. 259–285). New York: Routledge.

Chodorow, N. (1978). *The reproduction of mothering: Psychoanalysis and the sociology of gender.* Berkeley: University of California Press.

Collins, P. H. (1994). Shifting the center: Race, class, and feminist theorizing about motherhood. In E. N. Glenn, G. Chang, & L. N. Forcey (Eds.), *Mothering: Ideology, experience, and agency* (pp. 45–64). New York: Routledge.

Coontz, S. (1992). *The way we never were: American families and the nostalgia trap.* New York: Basic Books.

DiLapi, E. (1989). Lesbian mothers and the motherhood hierarchy. *Journal of Homosexuality, 18,* 101–121.

Dill, B. T. (1988). Our mother's grief: Racial ethnic women and the maintenance of families. *Journal of Family History, 13,* 415–431.

Eyer, D. E. (1992). *Mother-infant bonding: A scientific fiction.* New Haven, CT: Yale University Press.

Eyer, D. E. (1996). *Motherguilt: How our culture blames mothers for what's wrong with society.* New York: Times Books.

Glenn, E. N. (1992). From servitude to service work: Historical continuities in the racial division of women's work. *Signs, 18,* 1–43.

Hays, S. (1996). *The cultural contradictions of motherhood.* New Haven, CT: Yale University Press.

Hrdy, S. B. (2000). *Mother nature.* London: Vintage.

Hunter, B. (2000). *Home by choice: Raising emotionally secure children in an insecure world.* Sisters, OR: Multnomah.

Kenison, K. (2000). *Mitten strings for God: Reflections for mothers in a hurry.* New York: Warner Books.

Ladd-Taylor, M., & Umansky, L. (1998). *'Bad' mothers: The politics of blame in twentieth-century America.* New York: New York University Press.

Leach, P. (1995). *Children first.* New York: Vintage Books.

Lewin, E. (1994). Negotiating lesbian motherhood: The dialectics of resistance and accommodation. In E. N. Glenn, G. Chang & L. N. Forcey (Eds.), *Mothering: Ideology, experience, and agency* (pp. 333–354). New York: Routledge.

Maushart, S. (1999). *The mask of motherhood: How becoming a mother changes everything and why we pretend it doesn't.* New York: New Press.

McMahon, M. (1995). *Engendering motherhood: Identity and self-transformation in women's lives.* New York: Guilford Press.

Peters, J. (1997). *When mothers work: Loving our children without sacrificing our selves.* Reading, MA: Perseus Books.

Rich, A. (1976). *Of woman born: Motherhood as experience and institution.* New York: Norton.

Risman, B. (1998). *Gender vertigo: American families in transition.* New Haven, CT: Yale University Press.

Rothman, B. K. (1994). Beyond mothers and fathers: Ideology in a patriarchal society. In E. N. Glenn, G. Chang, & L. N. Forcey (Eds.), *Mothering: Ideology, experience, and agency* (pp. 139–160). New York: Routledge.

Ruddick, S. (1983). Maternal thinking. In J. Trebilcot (ed.), *Mothering: Essays in feminist theory* (pp. 213–230). Savage, MD: Rowman & Littlefield.

Ruddick, S. (1989). *Maternal thinking: Toward a politics of peace.* New York: Ballantine Books.

Sanders, D., & Bullen, M. (1992). *Staying home: From full-time professional to full-time parent.* Boston: Little, Brown.

Schlessinger, L. (2000). *Parenthood by proxy: Don't have them if you won't raise them.* New York: HarperCollins.

Solinger, R. (1994). Race and 'value': Black and White illegitimate babies, 1945–1965. In E. N. Glenn, G. Chang, & L. N. Forcey (Eds.), *Mothering: Ideology, experience, and agency* (pp. 287–310). New York: Routledge.

Thurer, S. (1995). *The myths of motherhood: How culture reinvents the good mother*. New York: Penguin.

Trebilcot, J. (1983). *Mothering: Essays in feminist theory*. Savage, MD: Rowman & Littlefield Publishers.

## READING FOR CONTENT

1. How do the authors define "mother war" in paragraph 2?
2. How does the last sentence of paragraph 5 convey a thesis statement for the authors' synthesis of research?
3. Draw a schematic diagram of the ways in which the authors distinguish the categories of "employed mothers" and "at-home" mothers in paragraph 7.

## READING FOR GENRE, ORGANIZATION, AND STYLISTIC FEATURES

1. Consult the list of References at the end of the article. Have the authors managed to convey the variety of topics and approaches represented in this list? What are the advantages of their topical approach to discussing this list, instead of proceeding through the list in some alphabetical or chronological order?
2. How does paragraph 6 provide a linkage between the first and second parts of this review? In your own words, describe the relationship between "ideology" and "myth."
3. In addition to categorizing the References entries according to topic and then briefly alluding to their content, do the authors provide other information about these works? What other sorts of information would you find useful in such a literature review and synthesis of research?

## READING FOR RHETORICAL CONTEXT

1. If the last sentence of paragraph 5 implies a thesis statement about the divergence between ideology and lived social reality, which books mentioned in this review would seem most useful for the author's argument? Underline the important titles.
2. If you were preparing to write a paper on the "Mommy Wars," which titles would seem most useful for your purposes? Circle these titles and collect some additional information about them by doing a brief Internet search. Using a search engine such as Google or Yahoo, type in the author's name and the title of the book and follow the links to a publisher's or bookseller's description of the book.

## WRITING ASSIGNMENTS

1. Using the titles that you have underlined and circled in the preceding questions on Reading for Rhetorical Context, consult the online catalogue of your college library to find which books your library has or doesn't have. Then write a two-page letter to the acquisitions director of your library requesting that he or she purchase for the collection titles not currently catalogued. Explain what kind of literature review has brought these titles to your attention, how they seem appropriate

to your research in the "Mommy Wars," and why they would be good additions to the college library.

2. Read through the remaining articles in this chapter and write a 750-word literature review and synthesis of research that explains their focus and describes their points of view on the topic of the "Mommy Wars."

■ ■ ■ ■ ■ ■ ■ ■ ■ ■ ■

# The Least Worst Choice: Why Mothers "Opt" Out of the Workforce

## *Judith Stadtman Tucker*

*Judith Stadtman Tucker is editor and publisher of* The Mothers Movement Online. *She has served as senior manager of the national advocacy for Mothers & More and other groups devoted to mobilizing mothers for change. She has contributed several articles on women's issues to various national associations about mothering and to many media interviews.*

## PREREADING

In mounting her argument, Stadtman Tucker surveys arguments by other writers about why educated women should or should not continue to work when they are mothers. Form collaborative groups of five students each and commission participants to make a list of friends or family members—possibly including some students themselves—who have become mothers in the past ten years. Participants should then discuss how many have been stay-at-home moms—and where possible include reasons why they made their choice. How many had returned to work on a part-time basis within six months of giving birth to their last child? How many had returned to work on a full-time basis within six months of giving birth to their last child? How many plan on returning to work before their children are in school? How many altered their plans as time went on? Students should then discuss the conclusions they can derive from these data.

W hy don't women get to the top? According to a recent cover story for the *New York Times* magazine, it's because the bright young women who were poised to take over the world would rather be at home with their kids than climbing the corporate ladder (Lisa Belkin, *The Opt-Out Revolution*, October 26, 2003).

The *New York Times* could have featured a serious investigation of systemic factors that limit the upward mobility of mothers in the workplace. Or a more philosophical piece about why our society is still locked into the idea that mothers, above all others, are responsible for caring for the nation's children and how this attitude impacts women both in and outside the workplace. Even an in-depth commentary about how U.S. social policy lets down working families, time and time again, would be welcome. Instead, the *Times* gave pride of place to an article which resorts to pop science to make the case that mothers—even the really brainy ones—are biologically hard-wired to prioritize caregiving over competition.

Perhaps the editors were hungry for the controversy that followed the publication  3 of Belkin's story,[1] or perhaps they were simply content to write off reports of women's inequality in the professional arena as a product of maternal behavior. Either way, *The Opt-Out Revolution* fails to shed new light on the issue it purports to address: the scarcity of women in political, corporate and academic leadership. "Why don't women run the world?" Belkin ponders. "Maybe it's because they don't want to."

Or maybe it's because the world doesn't want women in charge.  4

## The Motherhood Factor

Belkin's article—and other recent reports in the popular media[2]—might have us con-  5 vinced there is indeed an Alarming National Trend of educated, middle-class mothers abandoning professional careers to take over the messy business of raising children at home. In reality, the probability a mother will participate in the paid labor force increases with her level of education—over 78 percent of mothers with a graduate or professional degree are in the paid workforce, and they are three times as likely to work full-time as to work part-time. So if the fundamental question about the future of women's leadership is "What's become of our best and brightest young women?," it appears most of them are at the office, whether they happen to have had a baby or not.[3]

However, as Joan Williams notes in her book *Unbending Gender: Why Family*  6 *and Work Conflict and What To Do About It*, having all the right talent and training to excel in a career may not be enough to bring mothers into the mainstream of professional achievement. Success in today's workplace depends on an employee's capacity to meet her employer's need for labor on demand—meaning that the most valued workers are those who can work long hours any day of the week, at any time of day or night, without risk of interruption from personal responsibilities outside the job.

For mothers—who, by contemporary cultural standards, are still expected to take  7 the lead in child rearing and homemaking—conforming to the uncompromising grind of the "ideal" worker is nearly impossible. According to Williams, mothers on the professional career track face "Three unattractive choices. They remain in a good job that keeps them away from home 10 to 12 hours a day, or they take a part-time [job] with depressed wages, few benefits and no advancement. Or they quit."[4]

Women continue to enter elite professions at a growing rate; a recent study on  8 transitions in the U.S. workforce found that women are now more likely than men to work at "professional or managerial" occupations.[5] But only a fraction of these women are reaching the upper ranks—partly due to garden-variety gender discrimination, but they may also run into a barrier Williams describes as "the maternal wall." Williams and other scholars who study work-life conflict are adamant that paid work and motherhood are not inherently incompatible, and argue that cultural attitudes about women, work and family have generated workplace practices that consistently marginalize mothers and other workers with normal caregiving obligations.[6]

Cultural resistance to mothers remaining in the paid workforce is less strident  9 today than it was in the 1970s and '80s, but it hasn't disappeared. A 2002 survey of wage and salaried workers found that two out of every five male employees—and almost as many female employees—agreed with the statement "men should earn the money and women should stay at home minding the house and children." (In 1977, only 26 percent of men felt it was appropriate for women to work outside the home.)

The same study found that women in dual-earners couples *with* children were considerably more likely than women in dual-earner couples *without* children to feel that mom should handle the care work while dad manages the money work (48 percent versus 34 percent). The authors duly noted that "the challenge or anticipated challenge of raising children apparently induces a change of attitude, if not employment behavior, in some people."[7]   10

## "It is Really About Work"

As one of the Ivy League educated mothers Belkin interviewed for her *Opt-Out Revolution* story observes. "The exodus of professional women from the workplace isn't really about motherhood at all. It is really about work." Several other women profiled in Belkin's article openly admitted their departure from the workforce was precipitated by an employer's refusal to negotiate a more family-friendly schedule. Even for women contemplating an exit from less prestigious jobs, the inexorable pull of maternal love may only play a small role in the decision to leave the workforce.   11

As Americans advance into the 21st century, access to new technology lets us work smarter—but we are also working harder. Despite a consistent preference among employed adults for shorter working hours—most would like to spend around 35 hours a week on the job[8]—hours of work continue to increase in the U.S. as companies trim down staffing (and payroll costs) in order to survive today's economic conditions. Dual-earner couples with children under 18 worked an average of 91 hours a week in 2002, up from 81 hours a week in 1977. Fathers in dual-earner couples spend an average of 51 hours a week of paid and unpaid time on work related to their jobs, and mothers' weekly hours of job-related work increased from 38 in 1977 to 43 in 2002.[9]   12

Not surprisingly, levels of stress from work/life conflict are also on the rise. Employees with families report significantly higher levels of interference between their jobs and family lives than they did 25 years ago (45 percent in 2002 versus 34 percent in 1977), and men with families report higher levels of interference between their jobs and their family lives than women.[10]   13

It's not only moms and dads who are feeling the pain of the American way of work. A September 2003 report from The Conference Board, an international organization tracking corporate and employment issues, found that less than half of all U.S. workers are happy with their jobs. Employees reported the least satisfaction with their employer's promotion policy and bonus plan. But only one out of every three workers was satisfied with their company's plans for health care coverage, pensions, flexible time or family leave.   14

While all groups of workers reported lower levels of job satisfaction in 2003 than they had previous years, the steepest decline occurred for those between the ages of 35 and 44—job satisfaction for this group slipped from 61 percent in 1995 to 47 percent in 2003.[11] It may not be entirely coincidental that workers in this age range tend to be in the middle of their most active parenting years—and this is especially true for professional women, who are increasingly likely to delay child-bearing until their early or mid-30s.[12]   15

Workers employed by businesses with more supportive work/life practices and cultures are more likely to be satisfied with their jobs and life in general, and express   16 higher levels of commitment to their employers. However, the 2002 *National Study of the Changing Workforce* found that employers' progress in adopting family-friendly practices and attitudes has been steady over the last two decades, but slow. With the exception of additional services and programs to help workers balance their workload with responsibilities for elder care, the study found there has not been a significant increase in other types of employer-implemented programs to reduce work/family conflict in the last decade.[13]

Even if work-life supports on the job are gradually improving, a recent news report in *USA Today* highlighted several new industry studies suggesting nearly one-third of U.S. companies are downsizing their family-friendly programs in response to high levels of unemployment. As the pressure to retain talent recedes, employers are scaling back options for telecommuting, flexible schedules and job sharing. According to the article, a group of industry experts concluded that, "with 9 million people out of work, companies no longer need to offer varied benefits to attract and retain workers."[14]  17

As work hours escalate and the number of family-friendly programs employers offer remain stagnant or decline, employed mothers often find themselves in an untenable situation. For married couples, men's commitment to longer hours of paid work—and their limited contribution to carework at home[15]—is often justified by their higher earnings.[16] But something's got to give, and it's usually mom—her time, long-term economic security, general well-being, and aspirations for getting ahead on the job are all up for grabs in the dispiriting shuffle of priorities called "balancing" work and family.  18

Cutting back to a part-time schedule may seem like an ideal solution for easing work/life stress in families who can still make ends meet with one or both wage-earners working less than full-time. A 2000 survey by the Alfred C. Sloan Center at the University of Chicago found that nearly two-thirds of mothers who worked full-time would have preferred to work part-time, and one-half of all mothers who were out of the paid labor force would have preferred part-time paid employment to staying at home full-time.[17] But the part-time option is not without a downside. In 2002, three out of every five employees who worked for organizations employing part-time workers reported that part-timers received less than pro rata pay and benefits compared to full-time employees in the same positions *just because they work part-time*.[18]  19

When it comes to managing the conflicting demands of work and family, affluent married mothers who can afford to hop on and off the career track at will have a definite advantage—for most single-parent and dual-earner families, reducing or forgoing one parent's wages in the interest of "putting family first" is not a realistic option. As author and career coach Elizabeth Wilcox emphasizes in her 2003 book *The Mom Economy*, women with post-graduate education and advanced professional skills have considerably more bargaining power when it comes to negotiating family-friendly work arrangements. However, she also notes that even the most qualified workers must be prepared to make substantial trade-offs in terms of wages, professional prestige and quality of assignments in order to land a good part-time or flexible time position.[19]  20

In other words: no matter what you bring to the table, if you want a good job with good pay and reasonable opportunities for advancement – and you also want time to have a fully developed family or personal life – you are pretty much out of luck. As Wilcox remarks, "I can't tell you how many women I come across who are so disgruntled with the state of the workforce and the existing inequalities that it leaves them in a state of paralysis."  21

# The Other Big Picture

One major reason work and family conflict in America is because our social policies— 22 which are a direct reflection of the national ethos—run contrary to having it any other way. Other than sustained efforts by feminist organizations to secure workers' rights to parental and medical leave and expand access to affordable child care, easing the strain the system puts on working women with children has not been a political priority.

The peculiar reluctance to actively address the needs of working families in the 23 United States results from a muddled confluence of ideology about women, work, family, children, personal responsibility and the power of the free market to serve the true needs of the people.[20] According to Dr. Sheila Kamerman of the Clearinghouse on International Developments in Child, Youth & Family Policies at Columbia University, the U.S. sends

> "mixed messages about how to balance work and family life. We believe that it is in the best interest of our children to be with their mothers when they are very young, and more recently, have come to see the benefits of fathers spending time with their young children. We also believe that it is the responsibility of both parents to contribute to the economic well being of their families. Yet we continue to hold back from putting policies in place that will allow working mothers, and fathers, to succeed in both the workplace and at home."[21]

Although a 1998 survey found that 82 percent of women and 75 percent of men 24 "favored the idea of developing a new insurance program that would give families some income when a worker takes a family or medical leave,"[22] the U.S. remains one of only two wealthy nations lacking a national program of paid parental leave for working men and women. Australia, the other laggard in the paid leave department, offers working women up to 52 weeks of unpaid, job protected leave for the birth and care of a newborn. The 12 weeks of unpaid parental leave guaranteed to American workers who qualify under the provisions of the 1993 Family and Medical Leave Act[23] look downright skimpy compared to the benefits provided to working families in Western Europe.[24]

31 states are currently studying the feasibility of implementing paid leave pro- 25 grams. In 2002, California became the first state in the nation to pass legislation providing up to 6 weeks of wage replacement benefits to workers who take time off work to care for a seriously ill child, spouse, parent, domestic partner, or to bond with a new child. However, the national campaign for paid leave—which is coordinated by the National Partnership for Women and Families, an organization which was instrumental in securing the passage of the FMLA—suffered a serious setback in October 2003 when President George W. Bush revoked the "Baby UI" rule—an experimental regulation allowing states to tap into unemployment funds to cover wage replacement for leave takers who were caring for a newborn or newly adopted child.

The campaign for universal, affordable child care—which was a centerpiece of 26 the feminist agenda in the 1960s—is now so politically untouchable that advocates have been forced to "reframe" the public debate to focus on universal access to "early childhood education."[25] Child care remains a problem issue, and not just because Americans remain uneasy about young children being cared for by someone other than their mothers. (Despite the regular bashing child care takes in the media, nearly every reliable study has shown that a moderate amount of high-quality non-parental care is, in many cases, beneficial to the learning readiness and social development of young children.) A more immediate concern is the economic marginalization of low-income female workers—often mothers themselves—who typically provide child care for more affluent families. On the other hand, low-income families spend as much as 25 percent of their household earnings on child care, and in some urban areas, low-income families spend more on center-based day care for their young children than they do on housing.[26]

So far, the private sector has failed to produce an acceptable solution to address 27 the fact that when parents must work, someone else has to take care of their kids. But don't expect the state to step in to pick up the slack any time soon. Lurking in the shadows of our national mentality is the unhealthy fiction that if we could just get every working mother happily married and send her back home to stay, some of our more pressing economic and social problems would magically evaporate.[27] But the old "normal"— that idealized retroland of 1950s family life—is gone for good. We're living in the new normal now, and it's high time we figured out how to do a better job of it. Meanwhile, the pressures on working families are only getting worse, and mothers are especially likely to feel the squeeze.

## Push Comes to Shove

There will always be women—and men—from all walks of American life who passion- 28 ately believe that the only way to bring up happy, healthy children is to do it the "old fash- ioned" way: mom taking care of things on the homefront, dad out bringing home the bacon. Couples who hold this view are not necessarily anti-feminist reactionaries longing for a bygone era where men were men and women were housewives (although some of the most vocal proponents of traditional "family values" definitely fall into this camp).

Anecdotal accounts suggest that a number of single-earner couples with children 29 share a more enlightened understanding that unpaid care work and wage-earning work contribute equally to the security and well-being of the family. Some mothers and fathers ultimately decide the most realistic way to manage the range of responsibilities that come with the job-marriage-children package is for each parent to "specialize" in a different kind of work. While dual-earner families are by far the norm, the number of children being raised by full-time stay-at-home mothers in the U.S. rose 13 percent between 1994 and 2002. Analysts believe both economic and cultural factors fed this trend.

In families with two married parents and children under 15, the parent that special- 30 izes in caregiving is predictably more likely to be the female one. In 2002, 5.2 million married mothers stayed at home to care for their families while their spouse was in the full-time labor force. Young children living in two parent households are 56 times more likely to live with a stay-at-home mother/employed father than they are to live with a stay- at-home dad.[28]

While cultural attitudes about male and female roles contribute to this disparity, 31 there are also economic considerations. Women's earnings are, on average, 23 percent lower than those of men with the same qualifications in comparable jobs. Of married mothers who worked for pay in 2002, 46 percent of those with at least one child under 6 years old and one or more children aged 6 to 17 earned less than $5,000 in wages or salary; 80 percent earned less than $30,000 a year—in other words, less than the base- line living wage for a family of four in most U.S. communities.[29,30]

When the cost of child care and the rate of taxation on the wages of secondary 32 earners is factored in—not to mention the advantage of having one parent available to act as a buffer when the primary breadwinner brings home negative spillover from paid work—some middle-class couples with children may conclude that it's more cost effective and better for all concerned if mom quits her job.

Plenty of women who trade in fast-paced careers for a life lived on child time are 33 happy with their decision. They see the work of child rearing as personally rewarding and socially important and take enormous pride in being the primary caregiver for their families. However, not every mother who's retreated from the paid labor force—temporarily or for the long haul—is prepared to describe the stay-at-home arrangement as her first, best choice.

Joan, a 38-year-old mother of one living in the Midwest, left her well-paid IT job 34 four years ago when her son was born—not because she felt caregiving was a higher calling, but because she was convinced there were no other realistic alternatives. "In my utopia, benefits like health care and retirement wouldn't be attached to a particular job—they'd be available to all citizens. The workweek would be 30 hours and there would be state-funded child care. Part-time jobs employing high-education skills (with prorated advancement possibility) would be available," she says. "If I lived in my utopia, I would not be a stay-at-home mom. But the way things are now, being the stay-at-home mom is simply the least worst choice for our family."

Joan doesn't know when she will return to paid work, or what kind of work she may 35 be doing when she does. "After four years out of the IT workforce, my skills are obsolete. But I can't see myself wasting my time working for a minimum wage at WalMart."

Moms determined to stick it out in the paid labor force hold another piece of the 36 motherhood-and-work puzzle.[31] Julie, an architect living in Southern California, is expecting her second child. She works 32 hours a week in an office of 70 people. "Half of the employees are women. I am one of two women with children. My male co-workers who have children (about 20) have wives who stay home. Many of these men have said to me, 'I wish my wife could work part-time so I could spend more time with my children, but as the single bread winner I cannot push for family-friendly work options for fear that I will be out of a job.'"

Julie worries that no one will be left to agitate for a change in the workplace if 37 more high-powered women opt out. "What do I tell the younger women I work with now? '. . . Don't focus on your work, honey, you better get yourself married to a guy who can provide'? Furthermore, what do I tell my daughter?" Julie says that she battles thoughts of leaving the workforce versus staying with it every day. But she adds, "It's hard for me to see how the women who 'opt-out' will lead a revolution in the workplace when they are not there to push for things to be different. I think that everyone's choice has a place, I just think a complete rejection of the system has the potential to create a different (perhaps parallel) system rather than changing the one we have.

## Back into the Fray

What happens to women who gear down their commitment to paid employment when 38 they're ready to pick up where they left off is another issue altogether, and so far the news on that front is not exactly encouraging. Some advisors warn it's extremely unlikely that women who've been out of the workforce for three to five years will be hired for positions offering the same level of responsibility or compensation they had in their previous occupations. Others feel the employment patterns of the downsizing culture—where most experienced workers have periods of unemployment, as well as several jobs listed on their resume—may be more favorable to women who have an extended gap in their employment record.[32]

According to Ann Crittenden, author of *The Price of Motherhood*, much depends 39 on the strength of the labor market, but it's not impossible for moms re-entering the workforce to find exactly the job they really want—if they persevere and are prepared to do whatever it takes to show employers they have the skills and experience to do the work. "Mothers returning to the workforce also face a tremendous cultural bias against women who stay at home," says Crittenden, who is working on a new book about job skills and motherhood. "Employers are not immune to negative stereotyping that characterizes homemakers as incompetent individuals."

Wilcox is cautiously optimistic that mothers who return to the workforce may have 40 their best years ahead of them. "The highest proportion of overall work/life success— meaning success at home, at work, and with balancing the two—is reported by women ages 50–64 with no children at home. That is the only time that the rate of overall feelings of success of women with children exceeds that of men with children." Wilcox notes that both men and women feel least successful when they've got preschoolers at home.

The trend Wilcox finds the most promising, though, is the explosion of woman- 41 owned businesses. "Women are starting businesses at twice the rate of men. And I'll be very interested to see what sort of impact these businesses have in the future, particularly as women are more able to give their time and energy toward them." Wilcox hopes that these new women-led businesses will provide a more receptive conduit for women re-entering the workforce. "After all, as the Families and Work Institute has found, women in senior management can be an important indicator in determining the relative family-friendliness of an employer."

Only time will tell if the resurgence of "sequencing" mothers into the market- 42 place will merit attention as another stage of the family and work "revolution." But in so very many ways, the media-driven focus on the fate of well-to-do mothers who bag the full-time-plus-overtime treadmill in favor of the joys of family life is utterly irrelevant. Of course, it's a pot shot at feminism—a smug "we told you so" aimed at those of us who still believe a woman should be able to combine public achievement and personal happiness without making inordinate compromises in any important area of her life. It's also a sleight of hand, a misdirection of our cultural angst about the changing meaning of family, that deflects public attention away from truly serious social problems that put millions of mothers and fathers and kids at risk every single day—social problems that could be resolved if not for a pathetic shortage of political will.

## Notes

1. Perhaps the best outcome of the publication of Lisa Belkin's *The Opt-Out Revolution* is that it spawned a deluge of intelligent criticism discussing the realities of motherhood, work, and barriers to women's leadership, including articles by Joan Walsh of *Salon*, Katha Pollitt of *The Nation*, Bee Lavender of *HipMama*, and Susan J. Douglas for *In These Times*. An online discussion board at nytimes.com also generated over 900 reader comments in the week following the publication of Belkin's article.

   "Clueless in Manhattan" by Joan Walsh
   "There They Go Again" by Katha Pollitt
   "Revolution or Regression" by Bee Lavender
   "Mommas in the Marketplace" by Susan J. Douglas

2. Reports about mothers leaving the professional workforce to focus on family crop up in work-life columns and lifestyle pages of major and local dailies, popular magazines, and television

news segments at regular intervals, but particularly in the weeks before Mother's Day. More recently, the *Washington Times* ran a feature by Gabriella Boston, *Home from the Office* (November 16, 2003) and in early October 2003 Sue Shellenbarger, the work-life columnist for the *Wall Street Journal*, wrote an article about the stress on breadwinners in single-earner families. Also: *Family Time: Why some women quit their coveted tenure-track jobs*, Piper Fogg, *The Chronicle of Higher Education*, June 13, 2003; *A Labor of Love, Star Tribune*, May 9, 2003; *Full-time moms trade careers for kids*, Bill Torpy, *The Atlanta Journal-Constitution*, April 8, 2003; *What moms want now, Redbook Magazine*, March 2003, which reports on a survey that found "Sixty-five percent of stay-at-home moms are pleased with their choice, while a mere 27 percent of mothers who work full-time say they have jobs because they want them and find them fulfilling"; *Mommy Me and an Advanced Degree*, Ann Marsh, *The Los Angeles Times*, January 6, 2002.

3. Data on mothers' workforce participation is from the U.S Census Bureau, Current Population Survey, *Fertility of American Women: June 2002*, issued October 2003. Overall, the number of mothers who return to paid employment within 12 months of a child's birth has declined slightly since an all-time high of 59 percent in 1998. Today, 54 percent of mothers with infants and 72 percent of other mothers between the ages of 15 and 44 work for pay—rates of maternal employment that have been relatively stable since the early 1990s.

4. *Why Moms Stay Home*, Joan C. Williams, *The Washington Post*, July 17, 2003.

5. *2002 National Study of the Changing Workforce*, The Families and Work Institute, 2003. The authors of the 2002 NSCW do note that jobs classified as "managerial" include "people who manage fast-food outlets and small retail stores as well as CEOs of major corporations," and "professionals" include "high-earning physicians and lawyers as well as low-earning nurses and school teachers." According to the study, two out of every three women work in "other" occupations—primarily in the service and manufacturing sectors.

6. For example, see *Shared Work, Balanced Care: New Norms for Organizing Market Work and Unpaid Care Work* by Eileen Appelbaum, Thomas Bailey, Peter Berg, and Arne L. Kalleberg, Economic Policy Institute, 2002.

7. *2002 National Study of the Changing Workforce*. The Families and Work Institute, 2003. One of the things that may change married women's mind about the "fair" distribution of care work and paid work is that they are typically responsible for over two-thirds of the unpaid labor that goes into housekeeping and child-rearing, and the tasks they regularly do—such as the household shopping, preparing and serving food, and helping children with schoolwork—tend to be more time sensitive than the domestic tasks men take responsibility for.

8. Gallinsky, et al., *Feeling Overworked: When Work Becomes Too Much*. The Families and Work Institute, 2001.

9. *2002 National Study of the Changing Workforce*, The Families and Work Institute, 2003.

10. *Ibid.*

11. The Conference Board, Executive Action Brief No. 69, September 2003, *America's Unhappy Workforce: Job Satisfaction Continues to Wither* by Lynn Franco. The organization has been tracking the job satisfaction of U.S. workers since 1995.

12. U.S. Census Bureau, Current Population Survey, *Fertility of American Women: June 2003*, October 2003.

13. *2002 National Study of the Changing Workforce*, The Families and Work Institute, 2003.

14. *More Companies Downsize Family Friendly Programs*, Stephanie Armour, *USA Today*, October 19, 2003.

15. Men are doing more around the house than they were 25 years ago, but in most dual-earners couples with children, dad is not carrying anywhere near half of the carework load. The *2002 National Study of the Changing Workforce* (The Families and Work Institute, 2003) found that 77 percent of women in dual-earner families with children take greater responsibility for cooking, 78 percent take greater responsibility for cleaning and 70 percent take greater responsibility for routine childcare. The "second shift" lives, and the prospect of reducing the daily grind of double-duty may be enough to convince some mothers that it's time to reassess their commitment to paid work.

16. According to the *2002 National Survey of the Changing Workforce* (The Families and Work Institute, 2003), wives in dual-earner couples contribute an average of 42 percent of the household income.

17. *Work and Family: The Balancing Act*, Alfred P. Sloan Center Newsletter, University of Chicago, June 2001. Preliminary results from the 500 Family Survey.
18. *2002 National Study of the Changing Workforce*, The Families and Work Institute, 2003.
19. *The Mom Economy: The Mothers' Guide to Getting Family-Friendly Work*, Elizabeth Wilcox, 2003. http://www.themomeconomy.com
20. See Sharon Hays, *The Cultural Contradictions of Motherhood*, 1996 and *Motherhood and its discontents: Why mothers need a social movement of their own*, Judith Stadtman Tucker, The Mothers Movement Online, 2003.
21. Clearinghouse on International Developments in Child, Youth & Family Policies at Columbia University, Issue Brief, Spring 2002 *Mother's Day: More Than Candy And Flowers, Working Parents Need Paid Time-Off*.
22. *Family Matters: A National Survey of Women and Men conducted for The National Partnership for Women & Families*, February 1998.
23. Two out of every 5 U.S. workers are not protected by the FMLA. U.S. Department of Labor, *Family and Medical Leave Surveys 2000 Update*.
24. The Clearinghouse on International Developments in Child, Youth and Family Policies at Columbia University, Maternity, Paternity, and Parental Leaves in the OECD Countries 1998–2002.
25. Susan Nall Bales, *Early Childhood Education and the Framing Wars*, 1998.
26. *Child Care Costs Busting NJ Family Budgets*, Peggy O'Crowley, *The Star-Ledger*, April 11, 2003.
27. *Conservatives Push for Marriage Promotion Programs*, Betty Holcomb, Women's Enews, October 15, 2002.
28. U.S. Census Bureau, Current Population Survey, *Children's Living Arrangements and Characteristics: March 2002*, June 2003.
29. U.S. Census Bureau, Current Population Survey, *Children's Living Arrangements and Characteristics: March 2002*, June 2003.
30. *Hardships in America: The Real Story of Working Families*, Economic Policy Institute, July 2001.
31. Read the MMO commentary by Sara Eversden, *Wake up call: Think family-friendly workplace policies are the new norm? Think again*.
32. CNN.com, *Tips for workforce re-entry*, by Shelly K. Schwartz, May 11, 2001.

## READING FOR CONTENT

1. What does the heading before paragraph 11, "It is really about work," mean in the context of Stadtman Tucker's survey of writing about working mothers?
2. What does the heading before paragraph 22, "The other Big Picture," refer to?
3. What does the heading before paragraph 28, "Push comes to shove," refer to?

## READING FOR GENRE, ORGANIZATION, AND STYLISTIC FEATURES

1. In paragraphs 5–10, underline such qualifying transitional words and phrases as "in reality," "however," and "but." How do these words shape Stadtman Tucker's conversation with the writing that she reports in this section?
2. In paragraphs 11–21, underline such transitional words and phrases as "not surprisingly," "not only," "even if," and "in other words." How do these words shape Stadtman Tucker's conversation with the writing that she reports in this section?
3. Consult the footnotes that Stadtman Tucker includes in paragraphs 22–27. What genres do they represent? What cumulative weight do they lend to her argument?

## READING FOR RHETORICAL CONTEXT

1. Why does Stadtman Tucker begin her inquiry into social and economic issues affecting working mothers with a summary and criticism of Lisa Belkin's article "The Opt-Out Revolution" in *The New York Times?* How does she relate this article to facts and figures drawn from specialized scholarship and research on the topic?

2. Underline phrases that cite other authors or publications such as "Williams notes that" (paragraph 6), "a 2002 survey . . . agreed that" (paragraph 9), "a September 2003 report . . . found that" (paragraph 14), and the like. What do their verbs suggest about Stadtman Tucker's attitudes toward these authors and publications? Does she approve or disapprove of the insights that they provide?

3. What is the rhetorical effect of incorporating into paragraphs 28–37 various anecdotes and the personal experiences of Joan and Julie?

## WRITING ASSIGNMENTS

1. Write a three-page essay that briefly reviews the review of opinions and conclusions presented in Stadtman Tucker's article. After noting and summarizing what you take to be the most important of these opinions and conclusions, explain how they might relate to one another as sides taken in a possible debate. Who agrees with whom? Who disagrees? What personal remarks might you contribute to the conversation?

2. Interview an individual or couple who is coping with motherhood and either full-time or part-time work. Based on what your interviewees tell you, write a three-page essay in which you compare their accounts with the picture of working motherhood that Stadtman Tucker presents.

3. Drawing upon the data that Stadtman Tucker reports in her article, write a three-page essay addressed to your classmates about the current crisis besetting working moms in our society. As you write, bear in mind different arguments that you might make for classmates who might have children as opposed to those who do not, and weave these arguments into your essay.

■ ■ ■ ■ ■ ■ ■ ■ ■ ■

# Many Women at Elite Colleges Set Career Path to Motherhood

## Louise Story

*Graduated from Yale University in 2003, Louise Story based her report on comments by members of her graduating class on whether they would prefer stay-at-home motherhood to balancing careers and motherhood.*

## PREREADING

As she approached graduation, Louise Story interviewed female friends and classmates at Yale University about their plans to juggle professional careers with marriage and mother-hood. Some critics have pointed out that the elite environment at Yale harbors opportunities unavailable elsewhere. Others have argued that Story's report misrepresents the majority view at Yale. Form collaborative groups among your own classmates to poll what their post-graduation plans might be. In each group of five or six students, appoint an "interviewer" who will record the views articulated by the group. Reassemble the class and have each interviewer report on the results. What diversity emerges from these reports? What similari-ties? What trends? Do male views differ notably from female views? Write a paragraph or two summarizing your impression of results from this exercise.

Cynthia Liu is precisely the kind of high achiever Yale wants: smart (1510 SAT), dis-  1
ciplined (4.0 grade point average), competitive (finalist in Texas oratory competition), musical (pianist), athletic (runner) and altruistic (hospital volunteer). And at the start of her sophomore year at Yale, Ms. Liu is full of ambition, planning to go to law school.

So will she join the long tradition of famous Ivy League graduates? Not likely. By  2
the time she is 30, this accomplished 19-year-old expects to be a stay-at-home mom.

"My mother's always told me you can't be the best career woman and the best  3
mother at the same time," Ms. Liu said matter-of-factly. "You always have to choose one over the other."

At Yale and other top colleges, women are being groomed to take their place in  4
an ever more diverse professional elite. It is almost taken for granted that, just as they make up half the students at these institutions, they will move into leadership roles on an equal basis with their male classmates.

There is just one problem with this scenario: many of these women say that is not  5
what they want.

Many women at the nation's most elite colleges say they have already decided  6
that they will put aside their careers in favor of raising children. Though some of these students are not planning to have children and some hope to have a family and work full time, many others, like Ms. Liu, say they will happily play a traditional female role, with motherhood their main commitment.

Much attention has been focused on career women who leave the work force to  7
rear children. What seems to be changing is that while many women in college two or three decades ago expected to have full-time careers, their daughters, while still in college, say they have already decided to suspend or end their careers when they have children.

"At the height of the women's movement and shortly thereafter, women were  8
much more firm in their expectation that they could somehow combine full-time work with child rearing," said Cynthia E. Russett, a professor of American history who has taught at Yale since 1967. "The women today are, in effect, turning realistic."

Dr. Russett is among more than a dozen faculty members and administrators at  9
the most exclusive institutions who have been on campus for decades and who said in interviews that they had noticed the changing attitude.

Many students say staying home is not a shocking idea among their friends. 10
Shannon Flynn, an 18-year-old from Guilford, Conn., who is a freshman at Harvard,
says many of her girlfriends do not want to work full time.

"Most probably do feel like me, maybe even tending toward wanting to not work 11
at all," said Ms. Flynn, who plans to work part time after having children, though she is
torn because she has worked so hard in school.

"Men really aren't put in that position," she said.                                  12

Uzezi Abugo, a freshman at the University of Pennsylvania who hopes to become a 13
lawyer, says she, too, wants to be home with her children at least until they are in school.

"I've seen the difference between kids who did have their mother stay at home 14
and kids who didn't, and it's kind of like an obvious difference when you look at it," said
Ms. Abugo, whose mother, a nurse, stayed home until Ms. Abugo was in first grade.

While the changing attitudes are difficult to quantify, the shift emerges repeat- 15
edly in interviews with Ivy League students, including 138 freshman and senior females
at Yale who replied to e-mail questions sent to members of two residential colleges over
the last school year.

The interviews found that 85 of the students, or roughly 60 percent, said that 16
when they had children, they planned to cut back on work or stop working entirely.
About half of those women said they planned to work part time, and about half wanted
to stop work for at least a few years.

Two of the women interviewed said they expected their husbands to stay home 17
with the children while they pursued their careers. Two others said either they or their
husbands would stay home, depending on whose career was furthest along.

The women said that pursuing a rigorous college education was worth the time 18
and money because it would help position them to work in meaningful part-time jobs
when their children are young or to attain good jobs when their children leave home.

In recent years, elite colleges have emphasized the important roles they expect 19
their alumni—both men and women—to play in society.

For example, earlier this month, Shirley M. Tilghman, the president of Prince- 20
ton University, welcomed new freshmen, saying: "The goal of a Princeton education is
to prepare young men and women to take up positions of leadership in the 21st century. Of course, the word 'leadership' conjures up images of presidents and C.E.O.'s,
but I want to stress that my idea of a leader is much broader than that."

She listed education, medicine and engineering as other areas where students 21
could become leaders.

In an e-mail response to a question, Dr. Tilghman added: "There is nothing 22
inconsistent with being a leader and a stay-at-home parent. Some women (and a handful of men) whom I have known who have done this have had a powerful impact on
their communities."

Yet the likelihood that so many young women plan to opt out of high-powered 23
careers presents a conundrum.

"It really does raise this question for all of us and for the country: when we work so 24
hard to open academics and other opportunities for women, what kind of return do we
expect to get for that?" said Marlyn McGrath Lewis, director of undergraduate admissions at Harvard, who served as dean for coeducation in the late 1970's and early 1980's.

It is a complicated issue and one that most schools have not addressed. The 25
women they are counting on to lead society are likely to marry men who will make

enough money to give them a real choice about whether to be full-time mothers, unlike those women who must work out of economic necessity.

It is less than clear what universities should, or could, do about it. For one, a person's expectations at age 18 are less than perfect predictors of their life choices 10 years later. And in any case, admissions officers are not likely to ask applicants whether they plan to become stay-at-home moms. 26

University officials said that success meant different things to different people and that universities were trying to broaden students' minds, not simply prepare them for jobs. 27

"What does concern me," said Peter Salovey, the dean of Yale College, "is that so few students seem to be able to think outside the box; so few students seem to be able to imagine a life for themselves that isn't constructed along traditional gender roles." 28

There is, of course, nothing new about women being more likely than men to stay home to rear children. 29

According to a 2000 survey of Yale alumni from the classes of 1979, 1984, 1989 and 1994, conducted by the Yale Office of Institutional Research, more men from each of those classes than women said that work was their primary activity—a gap that was small among alumni in their 20's but widened as women moved into their prime child-rearing years. Among the alumni surveyed who had reached their 40's, only 56 percent of the women still worked, compared with 90 percent of the men. 30

A 2005 study of comparable Yale alumni classes found that the pattern had not changed. Among the alumni who had reached their early 40's, just over half said work was their primary activity, compared with 90 percent of the men. Among the women who had reached their late 40's, some said they had returned to work, but the percentage of women working was still far behind the percentage of men. 31

A 2001 survey of Harvard Business School graduates found that 31 percent of the women from the classes of 1981, 1985 and 1991 who answered the survey worked only part time or on contract, and another 31 percent did not work at all, levels strikingly similar to the percentages of the Yale students interviewed who predicted they would stay at home or work part time in their 30's and 40's. 32

What seems new is that while many of their mothers expected to have hard-charging careers, then scaled back their professional plans only after having children, the women of this generation expect their careers to take second place to child rearing. 33

"It never occurred to me," Rebecca W. Bushnell, dean of the School of Arts and Sciences at the University of Pennsylvania, said about working versus raising children. "Thirty years ago when I was heading out, I guess I was just taking it one step at a time." 34

Dr. Bushnell said young women today, in contrast, are thinking and talking about part-time or flexible work options for when they have children. "People have a heightened awareness of trying to get the right balance between work and family." 35

Sarah Currie, a senior at Harvard, said many of the men in her American Family class last fall approved of women's plans to stay home with their children. 36

"A lot of the guys were like, 'I think that's really great,'" Ms. Currie said. "One of the guys was like, 'I think that's sexy.' Staying at home with your children isn't as polarizing of an issue as I envision it is for women who are in their 30's now." 37

For most of the young women who responded to e-mail questions, a major factor shaping their attitudes seemed to be their experience with their own mothers, about three out of five of whom did not work at all, took several years off or worked only part time. 38

"My stepmom's very proud of my choice because it makes her feel more valuable," 39 said Kellie Zesch, a Texan who graduated from the University of North Carolina two years ago and who said that once she had children, she intended to stay home for at least five years and then consider working part time. "It justified it to her, that I don't look down on her for not having a career."

Similarly, students who are committed to full-time careers, without breaks, also 40 cited their mothers as influences. Laura Sullivan, a sophomore at Yale who wants to be a lawyer, called her mother's choice to work full time the "greatest gift."

"She showed me what it meant to be an amazing mother and maintain a career," 41 Ms. Sullivan said.

Some of these women's mothers, who said they did not think about these issues so 42 early in their lives, said they were surprised to hear that their college-age daughters had already formed their plans.

Emily Lechner, one of Ms. Liu's roommates, hopes to stay home a few years, 43 then work part time as a lawyer once her children are in school.

Her mother, Carol, who once thought she would have a full-time career but gave 44 it up when her children were born, was pleasantly surprised to hear that. "I do have this bias that the parents can do it best," she said. "I see a lot of women in their 30's who have full-time nannies, and I just question if their kids are getting the best."

For many feminists, it may come as a shock to hear how unbothered many young 45 women at the nation's top schools are by the strictures of traditional roles.

"They are still thinking of this as a private issue; they're accepting it," said Laura 46 Wexler, a professor of American studies and women's and gender studies at Yale. "Women have been given full-time working career opportunities and encouragement with no social changes to support it.

"I really believed 25 years ago," Dr. Wexler added, "that this would be solved 47 by now."

Angie Ku, another of Ms. Liu's roommates who had a stay-at-home mom, talks 48 nonchalantly about attending law or business school, having perhaps a 10-year career and then staying home with her children.

"Parents have such an influence on their children," Ms. Ku said. "I want to have 49 that influence. Me!"

She said she did not mind if that limited her career potential.                         50

"I'll have a career until I have two kids," she said. "It doesn't necessarily matter 51 how far you get. It's kind of like the experience: I have tried what I wanted to do."

Ms. Ku added that she did not think it was a problem that women usually do most 52 of the work raising kids.

"I accept things how they are," she said. "I don't mind the status quo. I don't see 53 why I have to go against it."

After all, she added, those roles got her where she is.                              54

"It worked so well for me," she said, "and I don't see in my life why it wouldn't work." 55

## READING FOR CONTENT

1. What is the effect of the phrase "Not likely" in paragraph 2? What is the effect of the sentence beginning "Yet the likelihood that" in paragraph 23?

2. What is the effect of the sentence beginning "There is, of course, nothing new" in paragraph 29?

## READING FOR GENRE, ORGANIZATION, AND STYLISTIC FEATURES

1. Mark off in the text each instance of direct quotation. Reread the author's statements preceding and following each quotation. Does she appear to frame quotations with remarks that lead you to accept or reject their claims? Which genre of reporting does she seem to represent: personal? scientific? argumentative? objective?

2. What is the effect of presenting data from surveys of Yale and Harvard graduates in paragraph 4? Do the categories that the data fit into exactly match the category of the topic about stay-at-home moms?

3. Does the author present any diversity of view or change of attitude among her respondents? Does her report register any controversy?

## READING FOR RHETORICAL CONTEXT

1. What is the effect of the sentence that begins "For most of the young women" in paragraph 38? What does this sentence imply about the social backgrounds of the young women interviewed for this article?

2. What is the effect of the sentence that begins "For many feminists" in paragraph 45? What does this sentence imply about the audience of readers who might take this article seriously?

## WRITING ASSIGNMENTS

1. Write a two-page letter to the editor of the newspaper that printed this report in which you state your agreement with its findings and your perception that its views are more commonly held than many people imagine.

2. Write a two-page letter to the editor of the newspaper that printed this report in which you state your disagreement with its findings on the grounds of your own conversations with college-age women about their plans for motherhood and careers.

■ ■ ■ ■ ■ ■ ■ ■ ■ ■ ■

# Weasel-Words Rip My Flesh!

### *Jack Shafer*

*Jack Shafer is a writer for* Slate *online magazine. Before joining* Slate, *he edited two city weeklies,* Washington City Paper *and* San Francisco Weekly. *He has also written on new media, the press, and drug policy for the* New York Times Magazine *and* Inquiry.

## PREREADING

Good or bad writing brings into play not just what writers say but how they say it. Some literary critics who analyze style would say that you cannot divorce what someone says (usually referred to as content) from how that person says it (usually referred to as style). Taking this approach, Shafer demonstrates the flaws in Story's argument (in her article, "Many Women at Elite Colleges Set Career Path to Motherhood," on pages 91–95) from her stylistic choices in articulating that argument. As a prewriting exercise, examine Story's major claim that "many women at the nation's most elite colleges say they have already decided that they will put aside their careers in favor of raising children." Ask yourself, what does "many" mean? Most? Some? A good number? A vocal minority? What does "elite" mean? Highly selective (the dictionary definition of the term)? Expensive (though many expensive colleges are not highly selective)? Competitive (though many competitive colleges are not expensive)? High-achieving (though many high-achieving colleges are not selective)? And so the argument runs. There are few ways of predicting real professional success on the basis of a college's presumed reputation. You could continue this analysis by asking what "already decided" means: Are those who have "already decided" irrevocably committed to their decisions? What does "will put aside" mean? Does the phrase suggest "totally jettison" or rather "merely softpeddle"? And when does "raise children" begin (presumably at birth, though some retain full-time nannies for the preschool years) or end (presumably upon high-school graduation, though some enter into career-long partnerships with their adult children that extend until late retirement). Jot down some of the "weasel" terms that, when unexamined, can mean many things in the first few paragraphs of Story's report, and speculate about their possible applications. Afterward, form collaborative groups to compile a master list of such weasel terms.

How many "many's" are too many for one news story?    1

Like its fellow weasel-words—*some, few, often, seems, likely, more*—*many* serves    2
writers who haven't found the data to support their argument. A light splash of weasel-words in a news story is acceptable if only because journalism is not an exact science and deadlines must be observed. But when a reporter pours a whole jug of weasel-words into a piece, as Louise Story does on Page One of today's (Sept. 20) *New York Times* in "Many Women at Elite Colleges Set Career Path to Motherhood," she needlessly exposes one of the trade's best-kept secrets for all to see. She deserves a week in the stockades. And her editor deserves a month.

Story uses the particularly useful weasel-word "many" 12 times—including once    3
in the headline—to illustrate the emerging trend of Ivy League-class women who attend top schools but have no intention of assuming the careers they prepared for.

She informs readers that "**many of these women**" being groomed for the occupa-    4
tional elite "say that is not what they want." She repeats the weasel-word three more times in the next two paragraphs and returns to it whenever she needs to express impressive quantity but has no real numbers. She writes:

**Many women** at the nation's most elite colleges say they have already decided that    5
they will put aside their careers in favor of raising children. Though some of these students are not planning to have children and some hope to have a family and work full time, **many others**, like Ms. Liu, say they will happily play a traditional female role, with motherhood their main commitment.

Much attention has been focused on career women who leave the work force    6
to rear children. What seems to be changing is that while **many women in college** two or three decades ago expected to have full-time careers, their daughters, while still in college, say they have already decided to suspend or end their careers when they have children. . . .

**Many students** say staying home is not a shocking idea among their friends. 7
Shannon Flynn, an 18-year-old from Guilford, Conn., who is a freshman at Harvard,
says **many of her girlfriends** do not want to work full time. . . .

Yet the likelihood that so **many young women** plan to opt out of high-powered 8
careers presents a conundrum. . . .

What seems new is that while **many of their mothers** expected to have hard- 9
charging careers, then scaled back their professional plans only after having children, the
women of this generation expect their careers to take second place to child rearing. . . .

Sarah Currie, a senior at Harvard, said **many of the men** in her American Fam- 10
ily class last fall approved of women's plans to stay home with their children. . . .

**For many feminists** it may come as a shock to hear how unbothered **many** 11
**young women** at the nation's top schools are by the strictures of traditional roles. . . .

None of these *many*'s quantify anything. You could as easily substitute the word 12
*some* for every *many* and not gain or lose any information. Or substitute the word *few*
and lose only the wind in Story's sails. By fudging the available facts with weasel-words,
Story makes a flaccid concept stand up—as long as nobody examines it closely.

For instance, Story writes that she interviewed "Ivy League students, including 13
138 freshman and senior females at Yale who replied to e-mail questions sent to members of two residential colleges over the last school year." Because she doesn't attribute
the preparation of the e-mail survey to anyone, one must assume that she or somebody at
the *Times* composed and sent it. A questionnaire answered by 138 Yale women sounds
like it may contain useful information. But even a social-science dropout wouldn't consider the findings to be anything but anecdotal unless he knew 1) what questions were
asked (Story doesn't say), 2) how many questionnaires were distributed, and 3) why
freshman and seniors received the questionnaires to the exclusion of sophomores and
juniors. Also, 4) a social-science dropout would ask if the *Times* contaminated its e-mailed
survey with leading questions and hence attracted a disproportionate number of respondents who sympathize with the article's underlying and predetermined thesis.

To say Story's piece contains a thesis oversells it. Early on, she squishes out on the 14
whole concept with the weasel-word *seems*. She writes, "What **seems** to be changing is
that while many women in college two or three decades ago expected to have full-time
careers, their daughters, while still in college, say they have already decided to suspend
or end their careers when they have children."

To say the piece was edited would also be to oversell it. Story rewrites this *seems* 15
sentence about two-thirds of the way through the piece without adding any new information. "What **seems** new is that while many of their mothers expected to have hard-
charging careers, then scaled back their professional plans only after having children,
the women of this generation expect their careers to take second place to child rearing."
[Emphasis added.]

Halfway through, Story discounts her allegedly newsworthy findings by acknowl- 16
edging that a "person's expectations at age 18 are less than perfect predictors of their life
choices 10 years later." If they're less than perfect predictors, then why are we reading
about their predictions on Page One of the *Times*?

While bogus, "Many Women at Elite Colleges Set Career Path to Motherhood" 17
isn't false: It can't be false because it never says anything sturdy enough to be tested. So,
how did it get to Page One? Is there a *New York Times* conspiracy afoot to drive feminists
crazy and persuade young women that their place is in the home? Did the paper dispatch

*Times* columnist John Tierney to write a pair of provocative columns on this theme earlier this year (early May and late May) and recruit Lisa Belkin to dance the idea around in an October 2003 *Times Magazine* feature titled "The Opt-Out Revolution"?

Nah.

I suspect a *Times* editor glommed onto the idea while overhearing some cocktail party chatter—"Say, did you hear that Sam blew hundreds of thousands of dollars sending his daughter to Yale and now she and her friends say all they want in the future is to get married and stay at home?"—and passed the concept to the writer or her editors and asked them to develop it.

You can see the editorial gears whirring: The press has already drained our collective anxiety about well-educated women assuming greater power in the workplace. So, the only editorial vein left to mine is our collective anxiety about well-educated women deciding *not* to work instead. Evidence that the *Times* editors know how to push our buttons can be found in the fact that as I write, this slight article about college students is the "Most E-Mailed" article on the newspaper's Web site.

## READING FOR CONTENT

1. Why does Shafer focus upon the word "many" as an especially slippery "weasel-word"?
2. What other "weasel-words" does Shafer flag for analysis?
3. What does Shafer mean in paragraph 13 when he writes "even a social-science dropout wouldn't consider the findings to be anything but anecdotal unless he knew . . ."?

## READING FOR GENRE, ORGANIZATION, AND STYLISTIC FEATURES

1. How does the emphasis on Story's choice of words identify Shafer's article as rhetorical analysis?
2. How does Shafer develop his analysis?
3. Why does Shafer claim in paragraph 14 that the report has no thesis?

## READING FOR RHETORICAL CONTEXT

1. Whom does Shafer address?
2. Why does Shafer claim in paragraph 15 that "to say the piece was edited would also be to oversell it"?
3. What considerations might Shafer's analysis prompt his own readers to reflect upon?

## WRITING ASSIGNMENTS

1. Write a two-page letter to the editor of the newspaper that published Story's report protesting the sloppy writing and nonexistent editing that brought this article into print. Draw upon Shafer's analysis to strengthen your claims.
2. Take an article or editorial from a recent newspaper or magazine and analyze its language in the same terms that Shafer does. Write a two-page analysis of its rhetoric exposing its "weasel words," inexact formulations, and misleading arguments.

3. Write a two-page defense of Story's report arguing that, although its writing might be flawed, her argument still reflects careful thinking by many people in her generation.

■ ■ ■ ■ ■ ■ ■ ■ ■ ■ ■

# Critique of "Many Women at Elite Colleges Set Career Path to Motherhood"

## Tracey Meares

*Tracey Meares joined the University of Chicago Law School faculty in 1994 after serving as an Honors Program Trial Attorney in the Antitrust Division of the United States Department of Justice. She is also a faculty member of the University of Chicago Center for the Study of Race, Politics and Culture and an executive committee member of the Northwestern/University of Chicago Joint Center for Poverty Research.*

## PREREADING

Previous articles in this chapter have used the word "elite" to describe the undergraduate environment that Louise Story reports upon in "Many Women at Elite Colleges Set Path to Motherhood," on pages 91–95. What does this word mean in the context of a college education? What does it mean in the broader social context of families and working mothers? Though Story's article focuses on an issue apparently concerned with gender, what other social and cultural issues does it raise? Jot down provisional answers to these questions in your notebook. Afterward dedicate a brief class discussion to definitions of "elite" that have emerged from student notebooks.

Yesterday, *The New York Times* published an article called, "Many Women at Elite  1
Colleges Set Career Path to Motherhood." The basic premise of the article is that young women at colleges such as Yale (the focus of the piece) expect to be stay-at-home mothers by the time they are 30—including those young women who plan to go to law school.

"My mother's always told me you can't be the best career woman and the best  2
mother at the same time," says one student interviewed for the piece.

There are many things I find perplexing, indeed troubling, about the article, but  3
I'll mention only a few here.

First, there is the obvious race and class dynamic at play. While the article men-  4
tions that the women interviewed are "likely to marry men who will make enough money to give them a real choice about whether to be full-time mothers, unlike those women who must work out of economic necessity," nowhere does the article mention the racial cleavages present between the groups of women, even at elite colleges, poised to make such a choice.

Second, the authors of the article seem to lack any self-awareness that this is a social  5
structural issue as much as a cultural one. Changes in workplace structure, provision of

public pre-school and daycare, as well as changes in the tax structure generally can impact these decisions across gender groups.

Finally, while the article focuses upon the choices that the young women are 6 making (or think that they will) and the approval of the mothers of these women, nowhere does the article explore what the fathers of these women think or the opinions of their male peers, save the comment of one young man who piped up that his class-mates' decision to stay at home was "sexy." One wonders how sexy he will believe the decision to be when he's out working 3000 hours a year and spending little time with his partner or his children.

## READING FOR CONTENT

1. Summarize the author's three dominant points in one sentence for each point.
2. In paragraph 6, what social or cultural impact might feedback from Story's male peers produce?

## READING FOR GENRE, ORGANIZATION, AND STYLISTIC FEATURES

1. This article originated on a blog. What stylistic and organizational features characterize it?
2. Does this article convey a strong sense of organization? Or does it instead mimic the flow of casual conversation?
3. How informal is Meares's style? Does informality weaken or trivialize her argument?

## READING FOR RHETORICAL CONTEXT

1. What readership does the author address?
2. Does the nature of this readership and the format in which the article appeared help to explain the author's tone or point of view? How?

## WRITING ASSIGNMENT

Adopting the kind of style and organization that you would use on a blog, write a single-page response to Tracey Meares in which you elaborate upon her three points either in support or in opposition.

■ ■ ■ ■ ■ ■ ■ ■ ■ ■ ■

# Desperate Housewives of the Ivy League?

## Katha Pollitt

*Katha Pollitt is a well-known poet and a biweekly contributor of the column "Subject to Debate" to* The Nation *magazine. Her collected essays appear in three volumes;* Reasonable Creatures *(1995),* Subject to Debate *(2001), and* Virginity or Death! *(2006).*

## PREREADING

The preceding article has drawn attention to issues beyond gender that affect a woman's decision whether or not to be a stay-at-home mom. Form collaborative groups of five students each and ask participants to summon concrete issues that play into the dynamics of such a decision. Students may draw upon the experiences of friends, family members, or possibly themselves, or they may introduce issues that they have encountered in newspaper reports, talk-show discussions, or work for other courses. Each participant should jot down some considerations that have influenced people in making such decisions.

September 20's prime target for press critics, social scientists and feminists was the New York Times front-page story "Many Women at Elite Colleges Set Career Path to Motherhood," by Louise Story (Yale '03). Through interviews and a questionnaire e-mailed to freshmen and senior women residents of two Yale colleges (dorms), Story claims to have found that 60 percent of these brainy and energetic young women plan to park their expensive diplomas in the bassinet and become stay-home mothers. Over at Slate, Jack Shafer slapped the Times for using weasel words ("many," "seems") to make a trend out of anecdotes and vague impressions: In fact, Story presents no evidence that more Ivy League undergrads today are planning to retire at 30 to the playground than ten, twenty or thirty years ago. Simultaneously, an armada of bloggers shredded her questionnaire as biased (hint: If you begin with "When you have children," you've already skewed your results) and denounced her interpretation of the answers as hype. What she actually found, as the writer Robin Herman noted in a crisp letter to the Times, was that 70 percent of those who answered planned to keep working full or part time through motherhood. Even by Judith Miller standards, the Story story was pretty flimsy. So great was the outcry that the author had to defend her methods in a follow-up on the Times website three days later.

With all that excellent insta-critiquing, I feared I'd lumber into print too late to add a new pebble to the sling. But I did find one place where the article is still Topic No. 1: Yale. "I sense that she had a story to tell, and she only wanted to tell it one way," Mary Miller, master of Saybrook, one of Story's targeted colleges, told me. Miller said Story met with whole suites of students and weeded out the women who didn't fit her thesis. Even among the ones she focused on, "I haven't found that the students' views are as hard and fast as Story portrayed them." (In a phone call Story defended her research methods, which she said her critics misunderstood, and referred me to her explanation on the web.) One supposed future homemaker of America posted an anonymous dissection of Story's piece at www.mediabistro.com. Another told me in an e-mail that while the article quoted her accurately, it "definitely did not turn out the way I thought it would after numerous conversations with Louise." That young person may be sadder but wiser—she declined to let me interview her or use her name—but history professor Cynthia Russett, quoted as saying that women are "turning realistic," is happy to go public with her outrage. Says Russett, "I may have used the word, but it was in the context of a harsh or forced realism that I deplored. She made it sound like this was a trend of which I approved. In fact, the first I heard of it was from Story, and I'm not convinced it exists." In two days of interviewing professors, grad students and

*The Nation*, 281.12 (October 17, 2005): 14. http://www.thenation.com/doc/20051017/pollitt. Reprinted with permission of the author.

undergrads, I didn't find one person who felt Story fairly represented women at Yale. Instead, I learned of women who had thrown Story's questionnaire away in disgust, heard a lot of complaints about Yale's lack of affordable childcare and read numerous scathing unpublished letters to the *Times*, including a particularly erudite one from a group of sociology graduate students. Physics professor Megan Urry had perhaps the best riposte: She polled her class of 120, using "clickers" (electronic polling devices used as a teaching tool). Of forty-five female students, how many said they planned "to be stay-at-home primary parent"? Two. Twenty-six, or 58 percent, said they planned to "work full time, share home responsibilities with partner"—and good luck to them, because 33 percent of the men said they wanted stay-home wives.

The most interesting question about Story's article is why the *Times* published     3
it—and on page one yet. After all, as Shafer pointed out, it had run an identical story, "Many Young Women Now Say They'd Pick Family Over Career," on the front page December 28, 1980. (He even turned up one of its star subjects, Princeton alum Mary Anne Citrino, who says she was completely misrepresented by the *Times:* She never wanted to stay home and never did.) I'm particularly grateful to Shafer for digging up that old clip, because somehow I had formed the erroneous impression that the *Times* used to be less sexist than it is now—the week Story made the front page also saw an article uncritically reporting a drug-company study that claimed female executives are addled by menopause, and a Styles piece about the menace to society posed by mothers pushing luxury strollers on Manhattan sidewalks. All that was missing was one of those columns in which John Tierney explains that women, bless their hearts, lack the competitive drive to win at Scrabble.

Story's article is essentially an update on Lisa Belkin's 2003 *Times Magazine*     4
cover story about her Princeton classmates, whose marginalization at work after having children was glowingly portrayed as an "opt-out revolution" and which claimed that women "don't run the world" because "they don't want to." What's painful about the way the *Times* frames work-family issues is partly its obsessive focus on the most privileged as bellwethers of American womanhood—you'd never know that most mothers who work need the money. But what's also depressing is the way the *Times* lumps together women who want to take a bit of time off or work reasonable hours—the hours that everybody worked not so long ago—with women who give up their careers for good. Cutting back to spend time with one's child shouldn't be equated with lack of commitment to one's profession. You would not know, either, that choices about how to combine work and motherhood are fluid and provisional and not made in a vacuum. The lack of good childcare and paid parental leave, horrendous work hours, inflexible career ladders, the still-conventional domestic expectations of far too many men and the industrial-size helpings of maternal guilt ladled out by the media are all part of it.

Wouldn't you like to read a front-page story about that?     5

## READING FOR CONTENT

1. What argument does Pollitt launch in paragraph 2 with the sentence, "But I did find one place where the article is still Topic No. 1: Yale"?

2. In paragraph 4, how does Pollitt expand her statement that "choices . . . are fluid and provisional and not made in a vacuum" into her most powerful claim?

# READING FOR GENRE, ORGANIZATION, AND STYLISTIC FEATURES

1. What features of style, tone, and voice relate to this article's first appearance in its author's biweekly column in a national magazine?
2. Does each paragraph make a separate point? What advantage does this organization have for casual readers of a national magazine?

# READING FOR RHETORICAL CONTEXT

1. As she reports her interviews with Story and other women at Yale, Pollitt draws upon a template of strong verbs to convey what they said: "Miller told me," "Story defended," Russet "goes public with her outrage," "Urry had perhaps the best riposte." What effect do these verbs have on her argument?
2. Reread Pollitt's article and underline its transitional words, phrases, and clauses, such as "Instead, I learned of women," "After all, as Shafer pointed out," and "What's painful about the way." What effect do these transitions have on Pollitt's argument?

# WRITING ASSIGNMENTS

1. Write a one-page letter to the editor of the magazine that published this article either commending Pollitt for setting the record straight or arguing that she has missed Story's larger point about the widespread wish of many women to be stay-at-home moms.
2. Write a one- or two-page essay that expands the last sentence of paragraph 4. Argue whether or not that sentence accurately describes the workplace conditions of our present society.

■ ■ ■ ■ ■ ■ ■ ■ ■ ■ ■

# Homeward Bound

## Linda R. Hirshman

*Linda R. Hirshman has been Distinguished Visiting Professor at Brandeis University and is currently writing a book about marriage after feminism. She is the author of* Hard Bargains: The Politics of Sex *(1998),* A Woman's Guide to Law School *(1999), and most recently* Get to Work: A Manifesto for Women of the World.

## PREWRITING

Some critics of Louise Story's "Many Women at Elite Colleges Set Career Path to Motherhood" (91–95) have argued that affluent beneficiaries of an elite education should feel obliged to serve as role models for less-affluent, less-elite contemporaries. If you agree with this claim, jot down a few reasons why you believe in it. If you disagree, jot down a few reasons why not. If you can think of exceptions to either position, take note of them with pertinent examples. Students should then form collaborative groups to discuss the exceptions they have noted.

## I. The Truth About Elite Women

Half the wealthiest, most-privileged, best-educated females in the country stay home  1
with their babies rather than work in the market economy. When in September *The New York Times* featured an article exploring a piece of this story, "Many Women at Elite Colleges Set Career Path to Motherhood," the blogosphere went ballistic, countering with anecdotes and sarcasm. *Slate's* Jack Shafer accused the *Times* of "weasel-words" and of publishing the same story—essentially, "The Opt-Out Revolution"—every few years, and, recently, every few weeks. (A month after the flap, the *Times'* only female columnist, Maureen Dowd, invoked the elite-college article in her contribution to the *Times'* running soap, "What's a Modern Girl to Do?" about how women must forgo feminism even to get laid.) The colleges article provoked such fury that the *Times* had to post an explanation of the then–student journalist's methodology on its Web site.

There's only one problem: There is important truth in the dropout story. Even  2
*though* it appeared in *The New York Times.*

I stumbled across the news three years ago when researching a book on marriage  3
after feminism. I found that among the educated elite, who are the logical heirs of the agenda of empowering women, feminism has largely failed in its goals. There are few women in the corridors of power, and marriage is essentially unchanged. The number of women at universities exceeds the number of men. But, more than a generation after feminism, the number of women in elite jobs doesn't come close.

Why did this happen? The answer I discovered—an answer neither feminist lead-  4
ers nor women themselves want to face—is that while the public world has changed, albeit imperfectly, to accommodate women among the elite, private lives have hardly budged. The real glass ceiling is at home.

Looking back, it seems obvious that the unreconstructed family was destined to  5
re-emerge after the passage of feminism's storm of social change. Following the original impulse to address everything in the lives of women, feminism turned its focus to cracking open the doors of the public power structure. This was no small task. At the beginning, there were male juries and male Ivy League schools, sex-segregated want ads, discriminatory employers, harassing colleagues. As a result of feminist efforts—and larger economic trends—the percentage of women, even of mothers in full- or part-time employment, rose robustly through the 1980s and early '90s.

But then the pace slowed. The census numbers for all working mothers leveled  6
off around 1990 and have fallen modestly since 1998. In interviews, women with enough money to quit work say they are "choosing" to opt out. Their words conceal a crucial reality: the belief that women are responsible for child-rearing and homemaking was largely untouched by decades of workplace feminism. Add to this the good evidence that the upper-class workplace has become more demanding and then mix in the successful conservative cultural campaign to reinforce traditional gender roles and you've got a perfect recipe for feminism's stall.

*The American Prospect* [Princeton, N.J.], 16.12 (December 2005): 20–26.

People who don't like the message attack the data. True, the *Times* based its    7
college story on a survey of questionable reliability and a bunch of interviews. It is not
necessary to give credence to Dowd's book, from which her *Times Magazine* piece was
taken and which seems to be mostly based on her lifetime of bad dates and some e-mails
from fellow *Times* reporters, to wonder if all this noise doesn't mean something important is going on in the politics of the sexes.

What evidence *is* good enough? Let's start with you. Educated and affluent    8
reader, if you are a 30- or 40-something woman with children, what are you doing? Husbands, what are your wives doing? Older readers, what are your married daughters with
children doing? I have asked this question of scores of women and men. Among the
affluent-educated-married population, women are letting their careers slide to tend the
home fires. If my interviewees are working, they work largely part time, and their part-
time careers are not putting them in the executive suite.

Here's some more evidence: During the '90s, I taught a course in sexual bargain-    9
ing at a very good college. Each year, after the class reviewed the low rewards for child-
care work, I asked how the students anticipated combining work with child-rearing. At
least half the female students described lives of part-time or home-based work. Guys
expected their female partners to care for the children. When I asked the young men
how they reconciled that prospect with the manifest low regard the market has for child
care, they were mystified. Turning to the women who had spoken before, they said, uni-
formly, "But she chose it."

Even Ronald Coase, Nobel Prize–winner in economics in 1991, quotes the apho-    10
rism that "the plural of anecdote is data." So how many anecdotes does it take to make
data? I—a 1970s member of the National Organization for Women (NOW), a donor to
EMILY's List, and a professor of women's studies—did not set out to find this. I stumbled
across the story when, while planning a book, I happened to watch *Sex and the City*'s
Charlotte agonize about getting her wedding announcement in the "Sunday Styles" section of *The New York Times*. What better sample, I thought, than the brilliantly educated
and accomplished brides of the "Sunday Styles," circa 1996? At marriage, they included
a vice president of client communication, a gastroenterologist, a lawyer, an editor, and a
marketing executive. In 2003 and 2004, I tracked them down and called them. I interviewed about 80 percent of the 41 women who announced their weddings over three
Sundays in 1996. Around 40 years old, college graduates with careers: Who was more
likely than they to be reaping feminism's promise of opportunity? Imagine my shock
when I found almost all the brides from the first Sunday at home with their children.
Statistical anomaly? Nope. Same result for the next Sunday. And the one after that.

Ninety percent of the brides I found had had babies. Of the 30 with babies, five    11
were still working full time. Twenty-five, or 85 percent, were not working full time. Of
those not working full time, 10 were working part time but often a long way from their
prior career paths. And half the married women with children were not working at all.

And there is more. In 2000, Harvard Business School professor Myra Hart sur-    12
veyed the women of the classes of 1981, 1986, and 1991 and found that only 38 percent
of female Harvard MBAs were working full time. A 2004 survey by the Center for Work-
Life Policy of 2,443 women with a graduate degree or very prestigious bachelor's degree
revealed that 43 percent of those women with children had taken a time out, primarily
for family reasons. Richard Posner, federal appeals-court judge and occasional University of Chicago adjunct professor, reports that "the [*Times*] article confirms—what
everyone associated with such institutions [elite law schools] has long known: that a

vastly higher percentage of female than of male students will drop out of the workforce to take care of their children."

How many anecdotes to become data? The 2000 census showed a decline in the 13 percentage of mothers of infants working full time, part time, or seeking employment. Starting at 31 percent in 1976, the percentage had gone up almost every year to 1992, hit a high of 58.7 percent in 1998, and then began to drop—to 55.2 percent in 2000, to 54.6 percent in 2002, to 53.7 percent in 2003. Statistics just released showed further decline to 52.9 percent in 2004. Even the percentage of working mothers with children who were not infants declined between 2000 and 2003, from 62.8 percent to 59.8 percent.

Although college-educated women work more than others, the 2002 census 14 shows that graduate or professional degrees do not increase work-force participation much more than even one year of college. When their children are infants (under a year), 54 percent of females with graduate or professional degrees are not working full time (18 percent are working part time and 36 percent are not working at all). Even among those who have children who are not infants, 41 percent are not working full time (18 percent are working part time and 23 percent are not working at all).

Economists argue about the meaning of the data, even going so far as to contend 15 that more mothers are working. They explain that the the bureau changed the definition of "work" slightly in 2000, the economy went into recession, and the falloff in women without children was similar.

However, even if there wasn't a falloff but just a leveling off, this represents not a 16 loss of present value but a loss of hope for the future—a loss of hope that the role of women in society will continue to increase.

The arguments still do not explain the absence of women in elite workplaces. If 17 these women were sticking it out in the business, law, and academic worlds, now, 30 years after feminism started filling the selective schools with women, the elite workplaces should be proportionately female. They are not. Law schools have been graduating classes around 40-percent female for decades—decades during which both schools and firms experienced enormous growth. And, although the legal population will not be 40-percent female until 2010, in 2003, the major law firms had only 16-percent female partners, according to the American Bar Association. It's important to note that elite workplaces like law firms grew in size during the very years that the percentage of female graduates was growing, leading you to expect a higher female employment than the pure graduation rate would indicate. The Harvard Business School has produced classes around 30-percent female. Yet only 10.6 percent of Wall Street's corporate officers are women, and a mere nine are Fortune 500 CEOs. Harvard Business School's dean, who extolled the virtues of interrupted careers on *60 Minutes*, has a 20-percent female academic faculty.

It is possible that the workplace is discriminatory and hostile to family life. If firms 18 had hired every childless woman lawyer available, that alone would have been enough to raise the percentage of female law partners above 16 percent in 30 years. It is also possible that women are voluntarily taking themselves out of the elite job competition for lower status and lower-paying jobs. Women must take responsibility for the consequences of their decisions. It defies reason to claim that the falloff from 40 percent of the class at law school to 16 percent of the partners at all the big law firms is unrelated to half the mothers with graduate and professional degrees leaving full-time work at childbirth and staying away for several years after that, or possibly bidding down.

This isn't only about day care. Half my *Times* brides quit *before* the first baby 19 came. In interviews, at least half of them expressed a hope never to work again. None had realistic plans to work. More importantly, when they quit, they were already alienated from their work or at least not committed to a life of work. One, a female MBA, said she could never figure out why the men at her workplace, which fired her, were so excited about making deals. "It's only money," she mused. Not surprisingly, even where employers offered them part-time work, they were not interested in taking it.

## II. The Failure of Choice Feminism

What is going on? Most women hope to marry and have babies. If they resist the tradi- 20 tional female responsibilities of child-rearing and householding, what Arlie Hochschild called "The Second Shift," they are fixing for a fight. But elite women aren't resisting tradition. None of the stay-at-home brides I interviewed saw the second shift as unjust; they agree that the household is women's work. As one lawyer-bride put it in explaining her decision to quit practicing law after four years, "I had a wedding to plan." Another, an Ivy Leaguer with a master's degree, described it in management terms: "He's the CEO and I'm the CFO. He sees to it that the money rolls in and I decide how to spend it." It's their work, and they must do it perfectly. "We're all in here making fresh apple pie," said one, explaining her reluctance to leave her daughters in order to be interviewed. The family CFO described her activities at home: "I take my [3-year-old] daughter to all the major museums. We go to little movement classes."

Conservatives contend that the dropouts prove that feminism "failed" because it 21 was too radical, because women didn't want what feminism had to offer. In fact, if half or more of feminism's heirs (85 percent of the women in my *Times* sample), are not working seriously, it's because feminism wasn't radical enough: It changed the workplace but it didn't change men, and, more importantly, it didn't fundamentally change how women related to men.

The movement did start out radical. Betty Friedan's original call to arms com- 22 pared housework to animal life. In *The Feminine Mystique* she wrote, "[V]acuuming the living room floor—with or without makeup—is not work that takes enough thought or energy to challenge any woman's full capacity. . . . Down through the ages man has known that he was set apart from other animals by his mind's power to have an idea, a vision, and shape the future to it . . . when he discovers and creates and shapes a future different from his past, he is a man, a human being."

Thereafter, however, liberal feminists abandoned the judgmental starting point 23 of the movement in favor of offering women "choices." The choice talk spilled over from people trying to avoid saying "abortion," and it provided an irresistible solution to feminists trying to duck the mommy wars. A woman could work, stay home, have 10 children or one, marry or stay single. It all counted as "feminist" as long as she *chose* it. (So dominant has the concept of choice become that when Charlotte, with a push from her insufferable first husband, quits her job, the writers at *Sex and the City* have her screaming, "I choose my choice! I choose my choice!")

Only the most radical fringes of feminism took on the issue of gender relations at 24 home, and they put forth fruitless solutions like socialism and separatism. We know the story about socialism. Separatism ran right into heterosexuality and reproduction, to say nothing of the need to earn a living other than at a feminist bookstore. As feminist historian Alice Echols put it, "Rather than challenging their subordination in domestic life, the feminists of NOW committed themselves to fighting for women's integration into public life."

Great as liberal feminism was, once it retreated to choice the movement had no 25
language to use on the gendered ideology of the family. Feminists could not say,
"Housekeeping and child-rearing in the nuclear family is not interesting and not
socially validated. Justice requires that it not be assigned to women on the basis of their
gender and at the sacrifice of their access to money, power, and honor."

The 50 percent of census answerers and the 62 percent of Harvard MBAs and the 26
85 percent of my brides of the *Times* all think they are "choosing" their gendered lives.
They don't know that feminism, in collusion with traditional society, just passed the
gendered family on to them to choose. Even with all the day care in the world, the personal is still political. Much of the rest is the opt-out revolution.

## III. What is to be Done?

Here's the feminist moral analysis that choice avoided: The family—with its repetitious, 27
socially invisible, physical tasks—is a necessary part of life, but it allows fewer opportunities for full human flourishing than public spheres like the market or the government. This less-flourishing sphere is not the natural or moral responsibility only of
women. Therefore, assigning it to women is unjust. Women assigning it to themselves
is equally unjust. To paraphrase, as Mark Twain said, "A man who chooses not to read is
just as ignorant as a man who cannot read."

The critics are right about one thing: Dopey *New York Times* stories do nothing to 28
change the situation. Dowd, who is many things but not a political philosopher, concludes by wondering if the situation will change by 2030. Lefties keep hoping the
Republicans will enact child-care legislation, which probably puts us well beyond
2030. In either case, we can't wait that long. If women's flourishing does matter, feminists must acknowledge that the family is to 2005 what the workplace was to 1964 and
the vote to 1920. Like the right to work and the right to vote, the right to have a flourishing life that includes but is not limited to family cannot be addressed with language
of choice.

Women who want to have sex and children with men as well as good work in inter- 29
esting jobs where they may occasionally wield real social power need guidance, and they
need it early. Step one is simply to begin talking about flourishing. In so doing, feminism
will be returning to its early, judgmental roots. This may anger some, but it should
sound the alarm before the next generation winds up in the same situation. Next, feminists will have to start offering young women not choices and not utopian dreams but
*solutions* they can enact on their own. Prying women out of their traditional roles is not
going to be easy. It will require rules—rules like those in the widely derided book *The
Rules*, which was never about dating but about behavior modification.

There are three rules: Prepare yourself to qualify for good work, treat work seri- 30
ously, and don't put yourself in a position of unequal resources when you marry.

The preparation stage begins with college. It is shocking to think that girls cut off 31
their options for a public life of work as early as college. But they do. The first pitfall
is the liberal-arts curriculum, which women are good at, graduating in higher numbers
than men. Although many really successful people start out studying liberal arts, the
purpose of a liberal education is not, with the exception of a miniscule number of academic positions, job preparation.

So the first rule is to use your college education with an eye to career goals. 32
Feminist organizations should produce each year a survey of the most common job

opportunities for people with college degrees, along with the average lifetime earnings from each job category and the characteristics such jobs require. The point here is to help women see that yes, you can study art history, but only with the realistic understanding that one day soon you will need to use your arts education to support yourself and your family. The survey would ask young women to select what they are best suited for and give guidance on the appropriate course of study. Like the rule about accepting no dates for Saturday after Wednesday night, the survey would set realistic courses for women, helping would-be curators who are not artistic geniuses avoid career frustration and avoid solving their job problems with marriage.

After college comes on-the-job training or further education. Many of my *Times* 33 brides—and grooms—did work when they finished their educations. Here's an anecdote about the difference: One couple, both lawyers, met at a firm. After a few years, the man moved from international business law into international business. The woman quit working altogether. "They told me law school could train you for anything," she told me. "But it doesn't prepare you to go into business. I should have gone to business school." Or rolled over and watched her husband the lawyer using his first few years of work to prepare to go into a related business. Every *Times* groom assumed he had to succeed in business, and was really trying. By contrast, a common thread among the women I interviewed was a self-important idealism about the kinds of intellectual, prestigious, socially meaningful, politics-free jobs worth their incalculably valuable presence. So the second rule is that women must treat the first few years after college as an opportunity to lose their capitalism virginity and prepare for good work, which they will then treat seriously.

The best way to treat work seriously is to find the money. Money is the marker of 34 success in a market economy; it usually accompanies power, and it enables the bearer to wield power, including within the family. Almost without exception, the brides who opted out graduated with roughly the same degrees as their husbands. Yet somewhere along the way the women made decisions in the direction of less money. Part of the problem was idealism; idealism on the career trail usually leads to volunteer work, or indentured servitude in social-service jobs, which is nice but doesn't get you to money. Another big mistake involved changing jobs excessively. Without exception, the brides who eventually went home had much more job turnover than the grooms did. There's no such thing as a perfect job. Condoleezza Rice actually wanted to be a pianist, and Gary Graffman didn't want to give concerts.

If you are good at work you are in a position to address the third undertaking: the 35 reproductive household. The rule here is to avoid taking on more than a fair share of the second shift. If this seems coldhearted, consider the survey by the Center for Work-Life Policy. Fully 40 percent of highly qualified women with spouses felt that their husbands create more work around the house than they perform. According to Phyllis Moen and Patricia Roehling's *Career Mystique*, "When couples marry, the amount of time that a woman spends doing housework increases by approximately 17 percent, while a man's decreases by 33 percent." Not a single *Times* groom was a stay-at-home dad. Several of them could hardly wait for Monday morning to come. None of my *Times* grooms took even brief paternity leave when his children were born.

How to avoid this kind of rut? You can either find a spouse with less social power 36 than you or find one with an ideological commitment to gender equality. Taking the easier path first, marry down. Don't think of this as brutally strategic. If you are devoted to your career goals and would like a man who will support that, you're just doing what men throughout the ages have done: placing a safe bet.

In her 1995 book, *Kidding Ourselves: Babies, Breadwinning and Bargaining* 37 *Power*, Rhona Mahoney recommended finding a sharing spouse by marrying younger or poorer, or someone in a dependent status, like a starving artist. Because money is such a marker of status and power, it's hard to persuade women to marry poorer. So here's an easier rule: Marry young or marry much older. Younger men are potential high-status companions. Much older men are sufficiently established so that they don't have to work so hard, and they often have enough money to provide unlimited household help. By contrast, slightly older men with bigger incomes are the most dangerous, but even a pure counterpart is risky. If you both are going through the elite-job hazing rituals simultaneously while having children, someone is going to have to give. Even the most devoted lawyers with the hardest-working nannies are going to have weeks when no one can get home other than to sleep. The odds are that when this happens, the woman is going to give up her ambitions and professional potential.

It is possible that marrying a liberal might be the better course. After all, conser- 38 vatives justified the unequal family in two modes: "God ordained it" and "biology is destiny." Most men (and most women), including the liberals, think women are responsible for the home. But at least the liberal men should feel squeamish about it.

If you have carefully positioned yourself either by marrying down or finding 39 someone untainted by gender ideology, you will be in a position to resist bearing an unfair share of the family. Even then you must be vigilant. Bad deals come in two forms: economics and home economics. The economic temptation is to assign the cost of child care to the woman's income. If a woman making $50,000 per year whose husband makes $100,000 decides to have a baby, and the cost of a full-time nanny is $30,000, the couple reason that, after paying 40 percent in taxes, she makes $30,000, just enough to pay the nanny. So she might as well stay home. This totally ignores that both adults are in the enterprise together and the demonstrable future loss of income, power, and security for the woman who quits. Instead, calculate that all parents make a total of $150,000 and take home $90,000. After paying a full-time nanny, they have $60,000 left to live on.

The home-economics trap involves superior female knowledge and superior 40 female sanitation. The solutions are ignorance and dust. Never figure out where the butter is. "Where's the butter?" Nora Ephron's legendary riff on marriage begins. In it, a man asks the question when looking directly at the butter container in the refrigerator. "Where's the butter?" actually means butter my toast, buy the butter, remember when we're out of butter. Next thing you know you're quitting your job at the law firm because you're so busy managing the butter. If women never start playing the household-manager role, the house will be dirty, but the realities of the physical world will trump the pull of gender ideology. Either the other adult in the family will take a hand or the children will grow up with robust immune systems.

If these prescriptions sound less than family-friendly, here's the last rule: Have a 41 baby. Just don't have two. Mothers' Movement Online's Judith Stadtman Tucker reports that women who opt out for child-care reasons act only after the second child arrives. A second kid pressures the mother's organizational skills, doubles the demands for appointments, wildly raises the cost of education and housing, and drives the family to the suburbs. But cities, with their Chinese carryouts and all, are better for working mothers. It is true that if you follow this rule, your society will not reproduce itself. But if things get bad enough, who knows what social consequences will ensue? After all, the vaunted French child-care regime was actually only a response to the superior German birth rate.

## IV. Why do We Care?

The privileged brides of the *Times*—and their husbands—seem happy. Why do we care  42
what they do? After all, most people aren't rich and white and heterosexual, and they
couldn't quit working if they wanted to.

We care because what they do is bad for them, is certainly bad for society, and is  43
widely imitated, even by people who never get their weddings in the *Times*. This last is
called the "regime effect," and it means that even if women don't quit their jobs for
their families, they think they should and feel guilty about not doing it. That regime
effect created the mystique around *The Feminine Mystique*, too.

As for society, elites supply the labor for the decision-making classes—the senators,  44
the newspaper editors, the research scientists, the entrepreneurs, the policy-makers,
and the policy wonks. If the ruling class is overwhelmingly male, the rulers will make
mistakes that benefit males, whether from ignorance or from indifference. Media surveys reveal that if only one member of a television show's creative staff is female, the
percentage of women on-screen goes up from 36 percent to 42 percent. A world of
84-percent male lawyers and 84-percent female assistants is a different place than one
with women in positions of social authority. Think of a big American city with an
86-percent white police force. If role models don't matter, why care about Sandra Day
O'Connor? Even if the falloff from peak numbers is small, the leveling off of women in
power is a loss of hope for more change. Will there never again be more than one
woman on the Supreme Court?

Worse, the behavior tarnishes every female with the knowledge that she is almost  45
never going to be a ruler. Princeton President Shirley Tilghman described the elite colleges' self-image perfectly when she told her freshmen last year that they would be the
nation's leaders, and she clearly did not have trophy wives in mind. Why should society
spend resources educating women with only a 50-percent return rate on their stated
goals? The American Conservative Union carried a column in 2004 recommending
that employers stay away from such women or risk going out of business. Good psychological data show that the more women are treated with respect, the more ambition
they have. And vice versa. The opt-out revolution is really a downward spiral.

Finally, these choices are bad for women individually. A good life for humans  46
includes the classical standard of using one's capacities for speech and reason in a prudent way, the liberal requirement of having enough autonomy to direct one's own life,
and the utilitarian test of doing more good than harm in the world. Measured against
these time-tested standards, the expensively educated upper-class moms will be leading
lesser lives. At feminism's dawning, two theorists compared gender ideology to a caste
system. To borrow their insight, these daughters of the upper classes will be bearing
most of the burden of the work always associated with the lowest caste: sweeping and
cleaning bodily waste. Not two weeks after the Yalie flap, the *Times* ran a story of moms
who were toilet training in infancy by vigilantly watching their babies for signs of excre-
tion 24-7. They have voluntarily become untouchables.

When she sounded the blast that revived the feminist movement 40 years after  47
women received the vote, Betty Friedan spoke of lives of purpose and meaning, better
lives and worse lives, and feminism went a long way toward shattering the glass ceilings
that limited their prospects outside the home. Now the glass ceiling begins at home.
Although it is harder to shatter a ceiling that is also the roof over your head, there is no
other choice.

# READING FOR CONTENT

1. Can you find a single sentence that manages to express Hirshman's thesis? Or does the argument require paragraph 3 to do so? Does it also require paragraph 4 to complete the major claim that Hirshman makes in this article?

2. The four section headings stated before paragraphs 1, 20, 27, and 42 suggest that Hirshman moves from a critique of Story's report (sections I and II) to an advocacy for a particular solution (sections III and IV). List the measures that Hirshman advocates in paragraphs 28–36. How does her advocacy develop the critique she has made of Story's report?

3. What new phase of her argument does Hirshman initiate in paragraph 43? Does this phase follow directly from the preceding three sections about women's efforts to create equality in the workplace, or does it introduce a completely different set of problems about the role of models in society? How might these topics be related?

# READING FOR GENRE, ORGANIZATION, AND STYLISTIC FEATURES

1. Reconsider the four section headings stated before paragraphs 1, 20, 27, and 42. Do they imply that each section is addressing a separate topic and is consequently observing the form of a particular genre, such as critique in section I, history in section II, analysis in section III, and argument in section IV? If this article represents a composite genre, how does it relate its various parts to one another?

2. How does each of the four sections exemplify a different organizational plan? Why does section I include a great deal of data? Why does section II evoke personal anecdotes and statements made by prominent feminists? Why does section III propose several rules and then analyze them in sequence? Why does section IV ask a number of hard questions?

3. Underline the transitional sentences and paragraphs that introduce each of the four sections that begin in paragraphs 1, 20, 27, and 42. Which words, phrases, and clauses might you include in a template for expressing transitions?

# READING FOR RHETORICAL CONTEXT

1. Who is the implied audience as stated in paragraph 8? Does Hirshman strictly limit her address to this audience, or does she instead open her discussion to women of varying education and affluence, and to men as well as to women?

2. Do the comparisons between brides and grooms, husbands and wives in paragraphs 33–40 disparage men's contributions to marriage and family arrangements? How might Hirshman be trying to move her male readers to respond?

# WRITING ASSIGNMENTS

1. Write a two-page critique of section I in Hirshman's article in which you evaluate its data, judge its conclusions, and compare and contrast them with those of other articles in this chapter.

2. Write a two-page analysis of section III in Hirshman's article in which you evaluate its recommendations, judge its conclusions, and compare and contrast them with those of other articles in this chapter.

■ ■ ■ ■ ■ ■ ■ ■ ■ ■ ■

# The Year of Domesticity

## David Brooks

*David Brooks is a conservative columnist for* The New York Times. *He is the author of* Bobos in Paradise: The New Upper Class and How They Got There *(2003) and* How We Live Now (And Always Have) in the Future Tense *(2004).*

## PREREADING

If it is true that wives and mothers exercise dominant power over husbands and fathers in domesticity and parenting, what satisfactions and rewards might accompany that power? Do such satisfactions and rewards come with a safety net that assures the well-being of women when their domestic and parenting roles undergo change, as for example in the case of divorce or when children reach adulthood? Freewrite about whether women really do exercise such power, whether their satisfactions and rewards are commensurate with it, and whether safety nets guarantee their social and economic justice in times of change.

After a generation of feminist advance, women have more choices. They are freer 1
to pursue a career, stay home or figure out some combination of both. And this is progress, right?

Wrong, says Linda Hirshman, a retired Brandeis professor, in the December 2
issue of *The American Prospect*. Women who choose to stay home, she writes, stifle themselves and harm society. As she puts it, "The family—with its repetitious, socially invisible, physical tasks—is a necessary part of life, but it allows fewer opportunities for full human flourishing than public spheres like the market or the government."

Hirshman quotes Mark Twain, "A man who chooses not to read is just as ignorant 3
as a man who cannot read," and argues that a woman who chooses to stay home with her kids is just as weak as a woman who can't get out of the house.

Women need to be coached to make better choices, Hirshman advises. First, they 4
need to aim for careers that pay well: "The best way to treat work seriously is to find the money. Money is the marker of success in a market economy; it usually accompanies power, and it enables the bearer to wield power, including within the family."

Second, women need to find husbands who will share domestic drudgery 5
equally: "You can either find a spouse with less social power than you or find one with an ideological commitment to gender equality."

Finally, she writes, "Have a baby. Just don't have two." Women with two kids find 6
it harder to pursue a demanding career.

Women who stay home worrying about diapers have "voluntarily become untouch- 7
ables," Hirshman concludes. If these women continue to make bad choices, men will
perpetually dominate the highest levels of society. It is time, she says, to re-radicalize
feminism.

Hirshman's essay really clears the sinuses. It's a full-bore, unapologetic blast of 8
1975 time-warp feminism and it deserves one of the 2005 Sidney Awards, which I've
created for the best magazine essays of the year, because it is impossible to read this
manifesto without taking a few minutes to figure out why she is so wrong.

But of course, she is wrong.                                                  9

First, she's wrong with her astonishing assertion that high-paying jobs lead to 10
more human flourishing than parenthood. Look back over your life. Which memories
do you cherish more, those with your family or those at the office? If Hirshman thinks
high-paying careers lead to more human flourishing, I invite her to spend a day as an
associate at a big law firm.

Second, she's wrong to assume that work is the realm of power and home is the 11
realm of powerlessness. The domestic sphere may not offer the sort of brutalizing, dominating power Hirshman admires, but it is the realm of unmatched influence. If there is
one thing we have learned over the past generation, it is that a child's I.Q., mental
habits and destiny are largely shaped in the first few years of life, before school or the
outside world has much influence.

Children, at least, understand parental power. In "Eminem Is Right," a Sidney 12
Award-winning essay in *Policy Review*, Mary Eberstadt notes a striking change in pop
music. "If yesterday's rock was the music of abandon, today's is the music of abandonment." An astonishing number of hits, from artists ranging from Pearl Jam to Everclear
to Snoop Dogg, are about kids who feel neglected by their parents. This is a need
Hirshman passes over.

Her third mistake is to not even grapple with the fact that men and women are 13
wired differently. The Larry Summers flap produced an outpouring of work on the neuro-
logical differences between men and women. I'd especially recommend "The Inequality Taboo" by Charles Murray in *Commentary* and a debate between Steven Pinker and
Elizabeth Spelke in the online magazine *Edge*.

One of the findings of this research is that men are more interested in things and 14
abstract rules while women are more interested in people. (You can come up with your
own Darwinian explanation as to why.)

When you look back over the essays of 2005, you find many that dealt with the 15
big foreign policy issues of the year, but also an amazing number that dealt with domesticity. That's because the deeper you get into economic or social problems—national
competitiveness, poverty, school performance, incarceration—the more you realize
the answers lie with good parenting and good homes.

Hirshman has it exactly backward. Power is in the kitchen. The big problem is 16
not the women who stay there but the men who leave.

## READING FOR CONTENT

1. What three mistakes does Brooks attribute to Hirshman in paragraphs 10–13?
2. Elaborate upon Brooks's brief conclusion in paragraph 16. Has he justified his
   claim that "power is in the kitchen"? What sort of power? How much of it? Under

what conditions and with what guarantees? What does he mean when he identifies "the big problem" with "the men who leave"? Has he explained this last clause in the paragraphs that precede this conclusion?

## READING FOR GENRE, ORGANIZATION, AND STYLISTIC FEATURES

1. As a feature of its publication as a newspaper editorial, this article's sentence structures are simple and its paragraphs are brief. Is this feature conducive to nuanced reasoning?
2. This editorial is organized in two parts: first, a summary of Hirshman's three major claims (paragraphs 4–6); and second, a statement of her three major mistakes (paragraphs 10–13). Does the second set of three mistakes correspond exactly with the first set of three claims, or does Brooks venture into different topics in each part?
3. Why does Brooks end the first paragraph with a rhetorical question?

## READING FOR RHETORICAL CONTEXT

1. Brooks alludes to Mark Twain (paragraph 3), Mary Eberstadt (paragraph 12), Charles Murray (paragraph 13) and Steven Pinker and Elizabeth Spelke (paragraph 13). What role do these allusions play? Which names do you recognize? What sorts of positions—liberal or conservative—do you imagine these writers promote?
2. How specific is Brooks about the audience he addresses as "you" in paragraphs 14–15? Does this audience display a concrete personality?

## WRITING ASSIGNMENTS

1. Write a one-page letter to the editor of the newspaper that published this editorial either commending Brooks for setting the record straight or arguing that he has missed Hirshman's larger point about the need for mothers to enter the workforce.
2. Write a one- or two-page essay that expands the last sentence of paragraph 16. Argue whether or not this sentence accurately describes the domestic conditions of our present society.

■ ■ ■ ■ ■ ■ ■ ■ ■ ■ ■

# The Return of the Mommy Wars

## Cathy Young

*Cathy Young is the author of* Ceasefire! Why Women and Men Must Join Forces to Achieve Political Equality *(Free Press, 1999) and a Contributing Editor to* Reason *magazine.*

# PREREADING

What might it mean to claim that wives and mothers have a "choice" about whether to join the workforce or not? Is such a choice a luxury or a necessity? And, once made, can it be unmade? Think about wives and mothers whom you know in the workforce. Are their marital or domestic situations roughly equivalent, or do they instead represent a range of social and economic statuses characteristic of our society? When these women joined the workforce, or rejoined it after motherhood, have they clung to their early decisions, or have their career patterns changed and proved fluid over time? Make a list of the varieties you've encountered in your experience. Afterward dedicate a brief class discussion to the varieties of "choice" that have emerged from student notebooks.

After lying dormant for a while, the Mommy Wars reignited late last year with 1 "Homeward Bound," an article by the feminist legal scholar Linda Hirshman in the December *American Prospect*. Hirshman, who is not known for mincing words (she earned a spot in Bernard Goldberg's book *People Who Are Screwing Up America* by declaring that women who leave work to raise children are choosing "lesser lives"), boldly assailed the truism that, when it comes to full-time mothering vs. careers, it's a good thing for women to have a choice.

Hirshman surveyed 33 women whose wedding announcements had appeared in 2 *The New York Times* during a three-week period in 1996. Of the 30 with children, she found, half were not employed and only five were working fulltime.

Drawing on that and other studies, Hirshman argued that such choices by elite 3 women are a primary reason for the dearth of women in the corridors of political and economic power. Instead of "reaping feminism's promise of opportunity," she wrote, these former lawyers and executives are in the kitchen baking apple pies.

While Hirshman conceded that those "expensively educated upper-class moms" 4 seemed happy at home, she insisted that "what they do is bad for them [and] is certainly bad for society." It's bad for society, she argued, because it reinforces a "gendered ideology" of family roles, perpetuates male dominance in government and business, and deprives ambitious women of role models. It's bad for the women who give up careers, Hirshman suggested, because they fall short of a good life, which includes "using one's capacities for speech and reason in a prudent way," "having enough autonomy to direct one's own life," and "doing more good than harm in the world."

Interestingly, Hirshman blamed this state of affairs less on patriarchy or conser- 5 vatism than on feminism. Specifically, she damned its alleged failure to challenge male/female relations in the home, its embrace of the language of "choice," and its consequent refusal to be "judgmental" toward women who make "bad" choices.

Hirshman's article caused a splash from the blogosphere to *The New York Times*, 6 where David Brooks described her piece as an "unapologetic blast of 1975 time-warp feminism" and lamented her equation of careers with human flourishing, concluding his column with an unapologetic blast of 1955 time-warp feminine mystique: "Power is in the kitchen."

In fact, Hirshman's article raised important questions. The mantra of "choice" is too 7 simplistic, and it does evade the underlying conflicts of the Mommy Wars. And Hirshman doesn't even get to the real reasons for these tensions, forces far more concrete than the posited need for women in positions of power to promote other women's interests and to serve as role models.

Unquestionably, a working woman's lot would be much easier in a society where    8
stay-at-home motherhood was as rare as stay-at-home fatherhood is today. No mother would have to field a child's guilt-tripping question, "But Mommy, why do you have to work?" School-teachers and other parents would not assume that a mother was available for volunteering at school and sewing Halloween costumes. Working women would not have to deal with the lingering suspicion that, having started families, they will quit work or dramatically reduce their job commitments. Nor would they have to compete with men who have the advantage of a homemaker wife to handle most domestic responsibilities.

Conversely, a stay-at-home mother would have a far easier time in a society    9
where full-time motherhood was the norm. She would not have to contend with large numbers of women whose professional status might make her feel inadequate. She would not dread the question, "What do you do?" Single-earner families would face less economic pressure, and employers would probably be able to favor male breadwinners without facing legal or social sanctions.

The talk of choice also tends to downplay the fact that no personal choice is made    10
in a cultural vacuum. The belief that women who stay home are better mothers is definitely in the cultural bloodstream: In polls, at least two-thirds of Americans agree that it's better for the children if the mother stays home, a figure that has risen in recent years.

Surely these beliefs can translate into more or less subtle disapproval toward    11
working mothers, and guilt and self-blame on the part of mothers themselves. For all the talk of respecting choices, only half the stay-at-home moms in a recent *Washington Post* poll agreed that it's all right for the mother of a young child to get a job if she's happier working.

Hirshman rightly reminds us, too, of the peril of forgetting or dismissing the femi-    12
nist critique of full-time domesticity and motherhood. Financial dependency aside, I agree that it's not good for adult human beings to have no identity independent of personal relationships or to become too enmeshed in emotional intimacy. Freud was right that "love and work are the cornerstones of our humanness"; and while parenting involves a lot of work, it still belongs to the "love" half of that balance.

So Hirshman tackles some of the right issues; but she tackles them in so wrong-    13
headed a way as to sabotage her own argument. She absurdly overstates her case, claiming, for instance, that four decades of feminism have not changed relations between women and men in the family. (Women today spend twice as much time on housework as men—but 30 years ago, they did six times as much.)

Hirshman's "get thee to the office" hectoring has an obnoxiously patronizing    14
tone. She takes us back to the French feminist Simone de Beauvoir's assertion, in a 1976 interview with Betty Friedan, that "no woman should be authorized to stay at home to raise her children . . . because if there is such a choice, too many women will make that one." Friedan—whose 1964 classic *The Feminine Mystique* Hirshman invokes as a model of prowork feminism—was understandably appalled by this diktat.

Furthermore, one needn't lapse into hand-that-rocks-the-cradle clichés to be put    15
off by Hirshman's bilious contempt for anything traditionally femine—even for volunteerism and less-than-lucrative jobs tainted by "idealism" (though it's amusing to see so hearty an endorsement of capitalist values in a left-wing magazine).

Focusing only on the drudgery of home life, Hirshman misses the brighter side of    16
the female dilemma: When it comes to work-life balance, women have far more

options than men, including more freedom to choose lower-paying but more flexible and fulfilling jobs. Men, by contrast, are often trapped by more rigid social expectations and economic pressures.

While Hirshman deplores women's alleged slide into 1950s-style domesticity, her 17 vision of careers is itself of '50s vintage, with hardly any allowances for the flexibility of the modern workplace or the growth of self-employment and small businesses. Last November, *Fortune* ran a feature by Jia Lynn Yang on women who step off high rungs of the corporate ladder not to trade briefcases for diapers or to flee sexism but to pursue their ventures in business or in new fields. To these women, Yang noted, "taking control of one's own life can feel as bold as wielding power in a corporation."

Yang's article also suggested that, culturally, women have more freedom than 18 men to make such unorthodox choices. These greater choices can mean greater conflicts; but if there is an answer, it is to expand the choices available to men, not to narrow the options for women.

Hirshman wants to tell women to set aside their own preferences, including the 19 desire for more than one child, for the sake of the feminist revolution. It is resoundingly obvious this is not going to happen. Do we need a conversation about the downside of "opting out," the work and life expectations of women and men, and the benefits to both sexes of more flexible, less gender-bound roles? I think we do. But if Hirshman was hoping to initiate such a discussion, she started it off on the wrong note.

## READING FOR CONTENT

1. In paragraphs 7–12, which of Hirshman's claims does Young defend?
2. In paragraphs 13–19, which of Hirshman's claims does Young express skepticism about?
3. In paragraphs 13–19, which of Hirshman's claims does Young actively disagree with, and on what grounds?

## READING FOR GENRE, ORGANIZATION, AND STYLISTIC FEATURES

1. Young organizes her critique into a summary of Hirshman's article (paragraphs 1–5), a rehearsal of its strong points (paragraphs 6–12), and an attack on its weak points (paragraphs 13–19). Which section of the essay attracts your special attention?
2. Is Young even-handed when she assesses Hirshman's strong points and weak ones, or does she express greater force and stronger conviction with either approval or disapproval?

## READING FOR RHETORICAL CONTEXT

1. What does Young mean when she compares Hirshman's tone with that in feminist writings of the 1960s and 1970s in paragraph 14? What does she mean when she compares Hirshman's vision of domesticity with its counterpart in the 1950s? Is Young complimenting Hirshman with these comparisons?
2. Young alludes to an article by Jia Lynn Yang in paragraphs 17–18. Do you imagine that Yang's article represents a conservative or a liberal position on the topic?

## WRITING ASSIGNMENTS

1. Imagine a conversation between Young and Hirshman about the financial dependency of stay-at-home moms and jot down the points of agreement and disagreement that each would have. Write a two-page essay in which you recount the give-and-take of this imagined conversation.

2. Imagine a conversation between Young and David Brooks about Hirshman's article and jot down points of agreement and disagreement that each might have. Write a two-page essay in which you recount the give-and-take of this imagined conversation.

# Feminists to Women: Shut Up and Do As You're Told

## Don Feder

*Don Feder is a former syndicated columnist for the* Boston Herald *and the author of* A Jewish Conservative Looks at Pagan America. *As a conservative advocate, he earned small fame for his cynical attacks on President Clinton.*

## PREREADING

In the preceding article, which criticizes Linda Hirshman's "Homeward Bound" (on pages 104–112), Cathy Young reasons that by "focusing only on the drudgery of home life, Hirshman misses the brighter side of the female dilemma: When it comes to work-life balance, women have far more options than men." How do you respond to these observations? Which kinds of drudgery seem more onerous than others? What brighter side of the dilemma might you imagine? Do women in fact have more options than men? Do these questions strike you as antifeminist? What other sorts of antifeminist positions might you envision? Freewrite your responses to these questions.

$\mathrm{B}$ack in the 1980s, when conservative social critics suggested it was better for the mothers of young children to stay home (instead of consigning the kids to daycare gulags), feminists were furious.

"How dare you tell women what to do!" they screeched. "The nerve—trying to tell us how to live our lives!"

So, guess who's now telling women how to live and excoriating them for thinking independently? Feminists. Under a veneer of empowerment, the movement has always been fascistic. It's instructive to now see the sisters goose-stepping out of the totalitarian closet, truncheons raised to smash errant skulls.

Leading the charge is Linda Hirshman, lawyer, professor and scourge of stay-at-home moms.

*Human Events,* 62.9, March 13, 2006, p. 15. Reprinted with permission of the publishers.

Recently, ABC's "Good Morning America" (which my friends at the Media Research Center call "Good Morning Morons") showcased Hirshman's rant on two consecutive shows in segments titled "Mommy Wars: To Work or Stay at Home?" and "How to Raise Kids: Stay Home or Go to Work?"

Typical of what passes for balance on the networks, "Good Morning America" afforded roughly 80% of each segment to Hirshman's views. Dissenters got nodding notice to maintain the pretense of fairness.

## Feminism Threatened

Hirshman has attained celebrity status by alerting us to the under-reported crisis of our time: Despite decades of feminist indoctrination—delivered from the classroom to entertainment television, where what used to be called housewives are practically nonexistent—women are actually choosing to stay at home and nurture their children. Global terrorism, global warming—kids' stuff, by comparison.   2

ABC cited census data showing 54% of mothers with a graduate or professional degree no longer work full-time. This is bolstered by Hirshman's own study of 30 women whose wedding announcements appeared in the *New York Times* in 2003 and 2004. Only five are now working full-time outside the home, 10 work part time. The rest lead lives unsatisfactory to Hirshman and her allies.

Feminists are threatened by this phenomenon. It's ideology—and not the interests of women, individually or collectively—that drives them.

Hirshman's position: Stay-at-home moms are leading impoverished lives, wasting their educations, short-changing their children (who miss the joys of being raised by total strangers who are paid to care about them) and doing incalculable damage to the cause of women's rights.

"I think it's a terrible mistake for these highly educated and capable women to make that choice [choosing children and home over career]," Hirshman declares. "I am saying an educated, competent adult's place is in the office." Yes, I think we got that.

## Typical Elitism

The *Ms.* Magazine Poster Person isn't buying the argument that raising the next generation is in any way, shape or form fulfilling. "I would like to see a description of their daily lives that substantiates that," Hirshman harrumphs. "Their description of their lives does not sound particularly interesting or fulfilling for a complicated person, for a complicated, educated person," she adds.   3

What Hirshman means is: "I don't find their lives particularly interesting or fulfilling—and my judgment is the measure of all things." And to think, feminists have been accused of elitism.

Hirshman belittles those women who believe there's no substitute for mom. She pushes a proposition absurd on its face—that there is no difference in the "happiness levels" of children consigned to the Joyful Tots Detention Center versus those raised at home.

In the first place, only someone with a Ph.D. (a complicated, educated idiot) thinks happiness levels can be measured. And what about the disease and abuse (physical and sexual) rampant in daycare? How about the fact that children in daycare tend to be more aggressive and less socialized that their raised-at-home peers?

Have you ever witnessed the heartrending spectacle of a three-year-old crying and pushing its mother away—screaming that he wants to be taken to daycare? Nor will you.

As a counterpoint to Hirshman, "Good Morning America" presented Debbie Klett, a mother who left a job in ad sales and founded a magazine called *Total 180,* to spend more time with her kids.

Klett: "For me, I feel it is vital to be there for my children every day, to consistently tend to their needs, to grow their self-esteem, and to praise them when they're right, guide them when they're not, and to be a loving, caring mom every minute of the day."

Why, the anti-social wretch!

## Scare Tactic

To clinch her argument, Hirshman notes the divorce rate is over 40%. These ninnies, 4 says she, they devote themselves to hubby and kids, then they're cast aside in a divorce and see their standard of living take a nosedive.

But it was feminists in the '70s who pushed no-fault divorce, which, they maintained, would liberate women from stultifying marriages. Now they're using the divorce rate to scare women into the workforce. Talk about chutzpah.

Hirshman has a prescription for the ticking of biological clocks: "Have a baby. (If you must.) Just don't have two," which makes work outside the home difficult.

Also, Hirshman advises, find Mr. Mom—a guy who's into diapers and dirty dishes. "You can either find a spouse with less social power [read: money] than you or find one with an ideological commitment to gender equality [read: gender sameness]."

I can just picture the personal ad: "Feminist seeks socially inferior, self-neutered male who believes that men and women are emotionally androgynous. Objective: A matrimonial merger and the production of one child, who will be raised by the proverbial village on *The Feminist Mystique* and *Our Bodies, Our Selves* (between viewings of Thelma and Louise and G.I. Jane)."

In the '80s, young women had a word for such fine specimens: "wimps."

Linda Hirshman is doing a great service to humanity. She is glaringly obnoxious proof of what conservatives have been saying for decades—feminists hate the family. (Hirshman: "The family—with its repetitious, socially invisible, physical tasks—is a necessary part of life, but allows fewer opportunities for full human flourishing than public spheres like the market or government.")

In other words, the female insurance executive or the female junior college instructor (lecturing a roomful of bored freshmen in a 101 course) is engaged in stimulating, fulfilling, socially useful activity, while the mother who sees a human being developing on a daily basis, and shapes that life more than anyone else, is a brain-dead drudge and a dupe.

## Anti-Feminine

Here's the ultimate irony: Feminists are anti-feminine. They reject hearth and home, 5 procreation and child-rearing (unless it's done by "professionals"). They deny the maternal instinct. They condemn the feminine urge to nurture and to create a safe haven from the perils of modern life. (They also deny the male imperative to serve and protect.) Everything that's distinctive about their sex, they abhor.

Because they hate their nature, they are self-loathing. Most are miserable—and deservedly so.

For almost 20 years, I worked in a newsroom with these resentful, envious, humorless harpies. An uglier lot you will never find—this side of *Alien vs. Predator*.

Most were deeply unhappy with their lives, always ready to take offense at imaginary slights, convinced that any lack of advancement was due to a chauvinist conspiracy and angry at those who challenged feminist dogma. They were about as much fun as Hillary on a bad hair day (speaking of resentful, envious, humorless harpies).

Who in their right mind would take life advice from such spiritually misshapen creatures? ABC News, of course.

## READING FOR CONTENT

1. Examine the four section headings at the beginning of paragraphs 2, 3, 4, and 5. What topics do they cover, and does Feder's treatment of them expand the scope usually associated with them?

2. Mark off Feder's personal intrusions into his own argument, such as "Have you ever witnessed the heartrending spectacle . . ." and "I can just picture the personal ad." What claims is Feder trying to underscore with these intrusions?

## READING FOR GENRE, ORGANIZATION, AND STYLISTIC FEATURES

1. What elements of humor does Feder try to convey in this article? Is it good-natured humor or is it sarcastic humor?

2. Examine the four section headings at the beginning of paragraphs 2, 3, 4, and 5. Do these headings correspond with Feder's actual discussion of ideology, elitism, male wimps, and unmarried women in these paragraphs?

3. As an example of informal writing, Feder's article does not include footnote references to specific bits of source information. Are there particular examples of such citation that you wish Feder would have included so that you might check the information for yourself?

## READING FOR RHETORICAL CONTEXT

1. This article first appeared on a Web site called GrassTopsUSA.com. Look up this site and evaluate its purpose, intended audience, and point of view. Does Feder's article correspond with the mission of this venue?

2. Mark the statements that Feder punctuates with question marks or exclamation points. What effects, humorous or intentional, do they have in their specific contexts?

## WRITING ASSIGNMENTS

1. Imagine a conversation between Feder and Hirshman about the financial dependency of stay-at-home moms and jot down the points of agreement and disagreement that each would have. Write a two-page essay in which you recount the give-and-take of this imagined conversation.

2. Imagine a conversation between Feder and David Brooks about Hirshman's article and jot down the points of agreement and disagreement that each would have. Write a two-page essay in which you recount the give-and-take of this imagined conversation.

3. Imagine a conversation between Feder and Cathy Young about Hirshman's article and jot down points of agreement and disagreement that each might have. Write a two-page essay in which you recount the give-and-take of this imagined conversation.

■ ■ ■ ■ ■ ■ ■ ■ ■ ■ ■

# Paradise Lost

## *Terry Martin Hekker*

*Terry Martin Hekker is a writer who lives in Nyack, NY, where she has served as Deputy Mayor.*

## PREREADING

Skim through Terry Hekker's personal account of how her lifestyle changed dramatically upon the divorce of her long-term marriage. Think about how social conventions at one moment of time might affect choices that come to seem outdated at another moment. Form collaborative groups of five students each in order to compile a list of reasons why Hekker's account illustrates such a shift of values about women's work over the past three decades.

A while back, at a baby shower for a niece, I overheard the expectant mother being   1
asked if she intended to return to work after the baby was born. The answer, which rocked me, was, "Yes, because I don't want to end up like Aunt Terry."

That would be me.   2

In the continuing case of Full-Time Homemaker vs. Working Mother, I offer   3
myself as Exhibit A. Because more than a quarter-century ago I wrote an Op-Ed article for *The New York Times* on the satisfaction of being a full-time housewife in the new age of the liberated woman. I wrote it from my heart, thoroughly convinced that homemaking and raising my children was the most challenging and rewarding job I could ever want.

"I come from a long line of women," I wrote, "most of them more Edith Bunker   4
than Betty Freidan, who never knew they were unfulfilled. I can't testify that they were happy, but they were cheerful. They took pride in a clean, comfortable home and satisfaction in serving a good meal because no one had explained that the only work worth doing is that for which you get paid."

I wasn't advocating that mothers forgo careers to stay home with their children; 5
I was simply defending my choice as a valid one. The mantra of the age may have been
"Do your own thing," but as a full-time homemaker, that didn't seem to mean me.

The column morphed into a book titled "Ever Since Adam and Eve," followed 6
by a national tour on which I, however briefly, became the authority on homemaking
as a viable choice for women. I ultimately told my story on "Today" and to Dinah
Shore, Charlie Rose and even to Oprah, when she was the host of a local TV show in
Baltimore.

In subsequent years I lectured on the rewards of homemaking and housewifery. 7
While others tried to make the case that women like me were parasites and little more
than legalized prostitutes, I spoke to rapt audiences about the importance of being
there for your children as they grew up, of the satisfactions of "making a home," preparing family meals and supporting your hard-working husband.

So I was predictably stunned and devastated when, on our 40th wedding anniver- 8
sary, my husband presented me with a divorce. I knew our first anniversary would be
paper, but never expected the 40th would be papers, 16 of them meticulously detailing
my faults and flaws, the reason our marriage, according to him, was over.

We had been married by a bishop with a blessing from the pope in a country 9
church filled with honeysuckle and hope. Five children and six grandchildren later we
were divorced by a third-rate judge in a suburban courthouse reeking of dust and
despair.

Our long marriage had its full share of love, complications, illnesses, joy and stress. 10
Near the end we were in a dismal period, with my husband in treatment for alcoholism.
And although I had made more than my share of mistakes, I never expected to be served
with divorce papers. I was stunned to find myself, at this stage of life, marooned. And it
was small comfort that I wasn't alone. There were many other confused women of my age
and circumstance who'd been married just as long, sharing my situation.

I was in my teens when I first read Dickens's "Great Expectations," with the tale 11
of Miss Haversham, who, stood up by her groom-to-be, spent decades in her yellowing
wedding gown, sitting at her cobweb-covered bridal banquet table, consumed with
plotting revenge. I felt then that to be left waiting at the altar with a church full of
people must be the most crushing thing that could happen to a woman.

I was wrong. No jilted bride could feel as embarrassed and humiliated as a woman 12
in her 60's discarded by her husband. I was confused and scared, and the pain of being
tossed aside by the love of my life made bitterness unavoidable. In those first few bewil-
dering months, as I staggered and wailed though my life, I made Miss Haversham look
like a good sport.

Sitting around my kitchen with two friends who had also been dumped by their 13
husbands, I figured out that among the three of us we'd been married 110 years. We'd
been faithful wives, good mothers, cooks and housekeepers who'd married in the 50's,
when "dress for success" meant a wedding gown and "wife" was a tenured position.

Turns out we had a lot in common with our outdated kitchen appliances. Like 14
them we were serviceable, low maintenance, front loading, self-cleaning and (relatively) frost free. Also like them we had warranties that had run out. Our husbands
sought sleeker models with features we lacked who could execute tasks we'd either
never learned or couldn't perform without laughing.

Like most loyal wives of our generation, we'd contemplated eventual widowhood 15
but never thought we'd end up divorced. And "divorced" doesn't begin to describe the

pain of this process. "Canceled" is more like it. It began with my credit cards, then my health insurance and checkbook, until, finally, like a used postage stamp, I felt canceled too.

I faced frightening losses and was overwhelmed by the injustice of it all. He got to 16 take his girlfriend to Cancun, while I got to sell my engagement ring to pay the roofer. When I filed my first nonjoint tax return, it triggered the shocking notification that I had become eligible for food stamps.

The judge had awarded me alimony that was less than I was used to getting for 17 household expenses, and now I had to use that money to pay bills I'd never seen before: mortgage, taxes, insurance and car payments. And that princely sum was awarded for only four years, the judge suggesting that I go for job training when I turned 67. Not only was I unprepared for divorce itself, I was utterly lacking in skills to deal with the brutal aftermath.

I read about the young mothers of today—educated, employed, self-sufficient—who 18 drop out of the work force when they have children, and I worry and wonder. Perhaps it is the right choice for them. Maybe they'll be fine. But the fragility of modern marriage suggests that at least half of them may not be.

Regrettably, women whose husbands are devoted to their families and are good 19 providers must nevertheless face the specter of future abandonment. Surely the seeds of this wariness must have been planted, even if they can't believe it could ever happen to them. Many have witnessed their own mothers jettisoned by their own fathers and seen divorced friends trying to rear children with marginal financial and emotional support.

These young mothers are often torn between wanting to be home with their chil- 20 dren and the statistical possibility of future calamity, aware that one of the most poverty-stricken groups in today's society are divorced older women. The feminine and sexual revolutions of the last few decades have had their shining victories, but have they, in the end, made things any easier for mothers?

I cringe when I think of that line from my Op-Ed article about the long line of 21 women I'd come from and belonged to who were able to find fulfillment as homemakers "because no one had explained" to us "that the only work worth doing is that for which you get paid." For a divorced mother, the harsh reality is that the work for which you do get paid is the only work that will keep you afloat.

These days couples face complex negotiations over work, family, child care and 22 housekeeping. I see my children dealing with these issues in their marriages, and I understand the stresses and frustrations. It becomes evident that where traditional marriage through the centuries had been a partnership based on mutual dependency, modern marriage demands greater self-sufficiency.

While today's young women know from the start they'll face thorny decisions 23 regarding careers, marriage and children, those of us who married in the 50's anticipated lives similar to our mothers' and grandmothers'. Then we watched with bewilderment as all the rules changed, and the goal posts were moved.

If I had it to do over again, I'd still marry the man I married and have my children: 24 they are my treasure and a powerful support system for me and for one another. But I would have used the years after my youngest started school to further my education. I could have amassed two doctorates using the time and energy I gave to charitable and community causes and been better able to support myself.

But in a lucky twist, my community involvement had resulted in my being 25 appointed to fill a vacancy on our Village Board. I had been serving as titular deputy mayor of my hometown (Nyack, N.Y.) when my husband left me. Several weeks later the mayor chose not to run again because of failing health, and I was elected to succeed him, becoming the first female mayor.

I held office for six years, a challenging, full-time job that paid a whopping 26 annual salary of $8,000. But it consumed me and gave me someplace to go every day and most nights, and as such it saved my sanity. Now, mostly retired except for some part-time work, I am kept on my toes by 12 amazing grandchildren.

My anachronistic book was written while I was in a successful marriage that 27 I expected would go on forever. Sadly, it now has little relevance for modern women, except perhaps as a cautionary tale: never its intended purpose. So I couldn't imagine writing a sequel. But my friend Elaine did come up with a perfect title: "Disregard First Book."

## READING FOR CONTENT

1. What is the irony of the simple sentence in paragraph 2, "That would be me." Why would the mother of a newborn child not want to end up like Aunt Terry?
2. What shift in social values makes the author confess "I was wrong" in paragraph 12?
3. What advice does the author imply in paragraph 24?

## READING FOR GENRE, ORGANIZATION, AND STYLISTIC FEATURES

1. As a personal narrative, Hekker's account is especially courageous. Does the author prepare readers for a change in her viewpoint when she comments upon her origins and development in paragraphs 4, 7, 14, 18, and 21?
2. Underline the explicit changes in her lifestyle that the author describes in paragraphs 5, 10, 13, and 17.
3. How does the author convey her emotional reactions in paragraphs 8, 13, 16, 21, and 26?

## READING FOR RHETORICAL CONTEXT

1. According to the information in paragraph 6, what kind of audience has Terry Hekker addressed in the past? According to the information in paragraph 13, what kind of audience does she address in the present?
2. When she describes the shift in her audiences from paragraph 6 to paragraph 13, how does Hekker attempt to recruit members from her earlier readership to understand her current point of view?

## WRITING ASSIGNMENTS

1. Hekker is narrating how she came to write about herself and her life choices from a perspective radically different from one that she had embraced earlier. Summon a situation from you own life experiences to which you would respond today in a way completely different from your earlier response. Write a personal essay explaining your change of perspective.

2. Hekker writes about a conflict of values that developed over a span of forty years. Write a two-page essay about whether this conflict is still unfolding in our society in a speeded-up time frame, so that both sides of the issue about dependent stay-at-home wives and mothers are still a major problem. Draw upon personal experiences as well as upon experiences reported in various media.

■ ■ ■ ■ ■ ■ ■ ■ ■ ■ ■

# At Home with David Brooks

## *Rebecca Traister*

*Rebecca Traister is a staff writer at* Salon. *Her many articles cover topics on politics, the film industry, and issues of gender in various media.*

## PREREADING

Read the first paragraph of Rebecca Traister's "At Home with David Brooks" on page 128. Take note of her claim that Linda Hirshman's article (on pages 104–112) and David Brooks's response (on pages 114–115) could not have supplied "a bolder manifestation of two sides of the discussion." As you read through the next several paragraphs, underline the verbs Traister uses to introduce quotations from Brooks's response. They include: "Impressed by the 'full-bore . . .'"; "Brooks is able to write, 'of course . . .'"; "in response, Brooks urges"; "condescendingly inviting Hirshman to 'spend a day . . .'"; "Brooks gathers that"; "Brooks is also surprised that." What tone or attitude do these verbs convey? Might they furnish an effective template for you to use in writing your own critical analyses of essays in this anthology?

T hose of us mesmerized by the escalating debate about the relationship between  1 stay-at-home motherhood and feminism could not have asked for a balder manifestation of two sides of the discussion than this Sunday's *New York Times*.

First, Op-Ed columnist David Brooks weighed in on an *American Prospect* piece  2 about the fallacies of stay-at-home feminism by Brandeis professor Linda Hirshman. In Hirshman's December piece, she vociferously argued that so-called choice feminism — the ability to leave a career that many modern stay-at-home women describe as a perk of their emancipation — is in fact regressive, symptomatic not of the successes of the feminist movement but of its failures.

Hirshman's piece was an angry, troubling battle call that has provoked fierce  3 debate among feminists. Brooks answers her extremism with extremism. Impressed by the "full-bore, unapologetic blast of 1975 time-warp feminism," he bestows on the piece a "Sidney Award" as one of the best magazine essays of the year, on the grounds that it was so smart and dense that it took him a while to figure out how to poke holes in it. Finally, despite Hirshman's skill, Brooks is able to write, "of course, she is wrong."

Brooks takes issue with what he calls Hirshman's "astonishing" assertion that 4
high-paying jobs provide more visibility and opportunity for satisfaction than a purely
domestic existence. Hirshman originally wrote that "the family . . . allows fewer opportunities for full human flourishing than public spheres like the market or the government . . . assigning it to women is unjust. Women assigning it to themselves is equally
unjust. "To paraphrase, as Mark Twain said, 'A man who chooses not to read is just as
ignorant as a man who cannot read.'"

In response, Brooks urges, "look back over your life. Which memories do you 5
cherish more, those with your family or those at the office?" It seems there's only one
answer here; Brooks cherishes his memories with his family more, and in that he is
surely not alone. But couldn't he be failing to consider that perhaps the rewards of
child rearing are more fully appreciated when they are balanced by a professional existence? That those family dinners with the twins are especially sweet when you haven't
spent the previous 144 hours with the twins? Appreciation for both professional and
personal accomplishment often stems from the discovery in each realm of the satisfactions lacking in the other.

But Brooks staunchly maintains that the rewards of an outside job pale next to 6
the experience of parenthood, condescendingly inviting Hirshman to "spend a day as
an associate at a big law firm." Why? Because being a professor and researcher never
showed her what real professional work was like? Is it so hard to believe that a woman—
or man—might find pleasure in a job that also overextends and exhausts them? Maybe
Brooks should be invited to spend 18 years cleaning houses, ferrying children to play
dates, and having no other outlet for his ambitions, imagination, talents or acquisitive
desires.

According to Brooks, the "sort of brutalizing, dominating power that Hirshman 7
admires" may be available in the workplace, but the home is really "the realm of
unmatched influence." Here he's referring to the kind of influence that shapes "a child's
I.Q., mental habits, and destiny." Apparently, women are supposed to be thrilled, and fully
sated, by the chance to mold the lives of their children—the vessels for their identity—
and pine not at all for the economic or political force that they themselves might exert in
the outside world. Surely, David Brooks, *New York Times* Op-Ed columnist, must understand the pull of a public working life, the pleasures of influencing opinion. If he's really
so aggrieved by his lack of power as an IQ-builder for the next generation, perhaps he
should surrender his post to work full-time at a child-care facility.

But Brooks is a man. And, as he writes, Hirshman's biggest failing is in declining to 8
address "the fact that men and women are wired differently." Citing research by "Bell
Curve" co-author Charles Murray, Brooks gathers that "men are more interested in
things and abstract rules while women are more interested in people." (That's women,
folks. People who love people.)

Brooks is also surprised that in looking back over the essays of 2005, he noticed 9
many that addressed "the big foreign policy issues of the year"—(grunt, scratch)—"[but]
also an amazing number that dealt with domesticity"—(giggle, sigh). That's because,
according to the columnist, "the deeper you get into economic or social problems . . .
the more you realize the answers lie with good parenting and good homes." "Hirshman
has it exactly backward," Brooks writes. "Power is in the kitchen. The big problem is not
the women who stay there but the men who leave."

Central to Brooks' argument is the barely veiled suggestion that mothers who 10
work outside the home surrender influence in their households. The dark little melody

playing underneath his self-assured dismissal of Hirshman is that a breakdown of society can be pinned on all those women who have abandoned their rightful sphere of influence in exchange for the "brutalizing, dominating power" that he thinks Hirshman "admires."

It's a chorus that's been heard a lot recently, and at increasing volumes, as we  11 inch closer to a year in which many have speculated about the possibility of the ultimate working woman—a female president. It's as if critics like Brooks, petrified by the changes afoot, are urging us in silken tones to return quietly to our corners. "Back away from the White House," he seems to be saying. "You don't really want to be there anyway. You'll be so much happier, and more *powerful*, and *influential*, back home where you belong."

But Brooks should read his own paper, which on the same day his column was  12 published ran a piece in the "Modern Love" section by Terry Martin Hekker, a woman who did exactly as he recommends—stayed in the kitchen—and lived to regret her choice.

Hekker wrote a *Times* opinion column more than 25 years ago about the satisfac-  13 tions of full-time motherhood. That column led to a book, and a lifetime of proselytizing about the joys of housewifery. Having devoted decades to raising five children and celebrating the virtues and pleasures of "'making a home,' preparing family meals and supporting your hard-working husband," Hekker was stunned when, on her 40th wedding anniversary, her well-supported husband announced he wanted a divorce. Left not just emotionally bereft, but financially decimated in her 60s, Hekker was forced to pay insurance, taxes, a mortgage and car payments for the first time in her life.

Hekker's piece was problematic in its own ways. First, it did little to address a very  14 obvious contradiction: that a woman who writes for the *New York Times*, publishes a book, tours nationally and appears on television shows as an authority on domesticity is not quite the hausfrau she extolls.

She may be more an emblem of full-time motherhood than a true practitioner,  15 but Hekker proclaims that she is not alone. Several of her friends, women who'd "been faithful wives, good mothers, cooks and housekeepers," also found themselves discarded like "outdated kitchen appliances." Hekker now regrets a sentence from her original *Times* column mocking the feminist notion that "the only work worth doing is that for which you get paid." It turns out that that wasn't such a laughable idea after all. "For a divorced mother," she writes, "the harsh reality is that the work for which you do get paid is the only work that will keep you afloat."

And so Hekker, the preacher of post-feminist domesticity, has changed her mind.  16 "I read about the young mothers of today—educated, employed, self-sufficient—who drop out of the work force when they have children," she writes. "And I worry and wonder . . . Maybe they'll be fine. But the fragility of modern marriage suggests that at least half of them may not be."

Hekker observes that "the feminine and sexual revolutions of the last few decades  17 have had their shining victories, but have they, in the end, made things any easier for mothers?" Here, maybe unconsciously, she is echoing Hirshman's controversial thesis: that the persistent inequities of the home are the unspoken, buried failures of the feminist movement.

Perhaps Brooks is right about one thing: The number and intensity of pieces about  18 domestic life are increasing by the day. Maybe it's because women are being stirred from a self-justifying stupor and realizing that there remains a brigade of Americans who become increasingly nervous about women's professional and economic strides and deal with it by trying to scare them off the path.

For further evidence, look no further than John Tierney's Tuesday *Times* column 19 about how three women graduate from college for every two men, and his prediction that most will end up lonely spinsters. In it, he concludes that women's rights advocates have been "so effective politically" in their claims about "supposed discrimination against women: the shortage of women in science classes and on sports teams" that "the shortage of men period" had been forgotten. "You could think of this as a victory for women's rights," writes Tierney, "but many of the victors will end up celebrating alone." There it is again, that threat. Keep this up and you'll be punished, ladies. There is payback everywhere you turn: Leave the home and your kids will raise the crime rate, get those educations you've been fighting for and you'll drive men out of classrooms and become unmarriageable, and, as Hekker points out, give up your independence to wholly rely on the emotional and economic consistency of another human being, and you'll get screwed.

The good news is that we're talking about three stories in as many days. This 20 debate has in recent years been muffled—out of embarrassment or paralysis in the face of problems so thorny and personal that they are hard to parse, let alone solve. It's about time we all started taking the politics of the American home seriously again, remembering that the personal is absolutely political. If David Brooks is so quaintly fascinated by the number of pieces about domesticity in 2005, I urge him to buckle his seat belt in preparation for a bumpy 2006.

## READING FOR CONTENT

1. The first four paragraphs appear to summarize Hirshman's and Brooks's general arguments. Where does Traister actually begin to criticize Brooks's specific claims? Does the question in paragraph 5, beginning "But couldn't he be failing to consider," initiate her criticism? Does the question in paragraph 6, beginning "Is it so hard," initiate another criticism?

2. How does paragraph 15 portray Hekker as a foil to Brooks? What does Traister concede to Brooks in paragraph 18, and how does this concession deepen Traister's argument?

## READING FOR GENRE, ORGANIZATION, AND STYLISTIC FEATURES

1. Traister's comparative analysis derives its strength from the author's close examination of specific quotations from her sources. From your own critical reading of these sources in the preceding articles, do you find that Traister quotes fairly from major representative passages, or do you believe that she skews the evidence by focusing upon minor inconclusive details?

2. In paragraph 3, what critical point does Traister make as an organizing claim that shapes her own argument? In paragraph 12, how does she expand this point so as to extend her argument for the rest the essay?

3. In paragraphs 11 and 19, Traister summarizes Brooks's and Tierney's arguments in her own words by addressing women readers as though they hadn't detected

the messages of these arguments: "Back away from the White House" and "Keep this up and you'll be punished." How would you describe the tone of Traister's summaries? Are these summaries fair? How might the author deduce them from her sources?

## READING FOR RHETORICAL CONTEXT

1. In the URL for this article, observe that it was published on January 4, 2006. How does the final sentence of paragraph 20 capitalize on the context of its appearance close to New Year's Day?

2. In paragraph 11, Traister summarizes Brooks's article with the sentence "Back away from the White House," even though Brooks nowhere mentions the White House in his article. What broader context does Traister's summary introduce? What role might it play as her readers enter the midterm phase of the current presidency? What specific political figures does it evoke on the national Democrat and Republican scene?

## WRITING ASSIGNMENTS

1. Write a two-page critique of Traister's analysis of Brooks's editorial using your own analysis of Hirshman's and Hekker's sources. Try to engage Traister in a conversation about claims she might have missed or points of view she didn't take into account.

2. Using Traister's analysis as a template, rewrite her article by substituting different quotations from her sources in order to make different critical claims. You may consider your rewriting to amplify and reinforce Traister's argument, or else to correct its misrepresentations and produce a substantially different analysis and argument.

■ ■ ■ ■ ■ ■ ■ ■ ■ ■ ■

# Mother Yale

### *Frances Rosenbluth*

*Frances Rosenbluth is a Professor of Political Science at Yale University and the editor of* The Political Economy of Japan's Low Fertility *(Stanford University Press, 2006).*

## PREREADING

Form collaborative groups of five students each and read paragraph 1. Ask one another what kinds of information you might reasonably expect the ensuing article to provide as part of its argument and defense. If you were going to argue a similar claim in a longer term paper, what kinds of support would you want to include? Ask one another how each would go about designing such a term paper so as to incorporate the appropriate information and analysis.

Louise Story's *New York Times* feature stirred up much excitement over the idea   1
that women are retreating from the career trenches. Yet, if anything, Story's article showed the opposite: 70 percent of the women in her sample stated a preference for staying in the labor market, at least part-time. This is no massive rush for the door by a new generation disenchanted by the failures of the supermom.

What the article does underscore is the less than startling conclusion that change   2
is slow and incomplete. Put Story's survey results into the context of long-term trends in the U.S. economy, and then compare those with trends in other countries, and you have a more accurate picture of what our society calls "gender relations": our evolving division of labor in the family.

Female labor force participation in this country has risen steadily in the past   3
50 years, according to the U.S. Department of Labor. It currently stands at about 75 percent; most of the recent increases took place among mothers. In 2000, more than half of the mothers of small children were employed outside the home, at least on a part-time basis.

New mothers are, however, more likely than other women to leave their jobs—and   4
little wonder. Federal law (under the 1993 Family and Medical Leave Act) requires employers only to give new mothers 12 weeks' leave, without pay. Leaving a three-month-old baby in the care of others for a full day on the job is no one's idea of an ideal situation. By three months, the baby and mother may be in the full swing of a nursing relationship, the baby may not be sleeping through the night—leaving the mother as tired in the morning as when she went to bed—and the dad may or may not be helping with the night shift. As Yale professor Laura Wexler pointed out in an interview with Story, women have gained access to an ever-greater range of professional opportunities without a commensurate increase in social support for balancing family and career.

In Sweden, by contrast, employers pay a percentage of workers' salaries for an   5
18-month parental leave. (Some of that leave is take-it-or-leave-it for dads only.) Employers must also guarantee the possibility of part-time hours until the youngest child is 8 years old. Hardly surprising, then, that female labor force employment is even higher in Sweden than in the United States.

It is remarkable, in fact, that the U.S. rate is as high as it is. But there are several   6
reasons why the percentage remains substantial in the face of miserly government and employer support for parental leave. One is the high degree of intra-gender wage inequality in the United States, which allows women with high incomes to hire lower-income women to care for their children. Another reason is the fact that labor markets here are fluid for both men and women—unlike in the welfare states of Europe, where firms are given strong statutory encouragement to employ their workers for life.

Ironically, the European welfare state (and the Japanese and Korean lifetime   7
employment system) deals women an inadvertent blow. For firms that invest in lifetime employees, career interruptions of any kind are costly. As investments in human capital, therefore, women are expensive. The firms respond by trying to avoid hiring women and promoting women, and the result is that female labor force participation

rates are substantially lower in those countries: 58 percent for Japan, 62 percent for Germany, and 43.1 percent for Italy, for example. Even in Scandinavia, the percentage of women in private-sector jobs is substantially lower than that in the United States — though Scandinavian countries get around the problem by absorbing women into their large public sectors.

Some, no doubt, will wonder what all the fuss is about. If a woman wants to 8 take time out from her career to be with her young children, or if she wants to stay at home permanently, should she have to defend her choice? No: but she should know the consequences.

Young women should be aware that a decision to specialize in family work may 9 restrict their options on down the road. All else being equal, one's value on the market increases with experience. As the gap between the husband's and wife's labor market value increases, the potential loss of livelihood in the event of marital breakup grows larger for the wife, giving her a bigger stake in keeping the relationship going and leading to a loss of her bargaining stature at home.

This is, of course, a crass way of characterizing the marriage commitment. But it 10 is prudent for women to grasp the future range of possibilities, particularly in a society in which half of all marriages end in divorce.

Perhaps for these reasons, or perhaps because women find fulfillment in the 11 workplace, or perhaps because one-career incomes are insufficient for many families, all indications are that U.S. women are in the labor market to stay. Only when men are equally likely to be seen with banana puree on their suit lapels will we know we have arrived. But until then, women are keeping their eyes on their careers.

## READING FOR CONTENT

1. What does the last sentence of paragraph 3, "In 2000, more than half of the mothers of small children were employed outside the home," lead you to expect from the paragraphs that follow? Do these paragraphs fulfill your expectations?

2. What does the first sentence of paragraph 8, "Some, no doubt, will wonder what all the fuss is about," lead you to expect from the paragraphs that follow? Do these paragraphs fulfill your expectations?

## READING FOR GENRE, ORGANIZATION, AND STYLISTIC FEATURES

1. Rosenbluth's article is a brief contribution by an expert in the field to an alumni magazine that comments on a debate stirred up by one of its alumnae. How does Rosenbluth enter into the conversation in paragraph 2, and how does she urge us to frame the debate?

2. In paragraph 5, Rosenbluth offers the brief example of Sweden to compare U.S. policy on working mothers. What other comparisons, issues, and problems might she introduce if she were trying to organize a longer essay on this topic?

3. What effect does the triple use of "perhaps" have in the final paragraph? Does it weaken Rosenbluth's conclusions, or does it instead expand the range of possible variations on the problem of working mothers?

## READING FOR RHETORICAL CONTEXT

1. Rosenbluth is a leading scholar in the field of political economy and has written an important book on the topic. Can you infer that she might be able to back up her claims in this brief article by providing detailed data and arguments? Would you be inclined to consult her longer publications to find such data and argument?

2. What sources would you consult to engage other voices in this conversation about political economy? Might the footnotes and bibliographies of Rosenbluth's longer publications provide the names of other leading scholars who agree or disagree with her claims?

## WRITING ASSIGNMENTS

1. Write a two-page essay that responds to Rosenbluth's challenge in paragraph 2, "Put Story's survey results into the context of long-term trends in the U.S. economy." For research that might provide such a context, ask the librarians in your college library to direct you to appropriate materials.

2. Write a two-page essay that elaborates upon Rosenbluth's claim in paragraph 9, "Young women should be aware that a decision to specialize in family work may restrict their options on down the road." To determine what such options might be, use all the materials you have gathered from preceding articles on the problem in this chapter.

### WORKS CITED

Belkin, Lisa. "The Opt-Out Revolution." *The New York Times*, Sunday, October 26, 2003.
Thompson, Tracy. "A War Inside Your Head." *Washington Post*, 15 February 1998: W12.

# *Four*

# Critical Analysis

## ■■ PART I: CRITICAL ANALYSIS

Critical analysis appears in many guises in academic writing. Professors and college researchers exemplify it in their scholarly publications. Students exemplify it in their written reports, short essays, and term papers. Topics for critical analyses cover scientific issues, behavioral issues, literary or psychological questions, practical or procedural methodologies, and disciplinary and interdisciplinary concerns. For example:

- Donald French, a professor in the Department of Zoology at Oklahoma State University, writes a *policy analysis* of his university's proposal to add "rank in class" to grades on student transcripts.

- A student in American History 101 writes an *historical analysis* of the campaign for women's suffrage.

- A student in an art appreciation course writes a *critical analysis* of Renoir's "Luncheon of the Boating Party."

- Stephen J. Ceci, a professor of child development at Cornell, writes a *scientific analysis* of children's testimony in criminal child abuse trials.

- George Kuh, a professor of education at Indiana University, writes a *comparative analysis* of the impact colleges and universities have on students' character development.

- James Phelan, a professor of English at Ohio State University, writes a *literary analysis* of John Edgar Wideman's short story "Doc's Story."

- An economics major writes a *critical review* of Jeffrey Sachs's 2005 book *The End of Poverty.*

Analysis abounds in all fields of academia. As the preceding examples illustrate, academic writers analyze a wide range of topics, issues, and texts. Analysis is a habit of mind required for critical reading and academic writing. In Chapter 1, our chapter devoted to critical reading, the word *analysis* appears twenty-five times, and it figures predominantly throughout the rest of this book.

Yet, *analysis* is one of those ambiguous terms that often mystifies students. Whether the assignment is to analyze a literary text, a process, a trend, a policy, or two contrasting events, students are not sure how to proceed. Quite simply, **analysis** is *a process of breaking down something complex into simpler elements that will make it more understandable.* Analysis underpins a wide range of academic genres. Prior to writing a summary, a synthesis, an argument, or a research paper, one must engage in analysis. Analysis functions as a self-contained genre in forms of writing like the ones we've listed at the beginning of this chapter.

Analysis is frequently incorporated into other genres. A scientific lab report may contain a process analysis, and a sociolological/economic position paper may include a causal analysis explaining the relationships between antecedents and results.

## ■ Focus of the Chapter

The focus of this chapter is analytic reading and analytic writing. We cover a range of writing with emphasis on **critical analysis**, meaning *analysis with an argumentative and evaluative edge.* In keeping with the theme of this book, our focus is on the analysis of written texts. From the outset, it is important to understand the differences between straightforward analysis and critical analysis or evaluation. Figure 4–1 makes the distinctions clear.

The directives in your assignment will indicate whether your purpose is to analyze or to evaluate. The diagram in Figure 4–1 lists the verbs typically associated with each activity. The operations for analysis and evaluation are comparable, but critical analysis requires you to judge the effectiveness and worth of the text after you have dissected and interpreted it.

The reason to put an analysis in writing is to communicate your interpretation of data in hopes that it will heighten your readers' understanding and appreciation. Your analysis should enlighten your audience by revealing something that is not immediately obvious.

Writers of critical analysis have a sharpened purpose: to accompany their interpretation with an evaluation of the text's strengths and weaknesses. Figure 4–1 also displays genres typically associated with analysis.

## ■ Adopting a Questioning Frame of Mind

To become a successful academic writer, you have to adopt a way of thinking that favors analysis. You need to cultivate the frame of mind of a questioner. If you are not already someone who views texts with a critical eye, prepare yourself to assume this new disposition.

Analysis is stimulated by questions. Look back at Chapter 1 and you will find questions for analyzing the literal content of texts, questions for analyzing the stylistic features of texts, questions for analyzing rhetorical context, and questions for analyzing writing assignments. Questions promote analysis, as long as you know which questions to ask. Four basic questions apply to all texts: What is said? Why is it viewed that way? How is it said? Is the text comparable to another work with which the reader is familiar?

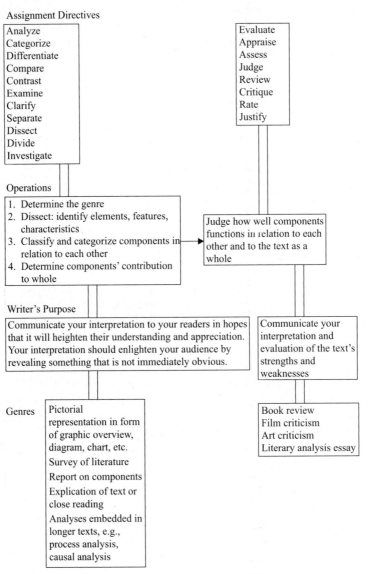

ANALYSIS                                    CRITICAL ANALYSIS/EVALUATION

Assignment Directives

| Analyze |
| Categorize |
| Differentiate |
| Compare |
| Contrast |
| Examine |
| Clarify |
| Separate |
| Dissect |
| Divide |
| Investigate |

| Evaluate |
| Appraise |
| Assess |
| Judge |
| Review |
| Critique |
| Rate |
| Justify |

Operations

1. Determine the genre
2. Dissect: identify elements, features, characteristics
3. Classify and categorize components in relation to each other
4. Determine components' contribution to whole

Judge how well components functions in relation to each other and to the text as a whole

Writer's Purpose

Communicate your interpretation to your readers in hopes that it will heighten their understanding and appreciation. Your interpretation should enlighten your audience by revealing something that is not immediately obvious.

Communicate your interpretation and evaluation of the text's strengths and weaknesses

Genres

Pictorial representation in form of graphic overview, diagram, chart, etc.
Survey of literature
Report on components
Explication of text or close reading
Analyses embedded in longer texts, e.g., process analysis, causal analysis

Book review
Film criticism
Art criticism
Literary analysis essay

**Figure 4–1    Comparison of Analysis and Critical Analysis**

## BROAD QUESTIONS FOR ANALYSIS

- What is said?
- Why is it viewed this way?
- How is it said?
- Is the text comparable to another work with which the reader is familiar?

The amount of emphasis you place on each of these questions will determine the type of analysis you will produce. Questions 1 and 2 focus on the text's argument and line of reasoning and lead to a **critical analysis**. Question 3 will examine the text's stylistic features and rhetorical context and result in a **rhetorical analysis** or a **literary analysis**. If you concentrate on Question 4, using another text as a lens to illuminate the focal test, you will write a **comparative analysis**.

In Chapter 1, you learned three sets of critical reading questions, the first for analyzing the literal content of a text; the second for analyzing the genre, organization, and stylistic features; and the third for analyzing the rhetorical context. These questions are the foundation for all types of analysis. In this chapter, you will learn how to build on these questions to probe further toward a more intellectually rigorous analysis and evaluation. In the three boxes below, we elaborate the original sets of questions by asking whether or not the text has accomplished its purpose.

---

### QUESTIONS FOR CRITICAL ANALYSIS OF CONTENT OF TEXTS

- What is the topic or focal point of the text?

- What is the main idea, major point, or central claim? Is it plausible, defensible, and illuminating? Is it a reasonable position, or does the author come across as someone with an axe to grind?

- What other ideas are important? Do they follow logically from the thesis?

- What aspects of the topic or issue are emphasized? Are these aspects appropriate and sufficient, or does the text fail to consider important aspects of the topic? Where are the gaps; what is not said? If the text were to address the issue in all its complexity, what would have to be added?

- How does the text support, qualify, and develop the claim or position? Is the evidence relevant, accurate, and substantial enough to support the thesis, or does it fall short and only partially support the thesis? Which points need more support and explanation?

- What inferences, judgments, or conclusions can be drawn? Do they follow logically from the evidence? Are they sound, valid, and justifiable? Are alternative inferences, judgments, and conclusions just as reasonable?

- What assumptions underlie the thesis and are explicitly stated or taken for granted? Will readers question these assumptions?

- Does the text position the reader as someone of a particular theoretical, political, or ideological persuasion? Is this a fair and accurate perception of the reader?

- Does the text anticipate and acknowledge other points of view, or does it fail to recognize that there are different ways of viewing the issue?

- What are the implications or consequences of the argument and reasoning presented in the text? Are the implications and consequences reasonable, accurate, and probable, or should we explore other possibilities?

## QUESTIONS FOR CRITICAL ANALYSIS OF GENRE, ORGANIZATION, AND STYLISTIC FEATURES OF TEXTS

- Does the text demonstrate an identifiable genre? Can you describe the special characteristics of that genre?
- Is the genre appropriate? Does it contribute to the argument? Would the writer have been better able to convey the message in a different form?
- How do the different components of the genre function in relation to the text as a whole? Are certain components stressed at the expense of others?
- How does the organization contribute to the meaning of the text? Would the meaning be better represented if the parts were arranged differently—for example, if the thesis were disclosed in the introduction instead of the conclusion; if the narrative had progressed from past to present instead of present to past; if reasons were ordered from most important to least important instead of vice versa?
- Does the language serve to heighten and illuminate the topic? Is it merely adequate? Does it detract?
- Does the writer use figurative language (for example, similes, metaphors, personification) to explore the subject? Is the figurative language appropriate or confusing, inexact, or misleading? Is the vocabulary unnecessarily formal or pompous? Does the writer use strange, unusual, or overly technical words where common ones would do? Does the writer clarify ideas when necessary?
- Are you struck by rhythmic, balanced, symmetrical, or graceful sentences, or are the sentences disorganized and awkward? Is the writer concise, or does he or she try to pack too many ideas into long, sprawling sentences?
- Do the writer's references or allusions illuminate or add significantly to the subject matter? Take account of the writer's formal references to other written sources as well as other types of references and allusions. (An allusion, not to be mistaken for "illusion," is a reference to some literary, cultural, or historical piece of information, whether through direct or indirect citation, that taps the reader's knowledge or memory.)
- Are the references to other written sources welcome additions to the text, or do they appear to be superfluous?

## QUESTIONS FOR CRITICAL ANALYSIS OF RHETORICAL CONTEXT OF TEXTS

- What effect does the author intend the text to have on the audience?
- For whom is the author writing? Where was the text first published? Who reads this publication?
- In what year was the text published? What was on people's minds? What prompted the author to write the text? Can you identify a circumstance, event, or social practice?
- Does the author supply the reader with sufficient background information, or does he or she make erroneous assumptions about the reader's previous knowledge?

- What is the writer's persona or stance (attitude or rhetorical posture), and how does it contribute to his or her point? Is it suitable, or does it detract from the piece?
- How does the writer's voice contribute to the text's effectiveness? Are the voice and tone appropriate or unnecessarily pompous or formal?
- What do we know about the author's background and credibility? Does the author come across as authoritative, creditable, and reliable, or are you left with questions about his or her background, prestige, political or religious orientation, or overall reputation?
- How is the author drawing on other writers and other texts? How does he or she view what others have said about the topic?

Whenever you read texts, especially sources that will inform your writing, systematically ask as many of the above questions as possible. In time, you will internalize the questions and cultivate a questioning frame of mind. When you receive an assignment that calls for written analysis, you will gravitate toward the questions that best serve your purpose. You will draw from a subset of the questions, and you may even focus your analysis on a small number of core questions.

## Types of Analyses You Will Be Asked to Write

College students analyze myriad topics and texts. Sometimes your analyses will take the form of **self-contained** essays, and other times they will be **embedded** in larger projects. Sometimes your goal is to give a close reading of a text simply to show your readers your interpretation. Other times your goal is to advance a particular interpretation: for example, a gender-based analysis of Ibsen's *A Doll's House*.

Critical analysis is both a self-contained genre and a pattern of development that is embedded in many other genres. It plays a dominant role in such professional genres as book reviews, movie reviews, art criticism, policy analyses, and comparative analyses, and in such academic genres as the literary analysis essay and the rhetorical analysis essay.

In this chapter, we will focus upon the genre of a self-contained critical analysis essay, though we will also discuss embedded analyses in other genres. You will learn how to write a critical analysis as we walk you through the academic reading-writing process of constructing such an essay, beginning with prereading and ending with editing. Chapter 5 covers rhetorical analysis, comparative analysis, literary analysis, process analysis, causal analysis, and the classic comparison and contrast essay. In Chapter 6 we cover analysis of visual texts and in Chapter 8 we delve deeper into analysis of formal arguments.

## Importance of Genre Knowledge

When you set out to analyze a text, if you don't know what you are looking for, you will be stymied from the start. Before you dissect the text, you need to identify the attributes, characteristics, or features most frequently associated with it. In English classes you'll have difficulty writing an analysis of a poem if you are unfamiliar with literary features such as narrative voice, imagery, figurative language, sound, and rhythm. In history classes you'll have difficulty analyzing an historical event if you lack information about the chronological context or background of the event, the primary decisions made, the key decision-makers, the secondary players, the advocates, and the dissenters.

The best way to discover the attributes, characteristics, or features most frequently associated with the text is to identify its genre. Genre knowledge is a topic we introduced in Chapter 1. We pointed out that the key to successful critical reading is identifying the genre, organization, and stylistic features of the text. Genre knowledge is also a key to intelligent analysis. Identify the genre, and you will unlock information about the text's organizing principle and constituent parts.

For illustration, let's say you are enrolled in an elective course in Children's Literature. One unit of the course concerns fairy tales, and you have decided to write your critical analysis paper on *Snow White*. You've been exposed to fairy tales since childhood, so you have ready knowledge of the genre. You know that because a fairy tale is a story, its organizing principle is narration. (To review organizing principles, see page 22). Thinking back to dozens of fairy tales you've read, you can easily identify characteristics of the genre: conflict between good and evil; heroes, heroines, and villains; magical elements; settings involving royalty (kings, queens, princes, princesses, and castles), peasants, fantastic characters (witches, monsters, dwarfs, giants), and nature (forests, mountains, streams); a dilemma; a happy ending; and typical phrases such as "once upon a time" and "they lived happily ever after." With knowledge of these elements, you are well on your way to analyzing the story of Snow White and her wicked stepmother.

Similar sorts of knowledge are required for other kinds of analyses. In order to analyze a piece of music, you need to know about melody, rhythm, harmony, dynamics, timbre, and form. In order to analyze an art work, you need to know about style, surfaces, colors, textures, shape, sizes, and volumes.

On the other hand, suppose you are enrolled in a course in American Government and you have been asked to analyze *Washington v. Glucksberg* (96–110) 521 U.S. 702 (1997) on the topic of physician-assisted suicide. You have not yet read the chapter of your textbook devoted to legal briefs, so you know nothing about the genre. You are flummoxed and you don't know where to begin. Before you can write an intelligent analysis, you will have to read a number of legal briefs in order to ascertain the organizing principle and determine the characteristics of the genre.

For any analysis assignment, early in the process you need to ask yourself the following questions:

- Can I identify the genre?
- What is the organizing principle or pattern for this genre?
- What are the constituent parts: the attributes, characteristics, or features most frequently associated with this genre?

### EXERCISE 4.1

Break into groups of three. Each group will read one of the selections in Chapter 3. As a homework assignment, one student will answer the questions for Critical Analysis of Content, the second will answer the questions for Critical Analysis of Genre, Organization, and Stylistic Features, the third will answer the questions for Critical Analysis of Rhetorical Context. When the group reconvenes, each student should summarize and share his or her responses. One student from each group will report to the class.

## ■ Approaches to Analysis

Another problem students encounter when they are assigned an analysis is they don't know what to do after they've dissected the text. After you've broken down the text, the next step is to examine the nature and function of the key components. Ask yourself:

- What is the nature of each component and what is its relationship to the other components?
- How does each component affect or function in the work as a whole?

This examination will result in a more sophisticated understanding and intelligent interpretation of the text.

If you wish, when you write an analysis essay, you can give equal weight to all of the components of the text you are examining. You might select this approach if you are writing an explication of the text or close reading of a piece of literature in an English class. It is more likely that you will zero in on a few key components, view the text through a critical lens, or compare the text to a source that is similar. You can use each of these approaches independently or in combination.

---

**APPROACHES TO ANALYSIS**

- Zero in on key elements
- View the text through a critical lens
- Compare the text to a source that is similar

---

## Zero In on Key Elements

After you examine the various components of the text, you may discover one or more features that have a special function or play a significant role in the way the work achieves its purpose. You can make these features the focal point of your analysis. You will still give consideration to other features, but you will focus on one feature or a small subset of features.

Returning to our earlier examples, instead of giving equal weight to all of the literary elements in a poem, you might focus on the role of imagery; instead of evaluating all aspects of an historical event, you might investigate the role of the advocates and the dissenters; instead of evaluating all of the characteristics of *Snow White*, you might analyze maternal conflict in the fairy tale.

Sometimes the focal point of your analysis is predetermined because your professors stipulate what they want you to do.

## View the Text Through a Critical Lens

Another approach is to use a **critical lens** to frame your analysis. The critical lens *focuses the analysis on certain aspects of the subject and enables you to discuss it from a particular perspective and point of view.* For example, instead of writing a broad-based analysis of the phrase *American dream*, you might analyze the concept of the American dream in terms of migrant workers' recent experiences in California. Examining the concept through migrant workers' eyes, you will focus the analysis on a certain group of immigrants at a particular point in time. The critical lens may be a person, theory, principle, concept, quotation, or any other controlling idea that frames the subject or text.

If you were to examine analysis assignments given by college professors, you would find that a large number of them provide students with a critical lens. Rarely are students asked "to analyze Barbie™." The assignment would be "Write a feminist analysis of Barbie as a female stereotype." Critical lens essays are sometimes taught in high school. One of the tasks on the New York State Regents Examination in English is called the Critical Lens Essay. In such a critical lens essay, high-school students are given a quotation and asked to interpret two works of literature through the perspective of the quotation. Given the quotation, "Love has no age, no limit; and no death" (John Galsworthy, *The Forsyte Saga*), a student might analyze *King Lear* and *Romeo and Juliet*.

Keep in mind that you must have in-depth knowledge of the critical frame you are applying to the text. In order to write an economic analysis of school tracking, you must have adequate knowledge of economic scholarship. Toward the beginning of the analysis, you would tell your readers what an economic analysis entails. Then, as you develop and support your thesis in the body paragraphs of the paper, you would use the principles of economic analysis to show how tracking reproduces class inequities.

## Compare the Text to a Source That Is Similar

Another way to analyze a text is through the lens of a source that is comparable. For example, you could analyze the representation of Dracula in the Bram Stoker novel, *Dracula*, and the Francis Ford Coppola film by the same name. In this type of analysis, your purpose would be more pointed than to show the similarities and differences between the novel and the film. You would make a claim, perhaps arguing that Coppola portrays Dracula by faithfully adapting the character in the novel.

For an example of comparative analysis, read how the drama critic Terry Teachout opens his review of *Well* and *Pen*, two plays that opened in spring 2006:

> No theatrical season can call itself complete without a new play about a weird mother. This week there are two and, not surprisingly, they bear certain family resemblances. Both have monosyllabic titles, both contain elements of fantasy, both are graced by splendid performances by the actresses who play the ladies in question—and neither is any good, though one is a good deal more ambitious than the other. (W9)

In the review, Teachout uses *Well*, the "more ambitious" play, as a lens for evaluating *Pen*, which he considers to be less successful.

> Except for Jayne Houdyshell's performance, I didn't like anything about *Well*. (I didn't laugh once.) Still, I freely admit that, as awful as it is, it's more interesting than David Marshall Grant's *Pen*, the latest in Playwrights Horizons' fast-growing string of excessively similar plays about family life. (W9)

Notice that Teachout begins the review by identifying three elements the two plays have in common: titles, fantasy, leading actor performances. The fourth commonality is that neither play is good. A difference between the two plays is that one is more "ambitious," and, as we discover later in the review, more "interesting" than the other.

The practice of using comparison to show the relative weight of one text as compared to another may be new to you. You are probably more familiar with the classic comparison and contrast essay in which you take two texts of seemingly equal value, make a list of their similarities and differences, and compose an essay comparing them along the lines of stated criteria. Comparative analysis is different in that one text becomes the lens for evaluating the other.

## EXERCISE 4.2

Select one of the texts in Chapter 3 and explain how you would analyze it with varying degrees of specificity. Identify the focus of analysis:

- Zero in on key elements
- View the text through a critical lens
- Compare the text to a source that is similar

Example: Suppose that the text is *To Kill a Mockingbird*.

*Zero in on key elements.* I would focus on characterization and analyze how the character of Scout evolves in the novel.

*View the topic or text through a critical lens.* I would use the principle of "social justice" as a lens for analyzing the novel.

*Compare the text to something similar.* I would analyze the courtroom scenes in John Grisham's *A Time to Kill* and Harper Lee's *To Kill a Mockingbird*.

For most analyses, you will not be using the three approaches discretely. You will be using them in combination. For example, in order to analyze the courtroom scenes in John Grisham's *A Time to Kill* and Harper Lee's *To Kill a Mockingbird*, you have to zero in on a key element such as setting. You also have to use your knowledge of courtroom procedures as a lens for analyzing the criminal trials.

## EXERCISE 4.3

Here is a list of typical analysis and evaluation assignments. Divide the class into groups and give a subset of the assignments to each group. Students will examine the extent to which each assignment affects the writer's scope. Does the topic restrict the writer to one or more of the three approaches?

- Zero in on key elements
- View the text through a critical lens
- Compare the text to a source that is similar

Or does it allow the writer freedom to use any approach or combination of approaches? A representative from each group will report to the class.

*Assignments*

- Write a critique of Vincent van Gogh's "Starry Night."
- Give your assessment of two arguments on stem-cell research.

- Write a book review of Philip Roth's historical novel, *The Plot Against America.*
- Relate one of Dickens's novels to the state of the class struggle in Victorian England.
- Write a critique of Martin Scorsese's film, *The Age of Innocence.*
- Use feminist theory to analyze one of the selections in Chapter 3 of this book.
- Write a critical analysis in which you focus on characterization in *Pride and Prejudice.*
- Select three poems and analyze e.e. cummings's use of space.
- Analyze two political candidates' positions on universal health care insurance.
- Write an economic analysis of how school tracking reproduces social class inequities.
- Write a rhetorical analysis of Martin Luther King's "I Have a Dream" speech.
- Evaluate nature imagery in two of the Seamus Heaney poems we have read.
- Analyze the role and quality of light in three paintings by Rembrandt.
- Write a comparative analysis of the architecture of Filippo Brunelleschi and Michelozzo di Bartolommeo in the Italian Renaissance.
- Analyze and evaluate Andreas Ronan's editorial on changes in U.S. immigration policies.
- Write a psychological analysis of the Islamist extremism.
- Analyze the presence of fate in *Romeo and Juliet.*

## ■ Purpose of Critical Analysis

A critical analysis of a text examines its argument by looking closely at the author's line of reasoning. When you receive an assignment that calls for critical analysis, think in terms of textual elements such as *thesis or major claim, evidence, point of view, assumptions, inferences, judgments, conclusions,* and *implications.* Examine what the text says and also what the text doesn't say: its *gaps, omissions,* and *oversights.*

The overall purpose of writing a critical analysis is to share your interpretation with your readers, and, ideally, to convince them that your enlightened reading of the text warrants their attention and should be taken seriously. A more focused purpose is to evaluate the author's argument in terms of its strengths and weaknesses.

## ■ Critical Analysis and the Academic Conversation

Critical analyses play a major role in intellectual debates and conversations waged in the public realm as well as in academia. These conversations focus on hot-button issues such as global warming, abortion, immigration, U.S. foreign policy, the war in Iraq, universal health care, and a host of other controversial topics. One such discussion is the controversy over a mother's choice to pursue a career or stay home to take care of her children. In Chapter 3 we presented a group of texts devoted to this debate. Among the reading selections were various forms of analysis, including critical analysis. These analyses served as touchstone texts because they exemplify many of the characteristics of their genres. By examining them closely, you will learn to master the genre conventions. Earlier, we advised you to read the selections in Chapter 3 prior to reading Chapters 4 through 9. If you have not already done so, please read the relevant articles.

We will illustrate critical analysis with two touchstone texts: Cathy Young's "The Return of the Mommy Wars" (pp. 116–19) and David Brooks's "The Year of Domesticity" (pages 114–16). Both authors analyze "Homeward Bound" (pages 104–12), an essay by

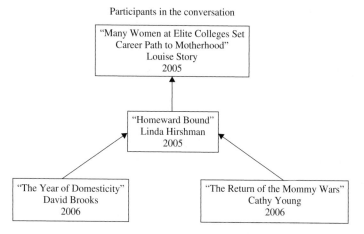

Participants in the conversation

"Many Women at Elite Colleges Set
Career Path to Motherhood"
Louise Story
2005

"Homeward Bound"
Linda Hirshman
2005

"The Year of Domesticity"
David Brooks
2006

"The Return of the Mommy Wars"
Cathy Young
2006

**Figure 4–2    Participants in the Conversation**

Linda Hirshman that originally appeared in *The American Prospect*. The article that sparked the conversation among Young, Brooks, and Hirshman is Louise Story's *New York Times* article, "Many Women at Elite Colleges Set Career Path to Motherhood" (pages 91–95). In Figure 4–2, we provide a graphic overview of the participants in the conversation.

In the article that began the conversation, Louise Story writes about women in elite colleges—Yale University in particular—who plan to abandon their careers when they have children. The attitude of these young women contrasts with that of women two and three decades ago who did not expect their careers to take second place to child rearing. Writing in response to Louise Story, Linda Hirshman says feminism is responsible for this new trend. She claims that feminism isn't radical enough because it offers women a choice between pursuing careers or becoming full-time mothers. Hirshman claims that women who pursue the latter option subordinate themselves to a domestic life that "allows fewer opportunities for full human flourishing than public spheres like the market or the government."

Before continuing, please take time to read: (1) Story's article, (2) Hirshman's article, and (3) Cathy Young's critical analysis.

## ■ Examination of "The Return of the Mommy Wars," Cathy Young's Critical Analysis of Linda Hirshman's "Homeward Bound"

Cathy Young is the author of *Ceasefire! Why Women and Men Must Join Forces to Achieve Political Equality* and a contributing editor at *Reason*, the magazine in which her analysis originally appeared. Young's critical analysis can easily be divided into three sections.

The first six paragraphs bring the reader into the conversation. Young describes the issue; introduces Linda Hirshman as a major voice in the debate; summarizes, paraphrases, and quotes the main points of Hirshman's article; and alludes to other critiques of Hirshman, including the one by David Brooks.

Each of the next six paragraphs is devoted to a strength of Hirshman's argument. Young begins this section of her analysis with the statement, "In fact, Hirshman's article raised important questions." Then she proceeds to discuss the questions one by one.

The final six paragraphs analyze the shortcomings of Hirshman's argument. Young begins this section with her thesis: "So Hirshman tackles some of the right issues, but she tackles them in so wrong-headed a way as to sabotage her own argument." Young goes on to discuss five weaknesses in Hirshman's argument: she "overstates her case"; she "has an obnoxiously patronizing tone"; she exhibits "bilious contempt for anything traditionally feminine"; she sees only one side of the problem; and her vision of women's careers is outdated. The five weaknesses correspond to the following criteria:

Criteria Used to Evaluate Argument

**reasonableness of author's position**: Hirshman is unreasonable and comes across as someone with an axe to grind.

**tone**: Hirshman's tone is unnecessarily pompous.

**anticipation of alternative views**: Hirshman fails to acknowledge readers who have a high regard for volunteerism and idealism.

**consideration of issue in all its complexity**: Hirshman "misses the brighter side of the female dilemma."

**evidence**: Some of Hirshman's evidence is outdated.

Young concludes the critical analysis by acknowledging that we need a discussion about the negative consequences of women opting out of the workforce. But she says Hirshman has "started it off on the wrong note."

When you write your own critical analysis, you might decide to follow the logic of Young's text.

### *Organization of Critical Analysis*

Bring your readers into the conversation:
explain issue, text, and author of text
↓

Summarize the text
↓

Discuss strengths of the text
↓

State your thesis
↓

Discuss weaknesses of the text
↓

Conclude with point about the larger conversation

Now we turn to another example of a critical analysis of Linda Hirshman's "Homeward Bound": David Brooks's "The Year of Domesticity." Please read the Hirshman selection and the Brooks selection before proceeding to our examination of Brooks.

# ■ Examination of "The Year of Domesticity," David Brooks's Critical Analysis of Linda Hirshman's "Homeward Bound"

Brooks's stance is evident from the start. In paragraph 1, he defines the issue as he sees it: Women have more choices today than in the past because "they are freer to pursue a career, stay at home or figure out some combination of both." In making this comment, Brooks argues that women's ability to make these choices is a sign of progress. He ends the paragraph with a rhetorical question "And this is progress, right?" that reveals his opposition to Hirshman.

In paragraphs 2 through 7, Brooks summarizes six of Hirshman's points, illustrating each point with a quotation from her essay. Paragraphs 8 and 9 contain Brooks's thesis: Hirshman's essay is a "blast of 1975 time-warp feminism" and it is downright wrong. Paragraphs 10 to 14 contain the meat of the critique:

| *Paragraph* | *Brooks's evaluation* | *Brooks's evidence* |
|---|---|---|
| 10 | Hirshman's *assertion* that "high-paying jobs lead to more human flourishing than parenthood" *is wrong.* | Brooks asks his readers to reflect on their own lives to decide which memories are more cherished: those of work or those of family. |
| 11 | Hirshman's *assumption* that "work is the realm of power and home is the realm of powerlessness" *is wrong.* | Brooks maintains that home is the realm of unmatched power because children's IQs and character are shaped in the first years of life. |
| 12 | Hirshman *neglects to consider* children's *views on the issue.* | Brooks cites an essay that describes how young pop musicians sing about abandonment. |
| 13–14 | Hirshman *disregards evidence* that explains why women choose to stay home. | Brooks cites neurological studies by Murray and Pinker and Spelke on the differences between men and women. |

Brooks ends the critique with an observation about the number of recent essays on topics related to domesticity and a concluding statement about power being in the kitchen rather than in the public sphere.

What can we take away from Brooks's critical analysis? Let us backtrack to speculate about his writing process. His response to Hirshman's article incorporates a subset of the analysis questions we presented on page 139:

- What is the topic or focal point of the text?

- What is the main idea, major point, or central claim? Is it plausible, defensible, and illuminating? Is it a reasonable position, or does the author come across as someone with an axe to grind?

- What aspects of the topic or issue are emphasized? Are these aspects appropriate and sufficient, or does the text fail to consider important aspects of the topic? Where are the gaps; what is not said? If the text were to address the issue in all its complexity, what would have to be added?

- What inferences, judgments, or conclusions can be drawn? Do they follow logically from the evidence? Are they sound, valid, and justifiable? Are alternate *inferences, judgments,* and *conclusions* just as reasonable?

- What assumptions underlie the thesis and are explicitly stated or taken for granted? Will readers question these assumptions?

- What are the implications or consequences of the argument or reasoning presented in the text? Are the implications and consequences reasonable, accurate, and probable, or should we explore other possibilities?

Brooks critiques Hirshman's line of reasoning by focusing on four evaluative criteria: **incorrect assertions, erroneous assumptions, omission of important viewpoints,** and **disregard for research**. And he substantiates each of his criticisms by referencing Hirshman's text.

How would you evaluate Brooks's analysis? Later in the chapter, we will discuss Rebecca Traister's evaluation of Brooks's critique. The intellectual debate continues.

Before you attempt the following exercise, read "Many Women at Elite Colleges Set Career Path to Motherhood" by Louise Story, pages 91–95.

## EXERCISE 4.4

On a blog called blackprof.com (www.blackprof.com), Tracey Meares, a professor of law at the University of Chicago, writes a brief critical analysis of "Many Women at Elite Colleges Set Career Path to Motherhood." Read Meares's analysis on pages 100–101, and then review the three sets of analysis questions on pages 139–41. Which questions is Meares responding to on her blog? List the evaluative criteria she uses to assess Louise Story's article.

Now that you have read three examples of critical analysis and have witnessed how the authors adapt the conventions of critical analysis to fit their purposes, we will guide you through the process of writing a critical analysis essay. First, we will review the defining characteristics of a critical analysis.

---

### REVIEW OF THE DEFINING CHARACTERISTICS OF A CRITICAL ANALYSIS

- Writer's purpose: Share your interpretation of a text with readers to convince them that your enlightened analysis and evaluation should be taken seriously.
- Elements of the text:

  Writer's thesis/appraisal of the text

  Thesis developed by focusing on evaluative criteria such as thesis/major claim of focal text, evidence, point of view, assumptions, inferences, judgments, conclusions, implications

  Emphasis on gaps, omissions, oversights in text

  Summary of major points in the text

  Use of paraphrase, quotation, and summary to support the critique

---

## ■ PART II: WRITING A CRITICAL ANALYSIS: A DETAILED DEMONSTRATION OF THE READING-WRITING PROCESS

The remainder of this chapter will illustrate the various stages of critical reading, textual analysis, pre-paper planning, rough-draft writing, comprehensive revision, and final editing that are involved in an academic paper.

Let us suppose that you received the following assignment:

Select an educational issue we have discussed this semester. The issue can be related to primary, secondary, or higher education. Choose an article dealing with the issue and critique its argument and line of reasoning.

For our purposes in this example, suppose you have chosen Ronna Vanderslice's article on grade inflation, "When I Was Young, an A Was an A: Grade Inflation in Higher Education," which we worked on in Chapter 2. You will find the article on pages 36–37.

## ■ Critical Reading

Your first steps are to clarify the assignment, set your rhetorical goal, and consider your audience.

*Clarify assignment.* The assignment is straightforward. It asks you to select a text and evaluate the argument and line of reasoning. As you already know from Figure 4–1 and our previous discussion, analysis goes hand in hand with evaluation.

*Set rhetorical goal.* The purpose of your critical analysis is to judge the effectiveness and worth of the text, after you have dissected and interpreted it, and to convey that judgment to your readers.

*Consider audience.* The assignment does not stipulate an audience, so you can assume your readers will be the professor and interested classmates.

### Prereading

You will recall from Chapter 1 that the next operation is prereading. Preview the text and derive questions that will help you set goals for close reading. Then recall your prior knowledge and express your feelings about the reading topic. Freewrite and brainstorm in your writer's notebook.

### *Preview the Text and Ask Questions About It*

Review the seven Prereading Questions on pages 6–7 and respond to the questions that are relevant. For our purposes, these questions are the following:

- What does the title indicate the text will be about? The title indicates that the author believes that when she was in college there was no grade inflation.

- Is there biographical information about the author? What does it tell me about the text? The documentation reveals that the author is a professor of education at Southwestern Oklahoma State University. The article was published in Phi Kappa Phi Forum. A Google search revealed that readers of this journal are faculty and student members of the national honor society, Phi Kappa Phi.

- Do any topic sentences of paragraphs seem especially important? The first sentence of the second paragraph mentions a problem, and the first sentence of the third paragraph says, "Universities must reform." The setup of the article is probably problem-solution.

- What type of background knowledge do I need to make sense of this text? *I need to know more about the history, causes, and effects of grade inflation.*

## Recall Your Prior Knowledge and Express Your Feelings About the Reading Topic

If you need some prompts to trigger your personal experiences, review the Prompts for Personal Response to the Text on page 36.

> *I question whether grade inflation is a problem. My writing teacher told the class not to expect high grades because the average grade for all sixty sections of the composition courses is between a B– and a C+.*

The Prereading operations will improve your comprehension and enable you to read more objectively. You will also be more conscious of your opinions and biases and less likely to confuse them inadvertently with those of the author.

## Close Reading

Turn back to page 36 and reread the Vanderslice article with pencil in hand, **annotating, marking**, and **elaborating on the text**. *Mark* the text by underlining, highlighting, circling, drawing arrows, boxing, and bracketing important ideas. *Annotate* by making marginal notes and recording brief responses. *Elaborate* by amplifying or supplementing the text with comments. We provide a complete set of strategies for elaborating on texts on pages 10–11.

The next operation, *pose and answer questions about the text*, lays the foundation for your critical analysis. Earlier in this chapter, we pointed out that the key to writing an effective analysis is acquiring a questioning frame of mind. Begin with the broad, preliminary questions we discussed earlier:

- What is said? *Grade inflation is getting worse and more widespread. Universities must institute reforms to combat this routine practice.*
- Why is it viewed this way? *Since the author is a professor, she thinks grade inflation is a serious problem.*
- How is it said? *With great urgency–she says universities must reform.*
- Is the text comparable to another work with which the reader is familiar? *In our textbook, we have other articles on grade inflation.*
- Does the text demonstrate an identifiable genre? *It seems to be a proposal. She states a problem and offers solutions.*
- What is the form or special characteristics of that genre, and how do the different components function in relation to each other and to the text as a whole? *There are data on why grade inflation is a growing problem and an explanation of the effects of grade inflation. Then Vanderslice urges universities to reform and she proposes a number of ways they can deal with the problem.*
- How is the text organized? *Problem–solution*

Your next step is to reread the text and ask any of the Questions for Critical Analysis (pp. 139–41) that you have not yet answered.

- What is the main idea, major point, or central claim? Is it plausible, defensible, and illuminating? Is it a reasonable position, or does the author come across as someone with an axe to grind? *Because grade inflation has increased and become a routine practice, universities must make explicit reforms that will raise standards. If, indeed, grade inflation is a serious, widespread problem, Vanderslice's position is reasonable.*

- What aspects of the topic or issue are emphasized? *The effects of grade inflation and ways to curtail it.*

- Are these aspects appropriate and sufficient, or does the text fail to consider important aspects of the topic? *More attention could be paid to the phenomenon of grade inflation itself. What is it? What are possible causes of grade inflation? Does everyone agree?*

- Where are the gaps; what is not said? If the text were to address the issue in all its complexity, what would have to be added? *I don't think all professors equate elevated grades with lower standards. Nor do they believe that they are rewarding mediocrity rather than excellence. I also question whether grade inflation is as widespread as the author claims.*

- How does the text support, qualify, and develop the claim or position? Is the evidence relevant, accurate, and substantial enough to support the thesis, or does it fall short and only partially support the thesis? Which points need more support and explanation? *The data in support of the rise in grade inflation are dated and limited. Haven't any surveys been published since 1993?*

- What inferences, judgments, or conclusions can be drawn? Do they follow logically from the evidence? Are they sound, valid, and justifiable? Are alternative inferences, judgments, and conclusions just as reasonable? *I could infer that higher grades are due to better teaching, easier exams, or brighter, better prepared students. Grade inflation might not be occurring everywhere.*

- What assumptions underlie the thesis and are explicitly stated or taken for granted? Will readers question these assumptions? *There are many assumptions. First, since V. doesn't mention alternative views, I assume that she thinks all her readers will concur with her assessment of the problem.*

- Does the text anticipate and acknowledge other points of view, or does it fail to recognize that there are different ways of viewing the issue? *Other views are not represented. I think students would view V's solutions differently. They wouldn't be in favor of the two-grade system, and they'd feel disempowered if their evaluations of professors weren't taken seriously.*

- What are the implications or consequences of the argument or reasoning presented in the text? Are the implications and consequences reasonable, accurate, and probable, or should we explore other possibilities? *I think we have to explore other possibilities. Why would the two-grade system raise standards and curtail grade inflation? How does ignoring student evaluations improve the quality of teaching?*

Notice that we did not respond to all of the Questions for Critical Analysis. In this book, we supply you with dozens of ways of questioning a text. You need not use all of them; select only the ones that best serve your purpose.

## Postreading

Now it is time to transform yourself from a reader to a writer. Before you make this transition, we recommend that you express your personal thoughts about the text. By relating your real-life experiences to the text, you will become more aware of what you can add to the argument.

### *PERSONAL RESPONSE*

*The solutions aren't very appealing. I'm already hyper about grades. I don't need two grades instead of one. I don't care if my B− in English is below the class average of B+. I do my best. I'm not trying to be better than everyone else. I feel the same about public grades and private grades. They focus on competition. Ever since kindergarten, I've been compared to my peers. I want to reduce the emphasis on grades. If we must have them, one is enough. I think the proposal to get rid of student evaluations is self-serving on the teachers' part. If they're going to do that, they should also get rid of professors' evaluations of students.*

## ■ Planning

The operations you have performed for critical reading—questioning the text, taking notes, annotating, elaborating on the text, and writing a personal response—will provide you with raw materials for your essay. Your next challenge is to give form to the raw materials. Find common threads among them, organize them, delete extraneous or inappropriate items, and, if necessary, return to the text to extract more information. This is the work of planning, the stage when you impose your own rhetorical goal and begin to exercise control over the material you have collected and generated.

### Formulate a Working Thesis and Decide on Your Approach

In a critical analysis essay, the writer's goal is to dissect and evaluate the text's argument and line of reasoning. The thesis will express this interpretation and evaluation of the text. Your first move is to arrive at a *working thesis* or preliminary understanding of the point you wish to make in your paper. Throughout the writing process, your thesis will evolve. It will be the product of a good deal of exploratory reading and prewriting. Eventually, you will arrive at the version of the thesis you will develop in your paper. Your thesis should reflect your rhetorical purpose—the effect you wish to have on your readers—and it may also reflect your organizational plan.

To form a working thesis, review the prewriting you have produced to date and ask yourself:

- Have I focused my responses on one feature of the text or on a small subset of features? Which critical analysis questions produced lengthy and substantive responses?

- Am I able to group responses that pertain to similar features of the text? Does a theme or pattern emerge?

Your answers to these questions will determine your approach; that is, whether you will zero in on key elements, view the text through a critical lens, or compare the text to a source that is similar.

When you sort through the writing you've produced so far, you find that your responses focus on weaknesses in the text: insufficient evidence, questionable assumptions, and lack of consideration of alternative ways of viewing the issue. You decide your approach will be to focus on this subset of features.

You jot down the following working thesis:

> *"When I Was Young, an A Was an A: Grade Inflation in Higher Education"* is problematic in that it has insufficient evidence, questionable assumptions, and lack of consideration of alternative ways of viewing the issue.

## Verify That You Have Support for Your Thesis

Return to the relevant parts of the text to check for supporting material. Each time you make a point about a textual feature, your essay should provide textual evidence in the form of a quotation, a paraphrase, or a summary. At this juncture, go back to the text and mark passages you will use to support your points. If you cannot find enough textual evidence, consider changing your focus.

## Decide On an Organizational Plan

After you come up with a working thesis and select an approach, your next step is to identify the organizational format you will use. Reexamine your prewriting. Categorize and try out several grouping schemes to find what works best. Review the organizational plans on page 22 to see which is most appropriate for critical analysis essays.

| | |
|---|---|
| Time order, narration, process | Example |
| Antecedent-consequent/cause-effect | Analysis/classification |
| Description | Definition |
| Statement-response | Analogy |
| Comparison/contrast | |

For example, if your purpose is to show the negative implications and consequences of the text's argument, you might develop your essay in a cause-and-effect format. If you wish to weigh the text's strengths against its weaknesses, you could use the comparison and contrast format.

- State your thesis and the criteria you are using to evaluate the text.
- Allocate one or more body paragraphs to each criterion, developing each point with specific evidence from the text.

The various patterns of organization may be used individually, or they may overlap. In "The Year of Domesticity," David Brooks uses statement-response as the overall pattern for his critical analysis, and in the second half of the article he uses the analysis pattern to classify Hirshman's "mistakes."

After studying your prewriting, you decide the argument format best suits your purpose. You sketch out the following loose plan:

"When I Was Young, an A Was an A: Grade Inflation in Higher Education" is problematic in that it has questionable assumptions, insufficient evidence, and lack of consideration of alternative ways of viewing the issue.

Write introduction. Summarize the article.

Make point about insufficient evidence: data only go up to 1993.

Make point about questionable assumptions:

- elevated grades = lowered standards
- two-grade system will raise standards; students use criteria of grades to evaluate professors.

Make point about lack of consideration of alternative ways of viewing the issue: no regard for students' point of view.

Write conclusion.

This loose plan suggests that the body of the essay will contain three paragraphs, each focusing on an evaluative criterion and each claiming a weakness in the text and supplying evidence to substantiate that claim.

If you prefer, display your plan as a *graphic overview* (see page 50) or as a formal outline. The graphic overview will depict major ideas and show how they are related. Some students are more comfortable with a *formal outline* than with loose plans or a graphic overview. Traditional outlines are based on the following structure:

I.
   A.
      1.
         a.
            i.
            ii.
         b.
      2.
   B.
II.

The formal outline provides a clear hierarchical structure useful for imposing order on a topic that is complicated and has a number of discrete subtopics. The following is a segment of a formal outline for the critical analysis:

   A. a basic assumption is that elevated grades indicate lower standards, but it could be that

      1. professors are doing a better job teaching

      2. students are better prepared

      3. teachers are using more suitable tests and exams

B. assumption that changing grading system will raise standards

How will two-grade device raise standards?

# ■ Drafting

When you sit down to write a draft of your essay, you will find that you've already generated a fair amount of material. Now comes the challenge as you have to weave together (1) the points you are making about the text and (2) the supportive textual evidence. You may find it necessary to change, rearrange, or eliminate some of the material you have assembled. This process will be less daunting if you observe the guidelines listed in the following box.

---

### ROUGH-DRAFT GUIDELINES

- You need not include all your preliminary work in your draft.
- You don't have to follow your outline religiously or incorporate it completely.
- You don't have to—and probably shouldn't—begin at the beginning. Many writers start with the body paragraphs and write the introduction and conclusion later. After all, you can't introduce a person until he or she is present, so you shouldn't expect to introduce a paper until you've finished writing the body paragraphs.
- As you revise, you should focus on higher-order concerns, such as ideas and organization, and not get bogged down with spelling, punctuation, and word choice. You can return to these lower-level concerns when you have completed the draft.

---

Keep these guidelines in mind as you consider the six strategies for drafting, shown in the following box. Apply these strategies liberally and flexibly; drafting does not necessarily follow a set procedure or a fixed sequence.

---

### DRAFTING STRATEGIES

- Select and use organizational plans for individual paragraphs.
- Weave direct quotations, paraphrases, and summaries in with your own ideas, and supply proper documentation.
- Decide on an introductory paragraph.
- Construct a conclusion.
- Develop a list of references or works cited.
- Title your essay.

---

For convenience, we describe the strategies in the order in which they appear in the boxed outline. You need not apply them in that order. For instance, you may find it easier to begin with the introduction and then compose the body of the essay. Whatever you do, don't get stymied by a particular sequence. Try another approach if you find yourself staring at a blank page or waiting for sentences to come to you. Move on to sections you can write readily. Later you can return to the parts that caused difficulty.

## Plan Individual Paragraphs

As you draft the body of your essay, follow the organizational plan you chose at the prewriting stage. For our illustration, it is the plan for an argument. Develop each paragraph in accordance with this top-level structure. Needless to say, as you compose individual paragraphs, other organizational patterns will come into play. Most writers use multiple patterns to organize their prose. Again, we should point out that if your prewriting plan proves unworkable, or if you discover a new direction for the paper in the process of drafting, don't hesitate to rethink the organizational format.

Your paragraphs should be unified and coherent. Each one should develop a central idea, and all the sentences should contribute to that idea in some way. You may need more than one topic sentence to express the paragraph's dominant ideas. You can achieve coherence by repeating words and ideas, rewording, and using transitional expressions ("also," "for example," "thus," "similarly," "consequently," and so on). All these devices show readers the logical links between sentences.

Here are the body paragraphs for the first draft of the critique of Ronna Vanderslice's "When I Was Young, an A Was an A: Grade Inflation in Higher Education":

> Vanderslice writes that "grades of C or less moved from 25 percent in 1969 to 9 percent in 1993" and today they continue to spiral upward (24). On what evidence is she basing this claim? And where are the statistics for the years between 1993 and 2004, when the article was written? My writing teacher told our class not to expect high grades because the average grade for all sixty sections of the composition courses is between a B− and a C+. This leads me to question Vanderslice's claim that "between 80 and 90 percent of all college students receive grades of A or B" (24). Is grade inflation occurring across the board, or are some colleges more guilty than others?
>
> The text's most basic problematic assumption is that elevated grades are indicative of lowered standards. But there are other reasonable explanations for higher grades. It could be that professors are doing a better job of teaching. Perhaps today's college students are better prepared and smarter than they were in previous decades. Maybe professors are using improved, more authentic, and more valid measures of assessment.
>
> A questionable assumption underlies Vanderslice's recommendation that professors change their grading practices by giving students two grades instead of one. The author assumes that this system will help to solve the problem of grade inflation, but she fails to explain how this practice will raise standards. The number of As and Cs will remain the same. The two-grade system also assumes that students are interested in how they stack up against their peers. This may not be the case at all. They may be less interested in competition than in mastery of subject matter.
>
> Another solution for curbing grade inflation is to reassess the practice of using student evaluations for personnel decisions involving faculty. This proposal assumes that students give high evaluations to professors that give high grades and low evaluations to professors that have rigorous standards. It also assumes that professors are so insecure that they cave in to student pressure. The implications of this proposal are dangerous: A professor who performs poorly in the classroom will be rewarded. If the personnel committee does not look at student evaluations, no one will ever know. One could argue that this proposal is also

*self-serving. Colleges should eliminate professors' evaluations of students as well as students' evaluations of professors? This would lead to a healthier, less competitive atmosphere.*

These are decent first-draft paragraphs, with one major exception: the last three fail to include direct references to the text. Each point that is made about the text needs to be backed up by a quotation, paraphrase, or summary.

## Use Quotations, Paraphrases, and Summaries

Quotations, paraphrases, and summaries are the principal ways to integrate material from sources into an essay. In Chapter 2, we covered in detail how to compose paraphrases and summaries and how to extract quotations as you take notes. If you need to supplement your notes with additional paraphrases, summaries, and quotations, return to those procedures. Remember that the reading-writing process is recursive. It is not uncommon for writers to read the source texts at the drafting stage.

When you employ quotations, paraphrases, or summaries in academic essays, be sure to differentiate them from your own words and document the text, as we described in Chapter 2. Always provide your readers with some identification of the source, usually the author and the page number (for printed sources) and, if necessary, the title. The reason for including this information is to allow interested readers to locate the complete reference in the list of sources at the end of the paper. Be sure you know which documentation style your professor requires.

Take note of how we incorporated quotations and paraphrases into the three paragraphs:

The text's most basic problematic assumption is that elevated grades are indicative of lowered standards. <u>The opening sentence places "low standards" side by side with "elevated grades," and the third paragraph states that the objective of the proposed reforms is to "increase standards instead of decreasing them."</u> But there are other reasonable explanations for higher grades. It could be that professors are doing a better job of teaching. Perhaps today's college students are better prepared and smarter than they were in previous decades. Maybe professors are using improved, more authentic, and more valid measures of assessment.

A questionable assumption underlies Vanderslice's recommendation that professors change their grading practices. <u>She recommends Harvard professor Harvey Mansfield's method of assigning two grades, a public grade for the registrar and a private grade for the student. Vanderslice explains, "the private grades give students a realistic, useful assessment of how well they did and where they stand in relation to others" (24).</u> The author assumes that this system will help to solve the problem of grade inflation, but she fails to explain how this practice will raise standards. The number of As and Cs will remain the same. The two-grade system also assumes that students are interested in how they stack up against their peers. This may not be the case at all. They may be less interested in competition than in mastery of subject matter.

Another solution for curbing grade inflation is to reassess the practice of using student evaluations for personnel decisions involving faculty. <u>Citing a moratorium at Indiana University, Vanderslice writes, "The university believes that removing concerns about student complaints about receiving lower grades might motivate all instructors to reset their standards, free from the pressures to give A's in exchange for high evaluations" (24).</u>

This proposal assumes that students give high evaluations to professors that give high grades and low evaluations to professors that have rigorous standards. It also assumes that professors are so insecure that they cave in to student pressure. The implications of this proposal are dangerous: A professor who performs poorly in the classroom will be accountable to no one. If the personnel committee does not look at student evaluations, no one will ever know. One could argue that this proposal is also self-serving. Colleges should eliminate professors' evaluations of students as well as students' evaluations of professors? This would lead to a healthier, less competitive atmosphere.

## Whether or Not to Include a Summary of the Text

When writing a critical analysis, you have to decide whether you will include a summary of the text or simply mention the main points you are critiquing. If you include a summary, its length depends on your purpose. You may want to provide your readers with a comprehensive summary that covers all the major aspects of the source, or you may want to focus on the aspects that concern you most. Refer to the summarizing strategies on page 49. You will find them very helpful.

Remember that your objective is to integrate the summary of the text with your own ideas on the topic. Once you order and classify your ideas and establish your direction, adapt the summary to your purpose. You need not summarize the entire text, only the sections that relate to your purpose. The summary should highlight the passages that prompted your evaluation and refer only incidentally to other portions of the text.

## Write Introductory Paragraphs

A strong introduction ought to interest readers, announce the text and topic, disclose your thesis or an attitude, and establish your voice. It may also, when appropriate, present background information essential to understanding the topic and indicate the organizational plan.

Here is the introductory paragraph for the draft of the critical analysis of "When I Was Young, an A Was an A: Grade Inflation in Higher Education."

> Is grade inflation a serious problem of college professors? Ronna Vanderslice, a professor of education at Southwestern Oklahoma State University, in her article "When I Was Young, an A Was an A: Grade Inflation in Higher Education," asserts that grade inflation is an increasingly serious problem that universities must counteract. Writing in *Phi Kappa Phi Forum*, the journal of a national honor society, she urges university faculty to reform their grading practices and offers various suggestions for doing so. Her argument is problematic in that it rests on insufficient evidence and questionable assumptions, and it neglects to consider alternative ways of viewing the issue.

The introduction presents the following components: *use of question as paper opener, identification of author and her major claim, title of the text, thesis of the critical analysis.*

The opening sentences of an essay are crucial. They should engage readers and encourage them to read on. These initial sentences also establish the writer's voice as formal or informal, academic or conversational. Some forms of academic writing require you to write in a very professional voice and open your paper in a designated way. For instance, research studies often begin with a one-paragraph abstract or summary of the study's principal findings. As we noted in Chapter 2, abstracts are written in formal, objective language. Other types of essays give you more freedom and allow you to use an informal opening that speaks directly to the reader.

There are several openers you could use. For example, if you were writing an essay on cloning human beings, you could open it with a *quotation from the reading source:*

Social critic Babara Ehrenreich warns, "Human embryos are life-forms, and there is nothing to stop anyone from marketing them now, on the same shelves with Cabbage Patch dolls" (86). Perhaps we are headed for a future where, as Ehrenreich suggests, we will purchase rather than bear our children.

You could start out with *an anecdote, a brief story,* or *a scenario:*

Imagine that you are a clone, an exact copy, of either your mother or your father rather than a combination of genetic material from both of them.

Or you could open with a *question:*

Is there any justification for reproductive cloning?

Alternatively, you can begin by *providing background information:*

Cloning, a genetic process that makes it possible to produce an exact, living replica of an organism, has been applied to simple organisms for years. Now it is possible to clone complex animals, even human beings.

Other opening strategies are to begin with a fact or a statistic, a generalization, a contradiction, or a thesis statement. *Avoid opening with clichés or platitudes* ("As we contemplate cloning, we should remember that fools rush in where angels fear to tread"), *dictionary definitions* ("According to *Webster's International Dictionary,* 'cloning' is . . ."), or *obvious statements* ("Cloning is a very controversial topic").

## Components of Introductory Paragraphs

Paper opener
>   Question
>   Quotation
>   Anecdote, brief story, or scenario
>   Background information
>   Fact or statistic
>   Generalization
>   Contradiction
>   Thesis

Identification of author and major claim
Title of text
Thesis of critical analysis

> **EXERCISE 4.5**
>
> Read the opening paragraphs of each of the selections in Chapter 3. For each selection, identify the components of the introductory paragraph and the type of paper opener the author uses.

## Recast the Thesis

As you write the introduction, leave open the possibility of revising the working thesis that you derived earlier in the process (see page 154). Make sure that the thesis still expresses your main idea. You don't have to situate the thesis in any particular place. Thesis statements often occur toward the end of the introduction, after the opening explanation of the general topic and identification of the source; however, they can occur elsewhere, even at the beginning of the introductory paragraph. For example, the thesis of Vanderslice's text, "Universities must initiate reforms that increase standards instead of decreasing them," appears in the third paragraph, and the thesis of David Brooks's "The Year of Domesticity" appears in the next-to-last sentence of his critical analysis: "Hirschman has it exactly backward. Power is in the kitchen."

Wherever you place the thesis, be sure that you express it adequately and provide your reader with enough context to understand it fully. In academic writing, a thesis statement may occupy several sentences. The complex issues that academic essays deal with cannot always be formulated adequately in a single sentence.

Just as the thesis statement can consist of more than one sentence, the introduction can comprise more than one paragraph. Notice how our student Maura Grady opens her essay on immigration with two introductory paragraphs. The first stresses the significance of her personal experience; the second identifies the key topic the paper will address and presents Maura's thesis statement.

> *I am a second-generation American. My grandparents emigrated to the United States from the west of Ireland in the 1920s to pursue the American Dream and make a better life for their children. Like most immigrants, they came to this country to labor in low-paying jobs, the Kellys as cab driver and domestic worker, the Gradys as longshoreman and laundress. I never read about "little people" like them in my history textbooks. Textbook writers must think along the same lines as the Irish maid in Ronald Takaki's* A Different Mirror: *"'I don't know why anybody wants to hear my history. . . . Nothing ever happened to me worth tellin'" (601).*
>
> *Historically, women fortunate enough to gain entry into the United States, women like my grandmothers—Irish maids, Chicana cleaners, and Japanese "wives who [did] much of the work in the fields" (606)—have been even more silenced than their male counterparts. The women whom male immigrants left behind—wives and lovers barred from entering the country—have never had the opportunity to tell their tales. As revisionist historians, Takaki and others relate the stories of the "little people," I hope they remember to give women a strong voice. I want my daughters to be able to look into the "'mirror' of history" and through the lens of the present to see "who [women] have been and hence are" (602) and what they have the potential to become.*

Lengthy articles in scholarly journals often have a multiparagraph subsection labeled "Introduction" that includes information needed to understand the thesis statement. Sometimes a complex paper opener requires a separate paragraph. For instance, an essay that evaluates the social consequences of cloning human beings might begin with a dramatized scenario, perhaps a description of a family in which the children were clones of their parents, to provide a test case for the author's argument. The details of this scenario might require one or more paragraphs. These opening paragraphs would be followed by a paragraph that zeroes in on the topic and presents the thesis.

## Write Conclusions

The concluding paragraph should do more than recapitulate the high points of the discussion that precedes it. A summary of the main points is justified, but you should also consider the techniques in the following box:

---

### TIPS FOR WRITING CONCLUSIONS

- Stress the significance of your thesis rather than simply repeating it.
- Predict the consequences of your ideas.
- Call your readers to action.
- End with a question, an anecdote, or a quotation.
- Summarize your main points.

---

Consider the conclusion of the critical analysis essay that we've been discussing:

*"When I Was Young, an A Was an A: Grade Inflation in Higher Education" tackles an important issue, but it is based on too many questionable assumptions. If Vanderslice had provided more data, addressed the issue of grade inflation in all its complexity, and given more consideration to the implications of her proposals, her readers would be better served and they would take her article more seriously.*

### EXERCISE 4.6

Reread the concluding paragraphs of each of the reading selections in Chapter 3. Identify the concluding technique each author uses. If it is not one of the four techniques listed above, do your best to describe the way the author ends the text.

## Prepare Lists of References or Works Cited

At the end of source-based papers, you need to construct a list of the texts you quote, paraphrase, summarize, or cite in your essay. The list should contain an entry for every source you use, and it should be alphabetized according to the authors' last names. The Appendix of this textbook provides guidelines for setting up the list of works cited for the MLA documentation style and the list of references for the APA style.

The work-cited list for the critical analysis, constructed according to MLA guidelines, contains only one source:

### Work Cited

Vanderslice, Ronna. "When I Was Young, an A Was an A: Grade Inflation in Higher Education," *Phi Kappa Phi Forum* 84 (2004): 24–25.

## Title the Essay

Your title should indicate your perspective and, if possible, capture the spirit of the issue you are addressing. A title such as "A Critique of 'When I Was Young, an A Was an A: Grade Inflation in Higher Education'" identifies the genre and text, nothing more. Another direct title, "Vanderslice's Problematic Solutions," is formed by *lifting key words* from the critical analysis. If you prefer a title that is less straightforward, you can choose from a number of options for deriving titles. One alternative is to *let the title reflect your organizational plan.* An essay that develops according to the comparison/contrast pattern might be titled "A Professor's View of Grade Inflation vs. the Perspective of the Silenced Student." Another alternative is to *use a hook* that will interest your reader, for example: "As Grades Go Up, Do Standards Go Down?" Still another option is a title that expresses a *generalization, followed by a specific point*; for example, "Grade Inflation: A Practice that Has Become Routine," or a *specific point followed by a generalization*; for example, the title Vanderslice uses for her essay. You could also title your paper with an *apt phrase* from the reading source or from your essay itself. A *catchy saying* or a *relevant quotation* from some other text could also be used.

The possibilities for titles are limited only by your creativity. Here is a title for the critical analysis essay: "Grade Inflation: Which Is More Questionable, the Problem or the Solutions?"

---

### TIPS FOR TITLING ESSAYS

- Identify the genre and text.
- Extract key words from your essay.
- Reflect your organizational plan.
- Use a hook to interest your readers.
- Express a generalization, followed by a colon, followed by a specific point.
- Express a specific point, followed by a colon, followed by a generalization.
- Use an apt phrase from a reading source.
- Use a catchy phrase.
- Use a relevant quotation.

---

### EXERCISE 4.7

Review the titles of the reading selections in Chapter 3. Explain the relevance of each title and describe the strategy the author uses.

At this point, you will have finished a complete draft of your paper. Congratulations! You are now entitled to take a break from your assignment. But remember that a paper presented only in first-draft form is unlikely to earn you a high grade. A conscientiously revised paper will display your writing to its best advantage. So, you must now turn to a full-scale revision of your paper before you hand it in. This last phase includes both reworking your ideas and your presentation and copyediting your paper for errors in standard form or usage. It can be the most rewarding phase of the writing process because you will see your ideas take stronger, clearer shape and hear your voice emerge with confidence and authority.

You will also find that cleaning up your grammar, spelling, punctuation, and other mechanics will reassure you about having written a good paper. It is wise to set your first draft aside for some time before you revise it. Experience shows that you will come back to it with freshness and alertness, keen to spot weak arguments, poor evidence, awkward transitions, and stylistic mistakes that you did not realize you had made.

## ■ Revise the Preliminary Draft

To varying degrees, writers revise while they are drafting as well as after they have produced fully formed papers. Those who do a great deal of revision as they are composing their drafts may come up with polished products that require minimal changes. Those who prefer to scratch out rough first drafts may make substantial changes as they rewrite in multiple versions. Whether you are an in-process reviser or a post-process reviser, you should keep in mind certain effective principles of revision.

---

### PRINCIPLES OF REVISION

- Do not allow your in-process revision to interfere with your draft.
- Restrict in-process revising to important elements, such as ideas and organization.
- Check that you have a clear thesis and convincing support, and as you move from one part of the paper to another, be sure you are progressing logically, maintaining your focus, and supplying appropriate transitions.
- Be sensitive to your readers' needs. But leave concerns like word choice, sentence structure, punctuation, spelling, and manuscript format until after you have finished a full draft of the paper.

---

The best revisions do more than correct errors in usage, punctuation, and spelling. Here is the revision of the first draft of the critical analysis essay.

## Student's Critical Analysis Essay: Revision of Preliminary Draft

### *Grade Inflation: Which Is More Questionable, the Problem or the Solutions?*

*[handwritten: should change the way they grade their students?]*

Is grade inflation a *such* serious ~~problem of~~ *concert that* college professors? Ronna

Vanderslice, a professor of education at Southwestern Oklahoma State

University, *[handwritten: The argument she presents in]* ~~in her article,~~ "When I was Young, an A Was an A: Grade

Inflation in Higher Education," ~~asserts~~ *claims* that grade inflation is an

increasingly serious problem. ~~that universities must counteract,~~

*[handwritten: According to Vanderslice, forty years ago very few students received high grades. Now most receive As and Bs. As a result, transcripts no longer give accurate information to students or to their potential employers.]*

add comp
underscore

Writing in _Phi Kappa Phi Forum_, the journal of a national honor

Vanderslice
society, ~~she~~ urges university faculty to reform their grading

she
practices and ∧offers various suggestions for doing so. ~~Her argument~~

is problematic in that it rests on insufficient evidence and

questionable assumptions, and it neglects to consider alternate

ways of viewing the issue.

comp
fix sp.

Vanderslice writes that "grades of C or less moved from 25 percent

74
~~000~~
in 1969 to 9 percent in 1993" ~~(74)~~ , and today they continue to spiral

upward. On what evidence is she basing this claim? And where are the

statistics for the years 1993 to 2004 when the article was written?

My writing teacher told our class not to expect high grades because the

average grade for all sixty sections of the composition courses is

between a B− and a C+. This leads me to question Vanderslice's claim

that "between 80 and 90 percent of all college students receive grades

~~000~~
(74)  Stet
of A or B"∧ Is grade inflation occurring across the board, or are some

colleges more guilty than others?

The text's most basic ~~problematic~~ assumption is that elevated

grades are indicative of lowered standards. The opening sentence

places "low standards" side by side with "elevated grades," and the

Vanderslice's
objective of ~~the proposed~~ reforms is to "increase standards instead

~~000~~
(74) 74
of decreasing them"∧ But there are other reasonable explanations

for higher grades. It could be that professors are doing a better

job of teaching. Perhaps today's college students are better prepared

Or m
and smarter than they were in previous decades.∧ Maybe professors

are using ~~improved~~, more authentic and more valid measures of

assessment.

puzzling
A ~~questionable~~ assumption underlies Vanderslice's recommendation

should                          Vanderslice proposes
that professors ∧change their grading practices. ~~She recommends~~

Harvard professor Harvey Mansfield's method of assigning two grades,

comp
fix sp.
registrar
a public grade for the ~~student~~ and a private grade for the student.

T
Vanderslice explains, "∧ the private grades give students a realistic,

useful assessment of how well they did and where they stand in

relation to others" ~~(24).~~ 24 The author assumes that this system will help

to solve the problem of grade inflation, but she fails to explain

how ~~this practice~~ *it* will raise standards. *Granted, students will learn how they rank in class, but* The number of *"public"* As and Cs,

*could very well* ~~will~~ remain the same. The two-grade system also assumes that

students ~~are interested in~~ *the ones that count on the transcript, want to know* how they stack up against their peers.

This may not be the case at all. They may be less interested in

competition than in mastery of subject matter.

Another *of Vanderslice's* solution~~s~~ for curbing grade inflation is to reassess the

practice of using student evaluations for personnel decisions

involving faculty. Citing a moratorium [comp: fix sp.] at Indiana University,

Vanderslice writes, "The university believes that removing

concerns about student complaints about receiving lower grades

might motivate all instructors to reset their standards, free

from the pressures to give A's in exchange for high evaluations" ~~(~~ 24.

*Underlying* This proposal ~~assumes~~ *are two assumptions. One is* that students give high evaluations to

professors ~~that~~ *who* give high grades and low evaluations to professors

*who give low grades and maintain* ~~that/have~~ rigorous standards. It also assumes that professors are so

*Is there any research that demonstrates that either of these assumptions is valid?*

*Another concern is*

insecure that they cave in to student pressure. *The dangerous* implications of

this proposal ~~are dangerous:~~ a professor who performs poorly in the

*could very likely receive promotion or tenure.*

classroom ~~will be rewarded.~~ If the personnel committee does not look

*the effect the professor has on students*

at ~~student~~ *course* evaluations, no one will ever know. One could *also* argue that

*Why shouldn't*

this proposal is ~~also~~ self-serving. *c*Colleges ~~should~~ eliminate

professors' evaluations of students as well as students' evaluations

of professors? This would lead to a healthier, less competitive

atmosphere.

> The issue of grade inflation is not new. If grades are increasing unjustifiably and if universities have lowered their standards, reforms are necessary.

```
 "When I Was Young, an A Was an A: Grade Inflation in Higher Education"
                        Too bad                          so
 tackles an important issue: but it is based on too many questionable

 assumptions. If Vanderslice had provided more data, addressed the

 issue of grade inflation in all its complexity, and given more

 consideration to the implications of her proposals, her readers

 would be better served and they would take her article more

 seriously.
```

### Work Cited

```
Vanderslice, Ronna. "When I Was Young, an A Was an A: Grade Inflation
    in Higher Education," Phi Kappa Phi Forum 84 (2004): 24-25.
```

We revised the first paragraph by sharpening the opening sentence and fleshing out our points with paraphrases from the text. We left paragraph two as is, and made a few editorial changes to paragraph three. In paragraph four, we made additional editorial changes, revising awkward or imprecise word choice, and we added a concession. We reworded parts of paragraph five, added clarifications, inserted a question about Vanderslice's evidence, and provided smoother transitions. Finally, in the conclusion we added an acknowledgement of the seriousness of the issue we discussed. Notice that throughout the draft, we adhere to special conventions that academic writers follow when writing about texts, shown in the box below.

---

**SPECIAL CONVENTIONS FOR WRITING ABOUT TEXTS**

- Use the present tense when explaining how the author uses particular procedures and writing techniques.
- Identify the author of the source by first and last name initially and thereafter only by the last name.
- Keep these conventions in mind at the beginning of the process and, if necessary, make the necessary changes at the time of revision.

---

## Revise Ideas

When you revise your draft, your first priority should be to make changes in meaning by reworking your ideas. You might *add information, introduce a new line of reasoning, delete extraneous information or details,* or *rearrange the order of your argument.* Revision should always serve to sharpen or clarify meaning for your readers. Ask yourself the questions in the following box.

---

### REVISING IDEAS

- Is my paper an adequate response to the assignment?
- Is my rhetorical purpose clear? How am I attempting to influence or affect my readers?
- Does everything in the draft lead to or follow from one central thesis? If not, which ideas appear to be out of place? Should I remove any material?
- Do individual passages of my paper probe the issues and problems implied by the thesis in sufficient detail? What do I need to add?
- Will the reader understand my central point?

---

The process of drafting stimulates your thinking and often brings you to new perspectives. You may see links among pieces of information and come to conclusions that had not occurred to you at the planning stage. As a result, first drafts are often inconsistent; they may start with one central idea but then depart from it and head in new directions.

Allow yourself to be creative at the drafting stage but when you revise, make sure that you express a consistent idea throughout your entire essay. Check to see if you have drifted away from your thesis in the subsequent paragraphs or changed your mind and ended up with another position. If you have drifted away from your original goal, examine each sentence to determine how the shift took place. You may need to eliminate whole chunks of irrelevant material, add more content, or reorder some of the parts. After you make these changes, read over your work to be sure that the new version makes sense, conforms to your organizational plan, and shows improvement.

## Revise Organization

When you are satisfied that your draft expresses the meaning you want to get across to your readers, check that your ideas connect smoothly with each other. Your readers should be able to follow your train of thought by referring back to preceding sentences, looking ahead to subsequent sentences, and paying attention to transitions and other connective devices. Ask yourself the questions in the following box.

---

### REVISING ORGANIZATION

- Is my organizational plan or form appropriate for the kind of paper I've been assigned? If not, can I derive another format?
- Do I provide transitions and connecting ideas? If not, where are they needed?
- Do I differentiate my own ideas from those of the text?
- What should I add so that my audience can better follow my train of thought?
- What can I eliminate that does not contribute to my central focus?
- What should I move that is out of place or needs to be grouped with material elsewhere in the paper?
- Do I use a paper opener that catches the reader's attention?

(continued on the next page)

- Does each paragraph include a topic sentence(s) and does all the material in this paragraph support it?
- Does my conclusion simply restate the main idea or does it offer new insights?
- Does my essay have an appropriate title?

## EXERCISE 4.8

Obtain a copy (photocopy or extra computer-generated copy) of at least two pages of a paper you have written. Select a paper written for any course, either a final draft or a rough draft. (Your instructor may elect to distribute a single essay to the entire class.)

Apply the questions listed in the boxes on Revising Ideas (page 169) and Revising Organization (pages 169–70) to the piece of writing. Ask yourself each question and hand-write on the essay any revisions that seem necessary.

Submit the original essay along with your revised version.

## EXERCISE 4.9

In preparation for this exercise, the instructor needs to copy a short student essay (not more than two pages) for each class member. A preliminary draft will work best. Form collaborative learning groups of five students each.

Select one student to read the essay aloud. Other group members should follow along, noting on their own copies passages that would profit from revision according to the principles of Revising Ideas and Organization discussed above.

Select another student to read aloud the questions from the Revising Ideas (page 169) and Revising Organization (pages 169–70) boxes. After each question is read, discuss whether it suggests any revisions that might improve the essay, and have the recorder write out the changes on which the group agrees.

Reconvene the entire class. Each group recorder should report the revisions the group made and explain why they are necessary. Try to account for differences in revisions.

## Revise Style

You may associate the term *style* with works of high literary art—the style, say, of a poem by John Keats or a novel by Emily Brontë. In actuality, however, every piece of writing displays a style of its own, whether it be a business report by a professional analyst or a note of reminders by a roommate or a family member. A style, a tone, a sense of voice and attitude, and above all a sense of liveliness and energy (or their absence) emerge from the writer's choice and use of words; the length and complexity of the writer's sentences; and the writer's focus on sharp, meaningful, reader-based expression. When you revise for style, you consider the effect your language choices have on your audience. We will discuss five ways to improve writing style.

### STRATEGIES FOR IMPROVING STYLE

- Move from writer-based prose to reader-based prose.
- Add your own voice.

- Stress verbs rather than nouns.
- Eliminate ineffective expressions.
- Eliminate sexist language.

## *Move from Writer-Based Prose to Reader-Based Prose*

Throughout this book, we continually stress the importance of audience. It is imperative to keep your readers in mind throughout the entire reading-writing process, and especially at the revising stage. Making a distinction between *writer-based prose* and *reader-based prose* will help you attend to audience needs as you revise. We already introduced you to these two concepts on page 39. Writer-based prose is egocentric because the writer records ideas that make sense to him or her, but the writer makes minimal if any effort to communicate those ideas to someone else. In contrast, reader-based prose clearly conveys ideas to other people. The writer does not assume anything; she provides information that will facilitate the reader's comprehension.

It is easy to forget about your readers amid all the complications in producing the first draft of an academic essay. That's why first drafts are quite often writer-based. An important function of revising is to convert this writer-based prose to something the reader can readily understand.

To illustrate writer-based prose, we have reproduced a student's reaction to two articles on computer intelligence. As you read the student essay, place checks next to the sentences that are writer-based.

> Both of these articles deal with the present and future status of computers. Carl Sagan tends to agree with Ulrich Neisser except that Sagan thinks computers are changing rapidly, whereas Neisser believes they will remain the same for quite some time.
>
> Both articles discuss differences between computer intelligence and human intelligence. To prove that human intelligence is different, Sagan uses the example with a U.S. Senator. Neisser agrees with Sagan by stating that a computer has no emotions, no motivation, and does not grow. Neisser feels that this is where humans have the advantage over computers. As stated in the introductory paragraph, the authors differ in one major way: Sagan thinks that the computer's ability will change soon, while Neisser thinks that it will be some time before that happens.
>
> The other issue the articles discuss concerns social decisions. Both writers feel that computers should not be allowed to make social decisions. Sagan believes a computer shouldn't make social decisions if it can't even pass the test in the example. Neisser also goes back to this example. He also states that the computer only deals with the problems that it is given. It has no room for thought, since it is confined just to finding the answer. Once again, the only place Sagan and Neisser seem to contrast is about the length of time it will take for the computer to be able to make social decisions.
>
> I agree more with Sagan than with Neisser. The rapid growth of computers will continue, and the issues will constantly change.

Notice that our writer assumes the audience is familiar with both the assignment and the articles on which it is based. For example, the introduction begins "Both of these articles . . ." as if the reader knows in advance which articles will be discussed (see Works Cited, p. 180). The first sentence tells us only that the articles discuss the computer's "status," a term that conveys little to anyone who has not read the texts. The second sentence states that Neisser and Sagan agree on something, but it does not indicate what ideas they supposedly share. The writer has simply failed to take into account that the reader may or may not be able to follow the train of thought. Similar failures to consider the audience occur throughout the essay. Below, we have transformed its introduction from writer-based prose to reader-based prose.

> The articles "In Defense of Robots" by Carl Sagan and "The Imitation of Man by Machine" by Ulrich Neisser both deal with the computer's potential to match the intellectual accomplishments of humans. Sagan and Neisser agree that there is currently a wide gap between machine and human intelligence. However, Sagan argues that the gap will quickly narrow, whereas Neisser maintains that computer and human intelligence will always be significantly different.

As you revise your first drafts, make sure that you have provided the necessary context or background for material taken from sources. Unless the assignment indicates that the audience has read the sources, do not assume that your readers will share your prior knowledge and experience.

## Add Your Own Voice

After you've written your paper, read it aloud. Better still, ask a friend to read it aloud to you. Does your writing sound like it's really yours? Or does it sound stiff, wooden, impersonal, colorless? Would your paper be better if it resonated with some of your spoken personality?

Richard Lanham devoted his book *Revising Prose* to helping writers project their own voices and breathe life into their writing. Among his suggestions are the following:

- If too many of the sentences wind endlessly around themselves without stopping for air, try dividing them into units of varying length.
- Give a rhythm to your prose by alternating short sentences with longer ones, simple sentences with complex ones, statements or assertions with questions or exclamations.
- Bring your readers into the essay by addressing them with questions and commands, expressions of paradox and wonderment, challenge and suspense.

Try these strategies. They can bring the sound of your own voice into otherwise silent writing and liven it considerably. Be careful, though. Some professors prefer a relentlessly neutral style devoid of any subjective personality. Proceed cautiously.

## Stress Verbs Rather Than Nouns

Pack the meaning in your sentences into strong verbs rather than nouns or weak verbs. See how the following example uses verbs and nouns. We have underlined the nouns and italicized the verbs.

*Original:* The <u>creation</u> of multiple <u>copies</u> of an <u>individual</u> through the <u>process</u> of <u>cloning</u> *is* now an actual <u>feasibility</u>.

*Revision:* <u>Scientists</u> can now *clone* multiple <u>copies</u> of a <u>human</u>.

The first version uses nouns to get the message across, but the revised version uses verbs. Notice that the first version contains only a single verb, *is*. *Is* and other forms of the verb *be* (*are, was, were, be, being, been*) are weak and lifeless because they draw their meaning from the nouns preceding and following them. Sentences that are structured around *be* verbs depend heavily on nouns to convey their central ideas. These "noun-style" sentences are characterized by forms of the verb *be* (*is, are,* and so on) and by nominalization. **Nominalization** is *the practice of making nouns from verbs or adjectives by adding suffixes (-ance, -ence, -tion, -ment, -ness, -sion, -ity, -ing).* For example, *preserve* becomes *preservation* and *careless* becomes *carelessness.*

An additional sign of nominalization is frequent use of prepositions and prepositional phrases. In the following example, we have underlined the *be* forms, the instances of nominalization, and the prepositions in the sentence we considered earlier. Notice that the revision does not rely on *be* verbs or nominalizations.

*Original:* The <u>creation of</u> multiple copies <u>of</u> an individual <u>through</u> the process <u>of</u> cloning <u>is</u> now an actual <u>feasibility</u>.

*Revision:* Scientists can now clone multiple copies <u>of</u> a human.

Of course, there are occasions when *be* verbs or nominalizations are appropriate. Problems arise only when these forms are overused. Although there is no absolute rule, you should look closely when you find more than one *be* verb or one nominalization per sentence. You need not analyze the nouns and verbs in every paper you write, but periodically you should check the direction in which your style is developing. Over time, you will find that less analysis is necessary because you will be using more active verbs and fewer prepositions and nominalizations.

## Eliminate Ineffective Expressions

Avoid ineffective expressions and words that do not contribute directly to the meaning of your paper. Notice how the underlined words and phrases in the following passage do not advance the writer's goals.

<u>Basically</u>, those in support of surrogate motherhood claim that this <u>particular</u> method of reproduction has brought happiness to countless infertile couples. It allows a couple to have a child of their own <u>despite the fact that</u> the woman cannot bear children. In addition, it is <u>definitely</u> preferable to waiting for months and sometimes years on <u>really</u> long adoption lists. <u>In my opinion</u>, however, surrogate motherhood exploits the woman and can be <u>especially</u> damaging to the child. <u>Obviously</u>, poor women are affected most. <u>In the event that</u> a poor couple cannot have a child, it is <u>rather</u> unlikely that they will be able to afford the services of a surrogate mother. <u>Actually</u>, it is fertile, poor women who will become "breeders" for the infertile rich. In any case, the child is <u>especially</u> vulnerable. The <u>given</u> baby may become involved in a custody battle between the surrogate mother and the adopting mother. If the <u>individual</u> child is born handicapped, he or she may be <u>utterly</u> rejected by both mothers. <u>Surely</u>, the child's welfare should be <u>first and foremost</u> in everyone's mind.

The underlined elements are either overused, hackneyed words and phrases or unnecessary qualifiers, intensifiers, or modifiers. None of these words further the writer's intentions. They are inherently vague. Check to see if ineffective expressions occur frequently in your writing.

## Eliminate Sexist Language

Always reread your drafts to be sure that you have avoided sexist language. Use the masculine pronouns "he" and "his" and nouns with -*man* and -*men* (*mailman, policemen,* and so on) only when they refer to a male or a group composed entirely of males. Don't use these forms to refer to women. Instead, use the techniques listed in the following box.

---

### TECHNIQUES FOR AVOIDING SEXIST LANGUAGE

- Use pronouns that recognize both sexes ("his or her" or "her or his").
- Use the plural rather than the singular. Plural pronouns by their very nature do not specify gender ("they" and "their").
- Use nouns that are not gender-specific ("mail carrier" and "police officer").

---

Observe how we use these techniques to revise sexist language in the following example:

*Original:* A physician must consider the broader social consequences of supplying new reproductive technologies to his patients. Likewise, each scientist working on genetic engineering must be aware of the potential social impact of his research.

*Revision:* Physicians must consider the broader social consequences of supplying new reproductive technologies to their patients. Likewise, scientists working on genetic engineering must be aware of the potential social impact of their research.

### EXERCISE 4.10

Obtain a copy (photocopy or extra computer-generated copy) of at least two pages of a paper you have written. Select a paper written for any course, either a final draft or a rough draft. (Your instructor may elect to distribute a single essay to the entire class.)

Revise the draft according to the advice in this chapter, keeping in mind the following guidelines:

- Move from writer-based to reader-based prose.
- Vary sentence length.
- Stress verbs rather than nouns.
- Use words effectively.
- Detect sexist language.
- Add your own voice.

Handwrite on the essay any revisions that seem necessary.
Submit the original version of the essay along with your revised version.

## EXERCISE 4.11

In preparation for this exercise, the instructor will need to copy a short student essay (not more than two pages) for each class member. A preliminary draft will work best. Form collaborative learning groups of five students each.

Select one student to read the essay aloud. Other group members should follow along, noting on their own copies words, phrases, sentences, and whole passages that would profit from revision and editing according to the principles of revising and editing signaled above.

Select another student to read aloud the following list of revising and editing concerns:

- Moving from writer-based to reader-based prose
- Varying sentence length
- Stressing verbs rather than nouns
- Using words effectively
- Detecting sexist language
- Adding your own voice

After each question is read, discuss whether it suggests any revisions that might improve the essay, and have the recorder write out the changes on which the group agrees.

Reconvene the entire class. Each group recorder should report the revisions the group made and explain why they are necessary. Try to account for differences in revisions.

## Conferences and Peer Review

When you are satisfied with your preliminary draft, make arrangements to share it with your teacher or a classmate. Before you proceed any further, you need to get some feedback on what you have written so far.

### Instructor Conferences

If your instructor invites students to schedule conferences, be sure to take advantage of this opportunity. The conference will be beneficial to you if you approach it with the correct mind-set and adequate preparation. Don't expect your instructor to correct your work or tell you what to do. You should assume a proactive role: Set the agenda and do most of the talking. After the teacher reads your draft—preferably, you should read it to the teacher—inquire about what worked well and what fell flat. Be prepared to explain what you are trying to achieve and point out the parts of the paper you feel good about and the parts you think need work. Most important, be ready to answer the teacher's questions.

### Peer Reviews

If your teacher agrees, make arrangements to have a classmate or a friend review your preliminary draft and give you feedback. If that is not possible, set the paper aside for a few days and then review it yourself. Respond to the questions listed in the box that follows.

**QUESTIONS FOR HELPING A WRITER REVISE A CRITICAL ANALYSIS ESSAY**

- What is the rhetorical purpose? Has the writer provided an insightful interpretation of the text and in so doing explained how certain characteristics contribute to its meaning?
- Does the writer move beyond interpretation to the strengths and weaknesses of the text?
- Does everything in the draft lead to or follow from the writer's thesis? If not, which ideas seem to be out of place?
- Is the writer sensitive to your concerns?
  a. Are you given sufficient background information, summary, title, and the author? If not, what is missing?
  b. Does the writer provide clear transitions and connecting ideas that differentiate his or her own ideas from those of the source text?
  c. Does the writer display an awareness of the author of the text by referring to the author by name or personal pronoun ("Smith states," "she explains"). Or does the writer personify the source ("the article states," "it explains")?
- Which organizational format does the writer use: cause and effect, comparison and contrast, or argument? If another pattern is used, is it appropriate for an analysis essay?
- Has the writer made you aware of the criteria for the evaluation? On which characteristics of the text is the analysis focused? If the bases for the analysis are unclear, explain your confusion.
- Does the writer support each of his or her points with direct evidence (quotations, paraphrases, summaries) from the source? If not, where are they needed?
- Does the writer provide smooth transitions and connecting ideas as he or she moves from one point of analysis to another? If not, where is evidence needed?
- Do you hear the writer's voice throughout the essay? Describe it.
- What type of paper opener does the writer use? Is it effective? Why or why not?
- Does the paper have an appropriate conclusion? Can you suggest an alternative way of ending the essay?
- Is the title suitable for the piece? Can you suggest an alternative title?
- Has the writer followed academic writing conventions, such as:
  a. Writing in present tense when explaining how the author of the source uses particular procedures and techniques?
  b. Identifying the author initially by first name and last name and thereafter only by last name?
  c. Indenting long quotations in block format?

## ■ Editing

When you have finished your revision, read your paper aloud once again to catch any glaring errors. Then reread the essay line by line and sentence by sentence. Check for correct usage, punctuation, spelling, mechanics, manuscript form, and typos. If you are especially weak in editing skills, and if it is all right with your instructor, go to your campus writing center or get a friend to read over your work.

This stage of revision encompasses the rules for usage, punctuation, spelling, and mechanics. We cannot begin to review all these rules in this textbook. You should think seriously about purchasing a few solid reference books, such as a good dictionary; a guide to correct usage, punctuation, and mechanics; and a documentation manual like the *MLA Handbook for Writers of Research Papers* or the *Publication Manual of the American Psychological Association.* Your campus bookstore and your college library will have self-help books for improving spelling, vocabulary, and usage. Browse through them and select the ones that best serve your needs.

Here are questions to ask yourself as you edit your paper. Remember that you need to abide by all the rules of standard written English.

---

### QUESTIONS FOR EDITING

- Are all my sentences complete?

  *Original:* Certain feminists claim that the new reproductive technologies exploit women. While other feminists argue that these same technologies help liberate women from traditional, oppressive roles.

  *Revision:* Certain feminists claim that the new reproductive technologies exploit women, while other feminists argue that these same technologies help liberate women from traditional, oppressive roles.

- Have I avoided run-on sentences, both fused sentences and comma splices?

  *Original:* Science fiction writers have long been fascinated with the prospect of cloning, their novels and short stories have sparked the public's interest in this technology.

  *Revision:* Science fiction writers have long been fascinated with the prospect of cloning, and their novels and short stories have sparked the public's interest in this technology.

- Do pronouns have clear referents, and do they agree in number, gender, and case with the words for which they stand?

  *Original:* A scientist who works on new reproductive technologies should always consider the social consequences of their work.

  *Revision:* A scientist who works on new reproductive technologies should always consider the social consequences of his or her work.

- Do all subjects and verbs agree in person and number?

  *Original:* Not one of the new reproductive technologies designed to increase couples' fertility have failed to incite controversy.

  *Revision:* Not one of the new reproductive technologies designed to increase couples' fertility has failed to incite controversy.

- Is the verb tense consistent and correct?

  *Original:* Some futurists claim that eugenics will provide the answers needed to ensure the survival of the human race. They predicted that by the year 2050, human reproduction will be controlled by law.

(continued on the next page)

*Revision:* Some futurists claim that eugenics will provide the answers needed to ensure the survival of the human race. They predict that by the year 2050, human reproduction will be controlled by law.

- Have I used modifiers (words, phrases, subordinate clauses) correctly and placed them where they belong?

*Original:* Currently, scientists across the nation work to clone various species with enthusiasm.

*Revision:* Currently, scientists across the nation work enthusiastically to clone various species.

- Have I used matching elements within parallel construction?

*Original:* Proposed reproductive technology projects include creating ways for sterile individuals to procreate, developing cures for genetic disease, and eugenic programs designed to improve the human species.

*Revision:* Proposed reproductive technology projects include creating ways for sterile individuals to procreate, developing cures for genetic disease, and designing eugenic programs to improve the human species.

- Are punctuation marks used correctly?

*Original:* The potentially dire social consequences of genetic engineering, must be examined carefully, before we embrace this powerful new frightening technology.

*Revision:* The potentially dire social consequences of genetic engineering must be examined carefully before we embrace this powerful, new, frightening technology.

- Are spelling, capitalization, and other mechanics (abbreviations, numbers, italics) correct?

*Original:* Research on Reproductive Technology is not often funded by The Government, since these innovations are so controversial.

*Revision:* Research on reproductive technology is not often funded by the government, since these innovations are so controversial.

## Manuscript Format

For this stage of revision, you need a great deal of patience and a good pair of eyes. Ask yourself the questions in the box below. They are based on the format recommended by the *MLA Handbook for Writers of Research Papers.* The format recommended by the APA is slightly different (see pages 673–78).

### MANUSCRIPT CHECKLIST

- Have I typed my last name and the page number in the upper right-hand corner of each page?
- Have I provided my full name, my professor's name, the course, and the date?
- Have I centered my title and typed it without underlining it?
- Have I indented the first line of each paragraph five spaces?

- Have I double-spaced and left one-inch margins on all sides throughout the paper?
- Are all typed words and corrections legible?
- Will my audience be able to tell which thoughts are mine and which are derived from sources?
- Are all quotations enclosed in quotation marks and properly punctuated?
- Have I properly documented all quotations, paraphrases, and summaries?
- Do I include all sources in a Works Cited list?

In Figure 4–3 on pages 179–182, we annotate the final draft of the critical analysis essay to show the important features of MLA manuscript format.

### STUDENT'S CRITICAL ANALYSIS ESSAY: FINAL DRAFT

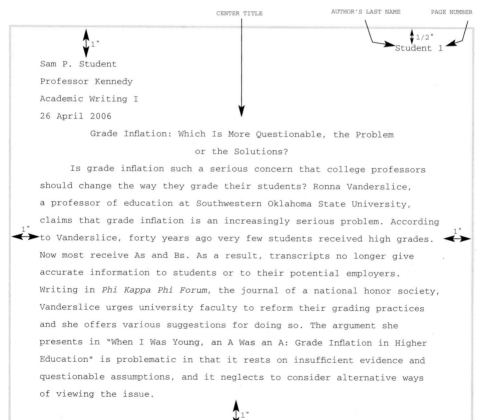

CENTER TITLE          AUTHOR'S LAST NAME          PAGE NUMBER

↕1"                                              ↕1/2"
                                              Student 1

Sam P. Student

Professor Kennedy

Academic Writing I

26 April 2006

Grade Inflation: Which Is More Questionable, the Problem
or the Solutions?

Is grade inflation such a serious concern that college professors should change the way they grade their students? Ronna Vanderslice, a professor of education at Southwestern Oklahoma State University, claims that grade inflation is an increasingly serious problem. According to Vanderslice, forty years ago very few students received high grades. Now most receive As and Bs. As a result, transcripts no longer give accurate information to students or to their potential employers. Writing in *Phi Kappa Phi Forum*, the journal of a national honor society, Vanderslice urges university faculty to reform their grading practices and she offers various suggestions for doing so. The argument she presents in "When I Was Young, an A Was an A: Grade Inflation in Higher Education" is problematic in that it rests on insufficient evidence and questionable assumptions, and it neglects to consider alternative ways of viewing the issue.

↕1"

USE 8½" BY 11" PAPER FOR EACH PAGE. USE DOUBLE SPACES BETWEEN ALL LINES. LEFT JUSTIFY ALL LINES IN THE TEXT OF THE PAPER. DO NOT RIGHT JUSTIFY, EVEN IF YOUR WORD PROCESSOR PROVIDES THIS FEATURE.

**Figure 4–3**

1"

1/2"
Student 2

Vanderslice writes that "grades of C or less moved from 25 percent in 1969 to 9 percent in 1993" (24) and today they continue to spiral upward. On what evidence is she basing this claim? And where are the statistics for the years 1993 to 2004 when the article was written? My writing teacher told our class not to expect high grades because the average grade for all sixty sections of the composition courses is between a B– and a C+. This leads me to question Vanderslice's claim that "between 80 and 90 percent of all college students receive grades of A or B" (24). Is grade inflation occurring across the board, or are some colleges more guilty than others?

The text's most basic assumption is that elevated grades are indicative of lowered standards. The opening sentence places "low standards" side by side with "elevated grades," and the objective of Vanderslice's reforms is to "increase standards instead of decreasing them" (24). But there are other reasonable explanations for higher grades. It could be that professors are doing a better job of teaching. Perhaps today's college students are better prepared and smarter than they were in previous decades. Or maybe professors are using more authentic and more valid measures of assessment.

A puzzling assumption underlies Vanderslice's recommendation that professors should change their grading practices. Vanderslice proposes Harvard professor Harvey Mansfield's method of assigning two grades, a public grade for the registrar and a private grade for the student. Vanderslice explains, "The private grades give students a realistic, useful assessment of how well they did and where they stand in relation to others" (24). The author assumes that this system will help to solve the problem of grade inflation, but she fails to explain how it will raise standards. Granted, students will learn how they rank in class, but the number of "public" As and Cs, the ones that count on the transcript, could very well remain the same. The two-grade system also assumes that students are interested in how they stack up against their peers. This may not be the case at all. They may be less interested in competition than in mastery of subject matter.

Another of Vanderslice's solutions for curbing grade inflation is to reassess the practice of using student evaluations for personnel decisions involving faculty. Citing a moratorium at Indiana University, Vanderslice writes, "The university believes that removing concerns about

1"                                                                          1"

1"

Student 3

student complaints about receiving lower grades might motivate all
instructors to reset their standards, free from the pressures to give A's
in exchange for high evaluations" (24). Underlying this proposal are two
assumptions. One is that students give high evaluations to professors who
give high grades and low evaluations to professors who give low grades
and maintain rigorous standards. It also assumes that professors are so
insecure that they cave in to student pressure. Is there any research
that demonstrates that either of these assumptions is valid? Another
concern is the dangerous implications of this proposal: a professor who
performs poorly in the classroom could very likely receive promotion and
tenure. If the personnel committee does not look at course evaluations,
no one will ever know the effect the professor has on students. One could
also argue that this proposal is self-serving. Why shouldn't colleges
eliminate professors' evaluations of students as well as students'
evaluations of professors? This would lead to a healthier, less
competitive atmosphere.

   The issue of grade inflation is not new. If grades are increasing
unjustifiably and if universities have lowered their standards, reforms
are necessary. "When I Was Young, an A Was an A: Grade Inflation in
Higher Education" tackles an important issue. Too bad it is based
on so many questionable assumptions. If Vanderslice had provided more
data, addressed the issue of grade inflation in all its complexity,
and given more consideration to the implications of her proposals,
her readers would be better served and they would take her article
more seriously.

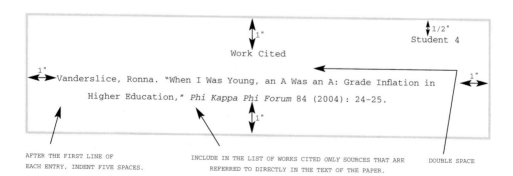

↑1"
Student 4    ↑1/2"

Work Cited

1"
→Vanderslice, Ronna. "When I Was Young, an A Was an A: Grade Inflation in
       Higher Education," *Phi Kappa Phi Forum* 84 (2004): 24–25.    ←→1"
↓1"

AFTER THE FIRST LINE OF            INCLUDE IN THE LIST OF WORKS CITED *ONLY* SOURCES THAT ARE        DOUBLE SPACE
EACH ENTRY, INDENT FIVE SPACES.           REFERRED TO DIRECTLY IN THE TEXT OF THE PAPER.

## WORKS CITED

Ehrenreich, Barbara. "The Economics of Cloning." *Time* 22 Nov. 1993: 86.

Lanham, Richard. *Revising Prose* 2nd ed. New York: Macmillan, 1987.

Neisser, Ulrich. "The Imitation of Man by Machine." *Science* 139 (1963): 193–97.

Sagan, Carl. "In Defense of Robots." *Broca's Brain*. New York: Ballantine, 1980. 280–92.

Teachout, Terry. "Mother Knows Worst." *The Wall Street Journal*. 7 April 2006: W9.

# *Five*

# Rhetorical, Comparative, Literary, Process, and Causal Analyses, and the Classic Comparison and Contrast Essay

This chapter deals with some kinds of analytical writing that address readings of specific texts. The analyses include rhetorical, comparative, literary, process, and causal. The chapter also covers the classic comparison and contrast essay.

## ■ RHETORICAL ANALYSIS

A **rhetorical analysis** examines *how a text is written*. It pays attention to what the text talks about, but its main focus is the strategies and devices the author uses to convey the meaning. As Chapter 1 demonstrated, rhetorical analysis is an important operation of critical reading. If you look back to pages 24–26, you can reread our rhetorical analysis of the stylistic features of Pauline Irit Erera and Barbara Ehrenreich's texts. When you receive an assignment that calls for rhetorical analysis, think in terms of rhetorical strategies that we presented in Chapter 1. Ask questions about *genre, organization, stylistic features,* and *rhetorical context*. In Chapter 4, we discussed three approaches to analysis: zero in on key elements, view the text through a critical lens, and compare the text to a source that is similar. A rhetorical analysis zeroes in on the rhetorical features of the target text.

Similar to the purpose of a critical analysis, the *overall purpose* of a rhetorical analysis is to share your interpretation with your readers, and, ideally, to convince them that your enlightened reading of the text warrants their attention and should be taken seriously. A more *focused purpose* is to evaluate the author's rhetorical context and strategies.

To illustrate rhetorical analysis, we will examine "Weasel-Words Rip My Flesh!" (pp. 96–99), a rhetorical analysis in which Jack Shafer critiques Louise Story's *New York Times* article, "Many Women at Elite Colleges Set Career Path to Motherhood" (pp. 91–95). Be sure to read the Story article and "Weasel-Words Rip My Flesh!" before moving on to our examination of Shafer's article.

## ■ Examination of "Weasel-Words Rip My Flesh!" Jack Shafer's Rhetorical Analysis and Critique of Louise Story's "Many Women at Elite Colleges Set Career Path to Motherhood"

As background, we should explain the title "Weasel-Words Rip My Flesh!" A weasel is a little animal with short legs, a long slender body, and a short tail. In winter the weasel's fur is white, and in summer it is brown. The changing color of the fur may account for the association of the weasel with deception, but the association is more likely related to the weasel's habit of sucking the contents out of eggs, leaving only their shells. In any case, "weasel words" are words and expressions that are vague and misleading. They are sometimes called *hedges* and *intensifiers*. Examples of hedges are *usually, often, sometimes, almost, most, many, some, might, seems, appears*, and examples of intensifiers are *very, quite, rather, major, essential, as everyone knows*.

Shafer argues that Louise Story presents a bogus argument when she claims that women from elite colleges are choosing to abandon their careers to pursue childrearing. He insists that she misleads her readers with weasel words that enable her to fudge her weak and inconclusive data. In addition to analyzing Story's language, Shafer appraises her thesis, the quality of the editing, and the motives of the publisher.

Shafer shows that Story's article is replete with weasel words. He points out that she uses the word "many" twelve times, and he documents each instance of "many" by quoting from her article. Shafer maintains that weasel words disguise the weak and inconclusive data supporting Story's argument. He goes on to say that the article contains a poorly stated, questionable thesis, and it suffers from lack of editing. He wonders how such a poorly written article could have been published on page one of the *New York Times*. He speculates that because the paper has already published a number of articles on the same theme, there might be a "conspiracy afloat to drive feminists crazy and persuade young women that their place is in the home." He ends the critique with another speculation: that the editors of the *Times* are simply trying to push their readers' buttons.

In Chapter 4, we presented three sets of analysis questions: Questions for the Critical Analysis of the Content of Texts; Questions for the Critical Analysis of Genre, Organization, Stylistic Features of Texts; and Questions for Critical Analysis of the Rhetorical Context of Texts (pages 139–41). We will hazard a guess that Shafer focused on the following subset of the three sets of analysis:

- What is the topic or focal point of the text?

- What is the main idea, major point, or central claim? Is it plausible, defensible, and illuminating? Is it a reasonable position, or does the author come across as someone with an axe to grind?

- How does the text support, qualify, and develop the claim or position? Is the evidence relevant, accurate, and substantial enough to support the thesis, or does it fall short and only partially support the thesis? Which points need more support and explanation?

- Does the text demonstrate an identifiable genre? Can you describe the special characteristics of that genre?
- Are certain components stressed at the expense of others?
- Does the language serve to heighten and illuminate the topic? Is it merely adequate? Does it detract?
- What effect does the writer intend the text to have on the audience?
- For whom is the author writing? Where was the text first published? Who reads this publication?
- In what year was the text published? What was on people's minds? What prompted the author to write the text? Can you identify a circumstance, event, or social practice?

As you can see, the list is derived from all three sets of questions. In published analyses, the genres of critical analysis, rhetorical analysis, and comparative analysis often overlap. In the case of "Weasel Words Rip My Flesh!" a rhetorical analysis is also a critical analysis. Later, when we discuss Rebecca Traister's article, we will see that comparative analysis is also critical analysis. Examples of pure analysis forms are hard to come by.

We present the process and questions for writing a rhetorical analysis essay in the box below.

---

### PROCESS OF WRITING A RHETORICAL ANALYSIS ESSAY

#### Critical Reading

*Prereading*

- Clarify the assignment: Is my assignment open-ended, or does it stipulate the rhetorical features I will analyze?
- Set your rhetorical goal: How will I give my readers an interpretation and evaluation of rhetorical features of the text?
- Consider your audience: What will my readers already know about the text, and how much of the text should I summarize?
- Review the eight Prereading Questions on pages 6–7 and respond to the questions that seem relevant.
- Recall your prior knowledge and express your feelings about the reading topic.

*Close Reading*

- Read with pencil in hand, annotating, marking, and elaborating on the text.
- Pose and answer questions about the text, beginning with the broad, preliminary questions: What is said? Why is it viewed this way? How is it said? Is the text comparable to another work with which the reader is familiar? Does the text demonstrate an identifiable genre? What is the form or special characteristics of that genre, and how do the different

(continued on the next page)

components function in relation to each other and to the text as a whole? How is the text organized?

- Reread the text and ask the three sets of analysis questions on pages 139–41.

*Postreading*

- Express your personal thoughts about the text you have just read.

*Planning*

- Formulate a working thesis and decide on your approach.
- Review the writing you have produced to date: responses to Prereading Questions; statement of your prior feelings and knowledge of the topic; annotations, markings, and elaborations; answers to preliminary questions; responses to the three sets of analysis questions; and your personal response. Then ask yourself:

  Have I focused my responses on one feature of the text or on a small subset of features? Which analysis questions produced lengthy and substantive responses?

  Am I able to group together responses that pertain to similar features of the text? Does a theme or pattern of response emerge?

- Verify that you have textual support for your thesis.
- Return to the relevant parts of the text to check for supporting textual evidence in the form of quotations, paraphrases, or summaries.
- Decide on an organizational plan.
- Sketch a loose plan for the essay or construct a formal outline or graphic overview.

**Drafting**

- Select and use organizational plans for individual paragraphs.
- Weave direct quotations, paraphrases, and summaries in with your own ideas, and supply proper documentation.
- Decide on an introductory paragraph.
- Construct a conclusion.
- Develop a list of references or works cited.
- Title your essay.

**Revising**

- Revise ideas, organization, and style, and check manuscript format.

**Editing**

- For specific strategies for revision and editing, see Chapter 4, pages 176–82.

## ◼️ COMPARATIVE ANALYSIS

A **comparative analysis** *analyzes a focal text through the lens of a text that is comparable.* The purpose is to show how one text corroborates or debates the other, not simply to show the similarities and differences between the two texts. An important factor is the basis for the comparison. When you write a comparative analysis, your readers need to know the grounds for your choice of Text A and Text B rather than Text A and Text C. Keep in mind that you may use the comparative analysis approach in combination with other approaches such as zeroing in on key elements and viewing the text through a critical lens.

To illustrate comparative analysis, we return to the conversation about stay-at-home and working mothers. Rebecca Traister joins the conversation when she responds to David Brooks. In her comparative analysis, "At Home with David Brooks" (pp. 128–31), she analyzes David Brooks's "The Year of Domesticity" (pp. 114–15) through the lens of a second article, Terry Martin Hekker's "Paradise Lost" (pp. 124–27). You will recall that Brooks's article, which is a critique of Linda Hirshman's essay, "Homeward Bound," is the touchstone text we examined when we discussed critical analysis in Chapter 4. Tracy Martin Hekker brings a new perspective to the debate over stay-at-home and working mothers by presenting the view of a woman who chose to become a full-time homemaker but later found herself in a desperate situation when her husband divorced her after forty years of marriage. In Figure 5–1, we present a graphic overview of the conversation among Traister, Brooks, Hekker, and Hirshman.

Be sure to read all four selections before moving on to our examination of Traister's comparative analysis.

## ■ Examination of "At Home with David Brooks," Rebecca Traister's Comparative Analysis of David Brooks's "The Year of Domesticity" and Terry Martin Hekker's "Paradise Lost"

The one-sentence summary under the title of Rebecca Traister's article cues the reader into the comparative nature of the analysis:

On the same day the right-wing *Times* columnist argued that women are happier at home, a mom who stayed home contradicted him.

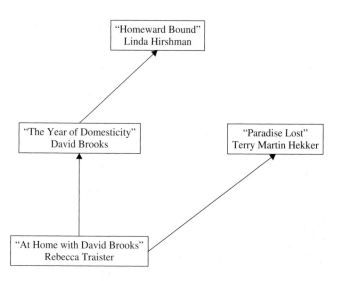

**Figure 5–1    Overview of the Conversation**

The focal text of Traister's review is David Brooks's critical analysis of Linda Hirshman's argument in "Homeward Bound." Hekker's text, which occupies only five of the twenty paragraphs in Traister's critique, functions as the lens for viewing Brooks's "The Year of Domesticity." Hekker's article stands in direct contrast to Brooks's because it illustrates the disastrous consequences of stay-at-home motherhood. As Traister points out, "Hekker did exactly as [Brooks] recommends—stayed in the kitchen—and lived to regret her choice."

Traister is not interested in comparing and contrasting elements in the two texts. In fact, her critique of Hekker's argument is minimal. Granted, she questions Hekker's credibility as a spokesperson for homemakers, pointing out that, as a published author and public speaker, she is "more an emblem of full-time motherhood than a true practitioner." Traister values Hekker's argument because it illustrates the negative consequences of Brooks's line of reasoning.

Traister uses seven criteria to evaluate Brooks's text: tone, questionable implications, limited point of view, erroneous assumptions, questionable inferences, contributions to the larger conversation, and perspectives he neglects to consider. If we retrace her writing process to the three sets of analysis questions on pages 139–41, we might speculate that the following list of questions became her focus:

- What is the main idea, major point, or central claim? Is it plausible, defensible, and illuminating? Is it a reasonable position, or does the author come across as someone with an axe to grind?

- What inferences, judgments, or conclusions can be drawn? Do they follow logically from the evidence? Are they sound, valid, and justifiable? Are alternative inferences, judgments, and conclusions just as reasonable?

- What assumptions underlie the thesis and are explicitly stated or taken for granted? Will readers question these assumptions?

- Does the text anticipate and acknowledge other points of view, or does it fail to recognize that there are different ways of viewing the issue?

- What are the implications or consequences of the argument or reasoning presented in the text? Are the implications and consequences reasonable, accurate, and probable, or should we explore other possibilities?

- In what year was the text published? What was on people's minds? What prompted the author to write the text? Can you identify a circumstance, event, or social practice?

- What is the writer's persona or stance (attitude or rhetorical posture), and how does it contribute to his or her point? Is it suitable, or does it detract from the piece?

- How does the writer's voice contribute to the text's effectiveness? Are the voice and tone appropriate or unnecessarily pompous or formal?

- What do we know about the author's background and credibility? Does the author come across as authoritative, creditable, and reliable, or are you left with questions about his or her background, prestige, political or religious orientation, or overall reputation?

As was the case with Jack Shafer's rhetorical analysis, Traister's comparative analysis draws upon questions relating to argument and reasoning; genre, organization, and stylistic features; and rhetorical context. Keep in mind that a comparative analysis may share features with essays that critically analyze an argument and essays that analyze the rhetorical strategies and context of a text.

## ■ Process of Writing a Comparative Analysis

To write a comparative analysis, follow the process outlined for critical analysis essays (see Chapter 4) and rhetorical analysis essays (see first part of this chapter), but pay attention to the following points:

- Keep in mind that early in the process, when you ask the four basic analysis questions: (1) What is said? (2) Why is it viewed that way? (3) How is it said? and (4) Is the text comparable to another work with which the reader is familiar?, you will be paying special attention to Question 4.

- Make your readers aware of the grounds for the comparison.

- View the second text as a lens for corroborating, debating, reinforcing, proving, or disproving the focal text. Do not examine all the points of similarity and difference between the texts.

- Include the correct amount of summary, paraphrase, and quotation. This will depend on the readers' knowledge of the second text.

- Organize the essay either in a block, text-by-text pattern, analyzing the focal text before turning to the text that serves as the lens (as Traister did in her critique), or in a point-by-point pattern, alternating points about the focal text with comparable points about the lens text. The block, text-by-text pattern is more widely used for comparative analyses of the type we have been discussing.

## ■ Differentiating Between Comparative Analysis Essays and Classic Comparison and Contrast Essays

As we noted earlier, in high school you probably wrote classic comparison and contrast essays in which you analyzed two objects, issues, or texts and discussed their points of similarity and difference. We want to be sure you understand how the comparative analysis essay we have been discussing differs from the classic comparison and contrast essay. To that end, we thought it would be useful for you to examine a graphic overview of Rebecca Traister's comparative analysis and compare it to a diagram of a classic comparison and contrast essay dealing with the same two texts.

Each box in the graphic overview represents a paragraph of Traister's critique. We have shaded the boxes to highlight the amount of space devoted to Hekker. A comparison and contrast essay would allocate roughly the same amount of space to each of the texts. Compare the graphic overview in Figure 5–2 to a diagram for a comparison and contrast essay based on the same two texts.

You could easily construct a comparison and contrast essay from the table in Figure 5–3 by using a point-by-point arrangement in which you contrast Brooks and Hekker's views on stay-at-home mothers' sense of fulfillment and success, power, and inclinations based on biology. Or you could organize the essay in a block pattern in which you first present Brooks's views on the three issues and then present Hekker's views. We will discuss comparison and contrast essays in more detail later in this chapter.

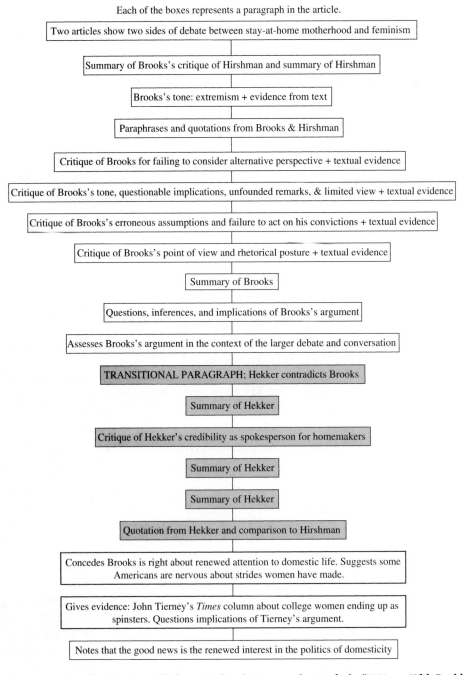

Each of the boxes represents a paragraph in the article.

Two articles show two sides of debate between stay-at-home motherhood and feminism

Summary of Brooks's critique of Hirshman and summary of Hirshman

Brooks's tone: extremism + evidence from text

Paraphrases and quotations from Brooks & Hirshman

Critique of Brooks for failing to consider alternative perspective + textual evidence

Critique of Brooks's tone, questionable implications, unfounded remarks, & limited view + textual evidence

Critique of Brooks's erroneous assumptions and failure to act on his convictions + textual evidence

Critique of Brooks's point of view and rhetorical posture + textual evidence

Summary of Brooks

Questions, inferences, and implications of Brooks's argument

Assesses Brooks's argument in the context of the larger debate and conversation

TRANSITIONAL PARAGRAPH; Hekker contradicts Brooks

Summary of Hekker

Critique of Hekker's credibility as spokesperson for homemakers

Summary of Hekker

Summary of Hekker

Quotation from Hekker and comparison to Hirshman

Concedes Brooks is right about renewed attention to domestic life. Suggests some Americans are nervous about strides women have made.

Gives evidence: John Tierney's *Times* column about college women ending up as spinsters. Questions implications of Tierney's argument.

Notes that the good news is the renewed interest in the politics of domesticity

**Figure 5–2    Graphic Overview of Rebecca Traister's Comparative Analysis, "At Home With David Brooks"**

**Working thesis**

STANDING IN STARK CONTRAST TO DAVID BROOKS'S "THE YEAR OF DOMESTICITY" IS TERRY MARTIN HEKKER'S "PARADISE LOST"

**Outline for body paragraphs**

| CRITERIA | BROOKS | HEKKER |
|---|---|---|
| Fulfillment and success | Parenthood is more "flourishing" than a high-paying job. | When a divorce occurs, the woman who hasn't worked is left with financial difficulties and limited employment opportunities. "For a divorced mother, the harsh reality is the work for which you do get paid is the only work that will keep you afloat." |
| Power | The realm of power is in the home, not in the public sphere. Home is of "unmatched influence" in the rearing of children.<br><br>"Power is in the kitchen. The big problem is not the women who stay there but the men who leave." | The power of the home may not last. "Wife" is not a tenured position. If the husband divorces the wife, she is stripped of much of her power.<br><br>The problem is the fragility of marriage; men leave the marriage. |
| Biology | Women are more comfortable in the home. "Men are more interested in things and abstract rules while women are more interested in people." | Interest in people will get you nowhere. Hekker gave a lot of time and energy to charitable and community causes as well as to family. She wishes she had used that time to further her education. |

**Figure 5–3    Diagram for a Comparison and Contrast of David Brooks's "The Year of Domesticity" and Terry Martin Hekker's "Paradise Lost"**

# ■ LITERARY ANALYSIS

We will focus our **literary analysis** upon a brief discussion of poetry. Poetry is the most concentrated of literary genres, and its major characteristics exemplify those of all the other genres. For this reason, the questions we might ask about reading poetry, the topics we might pursue in analyzing it, and the strategies we might adopt for writing about it bear much in common with those we might direct toward other literary forms such as the short story, drama, and novel.

Like fiction, poetry presents the voice of an imagined character as it offers a particularized expression of some thought, idea, emotion, or lived sensation. In poetry, we identify this character as **"the poem's speaker,"** a speaker who may or may not necessarily overlap with the individual poet who composed the poem.

Like drama, poetry presents the voice of this speaker in an imagined dialogue or conversation with another person or persons. It differs from drama in that it usually does not present the other person's voice as well—it allows us to hear only one side of the conversation and to imagine what the other side might be. In poetry, we identify this other person as the speaker's **"addressee"** (that is, the person whom the speaker addresses) or **"implied audience,"** and we are prompted to flesh out a concrete impression of this person's special characteristics.

Like fiction and drama, poetry also presents a rhetorical context, a moment in which its speaker interacts with the addressee or with some other individual who has brought the speaker to a crisis and has prompted him or her to suspend business as usual and perhaps to consider making a change.

## ■ Process of Writing a Literary Analysis Essay

Viewed in this way, poetry is not so different from other literary genres, nor is it really more difficult to read, enjoy, or comprehend. It presents us with the **voice** of a speaker, with some prompts to imagine other characters with whom the speaker interacts, with the suggestion of a **dramatic situation** that brings them together, and with the possibility of a crisis that will necessitate some change in the speaker's environment. Such features prevail, whether in a twelve-line poem, a twelve-page short story, a twelve-scene drama, or a twelve-chapter novel. Consequently, the tools that you use to analyze poetry will be the same that you use to analyze short fiction, plays, or long fiction.

The reading strategies and exercises that follow will focus on poetry, but their principles will pertain to other literary forms as well. To reinforce these principles, we present them with a set of collaborative discussion assignments based on analyzing the words of a popular song of your choosing. A song is a poem accompanied by music, and in analyzing the text of a song, we bring to it the same kind of questions about content, genre, organization, style, and rhetorical context that we bring to analyzing a literary text.

The following pages present a writing assignment based on a poem that a student named Ipek Kadife will analyze in a critical paper. We will examine Ipek's written responses to prompts for Prereading; Reading for Content; Reading for Genre, Organization, and Stylistic Features; and Reading for Rhetorical Context, and we will conclude with her finished and revised literary analysis.

The writing assignment asked Ipek to do the following:

> Select one of the poems in your Xeroxed course packet and analyze it as a dialogue between the poet and an interlocutor. What kind of "voice" characterizes the poem's speaker? What kind of interlocutor does it address? What kind of conversation does it suggest between them? How do the formal elements of meter, rhyme, "poetic license," and figurative diction project a specific tone that haunts this conversation?

Ipek has selected a well-known poem by the American poet, Emily Dickinson (1830–1886):

Me from Myself—to Banish

Me from Myself—to Banish—
Had I Art—
Impregnable my fortress
Unto All Heart—

But since Myself—assault Me—
How have I peace
Except by subjugating
Consciousness?

And since We're mutual Monarch
How this be
Except by Abdication—
Me—of Me?

Poem 642, (1862): *The Poems of Emily Dickinson*, ed. Thomas S. Johnson, 1955.

Here are general prompts for Prereading; Reading for Content; Reading for Genre, Organization, and Stylistic Features; and Reading for Rhetorical Context. Ipek's paper on literary analysis is based on them. So too is the set of exercises on the words of a popular song that you can find on the Internet.

## Prereading Questions

As you would with any other kind of writing, skim through the poem before you concentrate your attention on reading it word for word. What does its title suggest? What does its visual arrangement on the page—especially if it appears divided into sections or sub-sections—imply about its organization? From its first few lines, what can you deduce about the character of its speaker? What, if anything, can you provisionally assume about the character of the addressee? What hints does it provide about some dramatic situation that might have brought the speaker and the addressee into conversation?

### Ipek Kadife's Response to Prereading Emily Dickinson's "Me from Myself – to Banish"

> The speaker seems to be in conflict with herself. She would like to banish herself from herself. The addressee must be someone included within the pronoun "we" in line 9. The speaker and the addressee evidently share something important in common. This "we" might represent just some other aspect of the speaker's self. The poem is dated in 1862 and was written during the American Civil War. Might the "we" represent Dickinson's contemporaries?

### EXERCISE 5.1

Form collaborative groups of five students each that will search the Internet for the words of a contemporary song that the group agrees upon.

*Useful Hint:* To find the song's text on the Internet, use a search engine such as Google. Type in the name of the song and, for good measure, the name of the major performer with whom it is associated. The Web site for the group U2, for example, found at U2.com, offers the lyrics of every song the group has created. As with every sort of intellectual property, however, the site cautions that these lyrics are available only for personal research or limited educational use and are to be credited with the usual documentary information when they are quoted.

After locating the text, individuals in the group should report to one another how their impressions of the song might have changed after reading the lyrics. Each group should then examine and discuss the lyrics to ask what kind of person emerges from the song. Here are questions to consider:

- What kind of character does the song attribute to its singer or speaker?
- What kind of character does it attribute to the person whom the singer or speaker is addressing?
- What situation has brought them together, and what dimensions of this situation lend a dramatic depth to the song?

The recorder should take notes and present them to the class at the end of the exercise.

## Reading for Content

Since poems present the voice of a speaker who is engaged in some sort of dramatic situation that might unfold in a story, play, or novel, the questions that we ask of a particular poem's content should focus on the components of this situation:

- What kind of drama does the poem suggest?
- What is happening to the speaker?
- How does what is happening implicate the addressee or some presumed other person?
- How does the speaker react to what is happening?
- Does the speaker convey a consistent attitude toward the event? Or does the speaker's attitude evolve in some changing fashion?

### Ipek Kadife's Response to Reading for Content in Emily Dickinson's "Me from Myself – to Banish"

If the speaker is experiencing some conflict with herself, she feels uneasy about it. The other person implied in "we" seems part of the conflict. If this "we" represents some other aspect of the speaker's self, she has to learn to adapt to the situation. Her attitude seems to evolve from feeling puzzled about being unable to resolve the conflict to accepting that she must surrender part of herself to resolve it. If the conflict concerns something that happened in or around Amherst in 1862, what might it be?

### EXERCISE 5.2

Collaborative groups of five students each should continue to examine the lyrics of a popular song that they have located on the Internet. Here are some questions to consider:

- What is happening to the singer as he or she addresses the listener?
- How does the song express or imply some particular situation that has involved the singer in an emotional conflict?
- What is the singer's attitude toward this conflict?
- How does the singer's attitude change or develop during the course of the song?

The recorder should take notes and present them to the class at the end of the exercise.

## Reading for Genre, Organization, and Stylistic Features

### Genre

The specific markers of poetry as a genre are **meter**, or recurrent numbers of syllables and sound stresses on individual lines, and **rhyme**, or recurrent echoes of sound at the ends of lines. Both meter and rhyme may fall into patterns that repeat themselves throughout the poem. Or they may not. Many poems in "free verse" appear to have no pattern of meter or rhyme at all.

Questions to ask include: How many syllables appear on each line? Do they gather into rhythmic clusters of two, three, or four syllables on individual lines? Do they display a pattern of regular sound stresses? Do groups of lines display a pattern of repetition and/or variation? How many rhyme words punctuate the lines? Do these rhyme words gather into clusters? Do they display a regular pattern?

### Ipek Kadife's Response to Reading for Genre in Emily Dickinson's "Me from Myself – to Banish"

As I count the syllables on each line, I find that every odd-numbered line regularly has seven syllables. The even-numbered lines alternate between three and four syllables. These lines also rhyme in each stanza, though the rhyme in the middle stanza (peace/consciousness) is not exact.

---

#### EXERCISE 5.3

Collaborative groups of five students each should continue to examine the lyrics of a popular song that they have located on the Internet. Here are questions to consider:

- How many syllables appear on each line? Do they gather into any rhythmic clusters? Do they sustain any pattern?
- What about rhyme words in this song? Is there a distinct rhyming pattern?

The recorder should take notes and present them to the class at the end of the exercise.

---

### Organization

Poems with a strict metrical form repeat the same **rhythmic pattern** in each stanza. Poems with a strict **rhyme scheme** likewise repeat the same rhyming pattern in each **stanza**. Many poems vary these patterns with great subtlety. Others display no rhythmic or rhyming patterns at all. Questions to ask include:

- What metrical patterns emerge? How are they repeated or varied?
- What rhyming patterns emerge? How are they repeated or varied?
- Do these patterns appear in other poems by other authors, where they might be identified with such particular forms as sonnets, couplets, limericks, nursery rhymes, hymns, odes, and the like?

## Ipek Kadife's Response to Reading for Organization in Emily Dickinson's "Me from Myself — to Banish"

The poem has three stanzas that approximate each other, with the variations of three- and seven-syllable lines mentioned above. Such a regular pattern lends itself to musical accompaniment—the lyrics for many songs are written in stanzas so that the musical rhythm and tempo can be repeated with the same number of beats in each stanza. The short stanzas of Dickinson's poem remind me of the way hymns look when they are printed for churchgoers. That might seem right for the churchgoing population of Amherst in 1862.

---

### EXERCISE 5.4

Collaborative groups of five students each should continue to examine the lyrics of a popular song that they have located on the Internet. Questions to ask include:

- Is the song divided into stanzas with notable repetitions and variations of form?
- Are there any "openers" or recurring refrains? Or is the song instead "through-composed" in a single forward movement?
- What other songs does it resemble?

The recorder should take notes and present them to the class at the end of the exercise.

---

### Stylistic Features

The language and sentence structures of many poems take **poetic license** with diction and syntax as they deploy unusual words or unusual grammar for striking effects. Rare usage, compressed expression, and inverted word order exemplify this license. **Figures of speech** such as metaphor, simile, personification, synecdoche (or part-for-the-whole), and metonymy (or sign-for-the-thing meant) likewise galvanize poetic styles. Questions to ask include:

- What is strange or exceptional about the heightened use of language in this poem?
- What is strange or exceptional about its syntax?
- How does this strangeness complicate or qualify the poem's meaning? How does it multiply the possibilities of interpreting the poem's characters or dramatic action?

## Ipek Kadife's Response to Reading for Stylistic Features in Emily Dickinson's "Me from Myself — to Banish"

The first sentence is hard to understand as it is written because it is so compact. If I try to paraphrase it, I have to expand the sentence to get something like this: "If only I had the art to banish myself from myself; but my fortress of self-defense is so strong that it resists my own efforts to break it down." As for figures of speech, the words "fortress" and "peace" suggest that there's a war going on somewhere in the background. 1862 was the second year of the American Civil War, no? Do the military metaphors refer to this war?

### EXERCISE 5.5

Collaborative groups of five students each should continue to examine the lyrics of a popular song that they have located on the Internet. Here are questions to consider:

- Does its use of diction and grammar suggest ordinary language? Or do its selection of words and its combination of sentence structures transmit a special kind of expression?
- Do you find its lyrics "catchy" and unique? Why?

The recorder should take notes and present them to the class at the end of the exercise.

## Reading for Rhetorical Context

Since a poem usually records only a single speaker's discourse, it leaves his or her **conversation with other speakers** in the shadows. Reading such poetry invites you to fill in the gaps with your own imagination about what is left unsaid. In this way, as a reader of poetry you become part of the conversation. Questions to ask include:

- If this poem were recast in the form of a short story or drama, what would the rest of the dialogue record?
- What aspects of time, place, or situation would the context convey?
- Would we necessarily identify the poem's speaker with its historical author, or might we instead understand the poem as a fiction in its own right?
- What allusions does the poem make to other poems?

### Ipek Kadife's Response to Reading for Rhetorical Context in Emily Dickinson's "Me from Myself — to Banish"

After reading several poems by Emily Dickinson, I have no idea who she really was. As our professor told us, her contemporaries thought she was eccentric and they called her "the Myth of Amherst." She responded to their exaggerations about her by calling herself "a supposed person." This "supposed person" certainly wrote poems that portray quite a character. Her eccentricity stands out in the context of the Civil War.

### EXERCISE 5.6

Collaborative groups of five students each should continue to examine the lyrics of a popular song that they have located on the Internet. Here are questions to consider:

- What story or drama is the song working to portray?
- If the singer is a well-known entertainer, do we really think that the lyrics communicate a bare-all confession? Or do we instead participate in the conversation with the tacit understanding that the performance is instead a fiction?

The recorder should take notes and present them to the class at the end of the exercise.

Here is Ipek Kadife's completed and revised paper of literary analysis on Emily Dickinson's "Me from Myself—to Banish."

*STUDENT'S LITERARY ANALYSIS ESSAY*

Ipek Kadife

English 11

Prof. Orhan Mitchell

October 12, 2006

Emily Dickinson and America's Civil War

Emily Dickinson is one of the most enigmatic poets we've read
in our course packet. As we discussed in class, her neighbors in Amherst,
Massachusetts, regarded her as a reclusive eccentric and called her "the
Myth of Amherst" (class notes, October 24, 2006). She responded to their
stories about her by referring to herself as a "supposed person" (class
notes). As reclusive as she seemed to be, she still pursued a literary
career with ferocity and determination. This strange blend of passivity and
aggression characterizes her poetry. We may never know what "real person"
lurks behind the many voices that speak in her poetry. And we may never
know which real persons (if any) her poems address. But we can listen to
her poetry as it speaks in dialogue with the shared issues of her time.
"Me from Myself — to Banish" was written in 1862 during the earliest months
of the Civil War. I am going to argue that the divided voice banishing "Me
from Myself" addresses a nation suddenly at war with itself.

The poem begins with one wishful statement in a convoluted syntax —
"Me from Myself—to Banish—/Had I Art"—and follows it with two questions.
The opening statement amounts to a poetic license from ordinary language,
and its strained effect conveys the painful self-division that the speaker
senses within herself. Straightened out, the stanza means: "If only I had
the art to banish myself from myself; but my fortress of self-defense is
so strong that it resists my own efforts to break it down." Its dominant
metaphor depicts banishment from a fortress. This figure of a military
coup dominates the questions posed in the next stanza. Here the speaker
refers to an "assault" on herself and she asks how she might have "peace"
without "subjugating" herself. In the final stanza, the use of force
results in the "Abdication" of an authoritarian "Monarch" who has absorbed
the speaker and her partner as a "We" into some "mutual" conflict.

The poem's rhyme scheme and its rhythms express a similar sense of
strain. At first their patterns seem simple: each short line of seven
syllables is followed by a shorter line of three or four syllables.
Likewise, the rhyme scheme verges on free verse, as only the second and
fourth lines in each stanza seem to rhyme. On the printed page, the poem
looks like a hymn in some denominational song book. But if so, it's a
cracked hymn. The rhyme in the middle stanza is definitely off-key: "peace/
fortress" rhyme only if we make "peace" sound like "pess" or "fortress"

Kadife 2

sound like "fortrice." Did the townspeople of Amherst pronounce these
words like that in 1862? I doubt it. Likewise the poem's rhythms wage war
against each other. Instead of the expected three syllables, the fourth
and sixth lines offer four syllables. When in the sixth line the speaker
asks, "How have I peace," its disruption signals her inner confusion. The
third stanza does, I'll admit, convey a rhythmic regularity. But its
coordination appears elusive as its content refers to political unrest and
a monarch's abdication. Significantly, the total number of syllables in the
poem is 62, the cardinal numbers of the year in which Dickinson composed
the poem at the start of America's war against itself.

How, then, might the poem address the specter of this national war
and the conscience of its participants? Does its cracked hymn point to
discord in a confederated state? Does its "supposed person" offer her
own psychological self-division as an emblem of the social self-division
north and south of the newly created borders? I find it symptomatic that
the poem's pronouns move from "Me," "Myself," and "I" in the first two
stanzas to "We" at the beginning of the third stanza. Here the speaker
refers to the duality that she feels because of her internal conflict.
But the plural pronoun encompasses her readers and broader audience as
well. Nowhere does the poem effectuate itself as a dialogue. And yet its
passionate urgency everywhere suggests that it converses not just with
itself but with a nation against itself. The final metaphor of a
"Monarch" in "Abdication" reminds us that this nation believed it had
already thrown off the chains of an earlier monarchy, only to find itself
now enthralled to a greater threat. Was the poet who wrote these lines a
mad recluse or a mere eccentric? Come again?

Kadife 3

Works Cited

*The Poems of Emily Dickinson*, ed. Thomas S. Johnson, 3 vols. Cambridge,
    Mass.: The Harvard University Press, 1955.
Mitchell, Prof. Stuart. Class Notes, 16–18 October, 2006.

# ◼ PROCESS ANALYSIS

A **process analysis** *outlines the steps in an operation.* In so doing, it often explains and comments on the formation of these steps, emphasizes important relationships among them,
provides supplementary information, and includes caveats about what can go wrong.

# ■ Examination of Passages from Charles Krauthammer's "Crossing Lines: A Secular Argument Against Research Cloning"

We will illustrate a process analysis with a selection by Charles Krauthammer in Chapter 10. As the title, "Crossing Lines: A Secular Argument Against Research Cloning," indicates, Krauthammer is presenting an argument. He knows that before he defends his position he must explain the cloning procedure to his readers. He does this by embedding a *process analysis* into the larger argument. We have annotated the Krauthammer passage.

| *Krauthammer passage* | *Annotations* |
|---|---|
| This is how research cloning works. You take a donor egg from a woman, remove its nucleus, and inject the nucleus of, say, a skin cell from another person. It has been shown in animals that by the right manipulation you can trick the egg and the injected nucleus into dedifferentiating—that means giving up all the specialization of the skin cell and returning to its original state as a primordial cell that could become anything in the body. | *first three steps*<br><br>*further explanation* |
| In other words, this cell becomes totipotent. It becomes the equivalent of the fertilized egg in normal procreation, except that instead of having chromosomes from two people, it has chromosomes from one. This cell then behaves precisely like an embryo. It divides. It develops. At four to seven days, it forms a "blastocyst" consisting of about 100 to 200 cells. | *further information*<br><br>*explains term* |
| The main objective of cloning researchers would be to disassemble this blastocyst: Pull the stem cells out, grow them in the laboratory, and then try to tease them into becoming specific kinds of cells, say, kidney or heart or brain and so on. (353) | *additional steps in the process* |

Krauthammer simply might have described the sequence of steps in the procedure. In that case, he would have written a summary of the process rather than an analysis. For example:

> Take a donor egg from a woman, remove its nucleus, inject the nucleus of, say, a skin cell from another person. Allow the cell to divide and develop at four to seven days, to form a "blastocyst" consisting of about 100 to 200 cells. Disassemble this blastocyst: Pull the stem cells out, grow them in the laboratory. Then try to tease them into becoming specific kinds of cells, say, kidney or heart or brain and so on.

Unlike a summary, a process analysis explains the amount of time the process will take, defines unfamiliar terms, comments on the importance of selected steps, mentions the problems that might be encountered, and gives advice on how the problems could be overcome. In academic writing, you might occasionally be asked to write a self-contained, stand-alone process analysis essay, but more often you'll be called upon to embed a process analysis within other genres of writing.

## ■ Process of Writing a Process Analysis

Your first step in writing a process analysis is to identify your purpose. In the Krauthammer passage, the writer's purpose is to provide his readers with information about how research cloning works. Another purpose of a process analysis is to provide readers with directions for completing the process themselves. You may have written this type of essay in the earlier grades when you were asked to explain processes such as how to make a peanut butter sandwich or how to give your dog a bath. You may be called upon to write a self-contained process analysis essay in one of your college classes.

If so, a second consideration, aside from determining your purpose, is deciding how much background information to give your readers. If you are embedding the analysis in a larger project, the context is a given. If you are writing a self-contained analysis, you need to give your audience a reason for reading your analysis.

Here are questions that will prove helpful.

---

**QUESTIONS FOR WRITING A PROCESS ANALYSIS**

- Why am I analyzing the process? Do I want my readers to understand the process (supply information) or do I want them to perform the procedure (give directions)?
- Will I provide background information and motivate my readers to read my analysis, or will I be embedding the analysis in a larger piece of writing?
- If I am offering directions, have I made correct assumptions about my readers' level of expertise?
- Have I explained the amount of time the process will take, sequenced the steps, and provided an appropriate level of specificity (enough concrete, detailed explanation)?
- Have I provided supplementary information by:
  defining unfamiliar terms?
  commenting on the importance of selected steps?
  including precautions and warnings about what might go wrong and how to overcome the problems?
  giving follow-up or trouble-shooting advice?
- Have I used an adequate number of chronological transitions?

---

## ■ CAUSAL ANALYSIS

A **causal analysis**, also called cause-and-effect analysis, seeks *to identify the reasons why something happens.* It is often used to examine why a phenomenon or event is occurring, to investigate possible causes of a problem, or to examine effects. A causal analysis may be a self-contained essay or it may be embedded in a longer piece of writing. Chapter 3 contains a freestanding causal analysis, "Mother Yale" (pp. 132–34) by Frances Rosenbluth. Another example is "Isolated by the Internet" (pp. 392–98), by Clifford Stoll. Stoll analyzes the negative long-term effects the Internet has on people's social lives and development.

## ■ Examination of "Mother Yale": Frances Rosenbluth's Causal Analysis

To illustrate a causal analysis, we will examine Frances Rosenbluth's "Mother Yale" (pp. 132–34). Like a number of the authors in Chapter 3, Rosenbluth writes in response to Louise Story. Story wrote an article about undergraduate women who intend to stay home with their children rather than work full time. Rosenbluth, a professor of political science at Yale, points out that despite what Story says about women preferring to stay at home, female labor force participation stands at about 75 percent. Moreover, over 50 percent of mothers with small children are employed outside the home. In her causal analysis, Rosenbluth examines the causes and effects of this phenomenon. The pictorial representation in Figure 5–4 shows how Rosenbluth organized the causes and effects.

This sort of representation is called a fishbone diagram because it depicts relationships among parts of the whole as though they belonged to a skeletal trunk. Each major part is shown as though it were a "fish scale" on this osseous structure. A fishbone diagram is valuable for mapping causes and effects in texts you read and write.

## ■ Process of Writing a Causal Analysis

You already know a good deal about analyzing causes and effects. The analysis questions you have been using throughout this chapter emphasize the importance of examining reasons as well as implications, conclusions, and consequences. Investigating causes and effects is an operation of critical thinking as well as a format for writing.

Continuing with the debate over the "Mommy Wars," let's say you have received an open-ended assignment that allows you to examine any aspect of what Rebecca Traister

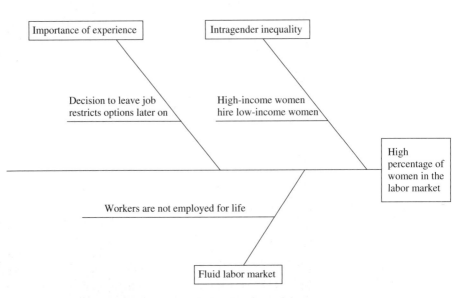

**Figure 5–4    Fishbone Diagram of Rosenbluth's "Mother Yale"**

calls "the politics of the American home." Thinking in terms of causes and effects, you could examine any number of topics; for example:

- The reasons many liberated men still leave the mothering and housework to women
- The factors that account for continued inequities in the home
- The reasons the Mommy Wars have been reignited
- The effect of interrupting a career to pursue child-rearing
- The effect of women's employment on the development of young children

The purpose of your causal analysis essay is to heighten your readers' awareness of the various causes and/or effects and to make a case that certain causes or effects are more plausible and convincing than others. As you conduct your analysis, map the relationships between the causes and effects by constructing a fishbone diagram like the one we presented on page 202. The fishbone allows you to trace the actual streams of the various causes. After you have conducted research, acquired ample knowledge, and progressed to the stage of planning your essay, formulate a thesis along the lines of "The Mommy Wars have been reignited because of [effect A], [effect B], and [effect C]" or "[Cause A] and [cause B] have resulted in liberated men leaving mothering and housework to women." Here are questions that will prove helpful.

---

**QUESTIONS FOR WRITING A CAUSAL ANALYSIS**

- Why am I writing this causal analysis — to heighten my readers awareness or also to argue that some causes or effects are more plausible and explanatory than others?
- Have I sufficiently narrowed the focus of the cause-effect investigation to focus on the most compelling aspects of the issue?
- Have I supplied my readers with sufficient background information about the issue I am analyzing?
- Have I supported my points with textual evidence?
- Have I been able to differentiate among different types of causes?
- Are the causes and effects spelled out, or will my readers have to make inferences?
- Have I used adequate cause-effect transitions (e.g., *accordingly, as a result, because, since, therefore, consequently, for this purpose, hence*)?

---

**EXERCISE 5.7**

Read Clifford Stoll's "Isolated by the Internet" (pp. 392–98) and draw a fishbone diagram that depicts the causes and effects that Stoll attributes to the impact of the Internet on people's social lives and development.

## ■■ CLASSIC COMPARISON AND CONTRAST ESSAY

All too often students think the object of a comparison and contrast essay is to list and report similarities and differences as an end in itself. They fall into the trap of doing too much summarizing, giving a synopsis of each text, and then simply explaining how the authors' views are alike and different. You need to take the process a step further. Analyze the texts, step back, and then reflect on what the similarities and differences represent, reveal, or demonstrate. Ask yourself the questions in the following box.

Answers to these questions will shape or expand on your goal.

---

### QUESTIONS TO ASK ABOUT SIMILARITIES AND DIFFERENCES

- How do the views in these two texts relate to one another — as though they were part of a conversation or a give-and-take of interdependent ideas?
- What happens when they qualify, contradict, or otherwise complicate one another?
- What angle or point of view emerges with regard to the material?

---

## ▥ Illustration of Comparison and Contrast

To illustrate how a published writer expresses an expanded goal, consider the opening paragraphs of "Two Views of Motherhood," a review essay in which sociologist Carol A. Brown compares and contrasts two books: *Engendering Motherhood: Identity and Self-Transformations in Women's Lives* by Martha McMahon and *Bearing Meaning: The Language of Birth* by Robbie Pfeufer Kahn. McMahon's book is pointedly academic whereas Kahn's includes personal experience.

> These books give opposing answers to a question: How do we study and how do we teach about any social relation, in this case motherhood, while taking into account both the personal experiences of the individuals involved and the macrosocial factors that create and vary the institution?
>
> Both books take a feminist perspective, understanding the historical significance of patriarchy and the extent to which gender and male domination affect current concepts and practices. Both recognize the conflicted meaning of childbirth and motherhood as a cause for women's devaluation in a masculist society and as a feminine domain that connects, empowers, and activates women's self-confidence and social presence.
>
> The difference is that between a monograph and a monologue. (355)

Brown frames the book review with a question and she uses the body paragraphs of the comparison and contrast essay to answer this question. She ends the essay with the following paragraphs:

> I find it ironic that when I sit back and think about what I have taken away from both books, I realize that Kahn, impassioned and personal, spoke to me as a sociologist, while McMahon, cool and academic, spoke to me as a mother.
>
> So the answer to my original question is that there are a variety of ways of teaching about a social relation while taking into account both the personal experiences of the individuals involved and the macrosocial factors that create and vary the institution. Both books are strong on data and analysis; both give us an individual perspective as well as

sociological analysis. McMahon's sociology is easier to see because it is in the classic format, but Kahn's sociology is just as suitable to her topic as McMahon's is for hers. (358)

Once you have analyzed the two texts with which you are working, step back to see if there is anything significant about the comparable and contrastable elements you have identified. As the passages from Brown's essay illustrate, what she finds interesting is the fact that despite the two books' different approaches, they are equally effective as studies of the sociology of motherhood.

## ■ Identifying Comparisons and Contrasts

As you read the texts that you intend to compare and contrast, annotate them to highlight correspondences between them. Then do a second reading for the purpose of identifying as many similarities and differences as you can. In the box below, we provide strategies that will help you discover how two reading sources can be similar and different.

---

### ELABORATING TO UNCOVER COMPARISONS AND CONTRASTS

- Identify points where one text

  agrees or disagrees with the other text

  says something relevant about the topic that the other text has neglected

  qualifies ideas stated by the other text

  extends a proposition made by the other text

- Validate one author's assertion with information provided by the other author
- Subsume similarities and differences between the texts under subordinate categories
- Create hierarchies of importance among ideas that are similar or different
- Make judgments about the relevance of one author's view in relation to the other's view

---

Many writers find it useful to create a pictorial representation of the similarities and differences. We used this technique in Figure 5–3 on page 191 when we constructed a graphic overview of the similarities and differences between the articles by Tracy Martin Hekker and David Brooks. Another useful technique for creating a visual display of similarity and difference is webbing (see Figure 5–5).

Once you have identified a point of similarity or difference, summarize it in a short phrase and place it in a box in the center of a sheet of paper. Spin out the web by writing each author's ideas around this key idea node. Circle each of these ideas and connect them with lines to the key idea and, where appropriate, to each other. When you are finished webbing, you will have a visual display of the points of similarity and difference.

## ■ Process of Writing a Comparison and Contrast Essay

To illustrate the process of composing a comparison and contrast essay, we will accompany our student Kathy Tryer as she works through an assignment based on Herbert Gans's

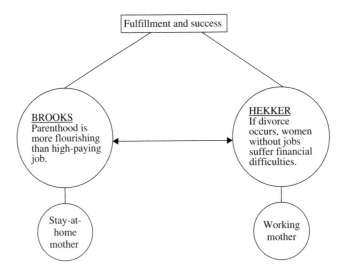

**Figure 5–5    Webbing**

"The War Against the Poor" and Myron Magnet's "Rebels with a Cause" asking her to compare and contrast a politically liberal view of poverty with a conservative view.

> Analyze Herbert Gans's and Myron Magnet's views of poor people. Write for an audience of classmates. Your essay should be three to four pages, and you should address it to your classmates.

> Gans's article, included in Chapter 14 of this book, was originally published in the liberal magazine, *Dissent.* Magnet's article was published in the conservative magazine, *National Review.*
> On her first reading, Kathy underlines and annotates the texts, jots down her reactions, and marks passages where one text relates to the other. On the second reading, she examines the texts for additional points of similarity and difference, and she takes notes. (See Figure 5–6.)

## Planning Comparison and Contrast Essays

Next, Kathy selects and orders her ideas and sketches out a blueprint for the essay. She creates two lists: one list for similarities between the sources and the other for differences. Another way you might do this is by marking the text wherever you've discovered similarities or differences (use symbols: = for similarities and ≠ for differences). Here are Kathy's two lists:

### Similarities:

- Both Gans and Magnet believe that poverty is a symptom of social decay.
- Both writers demonstrate that antisocial behavior may be used as a form of power, and that such behavior may be admired by certain groups or cultures.

*Gans, Paragraph 4*
True, some poor people are indeed guilty of immoral behavior—that is, murderers, street criminals, drug sellers, child abusers.

*Gans, Paragraph 5*
Then there are poor people whose anger at their condition cannot be defined as political protest. Even so, most of those labeled "undeserving" are simply poor people who for a variety of reasons cannot live up to mainstream behavioral standards, like remaining childless in adolescence, finding and holding a job, and staying off welfare. This does not make them immoral.

*Magnet, Paragraph 5*
. . . For though the governmental structure of force and threat—police, judges and prisons—is a key means by which society restrains aggression and crime, it isn't the principal means. The most powerful curb is the internal inhibition society builds into each man's character, the inner voice (call it reason, conscience, superego, what you will) that makes the social contract an integral part of our deepest selves.

*Kathy's Notes*
Gans uses the examples of criminality and morality, as does Magnet, but in different ways. Taking great pains to clarify his own perception of morality, Gans defensively pits the abject criminality of murderers and drug sellers against the merely antisocial behavior of teenage mothers and individuals incapable of remaining employed. Here Gans attempts to soften the argument of immorality against the less severe offenders of mainstream moral standards. In contrast to Magnet, who suggests preventative tactics and never raises the issue of morality, Gans proposes a band-aid approach to the problem that is only getting worse with time.

*Kathy's Notes*
Though the examples of government and control by authority are discussed by both Magnet and Gans, Magnet suggests that the true controlling factor in human life is the internal motivations of the individual. If such motivation is misguided or absent, criminal behavior may result. Magnet argues that within impoverished cultures, built-in inhibition is absent from the character makeup of many of its individuals. This approach, which holds each man or culture responsible for its own behaviors, differs greatly from Gans's. He states that antisocial behaviors are a symptom of poverty, which in turn, is a symptom of government policies and the social attitudes and beliefs of mainstream culture. Gans never suggests that individuals within a given culture can (or should) be responsible for their own beliefs and behaviors, unless they have demonstrated an ability to do so according to mainstream moral values.

**Figure 5–6    Text and Student's Notes**

Differences:

- Cultural mores serve as the basis of both writers' arguments, but whereas Gans blames government policies and the attitudes of society at large, Magnet finds the absence of traditional middle-class values to blame.

- Gans blames politics, the economy, and the cultural mores of the middle class as either unfair, outmoded, or not applicable to the real-life situations faced by impoverished peoples.

- Magnet uses a historical/theoretical model to demonstrate that impoverished peoples lack the internal guidance and discipline that characterize the "social contract" adhered to by the middle and upper classes.

- Whereas Gans writes of declining morality in terms of it being a recent phenomenon, Magnet suggests that moral standards have undergone continual change, and that, historically, moral decline has always been a part of human culture.

As Kathy analyzes the similarities and differences, she asks herself two questions: (1) What do the similarities and differences demonstrate? and (2) What do they tell me about each of the two texts? In response to the questions, Kathy forms a generalization about the similarities and differences.

When academic writers compare and contrast texts, their goal is to make a claim or propose a thesis. As we said earlier, sometimes student writers simply describe the similarities and differences. This is a limited rhetorical goal. A more powerful purpose requires the writer to compare and contrast the texts for a specific reason: for example, to describe, explain, or argue a point, or to communicate what the comparison reveals or demonstrates about the subject.

| Limited Goal | More Powerful Goal |
|---|---|
| Bring out similarities and differences in the subject matter. | 1. Use the comparison to describe, explain, or argue a position. |
| | 2. Show what the comparison reveals or demonstrates about the subject. |

When you read Kathy's essay on pages 211–13, you will see that as she lays out the similarities and differences between the two readings, she aligns herself more with Magnet than with Gans, leading up to paragraphs 5 and 6, where she argues that Magnet's analysis of poverty is more realistic and constructive than Gans's.

## Organizing the Comparison and Contrast Essay

Comparison and contrast essays are organized in a point-by-point format, a block arrangement, or a combination of the two.

---

### ORGANIZATIONAL PATTERNS

**Point-by-Point**

*Introduction*

1. Paper Opener. See techniques on pages 160–61.
2. Identify the texts and the issue(s) on which they focus.
3. Explain your rhetorical goal (your purpose for comparing the sources).

*Body Paragraphs*

1. Compare the texts with respect to a single characteristic.
2. Repeat Step 1 for each characteristic you intend to treat.

*Conclusion*

See the techniques on page 163.

## Block

*Introduction*

1. Paper Opener. See techniques on pages 160–61.
2. Identify the texts and the issue(s) on which they focus.
3. Explain your rhetorical goal (your purpose for comparing the sources).

*Body Paragraphs*

1. Identify and discuss the characteristics of the first text.

    Compare the characteristics of the second text with those of the first one.

*Conclusion*

See the techniques on page 163.

Kathy Tryer organizes her essay by using a combination of both patterns. Paragraphs 2 and 3 treat Magnet and Gans, respectively, in "blocks." In the remaining paragraphs (4, 5, and 6), Kathy compares both writers in point-by-point fashion. If Kathy had used the point-by-point pattern exclusively, she would have written her essay according to the outline that follows.

## OUTLINE FOR COMPARISON ESSAY WRITTEN IN POINT-BY-POINT ARRANGEMENT

*Paragraph 1:*    Introduction

### Objectivity (Point 1)

*Paragraph 2:*    Magnet's argument — a practical social and historical monograph explaining the causes of ills suffered by the poor.

Gans's argument — reactionary, reminiscent of a classic "knee-jerk" liberal response.

### Examples (Point 2)

*Paragraph 3:*    Gans — band-aid style approach to an age-old problem.

*Paragraph 4:*    Magnet — doesn't suggest a solution aimed at diminishing the ways the poor are viewed negatively, but does identify the conditions needed for the advancement of the poor.

### Rhetorical Stance (Point 3)

*Paragraph 5:*    Gans's and Magnet's arguments lie at opposite ends of the spectrum. Gans claims the cause of the prevailing view of the poor is mainstream political precepts.

*Paragraph 6:*    Magnet blames what he believes to be poverty's root itself: the values and character of individuals.

*Paragraph 7:*    Conclusion

If Kathy had relied solely on the block pattern instead of alternating between Magnet and Gans with each point of comparison, she would have contrasted the texts in blocks, dealing with one text in the first block and switching to the other in the second segment. Her essay would have conformed to the following outline:

---

### OUTLINE FOR COMPARISON ESSAY WRITTEN IN BLOCK ARRANGEMENT

*Paragraph 1:*   The introduction is the same as in the point-by-point essay.

**First Block: Magnet**

*Paragraph 2:*   Magnet's argument — not reactionary or desperate, objective and convincing.

*Paragraph 3:*   Magnet claims that antisocial behavior, poverty, and the other ills of the lower classes beget an underdeveloped "social contract." He cites examples from history, philosophy, and psychology.

*Paragraph 4:*   Magnet tries to persuade his audience that the condition of the poor is due to individual, not social, circumstances.

**Second Block: Gans**

*Paragraph 5:*   Gans — reactionary, reminiscent of a classic "knee-jerk" liberal response.

*Paragraph 6:*   Thorough in explaining his argument for social change, but he fails to convince the reader of either the problem or his proposed solution.

*Paragraph 7:*   Gans's attempts to elicit an emotional response from his readers further the overall perception that his arguments are biased and one-sided.

*Paragraph 8:*   Conclusion

---

## Drafting Comparison and Contrast Essays

After Kathy selects an organizational plan, she writes a draft of her essay. This first draft is preliminary. She will have an opportunity to change direction, sharpen her focus, and revise at a later date.

The box that follows lists conventions for comparison essays. As you read Kathy's essay, notice the extent to which she uses them.

---

### CONVENTIONS FOR COMPARISON AND CONTRAST ESSAYS

- Give your readers background about the topic.
- Identify the texts by title and author.

- Indicate the grounds for comparison; that is, the points you are using to compare and contrast the texts.
- Clearly state your thesis.
- Develop each point of comparison by paraphrasing, summarizing, or quoting relevant points in the readings and bringing your prior topic knowledge and experience to bear on the text.
- Clearly differentiate your own ideas from those in the texts.
- Correctly document material you have paraphrased, summarized, or quoted.

## SAMPLE COMPARISON AND CONTRAST ESSAY

Kathy Tryer

Professor Kennedy

English 131

16 September 2003

Poverty's Roots — The Environment versus the

Individual: Two Views

Myron Magnet and Herbert J. Gans, both writing about poverty in America, arrive at startlingly different conclusions concerning its roots, causes, and prevention. Magnet, in "Rebels with a Cause," argues that the poor are an inevitable by-product of advanced cultures. According to Magnet, those within advanced cultures incapable of the discipline or restraint necessary for social advancement become outcast, socially immobile, and poor. Magnet supports his argument with substantive examples and draws on historical, philosophical, and psychological literature. Gans, however, in "The War Against the Poor," proposes a means to end mistreatment of the poor rather than proposing methods by which to end poverty, and places the blame for the social condition of the poor and their mistreatment squarely on the shoulders of mainstream society itself. Neither writer suggests it is possible to end poverty entirely. Magnet, though, examines poverty's underlying causes, identifies the conditions necessary for its reduction, and offers the more sensible analysis of the condition.

Magnet points out that the personal values of the poor place them outside the social order. He discusses the importance of order in society, claiming, "the achievements of civilization rest upon the social order, which rests in turn upon a mutual agreement to foreswear aggression" (50). Magnet alludes to statements made by Plato, St. Augustine, Hobbes, Burke, and Freud and points out that each of these thinkers concludes that "as men come from the hand of nature, they are instinctively aggressive, with a built-in inclination to violence" (47). The underlying purpose of social order, a relatively recent phenomenon in history, Magnet explains, "is to restrain man's instinctual aggressiveness, so that human life can be something higher than a war of all against all" (47). Social order is the principal element lacking in poor society, Magnet claims, and this problem must be traced to the individual. To elaborate, "the hardest of hard realities — whether people commit crimes or not — comes down to a very large extent to nothing more than values and beliefs in the world within the individual," claims Magnet (48). The values and beliefs of the poor, according to Magnet, are out of step with those of the larger society, which is the direct cause of their socioeconomic conditions.

Gans sees things differently. He believes poverty is caused by mainstream society which, by design, suppresses the poor and creates a social climate hostile to the poor. He blames the economy, politics, and social policy toward the poor for their ills and for the creation of an environment conducive to their debasement. For example, he cites the economy as a culprit and claims that mainstream attitudes toward the poor were "initiated by dramatic shifts in the domestic and world economy which have turned more and more unskilled and semiskilled workers into surplus labor" (461). Individuals within the middle and upper classes, however, view the poor unsympathetically and see them "not as people without jobs but as miscreants who behave badly because they do not abide by middle-class or mainstream moral values" (461). He does allow, though, that some poor people are involved in criminal or indecent behavior, but suggests this is an insignificant segment of the underclass population. To counteract the problems created by the economy, politics, and existing social policy, Gans suggests enormous government programs such as a "new" New Deal for the poor, programs to find uses for stagnant or redundant private enterprise to raise levels of employment, and for those remaining who can't — or won't —work, a program of income grants. "Alas," concedes Gans, "when taxpayers discover how much cheaper it is to pay welfare than to create jobs, that remedy may end as it has before" (462). Gans's proposals do nothing to improve the condition of the poor, nor do they address the underlying causes of poverty. As he notes above, to implement such programs might actually increase the anger of mainstream culture toward the poor. In short, Gans proposes a band-aid approach to solving an age-old problem.

Magnet, while he doesn't suggest a solution aimed at diminishing the ways the poor are viewed negatively, does identify the conditions needed for the advancement of the poor. Unlike Gans, Magnet does not think that "society has so oppressed people as to bend them out of their true

Tryer 3

nature" (48). He believes instead that the plight of the poor is oftentimes attributable to social maladjustment of the poor themselves. "Examine the contents of their minds and hearts and what you find is free- floating aggression, weak consciences, anarchic beliefs, detachment from the community and its highest values," he states (48). Magnet attributes these defects to "unimaginably weak families, headed by immature irresponsible girls, who are at the margin of the community, pathological in their own behavior, and too often lacking the knowledge, interest and inner resources to be successful molders of strong characters in children" (48). Clearly then, to "adequately socialize" the members of the underclass who lack inner discipline and social order, their values and morals must change.

Gans's and Magnet's arguments are in direct opposition. Gans claims the cause of the prevailing view and the current condition of the poor is mainstream social and political precepts. Magnet blames the values and character of the individual alone. Gans proposes government intervention and an "intellectual and cultural defense" (463) on behalf of the poor. Magnet suggests uncovering the true basis for poverty and acting on a local level by attempting to understand poverty-stricken individuals themselves, of whom Gans admits "Americans accept so many untruths" (461). Gans's band-aid approach to artificially elevating the status of the poor through government programs and cash subsidies will do little toward changing mainstream society's negative view of the poor. Magnet's more comprehensive value-oriented approach to addressing the ills of the underclass, grounded in historical, philosophical, and psychological precedents, has a better chance of success.

Magnet, in suggesting a reexamination of the very mechanism which catalyzes poverty and crime, offers a possible solution that is far more realistic than that submitted by Gans. Gans's emotionally charged argument attempts to conjure enemies from inanimate entities: the government, politics, and the economy. Magnet's proposal provides a constructive, accountable approach to addressing the problems of the poor. Thus, Gans's suggestions amount to little more than a critique of mainstream American society and an unfounded claim that American institutions are responsible for the plight of the underclass.

Tryer 4

## Works Cited

Gans, Herbert. "The War Against the Poor." *Dissent* Fall 1992: 461–65.

Magnet, Myron. "Rebels with a Cause." *National Review* 15 March 1993: 46–50.

Notice that Kathy Tryer's essay follows many but not all of the guidelines we've suggested for comparison and contrast papers. No essay can ever be expected to observe all the guidelines for a particular form of writing, because each topic or issue introduces matters that require their own distinctive treatment. Nevertheless, you will note in Kathy's essay a consistent attention to detail that takes account of her readers' knowledge of the two texts and a careful assessment of the texts' argument, organization, and rhetorical context. The essay reveals that Kathy annotated the reading materials point by point, and it demonstrates that Kathy's argument is clear and systematic from her opening paragraph about the major differences between Magnet and Gans, through individual paragraphs that focus on each text, to her concluding paragraph about the texts' divergence.

We have presented Kathy's polished essay. Bear in mind that she produced this version after several preliminary drafts, a conference with her instructor, and a peer review. If your professor agrees, ask a classmate to review your essay. If this is not possible, review the essay yourself. We provide questions in the following box.

---

## QUESTIONS FOR HELPING A WRITER REVISE THE FIRST DRAFT OF A COMPARISON AND CONTRAST ESSAY

- Is the writer's rhetorical purpose clear? Explain how he or she is attempting to influence or affect readers.
- Does the writer explain what the similarities and contrasts reveal or demonstrate, or is the writer's purpose simply to show that similarities and differences exist? If the writer's goal is limited, suggest a more powerful goal.
- Does everything in the essay lead to or follow from one central meaning? If not, which ideas appear to be out of place?
- Will the reader understand the essay, and is the writer sensitive to the reader's concerns?

  Does the writer provide necessary background information about the subject matter, the sources, and their titles and authors? If not, what is missing?

  Throughout the essay, when the writer refers to the source text, does he or she supply the reader with necessary documentation?

  Does the writer provide clear transitions or connecting ideas that differentiate his or her own ideas from those expressed in the texts?

  Does the writer display an awareness of the authors by referring to them by name and personal pronoun ("Smith states," "she explains") rather than personifying the source ("the article states," "it explains")?

- Is the organizational format appropriate for a comparison and contrast essay? Is the writer using point-by-point or block arrangement?
- Has the writer revealed the points of comparison to the reader? Are these criteria or bases for comparison clear or confusing? Explain.
- Does the writer provide transitions and connecting ideas as he or she moves from one source to another or from one point of comparison to the next? If not, where are they needed?
- Do you hear the writer's voice throughout the entire essay? Describe it.

- Does the writer use an opener that catches the reader's attention?
- Does the conclusion simply restate the main idea, or does it offer new insights?
- Does the essay have an appropriate title?
- What other suggestions can you give the writer for improving this draft?

## EXERCISE 5.8

Reread Kathy Tryer's essay. After the introduction, Kathy summarizes the Magnet text. Then she summarizes Herbert Gans's article. She does not summarize, paraphrase, or quote from all sections of the texts; instead, she focuses on points where Magnet's argument relates specifically to Gans's. Evaluate her selection. Can you make any generalizations about her selective use of paraphrase and quotation?

## EXERCISE 5.9

In Chapter 4 you read two critical analyses of Linda Hirshman's argument, "Homeward Bound." One analysis was Cathy Young's "The Return of the Mommy Wars" (pp. 116–19) and the other was David Brooks's "The Year of Domesticity" (pp. 114–15). Write an essay in which you compare and contrast these two analyses.

## WORKS CITED

Brown, Carol A. "Two Views of Motherhood." *Qualitative Sociology* 23 (2000): 355–58.

Gans, Herbert. "The War Against the Poor." *Dissent* Fall 1992: 461–65.

Magnet, Myron. "Rebels with a Cause." *National Review* 15 March 1993: 46–50.

*Six*

# Visual Analysis

Cultural critics point out that ours is an age increasingly reliant upon **visual imagery** for communication, commentary, documentation, information, instruction, entertainment, and persuasion. Certainly the technology of visual representation over the past century-and-a-half has developed at an exponential rate from the earliest daguerreotype prints through motion pictures and television to digital photography, computer imaging, and multimedia presentation. Developments and improvements in technology are likely to reinforce the importance of visual representation in the workplace, marketplace, scientific sphere, recreational venues, and domestic environment. For these reasons, it is worthwhile to develop some analytical skills in viewing visual representations and in writing about them with expression and conviction.

## ◼◼ PRINCIPLES OF VISUAL ANALYSIS

The major **principles of visual analysis** hold much in common with other forms of analysis. Though this type of analysis will focus on **images** rather than words, it still requires us to concentrate on details and on the connections among them. It will ask us to look for **content** and meaning; to determine what **genre** the image belongs to, what sorts of **organization** give structure to the image, and what **stylistic features** characterize it; and finally to question **rhetorical contexts** concerning who created the image, for whom it was created, and what purpose it served.

As images can be dramatically manipulated through decisions based on **selection, arrangement, inclusion, omission, focus, differentiation**, and the like, we can assume that what we perceive in a picture is not the same as the reality that the picture represents. This assumption holds true whether the picture is a drawing, painting, etching, or cartoon produced by an artist's hand through memory, imagination, direct observation, or some combination of them; or whether it is a photograph, video image, computer-generated collage, or the like produced through the eye of a camera set up and controlled by a human being.

This chapter will concentrate on photographs or camera-generated images rather than on hand-crafted or computer-generated images. Not only are photographs amenable to **reproduction** in hard-copy textbooks such as the one in your hands, but they also pose a particularly forceful demonstration of the axiom that all pictures manipulate the **viewer's perception** in dramatic ways. We usually believe that a simple snapshot faithfully records what passed through the **camera's lens**. But we might challenge this belief by analyzing such factors as **distance, perspective, placement, lighting, contrast**, and the like.

After such an analysis, we might well develop a healthy skepticism about the alleged "realism" of photographs in newspapers, magazines, and history books that purport to show what actually happened; of photographs in training manuals, cookbooks, and do-it-yourself brochures that lead us to believe we can achieve the same results that are pictured; and of photographs in magazine ads, travel brochures, and supplier catalogues that entice us to buy what is presented for sale. In each case, we will be examining the **hidden persuasion** of photographs, even and especially when such photographs seem far from trying to manipulate their viewers.

## ◼ PORTFOLIO OF PHOTOGRAPHS

Here is a brief portfolio of four photographs that we will use to study visual analysis in this chapter. Each of the pictures depicts a parent, usually a mother, with a small child in a setting that suggests some components of a workplace environment. Each picture introduces an element of tension or strain associated with the presence of young children in the workplace. With these tensions and strains, the portfolio relates to the anthology section on the

**Photo 6–1    Young woman using a laptop.**
Courtesy of FOTOSEARCH.com.

**Photo 6–2    People, keyboard, telephone.**
Courtesy of FOTOSEARCH.com.

**Photo 6–3    Mother holding her daughter and using a computer.** Courtesy of FOTOSEARCH.com.

**Photo 6–4    A father wearing a business suit and holding his baby.** Courtesy of FOTOSEARCH.com.

"Mommy Wars" in Chapter 3. As we analyze these four photographs, you might think of the pictures as illustrating the arguments in the anthology section, and of the anthology section as creating a context for analyzing the pictures.

## ■ OVERVIEW OF VISUAL ANALYSIS

At the beginning of this chapter, we have used the words "dramatically" and "in dramatic ways." That's because visual analysis—to a significant extent—resembles literary analysis that focuses upon a **narrative or dramatic situation**, a story or poem with characters who conduct a **conversation** with one another. The genre that visual analysis most resembles is the **detective story**. In Edgar Allen Poe's tale, "The Purloined Letter," the detective-hero named Dupin prides himself upon his "lynx eye" that can ferret out details that appear "simple and odd," even "a little *too* plain" and "a little *too* self-evident" (Poe 250). Whereas other characters in the tale see only different parts of a puzzle, Dupin observes "the *radicalness* of these differences" and consequently unlocks their hidden logic (Poe 262).

Like Poe's hero, the viewer who analyzes a photograph is asked to imagine the story motivating the picture, the template that allows it to make sense, the features that make it distinctive, and the context that has set it in motion. This viewer will be bringing to the picture the kinds of questions about content, genre, organization, stylistic features, and rhetorical context that a reader who analyzes a literary text brings to a story, play, or poem.

Think of the picture as a text. Photo 6–1, for example, shows two women and a baby. What situation has brought them together? Is the woman in the background the baby's mother? Why does she concentrate upon the woman in the foreground while the other woman concentrates upon her laptop? What attitude does the woman in the background project toward what is going on? The tools that you use to analyze and write about this picture will be the same that you've used to analyze and write about other texts in this book.

# ◼◼ PROCESS OF WRITING A VISUAL ANALYSIS ESSAY

On pages 230–33 below, our student Lionel Essrog has written a visual analysis of these photographs. In what follows here, we will trace the steps he took in preparing to write this paper. Once again we will review these steps through our general prompts for Previewing; Viewing for Content; Viewing for Genre, Organization, and Stylistic Features; and Viewing for Rhetorical Context. Lionel's paper is based on these prompts. So too is the accompanying set of collaborative exercises on photographs that you and members of your group might gather from newspapers, magazines, or books; on the Web; or in your own family snapshot collections.

## ◼ Previewing

We begin with previewing the visual material selected for analysis. We might survey the broad **field** of the picture to isolate its major components, its dominant topic, and the positive or negative feelings that it evokes. We should look for a **title**, **caption**, or other verbal clue to define its context. We could ask ourselves whether we have encountered **other pictures like** it, such as those in mass publications, instructional manuals, advertising supplements, school textbooks, private photo albums, coffee table art books, and so forth. We might speculate about the **picture's purpose**—whether to document an event, illustrate a point, teach a lesson, summon the viewer to action, or some other purpose. If we can identify the topic of the picture, we might question whether its presentation corresponds to **what we know or have experienced** of the situation on which it focuses.

At this point, we will still be dealing with generalities, with broadly available issues or meanings. If we can, however, locate some appeal (or perhaps revulsion) that the picture has for us because of some still unknown, unexpected, as yet unarticulated reason, we should take note of this response, too. In Photo 6–1, for example, what relationship might the woman in the foreground bear to the woman and baby in the background? Is she a friend or relative of the woman and baby? Does the woman in the background envy or resent her freedom to use the laptop? Or is she actually the baby's mother and has entrusted the child to the care of someone else while she attends to work or to some emergency?

Lionel Essrog has been instructed to write an essay of 1,000 words analyzing one or more of the pictures in our visual portfolio on pages 217–18. Here is his specific assignment:

> In an essay of 1,000 words, analyze the form and content of one or more photographs from our visual portfolio on "Moms, Dads, and Babies." Discuss the relationships among the persons or objects pictured and offer a plausible argument about the rhetorical context of the picture or pictures you've selected.

Here is Lionel's first effort to address this topic by freewriting his response to previewing the visual portfolio:

> The cliche states, "A picture is worth a thousand words." But I think the opposite can be true. At least words can tell us exactly what is going on. In these pictures, we can only guess at what is happening. In "Young woman using a laptop," what are the other woman and the baby doing in the background? In "People, keyboard, telephone," is it good or bad that the baby is playing with the computer keyboard while the mother speaks on the telephone? Why is the father so well-dressed in "A father wearing a business suit holding

his baby"? Maybe it's the captions that are failing to tell us what is happening. If they were more informative, at least they could tell us what is going on. At first glance, the pictures are a mystery.

## EXERCISE 6.1

- Form collaborative groups of five students each. Have some members of the group search for eye-catching photographs in newspapers, magazines, and illustrated books. Have other members of the group search for pictures on such Web sites as http://fotosearch.com or http://ap.accuweather.com. Have still other members search through family snapshot collections or, if they are able, produce some on-the-spot pictures with their own cameras.

- When the group has assembled a couple of dozen photographs, sort them out into major categories. Which photographs document an event, illustrate a point, teach a lesson, entertain the viewer with a pleasant or odd perspective, or summon the viewer to specific and deliberate action? Which categories dominate among pictures in the public domain? Which categories dominate among pictures in private collections?

- Discuss as a group how accurately or faithfully each of these pictures corresponds to what we know about the situation or have experienced in our own lives?

- The group's recorder should take notes on this discussion and present a summary when the entire class reconvenes.

## ■ Viewing for Content

The content of a picture differs from that of a written text because its information appears all at once, enabling viewers to survey its **visual field** in different stages of perception, rather than sequentially in the prescribed order that would appear in a verbal text. It beguiles the viewer into assuming that its visible materials convey obvious, generally transparent, shared meanings. A careful viewer will nonetheless begin to question the picture's **details** and its **overall presentation** of meaning. Like Poe's Dupin, such a viewer will come to discover meanings and responses undetected by more casual viewers.

The careful viewer may regard the picture's details as a site where contested **meanings are produced** and the overall presentation as a site where these **meanings are argued**. He or she will then attend to the picture as though it were registering a silent **conversation** with us and other viewers, as perhaps an **argument** between competing claims, or a **drama** with sudden reversals of behavior and response, or a **story** with shifting patterns of action and meaning.

Like a conversation, a picture will project ideas, some dominant and **attention-getting**, others quiet and **subdued**. Like an argument, a picture will incorporate a **focus** that concentrates on some ideas while relegating others to supporting roles. Like a drama, it will show someone or something in a process of change, caught by the camera's shutter in a moment of **arrested time**. Like a story, it will suggest that the player or players in this moment of action have various **connections** to the scene of action, to one another, to what has preceded the picture, and to what will follow.

In Photo 6–2, for example, why is the mother holding her baby as she talks on the phone? Do her half-closed eyes suggest tiredness or concentration on the phone call? Is she fully aware that the baby is fingering the keyboard and perhaps deleting important data that she has just fed into her computer? What does the picture tell us about the stresses and strains of child-raising and attending to other affairs at the same time?

When you think of a picture as reporting a conversation or delivering a narrative, you will then have a framework for posing questions about its content. Here are some examples of questions you might ask.

---

### QUESTIONS FOR VIEWING CONTENT IN VISUAL ANALYSIS

- What is happening in this picture?
- What has preceded the particular action that is now frozen in time?
- What will follow this action?
- How probable is the scenario that a viewer might construct?
- Who or what are the participants in this action?
- Which participants does the picture include?
- Which participants does it omit? Is the omission casual, or is it an important part of the story?
- Does the particular selection of details result from careful planning (as in a studied pose)?
- Does the selection result from catching a spontaneous action in unplanned movement?
- Does the selection result from cropping or removing content from an already processed photo?
- Why does the picture make some participants seem natural, familiar, realistic, or understandable?
- Why does it make other participants seem unnatural, intensified, exaggerated, or ambiguous?
- Why does it situate some participants close to one another? Why does it situate others at a distance?
- Does it include elements that mirror or repeat one another in any significant way?
- Where does it position the action?
- Does it locate the participants in a likely or an unlikely setting?
- Does it depict a familiar or an unfamiliar cultural environment?
- Does it convey an action in the recent past or one in a remote past?

---

Here is Lionel Essrog's freewritten response to Questioning the Content of the Visual Portfolio. Notice especially how he makes a spontaneous connection between the pictures' collective content and the topic of his earlier reading in the chapter on the "Mommy Wars" in this anthology. Notice too how he questions whether he might be able to use arguments about the "Mommy Wars" to document his essay on the visual portfolio.

> The more I look at them, the more the puzzles in these pictures seem deliberate. In "Young woman using a laptop," the mother in the background seems annoyed at the woman using the computer. Does she want to attract her friend's attention? Does she resent being stuck with baby-care chores? Do we know whether she's really a friend, or even that she's the baby's mother? Is the picture trying to tell us something about the differences between the job of caring for children and the job of working at a computer?

Do the well-dressed parents in "Mother holding her daughter and using a computer" and "A father wearing a business suit and holding his baby" try to suggest that it's possible and even easy to have a career and raise children at the same time? These pictures might take part in the conversation about the "Mommy Wars" that we've been reading. I wonder whether I can use some of the arguments from that chapter to help my visual analysis in this chapter?

## EXERCISE 6.2

- Ask a friend or classmate to provide you with a snapshot of a family member whom you do not know. Study its details and the overall presentation and ask the questions suggested above. Construct a list of possible answers that point toward a specific scenario.
- Then, ask your friend to tell you the real story that explains the picture. Say, for example, that the picture represents a bride in her wedding gown sitting alone and crying or weeping. What has happened? Is she expressing nervous jitters? Where is the groom? Is he drowning jitters of his own with his pals at the reception bar? Is he eloping with a bridesmaid? Has a jealous rival just shot him? How do you respond when your friend tells you, "Oh, that's my mom's cousin when she got married in 1967. She just caught a piece of dust in her contact lens. Things like that happened in those days."
- What precautions might you take to correct your initial understanding of the picture?

## EXERCISE 6.3

- Form collaborative groups of five students each. Review the photographs that members have already culled from newspapers, magazines, books, Web sites such as Corbis.com, family snapshot collections, or on-the-spot pictures taken with personal cameras.
- Choose three or four pictures that typify diverse sorts of content, such as a news photo presenting an action shot of protest marchers, a magazine photo of last season's sportswear, a textbook photo of elected leaders shaking hands, and a family snapshot of dad doing the dishes.
- Examine and discuss the stories implied in these pictures, what has been selected and emphasized in them, what has been omitted, how the participants appear to relate to one another, what is likely or unlikely about the picture, and what is familiar or unfamiliar.
- If a written source has accompanied the picture, appoint a member of the group to read the source and evaluate how accurate the collaborative understanding of the picture proved to be.
- The group's recorder should take notes on this discussion and present a summary when the entire class reconvenes.

## ■ Viewing for Genre, Organization, and Stylistic Features

As we have seen in previous chapters of this book, genre, organization, and stylistic features largely reflect **conventions** that have been adopted by the **discourse community** that uses them. Like written texts, photographs have their own categories of genre, forms of organization, and range of stylistic features, all of which rely upon conventions that communities of photographers have established by imitation and example.

These conventions are not immutable—they do change over time. A century ago, for example, wedding portraits were stiffly posed compositions set indoors against artificial studio backdrops. At a later date, they became more relaxed in format and were often set outdoors against natural backgrounds in state parks or public gardens. In recent decades they have emulated "candid" shots sometimes arranged in highly informal situations. In any case, viewers recognize the photos as wedding portraits because they bear conventional characteristics associated with the form. Our recognition of these characteristics depends upon repeated encounters with their conventions. Like Poe's Dupin, we know what we see when we see it.

Recognizing conventions enables us better to assess the meanings and values at stake in the picture that embodies them. Misinterpreting a wedding portrait as a graduation photo, for example, would mean confusing the conventions of wedding gowns with those of academic gowns, of coupled pairings at weddings with those of individuals or mixed groups at graduations, of more or less formality at weddings with spontaneity and bustle at graduations.

The usefulness of applying conventions to both photographs and written texts is that they provide shortcuts that help communicate what is going on. We don't need to reinvent or reinterpret each element of the composition anew each time.

## Genre

The preceding paragraphs have already indicated some types of genre commonly encountered in photography, such as **documentary action photographs** in newspapers, magazines, and history books that purport to show what truly happened; **instructional photographs** in training manuals, cookbooks, and do-it-yourself brochures, which prompt us to achieve the same results depicted in them; **advertising photographs** in magazine ads, travel brochures, and supplier catalogues that encourage us to buy what's being sold; **recreational photographs** to entertain or amuse by depicting famous celebrities, unusual events, or far-off places; or **formal portraits** or **personal snapshots** to commemorate an event or help us recall a memory.

Photo 6–4, for example, presents an impeccably dressed and well-groomed young man in business attire improbably supporting a diapered baby; perhaps the photo marks a promotion that he has just received at work, or perhaps alternatively it reflects an advertising campaign to illustrate his company's friendly policies toward family values.

---

### QUESTIONS FOR VIEWING GENRE IN VISUAL ANALYSIS

- What principles of selection and omission govern the details?
- Which details are emphasized? Which ones are intensified? Which ones are exaggerated?
- What helps us to differentiate important from unimportant details?
- How do the images allow us to decipher hierarchies among the persons or actions represented?
- Which cultural values heighten the composition?
- Which historical values determine the details?
- Which positive and negative emotions are evoked by the picture?
- Which emotions are clearly legible? Which emotions seem ambiguous?
- How manipulated does the final result seem? Has the presenter manipulated the picture from the start by staging or posing it? Has the presenter manipulated it later by evidently adding to it, deleting from it, or rearranging what was there?

**EXERCISE 6.4**

- Form collaborative groups of five students each. Review the photographs that members have already culled or taken with their own cameras. Choose three or four pictures that typify diverse sorts of content, such as a news photo depicting a person or event of current interest; a magazine photo illustrating a do-it-yourself project; a textbook photo depicting features of the accompanying lesson; and a family portrait commemorating an event such as a graduation, an occasional reunion, or a milestone anniversary.

- Examine and discuss what purposes the pictures serve:
    - To document what happened?
    - To aid in instruction or installation?
    - To inform, advise, or warn?
    - To entertain?
    - To preserve personal or communal memories?

- The discussion should take account of what has been selected and emphasized in these pictures, what has been omitted, what is likely or unlikely about the details, and what is familiar or unfamiliar about them.

- If a written source has accompanied the picture, appoint a member of the group to read the source and evaluate how accurate the collaborative understanding of the picture proved to be.

- The group's recorder should take notes on this discussion and present a summary when the entire class reconvenes.


## Organization

Particular genres usually display specially marked features of organization appropriate for their content. News photos of current events, for example, may seem cluttered, haphazard, or occasionally awkward or distasteful, all in the interest of conveying the spontaneity of the moment and the surprise of being there when something unexpected happens. Photographs taken for instructional purposes may seem stripped down, focused on specific details, magnified in close-ups, and devoid of background distractions. Family snapshots taken on special occasions may favor poses and grouping found in professional images of the same sort: the recent graduate flanked by parents, the grandparents on their wedding anniversary surrounded by their grandchildren, the newborn held by one parent and supported by the other.

The conventions for such sorts of organization are so compelling that any variation in them—say, a too-stylized picture of an unruffled sports figure supposedly shown in the throes of performance, or of a bride surrounded by a dozen unrelated men in firefighting gear—would likely provoke comment. Poe's Dupin would certainly spin into action upon noting them. In Photo 6–3, for example, the baby appears unusually contented and the mother unusually engrossed in her computer; the lack of distraction in this picture focuses our attention on a moment of concentration in which the mother succeeds in double-tasking child-raising responsibilities with some other important activity.

---

**QUESTIONS FOR VIEWING ORGANIZATION IN VISUAL ANALYSIS**

- Which images are most legible in the picture?
- Which images receive the sharpest focus? Which ones appear blurred?
- Do commanding images appear in the center of the frame, or are they off to one side?
- What shapes or forms appear in the background?
- What shapes or forms appear in the foreground?
- What dominates the top of the picture?
- What dominates its bottom?
- What public images does this photograph evoke, such as well-known historical representations, celebrity shots, cultural landmarks, or advertising icons?
- Are there any parallels, duplications, or analogues within the picture, such as different people grouped in identical poses, or small children in the foreground imitating actions of adults in the background?
- Are there any contrasts, oppositions, or inversions within the picture, such as impoverished people mingling with wealthy people, or well-armed military men confronting ordinary women and children?
- What hierarchical relationships might we decipher in the picture?
- What parts present in the picture might suggest whole images that are not represented in it?

---

**EXERCISE 6.5**

- Form collaborative groups of five students each. Review the photographs that members have already culled or taken with their own cameras. Choose three or four pictures that typify different kinds of organization, such as a news photo presenting a candid shot of some current event, a magazine photo depicting a new line of seasonal clothing, an instructional photo illustrating some manual-operational process, and an entertainment photo parodying some promotional scheme or advertising gimmick.

- Examine and discuss what has been selected and emphasized in these pictures, what has been omitted, what appears focused or unfocused, what appears centered or uncentered, what familiar icons or representations seem implied in the particular arrangement, and what relationships of hierarchy or domination emerge among the various images.

- The discussion might also include some speculation about how the photographer may have manipulated the organization before taking the picture or while editing and printing it afterward.

- The group's recorder should take notes on this discussion and present a summary when the entire class reconvenes.

## Stylistic Features

Particular genres also display specially marked stylistic features appropriate for their content. Instructional photos aim toward low-contrast, blandly textured images in order to emphasize the major topic of instruction rather than idiosyncratic elements unrelated to it. Publicity photos incorporate high-contrast, strongly textured images in order to project a glamorous, attention-getting, one-of-a-kind ambience. These features usually make use of specific lighting techniques, high- or low-angle shots, elongated or foreshortened perspective, limited or exaggerated scale, and deliberately heightened or subdued color schemes.

Photo 6–1, for example, implies a strong tension between its background with the baby crying and its foreground with the young woman concentrating on her work. What is the picture telling us? As with principles of organization, certain features of style come to be associated with distinct genres, such as wide-angle shots for sports photography, medium close-up for entertainment photography, and telescopic close-up for scientific photography.

---

### QUESTIONS FOR VIEWING STYLISTIC FEATURES IN VISUAL ANALYSIS

- Does the picture appear posed, or is it spontaneous?
- How far away is the camera from the object photographed? Does the distance appear to be blown up or exaggerated through the use of a special lens or other special equipment?
- Is the camera placed above or below the object photographed? Is it tilted at an unusual angle?
- Does the lighting appear natural or artificial?
- Is the source of lighting in front of the object, behind it, or to one side of it?
- How do shadows emphasize (or perhaps deemphasize) the contours of the object?
- Were special filters used to heighten or soften the usual contrasts of texture and tone?
- Were some of these stylistic features achieved by using special printing, processing, or editing techniques after the picture was taken?
- What emotional effects do these stylistic choices evoke? Does the picture make us feel happy? sad? alienated? engaged?

---

### EXERCISE 6.6

- Form collaborative groups of five students each. Review the photographs that members have already culled or taken with their own cameras.
- Choose three or four pictures that typify different kinds of stylistic features, such as a news photo presenting an out-of-focus candid shot of some current event, a magazine photo depicting a resplendent new line of seasonal clothing, an instructional photo illustrating some intricate manual operation, and an entertainment photo parodying some already familiar advertising gimmick or promotional scheme.
- Examine and discuss how far the camera appears from the object photographed; whether it is placed above or below the object photographed; if it is tilted at an odd angle; whether the lighting appears natural or artificial; whether its source appears in front of the object, behind it, or to one side of it; how shadows emphasize (or perhaps deemphasize) the contours of the object?

- The discussion might also include some speculation about how the photographer might have manipulated the organization before taking the picture or while editing and printing it afterward.
- The group's recorder should take notes on this discussion and present a summary when the entire class reconvenes.

Here are Lionel Essrog's freewritten responses to Questions for Viewing Genre, Organization, and Stylistic Features in preparing for his paper on visual analysis. Notice especially how he begins to move from a negative mode of questioning the pictures to a positive mode of speculating about answers. In earlier freewritten responses, he expressed a great deal of bafflement about the photographs. Here he is actively searching for a way to formulate some positive argument about their meaning.

> The style of these pictures doesn't allow for too much information to define what's going on. The backgrounds in all of them are pretty bare and they tell us nothing in particular about where the actions are taking place. Their organization makes us concentrate on just the appearance of the people and a few objects (e.g., laptops, computers, telephones) that they are using. I wonder whether the genre of these pictures has something to do with advertising these objects? Or maybe advertising the clothes they are wearing? Perhaps that's true in Photos 3 and 4. But in Photos 1 and 2 the computer equipment and the clothes are not especially well defined. There the emphasis is on the people's faces. So perhaps the story about childraising and careers is what's most important after all. If only the outlines of this story might be clearer! Perhaps I could shuffle some of the possibilities so that, instead of trying to find the single master key, I could allow elements from each of them to shed light on the others.

## ■ Viewing for Rhetorical Context

Visual images have rhetorical contexts just as written texts do, and they also present arguments. First, they originate with **people who produced them** and who, like those who produce written texts, have ideas, emotions, and values that they want to communicate. Second, they aim at **viewers** whom they seek to inform, persuade, and perhaps motivate to action, just as written texts aim at readers for the same purposes. Third, like written texts, pictures themselves are embedded in social and cultural situations to which producers and viewers may react in agreement or in opposition—or in many ways in between.

The range of in-between reactions may be astonishingly broad. Some pictures purport to **gratify** viewers with soothing representations of pleasant and familiar situations: think of pictures in a church bulletin celebrating the community's achievements, or pictures in an alumni magazine recalling old friends in a festive mood. Flip ahead to Photo 17–1 in Chapter 17, with its image of a family representing three generations of children, parents, and grandparents. This example presents a highly idealized version of an attractive, intact, seemingly happy family unit.

Other images can **disturb** viewers with representations of violent or repulsive behavior: think of pictures in a sensationalist tabloid displaying the ravages of freak accidents or irresponsible conduct. For an example of disturbing social commentary, flip ahead to Photo 17–17 in Chapter 17, which depicts the harsh treatment accorded by U.S. Border

Control to illegal immigrants. Still other photographs may **attract** viewers in subtle and intriguing ways, persuading them to look closer and perhaps change their minds about a certain issue: think of pictures in commercial advertising that urge you to switch your brands of shampoo or footwear.

In each case, such pictures deploy **conventional or unconventional** images in a rhetorical context. Photo 10–17, for example, depicts a homeless man pushing a shopping cart filled with his belongings. The expected response to such an image would be sorrow for his plight. In the background, however, the photograph depicts the gleaming skyscrapers of downtown Denver, inviting a response of awe at their magnificence. Juxtaposed, the responses demand our reconsideration. What links homelessness to corporate America?

Pictures have an extraordinary persuasive power that may supplement, complement, or go far beyond the power of words **to compel action or assent**. The most familiar genres of photography have a cogent **normalizing effect**. A group photo of schoolmates in a classroom, for example, will show each child in presentable dress at his or her best behavior; the purpose is not just to offer parents a sweet picture of their offspring, or to afford children some memory of a classroom that in fact never appeared that way on a day-to-day basis, but rather to project an **idealized image** of what presentable dress and good behavior should be and of what each student could strive toward.

Photo 17–1, for example, might have appeared in a parenting magazine photo spread on how to unite three generations of a family. Families whose composition, temperament, and financial means differ from those in the photo might question what habits they need to change or cultivate so as to enjoy the same activities. Poe's Dupin would point out that few families match the "normal" description pictured in the article, even though the magazine is promoting the belief that everyone can aspire to this image.

Images that convey a normalizing effect contrast with those that convey an **alienating effect**. Such an effect serves to warn, admonish, or advise its viewers, as in photojournalism that documents the ramifications of alcohol or drug addiction. It can also serve to stigmatize persons or groups by evoking deformity, oddity, or even malevolence, as in tabloid depictions of obesity or political terrorism. Photo 17–16 shows that in some communities drivers are warned of illegal border crossings as though immigrants were stupefied wild animals. Sometimes the effect can be used for sheer entertainment, as in photo collages that celebrate nonconformity or stubborn eccentricity.

Normalizing and alienating effects converge in **advertising** photographs, which aim to convince viewers that it's normal to prefer one brand over another (especially when it identifies the customer as belonging to an admired group) yet attract the viewer's attention with incongruous, unconventional images. If normalizing effects persuade us to imitate certain behaviors and alienating effects persuade us to avoid others, advertising effects persuade us to buy a product (such as dish detergent) or buy into a movement (such as to vote for a political candidate).

Photo 6–3, for example, might serve as an illustration to advertise the desktop computer or the mother's clothing: the baby appears placid and the mother comfortable, as though her access to the computer and her semi-business attire made it possible for her to double-task while caring for her child. All three forms of photographic persuasion show how pictures can move viewers with a rhetoric of imagery instead of words, and how images conduct arguments by manipulating evidence, heightening emotions, changing attitudes, and summoning responses.

When you think of images as doing these things, you will then have a framework for posing questions about their rhetorical context. Imagine that such pictures are entering a conversation about an issue that prompts competing claims. The evidence for these claims is visual, and it can be interpreted from several perspectives. Try to determine what perspective the picture adopts on the information that it presents and how it invites viewers to accept such a perspective as reasonable and advantageous or to reject it as incongruous, invalid, or harmful. Construe the picture in the framework of an argument that challenges you to respond with your own argument about the information it presents.

---

### QUESTIONS FOR VIEWING RHETORICAL CONTEXT IN VISUAL ANALYSIS

- Who is the producer of the image and for whom does he or she work?
- Who are the intended viewers, and what experiences, expectations, preferences, and attitudes do they have?
- Does the picture seek to attract these viewers? Gratify them? Challenge their assumptions? Motivate them to some specific action?
- What might be controversial about the photo's attraction, gratification, confrontation, or motivation?
- What normalizing effects does the picture suggest? Do its images invite acceptance and imitation? Do they invite rejection or attack?
- What alienating effects does the picture suggest? Do its images invite consideration and appraisal? Do they invite resistance and criticism?
- Do its images suggest the drawbacks and limitations of standardized thinking?
- What advertising or promotional effects does the picture evoke? Do its images move us to buy a product or buy into ideas represented in them?
- Do the images convey options or alternatives to the outcomes suggested by what they represent?

---

Here are Lionel Essrog's freewritten responses to Viewing for Rhetorical Context in preparing for his essay on the visual portfolio. Notice how he comes close to expressing the thesis that he will eventually state in his essay on pages 230–33.

I don't know who the photographers of these pictures were, or where the photographs originally appeared. But their organization and stylistic features lead me to wonder whether they belong to the genre of advertising. Since I can't specify what kind of product they could be pushing, I wonder whether it's some more general normalizing effect that they're promoting. Despite all the chaos that could be going on with the babies, the parents seem pretty cool and collected. Their attitude seems pretty close to being ideal. In the context of the "Mommy Wars" essays that we read, these pictures could be poster–children (no pun intended) for a marriage of child–raising and the workplace. Still, the details are not exactly tidy. I could argue that they talk back to an idealizing attitude and even challenge the ideals imaged on the surface.

## EXERCISE 6.7

- Form collaborative groups of five students each. Review the photographs that members have already culled or taken with their own cameras. Choose three or four pictures that typify different kinds of persuasion, such as a photo from a school or social club depicting members pursuing a common activity, a photo from a health magazine depicting the effects of a high-cholesterol, low-exercise diet, and a news photo depicting a candidate for political election chatting up voters during his or her leisure time.
- Examine and discuss how the photographs represent desirable activities, undesirable activities, and activities that may be assessed either positively or negatively according to the particular context at the time. The discussion might also include some speculation about how the photographer might have manipulated the organization before taking the picture or while editing and printing it afterward.
- The group's recorder should take notes on the discussion, and when the entire class reconvenes, he or she should summarize these notes for the class.

Now turn back to the visual portfolio on pages 217–18 above and review these pictures again. Use your review to evaluate the following essay by Lionel Essrog based upon them. The assignment, as you remember, was as follows:

In an essay of 1,000 words, analyze the form and content of one or more photographs from our visual portfolio on "Moms, Dads, and Babies." Discuss the relationships among the persons or objects pictured and offer a plausible argument about the rhetorical context of the picture or pictures you've selected.

You've already read Lionel's freewritten responses to the questions for Previewing; for Viewing for Content; for Viewing for Genre, Organization, and Stylistic Features; and for Viewing for Rhetorical Context. Here is Lionel's completed essay, represented as a finished product after initial drafting, revisions, copy editing, and a final revision for presentation in this anthology.

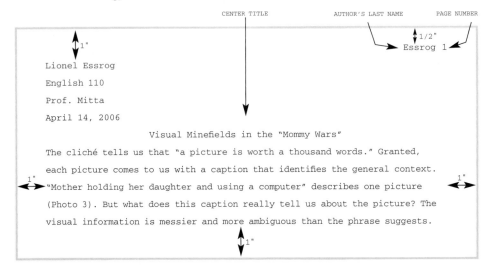

CENTER TITLE                    AUTHOR'S LAST NAME         PAGE NUMBER

1/2"
Essrog 1

1"

Lionel Essrog

English 110

Prof. Mitta

April 14, 2006

Visual Minefields in the "Mommy Wars"

The cliché tells us that "a picture is worth a thousand words." Granted, each picture comes to us with a caption that identifies the general context. "Mother holding her daughter and using a computer" describes one picture (Photo 3). But what does this caption really tell us about the picture? The visual information is messier and more ambiguous than the phrase suggests.

1"

Use 8½" by 11" paper for each page. Use double spaces between all lines. Left justify all lines in the text of the paper. Do not right justify, even if your word processor provides this feature.

INDENT FIVE SPACES                                    AUTHOR'S LAST NAME        PAGE NUMBER

1"
↕                                                        ↕ 1/2"
                                                    ➤ Essrog 2 ◄

Its details collide with one another, and that's a good thing because this
collision forces us to look closer at the picture for shades of meanings that
the caption glides over. A nicely dressed young mother seems in control while
she talks on the telephone with a baby in her lap, but she doesn't notice
that the child is toying with her computer and may be deleting important
documents that she has stored on it. While the caption might suggest what is
going on, the photo is doing much more. On the one hand, it wants to idealize
the mother's efficiency and smart-looking appearance and to present the
situation as something normal and expected. On the other, it leaves the
barn door open for chaos to break loose. I am going to argue that details in
these pictures talk back to their idealizing functions and pose a challenge
to the otherwise straightforward visual images on the surface.

    The picture captioned "Mother holding her daughter and using a
computer" (Photo 3) provides a clear contrast. Here the mother is well-
dressed, confident, and composed while she fingers the keyboard of her
computer. The baby is equally calm and composed, and even mimics her
mother's attention to the computer equipment. While the mother focuses on
the keyboard and the data that she is feeding into the computer, the baby
looks at the screen in amusement. Still, the picture is highly abstract.

1"
↔ Except for the mother, child, and computer, it offers no other details to    ↔ 1"
cement its narrative. The background is a flat white wall, and the table on
which the computer rests allows no clutter or confusion to divert anyone's
attention. Real life does not look like this. I wonder how or whether the
picture represents life as we or others know it. The picture's idealizing
function rules its organization. It seems to be saying that any young
mother can take charge and attend to her baby's needs (and note that it is
only one baby and not two or three or more) while also managing to catch up
on a bit of her professional work as she stands in front of her computer.

    The same can be said for "A father wearing a business suit and holding
his baby" (Photo 4). Whoever saw a businessman posing for a picture with a
child in diapers, unless someone wanted to use it as some photo-op for a
political campaign or for a better-business family-values blurb? This
picture's genre resembles a formal portrait, except for the baby's diapers.
Perhaps this young father wanted a household snapshot before running off
to the office one morning or upon returning from it one evening. As with
"Mother holding her daughter," the ambiance is idealized. The picture
almost screams at us that the good life is possible for everyone. And yet,
when push comes to shove, it's more likely than not that this father's wife
is a rather privileged stay-at-home mom. Since writers as diverse as the
feminist scholar Linda R. Hirshman in "Homeward Bound," the magazine

↕ 1"

commentator Katha Pollitt in "Desperate Housewives of the Ivy League?"
and law professor Tracey Meares in her "Critique of 'Many Women at Elite
Colleges Set Career Path to Motherhood'" point out that this option is
available to only a small minority of families, the picture has already
passed beyond the attainability of mainstream North America.

The fallout from the "Mommy Wars" dominates yet another picture in our
portfolio, "Young woman using a laptop." Here the caption only increases
the near-total ambiguity of the picture. The photograph depicts two women
and a baby. One woman is seated at a laptop. The other stands behind her
in soft focus holding the baby. Which woman is the baby's mother? In one
scenario, the seated woman might be the mother, and she has handed her baby
to a friend or relative while she catches up on some work at her computer.
The agitated look on the other woman's face suggests that she may be
uncomfortable taking care of the baby and is hoping that the computer
session will soon come to an end. The conflict in the picture pits a
nicelydressed, fairly self-assured young woman in the foreground against a
vaguely defined, semianxious counterpart with a baby in the background. Its
narrative suggests a tension between them, but no single detail or set of
details in the picture unlocks the exact source of this tension.

In another scenario, the standing woman could be the baby's mother,
and from the perspective of her child-care responsibilities she is looking
at her friend with some envy or regret at the relative freedom of her
computer work. In yet another scenario, the face of the standing woman may
betray neither discomfort nor envy or regret; instead, perhaps the baby has
developed a fever or a rash, and her friend is searching the Internet for
first-aid advice. In a fourth, but totally fictional scenario, the young
woman at the laptop may be day-dreaming about her friend with the baby
in a soft-focus background.

Which scenario is the most probable one? I'd shuffle them together to see
how one explanation might illuminate another one. Identifying the standing
woman with the baby's mother, I'd say that the picture presents a series of
conflicts that challenge her composure. It exposes her anxieties about caring
for her child while it also arouses her wish for the security that her friend
in the foreground seems to enjoy. At the same time it suggests that the woman
in the foreground inhabits her own private world, at least for the time
being, immune from the push and pull of emotions that accompany motherhood in
all its complex forms. The picture captures the complexity of these feelings
as it juxtaposes the two spheres of motherhood and working career woman.

One feature prominent in all four photographs is absolutely certain.
Taken together, this group of pictures illustrates the contradictions of the
"Mommy Wars" that we read about in Chapter 3 of our anthology. The women

with babies on the telephone in Photo 2 and at the computer in Photo 3 project competence, success, and career-oriented drive, even if the baby provides a realistic distraction in the first instance and an idealized accompaniment in the second. The father with the baby in Photo 4 stands in a clearly idealized portrait pose. All three pictures imply a normalizing effect as they depict working mothers and fathers taking care of young babies without too many stresses and strains that we know in the real world. Photo 1 by contrast sheds light upon a less tidy aspect of the contrast between the ideal and the real. It consequently draws the accompanying photos into a contemporary dialogue about parenthood, working adults, and stay-at-home moms. It seems to say that the simple assumptions about family life in a world that never really was are always subject to debate.

AFTER THE FIRST LINE OF EACH ENTRY,
INDENT FIVE SPACES.

DOUBLE SPACE

↕1/2"
Essrog 5

↕1"
Works Cited

Anonymous. *A Father Wearing a Business Suit and Holding His Baby.*
    fotosearch.com. 23 March 2006 <http://www.fotosearch.com/
    BCP102/bcp002-47/jpg.html>.

Anonymous. *Mother Holding Her Daughter and Using Her Computer.*
    fotosearch.com. 23 March 2006 <http://www.fotosearch.com/SBY258/
    306007rkn/jpg.html>.

Anonymous. *People, Keyboard, Telephone.* fotosearch.com. 23 March 2006
    <http://www.fotosearch.com/SPS108/1166r-4726a/jpg.html>.

Anonymous. *Young Woman Using a Laptop.* fotosearch.com. 23 March 2006
    <http://www.fotosearch.com/SBY258/306004rkn/jpg.html>.

Hirshman, Linda R. "Homeward Bound." *The American Prospect* 16.12 (December
    2005): 20-26.

Meares, Tracey. "Critique of 'Many Women at Elite Colleges Set Career Path
    to Motherhood.'" http://www.blackprof.com/archives/2005/09. Accessed
    April 4, 2006.

Pollitt, Katha. "Desperate Housewives of the Ivy League?" *The Nation*, 281.12
    (October 17, 2005): 14, 4 Apr. 2006 <http://www.the nation.com/
    doc/20051017/pollitt>.

↕1"

INCLUDE IN THE LIST OF WORKS CITED *ONLY* SOURCES THAT
ARE REFERRED TO DIRECTLY IN THE TEXT OF THE PAPER.

## EXERCISE 6.8

- Form collaborative groups of five students each. Members should review the notes the recorder has taken on the preceding exercises in this chapter. Each group should then summarize for itself which principles for Previewing; for Viewing for Content; for Viewing for Genre, Organization, and Stylistic Features; and for Viewing for Rhetorical Context are the most useful ones for writing a paper of visual analysis on the portfolio in this chapter. The group's recorder should organize this summary.

- One student in the group should read Lionel Essrog's paper aloud while the group's other members follow the paper in their textbooks. As the paper is read, each student should take note of features that he or she thinks could still profit from revision.

- After the paper has been read, the group's reporter should then repeat the principles that the group has emphasized for Previewing and Viewing, pausing after each one so that members can comment on how they might apply to features that Lionel Essrog might revise in his paper.

- The group's recorder should take notes on which features Lionel should revise, and when the entire class reconvenes, he or she should convey them to the class. The class should them compare recommendations for revision that the groups have formulated.

## WORK CITED

Poe Edgar Allan. *Selected Titles.* New York: Oxford University Press, 1998.

# Seven

# Synthesis

## ANALYSIS AND SYNTHESIS

Analysis, the topic of Chapters 4, 5, and 6, is the precursor of synthesis. Without it, the broad overview that sustains a synthesis cannot take place. Analysis requires you to perform two operations: (1) Break up the text into its component parts, and (2) Examine the relationship of the parts to each other and to the text as a whole. Synthesis asks you to (1) perform these analysis operations on two or more texts, (2) identify and group textual components that share common attributes, and (3) repackage these components in a new composition.

Let's say your professor asks you to synthesize the arguments presented in three reading selections in this book. First, you must unravel each author's line of reasoning. This analysis will enable you to extract threads—thematic elements, comparable features, similar ideas—that you can weave into the fabric of your synthesis essay.

---

### SYNTHESIS

To synthesize is to:

- Analyze two or more texts that share a topic or interest
- Identify grounds for grouping the textual components
- Organize this textual material under a controlling theme

---

A synthesis requires you to read and analyze an array of texts—for example, two articles from academic journals, a chapter from a book, and a column from a newspaper. As you read, you try to identify a controlling idea. Then you extract various bits of text and relate them to each other on the basis of thematic consistency. Your reason for performing these operations depends on your rhetorical purpose.

Suppose the purpose of your writing is to define poverty. You would read various texts on the topic, discover commonalities among the texts, select pertinent ideas from each text, mesh them together, and form a definition.

Let's take another purpose. Your politics professor asks you to chart the development of the Arab-Israeli controversy. You would read various texts dealing with the controversy, identify common elements among the texts, combine the historical perspectives, and construct a coherent narrative account.

The preceding examples reveal a distinction between synthesis assignments and comparison and contrast assignments. When you write a comparison-contrast essay, you will work with texts that converge on the same topic and share similarities and differences. For example, you might read two journal articles on the topic of health-care reform and compare and contrast the authors' views. The texts already converge on the same topic, however different their premises and conclusions may be. When you write a synthesis essay, you may be working with texts that focus on separate, discrete topics or issues. Your first task is to analyze the texts in order to identify constituent elements of the interlocking materials that you will be able to combine into a single, unified piece of writing.

## ■ PROCESS OF WRITING SYNTHESIS ESSAYS

### ■ Examine the Assignment

As with any assignment, when you receive a directive to write a synthesis essay, you need to ask yourself the Questions for Analyzing Writing Assignments (page 33). If the professor specifies the topic and supplies the readings, you will have much less work to do than if you have to do library-based research, select the readings, and limit the scope of the topic yourself. Assignment A is much less demanding than the open-ended Assignment B.

### ASSIGNMENT A

Are the "Mommy Wars" real, or do they represent a fictitious debate promoted by the media? Write a five-page essay in which you synthesize the arguments in Judith Stadtman Tucker's "The Least Worst Choice: Why Mothers 'Opt' Out of the Workforce," Katha Pollitt's "Dangerous Housewives of the Ivy League," and Linda Hirshman's "Homeward Bound."

### ASSIGNMENT B

Recently the topic of the "Mommy Wars" has received considerable attention in the press. Write a five-page essay in which you synthesize key arguments in this controversy.

Both assignments ask the student to synthesize. However, sometimes students do not receive such explicit clues as "synthesize the arguments." Many of the directives we list on page 33 might entail synthesis. The determining factor would be the number of sources the writer is expected to use. An important question to ask your professor is "Which sources am I to use?" If your professor expects you to draw upon multiple sources for your paper, then you know you will be writing a synthesis.

One of the biggest problems students encounter when they write synthesis essays is that instead of taking time to adequately analyze the readings and puzzle out the commonalities among the texts, they rush into the assignment and they end up producing a pastiche of summaries instead of a tightly woven synthesis. The result is that sources determine the purpose and direction of the paper instead of the writer determining the purpose. For example, in response to Assignment A, a student writes, "Recently, prominent journalists and scholars have written incisive arguments about the clash between stay-at-home mothers and career mothers." Working with the reading selections in Chapter 3, the writer develops this anemic thesis by summarizing Stadtman Tucker's, Pollitt's, and Hirshman's arguments, devoting two to three body paragraphs to each author. Then she concludes her essay with the comment, "Stadtman Tucker, Pollitt, and Hirshman agree that the Mommy Wars are real and continue to be controversial."

What the student should have done was examine the assignment to determine a firm rhetorical purpose, analyze the three texts to discover subtopics they share in common, establish grounds for the synthesis, formulate a thesis, and pluck from the sources only the sentences and passages that directly relate to the thesis. The student needed to go beyond a simplistic presentation of information in the reading sources. A synthesis is not a compilation of summaries.

## ■ Determine Your Rhetorical Purpose: Purposes for Synthesizing Sources

Writers produce syntheses for clear-cut reasons. One purpose is to *provide background and explain a topic, problem, or issue to readers.* We see this purpose realized in reports; for example, "Climate Change 2001: Synthesis Report," edited by Robert T. Watson of the Core Writing Team of the Cambridge Earth, Environment, and Atmospheric Sciences. In college writing classes, this genre of synthesis is called explanatory synthesis. An **explanatory synthesis** *offers thorough but relatively nonjudgmental analysis of the texts in order to present informative results in a straightforward manner.* Such a synthesis often tries to define a topic or issue in an expository style that emphasizes the coverage of data rather than any further questioning or interpretation of data. The writer makes a point; for example, "Here is some important information you should be aware of," but does not advance a firm thesis. The writer says to the reader: "You decide how you would like to interpret this information."

A related purpose for synthesizing sources is to *provide background and explain a topic, problem, or issue by examining a wide array of published research studies.* This genre of synthesis is called a **literature review**. In some cases, the writer's goal is simply to communicate the research findings to an interested audience. For example, Greg Druian and Jocelyn A. Butler, researchers at the Northwest Regional Educational Laboratory, published "Schooling Practices and At-Risk Youth: What the Research Shows" in order to inform teachers about educational research. In other cases, the writer's objective is to *demonstrate her grasp of a research field by reviewing a wide range of published research.* Occasionally, literature reviews written for this purpose are self-contained, stand-alone essays, but more often they are part of a larger project. They precede a report describing a research study the writer has carried out.

A third purpose for synthesizing is *to extract from the sources textual evidence and material that will support your thesis.* The thesis is the chief point you are making in your essay. Some refer to a thesis as a claim. We use "claim" to discuss the theses of the argument essays in this chapter. A thesis advances the writer's interpretation or position. It is not a neutral statement. In university classes, you will be writing about complex issues and in so doing entering conversations that are already underway. The best way to join these conversations is to read what others have written about the issues. After you have learned about the issues and thought enough about them to be able to formulate a thesis, you will then decide how you will synthesize these expert voices in you own text. We call this a **thesis-driven synthesis**.

A fourth purpose for synthesizing is *to extract from the sources textual evidence for an argument essay*. In this chapter, we discuss the explanatory synthesis, the literature review, and the thesis-driven synthesis. Chapter 8 is devoted to argument synthesis.

## ■ Ask Questions to Identify Relationships among the Sources

### Baseline Questions

In Chapter 4, we emphasized the importance of questions. Questioning, the frame of mind that favors analysis, is also the attitude of mind you need for synthesis. Whether your professor has presented you with a set of readings or you have conducted library research and discovered your own texts, at the time of your initial reading ask yourself the five baseline questions in the following box.

---

**BASELINE QUESTIONS FOR INITIAL READING**

- What is the major topic that is treated by all the texts?
- What subtopics run across some or all of the texts?
- Do the texts discuss a controversy or debate?
- How do the texts talk to each other with respect to the topic, subtopics, and/or controversy?
- How will my answers to Questions 1 through 4 help me fulfill my rhetorical purpose?

---

Responses to questions 1, 2, and 3 in the box above will inform an explanatory synthesis or a review of the literature, and responses to questions 1 through 4 will inform both a thesis-driven synthesis and an argument synthesis.

### EXERCISE 7.1

- Divide the class into groups of three.
- Each group will choose three reading selections from Chapter 3. Each member of the group will read the selection and respond to the five Baseline Questions for Initial Reading.
- Group members will compare their responses and reach consensus.
- Then a representative from each group will report to the class. The professor will use a graphic overview to map the various group findings.

### In-Depth Questions

After you have conducted an initial reading of the texts, reread each text searching for ways in which it relates to the other sources. Ask yourself the questions in the following box.

---

**IN-DEPTH QUESTIONS FOR IDENTIFYING RELATIONSHIPS AMONG TEXTS**

- Are there other common threads running through this text and the other texts?
- Do the texts contain similar key words or phrases?
- Does the text provide background or additional information about points that are presented in other sources? Additional details about points made in other sources? Evidence for points made in another text?
- Are there places where this text contradicts or disagrees with other texts I have read?
- Are there places where the text supports or agrees with other sources?
- Are there cause-and-effect relationships between this text and the other sources?
- Are there time relationships among the texts?
- Does this text contain elements that can be compared or contrasted with those in other sources?
- Are there any other ways I can categorize the ideas in the reading sources?

---

**EXERCISE 7.2**

- Reconvene the groups from the previous exercise.
- Each group should respond to the same set of readings using In-depth Questions for Identifying Relationships Among Texts.
- Appoint a representative from each group to report to the class.

## ■ Formulate a Thesis and Review the Texts

After you have responded to the questions and discovered the common elements in the sources, decide on the points you wish to communicate to your readers, and formulate a working thesis. Next, review the texts for the evidence and support you will need to develop each of your points. As you reread the texts, mark or copy into your writer's notebook the bits of information that relate to your argument. When you have located a sufficient amount of relevant information, draft your essay. As you write, you will return to the texts to decide whether to paraphrase, quote, or summarize the supporting material.

In the next section of this chapter, we will discuss the explanatory synthesis, the review of the literature, and the thesis-driven synthesis.

## ■ PROCESS OF WRITING AN EXPLANATORY SYNTHESIS

The purpose of an explanatory synthesis is to unfold or unravel a topic to make it clearer to readers. An explanatory synthesis might crack open a concept, place an issue in an historical context, or clarify the sides in a controversy. The synthesis is objective: The writer is reporting on the sources rather than interpreting or evaluating. It is important to remember that the "reporting" is selective. The writer identifies a subtopic running across the texts and then selects from the texts bits of information related to the subtopic. The writer does not summarize each text in its totality. Such an operation would result in a string of summaries rather than a synthesis.

To illustrate, let's return to the conversation about stay-at-home mothers and working mothers and follow our student, Megan Farr, as she writes an explanatory synthesis based on the reading selections in Chapter 3.

## ■ Decide on Rhetorical Purpose

Megan decides her purpose is to place the "Mommy Wars" controversy in an historical context. In response to the Baseline Questions for Initial Reading (p. 238), Megan has:

- Identified the major issue: whether mothers should return to work or stay at home to take care of their children
- Selected *"historical context" as a subtopic running across the texts* and decided that there are six reading selections in Chapter 3 that will be useful:

  Deirdre D. Johnston and Debra H. Swanson, "Motherhood Ideologies and Motherhood Myths"

  Judith Stadtman Tucker, "The Least Worst Choice: Why Women 'Opt' Out of the Workforce"

  Louise Story, "Many Women at Elite Colleges Set Career Path to Motherhood"

  Katha Pollitt, "Desperate Housewives of the Ivy League?"

  Linda R. Hirshman, "Homeward Bound"

  Frances Rosenbluth, "Mother Yale"

- Begun to analyze what each text contributes to the historical context and how the texts talk to each other with respect to the subtopic

Turning her attention to the In-Depth Questions for Identifying Relationships Among Texts (p. 239), Megan focuses on time relationships and references to historical context. Then, as she reexamines each text, she looks to see if one text:

- Provides background or additional information and details about the points in other texts
- Provides evidence for points made in another text
- Contradicts, disagrees, or supports another text

Megan marks the texts and copies passages into her writer's notebook. Then she studies the bits of text she has selected to see if she can impose some type of order on them. Since the purpose of her explanatory synthesis is to provide her readers with historical background, Megan decides to order the bits of text chronologically. She does this by constructing a timeline. (See Figure 7–1.)

## ■ Formulate Working Thesis

Megan's next step is to formulate a working thesis. Remember that an explanatory synthesis is a straightforward, objective reporting of the sources. Her thesis will be descriptive, not persuasive. As a preliminary thesis, she writes:

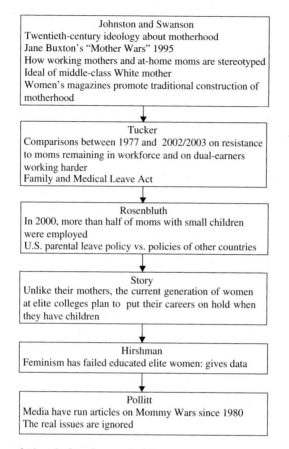

**Figure 7–1   Timeline of Historical Background on "Mommy Wars"**

*Whether women should stay at home or return to the workforce after having children is a long-standing debate that has recently been reignited.*

After she writes a draft of the essay, she may decide to sharpen this thesis. Consider other versions of theses she might write for an explanatory synthesis. If her subtopic was to clarify the sides in the controversy, she might have written:

*On the issue of the "Mommy Wars," Louise Story, David Brooks, and Don Feder advocate full–time motherhood whereas Judith Stadtman Tucker, Linda R. Hirshman, and Katha Pollitt argue that women should have the opportunity to return to the workforce after having children.*

Suppose her subtopic was the media's focus. Her thesis might be:

A number of pundits argue that the media's focus should be on issues such as affordable child care, parental leave, and flexible work hours, not on the so-called "Mommy Wars."

As Megan develops each of these theses, she would objectively describe the views of the various authors. She would not state her own position or make a claim.

We present Megan's exploratory synthesis in an annotated and highlighted version in order to illustrate how she draws together summaries, quotations, and paraphrases from a wide range of sources.

Megan Farr

Professor Kennedy

Academic Writing II

20 March 2006

The "Mommy Wars"

The long-standing debate over whether women should remain at home or resume their careers after having children has been reignited. One would have thought that this controversy had played itself out back in the Sixties when feminists were advocating for equal treatment in the workforce. Instead, the debate has been smoldering, and now it has been rekindled by a number of journalists, scholars, and academics. Luckily, for those of us who were not yet born in the Sixties, these writers have contextualized the issue and provided us with useful background.

*How Texts Talk to Each Other*

In the review-of-the-literature section of their research study, "Invisible Mothers: A Content Analysis of Motherhood Ideologies and Myths in Magazines," Deirdre D. Johnston and Debra H. Swanson discuss ideologies and myths related to motherhood. They point out that the white, middle class, stay-at-home mother is a "romanticized ideal" (21). They cite research to that effect, and as they put it, "Motherhood is a social and historical construction. . . . The 'traditional family' with a wage-earner father and a stay at home mother is an historical and cultural aberration" (21).

*Quotation*

Summarizing the work of Jane Buxton who in 1998 used the term "Mother Wars," Johnston and Swanson explain that working mothers are typically stereotyped as efficient but cold-hearted "Superwomen" and stay-at-home mothers as warm, smiling "Earth Mothers" (21-22). Johnston and Swanson review research that explores the ideologies behind these stereotypes and the extent to which those ideologies are influenced by patriarchal views. They go on to add that many people think the experiences of white, middle-class, stay-at-home mothers are the ideal, and the experiences of other types of mother are imperfect. They call attention to a contradiction, however, scholarship by Blair-Loy and by Chang that points out:

*Summary and paraphrase*

*Johnston and Swanson draw from Buxton*

*Johnston and Swanson draw from Blair-Loy and from Chang*

Farr 2

*Quotation* —
> Although the conventional motherhood ideology maintains that mothers should not work outside the home, economically or financially privileged mothers continue to hire working class women and Women of Color, who are often mothers themselves, to perform the more arduous childcare work. (22)

Johnston and Swanson's 2003 research study of the representations of women in contemporary women's magazines concluded *Quotation* — that these publications "persist in the promotion of traditional constructions of motherhood" (29).

The same year Johnston and Swanson published their research study, the *New York Times Magazine* featured a cover story entitled "The Opt-Out Revolution" by Linda Belkin. Belkin writes about Princeton alumnae who left their high-powered careers to pursue full-time child rearing. According to Judith Stadtman Tucker, who critiques Belkin's article *Tucker* in "The Least Worst Choice: Why Women 'Opt' Out of the *critique* Workforce," a positive outcome of Belkin's piece was that *Belkin* it "spawned a deluge of intelligent criticism discussing *Quotation* — the realities of motherhood, and barriers to women's leadership."

*Quotation* —
> Tucker observes, "Cultural resistance to mothers remaining in the paid workforce is less strident today than it was in the 1970s and 80s, but it hasn't disappeared."

*Summary and paraphrase* — Tucker explains that in 1977 only 26 percent of men thought women should work; by 2002 two out of five felt it was appropriate. Tucker also provides information about the changed conditions of the workplace. She reports that Americans are working harder. In 2001 dual-earner couples with children under eighteen worked over ninety-one hours a week whereas in 1977 they worked eighty-one hours. She goes on to add that "mothers' weekly hours of job-related work" jumped form thirty-eight hours in 1977 to forty-three hours in 2003. Tucker reminds us that the Family and Medical Leave Act, which grants women a mere twelve weeks of unpaid parental leave, was not passed until 1993. Tucker notes that *Quotation* — the provisions of this act are "downright skimpy compared to the benefits provided to working families in Western Europe."

Political scientist Frances Rosenbluth agrees that *Rosenbluth* government support is miserly, and she says this explains *agrees with* why "in 2000, more than half of the mothers of small children *Tucker* *Quotation* — were employed outside the home." Most women cannot afford to

Paraphrase — become full-time stay-at-home mothers. Rosenbluth comments, as did Johnston and Swanson before her, that wealthy women can afford careers because they hire low income women to take care of their children. She notes that there is serious

*Rosenbluth brings up point made by Johnston and Swanson*

Quotation — "intra-gender inequality in the United States."

Rosenbluth makes her remarks in the *Yale Magazine* in an article she wrote in response to a front-page feature in the *New York Times*, "Many Women at Elite Colleges Set Career Path to Motherhood," by Louise Story. According to Story, the current generation of women at elite colleges holds surprisingly traditional views about childrearing. The women plan to put their high-powered careers on hold in order to stay home to take care of their children. As Story puts it, this is a new trend because the mothers of these women planned to maintain full-time careers even though they may have modified their expectations after having children. Story bases her claim on a study of 138 freshmen and senior women at Yale. She uses as further evidence alumni surveys from both Yale and the Harvard Business School that reveal that for graduates of the past twenty to thirty years, work outside the home is the primary activity of men rather than women.

*Rosenbluth responds to Story*

Summary and paraphrase —

Story's article generated a vigorous response, including a very controversial critique by Brandeis legal scholar, Linda Hirshman. Writing in *The American Prospect*, Hirshman points out that census figures show "the percentage of women, even mothers in full- or part-time employment, rose robustly through the 1980s and early 90s." She goes on to add that the numbers for working mothers have decreased but only modestly since 1998.

*Hirshman responds to Story*

Quotation —

Hirshman contends that feminism has failed educated elite women because there are "few women in the corridors of power, and marriage is essentially unchanged." She cites data, her own study and other surveys, that show "elite women aren't resisting tradition." Hirshman blames these women's attitudes on feminism's desire to give women a choice between work and mothering. She argues, "They don't know that feminism, in collusion with traditional society, just passed the gendered family on to them to choose."

Quotation —

Quotation —

Writing in *The Nation*, Katha Pollitt observes that the press, especially the *New York Times*, has been highlighting

Farr 4

**Paraphrase** —
the "Mommy Wars" for over twenty-five years. She says Jack
Shafer, columnist for the online magazine Slate, discovered
that in 1980, the *Times* ran a story entitled "Many Women Now
Say They'd Pick Family over Career" which was comparable to
Linda Belkin's 2003 article and identical to Louise Story's
2005 piece. Pollitt concludes her own article, "Desperate
Housewives of the Ivy League?" by pointing out that a woman's

*Pollitt draws from Shafer*

*Shafer relates Belkin and Story*

**Quotation** —
choice to work or stay at home is not made in a vacuum: "The
lack of good childcare and paid paternal leave, horrendous
work hours, inflexible career ladders, the still-conventional
domestic expectations of far too many men and the industrial-size helpings of maternal guilt ladled out by the
media are all part of it."

The six articles I have discussed put the 2006 "Mommy
Wars" in an interesting perspective. For over twenty-five
years the "wars" have been enacted in the press but the
players have been highly educated women instead of the rest
of us.

---

Farr 5

## Works Cited

Hirshman, Linda. "Homeward Bound." *The American Prospect* December 2005: 16.
   15 Apr. 2006 <http://proquest.umi.com/pdqweb>.

Johnston, Deirdre D., and Debra H. Swanson. "Invisible Mothers: A Content
   Analysis of Motherhood Ideologies and Myths in Magazines." *Sex Roles*
   49 (2003): 21–33.

Pollitt, Katha. "Desperate Housewives of the Ivy League?" *The Nation* 17
   October 2005. 26 Apr. 2006 <http://www.thenation.com/doc/20051017/
   pollitt>.

Tucker, Judith Stadtman. "The Least Worst Choice: Why Women 'Opt' Out of
   the Workforce." The Mothers Movement Online. December 2003. 15 Apr.
   2006 <www.mothersmovement.org>.

Story, Louise. "Many Women at Elite Colleges Set Career Path to
   Motherhood." *The New York Times* 20 September 2005. Online.
   LexisNexis®Academic. 1 April 2006.

Rosenbluth, Frances. "Mother Yale." *Yale Magazine* November/December 2005.
   20 Apr. 2006 <http://www.yalealumni magazine.com/issues/2005_11/
   forum.html>.

As you can see, Megan's introduction and conclusion are the only paragraphs of the essay that do not contain material from source texts. The body of the essay is a mosaic of summaries, quotations, paraphrases, and textual associations. Make note of Megan's use of attribution words and the extent to which she provides background information about the authors. She follows the advice we give in Chapter 2, varying the ways she leads the reader into the textual material, for example:

Deirdre D. Johnston and Debra H. Swanson *discuss*

They *point out*

Johnston and Swanson *explain*

Johnston and Swanson *review*

They *go on to add*

They *call attention to*

Stadtman Tucker *observes*

Stadtman Tucker *also provides*

Stadtman Tucker *reminds us*

Stadtman Tucker *notes*

### EXERCISE 7.3

Review Megan's essay and make a list of additional attribution words. Also identify the spots where she offers background about a particular author.

In Chapter 2, we discussed *intertexuality*, which refers to the way writers relate other texts to their own text, often by weaving the other texts into their writing. In the left-hand margin of Megan's essay, we have identified Megan's use of direct quotations, paraphrases, summaries, and in the right-hand margin we have indicated how the source texts talk to each other. An explanatory synthesis is a quintessential example of intertextuality. We recap the strategies for writing an explanatory synthesis in the box below.

---

### RECAP OF STRATEGIES FOR WRITING AN EXPLANATORY SYNTHESIS

- Examine the assignment and decide on your rhetorical purpose.
- Ask Baseline Questions (p. 238) in order to identify the major issue treated by the various texts.
- Locate a theme or subtopic running across the sources.
- Analyze how the texts talk to each other with respect to the subtopic.
- Respond to In-Depth Questions for Identifying Relationships Among Texts (p. 239) to determine the points each text makes about the subtopic.
- Mark the texts and copy passages related to subtopic into your writer's notebook. Study the bits of text you have selected and impose some type of order on them.
- Formulate a working thesis. Remember that an explanatory synthesis is a straightforward, objective reporting of the sources.

- Write a draft of your essay, returning to source texts for paraphrases, quotations, and summaries.
- Ask a peer to review your paper. (Use questions on p. 176.)
- Revise and edit.

# ◼ PROCESS OF WRITING A LITERATURE REVIEW

The purpose of a literature review is to provide background and explain a topic, problem, or issue to readers by examining a wide array of published research studies. As we mentioned earlier, occasionally the writer's goal is simply to communicate the research findings to an interested audience. More typically, the writer seeks to demonstrate her knowledge of a research field in order to lay the foundation for her own research study. More so than with any other type of synthesis, a literature review requires the writer to engage in a sizable amount of library-based research and to sort and re-sort the textual material into manageable, workable categories.

## ◼ Examination of "Motherhood Ideologies and Motherhood Myths": Deirdre D. Johnston and Debra H. Swanson's Literature Review

To illustrate a literature review, turn to Deirdre D. Johnston and Debra H. Swanson's "Motherhood Ideologies and Motherhood Myths" in Chapter 3 (pp. 76–80). Johnston and Swanson's literature review is from their study, "Invisible Mothers: A Content Analysis of Motherhood Ideologies and Myths in Magazines." The objective of the study is to examine the representation of employed and at-home mothers in contemporary women's magazines. The focus of their inquiry is the ideologies and myths underlying these representations. In order to contextualize the issue and set the stage for their study, they give their readers background information and point out which facets of the topic have been studied and which still need to be investigated.

Read the literature review on pages 76–80, paying special attention to the various ways Johnston and Swanson organize the synthesis, and report on and cite the sources. Make note of the similarities and differences between this type of synthesis and the explanatory synthesis we described above. The comparison will reveal the following features of a literature review.

### FEATURES OF A LITERATURE REVIEW

- Gives readers workable theories as well as a thorough understanding of the issue.
- Moves one step beyond description and reporting to come to some conclusions about the research. That is, the writer explains the research questions that still have to be answered.
- Analyzes the sources along the lines of key subtopics or themes.

(continued on the next page)

- Organizes the synthesis to focus on ideas rather than sources.
- Uses parenthetical citation to list studies with similar finding; for example, Johnston and Swanson's citation "Motherhood is a social and historical construction (Bassin, Honey, & Kalan, 1994; Glenn, 1994; Risman, 1998)."
- Uses minimal quotation.

## ■ Organize the Literature Review to Focus on Ideas Rather Than Sources

Earlier in this chapter, we pointed out that when students write syntheses, one of their biggest pitfalls is to allow the sources to drive the paper instead of letting their own ideas take the lead. The temptation to let the sources take the lead is especially great when you are writing a review of the literature. It is easy to fall into the pattern of beginning each paragraph with "such and such a reseacher said." Turn to Johnston and Swanson's subsection, "Motherhood Myths," on pages 77–78 to see how the authors avoid this difficulty. Notice how each of the three paragraphs in this section begins with a topic sentence that states an idea before it goes on to cite the researchers' names.

"The building blocks of ideologies are myths."

"Myths of employed and at-home mothers abound in the culture."

"Scholars have sought to identify the underlying causes of maternal myths.…"

Zero in on the second paragraph and you will see that it is organized carefully according to ideas. Study the graphic representation in Figure 7–2. Note how the sources are used in the service of the ideas, not the other way around.

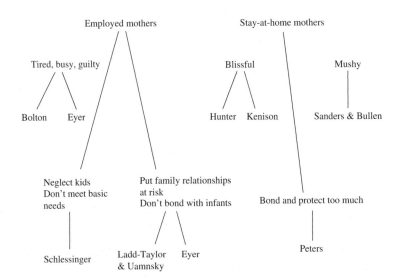

**Figure 7–2    Graphic Overview of "Motherhood Myths"**

When you are assigned a literature review, use the strategies in the following box.

---

**RECAP OF STRATEGIES FOR WRITING A LITERATURE REVIEW**

- Conduct a wide range of library-based research.
- Identify the subtopics addressed by the various sources.
- Analyze how the texts talk to each other with respect to the subtopics.
- Respond to In-Depth Questions for Identifying Relationships Among Texts (p. 239) to determine the points each text makes about the various subtopics.
- Mark the texts and copy passages into your writer's notebook. Study the bits of text you have selected and impose some type of order on them.
- Create a visual display of the subtopics and the sources related to each subtopic.
- Formulate a working thesis. In your introductory paragraphs, give your readers context and background for your topic and its various subdivisions.
- Organize the review with subdivisions devoted to sub-themes.
- In the body paragraphs, review the sources, being careful to subsume the research sources under the subtopic ideas, not the other way around.
- End the review by telling your readers what we know, what we don't know, what's been researched well, what is still up for speculation, and what needs to be done by future researchers
- Add a page of references.
- Ask a peer to review your paper (use questions on p. 176).
- Revise and edit.

---

# ■■ PROCESS OF WRITING A THESIS-DRIVEN SYNTHESIS

We have been examining various genres of academic writing with the tacit understanding that all forms of academic writing present arguments of one sort or another. By argument, we do not mean bickering, altercation, or verbal face-off. Instead, we mean a reasoned consideration that the writer has analyzed and explained by responding to earlier writing on the same topic. Such an analysis and explanation amounts to a conversation between one writer and another, and as such it inevitably registers the writer's point of view. This point of view is explicit in the writer's direct statement of judgment or opinion on the matter at hand. The writer is capable of making the direct statement or thesis because she has familiarized herself with the issue by becoming an active participant in the intellectual conversation.

## ■ Support Thesis with Evidence

Next, the writer has to decide how to support the thesis. This is where synthesis comes into play. She will return to the reading selections combing them for sentences and passages that relate directly to her thesis. She will look for support of two types:

- Background information that will enable her to contextualize the issue for her readers and inform them of the conversation
- Evidence that will support her thesis and major points

The most common types of evidence are facts, statistics, and other numerical information; observations based on data (e.g., surveys, polls, studies); examples and analogies; personal experience and anecdotal information; and viewpoints of competent authorities (e.g., testimonies, conclusions drawn from research).

## ■ Examination of Student's Thesis-Driven Synthesis

To illustrate the process of writing a thesis-driven synthesis, consider the following assignment:

> Drawing on Lillian B. Rubin's "'People Don't Know Right from Wrong Anymore,'" Frances K. Goldscheider and Linda J. Waite's "Alternative Family Futures," and Robert L. Griswold's "Fatherhood and the Defense of Patriarchy," write a four- to five-page essay explaining what American families are like today. Address your essay to an audience of peers.

What follows is an essay by a student, Siryal Benim, written in response to the above assignment.

### *SAMPLE THESIS-DRIVEN SYNTHESIS ESSAY*

Benim 1

Siryal Benim

Academic Writing I

Professor Smith

23 October 2000

New Conceptions of the Traditional Family

Our families today neither resemble nor function like those of just a few decades ago. In the past, American cultural norms suggested that upon finishing school, young adults would seek employment, get married, or live with their parents until they were prepared to enter the workforce or tie the knot. Lillian B. Rubin, in "'People Don't Know Right from Wrong Anymore,'" points out that the average age for marriage was earlier than it is today, 20.6 years for women and 22.5 years for men (17). The past few decades have seen three social upheavals, each popularly termed as sexual, gender, and divorce-related. And as Rubin notes, America has weathered "shifts in the economy, which forced increasing numbers of women into the labor force" (16). As a direct result of these changes, our families and lifestyles differ substantially from what they were thirty years ago. The new family structures and lifestyles, which are often described as "alternative," are occurring by

*Paraphrase of Rubin* [brace]

*Quotation from Rubin* [brace]

Benim 2

*Thesis*

default as often as by choice. It may be that the "alternative" has become the norm.

As the traditional nuclear family is diminishing and
different family systems are becoming more common,
traditional roles for men and women are changing as well. Men
are no longer the sole breadwinners for the family, and in
some cases, they may not even be the principal wage earners.
The ascension of women in the workforce and their growing
parity with men in terms of power and income have caused
problems for men who have difficulty facing the new realities
of economics and family. Goldschneider and Waite, in
"Alternative Family Futures" suggest, forebodingly, that "men

*Quotations
from
Goldsch-
neider and
Waite*

who still hold traditional definitions of their appropriate
adult role are increasingly having difficulty finding wives
willing to take the full burden of family obligations left by
a husband whose only responsibilities are to work" (208). The
authors go on to say, "It is also the case that pressures
have been building on men to become more involved in the
family and its tasks whether they want to or not" (208).
After a full day of work at the office, women are just as
exhausted as men. They look to their husbands to assist them
with household chores and childcare.

But will men willingly adopt this new role? According to

*Paraphrase
of Griswold*

Robert Griswold in "Fatherhood and the Defense of Patriarchy," signs of an emerging "new fatherhood" point
encouragingly toward a reaffirmation of shared values and an
effort toward renewed cohesiveness among family members
(257). As Griswold puts it, "Feminists and advocates for the

*Quotation
from
Griswold*

men's movement hope that the new fatherhood will be a
progressive step in redefining American manhood" (257). But
there is lack of enthusiasm for the so-called men's
movement, and this may suggest that men are not prepared to
adopt, en masse, any such feminist-driven ideology.

The dramatic change in men's roles over the past two
decades may indicate the rapid deterioration of the
traditional nuclear family as a cultural mainstay. Over
the past two decades, we have seen a high rate of divorce
and the rise of new "traditional" families: family units
still headed by adults, but these parents or guardians are
not necessarily biologically related to each other's
children.

Benim 3

Also, "step" parents have become more common. Previously married individuals remarry to create new, sometimes complex family units with various step relatives. Sometimes the second and third families are formed late in life. Rubin's interpretation is right on the mark: "Now, when, on the average, women live to nearly eighty and men to a little over seventy, we can marry and bear children very much later, safe in the knowledge that we'll be around to raise and nurture them as long as they need us" (17). Years ago, people died younger and very few families were created late in life.

*Quotation from Rubin*

Today, single-parent families, especially those headed by mothers, are subjected to increasingly demanding schedules and levels of stress. Goldschneider and Waite point out that women need more help than ever when raising families: "Despite the number of women who take on both parental and economic roles, not all women can do so; few can parent totally alone" (202). Indeed, the viability of single-parent families has become a major campaign issue in political campaigns. Political rhetoric aside, it would seem that children in single-parent households stand to suffer the greatest consequences when the pressures are too great for the family to bear.

*Quotation from Goldsch- neider and Waite*

An increasing number of families opt to remain childless. Historically, the absence of children in a family was less a matter of choice and more the result of physical limitations. Modern families make this choice based upon their own goals and the potential impact of these goals on family life. It would seem that such decisions are typically based on sound, rational judgments, and that they represent a morally responsible alternative to child-rearing.

Apprehensive about marriage due to high rates of divorce, many couples today postpone wedding plans indefinitely. Greater life expectancy through improved medical technology made postponement possible. This is a luxury our ancestors were not afforded. Nor were they afforded effective birth control or abortion. Unplanned pregnancies often led to marriage. As Rubin puts it, "Sometimes the young couple married regretfully; often one partner, usually the man, was ambivalent" (13). Rubin goes on to say that regardless of circumstances, "it didn't really matter; they did what was expected" (13). Such was the power exerted by cultural norms not long ago.

*Quotation from Rubin*

Benim 4

But have advances in human health practices devalued matrimony? Has the once time-honored principle of commitment been reduced to a mere buzzword among couples today? People today realize that even if their first or even second marriages don't succeed, they may take vows a third or possibly a fourth time, until they are satisfied. Certainly, today's families are very different from those of our ancestors. It remains to be determined, however, if these changes are for better or for worse.

Today couples and families have many more options to choose from when making decisions. This freedom comes with its own set of pros and cons. To debate the issue of today's fractured family using sound-bite styled catch phrases such as "family values" misses the point: values are widely held precepts based on accepted cultural norms which are usually grounded in history or tradition. Quite simply, it is precisely because of the absence of any consensus, morally, spiritually, or otherwise, that an understanding of what constitutes appropriate family behavior cannot be attained. Perhaps we are now creating a new concept of the "traditional" family that will be passed on to subsequent generations.

---

Benim 5

Works Cited

Goldschneider, Frances K., and Linda J. Waite. "Alternative Family Futures." *New Families, No Families? The Transformation of the American Home*. Berkeley: U of California P, 1991. 200–205.

Griswold, Robert L. "Fatherhood and the Defense of Patriarchy." *Fatherhood in America, A History*. New York: Basic Books, 1993. 257–60.

Rubin, Lillian B. "'People Don't Know Right from Wrong Anymore.'" *Families on the Fault Line*. New York: HarperCollins, 1994.

---

Siryal Benim successfully incorporates material from three reading sources, each of which addresses a different view of the topic. Drawing upon the three texts' perspectives on alternative family patterns, the role of fatherhood, and various moral points associated with these issues, Siryal discusses changes in contemporary family life, arguing that currently available options are very different from traditional family structures; however, these alternative structures may actually be the norm.

We have annotated Siryal's essay and highlighted the quotations and paraphrases from the three sources. We have also highlighted Siryal's verbs and phrases of attribution. Notice that he uses a variety of attribution verbs and avoids the monotonous mantra "he said-she said." A distinguishing characteristic of a thesis-driven synthesis essay is that it uses selective summary, paraphrase, and quotation. Place Siryal's essay next to Megan's (pp. 242–45) and you will see a major difference between a thesis-driven synthesis essay and an explanatory synthesis. Siryal uses fragments of the source texts but only insofar as they support his own thesis. The sources serve the thesis. Megan presents a mosaic of texts. She does not state her own position. Her goal is to tell her readers everything the texts say about the background and history of the current controversy over the "Mommy Wars."

---

### RECAP OF STRATEGIES FOR WRITING A THESIS-DRIVEN SYNTHESIS

- Firm up your rhetorical purpose: You are reading the texts with the goal of stating your position on the issue.
- Read all the texts to get a general impression of their treatment of the topic and respond to the five Baseline Questions for Initial Reading (p. 238).
- Reread each text to determine the elements it has in common with the other sources and respond to In-Depth Questions for Identifying Relationships Among Texts (p. 239).
- Decide what points you wish to get across to your readers and formulate a working thesis in which you state a position or make a claim.
- Review the texts to discover material you can use to develop each of your points.
- Draft your essay by quoting, paraphrasing, or summarizing relevant supporting information from the texts and by drawing on your knowledge of the basic features of writing: titles, introductions, sentences, paragraphs, transitions, and so on.

---

## ◼ REVISING SYNTHESIS ESSAYS

When you have completed a preliminary draft of your essay, schedule a conference with your professor, and if your professor agrees, ask a classmate or a friend to give you suggestions for revision. Use the questions in the box below. Then revise and edit your work.

---

### QUESTIONS FOR REVISING A SYNTHESIS ESSAY

- Is the title appropriate — objective for an explanatory synthesis and a literature review, and reflective of the writer's attitude for a thesis-driven synthesis? If not, can you suggest a more appropriate title?
- Is there an interesting lead that attracts the reader's attention? If not, can you suggest a more appropriate lead?
- Does the writer give you sufficient background information? If not, what else do you need to know?
- Does the writer make his or her overall purpose clear to the reader? If not, what remains fuzzy?
- What is the writer's thesis?

- As you read each paragraph, are you aware of the purpose that the writer is trying to accomplish? If not, where does your mind wander?
- Does the writer identify relationships among texts?
- In each paragraph, does the writer provide sufficient support from the texts? Is there too much summary?
- Does the writer include his or her own commentary when it is appropriate? Is there too much commentary?
- Does the conclusion do more than simply summarize the main points of the paper?
- Does the writer include parenthetical documentation where it is necessary and clearly differentiate among sources?
- Is there a Works Cited page?

## EXERCISE 7.4

- Reread Siryal Benim's paper.
- Note the structure of its presentation. After an introductory statement about changes in family patterns, Siryal discusses new roles for fathers, stepparents, couples without children, late marriages, and divorce, and then draws on information variously from three sources.
- Read the titles of these sources in the list of Works Cited. What separate topic does each appear to address? Can you make any generalization about Siryal's alternating and selective use of these sources?

## EXERCISE 7.5

- Form collaborative learning groups of three students each.
- Assign each member a single source to trace through Siryal's paper. Ask each to comment on the focus that Siryal puts on the material from that particular source.
- When the class reconvenes, have each group recorder explain the conclusions that individual members reached about Siryal's use of particular sources.

## WORKS CITED

Druian, Greg, and Jocelyn A. Butler. "Schooling Practices and At-Risk Youth: What the Research Shows." Northwest Regional Educational Laboratory. 23 Apr. 2006 <http://www.nwrel.org/scpd/sirs/1/topsyn1.html>.

Goldschneider, Frances K., and Linda J. Waite. "Alternative Family Futures." *New Families, No Families? The Transformation of the American Home.* Berkeley: U of California P, 1991. 200–05.

Griswold, Robert L. "Fatherhood and the Defense of Patriarchy." *Fatherhood in America, A History.* New York: Basic Books, 1993. 257–60.

Rubin, Lillian B. "'People Don't Know Right from Wrong Anymore.'" *Families on the Fault Line.* New York: HarperCollins, 1994.

Watson, Robert and the Core Writing Team of the Cambridge Earth, Environment, and Atmospheric Sciences, Eds. "Climate Change 2001: Synthesis Report," March 7th 2002. 15 Mar. 2006 <http://www.cambridge.org/uk/earthsciences/climatechange/reports.htm>.

CHAPTER

■ ■ ■ ■ ■ ■

*Eight*

# Argument

Arguing is an everyday activity. It is a practice that permeates many aspects of our lives. In a conversation among friends, a simple argument might range from whether one brand of shampoo is more effective in controlling bad-hair days than another to whether Saturday or Sunday is a better day to collaborate on a homework assignment. A more consequential argument among family members might concern whether excessive TV viewing interferes with family life. Depending on whose argument prevails, members may find themselves watching more or less TV. A serious argument for an entire community or an entire nation is whether one political candidate rather than another is better prepared to serve the public needs.

Those who argue well have learned how to examine the complexity of issues while maintaining respect for other people's positions. Those who do it poorly resort to simplistic thinking, tunnel vision, and verbal warfare. Argumentative skill is acquired. It is not innate. It is worth developing because it will increase your understanding of important issues that you encounter every day. As British scholar Aram Eisenschitz puts it:

> Argument gives students freedom — not the freedom of modularized choices — but the confidence and intellectual autonomy to interrogate academic fragmentation and thereby to reinterpret familiar landscapes and make abstract ideas real. Above all, it makes them aware of the wider implications of ideas that are in daily use and unafraid to challenge the conventions of wisdom. (25)

Learning to argue well in writing, as well as in speech, is a central concern of the university.

## ■ NATURE OF ACADEMIC ARGUMENT

Academic argument is less a dispute and more a polite exchange of ideas among interested parties. Imagine it as a conversation that you engage in with a group of acquaintances and friends, some of whom hold values and beliefs similar to your own and some of whom see things differently from the way you do. You put your ideas on the table. Some people nod in agreement. Others frown and purse their lips. When you have had your say, the Lip Pursers speak up. They proceed to poke holes in your argument and offer alternative ways of looking at the issue. You listen carefully. Then you respond to the Lip Pursers' objections tactfully, not in a belligerent manner. To be conciliatory, you use expressions such as

Some of what you say is true but . . .

Your recommendations have some merit, but . . .

You make a valid point about _____, but the more important issue is _____.

You make a good case about _____, but it overlooks _____.

Your argument addresses part of the problem, but it ought to consider _____.

Granted, _____ is important, but _____ is even more urgent to consider.

And you continue to make your case, bolstering it with evidence and using it to call upon your audience to take decisive action. When you commit an argument to paper, you need to imagine the same conversation and the same give and take between you and your readers.

For many students, writing an argument is a challenging task because they have not yet cultivated a disposition for arguing in this noncombative way. Like analyzing and synthesizing, arguing is a habit of mind. And, as with the other two operations, the way you develop a disposition for arguing is by learning to ask the right questions. Later in this chapter we will discuss this rhetorical strategy in more detail.

## ■ Argument in a Broad Sense and Argument in a Specialized Sense

In the broad sense, every college paper that expresses a thesis is an "argument" because the writer is motivating the reader to accept his or her perspective, position, or point of view. Even if a substantial portion of the essay is devoted to summarizing, paraphrasing, comparing, or contrasting sources, it can still form an argument that promotes a distinctive point of view. The choice of materials with their emphasis and arrangement will imply a perspective and demonstrate a position. All of the essays we have discussed up to this point in the book present an argument in the broad sense of the word. All of them set out or explain a particular idea, attitude, or speculative point of view.

A more specialized sense of the word *argument* evokes the goal of moving audiences to a particular action or persuasion. The word argument need not imply a quarrel or a polemic. It derives from a Greek word related to argent, "silver or white" (compare Ag, the chemical abbreviation for "silver"), denoting brilliance or clarity. From it comes the name of Argos, the mythological demigod with a hundred eyes. The word implies that a speaker or writer has seized upon an idea, clarified its point, and made its meaning strikingly visible.

The difference between written argument in the broad sense of getting your readers to see your point of view and argument in the narrower sense of persuading your readers to adopt your position is illustrated in the two thesis statements that follow. Both concern a popular social movement called "communitarianism." For some people, "community" is a contested concept. Many writers are embroiled in the controversy over whether it is more important to uphold community values or safeguard individual rights. Political philosophers and intellectuals who value identification with or membership in a community over private initiative or personal autonomy are referred to as "communitarians."

## THESIS A: ARGUMENT IN THE BROAD SENSE

The ideals set forth by communitarians are undemocratic, un-American, unconstitutional, and unfair.

## THESIS B: ARGUMENT IN THE SPECIALIZED SENSE

Although the academics who espouse communitarianism tout it as the panacea for our nation's ills, the ideals they set forth are undemocratic, un-American, unconstitutional, and unfair.

The difference between Thesis A and Thesis B is that B is trying to argue against a specific communitarian alternative. Writer B knows that some of her readers will not agree with her. She expects them to argue that restoration of community is a solution to America's social problems. When writer B says, "Although the academics who espouse communitarianism tout it as the panacea for our nation's ills," she anticipates her audience's opposing response. Later, in the body of her essay, she will give reasons why her view, expressed as that of "mainstream Americans," holds more weight than the view of her opponents. Writer A holds the same position as writer B, but she is more confident that her readers will agree with her position.

---

### ARGUMENT IN THE BROAD SENSE

- Your thesis states your position but it is not necessarily arguable and debatable.
- You don't acknowledge and weigh alternative views.
- Your purpose is to present your position. You are not intent on persuading your readers that your position is superior to other positions.

### ARGUMENT IN THE SPECIALIZED SENSE

- Your thesis is arguable and debatable.
- You anticipate alternative views, acknowledge them, and address them.
- You are intent on persuading your readers that your position is superior to other positions.

---

## ■ DEVELOPING SUPPORT FOR ARGUMENTS

To develop a strong argument, you must impart a breadth and depth to its focus. Try to make the argument two-dimensional. An argument that hammers away at one central idea until it has exhausted all available evidence and concludes by restating the original proposition, as in the following example, is not what you want to write.

The ideals set forth by communitarians are undemocratic, un-American, unconstitutional, and unfair. . . . Thus we see that communitarianism is undemocratic, un-American, unconstitutional, and unfair.

Instead, pursue a rounder, perhaps more oblique path by allowing the argument to recognize its own limitations. Multidimensional argument explicitly acknowledges competing hypotheses, alternative explanations, and even outright contradictions.

The ideals set forth by communitarianism are undemocratic, un-American, unconstitutional, and unfair even though its proponents tout it as the panacea for our nation's ills.

The value of this approach is that it widens the tunnel vision that repeats only one proposition. It implies that you have explored competing hypotheses and have weighed the evidence for and against each of them. Your readers may or may not agree with your conclusion, but they will certainly respect your effort to set it in a broader context.

## ■ **JOINING THE ACADEMIC CONVERSATION**

After reading the preceding section, you may well ask yourself, "How can I possibly explore and weigh the evidence against competing hypotheses if I have limited knowledge of the topic I am writing about?" Your question brings up an important point that student writers often overlook. You can't plunge into an argument and rush to take one side over the other. Before you put pen to paper, you must study the complexities of the issue. The issues you will write about in your college courses, even if they are current topics, are already being debated. Before your write a sentence of your argument essay, you have to become part of this debate. You need to enter into the conversation.

Kenneth Burke, a major philosopher and scholar of rhetoric, gives an apt, frequently quoted, description of the situation in which you find yourself:

Imagine that you enter a parlor. You come late. When you arrive, others have long preceded you, and they are engaged in a heated discussion, a discussion too heated for them to pause and tell you exactly what it is about. In fact, the discussion had already begun long before any of them got there, so that no one present is qualified to retrace for you all the steps that had gone before. You listen for a while, until you decide that you have caught the tenor of the argument; then you put in your oar. Someone answers; you answer him; another comes to your defense; another aligns himself against you, to either the embarrassment or gratification of your opponent, depending upon the quality of your ally's assistance. However, the discussion is interminable. The hour grows late, you must depart. And you do depart, with the discussion still vigorously in progress. (110–111)

We will concretize Burke's parlor discussion by looking at the debate about stay-at-home versus working mothers, the topic of the reading selections in Chapter 3. Let's say you've been assigned an argument essay and you've decided to write it on whether women should continue to work or quit their jobs when they have children. The point at which you select the issue is the moment you arrive at the parlor door. The guests who preceded you began discussing the issue over appetizers before dinner, and they continued to converse throughout the dinner. By the time you arrive, they have moved from the dining room to the parlor for dessert and coffee. They are scattered around the room chatting in small groups.

As you enter the parlor, you overhear Frances Rosenbluth, Jack Shafer, Tracy Meares, and Katha Pollitt talking about Louise Story's *New York Times* article about the trend among Yale undergraduates to opt out of the workforce when they have children. You make your way to the couch in front of the fireplace where you find Linda Hirshman defending her position on why women opt out of the workforce to David Brooks, Cathy Young, and Rebecca Traister. Later, you move over to the dessert table where you listen in on the heated discussion Judith Stadtman Tucker is having with Dan Feder. You listen carefully to what all these people are saying and then, as Burke observes, "You put in your oar." You articulate what you think is a reasonable position, but someone immediately challenges your claim. Another guest "comes to your defense; another aligns himself against you." You have become part of the academic conversation.

To extend Burke's metaphor to writing, you dip your oar into the water when you sit down to draft your paper. Before you arrive at this point, you have to

- Read what experts have already written about the issue.
- Examine the various dimensions of the issue by analyzing and evaluating the experts' arguments to determine which are the most convincing, which are reasonable but not terribly persuasive, and which are flawed.
- Articulate a thesis expressing your own position.
- Discover solid reasons to support your thesis.
- Return to the sources to extract evidence you will use to back up each of your reasons.
- Summarize alternative views and reasonable objections to your argument.
- Respond tactfully to these alternative views.
- Decide how you will structure your essay.

## ■ EXAMINATION OF "THE LEAST WORST CHOICE: WHY MOTHERS 'OPT' OUT OF THE WORKFORCE": JUDITH STADTMAN TUCKER'S ARGUMENT SYNTHESIS

As has been our practice, we will discuss a sample essay before we walk you through the process of writing an essay. The sample argument synthesis is Judith Stadtman Tucker's "The Least Worst Choice: Why Mothers 'Opt' Out of the Workforce" on pages 81–90. Be sure to read the selection before continuing.

Judith Stadtman Tucker joined the conversation about stay-at-home and working mothers in 2003 shortly after an article titled "The Opt-Out Revolution" by Lisa Belkin appeared in the *New York Times*. Belkin wrote about a small group of highly successful Princeton alumnae who abandoned their demanding careers to become full-time mothers. Belkin considers this exodus from the workforce to be a trend, and she concludes the reason women don't rule the world is "because they don't want to." Stadtman Tucker rejects the argument of Belkin and other journalists who share her views on the topic, saying that Belkin's story is superficial because it glosses over the real reasons women leave or remain in their jobs. Furthermore, Stadtman Tucker questions why the media have defined the issue in terms of well-to-do Ivy League graduates. She argues that the media are focusing on the wrong issue and the wrong women.

Before Stadtman Tucker makes her argument, she informs her readers about the ongoing conversation. Her opening paragraphs (1) familiarize her readers with the issue, (2) explain that she is responding to Belkin and journalists who have comparable viewpoints, and (3) state her claim that the reason women don't run the world is not that they don't want to but because "the world doesn't want women in charge." Essentially, what Stadtman Tucker says to her readers is "This is what people are talking about. This is what they're saying. And here is why they are wrong." Her reason for entering the conversation is to set her readers straight. She wants them to see the situation as she sees it. Similarly, your goal as a writer of argument essays is to give your readers a better understanding of an issue that interests them.

Stadtman Tucker's first move is to clarify the facts. Pointing out that the media have led people to believe that there is a trend of women leaving careers to raise children, Stadtman Tucker cites U.S. Census Bureau surveys that show no such trend exists. Then she proceeds to explain why women do not rise to leadership positions in the workforce. She offers five reasons to support her claim:

- Success in the workforce depends on employees' ability to meet employers' requests for labor on demand.
- Despite the fact that women are more likely than men to be professional managers, cultural attitudes about the incompatibility of women and work have led to workplace practices that marginalize mothers.
- There's a lack of family-friendly work arrangements.
- U.S. social policies do not address the needs of working mothers.
- When women reenter the workforce, they may not be hired at the same level of responsibility as when they left.

Stadtman Tucker substantiates each of these reasons with evidence she has obtained from a wide range of sources:

- U.S. Census Bureau, Current Population Survey
- Books
- Magazine and journal articles
- Newspaper articles
- National studies performed by the government
- An Executive Action Brief and other briefs issued by the government
- National surveys
- U.S. Department of Labor surveys
- Documents from university clearinghouse
- Web sites
- Online news services

All told, "The Least Worst Choice" contains thirty-two references to sources. But because it is an online text, it does not contain footnotes. Online texts are scrolled. There is no "foot" of the page. Stadtman Tucker cites sources by inserting numbers in parentheses within the text. The numbers link to corresponding content notes at the end of the document. If you were reading Stadtman Tucker's article online, you would see that the numbers are presented as hyperlinks.

> According to Williams, mothers on the professional career track face "three unattractive choices. They remain in a good job that keeps them away from home 10 to 12 hours a day, or they take a part time [job] with depressed wages, few benefits and no advancement. Or they quit." (**4**)

If you were to click on (**4**) in the above example, you would link to the end of the article to

> 4. *Why Moms Stay Home*, Joan C. Williams, *The Washington Post*, July 17, 2003.

Stadtman Tucker's system of documentation differs from the documentation styles your professors will expect you to use. We discuss the styles most commonly assigned in college courses, the MLA and APA documentation styles, in Chapter 9 and in the Appendix.

Before we move on, we will explain *content endnotes*. Content endnotes amplify or further explain material in a text. Because they are tangential to the text, the writer places them at the end of the text rather than interrupt the flow of the argument. Here is one of Stadtman Tucker's content endnotes:

### TEXT

> The peculiar reluctance to actively address the needs of working families in the United States results from a muddled confluence of ideology about women, work, family, children, personal responsibility and the power of the free market to serve the true needs of the people. (**20**)

### ENDNOTE

> See Sharon Hays, *The Cultural Contradictions of Motherhood*, 1996, and *Motherhood and its discontents: Why mothers need a social movement of their own*, Judith Stadtman Tucker, The Mothers Movement Online, 2003.

Stadtman Tucker uses the endnote to recommend additional sources to her readers. Her own article is hyperlinked; when readers click on the title, they link to the full text.

The hallmark of a strong argument is the writer's acknowledgement of alternative views. For example, in paragraph 27 Stadtman Tucker explains, "Lurking in the shadows of our national mentality is the unhealthy fiction that if we could just get every working mother happily married and send her back home to stay, some of our more pressing economic and social problems would magically evaporate" (86). She goes on to counter this view: "But the old 'normal'—that idealized retroland of 1950s family life—is gone for good." At another moment, Stadtman Tucker admits, "There will always be women—and men—from all walks of American life who passionately believe that the only way to bring up happy, healthy children is to do it the 'old fashioned' way: mom taking care of things on

Overview of Judith Stadtman Tucker's "The Least Worst Choice: Why Mothers 'Opt' Out of the Workforce"

### CENTRAL CLAIM

The *New York Time*'s focus on privileged women who opt out of the workforce to become full-time mothers is misplaced. It deflects attention away from serious discussion of the realities of motherhood and the systemic factors that limit women's leadership in the workforce. The reason women don't run the world is not because they don't want to but because "the world doesn't want them in charge."

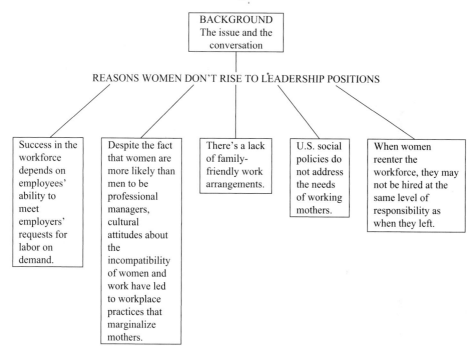

**Figure 8–1**

the homefront, dad out bringing home the bacon." She tactfully acknowledges, "Couples who hold this view are not necessarily anti-feminist reactionaries longing for a bygone era where men were men and women were housewives. . . ." Then Stadtman Tucker refutes the stay-at-home argument with objective evidence and anecdotal evidence. She describes the economic factors and cultural attitudes that cause mothers to give up their careers, and she quotes a stay-at-home mother who says, "'If I lived in my utopia, I would not be a stay-at-home mom. But the way things are now, being the stay-at-home mom is simply the least worst choice for our family.'"

In Figures 8–1, 8–2, and 8–3, we provide graphic overviews of Stadtman Tucker's argument. Study these maps. They are good templates for an argument synthesis essay. Figure 8–1 depicts Stadtman Tucker's claim, her presentation of background information, and the five reasons she uses to support the claim. In Figures 8–2 and 8–3, we flesh out two of these reasons by displaying the evidence she incorporates from the source texts.

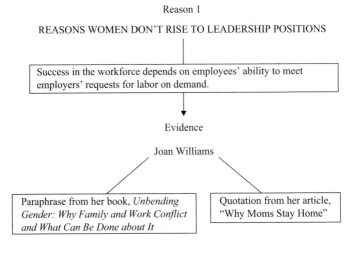

Reason 1

REASONS WOMEN DON'T RISE TO LEADERSHIP POSITIONS

Success in the workforce depends on employees' ability to meet employers' requests for labor on demand.

Evidence

Joan Williams

Paraphrase from her book, *Unbending Gender: Why Family and Work Conflict and What Can Be Done about It*

Quotation from her article, "Why Moms Stay Home"

**Figure 8–2**

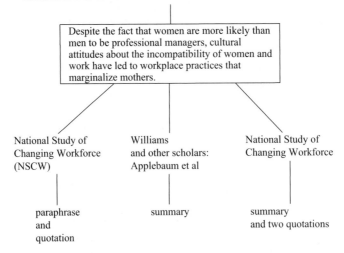

Reason 2

REASONS WOMEN DON'T RISE TO LEADERSHIP POSITIONS

Despite the fact that women are more likely than men to be professional managers, cultural attitudes about the incompatibility of women and work have led to workplace practices that marginalize mothers.

National Study of Changing Workforce (NSCW)

Williams and other scholars: Applebaum et al

National Study of Changing Workforce

paraphrase and quotation

summary

summary and two quotations

**Figure 8–3**

## EXERCISE 8.1

- Review Judith Stadtman Tucker's argument in "The Least Worst Choice: Why Mothers 'Opt' Out of the Workforce," pages 81–90. Then break into small groups. Assign one of the following reasons to each group:

  - There's a lack of family-friendly work arrangements (paragraphs 11–21).

  - U.S. social policies do not address the needs of working mothers (paragraphs 22–27).

  - When women reenter the workforce, they may not be hired at the same level of responsibility as when they left (paragraphs 38–42).

- Review Stadtman Tucker's claim and then reread the paragraphs devoted to the reason you have been assigned. The paragraph numbers are in parentheses.
- Ske tch out a map or graphic overview comparable to the ones we present in Figures 8–2 and 8–3. A member from each group will display the graphic overview and explain to the class the various ways Stadtman Tucker uses the sources to support her argument.

# ■ PROCESS OF WRITING AN ARGUMENT SYNTHESIS ESSAY

## ■ Differentiate Between Issues and Topics

Think of a debatable issue on which you have a strong opinion. Note that we use the word *issue* here rather than subject or topic. A *topic* maps out a general area for discussion or inquiry. In and of itself, it is not contestable. An *issue* involves a specific point or matter for contention and debate. Abortion is a topic. Whether or not women should have free choice in the matter of abortion is an issue. Some people will say "Yes"; others will say "No." On every issue, there are alternative views.

### EXERCISE 8.2

- Study the following list to be sure you understand the difference between a topic and an issue:

| Topic | Issue |
|---|---|
| 1. Imports | Whether we should buy American-made goods rather than imports |
| 2. Rap or heavy metal music | Whether rap or heavy metal music promotes violence |
| 3. Television | Whether excessive television viewing damages family life |
| 4. Extension of the school year | Whether the U.S. should extend the school year |
| 5. Experiments on animals | Whether cosmetics firms should experiment on animals |

- In your writer's notebook, jot down your views on one of the issues or on an issue of your choice.
- Next, state the primary reason you hold your position. Ask yourself two questions:
  - What is the basis or main reason for my view?
  - Based on this reason, would anyone disagree with my reasoning?

  For example, you might claim that excessive television watching does not damage family life because when you were growing up, the TV was always on in your house and this didn't interfere with your family life. Your classmate sees things differently, claiming that excessive television watching was a distraction that prevented him from having serious discussions with his family.

- Think about how your readers or a larger audience might react to your position, and you will see how difficult it can be to construct a persuasive argument defending your views.

  We will return to this activity in a collaborative exercise after we have considered some strategies and techniques for fashioning strong arguments.

## ■ Differentiate Between Opinions and Reasons

When you develop support for an argument, be sure to differentiate between opinions and reasons. An *opinion* is a belief that you cannot substantiate with direct proof, whereas a *reason* carries with it the weight of logic and reliable evidence. In the previous example, one student's opinion about television watching is as good as another's. But neither will win an argument. Here are two additional examples of opinions:

> The school year should be lengthened because young kids usually waste away their summers anyway.

> From the time I was thirteen, I worked hard at a job all summer long. Kids should work during the summer and not go to school.

In both examples, the writers are expressing opinions about the productivity of kids on vacation. Both individuals define their points of view, but neither gives firm grounds of support. On the other hand, the student who writes

> Because our school year is 180 days and Japan's and West Germany's extends from 226 to 243 school days, Japanese and German children have more time to learn science and math. A lengthened school year will allow our students to spend as much classroom time on science and math as students in other industrialized countries and perhaps "catch up" with the competition.

has provided a rational ground of support for his or her view. This is called a *reason*. To make a strong argument, you have to support your position with substantial reasons. This will be easy if you have ample background knowledge of the issue. But if you know little about the issue, even if you have very strong opinions about it, you must crack open reading sources that offer background information and present other people's arguments and views.

In some courses, professors will stipulate issues for you to discuss. At other times, you will be permitted to select your own issue. When this is the case, start with a topic and then convert your topic into an arguable issue by asking, "What is controversial about _____? What do people argue about?" Take "communitarianism," the topic we introduced earlier (see p. 258). If you have read about this social movement and know that it involves a conflict between individual claims and collective life, you will have no trouble delving beneath the surface and discovering a number of specific issues. Your background knowledge will enable you to refine the topic and come up with an innovative slant on it. If you know very little about communitarianism, however, you will have to learn more about it by carefully reading the texts your professor recommends or by conducting library research. (Chapter 9 will assist you with library work.)

When you have determined what it is that people argue about, convert that information into an issue: whether the interests of communities are more important than the interests of individuals. If you prefer, state your issue as a question: Which is more sacred, communal rights or individual rights?

Subject or Topic → What Do People Argue About? → Issue

You may have strong opinions on the issue from the outset ("No, communal rights are far less important than individual rights"; "Yes, people should honor the common good rather than the selfish individual"), but remember that opinions are not enough. To persuade someone else, you need convincing reasons. Unless you are well read and fully informed about the issue, you will have to consult reading sources.

## ■ Probe Both Sides of the Issue

As you read the sources, you may uncover so much information that you decide to redefine and narrow your issue. Remember to probe both sides and read with an open mind, even if you have already taken a stand. A useful activity is what writing professor Peter Elbow calls the "believing game." As you encounter views that conflict with your own, try to see them through the holder's eyes. Even if the views are absurd or directly opposite to yours, put yourself in the other person's place. As Elbow points out, "To do this requires great energy, attention, and even a kind of inner commitment. It helps to think of it as trying to get inside the head of someone who saw things this way. Perhaps even constructing such a person for yourself. Try to have the experience of someone who made the assertion" (149). The following exercise will give you practice.

### EXERCISE 8.3

To develop full, rich, rounded arguments requires some practice. You can get this practice by playing with controversial ideas in a creative and free-spirited way.

- Take a debatable issue, any issue, no matter how preposterous or absurd: for example, "Homelessness is a desirable way of life," "The U.S. government should allow no more immigrants to enter this country," "Recreational drugs should be freely available to anyone who wants them," "Communities should have the right to prohibit stores from selling questionable types of rock music," "Colleges and universities should enforce strict dress codes." Write down the issue in your own words.
- Write a statement expressing the opposite point of view.
- Brainstorm a list of possible reasons to explain the first statement. After that, brainstorm a list of possible reasons to explain the opposite point of view.
- Decide which reasons are most convincing for each position. Rank them in order of strength of importance.
- Decide which position is most convincing. State that position as the main clause of an independent sentence. Recast the other position as a subordinate clause linked to the main clause by "because," "although," "despite," or the like. Finally, try to express the relationship between both clauses: What is the connecting link that brings them together?

### EXERCISE 8.4

Here we return to the activity that we initiated earlier in the chapter.

- In your writer's notebook, jot down your views on one of the following issues or on an issue of your choice:
  - Whether we should buy American-made goods rather than imports.
  - Whether rap or heavy metal music promotes violence.
  - Whether excessive television watching damages family life.
  - Whether the United States should extend the school year.
  - Whether cosmetics firms should experiment on animals.

- Next, state the primary reason you hold your position. Ask yourself two questions:
  - What is the basis for my view?
  - Would someone agree or disagree with my reasoning?
- Form collaborative learning groups and share your positions and reasons with your classmates.
- As each student explains the issue and gives his or her position and reason for holding it, the other group members should remain noncommittal. For example, if a student in your group explains why she is in favor of lengthening the school year, pretend that you have no opinion on the issue. From your neutral stance, evaluate your classmate's argument. Have you been persuaded to accept her view?
- When each student's argument has been examined, come to a consensus on what characteristics made arguments either strong or weak. Have the group recorder note your group's conclusions.
- Reconvene the entire class. Each group recorder should explain the characteristics of strong and weak arguments that the group identified.

After you have read through the sources, write a clear-cut statement of your position. Returning to Kenneth Burke's metaphor of the parlor conversation (p. 259), you are like the person who has just entered a roomful of people who are engaged in a lively conversation. You may feel like an outsider as you read the first few texts. Remember the conversation started long before you arrived at the party, so you will have to hang in there until, as Burke says, you catch "the tenor of the argument." If your professor has supplied a set of readings as we have done in Chapter 3 and in the anthology section of this book, you will have a much easier job conceptualizing the argument and analyzing its complexities than if you have to obtain your own sources through library research.

In Chapter 3, we provide you with a graphic overview of the academic conversation on the Mommy Wars, and we map out the relationships among the texts indicating who is talking to whom. We suggest that you use the same approach to identify the major relationships among library sources that you obtain on your own.

## ■ Question the Reading Sources

Earlier in this chapter, we explained that arguing is a habit of mind. We said the best way to develop the disposition to argue is to ask questions. Essentially, argument synthesis relies on the same questions for identifying relationships among texts as other types of syntheses (see the questions on pp. 238–39), but argument synthesis also calls for more pointed questions, such as the ones we present in the box below.

---

### QUESTIONS FOR ARGUMENT SYNTHESIS

- How does each text position itself with regard to the issue? List each author's thesis or claim.
- Do one or more texts serve as catalysts for the other texts in the sense that they spark debate?
- How do the texts talk to each other about the controversy?
  Does one author critique other authors' arguments?

Does one author frame the issue in an entirely different way than the others?

Do some of the authors offer the same evidence?

Do some authors support their claims with weak or questionable evidence?

Which authors agree with each other and which differ?

Do some authors come to the same conclusions?

- Which authors present single-minded arguments and which acknowledge and respond to alternative views?
- Which claims are the most convincing? Which are reasonable? Which are flawed?
- Which texts do the best job of contextualizing the controversy?
- After synthesizing this background information, what aspects of the controversy still require further research?

## ■ State Your Claim

In the process of answering these questions, you will examine the complexities of the issue at hand, discover issues within the issue, and come to a deeper understanding. Your new understanding of the issue may lead you to formulate a position very different from the one you initially held. Or you may still hold the same position you expressed at the beginning of the process; however, you will have refined and solidified it. Either way, you are ready to point your oar toward the water, dip it in, and make a claim. To recap your progress, you have moved from a topic to an issue to a contestable claim.

*Claim* is another word for *thesis*; however, the claim of an argument synthesis is more inclusive than the types of theses we have discussed previously in this book. The bottom line is that your thesis should include your position on the issue, your central reason for holding that position, and your acknowledgement of alternative views. If you tried to stuff all three of these elements into a single statement, you would end up with an awkward, unwieldy thesis.

### EXAMPLE

CLAIM: The *New York Times* has misrepresented the controversy of whether mothers should work or stay at home to raise children.

CENTRAL REASON: The *New York Times* has presented frivolous feature articles about privileged, Ivy League white women's decisions to stay at home rather than stories about the cultural, social, and political factors that require large numbers of mothers to work.

ALTERNATIVE VIEW: At least the *Times* is devoting coverage to issues related to domesticity.

$$\downarrow$$

OVERSTUFFED THESIS: Even though we can credit the *New York Times* for devoting coverage to issues related to domesticity, the paper has misrepresented the controversy of whether mothers should work or stay at home to raise children because it has presented frivolous feature articles about privileged, Ivy League white women's decisions to stay at home rather than stories about the cultural, social, and political factors that require large numbers of mothers to work.

While we are not suggesting that you squeeze a detailed version of the three elements into one sentence, you should incorporate these elements into the introductory paragraph(s) of your essay. Here is a more manageable presentation of the three elements.

> Despite the *New York Times'* recent attention to work and motherhood, the paper has done women a disservice by misrepresenting the issue. Perhaps, women should be grateful that the *Times* is devoting space to domestic issues. Unfortunately, the newspaper is covering the wrong issue and the wrong women. The frivolous stories focus on privileged, Ivy League white women's decisions to opt out of the marketplace to become full-time moms. The real players are middle-class and poor women, especially women of color, and the real issues are the cultural, social, and political factors that require these mothers to work.

As you have been reading the selections in Chapter 3, you have probably noticed that authors' theses are not necessarily succinct and explicit, and sometimes authors make a series of claims that lead up to a major thesis. A glance back at our overview of Judith Stadtman Tucker's argument synthesis (pages 263–64) will make this clear.

Despite our caveats about overstuffed theses statements, we think it is good practice to use the graphic overview in Figure 8–4 to outline the major elements in your argument essay.

Your thesis—claim, main reason, and acknowledgement of alternative views—becomes an argument when you crack it open by adding two additional elements: *reasons* and *evidence*. Accordingly, your outline expands, as we illustrate in Figure 8–5.

Look back to our overview of Stadtman Tucker's argument synthesis for a version of a completed graphic overview (pp. 263–64).

## ■ Support Reasons with Evidence from Reading Sources

As we noted earlier, a *reason* carries the weight of reliable evidence. We gave you a list of various types of supporting evidence on page 252. Additional techniques for supporting reasons are presented in the following box:

---

**WAYS TO SUPPORT YOUR REASONS**

- Examples:
  Based on a similarity to something that happened in the past.
  Based on a similar case.
  Based on a hypothetical situation.
- Relevant information:
  Facts
  Statistics
  Points of interest
- Statements, testimony, or other relevant information from acknowledged authorities.
- Personal experience (be sure the experience relates directly to the reason you are developing).

---

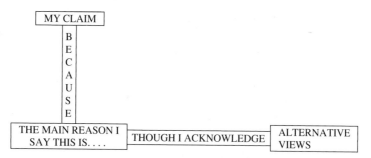

**Figure 8–4    Sample Outline of Major Elements of Thesis**

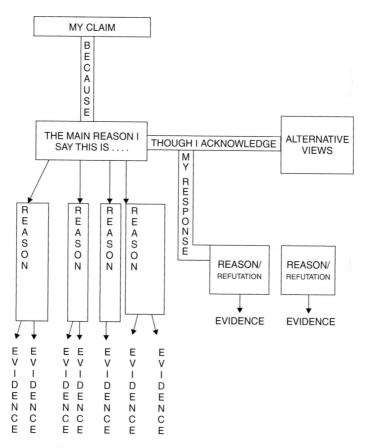

**Figure 8–5    Expanded Sample Outline of Major Elements of Thesis**

## ■ Acknowledge and Respond to Competing Claims

As Stadtman Tucker's synthesis illustrates, the supporting evidence comes from the reading sources. The challenge is to weave the evidence into your essay as gracefully and competently as you can. You can do this by using the vocabulary for attribution that we recommend on pages 65–66. When you are acknowledging and responding to competing claims, employ expressions comparable to the ones used by the authors in this book. In Figure 8–6, we list the authors and their expressions.

| AUTHOR | EXPRESSION |
|---|---|
| Stadtman Tucker | • This may seem like an ideal solution for _____, but _____. <br> • There will always be [people] who believe _____, but those who hold this view are _____. <br> • While _____ contributes to this _____, there are also other considerations such as _____. <br> • Some advisors warn _____. Others feel _____. |
| Hirshman | • Economists explain _____. However, this represents not _____ but _____. <br> • These arguments still do not explain _____. <br> • It is possible that _____, but it is also possible that _____. <br> • It defies reason to claim _____. <br> • The critics are right about one thing: _____. |
| Young | • _____ tackles some of the right issues, but _____. |
| Meares | • While _____ focuses on _____, nowhere does he explore _____. |
| Conley | • It is true that _____. Nonetheless, _____. <br> • The position argues _____. Such a critique refuses to discern _____. <br> • The [people with alternative views] legitimately highlight _____ . They suppress, however, _____. |
| Krauthammer | • These considerations raise serious questions about _____. <br> • This is an argument of _____. I happen not to share this view. <br> • These arguments are serious _____. Yet, in my view, insufficient to justify _____. <br> • Some have suggested _____, but this is plainly not so. <br> • Critics counter _____, but it makes no sense to _____. |
| Stoll | • It is true that _____, but _____. |
| Erera | • Contrary to claims of _____, there is no _____. <br> • _____ have it backwards when they argue _____. |
| Horn | • This, of course, is not without merit, but _____. <br> • Some advocate _____. Indeed, there is evidence that _____. Unfortunately, other research has found _____. <br> • The argument goes _____. Other research, however, suggests that _____. |

**Figure 8–6    Expressions for Acknowledging and Responding to Competing Claims**

In addition to the expressions gleaned from readings in this book, there are stock expressions of concession, such as:

Granted that _____, we still _____.

Even though _____, we nonetheless find that _____.

True _____. Yet, _____.

On the one hand, _____. On the other hand, _____.

If you have a vocabulary for acknowledging and responding to incompatible views, it will be easier to participate in a polite exchange of ideas in a gracious and intelligent way.

## Point-by-Point Arrangement of Alternative Views

One important feature of argument to consider before we move on to examine an argument synthesis paper written by a student concerns the point-by-point arrangement of alternative views. This point-by-point arrangement is usually the clearest way to present alternative views because it lists them in a summary format connected by transitional words or phrases, such as "some have suggested _____, but critics object _____"; "some propose _____, but we maintain _____"; and "some claim _____, yet evidence shows _____."

For an illustration of this point-by-point arrangement, read Charles Krauthammer's argument against human cloning, "Crossing Lines: A Secular Argument Against Research Cloning" on pages 351–58. We have excerpted five paragraphs from the article. As you read the paragraphs, examine the form, logic, and language. We have underlined the words and expressions Krauthammer uses to introduce and acknowledge alternative views and respond to them.

In the first paragraph, the "this" Krauthammer refers to is research cloning, which he describes as "the creation of nascent human life for the sole purpose of its exploitation and destruction" (357). Krauthammer supports stem-cell research but only if it uses embryos that are left over from fertility clinics.

How is this morally different from simply using discarded embryos from in vitro fertilization (IVF) clinics? <u>Some have suggested that it is not, that</u> to oppose research cloning is to oppose IVF and any stem-cell research that comes out of IVF. <u>The claim is made that because</u> in IVF there is a high probability of destruction of the embryo, it is morally equivalent to research cloning. <u>But this is plainly not so.</u> In research cloning there is not a high probability of destruction; there is 100 percent probability. Because every cloned embryo must be destroyed, it is nothing more than a means to someone else's end.

In IVF, the probability of destruction may be high, but it need not necessarily be. You could have a clinic that produces only a small number of embryos, and we know of many cases of multiple births resulting from multiple embryo implantation. In principle, one could have IVF using only a single embryo and thus involving no deliberate embryo destruction at all. In principle, that is impossible in research cloning.

<u>Furthermore</u>, a cloned embryo is created to be destroyed and used by others. An IVF embryo is created to develop into a child. <u>One cannot disregard</u> intent in determining morality. Embryos are created in IVF to serve reproduction. Embryos are created in research cloning to serve, well, research. <u>If</u> certain IVF embryos were designated as "helper embryos" that would simply aid an anointed embryo in turning into a child, <u>then we would have an analogy</u> to cloning. <u>But, in fact, we don't</u> know which embryo is

anointed in IVF. They are all created to have a chance of survival. And they are all equally considered an end.

Critics counter that this ends-and-means argument is really obfuscation, that both procedures make an instrument of the embryo. In cloning, the creation and destruction of the embryo is a means to understanding or curing disease. In IVF, the creation of the embryo is a means of satisfying a couple's need for a child. They are both just means to ends.

But it makes no sense to call an embryo a means to the creation of a child. The creation of a child is the destiny of an embryo. To speak of an embryo as a means to creating a child empties the word "means" of content. The embryo in IVF is a stage in the development of a child; it is no more a means than a teenager is a means to the adult he or she later becomes. In contrast, an embryo in research cloning is pure means. Laboratory pure.

---

### EXERCISE 8.5

- Select another subset of paragraphs from Charles Krauthammer's "Crossing Lines: A Secular Argument Against Research Cloning" on pages 351–58.
- Examine the form, logic, and language and underline the words and expressions Krauthammer uses to introduce and acknowledge alternative views and respond to them.

---

## ■ ILLUSTRATION OF STUDENT'S PROCESS IN WRITING AN ARGUMENT SYNTHESIS ESSAY

In the remainder of this chapter, we illustrate the process of composing an argument synthesis essay by following a student, Sarah Allyn, as she works on an essay entitled "Communitarianism Contested" (see pp. 279–83). For this assignment, Sarah read four texts: Amitai Etzioni's "Morality as a Community Affair"; Christopher Little's "Communitarianism, A New Threat for Gun Owners"; Barry Jay Seltser and Donald E. Miller's "Ambivalences in American Views of Dignity"; and Michael Walzer's "Multiculturalism and Individualism."

### ■ Consider Audience

An important consideration for Sarah is the likely audience for her essay. If the issue is highly controversial, readers will have opinions of their own. A writer who addresses a single reader—say, a college professor or a public official whose confidence one seeks to engage—should estimate what the reader already knows and thinks about the issue. Members of a larger audience may hold conflicting points of view. Writers who address such an audience need especially to rely on the power and conviction of their argued proofs.

---

#### QUESTIONS ABOUT AUDIENCE FOR AN ARGUMENTATIVE ESSAY

- Am I writing for my professor, my classmates, a broader audience, or a special group of readers?
- What do my readers already know about the issue? Will I have to explain basic concepts and provide background information for my point of view to make sense?

- How do I want to come across to my audience — as an objective, scholarly authority, or as someone who identifies with my readers and shares their concerns?
- Is my audience noncommittal, or have my readers already taken a stand on the issue I am discussing?

Answers to the questions in the box above tell writers a number of things: (1) how much effort they should expend to attract their audience's attention with the lead sentence and introduction; (2) how much background information they should provide so that their readers will thoroughly understand the issue; (3) how they will address their readers (whether they will be totally objective or use pronouns such as "I," "you," or "we"); and (4) how they will order their presentation and how much space they will devote to opposing views.

## ■ Determine Issue, Thesis, and Competing Positions

After Sarah contemplates the audience for her essay, she reads the four assigned texts looking first to identify the issue being discussed and second to determine how the texts are talking to each other.

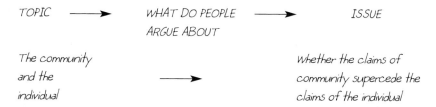

TOPIC  ⟶  WHAT DO PEOPLE ⟶  ISSUE
ARGUE ABOUT

The community and the individual  ⟶  Whether the claims of community supercede the claims of the individual

Sarah then rereads the four texts interrogating them with the Questions for Identifying Relationships among the Sources that appear on p. 239 and earlier in this chapter on pp. 268–69. In the process of answering these questions, Sarah refines the issue, stakes out her position, and acknowledges the major alternative position. Here is Sarah's schematic outline of the issue:

*Issue: Whether communitarianism is a panacea for the problems facing America.*

*My position: Few mainstream Americans will consider communitarianism a worthwhile solution to America's problems.*

*Alternative view: Communitarian principles will solve the nation's problems.*

Taking the two positions, Sarah composes a thesis statement that includes the main points of both sides:

*Even though some of the recommendations of communitarians are laudable, few, if any, mainstream Americans will see the resurgence of "community" as a panacea for our nation's ills.*

Then Sarah returns to the reading sources to locate reasons she can use to substantiate her own position as well as the alternative position. She asks herself, "Which facts, examples, pieces of evidence, and citations by reliable authorities support my views and the alternative views?" Sarah discovers reasons and jots them down in her writer's notebook.

## *SUPPORT FOR MY POSITIONS*

1. We should keep in mind that "communitarian writers are mainly academics, some of whom enjoy close connections to the Washington political community" (Little 30).
2. Etzioni himself admits that communitarian organizations can be excessive and corrupt, for example McCarthyism and the Ku Klux Klan (36).
3. How will the "common good" prevail and communitarianism function if, as Etzioni explains, "Americans don't like to tell others how to behave"?
4. Another conflict between individuals and communities is related to the issue of personal property. Seltser and Miller remind us that "property is defined as an extension of the self" (120).
5. Little: How can communitarianism be morally advantageous when it abrogates certain rights (30)?
6. Levinson in Yale Law Journal argues that most Americans will uphold individual rights, even at cost to others (Little 84).

## *SUPPORT FOR THE OTHER SIDE*

1. Walzer: "Individuals are stronger, more confident, more savvy, when they are participants in a common life, responsible to and for other people" (189).
2. Seltser and Miller: A common moral or ethical code is reasonable because society is formed "by a mixture of values and beliefs that both form its citizens and are in turn formed by them" (118).
3. Etzioni argues that the alternative to having the community voice sound moral principles is "state coercion or social and moral anarchy" (36).
4. Walzer: If we adopt communitarian principles, we will have "greater social and economic equality" (190).

Next, Sarah decides how to structure her argument synthesis essay.

## ■ Organize Argument Synthesis Essays

Some of the principles of argument that were taught in ancient Greece and Rome have been adapted for writers today. If you were a student in ancient times, you would have been taught to set up your argument in six parts:

1. Introduction (exordium)
2. Statement or exposition of the case under discussion (narratio)
3. Outline of the points or steps in the argument (divisio)
4. proof of the case (confirmatio)
5. refutation of the opposing arguments (confutatio)
6. conclusion (peroratio) (Corbett 25)

Today's principles of organization are not quite so rigid or formulaic. Nevertheless, most modern writers of arguments use some variation of the following divisions: introduction, explanation of the issue and background information, writer's thesis, presentation of and response to alternative views, reasons and evidence for writer's thesis, conclusion. Two standard organizational formats are (1) acknowledge and respond to alternative views in separate, self-contained sections of the essay and (2) acknowledge and respond to objections in a point-by-point fashion.

## Acknowledge and Respond to Alternative Views in Separate, Self-Contained Sections

---

### ARRANGEMENT: ACKNOWLEDGE AND RESPOND TO ALTERNATIVE VIEWS IN SEPARATE, SELF-CONTAINED SECTIONS OF THE ESSAY

The following template shows you how to construct an outline for sections of an essay in which you acknowledge and respond to alternative views.

#### Introductory Section

- Opener: Introduce the issue and invite your readers into the conversation.
- Explanation and background: Familiarize your readers with the controversy. Give them the information they need to understand the issue at hand and make sense of the conversation.
- Thesis: Give your stand on the issue—your main claim.

#### Body of the Essay

- Acknowledge and respond to alternative views and offer reasons, substantiated by evidence, for your main claim.

Individual sections of essay (as many as needed throughout the essay: Repeat template for each section):

| Variation A | Variation B |
|---|---|
| 1. Alternative view | 1. Reasons (#1, #2, #3, etc.) and evidence to support your claim |
| 2. Your response | 2. Alternative view |
| Reasons (#1, #2, #3, etc.) and evidence to support your claim | 3. Your response |

#### Conclusion

- Recap of argument
- Concluding technique

---

You can arrange your reasons in several different ways. Many writers prefer to present weaker reasons first and work to a climax by saving their strongest argument until the end of the composition. This movement from weak to strong provides a dramatic effect.

Weakest reason + evidence
Weaker reason + evidence
Fairly strong reason + evidence
Strongest reason + evidence
Alternative views and objections
Response to alternative views

Other writers start the body of the essay with the alternative views (Variation A in the preceding example); then, in sharp contrast, they present their strongest reasons; finally, they close with their weakest points. This movement begins the essay with an energetic claim that seizes the reader's attention.

Alternative views and objections
Response to alternative views
Strongest reason + evidence
Fairly strong reason + evidence
Weaker reason + evidence
Weakest reason + evidence

Still other writers think it best to present a relatively strong argument first, saving the strongest until last; in between, they arrange the weaker ones. This movement combines the dramatic effect of the first pattern with the attention-seizing aspect of the second.

Whether you choose to acknowledge and respond to alternative views before you give reasons for your own position or after you present your case depends on the situation and the nature of your audience. There is no hard rule that says that you must arrange your essay one way or the other.

## Acknowledge and Respond to Objections in a Point-by-Point Fashion

But what if you expect your readers to question or suggest alternative interpretations of multiple aspects of your argument? In that case, you may want to arrange the body of your essay in a different way. Instead of acknowledging and responding to alternative views in separate, self-contained sections of your essay, you can respond to the objections in a point-by-point fashion. The following box shows an outline of this alternating arrangement.

---

### ARRANGEMENT: ACKNOWLEDGE AND RESPOND TO OBJECTIONS IN A POINT-BY-POINT FASHION

**Introductory Section**

- Opener: Introduce the issue and invite your readers into the conversation.
- Explanation and background: Familiarize your readers with the controversy. Give them the information they need to understand the issue at hand and make sense of the conversation.
- Thesis: Give your stand on the issue—your main claim.

## Body of the Essay

- Alternative view on one aspect of the controversy
- Your refutation of this view
- Reason + evidence for your thesis
- Alternative view on another aspect of the controversy
- Your refutation of this view
- Reason + evidence for your thesis

(This pattern continues until you have covered all the aspects of the issue that you choose to focus on.)

## Conclusion

- Recap of the argument
- Concluding technique

As you read Sarah Allyn's essay, note especially that Sarah acknowledges and refutes opposing arguments in paragraphs 3, 4, and 5. Then in paragraphs 6 and 7, she provides further support for her own position. Here is Sarah's essay.

## STUDENT'S ARGUMENT SYNTHESIS ESSAY

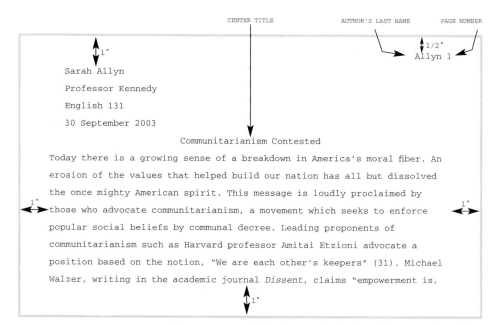

CENTER TITLE                    AUTHOR'S LAST NAME          PAGE NUMBER

1/2"
Allyn 1

1"
Sarah Allyn
Professor Kennedy
English 131
30 September 2003

Communitarianism Contested
Today there is a growing sense of a breakdown in America's moral fiber. An erosion of the values that helped build our nation has all but dissolved the once mighty American spirit. This message is loudly proclaimed by those who advocate communitarianism, a movement which seeks to enforce popular social beliefs by communal decree. Leading proponents of communitarianism such as Harvard professor Amitai Etzioni advocate a position based on the notion, "We are each other's keepers" (31). Michael Walzer, writing in the academic journal *Dissent*, claims "empowerment is,

1"

1"

1/2"
Allyn 2

with rare exceptions, a familial, class, or communal, not an individual achievement" (187). More than mere sloganeers, however, communitarians are working to realize a society bereft of many of the hard-fought liberties achieved in our Constitution, which set forth to ensure liberty for all Americans. Christopher Little reminds us, "Communitarian writers are mainly academics, some of whom enjoy close connections to the Washington political community" (30). Are these the voices mainstream Americans want speaking for them?

Are those of us from mainstream America as willing to sacrifice personal liberty for the greater welfare of the many as those from academia's privileged left wing? Are we willing to place our responsibil-

1"
1"

ity and duty to others in front of our personal rights, to uphold the safety of others and the liberty of the group before considering the claims of the individual, to sacrifice our Constitutional rights as an American citizen-and to do so in the name of a socialist political agenda devised by academics secure enough in their means to undertake such a radical experiment? Even though some of the recommendations of communitarian intellectuals are laudable, few, if any, mainstream Americans will consider the principles of communitarianism to be a worthwhile answer to our nation's ills.

As a system of organization, communitarianism is inherently impractical. In "Multiculturalism and Individualism," Walzer argues, "Individuals are stronger, more confident, more savvy, when they are participants in a common life, responsible to and for other people" (189). If the failure of Communism isn't enough to disprove Walzer's claim, consider the decline of a redundant form of communitarianism—labor unions. Labor unions haven't succeeded for the same reasons that any attempt to galvanize people according to structure reminiscent of Marxist principles would be doomed. First, in a democracy, the majority gets what it votes for, and most likely, existing forms of political leadership would be prepared to meet any challenge posed by a communitarian constituency. Second, communitarian organizations, much like labor unions, would be extremely vulnerable to excessiveness and corruption. Etzioni himself illustrates: "Forty years ago, for example, America experienced the nightmare of McCarthyism. Likewise the memory of the real Ku Klux Klan" (36). Consider also the disgraceful spectacle of organized labor's relationship with organized crime. These examples of communitarianism run awry remain fresh in the collective American consciousness. Furthermore,

1"

Allyn 3

according to Professor Sanford Levinson writing in the *Yale Law Journal*, Americans place such a high value on their individual rights that they "will honor them even when there is significant social cost in doing so" (quoted in Little 84). Lastly, to quote Etzioni again, "Americans do not like to tell others how to behave" (34). For communitarianism to function as it is intended, heavy emphasis has to be placed on people's ability to "police" one another. This monitoring of others is a troublesome and wholly undemocratic process.

Writing in "Ambivalences in American Views of Dignity," Barry J. Seltser and Donald E. Miller explain, "Societies are defined, in large part, precisely by the mixture of values and beliefs that both form [their] citizens and are in turn formed by them" (118). While Seltser and Miller may be correct, creating a factional, quasi-governmental system won't serve to advance Americans' common moral or ethical code. Moreover, along with the complexities inherent in forging relationships according to a communitarian model of social behavior, decisions to determine power accords and their regulation would be left up to a decentralized governing body. Such potentially great power represented without the benefit of definitive leadership could be dangerous. Seltser and Miller uncover a source of conflict that opposes communitarianism's principles. They explain, "In one important strand of the liberal political tradition, of course, property is defined as an extension of the self, as something of myself that has been mixed in with the physical world and therefore remains 'mine' in some important sense" (121). This contradiction alone between democratic and communitarian ideals makes the prospect of successfully managed communitarian environments all the more unlikely, at least as long as America intends to remain a democracy.

The advocates of communitarianism, in retreat, resort to hysteria. In "Morality as a Community Affair," Etzioni, admonishing his readers about the importance of catering to the whims and needs of the community, and in rare form, declares, "The alternative is typically state coercion or social and moral anarchy" (36). Claiming the only alternatives "to the exercise of moral voices" are either "a police state" or "a moral vacuum in which anything goes" (37), Etzioni neglects to mention that with a few rare exceptions in America's history, such alternatives have not been seriously considered. This is due to the fact that America's government, despite its tender age, has exhibited the greatest degree of stability and success in the annals of our planet's social order. Preying on what Walzer calls the nation's "strong egalitarian and populist strain" (186), some communitarians are determined to stress the negative aspects of our democratic society. An advocate of multiculturalism, Walzer believes

that "greater social and economic equality" will be the end result of
the adoption of communitarian principles (191). He goes on to admit,
however, that acting according to multicultural principles today may
bring more trouble than hope (191). He attributes this to America's
weak social agenda, but this rationalization serves merely as an
excuse.

The adoption of communitarianism in America would necessitate a
paradigm shift in our fundamental cultural construction, from individualism to collectivism. Though America is no longer a fledgling democracy,
there is still evidence of "rugged individualism" within our culture.
Individualism has played an important role in our national development.
And for many Americans, particularly recent immigrants, communitarian
principles may prove a barrier to pursuing the American dream. Clearly,
communitarianism, perhaps even in its mildest form, threatens the vitality
of the American populace and poses a potential challenge to American
democracy. Although advocates of communitarianism champion its principles
as morally advantageous, other people disagree. As Little puts it, "Its
public policy recommendations either implicitly or expressly call for the
attenuation or even abrogation of certain rights" (30). Doesn't communitarianism breach the moral foundations of our nation? Disturbingly, as
Little points out, "A recent issue of *The Communitarian Reporter* states
that the White House is 'seeking to move along communitarian lines,'
a fact well attested by the communitarian substance of many speeches
and writings of President Clinton" (31). "In fairness," Little continues,
"there are signs that Clinton is not a 'purist' communitarian," though
"nevertheless, his communitarian bent is by definition an anti-
constitutional bent" (84). Given the dubious morality and constitutionality of communitarianism, it is hard to account for its appeal.
Don't such radical principles actually serve the interests of the few
rather than the many?

Even if we were to agree with Etzioni that we ought to be "each
other's keepers" (31), democracy is indeed our efficient system of social
checks and balances. It is a system that enables Americans to determine
their collective progress or decline. We owe at least this much to one
another: to guard against the debasement of our personal freedoms, to
uphold our long-standing heritage of individualism and to never relinquish
our Constitutional rights. It is our responsibility, as privileged
citizens of this great nation, to oppose the undemocratic, un-American
ideals set forth by the immoral, unconstitutional, and unfair theories of
communitarianism.

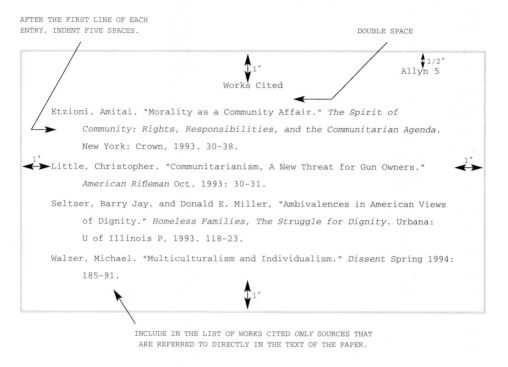

AFTER THE FIRST LINE OF EACH
ENTRY, INDENT FIVE SPACES.

DOUBLE SPACE

↕1"
Allyn 5

↕1/2"

Works Cited

Etzioni, Amitai. "Morality as a Community Affair." *The Spirit of*
    *Community: Rights, Responsibilities, and the Communitarian Agenda.*
    New York: Crown, 1993. 30-38.

Little, Christopher. "Communitarianism, A New Threat for Gun Owners."
    *American Rifleman* Oct. 1993: 30-31.

Seltser, Barry Jay, and Donald E. Miller, "Ambivalences in American Views
    of Dignity." *Homeless Families, The Struggle for Dignity.* Urbana:
    U of Illinois P, 1993. 118-23.

Walzer, Michael. "Multiculturalism and Individualism." *Dissent* Spring 1994:
    185-91.

INCLUDE IN THE LIST OF WORKS CITED *ONLY* SOURCES THAT
ARE REFERRED TO DIRECTLY IN THE TEXT OF THE PAPER.

Sarah Allyn's essay has followed many of the guidelines we've suggested for argumentative essays. It displays a broad knowledge of ideas that support the concept of communitarian ethics and related issues; it outlines major areas of controversy on the topic, such as the status of personal liberties, factional politics, and multicultural populism; and it articulates a strong thesis that expresses a particular point of view about the issues in question. Sarah's thesis is an oppositional one that takes the source readings to task for compromising personal liberties. An argumentative thesis need not and usually should not be so negative as this one. In general, a positive argument that expands one's understanding of the source materials succeeds much better than a wrangling altercation. Still, Sarah Allyn leaves no doubt that she has examined the issues and has considered how she wants her audience to respond.

## ■ Revising and Editing

Though we have presented Sarah's final draft, we want you to bear in mind that she produced this version of the paper after several preliminary drafts of its parts and their whole, and after a peer review session with a classmate. We present the peer review questions in the box on the following page.

## Editing the Preliminary Draft

When you are satisfied with your revision, read your paper aloud. Then reread it line by line and sentence by sentence. Check for correct usage, punctuation, spelling, mechanics, manuscript form, and typos. If you are especially weak in editing skills, try getting a friend to read over your work.

---

### QUESTIONS FOR HELPING WRITERS REVISE ARGUMENT ESSAYS

- Does the writer move beyond the purpose of simply synthesizing or comparing or contrasting opposing views? In other words, is the discussion around the discernible purpose of persuading or convincing an audience? If not, how might the writer sharpen the purpose?
- Is the argument two-dimensional, taking into account both sides of the issue or is it one-sided?
- Does the writer use the conventions (not necessarily in this order) that the reader expects to find in an argument essay?

  Explanation of the issue?
  Arguable thesis?
  Background information?
  Support for the position being argued?
  Acknowledgement and response to alternative views?
  Conclusion?

- Does the writer present a sufficient number of solid reasons to back up his or her main claim? If not, what should be added?
- Are the reasons substantiated with reliable evidence? If not, what should be added?
- Does the writer draw on reliable sources? If not, which sources are questionable?
- Does the writer create a favorable, creditable impression of himself or herself? If not, how might the writer do this?
- Does the writer display an awareness of the audience's needs and set a context for the reader by:

  Giving appropriate background information?
  Mentioning authors and titles of sources when necessary?
  Supplying necessary documentation for sources?
  Providing clear connectives that differentiate his or her ideas from those of the writers of the sources?

---

### EXERCISE 8.6

- Reread Sarah Allyn's paper.
- Note the structure of its presentation. After an introduction, Sarah questions whether mainstream America endorses communitarian thought; she points to shortcomings in quotations from its supporters; she cites criticism by its opponents; and she speculates about consequences that could follow from its adoption.
- Write a brief critical analysis in which you evaluate the strength of her argument. Guidelines for writing critical analysis essays are presented in Chapter 4.

## EXERCISE 8.7

- Form collaborative learning groups.
- Assign each member a paragraph from the body of Sarah Allyn's paper. Ask each to comment on Sarah's use of her sources.
- Reconvene the entire class. Each group recorder should read the members' evaluations and respond to inquiries from the rest of the class about the effectiveness of Sarah's argument.

## WORKS CITED

Burke, Kenneth. *The Philosophy of Literary Form.* 3rd ed. Berkeley: U of California P, 1941.

Corbett, Edward. *Classical Rhetoric for the Modern Student.* 3rd ed. New York: Oxford UP, 1990.

Eisenschitz, Aram. "Innocent Concepts? A Paradigmatic Approach to Argument." *Learning to Argue in Higher Education.* Eds. Sally Mitchell and Richard Andrews. Portsmouth, NH: Boynton/Cook Heinemann, 2000. 12–25.

Elbow, Peter. *Writing without Teachers.* New York: Oxford UP, 1973.

Etzioni, Amitai. "Morality as a Community Affair." *The Spirit of Community: Rights, Responsibilities, and the Communitarian Agenda.* New York: Crown, 1993. 30–38.

Little, Christopher. "Communitarianism, A New Threat for Gun Owners." *American Rifleman* Oct. 1993. 30–31.

Seltser, Barry Jay, and Donald E. Miller, "Ambivalences in American Views of Dignity." *Homeless Families, The Struggle for Dignity.* Urbana: U of Illinois P, 1993. 118–23.

Walzer, Michael. "Multiculturalism and Individualism." *Dissent* Spring 1994. 185–91.

■ ■ ■ ■ ■ ■

# *Nine*

# Writing Research Papers

## ◼▰ THE RESEARCH PAPER: AN INTRODUCTION

Research involves collecting information from multiple sources and then acting on that information by analyzing, organizing, synthesizing, generalizing, and applying what you have learned. Often, we connect the term *research* with scientific and medical discoveries, but it applies to systematic investigation in any discipline, including the humanities and the social sciences. Professors typically assign research papers to make you an active, independent scholar who is able to locate other people's ideas, analyze and synthesize those ideas, and come to an independent conclusion. Studying research methods is learning how to learn.

In Chapters 1 through 8, we have stressed that the writing process requires active engagement, careful thought, and hard work. The same is true for research. Research involves more than just finding and recording information. A collection of facts will mean little to your readers without explanation, organization, and commentary. To locate appropriate sources in the library, you must plan ahead and think carefully about what you want to find.

Writing a research paper involves many of the writing processes and strategies you have learned in this book. The clerical work of compiling a list of sources is only a small part of the overall process. At the same time, the research paper differs from the other essays you have been practicing in this book because it is lengthier, more complex, and more scholarly. Although research begins with examining other people's ideas, it can develop into an extremely creative activity. When you synthesize information from various texts, you come to new conclusions that are entirely your own.

In this chapter, we will explain the process of writing a research paper. When we speak of library-based research, we are referring to research conducted online in virtual libraries as well as in brick-and-mortar buildings. The process is outlined in the following box.

---

**PROCESS OF WRITING A RESEARCH PAPER**

- Identify a research topic.
- Develop a research strategy.
- Determine your rhetorical purpose.
- Set a schedule.
- Decide on the questions your research paper will answer.
- Determine where you will find the sources.

---

# ■ IDENTIFY A RESEARCH TOPIC: THE ROLE OF THE ASSIGNMENT

The process you go through to identify a research topic depends upon the specificity of your assignment. If your assignment defines the topic in pointed detail, you may be able to search for materials right away. If the assignment allows you to select your own topic, either from your personal storehouse of knowledge or from the professor's list, you'll have to choose a topic and narrow it before you begin your library search. Here are research assignments of varying degrees of specificity:

> *Specific assignment (from a psychology course)*: Write a six-page research paper in which you draw upon the psychological literature on dance therapy published during the past decade.

> *Focused assignment (from a psychology course)*: Write an eight- to ten-page research paper that expands upon one of the topics covered in our textbook or class lectures. Use at least ten sources of information, not including the textbook.

> *Open-ended assignment (from a first-year writing course)*: Select a topic that truly interests you. Narrow the topic, convert it into a research question, and write a ten-page research paper.

The first assignment asks you to consult psychological journals published in the last ten years for articles on dance therapy. The second assignment allows you to select a topic from among the topics covered in the course textbook or class lectures. The third assignment leaves the choice of topic entirely up to you.

To illustrate, let's say you receive Assignment 3 in your first-year writing class. A subject that has been in the news lately is steroid use among athletes. You're interested in learning more about this issue, so you select steroids as your topic. The first thing you have to do is learn the basic facts about steroids. Picture yourself standing on the threshold of a roomful of informed people who are discussing steroid use and athletes. As we explained in Chapter 8, you have to thoroughly familiarize yourself with the topic and issues before you can join the conversation.

For basic background information, consult a general encyclopedia and a specialized encyclopedia or other type of specialized reference work. Access you library homepage (we explain how to do this on page 296), click on the link for **references** or **reference tools**, and locate a general encyclopedia. Alternatively, you can go directly to The Internet Public Library <http://www.ipl.org>. Click first on *References* and then on *Encyclopedias*. Among the encyclopedias listed is the *Columbia Encyclopedia*. You look up *steroids*, read the entry, and narrow your topic to *anabolic steroids*, male hormones used to increase muscle mass.

Your next step is to look up the topic in a specialized encyclopedia that will give you more in-depth, detailed information. Your library probably offers a number of special encyclopedias in print; for example, *Encyclopedia of American History*, *Encyclopedia of Psychology*, and the *McGraw-Hill Encyclopedia of Science and Technology*.

You can also find specialized encyclopedias online. For example, the *A.D.A.M. Health Illustrated Encyclopedia Medline Medical Encyclopedia* is available from the United States National Library of Medicine at <http://www.nlm.nih.gov/>. A search for *anabolic steroids* produces eighteen entries. After reading a number of these entries, you narrow your topic to *consequences of the abuse of anabolic steroids.* (If you have difficulty locating a specialized encyclopedia, consult a reference librarian.)

When looking for online reference sources, students are quick to use Wikipedia (<http://en.wikipedia.org/wiki/Main_Page>). Wikipedia is worth consulting for general background information, but it is not a source you should include in your research paper. Anyone can contribute entries to Wikipedia; there is no academic oversight or review of its quality and accuracy. As a result, the usefulness of some of its articles is questionable and their validity is disputed.

## ■▤ ILLUSTRATION OF A STUDENT'S PROCESS OF WRITING A RESEARCH PAPER

Throughout the rest of this chapter, we will trace the process of our student, Jennifer Piazza. In an upper-level psychology course entitled "Counseling: Theory and Dynamics," Jennifer received the assignment we mentioned previously:

> Write an eight- to ten-page research paper that expands upon one of the topics covered in our textbook or class lectures. Use at least ten sources of information, not including the textbook.

### ■ Select a Research Topic

Jennifer narrows the focus of her assignment by reviewing the subject areas covered in her psychology class and isolating a topic or, better yet, several potential topics, for her paper. She already knows a certain amount about psychological topics, so she bypasses the initial reference searches. If that were not the case, however, her first move would be to consult a few general reference works, such as specialized encyclopedias (e.g., *Encyclopedia of Psychology*).

Two prewriting strategies that we described in Chapter 1, freewriting and brainstorming, will help Jennifer to identify possible research topics. She could brainstorm a list of words and phrases in response to the assignment and then read over the list for similarities, patterns, and connections. Alternatively, she could freewrite nonstop for ten minutes, using cues in the assignment to generate ideas. Then she would search her freewriting for useful topics. The following is an excerpt from Jennifer's freewriting.

> *The chapter on counseling trauma victims was especially interesting to me. I'm currently working as a volunteer with Suicide Prevention and Crisis Services, and many of the hotline calls I answer are from people who are coping with the result of a traumatic experience. Perhaps if I did my research paper on trauma, I would learn something that*

*would be of direct benefit to my hotline clients. But I'm not sure how I could add anything to what the textbook presented except maybe to add more details about the theory. Perhaps I could write about how current ideas about dealing with trauma are different from what was previously believed. Our textbook chapter started with Freud, so I could research what was believed about trauma before Freud and try to show how the theory developed over time. One topic that I wish the textbook had said more about was how talking through a traumatic experience is helpful in dealing with it. I know that my hotline clients feel better after they are able to get the experience off their chest by describing it. In my Personal Essay class, I wrote about a particularly traumatic event in my own life: When I was four, a close relative was diagnosed with cancer and in response to the news, my family really freaked out. I was terrified to see adults in this condition, and no one fully explained to me what was going on, so I couldn't make sense of it at all. I felt a strong sense of relief when, fifteen years later, I was able to relive the experience on paper and explain my emotions. Perhaps I could do research on the therapeutic effects of "reliving" traumatic experiences in conversation or on paper.*

In the process of rereading her freewriting, Jennifer decides she would like to learn more about the history of psychic trauma theory and current therapies for trauma, particularly the use of verbal expression as a therapeutic response. She decides to focus her initial research on these two areas.

Another way to zero in on a research topic is to consult general subject headings in periodical indexes related to your broad subject area (biology, music, psychology, and so forth). You could also ask your professor to suggest topics. Whichever strategy you use, follow your own interests. The research and writing process will be more successful and rewarding if you identify a topic that appeals to you.

It's a good idea to come up with several alternative subtopics because the one you initially select may not be practical for research. You might inadvertently select a topic that is treated only in scholarly texts that you would have difficulty understanding because of your unfamiliarity with their methodology, analytical techniques, and specialized vocabulary. You might choose a topic that requires a number of resources that are difficult to obtain from your college library. You might even identify a topic that cannot be researched because very few texts address it. If your preliminary research reveals that your initial research topic is naive and must be modified or abandoned, quickly turn to your alternative topics. We recap the procedure for selecting a topic in the box below.

---

### SELECTING A RESEARCH TOPIC

- Identify a topic that interests you by:

  - Reviewing topics covered in the course textbook, assigned readings, and class lectures
  - Consulting reference works such as general and specialized encyclopedias related to your broad subject area
  - Asking you professor to suggest a topic

(continued on the next page)

- Read up on your topic, narrow your focus, and come up with a list of alternative subtopics.
- Brainstorm a list of words or phrases associated with your topic. Then reread the list looking for similarities, patterns, and connections.

Or:

- Freewrite for ten minutes and then review your writing for useful ideas.

## EXERCISE 9.1

### Part A

Select a course you are taking this semester, excluding your writing course.

- Review the topics covered in the course textbook, readings, and lectures.
- Select a topic for a potential research paper.
- Brainstorm a list of words or phrases associated with your topic. Then reread the list looking for similarities, patterns, and connections.
- Write one or two pages explaining how you selected and narrowed your research topic.

### Part B

Select a topic you are interested in researching.

- First look up the topic in a general encyclopedia in your college library or in the online *Columbia Encyclopedia* (<http://www.ipl.org>).
- Then look up the topic in a specialized encyclopedia.
- Brainstorm a list of words or phrases associated with your topic. Then reread the list looking for similarities, patterns, and connections.

Or:

- Freewrite nonstop for ten minutes and then review your writing for useful ideas.
- Write one or two pages explaining how you selected and narrowed your research topic.

## ■ Develop a Research Strategy

You have a topic. Now you need a research strategy. Your most important consideration is your overall goal. Ask yourself the following questions:

- What am I trying to accomplish? What is my rhetorical purpose?
- What about a schedule? How long will the research and writing take me?
- What questions am I trying to answer?
- Where will I find sources for my paper?

## Determine Your Rhetorical Purpose

Research papers are synthesis essays such as the ones we discussed in Chapters 7 and 8. They will incorporate more research than those, but they will require the same operations.

Library research will locate texts related to your topic. As with any synthesis, you must analyze these texts to determine what each contributes to the ongoing academic conversation. You read to hear what various authors have to say about the topic, how they bounce ideas off one another, and how they zero in on subtopics that run across the texts.

When you are well informed, you stake out your own position. Then you revisit the sources to extract relevant bits of information that will support your thesis. In the process of writing the paper, you weave together your own ideas with those you've gleaned from the sources. Depending on the research paper assignment, you have three options: (1) to write an exploratory synthesis, (2) a thesis-driven synthesis, or (3) an argument synthesis. In the following box, we review each form of synthesis and its rhetorical purpose.

---

### SYNTHESIS: FORMS AND RHETORICAL PURPOSE

*Explanatory*

The writer's goal is to unfold or unravel a topic or question to make it clearer to the readers. The synthesis might crack open a concept, place an issue in historical context, or clarify sides in a controversy. The synthesis is broad and nonjudgmental. The writer presents informative results in a straightforward manner. Such a synthesis often tries to define a topic or issue in an expository style that emphasizes the coverage of data rather than any further questioning or interpretation of the data.

*Thesis-Driven*

The writer's goal is to get the readers to understand his or her thesis and point of view. The writer takes a position on the topic or issue. The writer's position is explicit in a direct statement of judgment or opinion on the matter at hand. The thesis is supported by reasons that are based on evidence.

*Argument*

The writer's goal is to persuade readers that his or her position is reasonable and worthy of support. The synthesis focuses on a debatable issue or arguable question. The writer anticipates, acknowledges, and addresses alternative views.

---

In college courses, students are seldom called upon to write research papers in the form of exploratory syntheses. The sample assignment we provided earlier, "Write a six-page research paper in which you draw upon the psychological literature on dance therapy published during the past decade," implies a goal of presenting the psychological literature in a straightforward manner. But even though the professor phrased the assignment in this way, he or she probably expects students to articulate and support a position. Before you write an exploratory synthesis, we strongly suggest that you consult with your professor. Most professors expect students to fashion research papers that are thesis-driven and/or argumentative.

Despite our caveats about explanatory synthesis, this form of writing serves as an excellent precursor to a thesis-driven synthesis or an argument synthesis. The student who presents straightforward coverage of ten years of research on dance therapy has already immersed herself in the academic conversation. She knows what the experts have said about dance therapy and she is aware of the issues they have yet to address and the questions they have yet to answer. She could easily propose an intelligent question or zero in on a pressing issue that would become the focal point of a research paper.

The preferred goal for research papers is either to get readers to understand your thesis or to persuade them of your argument. The goal you select depends on the assignment. If the assignment asks you to research a debatable issue—for example, whether the United States condones torture—then your paper will have an argumentative edge. If the assignment offers a topic rather than an issue, or if it leaves the choice of topic or issue up to you, you are free to determine your own purpose. Consider the progression we present below:

**Thesis:** Psychologists experiment with different forms of trauma therapy.

**Goal:** to inform readers about various forms of therapy.

**Thesis:** Oral and written communication therapies are effective for victims of trauma.

**Goal:** to get your readers to understand the effectiveness of oral and written therapies.

**Thesis:** Therapeutic writing has a more beneficial effect for victims of trauma than other forms of verbal communication.

**Goal:** to convince your readers that therapeutic writing has a more beneficial effect for victims of trauma than other forms of verbal communication.

The first statement lends itself to exploratory synthesis, the second to thesis-driven synthesis, and the third to argument synthesis.

Keep in mind that you may not be able to make a firm decision about your purpose until you complete your library research. The more you read, the more your purpose will evolve. Midway through the process, you might express the purpose of reviewing and evaluating the various therapies for victims of trauma. Later, after you have amassed and read more sources, you might decide your purpose is to argue that writing combined with oral communication is a more effective therapy than oral communication alone. Make sure that your research strategy is flexible enough to accommodate the unexpected. In practice, research often does not always proceed as planned. You may need to change your goals during the research process.

## Set a Schedule

A research paper is a major undertaking. Make sure you set aside enough time for it. The amount of time you need depends on the scope of your assignment. If your instructor provides a narrowed topic and requires only four or five sources, you may get by with a few visits to the library two or three weeks before the paper is due. If your instructor asks you to select your own topic and draw on ten or more sources, you need to begin six to eight weeks before the due date. Always allow for the unexpected in research assignments. Even knowledgeable researchers encounter difficulties that require more time than they had anticipated. You may discover your college library does not have important texts that you need. You will be able to obtain these sources through interlibrary loan, but you have to allow ample time for the transaction.

In our example, Jennifer has to select her own topic and locate at least ten sources, so she begins six weeks before the due date. She assumes that she will make at least five visits to the library. She establishes the following schedule:

### RESEARCH PAPER DEADLINES

| | |
|---|---|
| March 27 | Select topic |
| March 29 | Read entries from general and specialized encyclopedias and narrow topic |
| March 30 | Write a list of questions I want my research to answer and brainstorm a list of key terms |
| April 3–19 | Conduct online searches; visit library; locate sources (Leave time for interlibrary loan) |
| April 21 | Outline paper |
| April 22–28 | Write draft of paper; revisit library for needed sources |
| April 30 | Revise and edit draft |
| May 1 | Turn in final draft |

## Decide on the Question Your Research Will Answer

Throughout this book, we have emphasized the importance of developing a "questioning" frame of mind. Competent researchers do not merely look up information; they use research to answer questions about their topics. Before you begin the research process, at the point when you are reading entries in encyclopedias and reference sources or reviewing your course materials, list the questions that you hope your research will answer. Here are some of Jennifer's questions concerning trauma therapy:

1. To what extent do psychologists still accept Freud's theory concerning trauma?
2. How does current psychological theory explain the impact of traumatic experiences?
3. What therapies are available for victims of psychic trauma? Which are most effective?
4. According to psychologists and communication experts (writing and speech), what role does the verbal expression of traumatic experiences play in the recovery process?
5. Do victims of psychological trauma receive adequate attention in the mental health system?

In the process of conducting research, you will ask additional questions, refine the ones you started with, and drop questions that lead to dead ends. Questions will lead to questions and eventually you will have amassed enough information to write a draft of your paper.

## Brainstorm a Preliminary Search Vocabulary

Before you search for books and articles, you need to come up with a preliminary list of words or phrases associated with your topic. Brainstorm words or phrases that might be used to describe or categorize the subject. These are the terms you will look up when you search catalogs and databases. Jennifer brainstorms the following list of search terms related to trauma therapy:

- Trauma or shock
- Traumatic experiences
- Freud and trauma
- Psychology and trauma
- Writing and trauma
- Verbal expression (communication) and trauma
- Trauma therapy
- Trauma counseling
- Posttraumatic stress disorder (or syndrome)
- Traumatic neuroses
- Trauma and the mental health system

When you brainstorm for such a list, be expansive and jot down as many terms as you can. As you locate sources, you will refine this preliminary list and add new terms. You need a rich list of search terms because it is often hard to guess which ones will give you access to the information you want.

## EXERCISE 9.2

- Think of research papers you have written in the past. How did you select a topic? What planning did you do before attempting to locate sources? Were your activities during the early stages of the research process different from or similar to the ones we've described?
- Freewrite for ten minutes in response to these questions.
- Reread the paragraph you wrote for Exercise 9.1.
- Take the topic you already narrowed, speculate about the questions your research will answer.
- Write a list of at least five questions.
- Brainstorm a list of words and phrases you might use as search terms for your topic.

## EXERCISE 9.3

- Form small collaborative learning groups.
- Decide on a topic of mutual interest that your group might want to research. Do not take more than two or three minutes to come to a consensus. (The instructor may choose to assign research topics.)
- Working together, generate a list of research questions that pertain to your topic. Then brainstorm a list of search terms that will help you locate information on this topic.
- Reconvene the class. Each group recorder identifies the group's topic, reads the lists of research questions and search terms, and describes any problems that the group encountered.

## Determine How You Will Find the Sources

Your college library will enable you to connect to online catalogs and to periodical indexes and databases to which the library subscribes. Sitting at your computer, you can compile lists of books, articles, and other sources relevant to almost any topic. If your library's online system provides the complete texts of sources, you can complete all the research for relatively short projects without leaving your room. As the access to full-text periodicals grows and more book-length works become available online, it will become possible to conduct more extensive research from homes and offices.

The search engine Google is already scanning the contents of five major research libraries. The ultimate goal is to assemble a digital library of everything that was ever published. Writing about this new phenomenon in the *New York Times Magazine*, technology expert Kevin Kelly explains how books will eventually be linked to each other electronically:

> Once a book has been integrated into the new expanded library by means of this linking, its text will no longer be separate from the text in other books. For instance, today a serious nonfiction book will usually have a bibliography and some kind of footnotes. When books are deeply linked, you'll be able to click on the title in any bibliography or any footnote and find the actual book referred to in the footnote. The books referenced in that book's bibliography will themselves be available, and so you can hop through the library in the same way we hop through Web links, traveling from footnote to footnote to footnote until you reach the bottom of things. (45)

Although it will be a long time before the universal library moves from the realm of dream to the realm of reality, the explosive growth of technology has already affected how students conduct research. A vast collection of electronic texts, graphics, and sounds covers every imaginable topic, and sources that are appropriate for academic research are becoming available in full-text versions on the Web. A crucial word in the preceding sentence is "becoming." It will be a long time before we are able to access electronic versions of all the library sources we need. And some technology experts think this will never happen. So prepare yourself to visit the library and spend some time learning its ins and outs.

## ■ Locate Sources in an Academic Library

Before you launch your search, familiarize yourself with your college library. Libraries vary dramatically in how they organize their collections and how they provide access to materials. Before you attempt to do any research, get a guide or a map that shows how your campus library is organized. Make sure you know where the reference desk is located. Do not confuse it with the circulation desk, the place where items are checked out. The librarians at the reference desk can provide one-on-one research assistance.

Your library reference department may also offer library orientation sessions, reference-skills workshops, and credit-bearing courses on information resources. Take advantage of opportunities to learn about the library early in your academic career.

### EXERCISE 9.4

Take a self-guided tour of your college library.

- Start by locating the reference desk. Find out what days and hours reference librarians are available and what services they provide.

- Find out how the collection is organized. Are periodicals shelved with books or separately? Are other formats (recordings, microfilms, and so on) shelved separately?
- Are there any subject-specific (music, science, and so forth) libraries on your campus?

You should be able to answer these questions based on materials that you can obtain at the reference desk. Now tour the library and make sure you can find the principal units in the collection.

## EXERCISE 9.5

- Form collaborative learning groups.
- Pick an area of the library that your group will investigate from the following list. Groups should not duplicate one another's choices so that as many areas as possible will be covered.

  Reference collection
  Book collection (main stacks)
  Magazine and journal collection
  Sound recordings collection
  Video collection
  Newspaper collection
  Any discipline-specific collection

- Proceed to the library from class or arrange a time that your group can meet in the library for about an hour.
- When you arrive at the library, work together to answer the following questions concerning your area: What resources are available? What services are available?
- Reconvene the entire class. Each group recorder should read the group's answers to the two questions and respond to any inquiries from the class about the part of the library collection that the group investigated.

Your library houses computer workstations linked to the online catalog and databases. While you are at the library, sit down at a computer and click on the library home page. We have reproduced the SUNY Cortland library's home page below. (See Figure 9–1.)

Your library's home page is accessible from other computer workrooms across campus and from personal computers that can log into it with a network ID number. You will sign on using your ID number and a password. If you have questions about accessing the library from off-campus locations, ask a reference librarian to help you.

As we mentioned earlier, you might begin the research for your topic by finding background information in encyclopedias and other reference books. Next, you should move on to books. Then, you can search for more timely information in the form of articles. Finally, if you need still more information, use the Web to find Internet resources.

## How to Find Books

The catalog contains a description of each item in the library's collection and it indexes the items by subject, title, and author. Catalogs typically list books, periodicals (magazines, journals, and newspapers), pamphlets, sound recordings (reel-to-reel and cassette tapes, LPs, and compact discs), sheet music, microforms (microfilm, microfiche, and

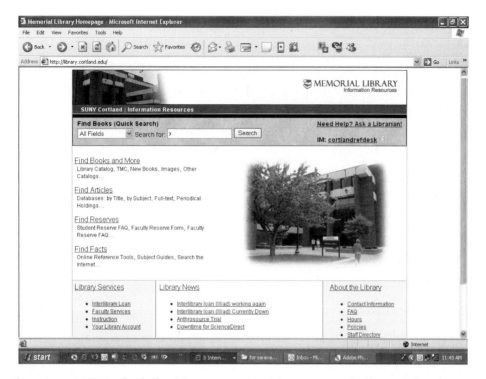

**Figure 9–1    SUNY Cortland Library Home Page.** Copyright © 2006. Used with permission of SUNY Cortland Memorial Library.

microcards), motion pictures, video recordings, computer data files, images (graphics and photos), three-dimensional artifacts, and maps.

The catalog provides titles of the journals and magazines the library subscribes to and the date range of holdings for periodicals, but it does not provide information about individual articles. In other words, if you look up *Newsweek* magazine, you may learn that the library includes the magazine in its collection. But in order to locate a particular article in *Newsweek,* you have to search a relevant index or database. We explain how to use these tools on page 299.

Online catalogs can be searched by subject, title, or author according to the principles described on pages 298–99. Figure 9–2 shows a computer catalog entry that Jennifer located in her research on trauma therapy.

The sample computer catalog entry includes a *call number* for the item: RC552.P67 H47 1997. This number indicates the item's subject area and its shelving location. You are probably familiar with the Dewey decimal call numbers used in most primary and secondary schools. College libraries typically use the Library of Congress system, which is more comprehensive than the Dewey decimal system. The call number in Figure 9–2 is based on the Library of Congress system. Print versions of the Library of Congress subject headings are located in the reference section of the library. They are also published in the "Library of Congress Classification Outline," available online at <http://www.loc.gov/catdir/cpso/lcco/lcco.html>. These subject headings provide a useful list of broad terms and narrow terms to use when searching for a topic. For example, "education" is divided into eleven categories, each of which is broken down into subtopics.

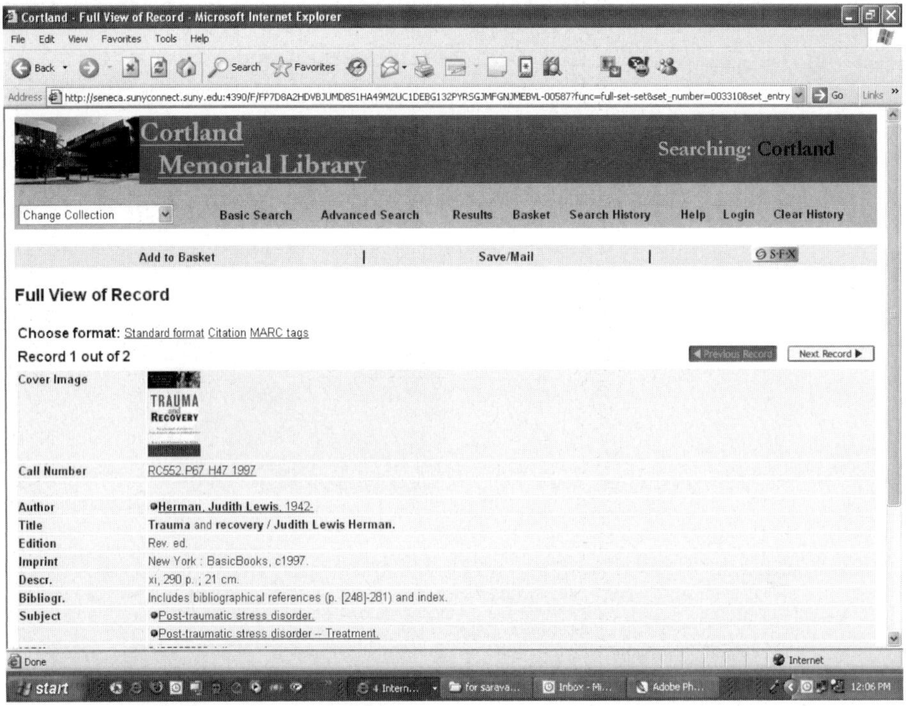

**Figure 9–2    Sample Computer Catalog Entry.** SUNY Cortland Memorial Library. Copyright © 2002 Ex Libris. Used with permission of SUNY Cortland Memorial Library.

Books and other materials are shelved systematically by call numbers. As an example, let's consider the parts of the call number for Herman's *Trauma and Recovery*: RC 552.P67 H47 1997. On the library shelves, books are alphabetized according to the letters indicating the general topic area—RC in the example above. Within each general topic area, items are arranged in ascending numerical order according to the topic subdivision, in this case 552.P67. For books, items within the subdivision are arranged alphabetically by the first letter of the author's last name and then numerically by an additional filing number. In our example, H is the first letter of Herman's name and 47 is the additional filing number. Finally, 1997 is the book's date of publication. Call numbers can get more complex than our example indicates, but the filing and shelving principles that we just described always apply. Call numbers provide a shelving address for an information source and they also assure that items on the same topic will be stored together. Thus, if you locate one item on your subject, you may find others shelved nearby.

College libraries differ in size. One of us teaches at SUNY Cortland, which has a single library collection of 412,000 volumes, and the other teaches at Cornell, where there are twenty different libraries containing more than seven million books. If your library does not own a source that you need, you will be able to acquire it through interlibrary loan. Your library probably has a link to Interlibrary Loan on its home page as the Web page does in Figure 9–1. Items may take anywhere from a day to a week or more to be delivered. That is why you must leave ample time when creating your research paper schedule.

In addition to searching your college's online catalog, you can also search the Library of Congress Online Catalog, a database of fourteen million records, at

<http://catalog. loc.gov/>. A search for *trauma therapy* yields the titles of 257 books. Your college won't have all these books, but you will be able to obtain the ones it lacks through interlibrary loan.

## Bibliographic Details for Electronic Books and Articles

As you locate sources that are potentially useful, be sure to keep a working bibliography that includes the elements we list in the Appendix on pages 662–65. Online sources require special attention because you must provide the date you access the electronic source. The URL (Web address) has to be included, and, in some cases, the name of the database and the library where the source was found. (See pages 664–65 in the Appendix.)

---

### EXERCISE 9.6

- Revisit the topic you narrowed in Exercise 9.1.
- Access the online catalog of your college library and locate at least five books related to your topic.
- Determine which books are available in your library and which you would have to apply for via interlibrary loan.
- Make a list of the books and include necessary bibliographic information.

---

## How to Find Articles

In academic libraries, you will find that magazines, journals, and newspapers are sometimes called *periodicals*. This term is used because they are published periodically—that is, at regular intervals (weekly, monthly, quarterly, annually) throughout the year.

To locate articles, you will access a periodical or article index, which is a searchable database containing thousands of articles. Article indexes provide bibliographic citations, abstracts, and occasionally, the full text of the articles. One such index is **OCLC First-Search**. OCLC stands for Online Computer Library Center, a computer library service and online database to which many college libraries subscribe. FirstSearch provides access to seventeen databases. One of the FirstSearch databases is **ArticleFirst**. ArticleFirst is a good place to begin your search because it is a general multidisciplinary database that provides information on articles from hundreds of academic and popular journals, magazines, and newspapers. Another good starting point is **EbscoHOST's Academic Search Premier**.

To access these databases, look on your library Web page for the listing "Articles," "Databases," "Reference Tools," or "Subject Guides." Individual libraries may designate these listings by different names. If you have trouble locating a general interdisciplinary database, consult a reference librarian. After you have searched the general database, look for a more specialized disciplinary databases, such as **ERIC (Educational Resource Information Center for Education)**, **PsycFirst** (for Psychology), and the **MLA International Bibliography** (for language courses and English), and search for your topic. Again, if you have difficulty locating a specialized database, ask a reference librarian for assistance.

When Jennifer accesses her college library home page, she clicks on the link "Find Articles." This link opens up a page with "Databases by Title" where she clicks on "Article-First." One of the citations she locates is:

### DISCLOSING TRAUMA THROUGH WRITING: TESTING THE MEANING-MAKING HYPOTHESIS

*Author*: *Park, Crystal L.; Blumberg, Carol Joyce* **Source**: *Cognitive Therapy and Research 26, no. 5 (2002): 597-616 (20 pages)* **Libraries Worldwide**: *529 See more details for locating this item.*

When she clicks on "See more details for locating this item," she obtains the detailed display shown in Figure 9–3.

We have annotated the entry to identify the various elements. The ArticleFirst entry provides a wealth of information including links to other articles published by the authors. There are also links that provide three options for locating the journal containing the article: (1) a link to the user's college library, (2) a link to the list of 529 libraries that subscribe to the journal, and (3) a link to services that will provide the article, including interlibrary loan.

---

**Availability: Check the catalogs in your library**

• Libraries worldwide that own item : 529 ——— link to a list of 529 libraries where you can obtain the article

• Search the catalog at your library ——— link to your library catalogue to see if your library has the article

**External Resources:** Find Fulltext ——— link to places where you can request the article, including interlibrary loan

**Copyright:** © Plenum Publishing Corporation

**Author(s):** Park, Crystal L. ; Blumberg, Carol Joyce ——— link to a list of articles written by each of the authors

**Affiliation:** Department of Psychology, University of Connecticut, Storrs, Connecticut; clpark@uconnum.uconn.edu; Department of ——— authors, college departments and email addresses — Mathematics and Statistics, Winona State University, Winona, Minnesota

**Title: Disclosing Trauma Through Writing : Testing the** ——— title of article
**Meaning-Making Hypothesis**

volume number | issue number | year of publication

**Source:** *Cognitive Therapy and Research 26, no. 5 (2002): 597-616 (20 pages)* ——— the article's page numbers

title of journal

**Additional Info:** Springer; 20021001

**Standard No: ISSN:** 0147-5916 ——— International Standard Serial Number, an 8-digit number assigned to periodical publications

**Language:** English

**Database:** ArticleFirst ——— database

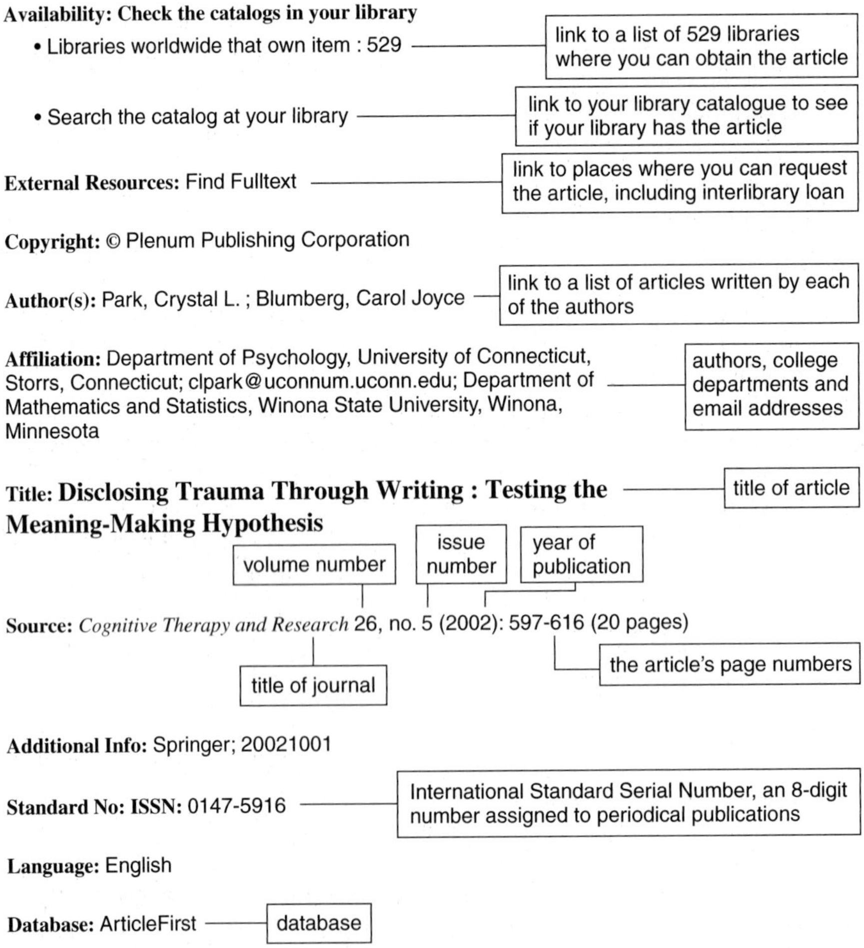

**Figure 9–3**   ArticleFirst Entry.

In addition to citations like the one we have presented for ArticleFirst, databases provide abstracts of articles. Abstracts are short summaries of articles' contents. Keep in mind that abstracts are intended to help researchers decide which articles are most relevant to their interests; they are not meant to circumvent careful reading of the complete text. Do not rely on abstracts as information sources; they are only access tools. You should not cite an article in a research paper if you have read only an abstract and did not obtain the article's full text. For a detailed discussion of abstracts, see pages 55–58.

## EXERCISE 9.7

- Select the topic you've been working on for Exercises 9.1, 9.2, and 9.6 or use a topic assigned by your professor.
- Go to the library and locate two books and two periodical articles on your topic.
- Use an online database to find two of these sources and print out the records.
- For the print sources, photocopy the table of contents of the book or periodical, and on the photocopy, circle the chapter or article that is relevant to your topic.
- Submit the computer printout and the photocopies to your instructor.

## EXERCISE 9.8

- Form small groups.
- Come to a consensus on a topic you would like to research, or use one assigned by your instructor.
- Assign each group member one type of information resource: general reference, discipline-specific book, magazine, newspaper, or professional journal.
- Proceed to the library from class or go individually outside of class time. Find a source on your topic that represents the particular type of information resource that you were assigned. Photocopy or print out the table of contents of the book or periodical, and on the photocopy or printout, circle the chapter or article that is relevant to your topic.
- Reconvene your group at the next class meeting. Have each group member report on the source he or she found. Then discuss which types of resources seemed most useful for your topic and what further research would be necessary to actually write on your topic.
- Reconvene the entire class. Each group recorder should explain the group's topic and summarize the group's discussion of sources on this topic.

## Which Articles Are Most Appropriate?

In your database searching, you will find articles from popular magazines as well as articles from scholarly journals. Early in the research process, ask your professor if you may use articles from the popular press in your paper. Sometimes it is difficult to distinguish between popular and scholarly sources. The Cornell University Library Web site offers a useful research guide to four categories of periodicals: scholarly, substantive news or general interest, popular, and sensational. The box below provides an overview of these categories.

---

## DISTINGUISHING SCHOLARLY FROM NONSCHOLARLY PERIODICALS

### Scholarly

- Scholarly journals generally have a sober, serious look. They often contain many graphs and charts but few glossy pages or exciting pictures.
- Scholarly journals always cite their sources in the form of footnotes or bibliographies.
- Articles are written by a scholar in the field or by someone who has done research in the field.
- The language of scholarly journals is that of the discipline covered. It assumes some scholarly background on the part of the reader.
- The main purpose of a scholarly journal is to report on original research or experimentation in order to make such information available to the rest of the scholarly world.
- Many scholarly journals, though by no means all, are published by a specific professional organization.
- Examples of scholarly journals:

    *American Economic Review*
    *Archives of Sexual Behavior*
    *JAMA: The Journal of the American Medical Association*
    *Journal of Marriage and the Family*
    *Modern Fiction Studies*
    *Sex Roles: A Journal of Research*

### Substantive News or General Interest

- These periodicals may be quite attractive in appearance, although some are in newspaper format. Articles are often heavily illustrated, generally with photographs.
- News and general interest periodicals sometimes cite sources, a scholar, or a freelance writer.
- The language of these publications is geared to any educated audience. There is no special training assumed, only interest and a certain level of intelligence.
- They are generally published by commerical enterprises or individuals, although some emanate from specific professional organizations.
- The main purpose of periodicals in this category is to provide information, in a general manner, to a broad audience of concerned citizens.
- Examples of substantive news or general interest periodicals:

    *Christian Science Monitor*
    *Economist*
    *National Geographic*
    *New York Times*
    *Scientific American*
    *Vital Speeches of the Day*

**Popular**

- Popular periodicals come in many formats, although they are often somewhat slick and attractive in appearance. There are usually lots of graphics (photographs, drawings, etc.).
- These publications rarely, if ever, cite sources. Information published in such journals is often second or third hand and the original source is sometimes obscure.
- Articles are usually very short, written in simple language, and are designed to meet a minimal education level. There is generally little depth to the content of these articles.
- Articles are written by staff members or freelance writers.
- The main purpose of popular periodicals is to entertain the reader, to sell products (their own or their advertisers'), and/or to promote a viewpoint.
- Examples of popular periodicals:

*Ebony*

*Parents*

*People Weekly*

*Reader's Digest*

*Sports Illustrated*

*Time*

*Vogue*

**Sensational**

- Sensational periodicals come in a variety of styles, but often use a newspaper format.
- The language is elementary and occasionally inflammatory or sensational. They assume a certain gullibility in their audience.
- The main purpose of sensational magazines seems to be to arouse curiosity and to cater to popular superstitions. They often do so with flashy headlines designed to astonish (e.g., "Half-man Half-woman Makes Self Pregnant").
- Examples of sensational periodicals:

*Globe*

*National Examiner*

*Star*

*Weekly World News*

Research guide from:
http://www.library.cornell.edu/t/help/res_strategy/evaluating/scholar.html. Copyright 2002, Cornell University. Courtesy of Cornell University Library, Reference Department; Instruction, Research, and Information Services (IRIS)

Whenever you are in doubt about the appropriateness of a particular newspaper or magazine, consult your professor or a reference librarian.

**EXERCISE 9.9**

- Break into small groups.
- Review the records for the articles you selected for the individual and collaborative exercises on locating sources on page 301.
- As a group, speculate about the appropriateness of the articles. Use the Cornell guide, "Distinguishing Scholarly from Nonscholarly Periodicals," to decide whether the articles are scholarly, substantive news or general interest, popular, or sensational.
- A reporter from each group will report the findings to the class.

## Using Electronic Retrieval Systems

Electronic retrieval systems do not possess artificial intelligence. They are merely word-matching tools; they cannot make even the simplest inferences about your intentions. Don't expect the system to do any of your thinking for you. In addition, most retrieval systems cannot correct for misspelling or adjust for variations in spelling. Distinctions that may seem insignificant to you, such as the difference between "first" and "1st," may be crucial when using a computerized system.

To put retrieval systems to best use, whether you are searching your library's online catalog, an electronic database, or the World Wide Web, you need to understand basic principles of online searching. Students are sometimes under the impression that electronic searching is simple, that all they have to do is type in words or phrases that describe their topic and, voilà, they will receive a wealth of valuable information sources. To take maximum advantage of online searching, you need to know how search software operates.

You search a database by typing in a *query*, which is typically several words related to your topic. In response, the retrieval system matches the query with relevant information sources in the system's database. While systems vary in their precise search strategies, most compare the specific words in queries to indexes or word lists compiled from all the information sources.

### Types of Searches

You can conduct either a **basic search** or a **guided, expert,** or **advanced search**. Basic searches allow you to search by keyword, author, title, source, and year. Guided, expert, or advanced searches permit you to search for other items, such as publication date, language, personal name, geographic name, and source type (book, video, sound recording, and so forth). Usually, you can examine several indexes with a single query; for example, you could search for sources on therapeutic writing that were published since the year 2000. In databases that provide the full texts of articles, the words used within each article are indexed so that you can search the articles' contents.

When you start a search on an electronic database, you see a template comparable to the ArticleFirst basic search template in Figure 9–4.

Returning to our student: Jennifer enters the words *trauma therapy* in the "Keyword" box and receives a list of 703 sources. She decides to narrow her search to sources published in recent years, so she repeats the search by adding 2003–2006 in the "Year" box. This search produces 161 sources. Jennifer wants to narrow her search even further, so she clicks on "Advanced Search." Figure 9–5 is a reproduction of the ArticleFirst Advanced Search template.

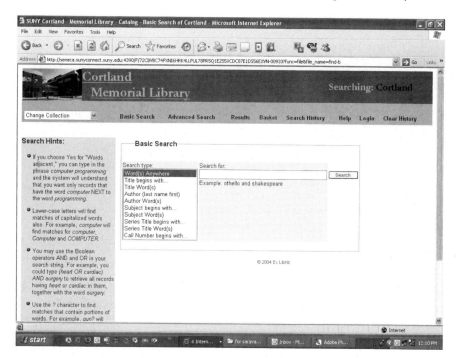

**Figure 9–4     Template for ArticleFirst Basic Search.** ArticleFirst screen capture ©1992–2007 Online Computer Library Center (oclc.org), reprinted with permission.

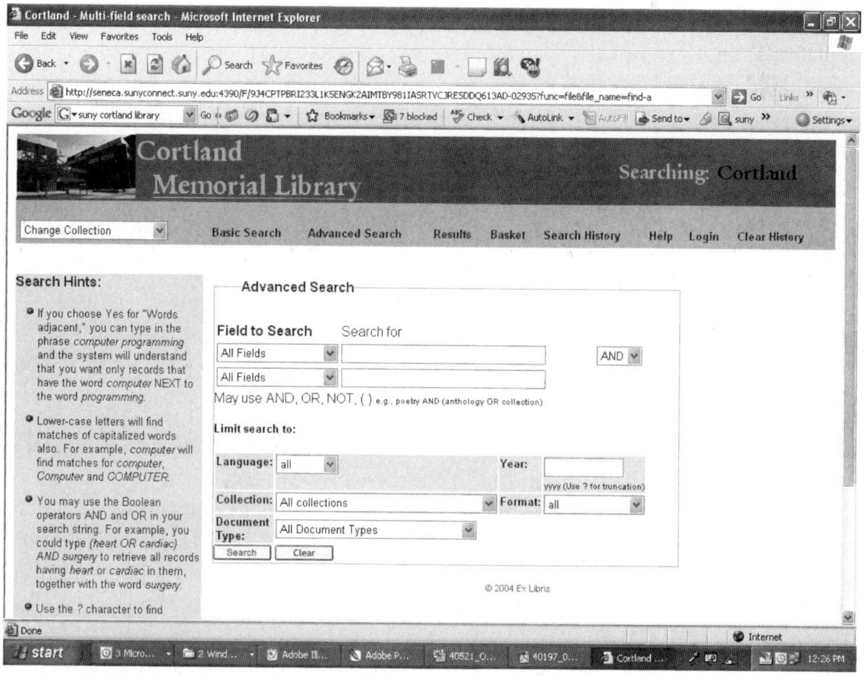

**Figure 9–5     Template for ArticleFirst Advanced Search.** ArticleFirst screen capture ©1992–2007 Online Computer Library Center (oclc.org), reprinted with permission.

The advanced search permits Jennifer to search by many other items in addition to keyword, author, title, source, and year. When she pulls down the menu bar, she sees that she can search by author phrase, first page, issue, issue identifier, publisher, publication date, source phrase, standard number, title phrase, and volume. She can also limit the search to periodicals held at her own college library.

Whenever you use a database for the first time, take a few minutes to familiarize yourself with it. In Figures 9–4 and 9–5, you see that the ArticleFirst template has a tab labeled "Home." When Jennifer clicks on this tab, she learns that the FirstSearch compendium of databases includes two other useful sources: the **ECO** database and the **WorldCat** database. A search of ECO will locate scholarly journal articles, and a search of WorldCat will retrieve the titles of books.

*Keyword Searching*  Unless you know the author or title of the source you are looking for, you will search by keyword. Keyword searches have advantages and disadvantages. A keyword search will locate one or more words in any position within the title or subject heading. When Jennifer types *trauma* in the title box of an electronic database, she will locate all titles that include the word *trauma*. It is often useful to search titles for key words or phrases since a title is a good indicator of a source's content. Keyword searching is also advantageous for subject indexes because it allows you to retrieve a reference without knowing the exact wording of the subject heading. For instance, a keyword search for *welfare reform* would retrieve the subject headings *public welfare reform*; *reform, welfare*; and *reform, public welfare*, as well as *welfare reform* and *Welfare Reform Reconciliation Act of 1996*.

A disadvantage of keyword searching is that it has the potential to draw in a great many irrelevant sources because the words in the query are matched to the index without regard to context. For instance, a keyword title search for *Grateful Dead* would retrieve the article entitled "Anti-Union Bill Dead in Committee: Autoworkers Grateful for Senator's Pivotal Vote." Some retrieval systems allow you to search for exact phrases—that is, for strings of words that appear in a particular order. For example, an exact phrase search for "Grateful Dead" would retrieve only the index items in which the word "Dead" immediately follows the word "Grateful." Exact phrase searches are usually specified by placing the target words in the query within quotation marks.

*Truncation*  Computerized retrieval systems often allow you to truncate or shorten search terms. Instead of typing in the search statement, *politically correct movement*, you might enter *political* and *correct*. This query would retrieve *politically correct movement*, *political correctness*, and other variations on this terminology. It is often wise to truncate words in search statements, particularly when you are unsure of the precise indexing terms used in the database.

*Refine Your Search by Using Boolean Logic*  Sometimes searches retrieve far more sources than you need, as well as many sources that are unrelated to your topic. At other times a search will yield only a handful of sources. Boolean logic will enable you to link words and phrases to create a very specific request that takes full advantage of electronic searching. Boolean logic is named after the nineteeth-century British mathematician George Boole. The logic has many applications, one of which is computer searching. All you need to know is a very simplified version of the logic: how to connect your search terms by using the three Boolean operators AND, OR, and NOT.

If your search produces too many results, you can limit it by inserting the word AND (some systems require the + sign instead of AND) between your search terms. Suppose you want information on the national debate over welfare reform that occurred in 1996.

You search with the term *welfare reform* and get hundreds of articles. If you enter *welfare reform* AND 1996, you will receive a list of all sources that have a subject heading "welfare reform" as well as a publication year of 1996. Don't let the Boolean AND confuse you. We usually associate AND with addition, so you would think that adding the word AND would increase the number of sources retrieved. The AND actually places more restrictions on searches and usually cuts down on the number of hits.

If your search produces a number of sources unrelated to the area you wish to study, insert the word NOT (some systems require the − sign instead of NOT) before words you would like to delete. Suppose your search for *welfare reform* results in a sizable number of articles dealing with occupational training, a topic you are not planning to investigate. If you enter *welfare reform* NOT *occupational training*, the computer will identify articles on welfare reform and exclude articles that concern job training.

If your search produces too few sources, insert the word OR between your search terms. Suppose you're interested in the topic of occupational training. The expression *welfare reform* OR *occupational training* will locate articles that focus just on welfare reform and articles that focus just on job training, along with articles that cover both topics.

You can also use Boolean operators in combination to piece together complex search statements such as the following: *welfare reform* OR *occupational training* AND 1996. Most of the templates you will be offered for guided, expert, or advanced searches already include Boolean operations (see Figure 9–5: ArticleFirst Advanced Search). Experiment with your search terms, but remember AND = narrow, NOT = limit, and OR = expand.

## EXERCISE 9.10

Return to the topic you have been working with in the previous exercises in this chapter.

- Go to your library's home page and access an article database.
- Look for a general interdisciplinary database such as ArticleFirst or EbscoHOST's Academic Search Premier or a database recommended by your professor or reference librarian.
- Perform the following operations:

  Conduct a basic search and record the number of articles the search retrieves.
  Conduct an advanced search and record the number of articles the search retrieves.
  If the database allows, experiment with the Boolean AND, NOT, and OR.

## ■ Conduct Research on the World Wide Web

### Advantages and Disadvantages of the Web

The explosion of the World Wide Web has made it easy to locate information on every imaginable topic. If you play the guitar, within seconds you can find Web sites that provide product information on new and used guitars, chords for the latest songs, and a discography for your favorite guitarist. This information would take hours to collect without the help of the Web. The Web works well in this case for several reasons. Since thousands of amateur musicians and music fans use the Web to share information, its popular music resources are vast and will probably cover any guitar, song, or guitarist that interests you. Search queries about guitars, guitar music, and guitarists are relatively easy to formulate, since they are based on straightforward names (Fender, "Voodoo Child," Jimi Hendrix) rather than descriptions of content. As an amateur guitarist, you are looking for information that is interesting or useful but you may not be concerned with precise accuracy. In other words, you'd be satisfied with playable chord progressions that sound acceptably close to the original songs rather than completely authentic musical transcriptions.

The World Wide Web does not work as well for scholarly research as it does for topics of general interest. Books and scholarly journals remain the standard vehicles for academic communication, and many of these publications are not available on the Web. Another problem is that academic research usually involves searching by subject matter rather than by proper name, and the Web is not arranged for efficient subject searching. Given the Web's huge size, haphazard organization, and poor indexing, it may be difficult to locate material on your research topic.

Another drawback of the Web is relevant information may be buried in long lists of information sources that contain the vocabulary in your search statement but are not actually useful to you. For example, if Jennifer, in her research on trauma therapy, used the search term *trauma* on the Web, it might steer her to the Web page of the Discoteca Trauma, a nightclub in Barcelona, Spain.

A final difficulty is that academic researchers care very much about reliability and accuracy, but the Web has no effective quality control. Any individual or group can establish a Web page and disseminate any information that they choose, except for content that is in clear violation of the law. Some Web pages use very professional graphics but include content that is merely uninformed opinion. Of course, print sources can also contain unreliable content, but the Web has expanded tremendously the opportunity for "publishing" material that has no basis in fact. Consequently, subject searches conducted on the Web often direct the researcher to Web sites that do not provide reliable information.

The issues of reliability and objectivity are further complicated by the commercial nature of many Web sites. For instance, the search term "trauma" will likely provide a great many links to the dot com (.com) business Web pages of psychologists, psychiatrists, and social workers who specialize in trauma therapy and use the Web to advertise their services. While some of these commercial sites may provide information that is useful to a researcher, others will be biased and manipulative. Keep in mind that standard Web search engines, the electronic retrieval systems that you use to search the Web, are commercial ventures. They may intentionally steer you to information providers who have paid the search engine companies to highlight their Web sites.

## Advantages of College Libraries

In contrast to the World Wide Web, a college library collection is developed specifically to serve the needs of academic researchers. Books, periodicals, and other materials are chosen either by librarians who specialize in collection development or by faculty members who are experts in their fields of study. Because an academic library collection is built systematically, it is much more likely to include the seminal works in a particular discipline, whereas the Web does not discriminate between expert and uninformed opinion. Your library may also include special collections for certain programs of study that are highlighted at your college. Currently, relatively few books are available in full-text online versions; thus, with the exception of periodicals, most of the scholarly sources in your college library's collection are probably not available online.

Another advantage of conducting research in your college library is that you can get help from the reference librarians. The major responsibility of these information professionals is to help students and faculty members with their research questions. Reference librarians can show you how to access sources that are available online from remote sites, including material on the World Wide Web. In most cases, a few minutes spent discussing your research needs with a reference librarian will be more productive than hours of surfing the Web.

A final advantage of academic libraries is that they provide the sophisticated tools you need to conduct scholarly research. In your college library, you will find an online catalog and electronic links to other libraries from which you can obtain material via interlibrary loan. Your library provides specialized electronic databases and academic indexes that will help you locate information in journals, magazines, and newspapers and, consequently, conduct far more precise searches than is possible with the general access tools available on the World Wide Web.

---

### ADVANTAGES OF THE WORLD WIDE WEB AND ACADEMIC LIBRARIES

**Advantages of the World Wide Web for Researchers**

- Uninterrupted availability
- Continuous updating
- Vast resources
- Coverage of virtually all topics (but without quality control)
- Convenience of one-stop shopping (but at risk of chaotic subject searching)

**Advantages of Academic Libraries for Researchers**

- Expert collection development and quality control
- Systematic organization and careful indexing of subject headings
- Increasingly available resources online for personal computer use at home
- Expert staff of reference librarians
- Extensive collections of book-length sources
- Commitment to scholarly inquiry and objectivity

---

## Find Digital Resources on the World Wide Web

After you have conducted research in the library, you will be able to use the Web to good advantage. The primary research tools on the Web are subject directories and search engines.

### Subject Directories

Subject directories are lists of Internet resources arranged by subject in a hierarchical order. For example, to use the Yahoo! Directory (<http://dir.yahoo.com/>) to search for *trauma therapy*, you would have to start by clicking on the broad subject, *Health*. This would bring you to a list of descriptors, one of which is "Procedures and Therapies." Under "Procedures and Therapies," you will find a link to "Mental Health." This link takes you to another page of descriptors, including "Journals" and "Narrative Therapy." When you select "Journals," you receive three resources and when you select "Narrative Therapy" you receive six. In other words, a search of subject directories uncovers layer after layer of material.

Subject directories are compiled by humans whereas search engine data are collected by computers and robots. Some subject directories are components of search engines; examples include the Google Directory (<http://www.google.com/dirhp>) and the Yahoo Search Directory (<http://dir.yahoo.com/>). Others, like the five we list in the box below, are compiled by librarians and subject specialists. Future generations of the Web, sometimes called the Semantic Web, will replace searches conducted by humans with searches conducted by computer software. The Semantic Web will enable intelligent computers to create hierarchical subject directories comparable to the ones listed in the box above. Until that time, however, we have to rely on human judgment.

---

### SUBJECT DIRECTORIES

**Academic Info**
<http://www.academicinfo.net/>

**Infomine**
<http://infomine.ucr.edu/>

**Librarians' Internet Index**
<http://lii.org/>

**The WWW Virtual Library**
<http://vlib.org/>

**Intute**
<http://www.intute.ac.uk/>

---

### EXERCISE 9.11

- Form groups of five students. Select a topic from among the topics the group members have been working on in the previous exercises.
- Each student in the group will search for the topic in a different subject directory.
- As you search, keep a record of the various links you click as you uncover the layers of material.
- When the group reconvenes, the members should review one another's work and decide which subject directory produced the best results.

## Search Engines

A Web search engine is a tool that combs the Internet looking for Web sites related to your search term. When you type your topic into a search engine, it responds with a list of Web sites that correspond as closely as possible to the words or phrases in your query. Search engines use a variety of methods for locating information. Entering the same words or phrases on two search engines can generate strikingly different search results. We suggest you begin with Google because it has the largest database. However, it does not search the entire Web. It is wise to search for your topic on two or three engines.

In the following box, we list five search engines and three metasearch engines. Metasearch engines search the databases of multiple search engines. For example, DogPile searches Google, Yahoo!, Windows Live, and Ask.

---

**SEARCH ENGINES**

**Google**
<http://www.google.com>

**Google Scholar**
<http://scholar.google.com/>

**Windows Live**
<http://www.live.com/>

**Ask**
<http://www.ask.com>

**Yahoo**
<http://search.yahoo.com>

**METASEARCH ENGINES**

**DogPile**
<http://www.dogpile.com>

**Mamma**
<http://www.mamma.com>

**Ixquick**
<http://www.ixquick.com>

---

The power of search engines is that they inspect billions of Web pages. The weakness is that they retrieve much more material than you need, and much of the material is inappropriate for college research papers. In the next section, we will explain how to increase the precision of your Web search and how to evaluate the sources you retrieve.

## How to Increase the Precision of Your Web Search

Our student Jennifer accesses Google (<http://www.google.com>), types the words *trauma therapy* into the search box, and in 0.26 seconds receives an overwhelming 17,700,000 results. Her first strategy for making the search more manageable is to move from a basic search to an advanced search. Jennifer clicks on the "Advanced Search" link. Before she

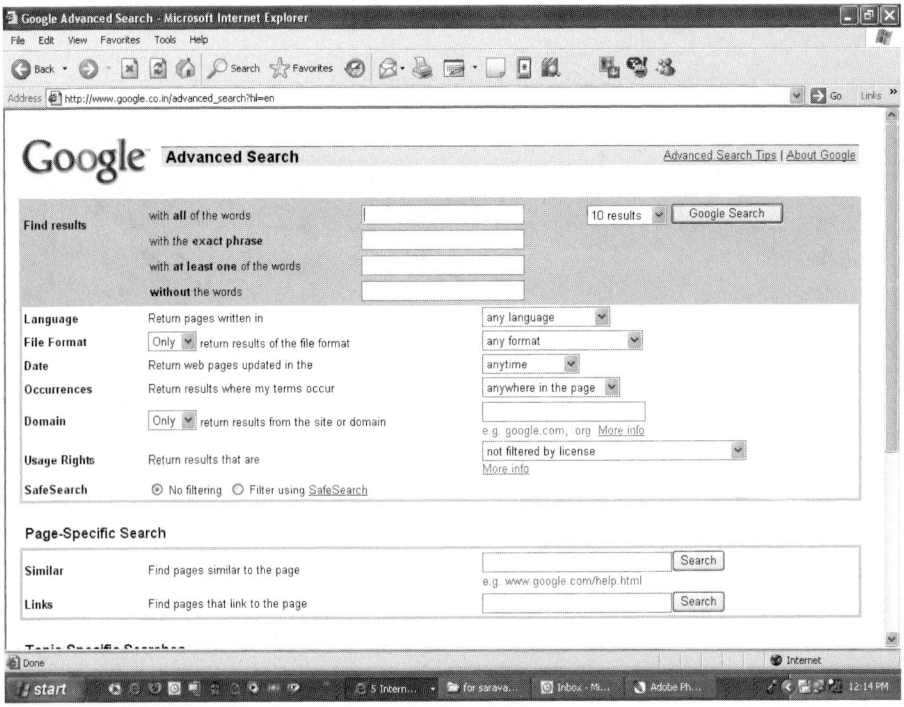

**Figure 9–6    Template for Google Advanced Search.** Google Scholar screen capture © Google Inc., reprinted with permission.

enters her search terms, she clicks on "Advanced Search Tips" in order to learn about advanced search operations. After reading the tips, she returns to the advanced search template and fills it in as we illustrate in Figure 9–6. The narrowed search produces 167 results.

Since Jennifer has already conducted library-based research, she has acquired a respectable search vocabulary. In the with-all-the-words box, she types *trauma therapy*. Google does not require her to type in the Boolean operator AND. The search is being narrowed because Google will locate documents that contain both the words *trauma* and *therapy*. In the with-exact-phrase box, she types *therapeutic writing*, which will ensure that the results contain this exact phrase. She narrows the search further, asking for documents written in English and updated within the past year. Lastly, in the "Domain" box, she excludes commercial Web sites with addresses ending in *.com*.

**Web Addresses**    Before we continue our discussion of search engines, we would like to say a few words about Web addresses. A Web address, also called a URL (uniform resource locator), reveals valuable information about the nature and purpose of the Web site. Let us look first at the composition of a URL, as detailed in Figure 9–7.

Sometimes you don't have to type in the abbreviations *http://* and *www*, though they are still part of the official Web address. An important component of the Web address is the three-letter suffix following the domain name. This suffix, called the "domain type," indicates the nature and purpose of the Web site, for example, whether it is a commercial site (com), an educational site (edu), or a government site (gov). We list some common domains in the box below.

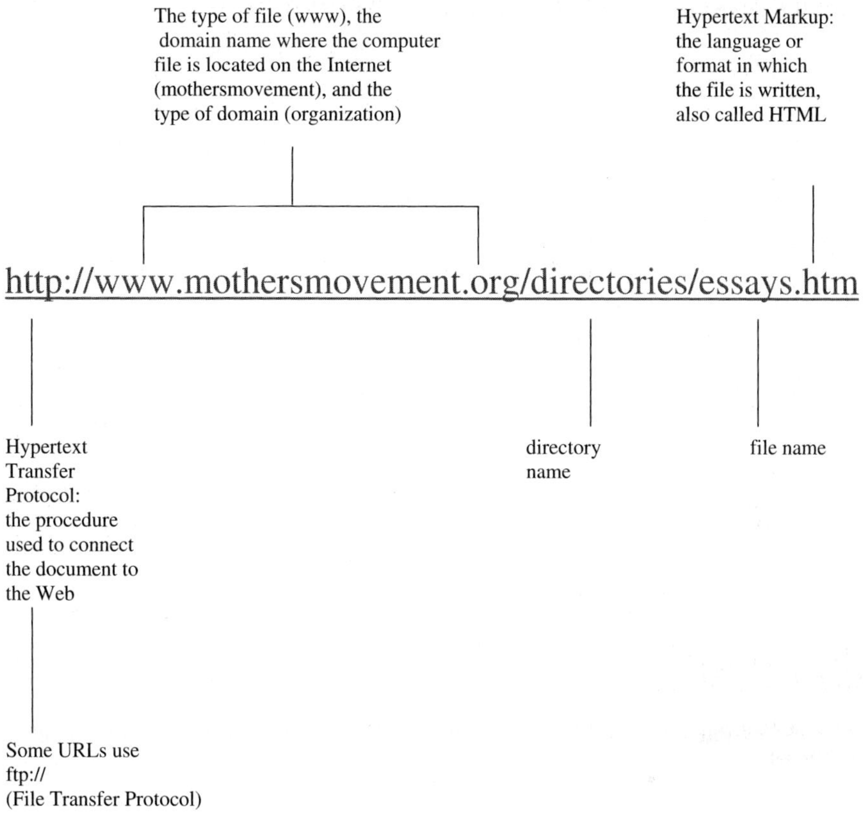

The type of file (www), the
  domain name where the computer
file is located on the Internet
(mothersmovement), and the
type of domain (organization)

Hypertext Markup:
the language or
format in which
the file is written,
also called HTML

## http://www.mothersmovement.org/directories/essays.htm

Hypertext
Transfer
Protocol:
the procedure
used to connect
the document to
the Web

directory
name

file name

Some URLs use
ftp://
(File Transfer Protocol)

**Figure 9–7    Composition of a URL.**

| COMMON DOMAIN TYPES | |
|---|---|
| **Domain Suffix** | **Nature** |
| .com | Commercial and business entities |
| .net | Network organization or network administration |
| .org | Public and nonprofit organizations, businesses, and groups |
| .info | Nonprofit; intended for informative sites |
| .edu | Education: reserved for educational institutions (most are postsecondary) |
| .gov | Federal and local U.S. Government sites |
| .mil | Department of Defense and military sites |

## EXERCISE 9.12

Access each of the sites in the following list. In each case, predict what the domain type reveals about the nature of the site and its rhetorical purpose.

<http://www.archiva.net/footnote/index.htm>

<http://catalog.loc.gov/>

<http://wildlifecontrol.info/chdp/reducingdeer4_05.htm>

<http://www.womensenews.org/>

<http://www.carlisle.army.mil/ahec/>

<http://www.eightimprov.biz/Improv-Off-Broadway.html>

<http://www.library.cornell.edu/library/libweb.html>

Let's return to our student: Jennifer conducts an additional search on Google Scholar (<http://scholar.google.com/>). The Google Scholar search retrieves 42 sources published between 1990 and 2006. Figure 9–8 shows a copy of her Google Scholar Advanced Search page.

Google Scholar may link you to sites that require you to pay a fee for articles that you can otherwise obtain for free from your college library. After you search Google Scholar,

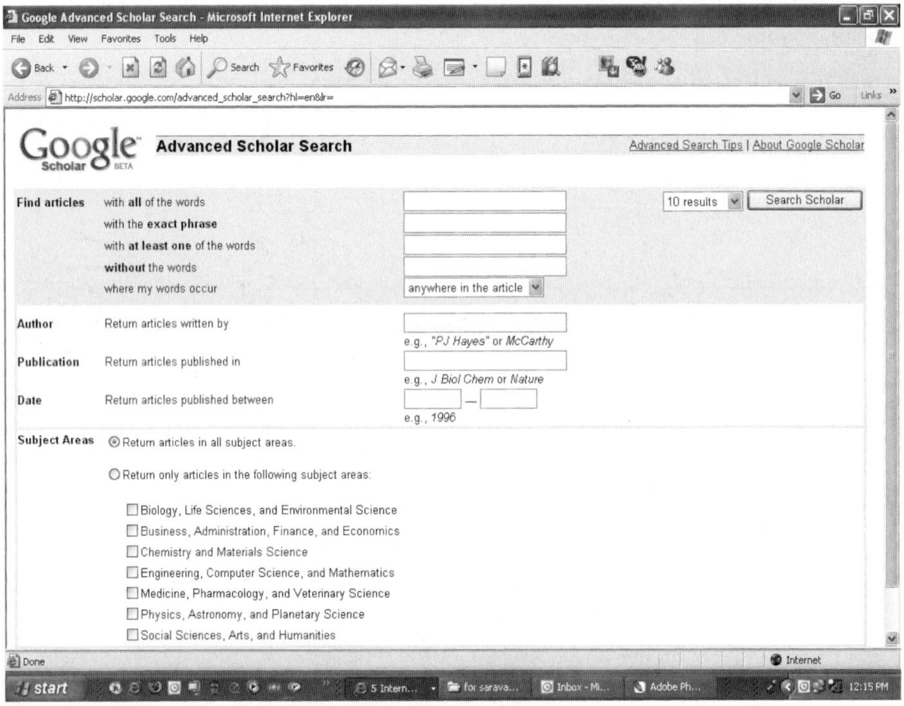

**Figure 9–8    Template for Google Advanced Scholar Search.** Google scholar screen capture © Google Inc., reprinted with permission.

return to your college library catalog to determine whether the articles that you've found on your Google search are also located there.

Another useful tool is the Google Book Search (http://books/google.com). As we mentioned earlier, Google has undertaken a library project that aims to digitalize the world's books. When Jennifer conducts an advanced book search, Google finds eleven books whose contents match her search terms, "trauma therapy" and "therapeutic writing." Google Book Search offers some books in their entirety and others with "previews" or "snippets." For each book, Google provides links to the libraries from which you may borrow the book.

**EXERCISE 9.13**

Reconvene the groups formed in Exercise 9.11 on page 310 and work with the same topic.

- As a group, decide which search terms and Boolean operations you will use to narrow or limit the topic.
- Each student will use these terms and operations to conduct an advanced search on one of the search engines we have listed on page 311. Assign a different search engine to each member of the group.
- When the group reconvenes, the members will review each other's work and decide which search engine produced the best results.

## How to Evaluate Web Sources

Question the reliability of all sources, even those that come from an academic library. It is particularly important to evaluate sources you obtain from the Web. Ask yourself the questions in the following box.

---

### QUESTIONS FOR EVALUATING WEB SITES

- What is the overall goal of the Web site? Do the authors of the Web site have motives other than presenting scholarly truth? For instance, does the site attempt to advocate for a particular political agenda or to sell a product?
- Is the site produced by a reputable organization? Does it provide a mailing address and phone number? Does it invite inquiries?
- Do the authors of the Web site identify themselves? Do they provide any evidence of their expertise or credibility? For example, do they possess training or experience in the topic area covered by their site? Do they demonstrate that they are aware of the standard scholarly or professional literature in the topic area?
- Do the authors distinguish between opinion and fact? Do they provide nonanecdotal evidence to substantiate their conclusions? Do they cite published sources?
- When was the site created? How often is it updated? When was it last updated?

## ■ Collect Information on Your Own: Surveys and Interviews

The bulk of the material you use in research papers will come from published sources; however, depending on your assignment, it may be appropriate to use information that you collect personally through informal interviews and surveys. For example, suppose you are writing a research paper for a psychology class on how birth order (only child, first born, last born, and so on) affects personality. The psychological literature contains numerous studies on this topic, but you decide to supplement these publications by interviewing selected students in your class who represent each of the birth order positions. You will use these cases as concrete illustrations of the conclusions reached in the psychological studies. You might also administer a survey to twenty-five students representing a range of birth orders to see if their perceptions of the relationship between birth order and personality match the research findings.

Informal surveys and interviews provide anecdotal information that is not a reliable basis for firm conclusions. You may recall the negative criticism Louise Story and Linda Hirshman received for basing their arguments on informal contacts (see Chapter 3 for Story's and Hirshman's articles and the critiques by Meares, Shafer, Young, and Brooks). Still, anecdotes are useful for explaining a concept to your readers or for framing an interesting introduction or closing for your research paper. Informal surveys may help you to sharpen your research question or identify trends that warrant more careful investigation. While an informal survey is not sufficient to challenge the conclusions of published studies, it can be useful to note a significant difference between informal and published research results. If the results of the informal classmate survey on the interaction between birth order and personality differ from published conclusions, then the student might suggest in his or her paper that additional formal research should be conducted to see whether the published conclusions still hold for the current college-age population.

A final advantage of conducting informal surveys and interviews is that they get you directly involved with the topic you are researching. This hands-on approach increases interest, particularly for topics that seem rather dry based on the published sources alone. Even if you do not end up using any of the anecdotal information, the experience of getting actively involved with the topic will lead to a better final product.

Whenever you conduct informal interviews or surveys, adhere to the guidelines in the following box.

---

### GUIDELINES FOR CONDUCTING INFORMAL INTERVIEWS AND SURVEYS

- Make sure you comply with college regulations concerning the use of human subjects. While these regulations typically apply to formal research studies, it is possible that your college has guidelines even for informal interviews and surveys. Check with your instructor if you are unsure of your college's human subject policies.

- Whatever your college's policies are, make sure you respect the privacy of your subjects. Do not repeat their responses in casual conversation, and do not use subjects' actual names in your research paper unless there is a clear reason to do so and you have their permission.

- Establish clear goals for your questions. Interview or survey questions should have one of the following goals:

To establish facts

To record beliefs about what is fact

To record personal feelings or values

- Ask the same question worded in several different ways. Sometimes, a slight change in wording will prompt a different response from a subject. It is often difficult to predict wording that will convey the question most effectively.

- Don't ask questions that betray a bias. For example, suppose you are interviewing last-born children to determine if there is a possible link between birth order and personality. You would indicate a bias whether you asked, "In what ways did your parents and older siblings spoil you?" A more neutral question would be, "What personality characteristics distinguish you from your older siblings?"

- Do not press anyone who is reluctant to undergo an interview or complete a survey. Many people do not want to discuss their personal lives, particularly when someone is taking notes on what they say.

## ■ Modify Your Research Strategy

Research, by its very nature, is a creative process that exposes new approaches and gives rise to new ideas. As your research proceeds, you may modify your topic (if the assignment allows you to define your own topic), your research schedule (you may require more trips to the library than you initially anticipated), your research questions, and your search vocabulary.

Consider how Jennifer modifies her search strategy. Recall her initial research questions:

1. To what extent do psychologists still accept Freud's theory concerning trauma?
2. How does current psychological theory explain the impact of traumatic experiences?
3. What therapies are available for victims of psychological trauma? Which are most effective?
4. According to psychologists and communication experts (writing and speech), what role does the verbal expression of traumatic experiences play in the recovery process?
5. Do victims of psychological trauma receive adequate attention in the mental health system?

Jennifer decides to drop Questions 3 and 5. She realizes that Question 3 is too broad for an eight- to ten-page paper, since it involves surveying and evaluating all the therapeutic techniques used in working with trauma victims, and she has found from her research that a wide range of treatments is available. She eliminates Question 5 because it is not addressed directly in any of the sources she has located so far. In addition, Jennifer has discovered that Questions 2 and 4 fit together because recent psychological theory, particularly theory grounded in research on brain physiology, highlights the therapeutic value of communication. And, as a result of the reading she has done so far, she has become particularly interested in these questions. She believes her research on Question 1 will fit into the introductory section of the paper where she will provide historical context.

## ■ Evaluate Information Sources

As you locate source material, judge whether it has direct relevance to your topic. Don't excerpt information that is only remotely related. Ask yourself how the source fits in with your overall goals for the research paper. To what facet of the topic does the source pertain? What perspective on the topic does it represent? Make sense of each source as you examine it. Don't wait until you have completed your library research.

In addition to evaluating the source's relevance to your topic, you should judge its comparative quality. As we mentioned on page 308, you need to examine the reliability of everything you find on the Web. You also need to evaluate library materials. Too many students have complete confidence in sources they find in the library. Library sources come with no absolute guarantees.

As you analyze your sources, examine the author's rhetorical purpose. As we suggested in Chapter 1, ask yourself the Questions for Analyzing the Rhetorical Context of Texts on pages 30–31. The answers to these questions will help you to understand the source better and figure out whether it is appropriate for your paper. For instance, if you are writing for a science course on the future of nuclear power, you may be skeptical of information from lobby groups for the nuclear industry. If you think about writers' motives, you will be able to put their ideas in the proper perspective.

## ■ Excerpt Information from Sources

The basic tools for excerpting information from sources—paraphrasing, summarizing, and quoting—are covered in Chapter 2. Here, we will discuss the special problems associated with the sheer number of sources required for a research paper.

One common problem is losing track of the exact source for an important piece of information. Each time you excerpt a passage from a source, whether you hand copy, reword, or photocopy, make sure that you carefully record a complete citation to the source. Be sure that you distinguish in your notes between passages that you have copied and passages that you have summarized or paraphrased in your own words (hint: always put direct quotations within quotation marks). Record the exact page numbers where specific pieces of text are located. Be especially careful about recording bibliographic information for electronic sources. (See our sample URL on page 313). When you draft your paper, you will cite the source as well as the page for each paraphrase, summary, and quotation. See the box below for information to record. (In the Appendix, we give more detailed information about citing and documenting sources including essential citation formats.)

---

**NECESSARY BIBLIOGRAPHIC INFORMATION**

- For books, record author(s), title, publisher, city of publication, date of publication, and pages where the information you excerpted is located.

> - For magazines and newspapers, record author(s), title of article, name of magazine, date (day, month, year), inclusive pages for entire article, and pages where the information you excerpted is located (the section number or letter is needed for multisectioned newspapers).
> - For scholarly journals, record the same information as for magazines and newspapers, as well as the volume number.
> - For online sources, in addition to recording the items listed above, copy down the title and date of the Web site, the Web address (URL), and the date you accessed the material online and, when applicable, the name of the database or online subscription service and the library where you accessed the database.

Another problem is failing to distinguish adequately between paraphrases and quotations in research notes and thus including an author's exact words in the research paper without quotation marks. This is an unintentional yet serious form of plagiarism. Be very meticulous about your use of quotation marks as you take notes. Reread our comments on plagiarism on pages 47 and 53.

Warning: There is a danger of excerpting too much information. Some students compulsively collect every scrap of information that is remotely related to their topic, thinking that they will make sense of it all at a later date. Don't bury yourself in paper, whether it consists of index cards, pages of notes, computer text files, or photocopies of sources. Excerpt only what you will use. Research is a sense-making process. It is hard to make sense when you are overwhelmed with information.

Much has been written on how students should record the information they excerpt from sources. Some textbooks strongly recommend hand-written index cards for research notes because cards can be grouped and regrouped easily. Of course, you may prefer to record your research notes on your computer and use word processing or outlining programs to organize the information. Try various methods of recording excerpts and decide what works best for you. In addition to research notes, keep a separate set of notes for preliminary thesis statements, organizational plans, or other important ideas that occur to you during the writing process.

## ■ Write a Working Thesis

After you have collected enough sources, formulate a working thesis. The purpose of the preliminary thesis or argument is to focus and direct your research. You may have a working thesis or argument in mind when you begin your research, or it may emerge as you collect information. The educational value of writing a research paper may in fact be to enable you to derive an important thesis or argument from what you have learned through research. You are no longer blowing hot air on an opinion you've conceived, but you're instead elaborating a thesis or argument based on careful research.

To generate a thesis from your research notes: (1) scan the notes for general trends, main concepts, or overall patterns; (2) freewrite for ten minutes on what you think your research will tell your readers; and (3) reduce your freewriting to several sentences that explain what you want to say to your readers.

After scanning her research notes, Jennifer writes the following paragraph:

> Freud's initial work on trauma led to the Seduction Hypothesis, the suggestion that hysteria resulted from the traumatic memories of sexual abuse. However, Freud abandoned this notion, and I don't want Freud to be the focus of my paper. Instead, I want to draw attention to the more current work by brain scientists that explains how trauma is etched into the human brain as an unprocessed memory. The research by van der Kolk best demonstrates this concept. Then I can go on to examine the evidence which shows that allowing these traumatic memories to be fully processed, through either speaking or writing, can provide relief from the trauma. The research done by Pennebaker will be helpful here. I still need more evidence on this point, but I think I will be able to back it up.

Jennifer rereads her freewriting and condenses it into a working thesis:

> In our society, people are discouraged from expressing their feelings about traumatic events that happen to them and instead are encouraged to "keep your chin up." Despite this, there is increasing evidence that it is psychologically helpful to express feelings about trauma. Based on studies of the human brain, it has been established that allowing verbal analysis of traumatic experiences may allow processing of the experiences to take place and may aid in recovering from the impact of trauma.

The thesis is still preliminary. Compare it with Jennifer's final thesis, excerpted from the final version of her research paper:

> While we live in a culture where personal trauma and the lasting psychological effects of traumatic events have been and continue to be silenced, current research suggests that verbal expression of pain, grief, and other responses to trauma speeds recovery. Psychologists and physiologists who study the brain have established that traumatic experiences are encoded in memory as images that are not fully processed by the conscious mind. Verbal analysis of the traumatic event, either through speech or writing, allows processing to take place and aids in recovering from the impact of trauma.

Jennifer's final thesis is refined, more fully developed, and more coherent than the earlier version. The main purpose of a working thesis is to focus your research activities, but you may find yourself departing from the initial thesis as you learn more about the topic.

## ■ Planning the Research Paper

### Select an Organizational Plan

A research paper can follow one organizational plan or a combination of the plans we have discussed in this book. Review the major organizational plans that we presented on pages 22–23. In many cases, a plan will occur to you as you conduct research. For instance, Jennifer has decided to write on how communicating about a traumatic event can help repair the psychological damage caused by the event. Thus, it occurs to her that a statement and response plan with a focus on problem and solution could work for her essay.

## Outline

Because research writers must juggle multiple sources and deal with issues in depth, they need an outline that will keep them on task and provide a framework that unifies information from various sources. Review our explanation of free-form and formal outlining on pages 156–57. A pitfall of writing research papers is to become so bogged down in the details from the reading sources that you fail to clarify the relationships among major ideas. Your research paper will be easier to write if you draft it working from a detailed outline. In the end, your train of thought will be more evident to your readers.

As an example of a free-form outline, consider the one Jennifer develops for her research paper on trauma:

### THESIS

- *Psychologists and physiologists who study the brain have established that traumatic experiences are encoded in memory as images that are not fully processed by the conscious mind. Verbal analysis of the traumatic event, either through speech or writing, allows processing to take place and aids in recovering from the impact of trauma.*

### BACKGROUND

- *After World War I, trauma came to attention of researchers in studies of shell shock victims. Rivers encouraged those victims to talk and write about wartime experiences (Herman).*
- *Later, a link was made between war-induced trauma and trauma which resulted from domestic violence and sexual abuse (Herman).*

### CURRENT PHYSIOLOGICAL RESEARCH ON TRAUMA

- *The brain responds to trauma through several distinct structures. The amygdala attaches emotional meaning to the experience, the hippocampus records the special dimensions of the experience and controls short-term memory of the experience, and the prefrontal cortex analyzes and categorizes the experience (van der Kolk, 1996).*
- *The information from a traumatic event goes first to the amygdala. If the emotional impact is too severe, the message cannot proceed to the hippocampus and prefrontal cortex for complete processing. Thus, the experience cannot be fully contextualized and understood (van der Kolk, 1996; LeDoux, Romanski, & Xagoraris). As a result, the traumatic experience is stored as images, not as a coherent narrative. The painful emotional feelings may remain over time, but the individual does not have a clear explanation for them and thus cannot cope with them.*

### RECOVERING FROM TRAUMA

– *Victims must first understand what makes the memories resurface (Rauch). Then, they must find a way to describe the memories verbally and give them meaning.*

### WRITING AS THERAPY FOR TRAUMA

– *Writing helps to integrate thoughts and feelings (Pennebaker).*

– *Writing can describe and give context to moments and images and help individuals make sense of incidents that initially were verbally indescribable.*

– *Writing has healing power and aids the immune system (Pennebaker).*

– *Writing provides an outlet to express the pain that our society masks in everyday life.*

– *Journaling is the most common form of writing. Focused Freewriting is another genre (Smith and Helm).*

### OPPOSITION AND RESPONSE

– *Some contemporary psychologists favor using beta-blockers to erase the memory of traumatic experience (Davis; Cahill). If this is done, the victims will never have a chance to fully process the experience, a necessary step on the road to recovery.*

## Write from Your Outline

Use your outline as a guide for drafting. Group your notes according to the points in your outline and draft the essay paragraph by paragraph. Be sure to record full bibliographic information in the first draft. It's easy to lose track of where the source information came from if you don't record it initially.

As you draft your essay, you may need to depart from your outline. An outline is supposed to guide your writing, but it should not be a straitjacket. If you discover new patterns or ideas in the process of writing, don't hesitate to include them in your essay.

## ■ Revising

If your teacher agrees, make arrangements to have a classmate review your paper. If that is not possible, set the paper aside for a few days and then review it yourself. Respond to the questions in the following box.

---

#### PEER REVIEW QUESTIONS FOR REVISING A RESEARCH PAPER

- Is the paper written on a sufficiently narrow topic? If not, how might the topic be narrowed?
- Can you understand the writer's research goals? If not, how might the writer make the rhetorical purpose clearer to the reader?
- Does the writer present a clear thesis? If not, how might the writer sharpen the thesis?
- Is the research paper a thesis-driven synthesis or an argument synthesis? If you are not sure, explain why.

---

- Are the writer's assertions substantiated with quotations, paraphrases, and summaries from sources? Which assertions need additional substantiation?
- Is the information from sources organized according to a clear plan? If not, what advice can you give the writer?
- Does the writer use information from sources convincingly? If not, what advice can you give the writer?
- Does the writer provide enough transitions and clearly differentiate between information from the sources and his or her own ideas? If not, what advice can you give the writer?
- Is the writer's voice appropriate for this type of essay? Why or why not?
- Is the paper opener satisfactory? Why or why not?
- Does the essay have an appropriate conclusion? Why or why not?
- Is the title suitable for the piece? Why or why not?
- Can you identify the source for each piece of information?
- Does the paper end with a list of works cited that includes all sources referred to in the text of the paper?

## ■ Editing

When you are satisfied with your revision, read your paper aloud. Then reread it line-by-line and sentence-by-sentence. Check for correct usage, punctuation, spelling, mechanics, manuscript form, and typos. If you are especially weak in editing skills, get a friend to read over your work. Ask yourself the Questions for Editing on pages 177–78.

### *SAMPLE RESEARCH PAPER*

The final draft of Jennifer Piazza's research paper appears on the following pages. Since Jennifer is writing her paper for a psychology class, she uses the American Psychological Association (APA) manuscript and documentation style rather than the MLA style given in our previous examples of student essays. APA style is used in many disciplines besides psychology.

Guidelines for the APA style are found in the *Publication Manual of the American Psychological Association*, 5th edition. In Figure 9–9, we annotate Jennifer's paper to show important features of this format. We list its major guidelines in the box below.

---

### **GUIDELINES FOR FORMATTING RESEARCH PAPERS IN THE APA STYLE**

1. Use a separate title page on which you center and double-space the title, your name, the course, the professor's name, and the date.
2. For each page, including the title page, use a shortened title and the page number as the header.

(continued on the next page)

3. Use a separate page for a concise (no more than 120 words) summary of the research paper. Title the summary "Abstract." See pages 55–57 on guidelines for writing abstracts.

4. Repeat the title before the introductory paragraph.

5. Introduce source material by citing the author's name followed by the publication date in parentheses. Or provide the same material followed by a parenthetical citation of the author, publication date, and page number.

6. Begin the list of references on a new page.

We provide information for documenting sources according to the APA style in the Appendix.

CENTER AND DOUBLESPACE THE TITLE, YOUR NAME,
THE COURSE, THE PROFESSOR, AND THE DATE

5 SPACES BETWEEN
TITLE AND PAGE NUMBER

↕ 1/2"

Effect of Therapeutic Writing          1

↔ 1"

The Effect of Therapeutic Writing

on the Recall of Traumatic Experiences

Jennifer R. Piazza

Counseling: Theory and Dynamics

Professor Nelson

April 24, 2005

↕ 1/2"

↕ 1"   Effect of Therapeutic Writing          2

Abstract

Though we live in a culture that does not encourage trauma victims to verbalize their suffering, research shows that verbal responses to trauma speed recovery. Trauma victims dissociate from or fail to recall the traumatic experience because they are unable to utilize explicit memory to tie past events to their present emotional states. Research has shown that writing serves to translate experiences individuals cannot express orally. Nonetheless, some psychologists question the value of verbal disclosure and advocate administering drugs that will erase memories of traumatic events.

↑ 1"

USE 8½" BY 11" PAPER FOR EACH PAGE. USE DOUBLE SPACES BETWEEN ALL LINES. LEFT JUSTIFY ALL LINES IN THE TEXT OF THE PAPER. DO NOT RIGHT JUSTIFY, EVEN IF YOUR WORD PROCESSOR PROVIDES THIS FEATURE.

The Effect of Therapeutic Writing on the
Recall of Traumatic Experiences

Trauma engulfs people suffering from abuse, grief, and loss of
self. From war to domestic violence, from the death of a loved one to
involvement in a tragic accident, from mental illness to physical
disabilities, from a host of factors, trauma infiltrates lives. Yet,
when trauma touches us on a personal level, we are sometimes taught that
disclosing personal information is undesirable and unacceptable. The
teachings come in the form of hushed words when a victim of trauma enters
the room; they are evident when people look the other way as the widow of
a spouse who committed suicide walks down the street; and the teachings are
strengthened when the media focus on how a victim of a traumatic event
could have prevented it. Those who contain their sorrow are viewed as the
strong and resilient, while those who display reactions to trauma become
the weak and insecure.

Though we live in a culture where personal trauma and the lasting
psychological effects of traumatic events are silenced, current research
suggests that it should be otherwise. Verbal expression of pain, grief, and
other responses to trauma speed recovery. Psychologists and physiologists
who study the brain have established that traumatic experiences are encoded
in memory as images that are not fully processed by the conscious mind.
Verbal analysis of the traumatic event, either through speech or writing,
allows processing to take place and aids the person in recovering from the
impact of trauma.

During the late nineteenth century, Jean-Martin Charcot studied
hysteria in an attempt to bring voices to those who have been silenced.
Two of his students, Pierre Janet and Sigmund Freud, sought to surpass
Charcot's work by finding the cause of hysteria (Herman, 1992). Both
determined that trauma precipitated neuroses and putting the traumatic
experience into words was essential to moving past the trauma and
dispelling neurotic symptoms. Freud discovered that everyday, trivial
experiences seemed to trigger memories of childhood trauma in his patients.
Freud stated that hysteria was the result of premature sexual experiences.
This became known as the Seduction Hypothesis.

At the same time Freud was exploring the Seduction Hypothesis in
Vienna, Janet was studying traumatic memory in France. Like Freud, he came
to the conclusion that hysteria was the result of early childhood trauma.
However, unlike Freud, Janet never abandoned his theory of hysteria and

remained faithful to his patients. Soon after, the medical and psychological establishments accepted Freud, while Janet and his ideas of hysteria
were forgotten. As a result, trauma research was halted for decades
(Herman, 1992).

It was not until after World War I that trauma was once again in the
forefront of research. Veterans who had undergone traumatic experiences
returned from the war displaying symptoms of hysteria, or what was then
called shell shock. A disease that was thought only to afflict women began to
victimize large numbers of men who were once considered glorious and brave.

War-related trauma was publicized as a result of war, but the traumas
of domestic violence, abuse, and rape were hidden. However, because both
men and women displayed similar behaviors after their own personal
traumas, the distinction between the trauma of war and the trauma of
sexual assault and abuse began to blur. As a result of the recognition of
psychological effects that occur both during and after traumatic events,
the diagnosis of post-traumatic stress disorder (PTSD) was included in the
*Diagnostic and Statistical Manual* in 1980 (Herman, 1992). Unfortunately,
the battle fought by trauma survivors did not end when psychologists
considered post-traumatic stress disorder legitimate. On the contrary,
victims of trauma are still being silenced, and to this day the rift still
exists between trauma survivors and those who do not understand the
psychological and biological effects of trauma.

Dennis Charney, head of the clinical neuroscience division of the
National Center for PTSD states:

> Victims of devastating trauma may never be the same, biologically. It
> does not matter if it was the incessant terror of combat, torture of
> repeated abuse in childhood, or a one-time experience, like being
> trapped in a hurricane or almost dying in an auto accident. All
> uncontrollable stress can have the same biological impact. (Butler,
> 1996, p. 41)

Individuals who have not experienced a major traumatic event or chronic
trauma have the natural ability to prepare their bodies for danger. In a
threatening situation, normal individuals' stress hormones increase, and
the fight or flight response prepares them to escape the danger, either by
resisting or by running. When the danger subsides, they return to a normal
state because hormones have leveled off, and the nervous system is no
longer in a state of arousal. It can be concluded, therefore, that normal,
everyday stress does not permanently alter an individual's neurobiology
(van der Kolk, McFarlene, & Weisaeth, 1996).

Unfortunately, this is not the case with trauma, especially trauma that occurs on a chronic basis. According to Bessel van der Kolk et al. (1996), "Chronic and persistent stress inhibits the effectiveness of the stress response and induces desensitization" (p. 222). Stress hormones in traumatized individuals are elevated because victims of trauma are in a state of constant hyperarousal and cannot modulate their bodies efficiently. Small stressors have the ability to trigger the release of a flood of hormones, which results in overreacting to everyday events. As a result, even in normal environments, the nervous system is always on alert.

It is evident that the neurochemistry of traumatized individuals is abnormal, and it is important to understand that traumatic experiences are also stored and processed differently from normal experiences. Bessel van der Kolk et al. (1996) state, "In the course of evolution, the human brain has developed three interdependent subanalyzers; the brainstem/hypothalamus, the limbic system and the prefrontal cortex" (p. 214). The authors go on to explain that the brainstem and hypothalamus are responsible for regulating internal homeostasis, and are partially dependent on the limbic system and prefrontal cortex to function properly. The limbic system, which maintains balance between the internal and external world, contains the hippocampus and the amygdala, two structures that are involved with processing traumatic events. The hippocampus records spacial dimensions of an experience and plays an important role in short-term memory; the amygdala is responsible for attaching emotional meaning to the sensory input of an experience. In other words, the hippocampus is responsible for the context of an experience, and the amygdala is responsible for the emotional weight of an experience. Finally, the prefrontal cortex analyzes the experience and categorizes it with past experiences (van der Kolk et al., 1996).

According to van der Kolk et al. (1996), all information that we receive through our five senses reaches the amygdala before it travels to the hippocampus and the prefrontal cortex. Therefore, emotional responses occur before an actual experience can be interpreted and evaluated. When we experience a normal event, this is not a problem because the emotional weight is too weak to outweigh the actual experience. However, when we experience a traumatic event, the emotional impact is too extreme for further processing to occur. As demonstrated in animal studies (LeDoux, Romanski, & Xagoraris, 1989), if the amygdala is excessively stimulated, it interferes with the functioning of the hippocampus. If there is interference of the hippocampus, as in the case of trauma, it is impossible for a person to form a context for his or her experience. Thus, integration of the traumatic memory with a wide store of other memories never occurs (van der Kolk et al., 1996).

Because integration does not occur, it is nearly impossible for people suffering from trauma to create a narrative that describes their traumatic memory. Instead, their experience exists in the form of images. Although the traumatic experience in its entirety may be hazy and difficult to retrieve, the images of certain moments remain frozen, untarnished. The pictures of the traumatic event are not organized. Traumatized victims cannot pick their mental photo albums off a shelf and note the manner in which the events occurred. Their pictures are scattered, bent, torn. There are no dates written on the back and no explanations as to why the event took place. Thus, trauma victims may dissociate from the experience. They are consciously unable to tie past events to their present emotional states.

This inability to be consciously aware of the connection between events and emotions can be explained by the theory of implicit and explicit memory. According to van der Kolk et al. (1996), explicit or declarative memory is utilized to remember a particular moment and enables people to consciously tie their present behavior to an incident that occurred in their past. It is the memory of context, and it is tied closely to the hippocampus. Implicit memory, unlike explicit memory, does not rely on the hippocampus. It is utilized when perceptions, thoughts, and actions are unconsciously influenced by past experiences.

Traumatic experience interferes with explicit memory but does not interfere with implicit memory. Interference with explicit memory can be attributed to the fact that the hippocampus does not function properly during traumatic experience, due to excessive amygdala stimulation and elevated levels of neurohormones, such as corticosteroids. Since the hippocampus is essential for short-term memory, any damage to the hippocampus results in a person's inability to establish context for his or her experiences. Due to damage to the hippocampus, explicit memory cannot function properly. However, implicit memory is intact (van der Kolk et al., 1996).

For trauma victims to navigate through the aftermath of a traumatic event, they must acquire an understanding of how memories resurface; the purpose of this is so they understand why only feelings and fragments can be recalled rather than the entire incident. An inability to narrate a traumatic experience was examined by Rauch et al. in 1996. By playing to combat veterans and sexual abuse survivors with PTSD a tape of their most horrific memory, the three researchers were able to stimulate flashbacks. During recollection, positron emission tomography (PET) scans were used to record brain activity in these individuals. Results showed that areas of the brain's cortex involved in sensory memory were active, while Broca's area, which plays a large part in verbal articulation of experience, was inactive. When asked to recall a mundane experience, the opposite trend emerged: The sensory areas were inactive, while Broca's area was active (Rauch et al., 1996).

For some trauma victims, writing is an effective vehicle for communication (MacCurdy, 1999). For this reason, therapeutic writing has become an essential form of therapy in the mental health field. As Pennebaker (2000) puts it, "The act of converting emotions and images into words changes the way the person organizes and thinks about the trauma" (8).

Writing is largely based on moments and images. Writers can make lists of things such as colors, feelings, and sounds. A piece of paper and a pen allow them to collect their thoughts; these inanimate objects, unlike people, are not impatient, nor do they become annoyed at images that do not form a story that makes sense. Writers have the power to write as quickly or as slowly as needed. Writers can arrange their pictures and take power over their prose until a story eventually emerges. The images are no longer uncontrollable; they are within the traumatized individual's control. The act of writing can be empowering to individuals as they try to make sense of incidents that initially seem indescribable.

Smyth and Helm (2003) point out that therapists have been using writing, especially journal writing, as a means of disclosure during the therapeutic process for decades. In addition to journaling, other types of writing may be valuable. Smyth and Helm are interested in a relatively recent type of therapeutic writing called Focused Free Writing (FEW):

> FEW involves asking participants to write about their deepest thoughts and feelings regarding the most stressful or traumatic event of their entire life. Typically, participants are brought into a research setting for several (typically three to five) sessions, usually on consecutive days. In these sessions, participants are asked to write about their assigned topic continuously for 20 to 30 min without regard for spelling or grammar. (p. 228)

Smyth and Helm believe FEW has great potential for trauma therapy.

In addition to the mental healing that writing provides, physical healing may also occur. Writing has been shown to enhance immune system functioning and reduce the number of physician visits (Pennebaker, Kiecolt-Glaser, & Glaser, 1988). Studies have shown that writing "increases antibody responses to the Epstein-Barr virus, and antibody response to hepatitis B vaccinations" (Pennebaker, 1997, p. 162). It also helps to increase t-helper cell growth (1997). Short-term changes in autonomic activity, such as lowered heart rate and electrodermal activity, are also produced by disclosure. Pennebaker (1997) has concluded that "the mere expression of trauma is not sufficient. Health gains appear to require translating experiences into language" (p. 164). Writing serves to translate experiences that an individual cannot express verbally. Writing also provides an outlet when no other outlet exists.

Without a supportive community, trauma victims bury their experiences beneath layers and layers of self-blame, guilt, and denial. The process of writing serves to integrate experience and document personal history. Memories, no matter how painful, make us who we are. By telling the story of our lives, we realize why we react the way we do in certain situations and why each of us is unique.

Unfortunately, some psychologists do not see the importance of community and disclosure. Instead, they would rather take the actual traumatic memory away by using drugs such as propranolol. According to Davis (1998), propranolol essentially blocks the ability to connect aversive emotions to traumatic memories by acting as an antagonist on the B-adrenergic receptor. During and after emotional experience, the B-adrenergic stress hormone systems are activated, resulting in enhanced memory for the emotional event. In a study conducted in 1994 (see Cahill, Prins, Weber, & McGaugh) participants were given either propranolol or a placebo an hour before being shown a series of slides accompanied by narratives. The emotionally neutral narrative described a mother taking her son to visit his father, who worked as a laboratory technician in a hospital. The emotionally charged narrative started with the boy and mother going to visit the boy's father at work, but in this version, the two never made it to the lab because the boy was struck by a car and suffered severe brain trauma. In addition, the boy's feet were severed, but a surgical team was able to reattach them. Participants were then given memory tests; results showed that participants in the emotionally neutral scenario, regardless of whether they had received the propranolol, had similar recall. In the emotionally charged condition, however, participants who were given propranolol scored significantly lower than participants who were given a placebo. The results of this study show the profound impact beta-blockers can have in the face of a traumatic event.

According to Davis, the next step is to use propranolol to conduct a controlled study with trauma victims. I think the thought of erasing a memory from another human being is terrifying. The neurobiology of trauma victims may leave them speechless, but with a supportive community and therapeutic writing, their voices can return. Unfortunately, our society does not recognize this. It was bad enough that we isolated victims from society; now we isolate them from themselves.

## References

Butler, K. (1996, March/April). The biology of fear. *Networker*, 39–45.

Cahill, L., Prins, B., Weber, M., & McGaugh, J. L. (1994). B-Adrenergic activation and memory for emotional events. *Nature*, 271, 702–704.

Davis, M. (1998). Neural systems involved in fear and anxiety. Symposium conducted at the University of Scranton, Scranton, PA.

Herman, J. L. (1992). *Trauma and recovery*. New York: HarperCollins.

LeDoux, J. E., Romanski, L., & Xagoraris, A. (1989). Indelibility of subcortical emotional memories. *Journal of Cognitive Neuroscience*, 1, 238–243.

MacCurdy, M. (1999). From trauma to writing: A theoretical model for practical use. In C. Anderson & M. MacCurdy (Eds.), *Writing and healing: Toward an informed practice*. Urbana, IL: National Council of Teachers of English.

Pennebaker, J. W. (2000). Telling stories: the health benefits of narrative. *Literature and Medicine*, 19(1), 3–18. Retrieved March 26, 2005, from Project Muse database.

Pennebaker, J. W. (1997). Writing about emotional experiences as a therapeutic process. *Psychological Science*, 8(3), 162–165.

Pennebaker, J. W., Kiecolt-Glaser, J. K., & Glaser, R. (1988). Disclosure of traumas and immune function: Health implications for psychotherapy. *Journal of Counseling and Clinical Psychology*, 56(2), 239–245.

Rauch, S. L., van der Kolk, B. A., Fisler, R. E., Alpert, N. M., Orr, S. P., Savage, C. R., et al. (1996). A symptom provocation study of posttraumatic stress disorder using positron emission tomography and scriptdriven imagery. *Archives of General Psychiatry*, 53, 380–387.

BEGIN YOUR ALPHABETICAL LIST OF REFERENCES ON A NEW PAGE. DOUBLE-SPACE THROUGHOUT. INCLUDE IN THE LIST OF REFERENCES ONLY SOURCES THAT ARE REFERRED TO IN THE TEXT OF THE PAPER.

Smyth, J., and R. Helm. (2003). Focused expressive writing as self-help for stress and trauma [Electronic version]. *Journal of Clinical Psychology* 59(2), 227-35. Retrieved March 26, 2005.

van der Kolk, B. A., McFarlane, A. C., & Weisaeth, L. (1996). *Traumatic Stress*. New York: Guilford Press.

## EXERCISE 9.14

Reread Jennifer Piazza's research paper and ask the following questions:

- What is her goal for writing?
- What is she trying to accomplish?
- What is the relationship between the sources of information she draws on and her own views?

Freewrite for ten minutes in response to these questions.

## EXERCISE 9.15

- Form collaborative learning groups.
- Within your group, discuss the following questions: To what extent is Jennifer Piazza's paper an explanation of her own conclusions about the topic? To what extent is it an argument? Have the recorder note the high points of your deliberations.
- Reconvene the entire class. Each group recorder should explain the group's answers to the two questions. Then, discuss any disagreements among groups.

## WORKS CITED

ArticleFirst Basic Search template. 24 May 2006 <http://libproxy.cortland.edu:2056/WebZ/FSPage?pagename=advanced:sessionid=fsapp1-51717-enm6xvb5-xheqji:entitypagenum=2:0>.

ArticleFirst Advanced Search template. 24 May 2006 <http://libproxy.cortland.edu:2056/html/webscript.html:%3Asessionid=fsapp1-51717-enm6xvb5-xheqji:sessionid=fsapp1-51717-enm6xvb5-xheqji:>.

"Distinguishing Scholarly from Non-Scholarly Periodicals." Research Strategy and Process: Evaluating Research Materials. 25 June 2006. Cornell Lib., Ithaca, NY. 24 May 2006 <http://www.library.cornell.edu/t/help/res_strategy/evaluating/scholar.html>.

Kelly, Kevin. "Scan This Book!" *The New York Times Magazine*. 14 May 2006: 43–49, 64, 71.

# An Anthology of Readings

# Natural Sciences and Technology

## ◼︎ SUBJECTS AND METHODS OF STUDY IN THE NATURAL SCIENCES AND TECHNOLOGY

### ◼︎ The Scientific Method

Science and technology are based on a **common methodology**, and thus scientific and technical researchers the world over share an approach to their work. Even though they may give conflicting answers to important questions in their disciplines, they rarely argue about the basic process of conducting scientific investigation. The specific means by which researchers discover, collect, and organize information is called **the scientific method**. This approach involves questioning, observing, experimenting, and theorizing. Drawing on previous knowledge and prior investigations, scientists ask questions not only about the unknown but also about phenomena that are supposedly understood. Often, they challenge commonly accepted beliefs as well as the conclusions of other scientists. Indeed, no fact or theory is exempt from legitimate inquiry. Even the most widely accepted ideas are continually reexamined. This questioning process helps make science self-correcting, since errors made by scientists can be detected and amended by subsequent investigation. The process is part of what we might call the "conversation" in scientific writing.

Scientific ideas must be confirmed through **verifiable observation** before they are considered fact. Assertions that cannot be supported by observation are generally greeted with skepticism by the scientific community. For phenomena that cannot be observed readily in nature, scientists design experiments that make events stand out more clearly. As with other information derived from observations, experimental findings are continually reexamined, and experiments are considered valid only if they can be repeated with identical results by different investigators. The "conversation" in scientific writing focuses upon this validation.

Scientists build **theories** to account for direct observations and experimental results. Theories are rules or models that explain a large body of separate facts. An example is the

335

Bohr model of the atom, in which electrons orbit around the nucleus like moons around a planet. The Bohr model explains many basic observations made by physicists and chemists, but it is by no means the only theoretical description of the atom; quantum theory suggests an atomic model that does not include electrons in discrete orbits. Scientists often weigh competing theories that purport to explain the same facts. The other parts of the scientific method—questioning, observing, and experimenting—contribute to constructing and testing theories.

# ■ WRITING ABOUT SCIENCE AND TECHNOLOGY

Texts concerning science and technology can be separated into two groups: (1) **reports of original research**, which focus on a narrow topic, and (2) **summary or speculative articles**, which generalize about a body of specific information. Research reports are typically written for experts in scientific or technical disciplines. Footnotes in research reports generally focus on earlier studies directly related to the experiment in question. Summary and speculative articles are often directed to less specialized audiences. The footnotes in such academic articles may range far and wide as they address social, cultural, political, moral, or historical issues related to the topic. Consider, for example, the different sorts of documentation in Raymond Kurzweil's speculative article (Chapter 11) which considers the ethical consequences of transferring the contents of a human mind into a computer and in Thomas Colbridge's summary article (Chapter 12) which reviews the constitutional issues that arise from police use of thermal imaging technology. Most of the articles in Chapters 10, 11, and 12 are summary and speculative articles written for a general audience rather than an audience of professional scientists. These articles engage in conversation with one another and also with various forms of writing in other branches of science and technology, the social sciences, philosophy, law, religion, public policy, and so forth.

## ■ Organization

Research reports share **a common rhetorical pattern**. Scientists within specific disciplines have established standard methods for organizing research reports, and most journals that publish research results accept only articles written according to these formats. Summary and speculative articles, however, vary widely in rhetorical structure. Nonscientists who think the only aim of science writing is to relate established facts fail to recognize that much science writing argues a point. As you read through the next three chapters, notice that the majority of the articles are organized as arguments in conversation with the arguments of other writers. For example, the title of Charles Krauthammer's article "Crossing Lines: A Secular Argument Against Research Cloning" (Chapter 10) indicates that the essay will touch upon religious concerns about ethics and morality, but that it will do so from a secular point of view. The pursuit of science often gives rise to intense debate over what questions should be investigated, what observations are accurate, and what theories best explain particular observations; as a result, argumentative writing is common in science. In addition to argumentation, the full range of rhetorical patterns can be found in popular science writing.

Writing research reports according to a set organizational formula does have its drawbacks. In some cases, scientists may become so obsessed with fitting their work into a research report formula that they lose sight of the central goal of scientific research: an active pursuit of the truth. A similar problem sometimes surfaces in popular science writing in which the rhetorical pattern becomes more important than scientific accuracy. For example, Joseph Weizenbaum, an internationally known computer scientist, states that most essays about the societal impact of computer technology follow a set pattern. First, they survey the benefits to society of computers; then, they consider some of the potential dangers of widespread computer use; finally, they claim that those dangers can be overcome with new technology and argue for a vigorous program to expand computer development and use. Weizenbaum implies that this simplistic, problem-solution approach to writing about computers may obscure the truth. Much popular writing about controversial science and technology follows a similar **problem-solution pattern**. To fit a set format, the science writer may ignore important facts or pass over alternative interpretations of certain facts. Consequently, analyzing rhetorical structure is an important element in comprehending science writing.

## ■ Style

Although the tone of research report writing is almost always unemotional and authoritative, the tone as well as style of summary and speculative science writing vary considerably. Once free from the constraints of the professional research report, scientists express emotions and personal attitudes, as do writers in other fields. As you read the article by Joshua Quittner in Chapter 12, notice that the writer uses a personal tone to discuss a technical issue: electronic information systems.

No matter what the tone, a science writer establishes authority by providing **concrete evidence**. Even the most eminent scientists must support their theories with **verifiable observations**. In Chapters 10, 11, and 12, you will find that most of the authors include objective evidence to support major assertions. That evidence often comes from scientific investigation, but it also comes from **informal observations, anecdotes**, and **hypothetical cases**. For example, in "Loving Technology" which appears in Chapter 11, Sherry Turkle lists a number of observations about children's interaction with electronic "pets" and then uses these observations as a basis for predicting how interactions between intelligent machines and humans will develop in the future. Most science writers are careful to build on evidence, even when they are writing for a general audience. Consequently, it is important for readers of science writing to identify and evaluate the evidence authors provide in support of their claims.

Nonscientists are often amazed to find that different sources may present **conflicting versions of scientific "fact."** The same body of experimental evidence can lead to several different notions of what the truth is. When the experts disagree, science writers enter the conversation by describing precisely the various versions of the facts, and if possible, by trying to explain reasons for the differences of opinion.

Sometimes, differences of opinion on scientific issues have nothing to do with scientific fact but, rather, reflect **conflicting personal or social values**. Science is not immune to the political and moral controversy that is part of other human activities. As you read the articles in Chapter 10 on human and animal cloning, you will see that the writers address social and moral issues. When writers do not support scientific claims with objective evidence, you should consider the moral, ideological, or emotional motivations behind their assertions.

Regardless of the specialized genre, writers in science and technology are expected to engage with one another in a sustained conversation on the topics they address. Most of the articles in the following chapters offer footnotes and bibliographies that report on the extent of their conversation with others. Student papers in science and technology are likewise expected to join this kind of conversation. Here are some typical writing assignments in the sciences, as taken from exercises in the following chapters:

> Drawing upon information about biotechnology in Andrews and Nelkin's "The Business of Bodies," write an essay of 750 words pro or con on the topic of the human body as a utilitarian object.

> Write a 750-word response to the editors of *Wired* magazine in which you develop your own commentary attacking the argument for relinquishing scientific developments in the new technologies in Bill Joy's article, "Why the Future Doesn't Need Us."

> Do the events of September 11, 2001, justify employing technology that may violate individual privacy? Answer this question in a 1,250-word essay that draws on at least three of the articles in the chapter on "Crime-Fighting Technology: Balancing Public Safety and Privacy."

Note that these assignments do not ask you to conduct original scientific research or even to draw inferences from scientific research or reports based on laboratory experiments. They do, however, require you to join the conversation about science and technology recorded in academic publications, summary and speculative studies, extended professional narratives, and journalistic reports.

Even nonscientists can evaluate intelligently many articles about science and technology addressed to a broad readership. As you read and think about the material in the next three chapters, keep in mind that many of the articles are organized as arguments and can be analyzed like other forms of argumentative writing. Ask yourself whether the article involves questioning, observing, experimenting, or theorizing—the basic components of the scientific method. Be sensitive to the author's tone. Look for evidence that supports the author's claims. Note the specific points on which the experts disagree, and try to account for those differences of opinion. Finally, consider the social or ethical questions that scientific advances raise. These procedures will help you read and write about science and technology with more understanding and better critical judgment.

# CHAPTER Ten

# Cloning

Intervention in reproductive processes is as old as civilization. Since prehistoric times, humans have selectively bred animals to enhance their usefulness: to make them pull heavier loads, produce more milk, have more offspring, and so forth. Ancient humans also tried to intervene in their own reproductive processes: for example, by trying to improve fertility through the use of amulets, rituals, and herbs. Certain cultures systematically controlled human reproduction: for instance, by putting some female babies to death to maintain a relatively high proportion of male laborers and warriors.

Modern technology provides new, dramatic ways of intervening in reproduction. Most domestic cattle now result from artificial insemination. Human couples with faulty eggs or sperm can now receive genetic material from donors to create an embryo outside the womb, a "test-tube baby" that can be implanted in the mother-to-be. Surrogate mothers incubate babies for women who are able to conceive but not bear children. And now, both animal and human embryos have been successfully cloned, opening up a range of new possibilities for reproduction.

Although interventions in reproductive processes have always been controversial, recent cloning experiments on animals and humans have intensified the debate. Is cloning just another reproductive technology, or does it raise unique ethical, political, or social issues? Should we allow asexual reproduction and the genetic duplication of particular individuals? Should childless couples or singles be allowed to use cloning to produce children to whom they are biologically related? Should individuals be allowed to produce genetic copies of themselves in a bid for "immortality"? Should we use cloning to reproduce the "best" individuals in our culture, the Einsteins and Mozarts? Should we clone endangered animal species to ensure their survival? Should we use cloning to bring back species that are already extinct? The topics in this debate cross boldly over social, cultural, political, and ethical boundaries and they recruit specialists from as many disciplines into the conversation.

The articles in Chapter 10 focus on controversies over human and animal cloning. Lee M. Silver's "Jennifer and Rachel," an excerpt from the author's book *Remaking Eden: Cloning and Beyond in a Brave New World*, describes the circumstances under which a human might opt for cloning and maintains that human cloning does not threaten society. Its style incorporates narrative, philosophical, and political features that sharpen its questions. Written in response to an experiment in which scientists cloned human cells, John J. Conley's "Narcissus Cloned" argues that cloning human embryos violates the sanctity of human life and undermines human relationships. Its style pursues a speculative philosophical line of reasoning. Charles Krauthammer argues that cloning should not be used in attempts to remove genetic defects from human embryos in his article "Crossing Lines: A Secular Argument Against Research Cloning." His style follows a question-and-answer model that appeals to a broad audience.

Lori Andrews and Dorothy Nelkin's "The Business of Bodies" offers an academic approach as it explores social and legal issues relating to biotechnology. It incorporates several academic footnotes that cut across the fields of sociology, law, and scientific research. Ian Wilmut concludes the conversation with his essay on "The Moral Imperative for Cloning." Though a research specialist who pioneered in the development of animal cloning, Wilmut undertakes an ethical argument that cites opposing arguments and acknowledges partial concessions to them.

■ ■ ■ ■ ■ ■ ■ ■ ■ ■ ■

# Jennifer and Rachel

## *Lee M. Silver*

*Lee M. Silver is a professor at Princeton University who holds appointments in the departments of Molecular Biology, Ecology, and Evolutionary Biology. He is a fellow of the American Association for the Advancement of Science and an expert on the social impact of reproductive technology. This article is excerpted from Silver's book* Remaking Eden: Cloning and Beyond in a Brave New World.

## PREREADING

What have you previously read or seen in the news concerning cloning? Brainstorm a list of specifics. Now read through your list. Based on the items in your list, would you say the news media present cloning in a positive, negative, or objective light? Do they sensationalize cloning, or do they provide balanced reporting?

Jennifer is a self-sufficient single woman who lives by herself in a stylish apartment    1
on Manhattan's Upper West Side. She has focused almost all her energies on her career since graduating from Columbia University, fourteen years earlier, and has moved steadily upward in the business world. In financial terms, she is now quite well

off. In social terms, she is happy being single. Jennifer has had various relationships with men over the years, but none was serious enough to make her consider giving up her single lifestyle.

And then on April 14, 2049, the morning of her thirty-fifth birthday, Jennifer 2 wakes up alone, in her quiet room, before the break of dawn, before her alarm is set to go off, and she begins to wonder. With her new age—thirty-five—bouncing around in her mind, a single thought comes to the fore. "It's getting late," she tells herself.

It is not marriage or a permanent relationship that she feels is missing, it is some- 3 thing else. It is a child. Not any child, but a child of her own to hold and to love, to watch and to nurture. Jennifer knows that she can afford to raise a child by herself, and she also knows that the firm she works for is generous in giving women the flexibility required to maintain both a family and a career. And now she feels, for the first time, that she will soon be too old to begin motherhood.

Jennifer is a decisive woman, and by the end of that day she decides to become a 4 single mother. It is the same positive decision that hundreds of thousands of other woman have made before her. But unlike twentieth-century women, Jennifer knows there is no longer any reason to incorporate a sperm donor into the process. An anony-mous sperm cell could introduce all sorts of unknown, undesirable traits into her child, and Jennifer is not one to gamble. Instead, she makes the decision to use one of her own cells to create a new life.

Jennifer is well aware that federal law makes cloning illegal in the United States 5 except in cases of untreatable infertility. She realizes that she could get around the law through a marriage of convenience with a gay friend, who would then be declared infertile by a sympathetic physician. But she decides to do what increasing numbers of other women in her situation have done recently—take an extended vacation in the Cayman Islands.

On Grand Cayman Island, there is a large reprogenetic clinic that specializes in 6 cloning. The young physicians and biologists who work at this clinic do not ask ques-tions of their clients. They will retrieve cells from any willing adult, prepare those cells for fusion to unfertilized eggs recovered from any willing woman, and then introduce the embryos that develop successfully into the uterus of the same, or another, willing woman. The cost of the procedure is $80,000 for the initial cell cloning and embryo transfer, and $20,000 for each subsequent attempt at pregnancy if earlier embryos fail to implant. When the clinic first opened, the fees were twice as high, but they dropped in response to competition from newly opened clinics in Jamaica and Grenada.

Since Jennifer is a healthy fertile woman, she has no need for other biological par- 7 ticipants in the cloning process. A dozen unfertilized eggs are recovered from her ovaries and made nucleus-free. One-by-one, each is fused with a donor cell obtained from the inside of her mouth. After a period of incubation, healthy-looking embryos are observed under a microscope, and two of these are introduced into her uterus at the proper time of her menstrual cycle. (The introduction of two embryos increases the probability of a successful implantation.) After the procedure, Jennifer stays on the island three more days to rest, then flies back to New York.

A week later, Jennifer is thrilled by the positive blue + symbol that appears on her 8 home pregnancy test. She waits another two weeks to confirm that the pregnancy has taken with another test, and then schedules an appointment with Dr. Steven Glassman, her gynecologist and obstetrician. Dr. Glassman knows that Jennifer is a single woman, and he doesn't ask—and Jennifer doesn't tell—how her pregnancy began. The following eight and a half months pass by uneventfully, with monthly, then weekly, visits to the doctor's office. Ultrasound indicates the presence of a single normal fetus, and amniocentesis confirms the absence of any known genetic problem. Finally, on March 15, 2050, a baby girl is born. Jennifer names her Rachel. To the nurses and doctors who work in the delivery room, Rachel is one more newborn baby, just like all the other newborn babies they've seen in their lives.

Jennifer, holding Rachel in her arms, is taken to a room in the maternity ward, 9 and shortly thereafter, the nurse on duty brings by the form to fill out for the birth certificate. Without a word, she enters Jennifer's name into the space for "the mother." She then asks Jennifer for the name of the father. "Unknown," Jennifer replies, and this is duly recorded. A day later, Jennifer is released from the hospital with her new baby girl.

Rachel will grow up in the same way as all other children her age. Occasionally, 10 people will comment on the striking similarity that exists between the child and her mother. Jennifer will smile at them and say, "Yes. She does have my facial features." And she'll leave it at that.

From time to time, Jennifer will let Rachel know that she is a "special" child, 11 without going into further detail. Then one day, when her daughter has grown old enough to understand, Jennifer will reveal the truth. And just like other children conceived with the help of reprogenetic protocols, Rachel will feel . . . special. Some day in the more distant future, when cloning becomes just another means of alternative reproduction, accepted by society, the need for secrecy will disappear.

Who is Rachel, and who really are her parents? There is no question that Jennifer 12 is Rachel's birth mother, since Rachel was born out of her body. But, Jennifer is not Rachel's genetic mother, based on the traditional meanings of mother and father. In genetic terms, Jennifer and Rachel are twin sisters. As a result, Rachel will constantly behold a glimpse of her future simply by looking at her mother's photo album and her mother herself. She will also understand that her single set of grandparents are actually her genetic parents as well. And when Rachel grows up and has children of her own, her children will also be her mother's children. Thus, with a single act of cloning, we are forced to reconsider the meaning of parents, children, and siblings, and how they relate to one another.

## Is Cloning Wrong?

Is there anything wrong with what Jennifer has done? The most logical way to approach 13 this question is through a consideration of whether anyone, or anything, has been harmed by the birth of Rachel. Clearly no harm has been done to Jennifer. She got the baby girl she wanted and she will raise her with the same sorts of hopes and aspirations that most normal parents have for their children.

But what about Rachel? Has she been harmed in some way so detrimental that it 14 would have been better had she not been born? Daniel Callahan, the Director of the Hastings Center (a bioethics think tank near New York City), argues that "engineering someone's entire genetic makeup would compromise his or her right to a unique identity." But no such "right" has been granted by nature—identical twins are born every day as natural clones of each other. Dr. Callahan would have to concede this fact, but he might still argue that just because twins occur naturally does not mean we should create them on purpose.

Dr. Callahan might argue that Rachel is harmed by the knowledge of her future 15 condition. He might say that it is unfair for Rachel to go through her childhood knowing what she will look like as an adult, or being forced to consider future medical ailments that might befall her. But even in the absence of cloning, many children have some sense of the future possibilities encoded in the genes they got from their parents. In my own case, I knew as a teenager that I had a good chance of inheriting the pattern baldness that my maternal grandfather expressed so thoroughly. Furthermore, genetic screening already provides people with the ability to learn about hundreds of disease predispositions. And as genetic knowledge and technology become more and more sophisticated, it will become possible for any human being to learn even more about their genetic future than Rachel can learn from Jennifer's past. In American society, it is generally accepted that parents are ultimately responsible for deciding what their children should, or should not, be exposed to. And there's no reason to expect that someone like Jennifer would tell Rachel something that was not in her best interest to know.

Just because Rachel has the same genes as Jennifer does not mean that her life 16 will turn out the same way. On the contrary, Rachel is sure to have a different upbringing in a world that has changed significantly since her mother's time. And there is no reason why she can't chart her own unique path through life. Furthermore, when it comes to genetic predispositions, they are just that and nothing more. Although their genetically determined inclinations may be the same, mother and daughter may choose to follow those inclinations in different ways, or not at all.

It might also be argued that Rachel is harmed by having to live up to the unrealis- 17 tic expectations that her mother will place on her. But there is no reason to believe that Jennifer's expectations will be any more unreasonable than those of many other parents who expect their children to accomplish in their lives what the parents were unable to accomplish in their own. No one would argue that parents with such tendencies should be prohibited from having children. Besides, there's no reason to assume that Jennifer's expectations will be unreasonable. Indeed, there is every reason to believe Rachel will be loved by her mother no matter what she chooses to do, as most mothers love their children.

But let's grant that among the many Rachels brought into this world, some *will* 18 feel bad that their genetic constitution is not unique. Is this alone a strong enough reason to ban the practice of cloning? Before answering this question, ask yourself another: Is a child having knowledge of an older twin worse off than a child born into poverty? If we ban the former, shouldn't we ban the latter? Why is it that so many politicians seem to care so much about cloning but so little about the welfare of children in general?

Some object to cloning because of the process that it entails. The view of the 19 Vatican, in particular, is that human embryos should be treated like human beings and should not be tampered with in any way. However, the cloning protocol does *not* tamper with embryos, it tampers only with *unfertilized* eggs and adult cells like those we scratch off our arms without a second thought. Only after the fact does an embryo emerge (which could be treated with the utmost respect if one so chooses).

There is a sense among some who are religious that cloning leaves God out of the 20 process of human creation, and that man is venturing into places he does not belong. This same concern has been, and will continue to be, raised as each new reprogenetic technology is incorporated into our culture, from in vitro fertilization twenty years ago to genetic engineering of embryos—sure to happen in the near future. It is impossible to counter this theological claim with scientific arguments. . . .

Finally, there are those who argue against cloning based on the perception that it 21
will harm society at large in some way. The *New York Times* columnist William Safire
expresses the opinion of many others when he says, "Cloning's identicality would restrict
evolution." This is bad, he argues, because "the continued interplay of genes . . . is
central to humankind's progress." But Mr. Safire is wrong on both practical and theoretical grounds. On practical grounds, even if human cloning became efficient, legal, and
popular among those in the moneyed classes (which is itself highly unlikely), it would
still only account for a fraction of a percent of all the children born onto this earth. Furthermore, each of the children born by cloning to different families would be different
from one another, so where does the identicality come from?

On theoretical grounds, Safire is wrong because humankind's progress has noth- 22
ing to do with unfettered evolution, which is always unpredictable and not necessarily
upward bound. H. G. Wells recognized this principle in his 1895 novel *The Time
Machine*, which portrays the natural evolution of humankind into weak and dimwitted,
but cuddly little creatures. And Kurt Vonnegut follows this same theme in *Galápagos*,
where he suggests that our "big brains" will be the cause of our downfall, and future
humans with smaller brains and powerful flippers will be the only remnants of a once
great species, a million years hence.

Although most politicians professed outrage at the prospect of human cloning 23
when Dolly [the first cloned sheep] was first announced, Senator Tom Harkin of Iowa
was the one lone voice in opposition. "What nonsense, what utter utter nonsense, to
think that we can hold up our hands and say, 'Stop,'" Mr. Harkin said. "Human cloning
will take place, and it will take place in my lifetime. I don't fear it at all. I welcome it."

As the story of Jennifer and Rachel is meant to suggest, those who want to clone 24
themselves or their children will not be impeded by governmental laws or regulations.
The marketplace—not government or society—will control cloning. And if cloning is
banned in one place, it will be made available somewhere else—perhaps on an underdeveloped island country happy to receive the tax revenue. Indeed, within two weeks of
Dolly's announcement, a group of investors formed a Bahamas-based company called
Clonaid (under the direction of a French scientist named Dr. Brigitte Boisselier) with
the intention of building a clinic where cloning services would be offered to individuals
for a fee of $200,000. According to the description provided on their Web page
(<http://www.clonaid.com>), they plan to offer "a fantastic opportunity to parents with
fertility problems or homosexual couples to have a child cloned from one of them."

Irrespective of whether this particular venture actually succeeds, others will cer- 25
tainly follow. For in the end, international borders can do little to impede the reproductive practices of couples and individuals.

## Surreptitious Cloning

In democratic societies, people have the right to reproduce and the right to *not* repro- 26
duce. This last "right" means that men and women cannot be forced to conceive a
child against their will. Until now, it has been possible to exercise this particular right
by choosing not to engage in sexual intercourse, and not to provide sperm or eggs for
use in artificial insemination or IVF [in vitro fertilization]. But suddenly, human
cloning opens up frightening new vistas in the realm of reproductive choice, or lack
thereof. Suddenly, it becomes possible to use the genetic material of others without
their knowledge or consent.

Let's reconsider the Jennifer and Rachel scenario in the light of reproductive 27
choice. At first glance, it might seem that nothing is amiss here because Jennifer obviously gave her consent to be cloned. But reproductive choice has been interpreted
traditionally to mean that people have the right not to be genetic parents against their
will. Does this mean that Jennifer should have asked her own parents for permission to
create a clone—her identical twin and their child—before proceeding? Actually, all
of *your* genes, as well, came from *your* mother and father. Does this mean that your
parents have the right to tell you how to use them?

At least Jennifer gave her consent to be cloned. But what are we to make of a situ- 28
ation in which someone is cloned without his or her knowledge, let alone consent? It
takes only a single living cell to start the cloning procedure, and that cell can probably
be obtained from almost any living part of the human body. There are various ways in
which cells could be stolen from a person. I will illustrate one here with what I will call
the Michael Jordan scenario.

Let's move to the near future. The year is 2009, and Jordan has now retired as a 29
professional basketball player. He goes into his doctor's office for his annual checkup,
during which a blood sample is taken into a standard tube. Jordan's sample, along with
others, is given over to a medical technician, who has been waiting for this moment
since Jordan scheduled his appointment a month before. After closing the lab door
behind her, she opens the tube of Jordan's blood and removes a tiny portion, which is
transferred to a fresh tube that is quickly hidden in her pocket. The original tube is
resealed, and no one will ever know that it has been tampered with.

At the start of her lunch break, the technician rushes the tube of blood to her 30
friend at a private IVF clinic on the other side of town. The small sample is emptied
into a laboratory dish, and there Jordan's white blood cells are bathed in nutrients and
factors that will allow them to grow and multiply into millions of identical cells, each
one ready for cloning. The cells are divided up into many portions, which are frozen in
individual tubes for later use.

And then the word goes out on the street. For a $200,000 fee, you can have your 31
very own Michael Jordan child. Would anyone buy? If not a Michael Jordan child,
would they be interested in a Tom Cruise, a Bill Clinton, or a Madonna (the singer, not
the saint)?

It's important to understand that what most people want more than anything else 32
is to have their *own* child, not someone else's child, no matter who that someone else
might be. And if cloning someone else is an option, then cloning oneself is also an
option. So what possible reason could exist for choosing a genetically unrelated child?

Perhaps heartless mothers will want a clone of someone famous in the belief
that they will prosper on the income that a clone could make, or the fame that he 33
would bring. But it would require an enormous investment in time and money to raise a
child over many years before there was even a chance of a payback. Clones of Michael
Jordan would likely be born with the potential to become outstanding athletes, and
clones of Tom Cruise or Madonna might have the same artistic talent as their progenitors. But the original Jordan, Cruise, and Madonna owe their success even more to
hard work than genetic potential.

Clones might not have the same incentive to train and exert themselves even 34
if—and perhaps because—unscrupulous parents and promoters try to force them in a
specified direction against their will. And while one Madonna clone might attract fame
and attention, the next dozen will almost certainly be ignored. It is hard to imagine that

many potential parents would be willing to take this gamble, with the wait being so long and the chances of success so small.

There will probably always be some infertile couples or individuals who will want 35 to clone simply for the opportunity to raise a child who is likely to be beautiful or bright, without any desire to profit from the situation themselves. These people will be able to reach their reproductive goals by cloning someone—who is not famous—*with* their consent. In the future, cell donors could be chosen from a catalog in the same way that sperm and egg donors are chosen today.

In contrast, cloning surreptitiously will almost certainly be frowned upon even by 36 those who accept other uses of the cloning technology. And those who participate will run the risk of serious litigation on the basis of infringing upon someone else's reproductive rights. This is not to say, however, that surreptitious cloning will never occur. On the contrary, if something becomes possible in our brave new reproductive world, someone will probably do it, somewhere, sometime.

## READING FOR CONTENT

1. What factors led Jennifer to decide to have herself cloned?
2. Why must Jennifer travel to the Cayman Islands for the cloning procedure?
3. Paraphrase Silver's description of the cloning process that Jennifer undergoes.
4. What is the biological relationship between Jennifer and Rachel? Between Rachel and Jennifer's parents?
5. In what ways will Rachel's and Jennifer's lives differ, even though the two individuals are genetically identical?
6. What might be the motive for "surreptitious cloning"?
7. Why does Silver think that relatively few people will want to raise clones of famous, talented individuals?

## READING FOR GENRE, ORGANIZATION, AND STYLISTIC FEATURES

1. Why does Silver begin his piece with an extended scenario?
2. Where does Silver respond to the views of those who oppose human cloning? Is that response successful?
3. Why does Silver choose to discuss "surreptitious cloning" at the end of the piece?
4. Would you characterize this as a piece of academic writing? Why, or why not? What types of sources and authorities does Silver cite?

## READING FOR RHETORICAL CONTEXT

1. How do Silver's credentials affect your reading of his essay?
2. What assumptions does Silver make about the general public's response to cloning? Why has he written this piece, and what is his attitude toward his readers?
3. What is Silver's rhetorical purpose? What does he want to get across to his readers?
4. Where does Silver indicate his own attitude toward Jennifer's use of cloning technology?

# WRITING ASSIGNMENTS

1.  In a 500-word essay, summarize the potential benefits and dangers of human cloning that are discussed in Silver's article. Write for an audience of nonscientists.
2.  Write a 1,000-word essay that attacks or defends Silver's suggestion that Jennifer's decision to use cloning technology is reasonable.
3.  Using Silver's article as a springboard, discuss the extent to which various segments of our society (scientists, the general public, elected officials, and so forth) should be involved in decisions about human cloning. Write at least 1,000 words.

■ ■ ■ ■ ■ ■ ■ ■ ■ ■ ■

# Narcissus Cloned

## John J. Conley

*John J. Conley, S.J., is a professor of philosophy at Fordham University.*

# PREREADING

Is human cloning immoral? Explain your answer in ten minutes of freewriting.

The recent experiment in human cloning in Washington, D.C., has provoked moral unease in the public. Both specialists and laypersons sense that this new technology is fraught with ethical and political peril. The discussion of the ethics of human cloning, however, rarely moves from intuitive praise and blame to careful analysis of the moral values—more frankly, the disvalues—presented by this practice. The discussion also reveals the moral impoverishment of our culture's categories for dealing with biotechnological challenges because the key ethical issues are often obscured by a bland subjectivism that reduces moral values to the simple desire of the parent or researcher.

Here I will sketch out the moral debits of the practice of cloning and criticize the narrow types of moral reasoning that have prevented our society from collectively facing the incipient ethical and political dangers in this practice.

First, human cloning violates respect for the life of each human being, which is due from the moment of conception. While empirical science as such cannot determine the nature and extension of the person, it is indisputable that conception marks the radical beginning of the personal history of each human being. Many of the physical characteristics that clearly influence our interpersonal relations, such as gender, height and somatic constitution, are clearly shaped in the moment of conception. Contemporary genetic research continues to reveal how profoundly other more "spiritual" traits of the person, such as intelligence and emotive temperament, are molded by one's conceptive history. The insistence that respect for human life begin at the time of conception is not a sectarian doctrine. Until quite recently, it formed the keystone of medical ethics, as witnessed by the influential doctor's oath designed by the World Medical Association in the aftermath of World War II: "I will maintain the utmost respect for human life from the moment of conception."

4    Current experimentation in human cloning deliberately conceives a human being for the sake of research and then designates this human embryo for destruction. It is true that this pre-embryo represents a human being in an extremely primitive state of development. Nonetheless, this minute being remains clearly human (it can belong to no other species), uniquely human (due to its singular corporeal occupation of space and time) and, if placed in the proper environment, a being with an internal capacity to develop the distinctly human faculties of intellect and will.

5    The fabrication and destruction of human embryos may appear a minor assault on life in a U.S. society numbed by 1.5 million abortions a year and Dr. Jack Kevorkian's house calls. The acid test of whether we corporately esteem human life, however, is not found primarily in our treatment of powerful adults. Rather, it emerges in our treatment of the vulnerable, like these fragile human beings at the dawn of gestation.

6    Second, the practice of cloning undermines one of the key values of social interaction: human diversity. Emmanuel Levinas, a contemporary French philosopher, argues that the central challenge in interpersonal contact is accepting the other person precisely as other, as something more than the mirror image of oneself. One of the oddest of the recent arguments in favor of human cloning went something like this: Childbearing will be easier for the parents if they can raise siblings hatched from the same egg, since the parents will always be dealing with children having the identical genetic code. (We could even save on the clothing bills.) It is hard to see how the family will benefit from becoming a hall of mirrors. The moral apprenticeship of family life consists precisely in the recognition of differences among siblings and the parents' recognition that their children are not simply the projection of their plans and wishes.

7    The possible reduction of human difference in a regime of routine cloning raises troubling political issues. Just who or what will constitute the model for the clonable human? Which race? Which physical composition? Which emotional temperament? Which kind of intelligence and at what level? The development of earlier biotechnologies, such as amniocentesis and eugenic abortion, has already begun to homogenize the human population.

8    Several sources indicate that up to 90 percent of fetuses with Down's Syndrome are currently aborted in the United States. The tendency to eliminate those ticketed as "disabled" contradicts the gains of the disability rights movement, which correctly urges us to respect and include those who are different because of physical or mental anomalies. Certain enthusiasts for cloning appear to dream Narcissus-like of a uniform humanity created in their own idealized image, an amalgam of Einstein and the Marlboro Man. Our aesthetic values, which focus so frequently on the unique timbre of a human voice or the difference between two human faces, would fade in such a monocolor regime. One can only marvel at the moral dexterity of our generation, which valiantly defends everything from the whale to the snail-darter lest bio-diversity be lost, yet calmly greets our growing destruction of the human other through eugenic technology.

Third, the practice of cloning undermines the integrity of human love. Human  9
beings, until quite recently, have usually been conceived in the conjugal embrace of
their parents. In marital intercourse, the two values of union between the spouses
and the procreation of the family's children remain indissoluble. It is the same act
unifying the couple and bringing forth the nascent child. Cloning, however, stands to
radicalize the divorce between conjugal union and procreation already introduced by
in vitro fertilization. A third person, the scientist in the laboratory, invades the once-
intimate drama of the generation of children.

I have long been haunted by the remark of Louise Brown, the first child success-  10
fully conceived in vitro, when the doctor who had artificially conceived her died.
Louise was plunged into grief. She told the press: "I feel that I have lost the person who
made me"—as if the role once reserved to God and parent had now passed to the scientist in the white coat. The ancient setting of procreation, the sacramental embrace of
spouses, is abandoned in favor of the fertile/sterile laboratory.

The initial experiment in human cloning indicates how radically procreation has  11
been divorced from conjugal union. The sperm and egg, provided by anonymous
donors, were deliberately fused to fabricate a human embryo that would deteriorate
within several days. It is true that in the future married couples struggling with infertility might resort to cloning technology. Even in this case, however, the wedge between
unitive and procreative values remains. The intimate union between the conjugal gift
of love and life remains severed.

The language employed by journalists to describe these new means of generation  12
also indicates the sea change wrought by cloning and related techniques. "Procreation"
becomes "reproduction." "The glimmer in my parents' eyes" becomes "the product of
conception." "The act of love" becomes "reproductive technology." The reduction of
the child, once the immediate evidence of romance, to a product of the laboratory suggests the assault on the integrity of human love implicit in this practice.

Cloning's infringements on the basic goods of life, love, and otherness ultimately  13
challenge human dignity itself. Immanuel Kant argues that human dignity entails the
recognition that other human beings are ends in themselves, worthy of respect, rather
than means to the ends of individual persons or society as a whole. Widespread cloning,
however, would radically reduce humans to a eugenic mean. The human embryo
would lose all claim to moral respect and legal protection by serving as an object of scientific curiosity or as an aid, easily discarded, to human fertility. In such a eugenic
regime, human beings would increasingly be valued only for possessing certain socially
desirable traits rather than for the simple fact that they exist as humans. By reducing the
human person to an object stripped of intrinsic worth, routine cloning could threaten
the ensemble of human rights itself.

The task of developing a moral response to the advent of human cloning is ren-  14
dered all the more problematic by the superficial debate our society is currently conducting on this issue. Whether on the editorial page of *The New York Times* or on Phil
and Oprah's television screen, the discussion tends to obscure the key moral problems
raised by this practice. Certain popular types of reasoning prevent, rather than assist,
the careful debate we deserve on this issue.

One common approach is the Luddite condemnation of all genetic engineering.  15
Jeremy Rifkin, the most visible critic of the cloning experiment, exemplifies this
approach. This position argues that the moral and political risks of genetic engineering
are so grave that we should simply censure and, where possible, ban all such technology.

References to Pandora's Box, Frankenstein, and the Third Reich decorate this blanket condemnation of all scientific intervention into human gestation. Such a categorical critique of biotechnology refuses to discern the different moral values present in the quite varied operations of genetic technology. While human cloning quite clearly appears to distort basic human goods, other therapeutic interventions can legitimately heal infertility and help an individual struggling with a genetic malady. Moral panic cannot ground a nuanced discernment of these disparate technological interventions.

Another approach, frequently offered by the proponents of cloning, contends that 16 the current experiments are simply "scientific research." Since they are just research, they should not be the object of moral critique. In other words, the Pope & Co. should chill out. This aura of value-free science seriously constricts the scope of the moral enterprise. The object of moral judgment is any human action, i.e., any act of human beings rooted in intellect and will. Moral scrutiny of scientific action is eminently justified inasmuch as such action is patently the result of rational deliberation and choice. The effort to sequester human cloning from ethical judgment, like the earlier attempt to "take morality and politics out of fetal tissue research," simply blinds us to the moral values at stake.

Perhaps the most common reasoning used to justify human cloning is the subjec- 17 tivist approach. As the editors of *The New York Times* argued, the producers of the material for cloning—I presume they mean the parents—should be the only ones to decide how the product is to be used. A thousand callers on radio talk shows claimed that "Father (or mother) knows best" and that no one could judge the clients and doctors who resort to this practice. Several proponents piously argued that these researchers sincerely wanted to help infertile couples. Such noble motives exempted them from moral censure.

In such a subjectivist perspective, the only relevant moral value is the motive of 18 the parties concerned, and the only virtue is unqualified tolerance for the desire of the scientist or the parent. Such subjectivism systematically averts its gaze from the action of cloning itself, and the question of whether or how this practice destroys human goods can never be raised. Moral scrutiny of this action is suffocated under a sentimental veil of compassion or, worse, under the steely curtain of private property rights.

The subjectivists legitimately highlight the psychological plight of infertile 19 couples who desire to bear children. They suppress, however, the salient ethical issue of which means, under what conditions, can properly be used to remedy this problem of infertility. An ancient moral and legal tradition rightly censures the buying and selling of infants as a just solution. There is a growing moral consensus that the violent battles over legal custody, not to mention the destruction of surplus embryos, have revealed the moral disvalues of surrogate mothering. Sentimental appeals to the pain of infertile couples "open to life" easily mask the ethical dangers of technologies that attempt to remedy infertility by the calculated manipulation and destruction of human lives.

The accompanying political debate must squarely question whether this practice 20 promotes or vitiates the common good. Conducting such a trenchant debate, however, is problematic in a society that increasingly perceives moral judgments as the arbitrary product of emotion or preference.

## READING FOR CONTENT

1. What is Conley's opinion on the public debate over cloning humans?
2. When does Conley believe that life begins?
3. What is Conley's opinion on abortion? Where is that opinion indicated?

4. Outline Conley's three main reasons for opposing cloning.
5. Outline the three popular responses to cloning humans that Conley criticizes.
6. What does Conley mean by the "subjectivist" position? What disturbs Conley about that position?

## READING FOR GENRE, ORGANIZATION, AND STYLISTIC FEATURES

1. What is the purpose of Conley's second paragraph?
2. Outline the main elements in Conley's argument. How does Conley signal the boundaries between those elements?
3. What is Conley's opening strategy?

## READING FOR RHETORICAL CONTEXT

1. What does the "S.J." title that follows Conley's name indicate? How might that affiliation influence his views on reproductive technology?
2. In the first paragraph, how does Conley describe his purpose in writing?
3. How does Conley treat the arguments of those he disagrees with?

## WRITING ASSIGNMENTS

1. In a 1,000-word essay, summarize and respond to Conley's argument against cloning humans.
2. Write a 1,000-word argumentative essay that supports or takes issue with Conley's assertion that "the subjectivists legitimately highlight the psychological plight of infertile couples who desire to bear children. They suppress, however, the salient ethical issue of which means, under what conditions, can properly be used to remedy this problem of infertility."
3. Write a 1,000-word analysis of Conley's rhetorical purpose and technique. Describe his goals, his intended audience, and the techniques he uses to influence that audience.

■ ■ ■ ■ ■ ■ ■ ■ ■ ■ ■

# Crossing Lines: A Secular Argument Against Research Cloning

### Charles Krauthammer

*Charles Krauthammer is a syndicated columnist and a contributing editor of the* New Republic. *He is a medical doctor and a member of the President's Council on Bioethics.*

## PREREADING

What have you read or heard about stem-cell research? What have you read or heard about the use of cloning technology to develop treatments for human diseases? Freewrite for ten minutes in response to these questions.

## The Problem

You were once a single cell. Every one of the 100 trillion cells in your body today is a    1
direct descendent of that zygote, the primordial cell formed by the union of mother's egg and father's sperm. Each one is genetically identical (allowing for copying errors and environmental damage along the way) to that cell. Therefore, if we scraped a cell from, say, the inner lining of your cheek, its DNA would be the same DNA that, years ago in the original zygote, contained the entire plan for creating you and every part of you.

Here is the mystery: Why can the zygote, as it multiplies, produce every different    2
kind of cell in the body—kidney, liver, brain, skin—while the skin cell is destined, however many times it multiplies, to remain skin forever? As the embryo matures, cells become specialized and lose their flexibility and plasticity. Once an adult cell has specialized—differentiated, in scientific lingo—it is stuck forever in that specialty. Skin is skin; kidney is kidney.

Understanding that mystery holds the keys to the kingdom. The Holy Grail of    3
modern biology is regenerative medicine. If we can figure out how to make a specialized adult cell dedifferentiate—unspecialize, i.e., revert way back to the embryonic stage, perhaps even to the original zygotic stage—and then grow it like an embryo under controlled circumstances, we could reproduce for you every kind of tissue or organ you might need. We could create a storehouse of repair parts for your body. And, if we let that dedifferentiated cell develop completely in a woman's uterus, we will have created a copy of you, your clone.

That is the promise and the menace of cloning. It has already been done in    4
sheep, mice, goats, pigs, cows, and now cats and rabbits (though cloning rabbits seems an exercise in biological redundancy). There is no reason in principle why it cannot be done in humans. The question is: Should it be done?

Notice that the cloning question is really two questions: (1) May we grow that    5
dedifferentiated cell all the way into a cloned baby, a copy of you? That is called reproductive cloning. And (2) may we grow that dedifferentiated cell just into the embryonic stage and then mine it for parts, such as stem cells? That is called research cloning.

Reproductive cloning is universally abhorred. In July 2001 the House of Repre-    6
sentatives, a fairly good representative of the American people, took up the issue and not a single member defended reproductive cloning. Research cloning, however, is the hard one. Some members were prepared to permit the cloning of the human embryo in order to study and use its component parts, with the proviso that the embryo be destroyed before it grows into a fetus or child. They were a minority, however. Their amendment banning baby-making but permitting research cloning was defeated by 76 votes. On July 31, 2001, a bill outlawing all cloning passed the House decisively. . . .

Krauthammer, Charles. "Crossing Lines: A Secular Argument Against Research Cloning." *New Republic* 29 April 2002: 20+. Reprinted by permission of Dr. Charles Krauthammer.

## The Promise

This is how research cloning works. You take a donor egg from a woman, remove its 7
nucleus, and inject the nucleus of, say, a skin cell from another person. It has been
shown in animals that by the right manipulation you can trick the egg and the injected
nucleus into dedifferentiating—that means giving up all the specialization of the skin
cell and returning to its original state as a primordial cell that could become anything
in the body.

In other words, this cell becomes totipotent. It becomes the equivalent of the fer- 8
tilized egg in normal procreation, except that instead of having chromosomes from two
people, it has chromosomes from one. This cell then behaves precisely like an embryo.
It divides. It develops. At four to seven days, it forms a "blastocyst" consisting of about
100 to 200 cells.

The main objective of cloning researchers would be to disassemble this blasto- 9
cyst: Pull the stem cells out, grow them in the laboratory, and then try to tease them
into becoming specific kinds of cells, say, kidney or heart or brain and so on.

There would be two purposes for doing this: study or cure. You could take a cell 10
from a person with a baffling disease, like Lou Gehrig's, clone it into a blastocyst, pull
the stem cells out, and then study them in order to try to understand the biology of the
illness. Or you could begin with a cell from a person with Parkinson's or a spinal cord
injury, clone it, and tease out the stem cells to develop tissue that you would reinject
into the original donor to, in theory, cure the Parkinson's or spinal cord injury. The
advantage of using a cloned cell rather than an ordinary stem cell is that, presumably,
there would be no tissue rejection. It's your own DNA. The body would recognize it.
You'd have a perfect match.

(Research cloning is sometimes called therapeutic cloning, but that is a misleading 11
term. First, because therapy by reinjection is only one of the many uses to which this
cloning can be put. Moreover, it is not therapeutic for the clone—indeed, the clone is
invariably destroyed in the process—though it may be therapeutic for others. If you
donate a kidney to your brother, it would be odd to call your operation a therapeutic
nephrectomy. It is not. It's a sacrificial nephrectomy.)

The conquest of rejection is one of the principal rationales for research cloning. 12
But there is reason to doubt this claim on scientific grounds. There is some empirical
evidence in mice that cloned tissue may be rejected anyway (possibly because a clone
contains a small amount of foreign—mitochondrial—DNA derived from the egg into
which it was originally injected). Moreover, enormous advances are being made elsewhere in combating tissue rejection. The science of immune rejection is much more
mature than the science of cloning. By the time we figure out how to do safe and reliable research cloning, the rejection problem may well be solved. And finally, there are
less problematic alternatives—such as adult stem cells—that offer a promising alternative to cloning because they present no problem of tissue rejection and raise none of
cloning's moral conundrums.

These scientific considerations raise serious questions about the efficacy of, and 13
thus the need for, research cloning. But there is a stronger case to be made. Even if the
scientific objections are swept aside, even if research cloning is as doable and promising as its advocates contend, there are other reasons to pause.

The most obvious is this: Research cloning is an open door to reproductive cloning. 14
Banning the production of cloned babies while permitting the production of cloned

embryos makes no sense. If you have factories all around the country producing embryos for research and commerce, it is inevitable that someone will implant one in a woman (or perhaps in some artificial medium in the farther future) and produce a human clone. What then? A law banning reproductive cloning but permitting research cloning would then make it a crime not to destroy that fetus—an obvious moral absurdity.

This is an irrefutable point and the reason that many in Congress will vote for the total ban on cloning. Philosophically, however, it is a showstopper. It lets us off too early and too easy. It keeps us from facing the deeper question: Is there anything about research cloning that in and of itself makes it morally problematic? 15

## Objection I: Intrinsic Worth

For some people, life begins at conception. And not just life—if life is understood to mean a biologically functioning organism, even a single cell is obviously alive—but personhood. If the first zygotic cell is owed all the legal and moral respect due a person, then there is nothing to talk about. Ensoulment starts with Day One and Cell One, and the idea of taking that cell or its successor cells apart to serve someone else's needs is abhorrent. 16

This is an argument of great moral force but little intellectual interest. Not because it may not be right. But because it is unprovable. It rests on metaphysics. Either you believe it or you don't. The discussion ends there. 17

I happen not to share this view. I do not believe personhood begins at conception. I do not believe a single cell has the moral or legal standing of a child. This is not to say that I do not stand in awe of the developing embryo, a creation of majestic beauty and mystery. But I stand in equal awe of the Grand Canyon, the spider's web, and quantum mechanics. Awe commands wonder, humility, appreciation. It does not command inviolability. I am quite prepared to shatter an atom, take down a spider's web, or dam a canyon for electricity. (Though we'd have to be very short on electricity before I'd dam the Grand.) 18

I do not believe the embryo is entitled to inviolability. But is it entitled to nothing? There is a great distance between inviolability, on the one hand, and mere "thingness," on the other. Many advocates of research cloning see nothing but thingness. That view justifies the most ruthless exploitation of the embryo. That view is dangerous. 19

Why? Three possible reasons. First, the Brave New World Factor: Research cloning gives man too much power for evil. Second, the Slippery Slope: The habit of embryonic violation is in and of itself dangerous. Violate the blastocyst today and every day, and the practice will inure you to violating the fetus or even the infant tomorrow. Third, Manufacture: The very act of creating embryos for the sole purpose of exploiting and then destroying them will ultimately predispose us to a ruthless utilitarianism about human life itself. 20

## Objection II: The Brave New World Factor

The physicists at Los Alamos did not hesitate to penetrate, manipulate, and split uranium atoms on the grounds that uranium atoms possess intrinsic worth that entitled them to inviolability. Yet after the war, many fought to curtail atomic power. They feared the consequences of delivering such unfathomable power—and potential evil— into the hands of fallible human beings. Analogously, one could believe that the cloned 21 blastocyst has little more intrinsic worth than the uranium atom and still be deeply troubled by the manipulation of the blastocyst because of the fearsome power it confers upon humankind.

The issue is leverage. Our knowledge of how to manipulate human genetics 22 (or atomic nuclei) is still primitive. We could never construct ex nihilo a human embryo. It is an unfolding organism of unimaginable complexity that took nature three billion years to produce. It might take us less time to build it from scratch, but not much less. By that time, we as a species might have acquired enough wisdom to use it wisely. Instead, the human race in its infancy has stumbled upon a genie infinitely too complicated to create or even fully understand, but understandable enough to command and perhaps even control. And given our demonstrated unwisdom with our other great discovery—atomic power: As we speak, the very worst of humanity is on the threshold of acquiring the most powerful weapons in history—this is a fear and a consideration to be taken very seriously.

For example, female human eggs seriously limit the mass production of cloned 23 embryos. Extracting eggs from women is difficult, expensive, and potentially dangerous. The search is on, therefore, for a good alternative. Scientists have begun injecting human nuclei into the egg cells of animals. In 1996 Massachusetts scientists injected a human nucleus with a cow egg. Chinese scientists have fused a human fibroblast with a rabbit egg and have grown the resulting embryo to the blastocyst stage. We have no idea what grotesque results might come from such interspecies clonal experiments.

In October 2000 the first primate containing genes from another species was 24 born (a monkey with a jellyfish gene). In 1995 researchers in Texas produced headless mice. In 1997 researchers in Britain produced headless tadpoles. In theory, headlessness might be useful for organ transplantation. One can envision, in a world in which embryos are routinely manufactured, the production of headless clones—subhuman creatures with usable human organs but no head, no brain, no consciousness to identify them with the human family.

The heart of the problem is this: Nature, through endless evolution, has pro- 25 duced cells with totipotent power. We are about to harness that power for crude human purposes. That should give us pause. Just around the corner lies the logical by-product of such power: human-animal hybrids, partly developed human bodies for use as parts, and other horrors imagined—Huxley's Deltas and Epsilons—and as yet unimagined. This is the Brave New World Factor. Its grounds for objecting to this research are not about the beginnings of life, but about the ends; not the origin of these cells, but their destiny; not where we took these magnificent cells from, but where they are taking us.

## Objection III: The Slippery Slope

The other prudential argument is that once you start tearing apart blastocysts, you get 26 used to tearing apart blastocysts. And whereas now you'd only be doing that at the seven-day stage, when most people would look at this tiny clump of cells on the head of a pin and say it is not inviolable, it is inevitable that some scientist will soon say: Give me just a few more weeks to work with it and I could do wonders.

That will require quite a technological leap because the blastocyst will not develop 27 as a human organism unless implanted in the uterus. That means that to go beyond that seven-day stage you'd have to implant this human embryo either in an animal uterus or in some fully artificial womb. Both possibilities may be remote, but they are real. And then we'll have a scientist saying: Give me just a few more months with this embryo, and I'll have actual kidney cells, brain cells, pancreatic cells that I can transplant back into the donor of the clone and cure him. Scientists at Advanced Cell Technology in Massachusetts have already gone past that stage in animals. They have taken cloned cow embryos past the blastocyst stage, taken tissue from the more developed cow fetus, and reimplanted it back into the donor animal.

The scientists' plea to do the same in humans will be hard to ignore. Why grow 28 the clone just to the blastocyst stage, destroy it, pull out the inner cell mass, grow stem cells out of that, propagate them in the laboratory, and then try chemically or otherwise to tweak them into becoming kidney cells or brain cells or islet cells? This is Rube Goldberg. Why not just allow that beautiful embryonic machine, created by nature and far more sophisticated than our crude techniques, to develop unmolested? Why not let the blastocyst grow into a fetus that possesses the kinds of differentiated tissue that we could then use for curing the donor?

Scientifically, this would make sense. Morally, we will have crossed the line 29 between tearing apart a mere clump of cells and tearing apart a recognizable human fetus. And at that point, it would be an even smaller step to begin carving up seven- and eight-month-old fetuses with more perfectly formed organs to alleviate even more pain and suffering among the living. We will, slowly and by increments, have gone from stem cells to embryo farms to factories with fetuses in various stages of development and humanness, hanging (metaphorically) on meat hooks waiting to be cut open to be used by the already born.

We would all be revolted if a living infant or developed fetus were carved up for 30 parts. Should we build a fence around that possibility by prohibiting any research on even the very earliest embryonic clump of cells? Is the only way to avoid the slide never to mount the slippery slope at all? On this question, I am personally agnostic. If I were utterly convinced that we would never cross the seven-day line, then I would have no objection on these grounds to such research on the inner cell mass of a blastocyst. The question is: Can we be sure? This is not a question of principle; it is a question of prudence. It is almost a question of psychological probability. No one yet knows the answer.

## Objection IV: Manufacture

Note that while, up to now, I have been considering arguments against research 31 cloning, they are all equally applicable to embryonic research done on a normal—i.e., noncloned—embryo. If the question is tearing up the blastocyst, there is no intrinsic moral difference between a two-parented embryo derived from a sperm and an egg and a single-parented embryo derived from a cloned cell. Thus the various arguments against this research—the intrinsic worth of the embryo, the prudential consideration that we might create monsters, or the prudential consideration that we might become monsters in exploiting post-embryonic forms of human life (fetuses or even children)— are identical to the arguments for and against stem-cell research.

These arguments are serious—serious enough to banish the insouciance of the 32 scientists who consider anyone questioning their work to be a Luddite—yet, in my view, insufficient to justify a legal ban on stem-cell research (as with stem cells from discarded embryos in fertility clinics). I happen not to believe that either personhood or ensoulment occurs at conception. I think we need to be apprehensive about what evil might arise from the power of stem-cell research, but that apprehension alone, while justifying vigilance and regulation, does not justify a ban on the practice. And I believe that given the good that might flow from stem-cell research, we should first test the power of law and custom to enforce the seven-day blastocyst line for embryonic exploitation before assuming that such a line could never hold.

This is why I support stem-cell research (using leftover embryos from fertility 33 clinics) and might support research cloning were it not for one other aspect that is unique to it. In research cloning, the embryo is created with the explicit intention of its eventual destruction. That is a given because not to destroy the embryo would be to produce a cloned child. If you are not permitted to grow the embryo into a child, you are obliged at some point to destroy it.

Deliberately creating embryos for eventual and certain destruction means the 34 launching of an entire industry of embryo manufacture. It means the routinization, the commercialization, the commodification of the human embryo. The bill that would legalize research cloning essentially sanctions, licenses, and protects the establishment of a most ghoulish enterprise: the creation of nascent human life for the sole purpose of its exploitation and destruction.

How is this morally different from simply using discarded embryos from in vitro fertil- 35 ization (IVF) clinics? Some have suggested that it is not, that to oppose research cloning is to oppose IVF and any stem-cell research that comes out of IVF. The claim is made that because in IVF there is a high probability of destruction of the embryo, it is morally equivalent to research cloning. But this is plainly not so. In research cloning there is not a high probability of destruction; there is 100 percent probability. Because every cloned embryo must be destroyed, it is nothing more than a means to someone else's end.

In IVF, the probability of destruction may be high, but it need not necessarily be. 36 You could have a clinic that produces only a small number of embryos, and we know of many cases of multiple births resulting from multiple embryo implantation. In principle, one could have IVF using only a single embryo and thus involving no deliberate embryo destruction at all. In principle, that is impossible in research cloning.

Furthermore, a cloned embryo is created to be destroyed and used by others. An 37 IVF embryo is created to develop into a child. One cannot disregard intent in determining morality. Embryos are created in IVF to serve reproduction. Embryos are created in research cloning to serve, well, research. If certain IVF embryos were designated as "helper embryos" that would simply aid an anointed embryo in turning into a child, then we would have an analogy to cloning. But, in fact, we don't know which embryo is anointed in IVF. They are all created to have a chance of survival. And they are all equally considered an end.

Critics counter that this ends-and-means argument is really obfuscation, that 38 both procedures make an instrument of the embryo. In cloning, the creation and destruction of the embryo is a means to understanding or curing disease. In IVF, the creation of the embryo is a means of satisfying a couple's need for a child. They are both just means to ends.

But it makes no sense to call an embryo a means to the creation of a child. The 39 creation of a child is the destiny of an embryo. To speak of an embryo as a means to creating a child empties the word "means" of content. The embryo in IVF is a stage in the development of a child; it is no more a means than a teenager is a means to the adult he or she later becomes. In contrast, an embryo in research cloning is pure means. Laboratory pure.

And that is where we must draw the line. During the great debate on stem-cell 40 research, a rather broad consensus was reached (among those not committed to "intrinsic worth" rendering all embryos inviolable) that stem-cell research could be morally justified because the embryos destroyed for their possibly curative stem cells were derived from fertility clinics and thus were going to be discarded anyway. It was understood that human embryos should not be created solely for the purpose of being dismembered and then destroyed for the benefit of others. Indeed, when Senator Bill Frist made his impassioned presentation on the floor of the Senate supporting stem-cell research, he included among his conditions a total ban on creating human embryos just to be stem-cell farms.

Where cloning for research takes us decisively beyond stem-cell research is in 41 sanctioning the manufacture of the human embryo. You can try to regulate embryonic research to prohibit the creation of Brave New World monsters; you can build fences on the slippery slope, regulating how many days you may grow an embryo for research; but once you countenance the very creation of human embryos for no other purpose than for their parts, you have crossed a moral frontier.

Research cloning is the ultimate in conferring thingness upon the human 42 embryo. It is the ultimate in desensitization. And as such, it threatens whatever other fences and safeguards we might erect around embryonic research. The problem, one could almost say, is not what cloning does to the embryo, but what it does to us. Except that once cloning has changed us, it will inevitably enable further assaults on human dignity. Creating a human embryo just so it can be used and then destroyed undermines the very foundation of the moral prudence that informs the entire enterprise of genetic research: the idea that while a human embryo may not be a person, it is not nothing. Because if it is nothing, then everything is permitted. And if everything is permitted, then there are no fences, no safeguards, no bottom.

## READING FOR CONTENT

1. What is "the mystery" that Krauthammer refers to in the first sentence of paragraph 2?
2. What is the goal of regenerative medicine?
3. What is the distinction between reproductive cloning and research cloning?
4. According to Krauthammer, what do most Americans think about reproductive cloning?
5. Describe how research cloning might be used to develop treatments for diseases.
6. Summarize the argument Krauthammer presents against research cloning in paragraphs 14 and 15.
7. Summarize the argument Krauthammer presents against research cloning in paragraphs 21 to 25.
8. Summarize the argument Krauthammer presents against research cloning in paragraphs 26 to 30.
9. Summarize the argument Krauthammer presents against research cloning in paragraphs 31 to 41.
10. What are "Huxley's Deltas and Epsilons" that Krauthammer refers to in paragraph 25?
11. Why does Krauthammer support stem-cell research but not research cloning?

## READING FOR GENRE, ORGANIZATION, AND STYLISTIC FEATURES

1. How does Krauthammer use subheadings to signal the parts of his argument?
2. What is the relationship between the content under the subheading "Objection I: Intrinsic Worth" and the content under the next three subheadings?
3. Krauthammer uses two sentence fragments in paragraph 20. Comment on his decision to use sentence structures that are technically incorrect. Is this decision consistent with his other stylistic choices?
4. What do you think is Krauthammer's target audience? What aspects of the article seem to be designed for that particular audience?

## READING FOR RHETORICAL CONTEXT

1. Krauthammer does not provide a compact thesis statement at the outset of the article but rather in his last paragraph. Comment on that strategy.
2. To what extent does Krauthammer draw on his expertise as a medical doctor to support his argument against research cloning?
3. In paragraphs 14 and 15, Krauthammer presents an argument against research cloning that he believes is "irrefutable." What is his rationale for continuing the essay after delivering what he considers to be a decisive blow against research cloning?
4. To what extent does Krauthammer acknowledge and examine the arguments of his opponents?

## WRITING ASSIGNMENTS

1. Draw on Krauthammer's article to write a 500-word objective explanation of the goals of research cloning.
2. In a 1,000-word essay, either attack or support Krauthammer's assertion that research cloning should be banned. Make sure that you summarize the principal points in Krauthammer's argument.
3. Write a 750-word essay of personal response in which you balance Krauthammer's objections to research cloning with the concerns of people who suffer from terminal and disabling illnesses.

■ ■ ■ ■ ■ ■ ■ ■ ■ ■ ■

# The Business of Bodies

### Lori Andrews and Dorothy Nelkin

*Lori Andrews is a Distinguished Professor of Law at Chicago-Kent College of Law and Director of the Institute for Science, Law and Technology at the Illinois Institute of Technology. She has been an advisor on biomedical law to Congress, foreign governments, and various federal agencies. Her books include* Genetics: Ethics, Law and Policy *(2002) (coauthored with Mark Rothstein and Maxwell Mehlman),* Body Bazaar: The Market for Human Tissue in the Biotechnology Age *(2001) (coauthored with Dorothy Nelkin),* Future Perfect: Confronting Decisions about Genetics *(2001), and* The Clone Age: Adventures in the New World of Reproductive Technology *(2000). Dorothy Nelkin was University Professor of Sociology at New York University until her death in 2003. Her books include* Controversy: Politics of Technical Decisions *(1992),* The DNA Mystique: The Gene as a Cultural Icon *(1995), and* The Molecular Gaze: Art in the Genetic Age *(2003).*

## PREREADING

Corporate funding of academic research, especially in profitable areas of medicine and public health, opens the way for researchers and corporations to enrich themselves by treating the body as a commodity in a market economy. Jot down a list of bodily properties—such as tissue, blood, sperm, and other parts—that might be bought and sold in such a market. Compare this list with properties that Andrews and Nelkin mention in their writing.

When John Moore, a Seattle businessman, fell ill with hairy cell leukemia, he 1 went to a top specialist at the UCLA School of Medicine. He followed his doctor's orders, submitting to surgery to remove his spleen and other treatments. Afterward he returned to Seattle, thinking his disease was cured. But for the next seven years, the UCLA doctor told him to keep flying back to Los Angeles for tests. Moore thought these visits were necessary to monitor his condition, and he complied out of fear that the leukemia might reappear. But his physician had additional interests. The physician was not concerned only with his health, but was patenting certain unique chemicals in Moore's blood and setting up contracts with a Boston company, negotiating shares worth an estimated $3 million. Sandoz, the Swiss pharmaceutical company, paid a reported $15 million for the right to develop the cell line taken from Moore—which the doctors had named the Mo-cell line.

Moore began to suspect that his tissue was being used for purposes beyond his per- 2 sonal care when his UCLA doctor continued to take samples not only of blood but of bone marrow, skin, and sperm. When Moore discovered that he had become patent number 4,438,032, he sued the doctors for malpractice and property theft.[1] Moore felt that his integrity was violated, his body exploited, and his tissue turned into a product: "My doctors are claiming that my humanity, my genetic essence, is their invention and their property. They view me as a mine from which to extract biological material. I was harvested."[2]

Considering Moore's case in 1990, the California Supreme Court held that doc- 3 tors must inform patients, in advance of surgical procedures, that their tissue could be used for research. But the court denied Moore's claim that he owned his tissue. He had no property rights in his body, the court said—so the profits should belong to the doctor and the biotechnology company. This was necessary, said the court, to encourage venture capital investment. The future of scientific progress was at stake.

Judge Stanley Mosk dissented, expressing concern about giving companies "the 4 right to appropriate and exploit a patient's tissue for their sole economic benefit—the

From: *Body Bazaar: The Market for Human Tissue in the Biotechnology Age* (New York: Crown Publishers, 2001), pp. 1–8.

right, in other words, to freely mine or harvest valuable properties of the patient's body."[3]

At a time when the techniques of biotechnology have enhanced the value of human tissue, Mosk was right to be concerned. Profound changes in federal law during the 1980s had encouraged corporate investment in academic research, especially in potentially profitable areas of biotechnology. Laws enacted at that time also allowed university medical researchers to profit from research they undertook, often with public funds. Following a pivotal 1980 U.S. Supreme Court case allowing the patenting of new life-forms, academic and government researchers as well as biotechnology companies rushed not only to publish their findings but also to patent them. This meant claiming ownership of the cell lines and genes of research subjects. The potential for profit from research on human tissue is turning people like John Moore into potential treasure troves.

The business of human bodies is a growing part of the $17 billion biotechnology industry comprising more than thirteen hundred biotechnology firms.[4] Those companies extract, analyze, and transform tissue into products with enormous potential for future economic gain. Their demands for skin, blood, placenta, gametes, biopsied tissue, and sources of genetic material are expanding. The blood that we all provide routinely for diagnostic purposes is now useful for the study of biological processes and the genetic basis of disease. Infant foreskin can be used to create new tissue for artificial skin. Umbilical cords are valued as a source of stem cells—a substitute for bone marrow transplants. Eggs and sperm are bought and sold for both research and in vitro fertilization, and embryos have been stolen. Cell lines derived from the kidneys of deceased babies are used to manufacture a common clot-busting drug. Human bones, valued today as a means to study human history and satisfy curiosity, are stored in museums and sold in shops as biocollectibles. Human tissue such as blood, hair, and DNA is a medium for artists. And human DNA can even be used to run computers, since the four chemicals—represented by the letters CATG—provide more permutations than the binary code.

Researchers study specific human tissues in order to understand individuals' behavior and personality traits. To nineteenth-century and early-twentieth-century phrenologists, the size and shape of the brain were clues to behavior and intelligence. Scientists have also studied brain tissue to understand the behavior of individuals with special traits—from the genius of Albert Einstein to the violence of serial killer Ronald Kray. During the eugenics movement in the early twentieth century, researchers looked to the "germ plasm" as a determinant of behaviors, including criminality, mental illness, intelligence, alcoholism, and poverty.[5] In the 1940s, hormones became the body substances defining personality and behavior.

In the age of biotechnology, the body is speaking in new ways. Waste tissue such as hair, blood, and saliva, when subjected to DNA analysis, can reveal intimate and detailed—and predictive—information about a person. According to recent scientific claims, genes will reveal information about behavioral traits and future disorders, ranging from sexual preference to manic-depression, from colon cancer to shyness, from Alzheimer's disease to a tendency to take risks.

Genetic information about the diseases an individual may develop during the course of his or her life may allow for the creation of beneficial therapeutic or remedial options, but it may also lead to employment or insurance discrimination.[6] Institutions have already used human tissue for purposes of social control. Law enforcement agencies extract DNA from tissue samples to identify the perpetrators of crimes. Body tissue is frequently used to identify suspected criminals, soldiers killed in action, Alzheimer's wanderers, illegal immigrants, putative fathers, those people likely to require extra health care dollars, descendants entitled to inheritance claims, and even the sexual liaisons of past and current presidents.

Where do all these tissue samples come from? The range of sources is extraordi- 10 nary. All babies born in the United States since the late 1960s have had blood taken at birth as part of a government-mandated newborn screening program intended to pinpoint diseases, such as PKU (phenylketonuria), for which early detection allows the possibility of remedial therapy. Some state public health departments keep those blood spots on file, and some have contracted with private companies to store them. Hospitals, research centers, and private depositories retain pathology samples and genetic data collected in the course of surgical procedures or research projects—a fact unknown to most patients. The U.S. Armed Forces runs an Institute of Pathology that has stored tissue samples since 1917 and is still used as a research and clinical resource. Today the U.S. Department of Defense stores blood samples collected from all military personnel through its mandatory genetic testing program. This military repository, expanding at a rate of ten thousand specimens each day, will have more than 3.5 million specimens by 2001. The Centers for Disease Control stores tissue samples that were collected for public health surveys. Forensic DNA banks—established in every state—contain the DNA not only of convicts who have committed violent crimes, but in some cases of misdemeanants, victims, and family members as well.

Private genetic testing companies are another source of tissue samples. Attracted 11 by the lucrative possibilities of paternity testing, about fifty DNA laboratories have been accredited in the United States,[7] and the number of paternity tests has grown from 76,000 in 1988 to 247,000 in 1998.[8]

There are now brain tissue banks, breast tissue banks, blood banks, umbilical 12 cord banks, sperm banks, and tissue repositories for studying AIDS, Alzheimer's, mental illnesses, and aging. More than 282 million archived and identifiable pathological specimens from more than 176 million individuals are currently being stored in United States repositories.[9] At least 20 million new specimens are added each year. Some specimens are anonymized or coded and not identified with specific individuals; others carry patient names or codes that allow for personal identification.[10] Virtually everyone has his or her tissue "on file" somewhere.

Expanding markets have increased the value of this tissue, and institutions— 13 hospitals, research laboratories, and the state and federal repositories that store tissue samples—find they possess a capital resource. Access to stored tissue samples is sometimes included in collaborative agreements between hospitals and biotechnology firms. In one joint venture agreement, Sequana Therapeutics, a California biotechnology firm, credited the New York City cancer hospital, Sloan-Kettering, with $5 million in order to obtain access to its bank of cancer tissue biopsies, which could be useful as a source of genetic information.[11]

An entire country has put its genome on the block. DeCode Genetics has gained 14 the rights to investigate, store, and commercialize the genes of the entire population of Iceland. Not only have Icelanders been isolated for centuries, they have maintained excellent genealogical and medical records. It is easier to locate genetic mutations linked to diseases by testing an isolated, homogeneous population like the Icelanders' than by testing a more diverse population. A Swiss company has already paid $200 million to access the results of this research.[12]

The value of human body tissue in the biotechnology age—and the potential for 15 profitable patents derived from it—encourages doctors and researchers to think about people differently. Some scientists refer to the body as a "project" or "subject," a system that can be divided and dissected down to the molecular level.

The language of science is increasingly permeated with the commercial language 16 of supply and demand, contracts, exchange, and compensation. Body parts are *extracted* like a mineral, *harvested* like a crop, or *mined* like a resource. Tissue is *procured*—a term more commonly used for land, goods, and prostitutes. Cells, embryos, and tissue are frozen, banked, placed in libraries or repositories, marketed, patented, bought, or sold. Umbilical cords, whose stem cells are useful for therapeutic purposes, are described as a "hot clinical property." The physician who patented John Moore's cell line apparently referred to his patient's body as a "gold mine."[13]

Such language reflects a set of cultural assumptions about the body: that it can be 17 understood in terms of its units, and that these units can be pulled from their context, isolated, and abstracted from real people who live in a particular time, at an actual location, in a given society.[14] The body has become commodified, reduced to an object, not a person.

That the body has utilitarian value has long been recognized. Nineteenth- 18 century philosopher Jeremy Bentham believed that corpses would be of greater use to society if they were studied or displayed rather than simply buried away. Preserved, exhibited, and studied, a corpse, he said, could serve "moral, political, honorific, dehonorific, money-saving, money-getting, commemorative, genealogical, architectural, theatrical, and phrenological" ends.[15] Following his instructions, Bentham's own body was preserved and placed on public display in a glass case at University College, London.

Certainly the living body has long been exploited as a commercial and mar- 19 ketable entity, as athletes, models, prostitutes, surrogate mothers, and beauty queens are well aware. But there is something new, strange, and troubling about the traffic in body tissue, the banking of human cells, and the patenting of genes. In the 1984 congressional hearings concerning anatomical gifts, Albert Gore, then a U.S. congressman, was troubled by a growing tendency to treat the body as a commodity in a market economy: "It is against our system of values to buy and sell parts of human beings. . . . The notion has perhaps superficial attraction to some because we have learned that the market system will solve lots of problems if we just stand out of the way and let it work. It is very true. This ought to be an exception because you don't want to invest property rights in human beings. . . . It is wrong."[16]

But what *is* troubling about the fragmentation and commodification of the body? 20 What is the problem with the growing interest in human tissue? Why shouldn't body parts be economic units of trade? Clearly the business of bodies is driven by instrumental and commercial values; but so too, as Gore suggested, are most technological endeavors. Moreover, much of the body tissue that is useful for biotechnology innovation—hair, blood, sperm—is replenishable. The average person loses two hundred hairs each day. Blood and sperm are constantly regenerated. And body materials such as umbilical cord blood, infant foreskin, or biopsied tissue discarded after surgery are normally regarded as refuse, like bloodied bandages and other medical wastes. Why not, then, view the body as a useful and exploitable resource if these tissues can be used to advance scientific research, contribute to progress, or provide life-saving benefits to others? Why are developments in the removal, storage, and transformation of human tissue becoming controversial? Why are there lawsuits against the commercialization of cell lines and protests against the patenting of genes?

The body is more than a utilitarian object: it is also a social, ritual, and metaphorical [21] entity, and the only thing many people can really call their own.[17] Indeed, our bodies and body parts are layered with ideas, images, cultural meanings, and personal associations.[18] Definitions of the body that reduce and decontextualize it, are what allow scientists or biotechnology firms to extract, use, and patent body tissue without reference to the individual or consideration of his or her personal desires and social needs. Biotechnological uses risk running roughshod over social values and personal beliefs.

The expanding use of human body materials poses basic and difficult dilemmas. [22] The removal of body tissue contributes to scientific research, but it also intrudes on body boundaries, imposing on individual autonomy. Collecting samples for the expanding DNA identification systems may be an efficient means to combat crime, but it also increases the risk of a surveillance society. Storing tissue samples and extracting information from them provides a clinically useful database for health information, but using tissue without the consent of the people who provided it may violate their personal privacy. Often little thought is given to people, like Moore, who are the unwitting sources of this material. And while patenting genes encourages the venture capital necessary to support costly research, the possibility of gaining a patent can also encourage predatory behavior. Biologist Erwin Chargoff has warned that the growing ability of doctors and scientists to profit from patients' tissue can be a slippery slope to social disaster, "an Auschwitz in which valuable enzymes, hormones, and so on will be extracted instead of gold teeth."[19]

The creation of commercial products from human tissue has raised questions of [23] profit and property, of consent and control. Participants in a range of legal and social disputes over body parts are asking whether tissue and genes are the essence of an individual and a sacred part of the human inheritance—or whether they are, as a director of Smith-Kline Beecham purportedly claimed, "the currency of the future."[20]

## Notes

1. *Moore v. Regents of the University of California*, 793 P.2d 479 (Cal. 1990).
2. John Vidal and John Carvel, "Lambs to the Gene Market," *Guardian* (London), November 12, 1994, 25.
3. *Moore v. Regents of the University of California*, 793 P.2d 479, 515 (1990) (J. Mosk, dissenting).
4. Craig Schneider, "An Ideal Medium for Growth of Biotechnology," *Atlanta Journal*, November 5, 1998, 01JH. See also http://www.busfac.com/99_10_cover.cfm.
5. Daniel B. Kevles, *In the Name of Eugenics* (New York: Knopf, 1983).
6. Dorothy Nelkin and Lawrence Tancredi, *Dangerous Diagnostics: The Social Power of Biological Information*, 2d ed. (Chicago: University of Chicago Press, 1995).
7. Pain Belluck, "Everybody's Doing It: Paternity Testing for Fun and Profit," *New York Times*, August 3, 1997, sec. 4, p. 1; Matthew Campbell and Jack Grimston, "Paternity Tests Are Now Available by Post. But Will They Give Birth to More Unhappiness Than They Cure?" *Sunday Times* (London), July 19, 1998.
8. Richard Willing, "DNA and Daddy: Explosion of Technology Is Straining Family Ties," *USA Today*, July 29, 1999, p. A1.
9. National Bioethics Advisory Commission, "The Use of Human Biological Materials in Research: Ethical Issues and Policy Guidelines," December 3, 1998.
10. Meredith Wadman, "Privacy Bill Under Fire from Researchers," *Nature* 392 (March 5, 1998), 6.

11. "Cancer Joint Venture Completed by Memorial Sloan-Kettering and Sequana," *Business Wire*, August 20, 1996.
12. Robert Kunzig, "Blood of the Vikings," *Discover* 19 (1998), 90–99.
13. Testimony of John Moore to the Committee on Human Genome Diversity of the National Academy of Sciences, September 16, 1996.
14. Margaret Lock, *Encounters with Aging* (Berkeley: University of California Press, 1993), 370–71; see also Renee Fox, "Regulated Commercialism of Vital Organ Donation," *Transplantation Proceedings* 25 (1993), 55–57.
15. Jeremy Bentham, quoted in Harvey Rachlin, *Lucy's Bones, Sacred Stones, and Einstein's Brain: The Remarkable Stories Behind the Great Objects and Artifacts of History, from Antiquity to the Modern Era* (New York: Henry Holt & Co., 1996), 205.
16. House Committee on Energy and Commerce, Subcommittee on Health and the Environment, *Hearing on H.R. 4080, "National Organ Transplant Act,"* 98th Cong. (1984), 128.
17. Leonard Barkan, "Cosmas and Damian: Of Medicine, Miracles, and the Economics of the Body," in Stuart Younger, Renee Fox, and Lawrence O'Connell, eds., *Organ Transplantation: Meanings and Realities* (Madison: University of Wisconsin Press, 1977), 242, 246.
18. Anthony Synnott, *The Body Social* (London: Routledge, 1993).
19. Quoted in Andrew Kimbrell, *The Human Body Shop: The Engineering and Marketing of Life* (New York: HarperCollins, 1993), 284.
20. George Monbiot, "A Corporate Great Blob Coalesces," *Guardian* (London), January 20, 2000.

## READING FOR CONTENT

1. What legal implications concerning property theft arise in paragraph 2?
2. As biotechnology develops, what further implications concerning social prejudice, group discrimination, and public law enforcement arise in paragraph 9?
3. Paraphrase the authors' definition of the problem in paragraphs 21–22.

## READING FOR GENRE, ORGANIZATION, AND STYLISTIC FEATURES

1. How does the essay exemplify the genres of scientific argument? of legal argument? of sociological argument? of moral argument?
2. Underline in the text the most important features of the new biotechnology that have social, economic, and moral consequences in paragraphs 6, 9, 12, and 16. Do these paragraphs present the major organizational features of Andrews and Nelkin's argument?
3. How do the footnotes exemplify the style of academic writing? Do they help to answer the questions raised in paragraph 20?

## READING FOR RHETORICAL CONTEXT

1. In paragraphs 10–14, how do the authors frame the problem in public, private, corporate, and medical terms?
2. In paragraphs 21–22, how do the authors frame the problem in social, cultural, moral, and economic terms?

## WRITING ASSIGNMENTS

1. Drawing upon information about biotechnology in this article, write an essay of 750 words—pro or con—on the topic of the human body as a utilitarian object.

2. Drawing upon information about biotechnology in this article, write an essay of 750 words on the risks that medical science takes in abusing social, cultural, moral, and personal values.

■ ■ ■ ■ ■ ■ ■ ■ ■ ■ ■ ■

# The Moral Imperative for Human Cloning

## Ian Wilmut

*Ian Wilmut is a Scottish embryologist who with his colleague Keith Campbell in 1996 produced the first clone from adult animal cells, a Finn Dorset lamb named Dolly. A year later they created Polly, a sheep cloned from fetal skin cells that had been genetically altered to contain a human gene. Wilmut pursues his work in animal research at the Roslin Institute in Edinburgh.*

## PREREADING

Wilmut's pioneering research in animal and human cloning touched off an international debate on the social, scientific, and moral consequences of cloning. From what you have read about cloning in other articles in this chapter and elsewhere, jot down a list of pro and con features associated with human cloning. Speculate on which side of the debate Wilmut would take and on reasons that he would give for doing so.

Human cloning is finally here. But while the Korean team has overcome some technical obstacles, the political barriers to realising cloning's medical potential remain. Many people object to the idea of any human cloning research, even for medical reasons, claiming it will inevitably open the door to reproductive cloning or, more generally, that experimenting with embryos is immoral. I believe the opposite: cloning promises such great benefits that it would be immoral not to do it.     1

That is why a number of UK labs, including my own, plan to apply to the relevant authorities for permission to study human cloning here in the UK. And while I remain implacably opposed to reproductive cloning per se, I do envisage that producing cloned babies would be desirable under certain circumstances, such as preventing genetic disease.     2

The therapeutic promise of human cloning lies in embryonic stem cells, or ES cells. Derived from 6-day-old embryos, ES cells can form any cell type in the body,     3

From: "The Moral Imperative for Human Cloning," *The New Scientist*, vol, 181, Iss. 2435, Feb. 21, 2004, pp. 16–17.

such as nerve or blood cells. It is possible to extract such cells from spare IVF embryos. But this has a drawback. Researchers have no control over the genetic make-up of the cells in these embryos. This presents a problem if such stem cells are used to regenerate tissue destroyed by accident or disease: if they don't genetically match the patient, they could trigger an immune response.

Cloning, however, could overcome this problem and provide patients with tissue-   4
matched stem cells. Although critics often claim therapeutic cloning would be too expensive and impractical, I think many of the problems can be tackled. But even if therapeutic cloning doesn't make it to the clinic, there are other compelling reasons why we need to develop human cloning technology.

The most imminent development is likely to be using cloning to study disease,   5
particularly inherited conditions. At present, it is often impossible to safely take samples of affected cells from living patients, especially those suffering from genetic diseases that affect the brain and heart such as Parkinson's disease or inherited heart arrhythmias. What's more, by the time a patient develops symptoms, their disease has been progressing for some time. This makes it hard to find out whether the changes we see in their cells are directly related to the cause of that disease, or whether they are merely secondary effects. Ideally, we would like to be able to monitor the progress of the disease as it develops inside the cells, so that we can home in on its cause.

Cloning would allow us to recreate these diseased cells, with the same genetic   6
make-up, outside the patient's body, and watch them develop from scratch. In principle, we could take, say, a skin cell, make a cloned embryo and then use its stem cells to create cultures of any cell type we wanted. These cell cultures would give us the power to do the kind of sophisticated genetics that we can often only do in animals.

Our team plans to start cloning ES cells from people with the neurodegenerative   7
condition ALS, or Lou Gehrig's disease. This progressive and fatal paralysis strikes people in middle age, robbing them of their ability to move, speak or breathe unaided. It is incurable and most victims die within five years of being diagnosed.

The disease affects nerve cells called motor neurons, which are found in the brain   8
and spine. Owing to their location, it is impossible to remove living motor neurons for study. Partly because of this, we have little idea of what causes ALS. We do know that about 10 percent of cases are inherited and that a fifth of these are caused by mutations in a gene called SOD1. But the cause of the majority of cases is a mystery.

Using cloning to create cultures of motor neurons from such patients would help   9
us to track down the causes of the disease. What damages these cells? Does the damage come from within, or from faulty interactions with other cells? What's more, being able to study which genes are switched on or off in such cells could tell us what might be going wrong in the 90 percent of ALS patients who did not inherit their condition. Cloning might even give us the chance to test new therapies.

For all these reasons, my colleagues and I are preparing to apply for a licence to   10
clone cells from ALS patients in the UK. As well as benefiting ALS research, we hope our techniques could be adapted for research into other neurodegenerative diseases, such as Parkinson's and Alzheimer's.

Human cloning also has the potential to revolutionise other areas of biomedical   11
research. One key area is developing and testing new drugs. It is a surprising fact that bad reactions to prescription drugs, even when those drugs are used correctly, kill thousands of people every year. At the moment, drug companies have no reliable way of predicting who will react badly.

In most cases, the variation from person to person is due to differences in the 12 genes that code for the liver enzymes that break down drugs. Human cloning could help in a number of ways. Researchers could clone and create cultures of liver cells from families who had suffered bad reactions to drugs. Such reactions often involve many different enzymes, and being able to study gene activity in the liver cells of susceptible people would let researchers identify variations in the key enzymes.

Findings from such research could allow drug companies to test their new drugs 13 more safely and effectively by letting them screen out susceptible individuals from their trials. Such patients could also be warned that certain drugs are not suitable for them. Drug companies currently use post-mortem liver samples as part of their extensive pre-clinical drug safety tests. However, these samples are often pooled, and the drug sensitivities of the donors are unknown.

Although research is likely to be the first beneficiary of human cloning, the most 14 exciting developments will come as "therapeutic" cloning: ways to repair or cure diseased organs or repair genetic defects. Transplants of stem cells that are genetically identical to their recipients promise new treatments, such as repairing damaged heart muscle following a heart attack.

Of course, this is still some way off. We have technical problems to solve, such as 15 how to get human ES cells to reliably form different cell types. There are safety aspects, too: we need to know these cells won't cause problems such as cancer. Lastly, human eggs are in short supply and this threatens to limit the use of therapeutic cloning. However, these problems can be addressed.

It is true that therapeutic cloning is unlikely to be practical for routine use. But not 16 all diseases are equal in terms of expense, and treatments could be targeted to maximise benefit. An older person with heart disease, for example, could be treated with stem cells that are not a genetic match, take drugs to suppress their immune system for the rest of their life, and live with the side-effects. A younger person might benefit more from stem cells that match exactly.

What's more, therapies are likely to become cheaper and easier to use as the tech- 17 nology progresses. One way of overcoming the human egg shortage could be to use cow eggs, strictly for making stem cells. I personally wouldn't have an issue with it from a moral point of view because essentially, you can just see eggs as bags of proteins. But you would have to be even more careful about the safety aspect.

The most radical use of human cloning technology is to treat inherited disease— 18 particularly those affecting whole organs that can't be replaced by stem cells, such as the lungs. It would also solve many of the problems that have recently plagued gene therapy, such as the risk of causing cancer.

At the moment, people carrying certain genetic diseases can try to avoid passing 19 them on by undergoing IVF and having the embryos tested so that only healthy ones are implanted. But if none of the embryos created is suitable, the couple face another round of invasive treatment to create more.

There is another way. In March 2003, Thomas Zwaka and James Thomson at the 20 University of Wisconsin in Madison reported that they had found a way of precisely replacing faulty genes in ES cells with healthy copies. This precision means there is little chance of a gene landing in the wrong place and causing problems. But how can the therapeutic gene be sent to every cell in the body?

This is where cloning could help. First, you would create an ordinary embryo 21 using IVF. Then you would take the ES cells from it and correct the diseased gene with genetic engineering. However, ES cells by themselves cannot be used to reconstitute the embryo they came from. To do this, you would take the nucleus from one of these corrected ES cells and transfer it into an egg. The resulting embryo would be the identical twin of the original embryo, but with the diseased gene corrected in every one of its cells. This embryo could then be implanted in its mother's womb to develop into a baby. Although such a child would be a human clone, it would be a clone of a new individual, not a clone of one of its parents. This form of cloning would not create the same ethical and social problems as reproductive cloning.

Of course the question of safety still applies. For now, we still know far too little 22 about what happens to the genes in a nucleus during cloning to consider creating a child in this way. But that should not hold us back from developing a technology that has such great potential to help so many people. Human cloning must not be banned. It could save many thousands of lives.

# READING FOR CONTENT

1. What specific benefits from human cloning does Wilmut cite in paragraphs 5, 9, and 11? Underline your answers in the text, and point to other benefits implied in the article.

2. What examples of therapeutic cloning does Wilmut cite in paragraphs 14, 16, and 17? Underline your answers in the text.

3. How does Wilmut propose that cloning might treat inherited diseases in paragraph 21? Does this proposal substantially differ from the ones that he makes earlier?

# READING FOR GENRE, ORGANIZATION, AND STYLISTIC FEATURES

1. How does the essay exemplify the genres of scientific argument? of moral argument? of social commentary?

2. While paragraph 6 argues briefly for the benefits of cloning and paragraphs 7–8 state the author's plans for research, paragraphs 10–22 focus on specific benefits that the author foresees in his research. How effective is this organization for presenting Wilmut's commentary?

3. In paragraphs 4, 15, and 16 Wilmut makes some concessions to opposing arguments about the dangers of cloning. How effective are his stylistic prompts such as "Although . . . , I think . . ."; "But even if . . ."; "Of course . . . , However . . ."; and "It is true . . . , But not all . . ."?

# READING FOR RHETORICAL CONTEXT

1. In paragraphs 7–8, Wilmut focuses on his immediate research plans and on questions that he hopes they might answer. How compelling are these questions as reasons for pursuing such research?

2. In paragraphs 15–17, Wilmut points to some technical difficulties in pursuing his research. How compelling are these difficulties as reasons for modifying his plans?

# WRITING ASSIGNMENTS

1. Write a 500-word response to Wilmut's commentary in support of his research and of the results that he hopes to obtain from it.

2. Write a 500-word response to Wilmut's commentary arguing against the unintended moral consequences that may derive from his research.

# SYNTHESIS WRITING ASSIGNMENTS

1. Imagine how it would be to have a younger brother or sister who was cloned from one of your cells. Write a 1,000-word essay that comments on the desirability of living with a clone sibling. Draw on at least two articles from Chapter 10 to support your commentary.

2. Design a scenario that illustrates the complex controversies over child custody that can develop when parents use cloning for reproduction. Write a 1,000-word essay in which you describe your scenario and weigh the various ethical considerations that the scenario involves.

3. Write a 1,250-word essay that argues for or against the legalization of human cloning. Make use of sources from Chapter 10 to support your viewpoint.

4. Synthesize material from Chapter 10 readings to describe, in a 1,250-word essay, how human and animal cloning technology might change our society. Evaluate these potential changes.

5. Imagine that in the future you and your partner are unable to conceive a child through either sexual intercourse or in vitro fertilization. Write a 1,000-word essay of personal reflection in which you explain why you would or would not resort to cloning in an effort to have a child.

6. Draw on articles by Silver, Conley, and Wilmut to discuss, in a 1,000-word essay, the pros and cons of cloning humans.

7. Use material from Chapter 10 readings to write a 1,500-word essay that analyzes the presentation of cloning technology in one or more science fiction movies, such as *Jurassic Park*, *The Boys from Brazil*, and *Godsend*.

*Eleven*

# Human/Machine Interaction

Most Americans are accustomed to relationships with machines. For example, we talk to our cars, feel betrayed when they break down, and sometimes grieve when they are hauled to the junkyard. As a nation, we spend more time in front of televisions than we do with family and friends. Video games have captivated a generation of adolescents, and many of their parents spend workdays in front of computer screens. The development of virtual-reality systems that emulate the real world may signal a new era in our relationship with machines, wherein circuitry may be an important source of "life" experiences.

Technology is often described as a double-edged sword that can work to our benefit or detriment, depending upon how it is applied. Some commentators argue that our relationship to machinery and electronics will provide us with greater control over our lives; others claim it will alienate us from human experience. These viewpoints and others are presented in the conversation about human/machine interaction in this chapter. The first selection, Carl Sagan's "In Defense of Robots," presents an important argument developed in the early 1970s about the usefulness of intelligent machines. Though it was written over three decades ago when artificial intelligence technology was in its infancy, it nonetheless rewards our attention by defining with exceptional clarity the contours of the field and the problems associated with it. Sagan's writing exemplifies a perennial style of scientific summary and speculation that brings us up to date not only with developments in the past but with ones on the horizon of the future as well. The potential for intimacy between humans and intelligent machines is explored in Sherry Turkle's "Loving Technology." This article summarizes her research in information technology in a user-friendly style that draws nonscientists into a vigorous conversation about developments in the field. In "Live Forever," Raymond Kurzweil predicts the consequences of being able to transfer the contents of a human mind into a computer. His sober consideration of what may now seem remote scientific possibilities expands the horizon of our understanding about computer technology even as it may prompt us to wonder whether such developments may come to pass. Clifford Stoll argues that technology cuts us off from contact with other humans in an excerpt from his book *High Tech Heretic*. His style is personal and idiosyncratic as it offers anecdotes, refers to uncited research and unspecified information, and alludes to complex scientific concepts in a breezy shorthand. Bill Joy, a pioneer in information technology, stands back from his own contributions to science and argues "Why the Future Doesn't Need Us." Like Stoll, but nonetheless detailing his references with academic footnotes where needed, he spins anecdotes, recounts personal conversations with other scientists, and dismisses many commonly held beliefs about science as though to repudiate his own earlier work in the field.

■ ■ ■ ■ ■ ■ ■ ■ ■ ■ ■

# In Defense of Robots

## *Carl Sagan*

*Carl Sagan was a professor of astronomy and space science at Cornell University and a Pulitzer Prize–winning science writer. His books include* Broca's Brain, Cosmos, *and* The Dragons of Eden.

## PREREADING

Sagan's title indicates that his essay will discuss robots. Consider both actual and fictitious robots that you are aware of. In ten minutes of freewriting, compare and contrast robots and humans.

The word "robot," first introduced by the Czech writer Karel Capek, is derived 1
from the Slavic root for "worker." But it signifies a machine rather than a human worker. Robots, especially robots in space, have often received derogatory notices in the press. We read that a human being was necessary to make the terminal landing adjustments on Apollo 11, without which the first manned lunar landing would have ended in disaster; that a mobile robot on the Martian surface could never be as clever as astronauts in selecting samples to be returned to Earth-bound geologists; and that machines could never have repaired, as men did, the Skylab sunshade, so vital for the continuance of the Skylab mission.

But all these comparisons turn out, naturally enough, to have been written by 2
humans. I wonder if a small self-congratulatory element, a whiff of human chauvinism, has not crept into these judgments. Just as whites can sometimes detect racism and men can occasionally discern sexism, I wonder whether we cannot here glimpse some comparable affliction of the human spirit—a disease that as yet has no name. The word "anthropocentrism" does not mean quite the same thing. The word "humanism" has

been pre-empted by other and more benign activities of our kind. From the analogy with sexism and racism I suppose the name for this malady is "speciesism"—the prejudice that there are no beings so fine, so capable, so reliable as human beings.

This is a prejudice because it is, at the very least, a prejudgment, a conclusion drawn ₃ before all the facts are in. Such comparisons of men and machines in space are comparisons of smart men and dumb machines. We have not asked what sorts of machines could have been built for the $30-or-so billion that the Apollo and Skylab missions cost.

Each human being is a superbly constructed, astonishingly compact, self- ₄ ambulatory computer—capable on occasion of independent decision making and real control of his or her environment. And, as the old joke goes, these computers can be constructed by unskilled labor. But there are serious limitations to employing human beings in certain environments. Without a great deal of protection, human beings would be inconvenienced on the ocean floor, the surface of Venus, the deep interior of Jupiter, or even on long space missions. Perhaps the only interesting results of Skylab that could not have been obtained by machines is that human beings in space for a period of months undergo a serious loss of bone calcium and phosphorus—which seems to imply that human beings may be incapacitated under 0 g for missions of six to nine months or longer. But the minimum interplanetary voyages have characteristic times of a year or two. Because we value human beings highly, we are reluctant to send them on very risky missions. If we do send human beings to exotic environments, we must also send along their food, their air, their water, amenities for entertainment and waste recycling, and companions. By comparison, machines require no elaborate life-support systems, no entertainment, no companionship, and we do not yet feel any strong ethical prohibitions against sending machines on one-way, or suicide, missions.

Certainly, for simple missions, machines have proved themselves many times over. ₅ Unmanned vehicles have performed the first photography of the whole Earth and of the far side of the Moon; the first landings on the Moon, Mars and Venus; and the first thorough orbital reconnaissance of another planet, in the Mariner 9 and Viking missions to Mars. Here on Earth it is increasingly common for high-technology manufacturing—for example, chemical and pharmaceutical plants—to be performed largely or entirely under computer control. In all these activities machines are able, to some extent, to sense errors, to correct mistakes, to alert human controllers some great distance away about perceived problems.

The powerful abilities of computing machines to do arithmetic—hundreds of ₆ millions of times faster than unaided human beings—are legendary. But what about really difficult matters? Can machines in any sense think through a new problem? Can they make discussions of the branched-contingency tree variety which we think of as characteristically human? (That is, I ask Question 1; if the answer is A, I ask Question 2; but if the answer is B, I ask Question 3; and so on.) Some decades ago the English mathematician A. M. Turing described what would be necessary for him to believe in machine intelligence. The condition was simply that he could be in teletype communication with a machine and be unable to tell that it was not a human being. Turing imagined a conversation between a man and a machine of the following quality:

> *Interrogator:* In the first line of your sonnet which reads "Shall I compare thee to a Summer's day," would not "a Spring day" do as well or better?
>
> *Witness:* It wouldn't scan.
>
> *Interrogator:* How about "a Winter's day"? That would scan all right.

*Witness:* Yes, but nobody wants to be compared to a Winter's day.

*Interrogator:* Would you say Mr. Pickwick reminded you of Christmas?

*Witness:* In a way.

*Interrogator:* Yet Christmas is a Winter's day, and I do not think Mr. Pickwick would mind the comparison.

*Witness:* I don't think you're serious. By a Winter's day one means a typical Winter's day, rather than a special one like Christmas.

No device of this sophistication has yet been built, although I am not sure how   7
many humans would pass Turing's human test. But the amount of effort and money put into artificial intelligence has been quite limited, and there are only about a half-dozen major centers of such activity in the world. One of the more striking results obtained in a very limited universe of discourse—that of children's blocks—has come from the work of Terry Winograd, then at the Massachusetts Institute of Technology. Here is a dialogue between man and machine, the machine having been programmed by Winograd:

*Q:* What does the box contain?

*A:* The blue pyramid and the blue box.

*Q:* How many blocks are not in the box?

*A:* Four of them.

*Q:* Is at least one of them narrower than the one which I told you to pick up?

*A:* Yes, the red cube.

*Q:* Is there a steeple?

*A:* Sorry, I don't know the word "steeple."

*Q:* A steeple is a stack which contains two green cubes and a pyramid, for example.

*A:* I understand.

*Q:* Are there any steeples now?

*A:* No.

*Q:* Build one.

The machine does. It reaches out its mechanical hand, moves the cubes and   8
builds the structure that has just been described.

*Q:* When did you pick up the pyramid?

*A:* While I was stacking up the red cube, the large red block and the large green cube.

*Q:* Why?

*A:* To get rid of it.

*Q:* Why did you clear off that cube?

*A:* To put it on the large green cube.

As another example, a machine psychiatrist has been developed by Joseph   9
Weizenbaum, also at MIT. This is a much simpler program than Winograd's, since it involves nondirective psychotherapy, which, generally speaking, requires extremely

simple-minded computer programs. Here is a striking dialogue between a human being and a computer psychotherapist. (There is certainly a selection effect here. Many other such machine/human psychiatric dialogues are not nearly so striking. But I suppose most human/human psychiatric dialogues are not very striking either.) In this interaction, in order to spell out clearly the respective roles of therapist and patient, the computer therapist types upper case while the patient types lower case:

men are all alike
IN WHAT WAY

they're always bugging us about something or other
CAN YOU THINK OF A SPECIFIC EXAMPLE

well, my boy friend made me come here
YOUR BOY FRIEND MADE YOU COME HERE

he noticed that i'm depressed much of the time
I AM SORRY TO HEAR YOU ARE DEPRESSED

he's right i am unhappy
DO YOU THINK COMING HERE WILL HELP YOU NOT TO BE UNHAPPY

i need some help, that much is clear
WHAT WOULD IT MEAN TO YOU IF YOU GOT SOME HELP

perhaps i could learn to get along with my mother
TELL ME MORE ABOUT YOUR FAMILY

my mother takes care of me
WHO ELSE IN YOUR FAMILY TAKES CARE OF YOU

my father
YOUR FATHER

you are like my father in some ways
WHAT RESEMBLANCE DO YOU SEE

you are not very aggressive, but i don't think you want me to notice that
WHAT MAKES YOU THINK I AM NOT VERY AGGRESSIVE

you don't argue with me
WHY DO YOU THINK I DON'T ARGUE WITH YOU

you are afraid of me
DOES IT PLEASE YOU TO BELIEVE I AM AFRAID OF YOU

it pleases my father to think i am afraid of him
WHAT ELSE COMES TO MIND WHEN YOU THINK OF YOUR FATHER
bullies
DOES THAT HAVE ANYTHING TO DO WITH THE FACT THAT YOUR
   BOY FRIEND MADE YOU COME HERE

This astonishing—one is very tempted to say "perceptive"—response from the 10 computer is, of course, preprogrammed. But, then, so are the responses of human psychotherapists. In a time when more and more people in our society seem to be in need of psychiatric counseling, and when time-sharing of computers is widespread, I can even imagine the development of a network of computer psychotherapeutic terminals, something like arrays of large telephone booths, in which, for a few dollars a session, we are able to talk to an attentive, tested and largely nondirective psychotherapist. Ensuring the confidentiality of the psychiatric dialogue is one of several important steps still to be worked out.

Another sign of the intellectual accomplishments of machines is in games. Even 11 exceptionally simple computers—those that can be wired by a bright ten-year-old—can be programmed to play perfect tic-tac-toe. Some computers can play world-class checkers. Chess is of course a much more complicated game than tic-tac-toe or checkers. Here programming a machine to win is more difficult, and novel strategies have been used, including several rather successful attempts to have a computer learn from its own experience in playing previous chess games. Computers can learn, for example, empirically the rule that it is better in the beginning game to control the center of the chessboard than the periphery. The ten best chess players in the world still have nothing to fear from any present computer. But the situation is changing. Recently a computer for the first time did well enough to enter the Minnesota State Chess Open. This may be the first time that a nonhuman has entered a major sporting event on the planet Earth (and I cannot help but wonder if robot golfers and designated hitters may be attempted sometime in the next decade, to say nothing of dolphins in free-style competition). The computer did not win the Chess Open, but this is the first time one has done well enough to enter such a competition. Chess-playing computers are improving extremely rapidly.

I have heard machines demeaned (often with a just audible sigh of relief) for the 12 fact that chess is an area where human beings are still superior. This reminds me very much of the old joke in which a stranger remarks with wonder on the accomplishments of a checker-playing dog. The dog's owner replies, "Oh, it's not all that remarkable. He loses two games out of three." A machine that plays chess in the middle range of human expertise is a very capable machine; even if there are thousands of better human chess players, there are millions who are worse. To play chess requires strategy, foresight, analytical powers, and the ability to cross-correlate large numbers of variables and to learn from the experience. These are excellent qualities in those whose job it is to discover and explore, as well as those who watch the baby and walk the dog.

With this as a more or less representative set of examples of the state of develop- 13 ment of machine intelligence, I think it is clear that a major effort over the next decade could produce much more sophisticated examples. This is also the opinion of most of the workers in machine intelligence.

In thinking about this next generation of machine intelligence, it is important to 14 distinguish between self-controlled and remotely controlled robots. A self-controlled robot has its intelligence within it; a remotely controlled robot has its intelligence at some other place, and its successful operation depends upon close communication between its central computer and itself. There are, of course, intermediate cases where the machine may be partly self-activated and partly remotely controlled. It is this mix of remote and *in situ* control that seems to offer the highest efficiency for the near future.

For example, we can imagine a machine designed for the mining of the ocean 15 floor. There are enormous quantities of manganese nodules littering the abyssal depths. They were once thought to have been produced by meteorite infall on Earth, but are now believed to be formed occasionally in vast manganese fountains produced by the internal tectonic activity of the Earth. Many other scarce and industrially valuable minerals are likewise to be found on the deep ocean bottom. We have the capability today to design devices that systematically swim over or crawl upon the ocean floor; that are able to perform spectrometric and other chemical examinations of the surface material; that can automatically radio back to ship or land all findings; and that can mark the locales of especially valuable deposits—for example, by low-frequency radio-homing devices. The radio beacon will then direct great mining machines to the appropriate locales. The present state of the art in deep-sea submersibles and in spacecraft environmental sensors is clearly compatible with the development of such devices. Similar remarks can be made for off-shore oil drilling, for coal and other subterranean mineral mining, and so on. The likely economic returns from such devices would pay not only for their development, but for the entire space program many times over.

When the machines are faced with particularly difficult situations, they can be  16 programmed to recognize that the situations are beyond their abilities and to inquire of human operators—working in safe and pleasant environments—what to do next. The examples just given are of devices that are largely self-controlled. The reverse also is possible, and a great deal of very preliminary work along these lines has been performed in the remote handling of highly radioactive materials in laboratories of the U.S. Department of Energy. Here I imagine a human being who is connected by radio link with a mobile machine. The operator is in Manila, say; the machine in the Mindanao Deep. The operator is attached to an array of electronic relays, which transmits and amplifies his movements to the machine and which can, conversely, carry what the machine finds back to his senses. So when the operator turns his head to the left, the television cameras on the machine turn left, and the operator sees on a great hemispherical television screen around him the scene the machine's searchlights and cameras have revealed. When the operator in Manila takes a few strides forward in his wired suit, the machine in the abyssal depths ambles a few feet forward. When the operator reaches out his hand, the mechanical arm of the machine likewise extends itself; and the precision of the man/machine interaction is such that precise manipulation of material at the ocean bottom by the machine's fingers is possible. With such devices, human beings can enter environments otherwise closed to them forever.

In the exploration of Mars, unmanned vehicles have already soft-landed, and  17 only a little further in the future they will roam about the surface of the Red Planet, as some now do on the Moon. We are not ready for a manned mission to Mars. Some of us are concerned about such missions because of the dangers of carrying terrestrial microbes to Mars, and Martian microbes, if they exist, to Earth, but also because of their enormous expense. The Viking landers deposited on Mars in the summer of 1976 have a very interesting array of sensors and scientific instruments, which are the extension of human senses to an alien environment.

The obvious post-Viking device for Martian exploration, one which takes advan-  18 tage of the Viking technology, is a Viking Rover in which the equivalent of an entire Viking spacecraft, but with considerably improved science, is put on wheels or tractor treads and permitted to rove slowly over the Martian landscape. But now we come to a new problem, one that is never encountered in machine operation on the Earth's surface. Although Mars is the second closest planet, it is so far from the Earth that the light travel time becomes significant. At a typical relative position of Mars and the Earth, the planet is 20 light-minutes away. Thus, if the spacecraft were confronted with a steep incline, it might send a message of inquiry back to Earth. Forty minutes later the response would arrive saying something like "For heaven's sake, stand dead still." But by then, of course, an unsophisticated machine would have tumbled into the gully. Consequently, any Martian Rover requires slope and roughness sensors. Fortunately, these are readily available and are even seen in some children's toys. When confronted with a precipitous slope or large boulder, the spacecraft would either stop until receiving instructions from the Earth in response to its query (and televised picture of the terrain), or back off and start off in another and safer direction.

Much more elaborate contingency decision networks can be built into the onboard 19 computers of spacecraft of the 1980s. For more remote objectives, to be explored further in the future, we can imagine human controllers in orbit around the target planet, or on one of its moons. In the exploration of Jupiter, for example, I can imagine the operators on a small moon outside the fierce Jovian radiation belts, controlling with only a few seconds' delay the responses of a spacecraft floating in the dense Jovian clouds.

Human beings on Earth can also be in such an interaction loop, if they are willing 20 to spend some time on the enterprise. If every decision in Martian exploration must be fed through a human controller on Earth, the Rover can traverse only a few feet an hour. But the lifetimes of such rovers are so long that a few feet an hour represents a perfectly respectable rate of progress. However, as we imagine expeditions into the farthest reaches of the solar system—and ultimately to the stars—it is clear that self-controlled machine intelligence will assume heavier burdens of responsibility.

In the development of such machines we find a kind of convergent evolution. 21 Viking is, in a curious sense, like some great outsized, clumsily constructed insect. It is not yet ambulatory, and it is certainly incapable of self-reproduction. But it has an exoskeleton, it has a wide range of insectlike sensory organs, and it is about as intelligent as a dragonfly. But Viking has an advantage that insects do not: it can, on occasion, by inquiring of its controllers on Earth, assume the intelligence of a human being—the controllers are able to reprogram the Viking computer on the basis of decisions they make.

As the field of machine intelligence advances and as increasingly distant objects 22 in the solar system become accessible to exploration, we will see the development of increasingly sophisticated onboard computers, slowly climbing the phylogenetic tree from insect intelligence to crocodile intelligence to squirrel intelligence and—in the not very remote future, I think—to dog intelligence. Any flight to the outer solar system must have a computer capable of determining whether it is working properly. There is no possibility of sending to the Earth for a repairman. The machine must be able to sense when it is sick and skillfully doctor its own illnesses. A computer is needed that is able either to fix or replace failed computer, sensor or structural components. Such a computer, which has been called STAR (self-testing and repairing computer), is on the threshold of development. It employs redundant components, as biology does—we have two lungs and two kidneys partly because each is protection against failure of the other. But a computer can be much more redundant than a human being, who has, for example, but one head and one heart.

Because of the weight premium on deep space exploratory ventures, there will be 23 strong pressures for continued miniaturization of intelligent machines. It is clear that remarkable miniaturization has already occurred: vacuum tubes have been replaced by transistors, wired circuits by printed circuit boards, and entire computer systems by silicon-chip microcircuitry. Today a circuit that used to occupy much of a 1930 radio set can be printed on the tip of a pin. If intelligent machines for terrestrial mining and space exploratory applications are pursued, the time cannot be far off when household and other domestic robots will become commercially feasible. Unlike the classical anthropoid robots of science fiction, there is no reason for such machines to look any more human than a vacuum cleaner does. They will be specialized for their functions. But there are many common tasks, ranging from bartending to floor washing, that involve a very limited array of intellectual capabilities, albeit substantial stamina and patience. All-purpose ambulatory household robots, which perform domestic functions as well as a proper nineteenth-century English butler, are probably many decades off. But more specialized machines, each adapted to a specific household function, are probably already on the horizon.

It is possible to imagine many other civic tasks and essential functions of everyday 24 life carried out by intelligent machines. By the early 1970s, garbage collectors in Anchorage, Alaska, and other cities won wage settlements guaranteeing them salaries of about $20,000 per annum. It is possible that the economic pressures alone may make a persuasive case for the development of automated garbage-collecting machines. For the development of domestic and civic robots to be a general civic good, the effective re-employment of those human beings displaced by the robots must, of course, be arranged; but over a human generation that should not be too difficult—particularly if there are enlightened educational reforms. Human beings enjoy learning.

We appear to be on the verge of developing a wide variety of intelligent machines 25 capable of performing tasks too dangerous, too expensive, too onerous or too boring for human beings. The development of such machines is, in my mind, one of the few legitimate "spin-offs" of the space program. The efficient exploitation of energy in agri-culture—upon which our survival as a species depends—may even be contingent on the development of such machines. The main obstacle seems to be a very human prob-lem, the quiet feeling that comes stealthily and unbidden, and argues that there is something threatening or "inhuman" about machines performing certain tasks as well as or better than human beings; or a sense of loathing for creatures made of silicon and germanium rather than proteins and nucleic acids. But in many respects our survival as a species depends on our transcending such primitive chauvinisms. In part, our adjust-ment to intelligent machines is a matter of acclimatization. There are already cardiac pacemakers that can sense the beat of the human heart; only when there is the slightest hint of fibrillation does the pacemaker stimulate the heart. This is a mild but very useful sort of machine intelligence. I cannot imagine the wearer of this device resent-ing its intelligence. I think in a relatively short period of time there will be a very similar sort of acceptance for much more intelligent and sophisticated machines. There is nothing inhuman about an intelligent machine; it is indeed an expression of those superb intellectual capabilities that only human beings, of all the creatures on our planet, now possess.

## READING FOR CONTENT

1. Paraphrase Sagan's definition of "speciesism" in paragraph 2.
2. Summarize the criticisms of robots and computers that Sagan responds to in his essay.
3. List the tasks that Sagan suggests we will assign to intelligent machines in the future.
4. List the advantages of robots and computers over human workers.
5. List the aspects of human intelligence that Sagan feels can be copied by machines.
6. In the last sentence, Sagan states, "There is nothing inhuman about an intelli-gent machine." What does he mean by that statement?

## READING FOR GENRE, ORGANIZATION, AND STYLISTIC FEATURES

1. What does Sagan attempt to achieve in his opening paragraph? How does this paragraph fit in with the rest of the essay?
2. How does the last paragraph mirror the organizational plan of the entire essay?
3. Why do you think Sagan chooses a pacemaker as his concluding example of an intelligent machine? Is this a good example? Why?

## READING FOR RHETORICAL CONTEXT

1. How would you characterize the style of Sagan's essay? Is it appropriate for his intended audience? Why?
2. What feelings does Sagan want his audience to develop toward computers? Does he achieve that effect on you? Why or why not?
3. Does Sagan respond adequately to the criticisms of robots that he mentions?
4. Sagan stresses the use of robots for space exploration, one of his personal and professional interests. Does Sagan convince you that robots have more practical, everyday applications? Which everyday applications impress you the most?

## WRITING ASSIGNMENTS

1. In a four-page essay, agree or disagree with Sagan's position that current machines do possess a form of intelligence. Do his examples of intelligent machines convince you? If not, what further evidence would you need?
2. Using Sagan's essay as a source, write a two-page description of what society will be like fifty years from now. Focus on the social roles that humans and robots will occupy and on what the interaction between people and machines will be like. Write for an audience of sociology students.
3. In paragraph 24, Sagan suggests that robots may take over from human workers such tasks as garbage collection. Describe some social problems that might arise from robotization of the workforce. Can those problems be solved? Are the social costs of robotization worth the potential social benefits?

# Loving Technology

*Sherry Turkle*

*Sherry Turkle is Abby Rockefeller Mauzé Professor in the Program in Science, Technology, and Society at MIT and the founder and current director of the MIT Initiative on Technology*

Reprinted with the permission of Sherry Turkle. This article appeared in *Technos*, Fall 2001.

*and Self. She is the author of* Psychoanalytic Politics: Jacqes Lacan and Freud's French Revolution, The Second Self: Computers and the Human Spirit, *and* Life on the Screen: Identity in the Age of the Internet.

## PREREADING

Think of a machine with which you have a "relationship" — perhaps a car, a computer, or an electronic "pet." In what ways, if any, do you treat that machine as if it were more than just a collection of metal and plastic? Freewrite for ten minutes in response to this question.

One of the questions posed by the recent Stephen Spielberg movie A.I.: *Artificial* 1
*Intelligence* is whether a humanoid robot could "really" be developed, with the focus on the reality of the new machine. I am going to turn that question around. There is an unstated question that lies behind much of our historic preoccupations with the computer's capabilities. That question is not what computers can do or what will the computer be like in the future, but instead, what will we be like? What kind of people are we becoming as we develop increasingly intimate relationships with machines?

In this context, the central character of the story on which A.I. is based is not the 2
"reality" of the boy, the nonbiological son, but of his adoptive, biological mother — this mother whose response to a machine who asks for her nurturance is the desire to nurture the machine; whose response to a creature who reaches out to her is to feel attachment and horror and confusion.

The question for the mother is, "What kind of relationship is it appropriate to 3
have with a machine?" I want to suggest that in terms of the "reality" of the film, that question is not science fiction but is current and urgent, and in this sense totally "real."

It is current and urgent, and not because AI [artificial intelligence] designers 4
have yet built machines that are "really" intelligent ... but because they have built machines that can bypass this essentialist question of what is innate in the machine and go straight to doing things that cause us to treat them as sentient, even emotional. So, even today we are faced with relational artifacts that — even when they are as simple as digital pets and dolls, the simple robotic creatures that are marketed to children — have people responding to them in ways that have something in common with the mother in the film. When a robotic creature makes eye contact, follows your gaze, and gestures towards you, what you feel is the evolutionary button being pushed to respond to that creature as a sentient and even caring other. I will come back to this.

### First, a Little History

Let me step back a moment to a historical view of twentieth-century thinking about 5
how we develop our notions of what is alive and what is not.

When the Swiss developmental psychologist Jean Piaget interviewed children in 6
the 1920s and 1930s about which objects were alive and which were not, he found that children honed their definition of life by developing increasingly sophisticated notions about motion, the world of physics. In contrast, when I began to study the nascent computer culture in the early 1980s, children argued about whether a computer was alive through discussions about its psychology. Did the computer know things on its own, or did it have to be programmed? Did it have intentions, consciousness, feelings? Did it

cheat? Did it know it was cheating? Faced with intelligent machines, children took a new world of objects and imposed a new world order. To put it too simply, motion gave way to emotion and physics gave way to psychology as criteria for aliveness.

By the 1990s, that order had been strained to the breaking point. Children spoke    7
about computers as just machines but then described them as sentient and intentional. They talked about biology, evolution. They said things like, *The robots are in control but not alive, would be alive if they had bodies, are alive because they have bodies, would be alive if they had feelings, are alive the way insects are alive but not the way people are alive; the simulated creatures are not alive because they are just in the computer, are alive until you turn off the computer, are not alive because nothing in the computer is real; the Sim creatures are not alive but almost alive, they would be alive if they spoke, they would be alive if they traveled, they're not alive because they don't have bodies, they are alive because they can have babies, would be alive if they could get out of the game and onto America Online.*

There was a striking heterogeneity of theory here: Children cycled through dif-    8
ferent theories to far more fluid ways of thinking about life and reality to the point that my daughter, upon seeing a jellyfish in the Mediterranean, said, "Look, Mommy, a jellyfish; it looks so realistic"; and visitors to Disney's Animal Kingdom in Orlando complained that the biological animals that populated the theme park were not "realistic" enough compared to the animatronic creatures across the way at Disney World.

## Feelings

Most recently, there is a new development in the story. A new kind of computational    9
object, a production of artificial intelligence, is raising new questions about what kinds of relationships seem appropriate to have with machines.

There are robot cats for lonely elders; at the MIT AI lab, Bit, a robot infant, now on    10
the market as My Real Baby®, makes baby sounds and even baby facial expressions, shaped by mechanical musculature under its artificial skin. Most significant, this computationally complex doll has baby "states of mind." Bounce the doll when it is happy, and it gets happier. Bounce it when it is grumpy, and it gets grumpier. At the MIT Media Lab, Rosalind Picard's research group are developing affective computers, machines that are programmed to assess their users' emotional states and respond with emotional states of their own. In the case of the robotic doll and the affective machines, the user is confronted with a relational artifact. It demands that the user attend to its psychology.

During the more than two decades in which I have explored people's relationships    11
with computers, I have used the metaphor of "computer as Rorschach"—the computer as a screen that allowed people to project their thoughts and feelings, their very different cognitive styles. With relational artifacts, the Rorschach model of a computer/human relationship breaks down. People are learning that to relate successfully to a computer you have to assess its emotional "state"; people are learning that when you confront a computational machine, you do not ask how it "works" in terms of any underlying process, but take the machine "at interface value," much as you would another person. Perhaps most important, a first generation of children are learning that artifacts have a life cycle and that they need care, even emotional nurturance.

To grow and be healthy, even the first popular relational artifacts, the very primi-    12
tive Tamagotchis® (little screen creatures), need to be fed, they need to be cleaned, and amused. Furbies® (a cuddly owl-like creature) simulate learning and loving. Furbies arrive in the child's life speaking "Furbish." They "learn" to speak English. They play

hide and seek. They communicate with each other and join together in song. They say, "I love you."

In my research on children and Furbies, I have found that when children play 13 with these new objects, they want to know their "state," not to get something "right" but to make the Furbies happy. Children want to understand Furby language, not to "win" in a game over a Furby, but to have a feeling of mutual recognition. Children are not concerned with how Furbies "work" or what they "really" know, but are very concerned with the toys' health and well-being. In sum, a new generation of objects push on our evolutionary buttons to respond to certain forms of interactivity by experiencing ourselves as being with a kindred "other."

Historically, in my studies of children and computer toys, children described the 14 lifelike status of machines in terms of their cognitive capacities (the toys could "know" things, "solve" puzzles). In my studies on children and relational artifacts, I have found that children describe these new toys as "sort of alive" because of the quality of their emotional attachments to the Furbies and because of their fantasies about the idea that the Furby might be emotionally attached to them. So, for example, when I ask the question, "Do you think the Furby is alive?" children answer not in terms of what the Furby can do, but how they feel about the Furby and how the Furby might feel about them.

> *Ron (6):* Well, the Furby is alive for a Furby. And you know, something this smart 15 should have arms. It might want to pick up something or to hug me.
>
> *Katherine (5):* Is it alive? Well, I love it. It's more alive than a Tamagotchi because it 16 sleeps with me. It likes to sleep with me.
>
> *Jen (9):* I really like to take care of it. So, I guess it is alive, but it doesn't need to really 17 eat, so it is as alive as you can be if you don't eat. A Furby is like an owl. But it is more alive than an owl because it knows more and you can talk to it. But it needs batteries, so it is not an animal. It's not like an animal kind of alive.

Children talk about "an animal kind of alive and a Furby kind of alive." Will they 18 also talk about a "people kind of love" and a "computer kind of love"?

## What is "Real"?

We are in a different world from the old "AI debates" of the 1960s to 1980s in which 19 researchers argued about whether machines could be "really" intelligent. The old debate was essentialist; the new objects sidestep such arguments about what is inherent in them and play instead on what they evoke in us. When we are asked to care for an object, when the cared-for object thrives and offers us its attention and concern, we experience that object as intelligent, but more important, we feel a connection to it. So, my goal here is not to enter a debate about whether objects "really" have emotions, but to reflect on what relational artifacts evoke in the user.

How will interacting with relational artifacts affect people's way of thinking about 20 themselves, their sense of human identity, of what makes people special? Children have traditionally defined what makes people special in terms of a theory of "nearest neighbors." So, when the nearest neighbors (in children's eyes) were their pet dogs and cats, people were special because they had reason. The Aristotelian definition of man as a rational animal made sense, even for the youngest children. But when, in the 1980s, it seemed to be the computers that were the nearest neighbors, children's approach to the problem changed. Now, people were special not because they were rational animals but because they were emotional machines. So, in 1983, a 10-year-old told me, "When there are robots that are as smart as the people, the people will still run the restaurants, cook the food, have the families, I guess they'll still be the only ones who'll go to church." He rendered unto the machines the domains of reason; he rendered unto the people the realms of emotionality and sociability.

Now, in a world where machines present themselves as emotional and sociable, 21 what is left for us?

The media reported a comment on AIBO®, Sony's household entertainment 22 robot, that startled me in what it might augur for the future of person-machine relationships: "[AIBO] is better than a real dog. . . . It won't do dangerous things, and it won't betray you. . . . Also, it won't die suddenly and make you feel very sad."

Mortality has traditionally defined the human condition. A shared sense of mor- 23 tality has been the basis for feeling a commonality with other human beings, a sense of going through the same life cycle, a sense of the preciousness of time and life, of its fragility. Loss (of parents, of friends, of family) is part of the way we understand how human beings grow and develop, and bring the qualities of other people within themselves. The possibilities of engaging emotionally with creatures that will not die, whose loss we will never need to face, presents dramatic questions that are based on current technology—not issues of whether the technology depicted in A.I. could "really" be developed.

## By Any Other Name

The question, "What kinds of relationships is it appropriate to have with machines?" 24 has been explored in science fiction, including A.I., and in technophilosophy. But the sight of children and, for that matter, the elderly exchanging tendernesses with robotic pets brings technophilosophy down to earth. It concretizes it in a new, more urgent posing of the question of what kinds of relationships are appropriate to have with a machine. In the end, the question is not just whether our children will come to love their toy robots more than their parents, but what will loving itself come to mean?

When I began studying popular responses to the idea of AI in the late 1970s, the 25 dominant models of AI were based on models of information processing, of symbols, of top-down instructions. At the time, I found that people tended to respond to the field with a kind of romantic reaction, saying, for example, that simulated thinking might be thinking, but simulated thinking could never be thinking, and simulated love could never be love. People's sense of personal identity often became focused on whatever they defined as "not cognition" or "beyond information."

Models of AI changed from those information-processing ideas. By the late 1980s 26 and early 1990s, AI models that looked to the brain and nervous system for their underlying images, models that looked to the behavior of insects and simple creatures, began to dominate the field. (They had been popular in the early days of AI, had gone out of favor, and were now in a period of restoration.) These more biological and behavioral models provoked a very different response. Once AI suggested that its creatures would be unpredictable and nondeterministic, they met the romantic reaction to artificial intelligence with their own "romantic machines." AI started to encourage a language of nature as a computer and of the computer as part of nature. It encouraged a way of thinking in which traditional distinctions between the natural and artificial, the "real" and simulated, might dissolve. Children described computers, machines, and people as made of the same stuff: "Just yucky computer cy-dough-plasm." By the 1990s, we were in the midst of an evolving cyborg consciousness.

Let me put this history somewhat differently: When, in the heyday of information- 27 processing AI, Marvin Minsky justified the AI enterprise with the quip, "The mind is a meat machine," the remark often was cited with irritation, even disgust. History has shown us that much of what seemed unacceptable about Minsky's words had to do with the prevailing images of what kind of meat machine the mind might be. The images were mechanistic and deterministic. But today's AI models suggest an artificiality made up of biologically or psychologically resonant components. With a changed image of machines, the idea that the mind could be one became far less problematic.

Walt Whitman said, "A child goes forth every day/And the first object he look'ed 28 upon/That object he became." We make our technologies, and our technologies make and shape us. We are not going to be the same people we are today on the day we are ever faced with "loving" machines.

## READING FOR CONTENT

1. Paraphrase the question Turkle poses in paragraph 1.
2. If you have not seen the film *A.I.: Artificial Intelligence*, ask a classmate to explain its plot.
3. What is the meaning of the word "sentient" that Turkle uses in paragraph 4?
4. Summarize the confusion between what is real and what isn't that Turkle describes in paragraph 8.
5. What is a Tamagotchi? A Furby?
6. Summarize how children respond to Furbies as described by Turkle in paragraphs 13 through 18.
7. In what sense does Turkle believe that the debate over artificial intelligence changed in the 1990s?
8. Summarize Turkle's comments in paragraph 27 on viewing the mind as a machine.

## READING FOR GENRE, ORGANIZATION, AND STYLISTIC FEATURES

1. Comment on Turkle's use of subheadings.
2. Paragraphs 2, 5, 18, and 21 are only one or two sentences long. Comment on how Turkle uses short paragraphs.
3. Describe Turkle's organizational plan.
4. What conventions of academic writing are exhibited in Turkle's article?

## READING FOR RHETORICAL CONTEXT

1. What is Turkle's goal in writing?
2. What is the basis of Turkle's authority on her topic?
3. Where does Turkle draw conclusions?

## WRITING ASSIGNMENTS

1. In paragraph 3, Turkle poses the following question: "What kind of relationship is it appropriate to have with a machine?" Write a 750-word essay of personal response that answers Turkle's question.
2. Write a 1,000-word essay that draws on Turkle's article and attempts to define "criteria for aliveness" (paragraph 6).
3. In a 1,000-word essay, compare and contrast Turkle's and Raymond Kurzweil's views on the potential for developing machines that exhibit emotion.

■ ■ ■ ■ ■ ■ ■ ■ ■ ■ ■

# Live Forever

## *Raymond Kurzweil*

*Raymond Kurzweil is responsible for a number of significant innovations in computer technology, including the first print-to-speech reading machine for the blind. He is the author of* The Age of Spiritual Machines: When Computers Exceed Human Intelligence.

## PREREADING

What is your response to the idea behind Kurzweil's title, "Live Forever"? Does immortality seem desirable to you? Freewrite for ten minutes in response to those questions.

Within 30 years, we will be able to scan ourselves—our intelligence, personalities, feelings and memories—into computers. Is this the beginning of eternal life?    1

Thought to Implant 4: OnNet, please.    2

Hundreds of shimmering thumbnail images mist into view, spread fairly evenly across the entire field of pseudovision.    3

Thought: Zoom upper left, higher, into Winston's image.    4

Transmit: It's Nellie. Let's connect and chat over croissants. Rue des Enfants, Paris in the spring, our favorite table, yes?    5

Four-second pause.    6

Background thought: Damn it. What's taking him so long?    7

Receive: I'm here, ma chère, I'm here! Let's do it!    8

The thumbnail field mists away, and a cafe scene swirls into place. Scent of honeysuckle. Pâté. Wine. Light breeze. Nellie is seated at a quaint table with a plain white tablecloth. An image of Winston looking twenty and buff mists in across from her. Message thumbnails occasionally blink against the sky.    9

Winston: It's so good to see you again, ma chère! It's been months! And what a 10
gorgeous choice of bodies! The eyes are a dead giveaway, though. You always pick those
raspberry eyes. Tres bold, Nellita. So what's the occasion? Part of me is in the middle of
a business meeting in Chicago, so I can't dally.

Nellie: Why do you always put on that muscleman body, Winston? You know 11
how much I like your real one. Winston morphs into a man in his early 50s, still overly
muscular.

Winston: (laughing) My real body? How droll! No one but my neurotechnician 12
has seen it for years! Believe me, that's not what you want. I can do much better! He
fans rapidly through a thousand images, and Nellie grimaces.

Nellie: Damn it! You're just one of Winston's MIs! Where is the real Winston? 13
I know I used the right connection!

Winston: Nellie, I'm sorry to have to tell you this. There was a transporter acci- 14
dent a few weeks ago in Evanston, and . . . well, I'm lucky they got to me in time for the
full upload. I'm all of Winston that's left. The body's gone.

When Nellie contacts her friend Winston through the Internet connection in her 15
brain, he is already, biologically speaking, dead. It is his electronic mind double, a virtual reality twin, that greets Nellie in their virtual Parisian cafe. What's surprising here is
not so much the notion that human minds may someday live on inside computers after
their bodies have expired. It's the fact that this vignette is closer at hand than most people
realize. Within 30 years, the minds in those computers may just be our own.

The history of technology has shown over and over that as one mode of technol- 16
ogy exhausts its potential, a new, more sophisticated paradigm emerges to keep us moving at an exponential pace. Between 1910 and 1950, computer technology doubled in
power every three years; between 1950 and 1966, it doubled every two years; and it has
recently been doubling every year.

By the year 2020, your $1,000 personal computer will have the processing power of 17
the human brain—20 million billion calculations per second (100 billion neurons times
1,000 connections per neuron times 200 calculations per second per connection). By
2030, it will take a village of human brains to match a $1,000 computer. By 2050, $1,000
worth of computing will equal the processing power of all human brains on earth.

Of course, achieving the processing power of the human brain is necessary but 18
not sufficient for creating human-level intelligence in a machine. But by 2030, we'll
have the means to scan the human brain and re-create its design electronically.

Most people don't realize the revolutionary impact of that. The development of 19
computers that match and vastly exceed the capabilities of the human brain will be no
less important than the evolution of human intelligence itself some thousands of generations ago. Current predictions overlook the imminence of a world in which machines
become more like humans—programmed with replicated brain synapses that re-create
the ability to respond appropriately to human emotion, and humans become more like
machines—our biological bodies and brains enhanced with billions of "nanobots,"
swarms of microscopic robots transporting us in and out of virtual reality. We have
already started down this road: Human and machine have already begun to meld.

It starts with uploading, or scanning the brain into a computer. One scenario is 20
invasive: One very thin slice at a time, scientists input a brain of choice—having been
frozen just slightly before it was going to die—at an extremely high speed. This way,
they can easily see every neuron, every connection and every neurotransmitter concentration represented in each synapse-thin layer.

Seven years ago, a condemned killer allowed his brain and body to be scanned in   21
this way, and you can access all 10 billion bytes of him on the Internet. You can see for
yourself every bone, muscle, and section of gray matter in his body. But the scan is not
yet at a high enough resolution to recreate the interneuronal connections, synapses,
and neurotransmitter concentrations that are the key to capturing the individuality
within a human brain.

Our scanning machines today can clearly capture neural features as long as the   22
scanner is very close to the source. Within 30 years, however, we will be able to send
billions of nanobots—blood cell-size scanning machines—through every capillary of
the brain to create a complete noninvasive scan of every neural feature. A shot full of
nanobots will someday allow the most subtle details of our knowledge, skills, and personalities to be copied into a file and stored in a computer.

We can touch and feel this technology today. We just can't make the nanobots   23
small enough, not yet anyway. But miniaturization is another one of those accelerating
technology trends. We're currently shrinking the size of technology by a factor of 5.6
per linear dimension per decade, so it is conservative to say that this scenario will be
feasible in a few decades. The nanobots will capture the locations, interconnections,
and contents of all the nerve cell bodies, axons, dendrites, presynaptic vesicles, neurotransmitter concentrations, and other relevant neural components. Using high-speed
wireless communication, the nanobots will then communicate with each other and
with other computers that are compiling the brain-scan database.

If this seems daunting, another scanning project, that of the human genome, was   24
also considered ambitious when it was first introduced twelve years ago. At the time,
skeptics said the task would take thousands of years, given current scanning capabilities. But the project is finishing on time nevertheless because the speed with which we
can sequence DNA has grown exponentially.

Brain scanning is a prerequisite to Winston and Nellie's virtual life—and appar-   25
ent immortality.

In 2029, we will swallow or inject billions of nanobots into our veins to enter a three-   26
dimensional cyberspace—a virtual reality environment. Already, neural implants are
used to counteract tremors from Parkinson's disease as well as multiple sclerosis. I have a
deaf friend who can now hear what I'm saying because of his cochlear implant. Under
development is a retinal implant that will perform a similar function for blind people,
basically replacing certain visual processing circuits of the brain. Recently, scientists from
Emory University placed a chip in the brain of a paralyzed stroke victim who can now
begin to communicate and control his environment directly from his brain.

But while a surgically introduced neural implant can be placed in only one or at   27
most a few locations, nanobots can take up billions or trillions of positions throughout
the brain. We already have electronic devices called neuron transistors that, noninva-
sively, allow communication between electronics and biological neurons. Using this
technology, developed at Germany's Max Planck Institute of Biochemistry, scientists
were recently able to control from their computer the movements of a living leech.

By taking up positions next to specific neurons, the nanobots will be able to   28
detect and control their activity. For virtual reality applications, the nanobots will take
up positions next to every nerve fiber coming from all five of our senses. When we want
to enter a specific virtual environment, the nanobots will suppress the signals coming
from our real senses and replace them with new, virtual ones. We can then cause our
virtual body to move, speak, and otherwise interact in the virtual environment.

The nanobots would prevent our real bodies from moving; instead, we would have a virtual body in a virtual environment, which need not be the same as our real body.

Like the experiences Winston and Nellie enjoyed, this technology will enable us 29 to have virtual interactions with other people—or simulated people—without requiring any equipment not already in our heads. And virtual reality will not be as crude as what you experience in today's arcade games. It will be as detailed and subtle as real life. So instead of just phoning a friend, you can meet in a virtual Italian bistro or stroll down a virtual tropical beach, and it will all seem real. People will be able to share any type of experience—business, social, romantic, or sexual—regardless of physical proximity.

The trip to virtual reality will be readily reversible, since, with your thoughts 30 alone, you will be able to shut the nanobots off or even direct them to leave your body. Nanobots are programmable in that they can provide virtual reality one minute and a variety of brain extensions the next. They can change their configuration and even alter their software.

While the combination of human-level intelligence in a machine and a com- 31 puter's inherent superiority in the speed, accuracy, and sharing ability of its memory will be formidable—this is not an alien invasion. It is emerging from within our human-machine civilization.

But will virtual life and its promise of immortality obviate the fear of death? Once 32 we upload our knowledge, memories, and insights into a computer, will we have acquired eternal life? First, we must determine what human life is. What is consciousness, anyway? If my thoughts, knowledge, experience, skills, and memories achieve eternal life without me, what does that mean for me?

Consciousness—a seemingly basic tenet of "living"—is perplexing and reflects 33 issues that have been debated since the Platonic dialogues. We assume, for instance, that other humans are conscious, but when we consider the possibility that nonhuman animals may be conscious, our understanding of consciousness is called into question.

The issue of consciousness will become even more contentious in the twenty-first 34 century because nonbiological entities—read: machines—will be able to convince most of us that they are conscious. They will master all the subtle cues that we now use to determine that humans are conscious. And they will get mad if we refute their claims.

Consider this: If we scan me, for example, and record the exact state, level, and 35 position of my every neurotransmitter, synapse, neural connection, and other relevant details, and then reinstantiate this massive database into a neural computer, then who is the real me? If you ask the machine, it will vehemently claim to be the original Ray. Since it will have all of my memories, it will say, "I grew up in Queens, New York, went to college at MIT, stayed in the Boston area, sold a few artificial intelligence companies, walked into a scanner there, and woke up in the machine here. Hey, this technology really works."

But there are strong arguments that this is really a different person. For one thing, 36 old biological Ray (that's me) still exists. I'll still be here in my carbon, cell-based brain. Alas, I (the old biological Ray) will have to sit back and watch the new Ray succeed in endeavors that I could only dream of.

But New Ray will have some strong claims as well. He will say that while he is not 37 absolutely identical to Old Ray, neither is the current version of Old Ray, since the particles making up my biological brain and body are constantly changing. It is the patterns of matter and energy that are semi-permanent (that is, changing only gradually), while the actual material content changes constantly and very quickly.

Viewed in this way, my identity is rather like the pattern that water makes when 38
rushing around a rock in a stream. The pattern remains relatively unchanged for hours,
even years, while the actual material constituting the pattern—the water—is replaced
in milliseconds.

This idea is consistent with the philosophical notion that we should not associate 39
our fundamental identity with a set of particles, but rather with the pattern of matter
and energy that we represent. In other words, if we change our definition of consciousness to value patterns over particles, then New Ray may have an equal claim to be the
continuation of Old Ray.

One could scan my brain and reinstantiate the new Ray while I was sleeping, and 40
I would not necessarily even know about it. If you then came to me, and said, "Good
news, Ray, we've successfully reinstantiated your mind file so we won't be needing your
old body and brain anymore," I may quickly realize the philosophical flaw in the argument that New Ray is a continuation of my consciousness. I may wish New Ray well,
and realize that he shares my pattern, but I would nonetheless conclude that he is not
me, because I'm still here.

Wherever you wind up on this debate, it is worth noting that data do not neces- 41
sarily last forever. The longevity of information depends on its relevance, utility, and
accessibility. If you've ever tried to retrieve information from an obsolete form of data
storage in an old obscure format (e.g., a reel of magnetic tape from a 1970s minicom-
puter), you understand the challenge of keeping software viable. But if we are diligent
in maintaining our mind file, keeping current backups and porting to the latest formats
and mediums, then at least a crucial aspect of who we are will attain a longevity independent of our bodies.

What does this super technological intelligence mean for the future? There will 42
certainly be grave dangers associated with twenty-first-century technologies. Consider
unrestrained nanobot replication. The technology requires billions or trillions of
nanobots in order to be useful, and the most cost-effective way to reach such levels is
through self-replication, essentially the same approach used in the biological world, by
bacteria, for example. So in the same way that biological self-replication gone awry
(i.e., cancer) results in biological destruction, a defect in the mechanism curtailing
nanobot self-replication would endanger all physical entities, biological or otherwise.

Other salient questions are: Who is controlling the nanobots? Who else might 43
the nanobots be talking to?

Organizations, including governments, extremist groups, or even a clever individ- 44
ual, could put trillions of undetectable nanobots in the water or food supply of an
entire population. These "spy" nanobots could then monitor, influence, and even control our thoughts and actions. In addition, authorized nanobots could be influenced by
software viruses and other hacking techniques. Just as technology poses dangers today,
there will be a panoply of risks in the decades ahead.

On a personal level, I am an optimist, and I expect that the creative and construc- 45
tive applications of this technology will persevere, as I believe they do today. But there
will be a valuable and increasingly vocal role for a concerned movement of Luddites—
those anti-technologists inspired by early nineteenth-century weavers who in protest
destroyed machinery that was threatening their livelihood.

Still, I regard the freeing of the human mind from its severe physical limitations 46
as a necessary next step in evolution. Evolution, in my view, is the purpose of life,
meaning that the purpose of life—and of our lives—is to evolve.

What does it mean to evolve? Evolution moves toward greater complexity, elegance,  47
intelligence, beauty, creativity, and love. And God has been called all these things, only
without any limitation, infinite. While evolution never reaches an infinite level, it
advances exponentially, certainly moving in that direction. Technological evolution,
therefore, moves us inexorably closer to becoming like God. And the freeing of our
thinking from the severe limitations of our biological form may be regarded as an
essential spiritual quest.

By the close of the next century, nonbiological intelligence will be ubiquitous.  48
There will be few humans without some form of artificial intelligence, which is growing at a double exponential rate, whereas biological intelligence is basically at a stand-
still. Nonbiological thinking will be trillions of trillions of times more powerful than
that of its biological progenitors, although it will be still of human origin.

Ultimately, however, the earth's technology-creating species will merge with its  49
own computational technology. After all, what is the difference between a human brain
enhanced a trillion-fold by nanobot-based implants and a computer whose design is
based on high resolution scans of the human brain and then extended a trillion-fold?

This may be the ominous, existential question that our own children, certainly  50
our grandchildren, will face. But at this point, there's no turning back. And there's no
slowing down.

## READING FOR CONTENT

1. What point is Kurzweil trying to make in the scenario he presents in paragraphs 2
   through 16?
2. Summarize Kurzweil's description in paragraphs 19 through 24 of the technology that may be used in the future to duplicate an actual human brain within a
   computer.
3. What are nanobots?
4. Summarize Kurzweil's description in paragraphs 27 through 31 of the technology that may be used in the future to provide humans with the ability to slip in
   and out of virtual reality at will.
5. Summarize Kurzweil's explanation in paragraphs 36 through 42 of the ways in
   which an electronic download of a human's brain would be similar to and different from the original.
6. What dangers of nanobot technology does Kurzweil mention in paragraphs 44
   and 45?
7. Explain "evolution" as Kurzweil defines it in paragraphs 47 and 48.

## READING FOR GENRE, ORGANIZATION,
## AND STYLISTIC FEATURES

1. Explain Kurzweil's opening strategy. Does it work?
2. What is the organizational plan for Kurzweil's article?
3. Is the vocabulary Kurzweil uses to describe computer technology appropriate for
   an audience that does not have special expertise? Use examples to explain your
   answer.

## READING FOR RHETORICAL CONTEXT

1. Why do you think the editors of *Psychology Today* were interested in printing Kurzweil's article?
2. How does Kurzweil attempt to lend authority to his predictions?
3. How does Kurzweil want his readers to feel about the concept of downloading human intelligence? Does he achieve that effect? Why, or why not?
4. Does Kurzweil address the views of those whose predictions for the future of human/machine interaction differ from his own?

## WRITING ASSIGNMENTS

1. Write a detailed 750-word summary of Kurzweil's predictions for the future.
2. Does Kurzweil's description of what he terms a "human-machine civilization" appeal to you? Write a 1,000-word essay of personal response in answer to that question. Include a brief explanation of the human-machine civilization that Kurzweil envisions.
3. Write a 1,000-word scenario set in the future that explores the consequences of the technology that Kurzweil predicts will be developed.

■ ■ ■ ■ ■ ■ ■ ■ ■ ■ ■ ■

# Isolated by the Internet

## *Clifford Stoll*

*Clifford Stoll is an astronomer, an expert on computer security, and the author of* The Cuckoo's Egg *and* Silicon Snake Oil: Second Thoughts about the Information Highway. *The article that follows is taken from Stoll's book* High Tech Heretic.

## PREREADING

Think of the ways you use the Internet to contact other people. Do you believe technology improves the quality of your social interactions? Freewrite for ten minutes in response to that question.

For all my grinching about the soul-deadening effects of the Internet, most Internet   1
users speak positively about it. One friend tells how she found a support group for an obscure medical condition. Another tells me that his modem provides an escape from a dull world, providing a rich mixture of fantasy and role playing. One soon-to-be-married

couple writes how they met through postings to a Usenet news group. And one computer programmer confesses that although she's extremely shy in person, in her electronic chat room, she becomes a feisty, enchanting contessa. Meanwhile, wired families keep in touch via email, and new friendships blossom thanks to online special interest groups. Isolated hobbyists sign onto Web sites to exchange information and help each other. Surely the electronic virtual community is a positive social development.

Well, not necessarily. According to Carnegie Mellon University psychologists 2 Robert Kraut and Vicki Lundmark, there are serious negative long-term social effects, ranging from depression to loneliness. The result of a concerted research effort, their findings were surprising, since this research was funded by high-tech firms like AT&T, Apple Computer, Lotus, Intel, and Hewlett-Packard. Their report, "The Internet Paradox— A Social Technology That Reduces Social Involvement and Psychological Well-Being?" appeared in the September 1998 issue of the *American Psychologist*.

Kraut and Lundmark had asked how using the Internet affects connections 3 between people. They looked at both the extent and the depth of human links, and tried to understand how the Internet affected these connections. Deep social ties are relationships with frequent contact, deep feelings of involvement, and broad content. Weak ties have superficial and easily broken bonds, infrequent contact, and narrow focus. Weak ties link us to information and social resources outside our close local groups. But it's the strong social ties that buffer us from stress and lead to better social interactions.

Hardly surprising that strong personal ties come about when you're in close prox- 4 imity to someone . . . it's been that way for millennia. Suddenly, along comes the Internet, reducing the importance of distance and letting you develop new relationships through chat rooms, email, news groups, and Web pages.

To learn about the social effects of the Internet, Kraut and Lundmark followed 5 ninety-six families of various backgrounds for two years. They provided computers, software, modems, accounts, and training; in all, some 256 individuals entered the study, and two thirds of them completed it. The software allowed full Internet use but recorded how much time was spent in various online activities. Each participant answered questionnaires before they went online, after a year, and after two years of Internet use.

The researchers measured stress, loneliness, and depression using standardized 6 psychological tests like the UCLA Loneliness Scale and the Center for Epidemiologic Studies Depression Scale. Participants would agree or disagree with statements like "I feel everything I do is an effort," "I enjoy life," "I can find companionship when I want it," "There is someone I could turn to for advice about changing my job or finding a new one." Kraut and Lundmark then measured each participant's social circle and distant social network during the two-year study.

After following the study group, the psychologists found an average increase in 7 depression by about 1 percent for every hour spent online per week. Online activity resulted in increased loneliness as well. On the average, subjects began with sixty-six members in their nearby social circle. For every hour each week spent online, this group shrank by about 4 percent.

Depression. Loneliness. Loss of close friendships. This is the medium that we're 8 promoting to expand our global community?

It's true that many online relationships developed as well, but most represented 9 weak social ties rather than deep ones: a woman who exchanged mittens with a stranger, a man who exchanged jokes with a colleague he met over a tourist Web site.

A few friendships blossomed—one teenager met his prom date online—but these were rarities. And even though such friendships were welcomed when they happened, there was an overall decline in real-world interaction with family and friends.

The overwhelming majority of online friendships simply aren't deep. Online friends can't be depended on for help with tangible favors: small loans, baby-sitting, help with shopping, or advice about jobs and careers. One participant "appreciated the email correspondence she had with her college-aged daughter, yet noted that when her daughter was homesick or depressed, she reverted to telephone calls to provide support."

Kraut and Lundmark concluded that "greater use of the Internet was associated with small but statistically significant declines in social involvement as measured by communication within the family and the size of people's local social networks, and with increases in loneliness and depression. Other effects on the size of the distant social circle, social support, and stress did not reach standard significance levels but were consistently negative." Paradoxically, the Internet is a social technology used for communication, yet it results in declining social involvement and psychological well-being.

What's important to remember is that their research wasn't a collection of casual claims, but "an extremely careful scientific study," said Tora Bikson, a senior scientist at Rand Corporation. "It's not a result that's easily ignored." Despite a decade of concerns, it's the first time that professional psychologists have done such a longitudinal study.

"We were shocked by the findings, because they are counterintuitive to what we know about how socially the Internet is being used," said Dr. Kraut, who hypothesized that Internet use is "building shallow relationships, leading to an overall decline in feeling of connection to other people."

Not surprisingly, computer makers scoffed: One Intel psychologist replied that "This is not about the technology, per se; it's about how it is used. It points to the need for considering social factors in terms of how you design applications and services for technology." In other words, technology is just a neutral tool and social technologists will solve this problem. Uh, right.

According to computer scientists James Katz and Philip Aspden, there's no reason to be pessimistic about the social effects of Internet use. They telephoned six hundred Internet users to survey the social effects of computer use. Their 1997 report, "A Nation of Strangers," argues that the Internet augments existing communities. It's a medium for creating friendships and to stay in touch with family members. They cheerily suggest that some two million new meetings have taken place thanks to the Internet. Katz and Aspden happily conclude that "The Internet is creating a nation richer in friendships and social relationships."

Unfortunately, Katz and Aspden used a biased system of self-reporting, a phone survey in which those called judged themselves on whether they had gained or lost friends. Hardly anyone's going to tell a stranger on the phone, "Oh, I've lost friends because I spend too much time online." Also, while Katz and Aspden tallied all social ties made over the Internet, they didn't probe into the possible loss of strong local ties. Since they didn't ask about the depth, nature, or quality of online "friendships," naturally their phone survey delivered a happily optimistic conclusion.

Psychologists point out that the best predictor of psychological troubles is a lack of close social contacts. There's a surprisingly close correlation between social isolation and such problems as schizophrenia and depression. Long hours spent online undercut our local social support networks; this isolation promotes psychological troubles.

Kraut and Lundmark's work points to a serious problem looming for wired 18
generations: Will the proliferation of shallow, distant social ties make up for the loss of
close local links?

Stanford psychology professor Philip Zimbardo has part of the answer. Since the 19
mid-1970s, he's studied the psychology of shyness. In 1978, Dr. Zimbardo found that
some 40 percent of undergraduates said, "I think of myself as shy." By 1988, this number
had reached 45 percent. And by 1995, some 50 percent of undergrads saw themselves as
shy; some research suggests that 60 percent of the population now suffers from shyness.

Why this epidemic of shyness? At a 1997 conference, Professor Zimbardo 20
pointed to several reasons, many connected to technology. Television and computing
make us more passive . . . and passivity feeds into shyness. Now that many family members have separate televisions, watching TV is no longer a communal experience, but
rather an isolated, nonsocial nonencounter. One report suggested that parents, busy
from work which they've brought home, spend only six to eight minutes a day talking
with their children.

"The electronic revolution of emails and faxes means the medium has finally 21
become the message," said Professor Zimbardo. "With more virtual reality overtaking
real reality, we're losing ordinary social skills, and common social situations are becoming more awkward."

Yep, for better or worse, the only way to learn how to get along with others is to 22
spend plenty of time interacting with people. Email, telephones, and faxes all prevent
us from learning basic skills of dealing with people face to face. These electronic inter-
mediaries dull our abilities to read each other's gestures and facial expressions, to
express our feelings, to strike up conversations with strangers, to craft stories, to tell
jokes.* Those weaned on computer communications won't learn basic social rules of
conversation. How to interrupt. How to share time with another. How to speak to an
audience. When to be quiet.

In the past, shyness has been passed off as a trivial problem that children grow out 23
of. "Although we think of shy people as passive and easily manipulated, at the same
time there is a level of resentment, rage, and hostility," Zimbardo warned. I wonder if
that explains some of the anger pervading the anonymous chat rooms and postings to
Usenet news groups.

The notion that people can become addicted to the Internet was scoffed at by 24
professional psychologists. It was considered to be a joke in the same way that alcoholism, compulsive gambling, and obsessive shopping were thought laughable in the
1950s. After all, you can just stop. Only recently have a few psychologists asked questions about the seductive nature of the Internet and the type of person likely to become
hooked. They're finding that the clinical definitions of established addictions fit the
profiles of plenty of people who spend their lives online.

Psychologist Kimberly Young was among the first to investigate clinical cases of 25
Internet addiction. She tells of a Pennsylvania college student she calls Steve who's
online sixty to seventy hours a week. Steve's a wizard in the Multi-User Dungeons,
Internet fantasy games best known as MUDs.

---

*Once, people told stories—you'd pay attention to the homegrown comedian who knew how to tell a joke. Joke
telling meant timing, inflection, and expression. Now, thanks to jokes passed by email and Internet forums,
stale comedy routines constantly circulate online. People who can't tell jokes won't shut their mouths.

"MUDs are like a religion to me, and I'm a god there. I'm respected by all the  26
other MUDders. . . . Even when I'm not playing, I wonder if there will be more new-
bies for me to kill that night or which other guys will be playing. I am in control of my
character and my destiny in this world. My character is a legend and I identify with
him." Yet when Steve's not online, he's held back by low self-esteem. Shy and awkward
around people, he's uncomfortable around women and believes he doesn't fit in at
school. "When I'm playing the MUDs, I'm not feeling lonely or mopey. I'm not thinking about my problems. . . . I want to stay on the MUDs as long as I possibly can."

Where once Steve would have to work within the real world and slowly learn how  27
to deal with people, today he is able to turn to the Internet for solace and escape.

Compounding the withdrawal of individuals from their close social circle, tech-  28
nology also blurs the line between work and play. Thanks to telephones, pagers, and
cell phones, work seeps into our private time, forcing shallow, impersonal communication into quiet hours and intimate moments. Email reaches our desktops and laptops;
even our wristwatches have alarms and electronic reminders. At home, on the road, or
on the golf course, we can't escape an electronic bombardment.

Walking in Yosemite Park, I met a hiker with all the latest paraphernalia hanging  29
from his belt: pager, GPS locator, and electronic altimeter. Amid the quiet of the sugar
pines, his cell phone squawked and I overheard one side of his conversation with some
New York advertising firm: "Tell both clients that I won't be able to make Monday's
meeting," he told an unseen secretary. "I'll get them a proposal when I'm over this cold."

Here's a guy who's brought the stress of his office into the tranquillity of the forest.  30
He's never lost and always in reach. At the same time, he's utterly lost and out of touch.*

Office work tags along with homes equipped with fax machines. On the street,  31
drivers and pedestrians dodge each other while talking over cell phones. In cafes, nerds
type on laptops. Office managers bring their work home on floppy disks. The telecom-
muter merely represents one milestone in the blurring of home and office.

As work sneaks into playtime, play just isn't as much fun. Used to be that only stu-  32
dents brought classwork home; increasingly, everyone has homework, everyone's on
call. Our home provides little refuge from the stress of the outside world.

This isn't just the fault of technology—so many people want high-tech careers  33
and professions that they willingly latch onto jobs which demand twenty-four-hour
availability. And so we find the Webmaster who's on call all night, just in case the file
server crashes. The high school teacher who answers students' email all evening. The
gardener who polishes her Web site when she comes home. For them, home is simply
an extension of their workplace.

For children, home computers, instructional videotapes, and educational televi-  34
sion extend the school into their home. Forget the innocence of childhood: Our kids
are increasingly programmed as academic automatons.

The Internet is widely promoted as an aid for speed, profit, productivity, and effi-  35
ciency. These business goals simply aren't the aims of a home. Maybe there's such a
thing as kitchen productivity, but efficiency doesn't make much sense in my living
room, and exactly who considers profits in their bedroom?

---

*In response to the noise and interruptions, one Japanese symphony hall has installed special transmitters to
disable all cell phones and pagers in the audience. I hadn't realized it before, but one of the joys of speleology
is that none of my caving partners can be reached a hundred feet under the ground.

At home, our goals might include tranquillity, reflection, and warmth . . . hardly 36 the image brought up by the phrase "home computing." With houses increasingly wired for communications, electronic messages invade our home life. It's not just the telemarketers who disrupt dinner with sales and surveys. Rather, our private space is increasingly available to the outside world, whether it's a call from the boss, tonight's business news on the TV, or an email message about a business meeting.

Nor are the goals of business those of a school. Productivity doesn't map onto a 37 sixth-grade class in pre-algebra. It's absurd to speak of increasing the efficiency of an instructor teaching a third-grade student how salt melts ice. Will a 200-MHz computer educate a child twice as fast as a 100-MHz computer?

The way we communicate constrains how we interact. Computer networks pro- 38 vide chat rooms in which emotions must fit into eighty columns of ASCII text, punctuated by smiley faces. No longer need my correspondent begin a letter with a gratuitous "Dear Cliff." Rather, the header of the email describes recipient, sender, and subject. Any pretense of politeness is erased by the cold efficiency of the medium.

One survey reports that office workers typically receive 190 messages per day. Yet 39 computer network promoters tell us that we need ever faster links and constantly more connectivity. Will I get more work done today if I receive three hundred messages rather than two hundred?

Instead of encouraging me to concentrate on a single job, the constant stream of 40 electronic messages makes me constantly flip from one task to another. Computers are great at doing this, but people aren't. Promoters of electronic work-places may speak glowingly of living asynchronous lives, but most of my work requires concentration, thinking, and organization . . . hardly promoted by a river of electronic messages.

Getting a high-speed link to the Internet causes Web pages to load faster. At first 41 glance, you'd think that this would reduce the amount of time that students would spend online. Hardly. As connection speeds increase, college students spend more time surfing the Web and less time writing, studying, or whatever they don't want to do. Same's true for office workers—an Internet link is a license to goof off.

As Robert Kraut and Vicki Lundmark's study reveals, email enhances distant 42 communications while degrading local interactions. It perniciously gives us the illusion of making friends with faraway strangers while taking our attention away from our friends, family, and neighbors.

In the past, people in trouble relied on close, nearby friends for support. Today, 43 plenty of people turn to online support groups or chat rooms. Professor Mary Baker of Stanford reports that while she was expecting, she exchanged five email messages a day with a friend across the country . . . a woman she'd never met. Yet email pen pals can hardly provide the social support of a nearby friend or family member—if Professor Baker had to rush to the hospital, she could hardly get a ride from her email friend.

Today, it's natural enough to look to the Internet for a community, since our real 44 neighborhoods have been relentlessly undercut by television, automobiles, and urban renewal. Yet as more and more people turn to the Internet, our real communities receive even less human investment.

For the effect of instant electronic communications is to isolate us from our col- 45 leagues next door. I met two computer jocks at a television station who spent their free time playing an Internet game with each other. Even though they sat five feet from each other, they'd communicate via email and rarely so much as glanced at each other.

Professor Zimbardo tells me that sometimes he sticks his head into the office of a 46
friend down the hall, with nothing more important than to say, "Hi!" "On several occasions, my greeting has been received with the shock of 'What's so important that you're
invading my personal space? Why are you interrupting my productivity?'"

The price of computing at home—as in school and at work—is far more than the 47
cost of the hardware. The opportunity cost is our time, and it is taken out of our individual
lives and our very real neighborhoods. The time you spend behind the monitor could be
spent facing another person across a table or across a tennis court. Disguised as efficiency
machines, digital time bandits steal our lives and undermine our communities.

## READING FOR CONTENT

1. In paragraphs 3 through 13, Stoll describes research on Internet communication
   that was conducted by Kraut and Lundmark. Explain briefly the results of their
   research.
2. In paragraph 15, Stoll describes research on Internet communication that was
   conducted by Katz and Aspden. Explain briefly the results of their research.
3. Why does Stoll believe that Katz and Aspden's research is problematic?
4. In paragraphs 19 through 24, Stoll describes research on social skills that was
   conducted by Philip Zimbardo. Explain briefly the results of his research.
5. In paragraphs 25 through 27, Stoll describes research on Internet addiction that
   was conducted by Kimberly Young. Explain briefly the results of her research.
6. What are the functions of the "pager, GPS locator, and electronic altimeter" that
   Stoll mentions in paragraph 29?
7. In what ways does Stoll believe that electronic communication devices intrude
   on home life?
8. In what ways does Stoll believe that access to electronic messages affects productivity in the workplace?

## READING FOR GENRE, ORGANIZATION, AND STYLISTIC FEATURES

1. Describe Stoll's opening strategy.
2. Describe Stoll's style of writing. Do you find Stoll's style appealing or irritating?
   Explain your answer.
3. Comment on Stoll's use of examples. Does he need to use as many examples as
   he does? Are his examples effective?

## READING FOR RHETORICAL CONTEXT

1. Write a one- or two-sentence summary of Stoll's thesis.
2. What assumptions does Stoll make about his audience?
3. What is the primary support that Stoll provides for his thesis?
4. Where does Stoll summarize and respond to the viewpoints of his opponents?
   Does he respond effectively to his opponents?

# WRITING ASSIGNMENTS

1. Write a 1,000-word argument that draws support from your own experience with electronic communication to either defend or attack Stoll's thesis.

2. In a 750-word essay, explain and respond to Stoll's closing words: "The time you spend behind the monitor could be spent facing another person across a table or across a tennis court. Disguised as efficiency machines, digital time bandits steal our lives and undermine our community."

3. Electronic communication via the Internet increases dramatically the opportunities for human-to-human contact and improves the social lives of millions. Attack or defend this statement in a 750-word essay that draws on Stoll's article.

■ ■ ■ ■ ■ ■ ■ ■ ■ ■ ■ ■

# Why the Future Doesn't Need Us

## *Bill Joy*

*Bill Joy (William Nelson Joy) is coauthor of the* Berkeley UNIX *and* The Java Language Specification. *In 1982 he became the cofounder and Chief Scientist of Sun Microsystems. In 2003 he left that company and founded a capital venture firm, HighBar Ventures.*

## PREREADING

When a scientist responsible for many breakthrough developments in information technology wrote this article about the risks to humanity presented by genetic engineering, nanotechnology, and robotics, people took notice. Can you think of other historical examples in which scientists issued warnings about the negative consequences of technologies that they helped to develop? Read the first and last paragraphs of this article and freewrite about its informal tone. Is Joy issuing a scientific pronouncement or is he offering a personal commentary on the topic?

From the moment I became involved in the creation of new technologies, their ethical dimensions have concerned me, but it was only in the autumn of 1998 that I became anxiously aware of how great are the dangers facing us in the 21st century. I can date the onset of my unease to the day I met Ray Kurzweil, the deservedly famous inventor of the first reading machine for the blind and many other amazing things.

Ray and I were both speakers at George Glider's Telecosm conference, and I encountered him by chance in the bar of the hotel after both our sessions were over. I was sitting with John Searie, a Berkeley philosopher who studies consciousness. While we

Bill Joy, "Why the Future Doesn't Need Us," *Wired* issue 8.04, April 2000. Copyright Bill Joy. Originally published in *Wired*.

were talking, Ray approached and a conversation began, the subject of which haunts me to this day.

I had missed Ray's talk and the subsequent panel that Ray and John had been on,    3 and they now picked right up where they'd left off, with Ray saying that the rate of improvement of technology was going to accelerate and that we were going to become robots or fuse with robots or something like that, and John countering that this couldn't happen, because the robots couldn't be conscious.

While I had heard such talk before, I had always felt sentient robots were in the    4 realm of science fiction. But now, from someone I respected, I was hearing a strong argument that they were a near-term possibility. I was taken aback, especially given Ray's proven ability to imagine and create the future. I already knew that new technologies like genetic engineering and nanotechnology were giving us the power to remake the world, but a realistic and imminent scenario for intelligent robots surprised me.

It's easy to get jaded about such breakthroughs. We hear in the news almost every    5 day of some kind of technological or scientific advance. Yet this was no ordinary prediction. In the hotel bar, Ray gave me a partial preprint of his then-forthcoming book *The Age of Spiritual Machines*, which outlined a utopia he foresaw—one in which humans gained near immortality by becoming one with robotic technology. On reading it, my sense of unease only intensified; I felt sure he had to be understating the dangers, understating the probability of a bad outcome along this path.

I found myself most troubled by a passage detailing a *dys*topian scenario:    6

## The New Luddite Challenge

First let us postulate that the computer scientists succeed in developing intelligent machines that can do all things better than human beings can do them. In that case presumably all work will be done by vast, highly organized systems of machines and no human effort will be necessary. Either of two cases might occur. The machines might be permitted to make all of their own decisions without human oversight, or else human control over the machines might be retained.

If the machines are permitted to make all their own decisions, we can't make    7 any conjectures as to the results, because it is impossible to guess how such machines might behave. We only point out that the fate of the human race would be at the mercy of the machines. It might be argued that the human race would never be foolish enough to hand over all the power to the machines. But we are suggesting neither that the human race would voluntarily turn power over to the machines nor that the machines would willfully seize power. What we do suggest is that the human race might easily permit itself to drift into a position of such dependence on the machines that it would have no practical choice but to accept all of the machines' decisions. As society and the problems that face it become more and more complex and machines become more and more intelligent, people will let machines make more of their decisions for them, simply because machine-made decisions will bring better results than man-made ones. Eventually a stage may be reached at which the decisions necessary to keep the system running will be so complex that human beings will be incapable of making them intelligently. At that stage the machines will be in effective control. People won't be able to just turn the machines off, because they will be so dependent on them that turning them off would amount to suicide.

On the other hand it is possible that human control over the machines may be      8
retained. In that case the average man may have control over certain private machines
of his own, such as his car or his personal computer, but control over large systems of
machines will be in the hands of a tiny elite—just as it is today, but with two differences.
Due to improved techniques the elite will have greater control over the masses; and
because human work will no longer be necessary the masses will be superfluous, a useless burden on the system. If the elite is ruthless they may simply decide to exterminate
the mass of humanity. If they are humane they may use propaganda or other psychological or biological techniques to reduce the birth rate until the mass of humanity
becomes extinct, leaving the world to the elite. Or, if the elite consists of soft-hearted
liberals, they may decide to play the role of good shepherds to the rest of the human
race. They will see to it that everyone's physical needs are satisfied, that all children are
raised under psychologically hygienic conditions, that everyone has a wholesome hobby
to keep him busy, and that anyone who may become dissatisfied undergoes "treatment"
to cure his "problem." Of course, life will be so purposeless that people will have to be
biologically or psychologically engineered either to remove their need for the power
process or make them "sublimate" their drive for power into some harmless hobby.
These engineered human beings may be happy in such a society, but they will most
certainly not be free. They will have been reduced to the status of domestic animals.[1]

In the book, you don't discover until you turn the page that the author of this pas-      9
sage is Theodore Kaczynski—the Unabomber. I am no apologist for Kaczynski. His
bombs killed three people during a 17-year terror campaign and wounded many others.
One of his bombs gravely injured my friend David Gelemter, one of the most brilliant
and visionary computer scientists of our time. Like many of my colleagues, I felt that I
could easily have been the Unabomber's next target.

Kaczynski's actions were murderous and, in my view, criminally insane. He is      10
clearly a Luddite, but simply saying this does not dismiss his argument; as difficult as it
is for me to acknowledge, I saw some merit in the reasoning in this single passage. I felt
compelled to confront it.

Kaczynski's dystopian vision describes unintended consequences, a well-known      11
problem with the design and use of technology, and one that is clearly related to
Murphy's law—"Anything that can go wrong, will." (Actually, this is Finagle's law,
which in itself shows that Finagle was right.) Our overuse of antibiotics has led to what
may be the biggest such problem so far: the emergence of antibiotic-resistant and much
more dangerous bacteria. Similar things happened when attempts to eliminate malarial
mosquitoes using DDT caused them to acquire DDT resistance; malarial parasites
likewise acquired multi-drug-resistant genes.[2]

The cause of many such surprises seems clear: The systems involved are com-      12
plex, involving interaction among and feedback between many parts. Any changes to
such a system will cascade in ways that are difficult to predict; this is especially true
when human actions are involved.

. . .

While talking and thinking about Kurzwell, Kaczynski, and Moravec, I suddenly remem-      13
bered a novel I had read almost 20 years ago—*The White Plague*, by Frank Herbert—in
which a molecular biologist is driven insane by the senseless murder of his family. To seek
revenge he constructs and disseminates a new and highly contagious plague that kills

widely but selectively. (We're lucky Kaczynski was a mathematician, not a molecular biologist.) I was also reminded of the Borg of *Star Trek*, a hive of partly biological, partly robotic creatures with a strong destructive streak. Borg-like disasters are a staple of science fiction, so why hadn't I been more concerned about such robotic dystopias earlier? Why weren't other people more concerned about these nightmarish scenarios?

Part of the answer certainly lies in our attitude toward the new—in our bias 14 toward instant familiarity and unquestioning acceptance. Accustomed to living with almost routine scientific breakthroughs, we have yet to come to terms with the fact that the most compelling 21st-century technologies—robotics, genetic engineering, and nanotechnology—pose a different threat than the technologies that have come before. Specifically, robots, engineered organisms, and nanobots share a dangerous amplifying factor: They can self-replicate. A bomb is blown up only once—but one bot can become many, and quickly get out of control.

Much of my work over the past 25 years has been on computer networking, 15 where the sending and receiving of messages creates the opportunity for out-of-control replication. But while replication in a computer or a computer network can be a nuisance, at worst it disables a machine or takes down a network or network service. Uncontrolled self-replication in these newer technologies runs a much greater risk: a risk of substantial damage in the physical world.

Each of these technologies also offers untold promise: The vision of near immor- 16 tality that Kurzwell sees in his robot dreams drives us forward; genetic engineering may soon provide treatments, if not outright cures, for most diseases; and nanotechnology and nanomedicine can address yet more ills. Together they could significantly extend our average life span and improve the quality of our lives. Yet, with each of these technologies, a sequence of small, individually sensible advances leads to an accumulation of great power and, concomitantly, great danger.

What was different in the 20th century? Certainly, the technologies underlying 17 the weapons of mass destruction (WMD)—nuclear, biological, and chemical (NBC)— were powerful, and the weapons an enormous threat. But building nuclear weapons required, at least for a time, access to both rare—indeed, effectively unavailable—raw materials and highly protected information; biological and chemical weapons programs also tended to require large-scale activities.

The 21st-century technologies—genetics, nanotechnology, and robotics 18 (GNR)—are so powerful that they can spawn whole new classes of accidents and abuses. Most dangerously, for the first time, these accidents and abuses are widely within the reach of individuals or small groups. They will not require large facilities or rare raw materials. Knowledge alone will enable the use of them.

Thus we have the possibility not just of weapons of mass destruction but of 19 knowledge-enabled mass destruction (KMD), this destructiveness hugely amplified by the power of self-replication.

I think it is no exaggeration to say we are on the cusp of the further perfection of 20 extreme evil, an evil whose possibility spreads well beyond that which weapons of mass destruction bequeathed to the nation-states, on to a surprising and terrible empowerment of extreme individuals.

. . .

In designing software and microprocessors, I have never had the feeling that I was design- 21 ing an intelligent machine. The software and hardware is so fragile and the capabilities of the machine to "think" so dearly absent that, even as a possibility, this has always seemed very far in the future.

But now, with the prospect of human-level computing power in about 30 years, a 22 new idea suggests itself: that I may be working to create tools which will enable the construction of the technology that may replace our species. How do I feel about this? Very uncomfortable. Having struggled my entire career to build reliable software systems, it seems to me more than likely that this future will not work out as well as some people may imagine. My personal experience suggests we tend to overestimate our design abilities.

Given the incredible power of these new technologies, shouldn't we be asking how 23 we can best coexist with them? And if our own extinction is a likely, or even possible, outcome of our technological development, shouldn't we proceed with great caution?

The dream of robotics is, first, that intelligent machines can do our work for us, 24 allowing us lives of leisure, restoring us to Eden. Yet in his history of such ideas, *Darwin Among the Machines*, George Dyson warns: "In the game of life and evolution there are three players at the table: human beings, nature, and machines. I am firmly on the side of nature. But nature, I suspect, is on the side of the machines." As we have seen, Moravec agrees, believing we may well not survive the encounter with the superior robot species.

How soon could such an intelligent robot be built? The coming advances in 25 computing power seem to make it possible by 2030. And once an intelligent robot exists, it is only a small step to a robot species—to an intelligent robot that can make evolved copies of itself.

A second dream of robotics is that we will gradually replace ourselves with our 26 robotic technology, achieving near immortality by downloading our consciousnesses; it is this process that Danny Hillis thinks we will gradually get used to and that Ray Kurzwell elegantly details in *The Age of Spiritual Machines*. (We are beginning to see intimations of this in the implantation of computer devices into the human body, as illustrated on the cover of *Wired* 8.02.)

But if we are downloaded into our technology, what are the chances that we will 27 thereafter be ourselves or even human? It seems to me far more likely that a robotic existence would not be like a human one in any sense that we understand, that the robots would in no sense be our children, that on this path our humanity may well be lost.

Genetic engineering promises to revolutionize agriculture by increasing crop 28 yields while reducing the use of pesticides; to create tens of thousands of novel species of bacteria, plants, viruses, and animals; to replace reproduction, or supplement it, with cloning; to create cures for many diseases, increasing our life span and our quality of life; and much, much more. We now know with certainty that these profound changes in the biological sciences are imminent and will challenge all our notions of what life is.

Technologies such as human cloning have in particular raised our awareness of 29 the profound ethical and moral issues we face. If, for example, we were to reengineer ourselves into several separate and unequal species using the power of genetic engineering, then we would threaten the notion of equality that is the very cornerstone of our democracy.

Given the incredible power of genetic engineering, it's no surprise that there are 30 significant safety issues in its use. My friend Amory Lovins recently cowrote, along with Hunter Lovins, an editorial that provides an ecological view of some of these dangers. Among their concerns: that "the new botany aligns the development of plants with their economic, not evolutionary, success." Amory's long career has been focused on energy and resource efficiency by taking a whole-system view of human-made systems;

such a whole-system view often finds simple, smart solutions to otherwise seemingly difficult problems, and is usefully applied here as well.

After reading the Lovins' editorial, I saw an op-ed by Gregg Easterbrook in *The* 31 *New York Times* (November 19, 1999) about genetically engineered crops, under the headline: "Food for the Future: Someday, rice will have built-in vitamin A. Unless the Luddites win."

Are Amory and Hunter Lovins Luddites? Certainly not. I believe we all would agree 32 that golden rice, with its built-in vitamin A, is probably a good thing, if developed with proper care and respect for the likely dangers in moving genes across species boundaries.

Awareness of the dangers inherent in genetic engineering is beginning to grow, as 33 reflected in the Lovins' editorial. The general public is aware of, and uneasy about, genetically modified foods, and seems to be rejecting the notion that such foods should be permitted to be unlabeled.

But genetic engineering technology is already very far along. As the Lovins note, 34 the USDA has already approved about 50 genetically engineered crops for unlimited release; more than half of the world's soybeans and a third of its corn now contain genes spliced in from other forms of life.

While there are many important issues here, my own major concern with genetic 35 engineering is narrower: that it gives the power—whether militarily, accidentally, or in a deliberate terrorist act—to create a White Plague.

The many wonders of nanotechnology were first imagined by the Nobel-laureate 36 physicist Richard Feynman in a speech he gave in 1959, subsequently published under the title "There's Plenty of Room at the Bottom." The book that made a big impression on me, in the mid '80s, was Eric Drexler's *Engines of Creation*, in which he described beautifully how manipulation of matter at the atomic level could create a utopian future of abundance, where just about everything could be made cheaply, and almost any imaginable disease or physical problem could be solved using nanotechnology and artificial intelligences.

A subsequent book, *Unbounding the Future: The Nanotechnology Revolution*, 37 which Drexler cowrote, imagines some of the changes that might take place in a world where we had molecular-level "assemblers." Assemblers could make possible incredibly low-cost solar power, cures for cancer and the common cold by augmentation of the human immune system, essentially complete cleanup of the environment, incredibly inexpensive pocket supercomputers—in fact, any product would be manufacturable by assemblers at a cost no greater than that of wood—spaceflight more accessible than transoceanic travel today, and restoration of extinct species.

I remember feeling good about nanotechnology after reading *Engines of Cre-* 38 *ation*. As a technologist, it gave me a sense of calm—that is, nanotechnology showed us that incredible progress was possible, and indeed perhaps inevitable. If nanotechnology was our future, then I didn't feel pressed to solve so many problems in the present. I would get to Drexler's utopian future in due time; I might as well enjoy life more in the here and now. It didn't make sense, given his vision, to stay up all night, all the time.

Drexler's vision also led to a lot of good fun. I would occasionally get to describe 39 the wonders of nanotechnology to others who had not heard of it. After teasing them with all the things Drexler described I would give a homework assignment of my own: "Use nanotechnology to create a vampire; for extra credit create an antidote."

With these wonders came clear dangers, of which I was acutely aware. As I said at a 40 nanotechnology conference in 1989, "We can't simply do our science and not worry about these ethical issues."[3] But my subsequent conversations with physicists convinced me that nanotechnology might not even work—or, at least, it wouldn't work anytime soon. Shortly thereafter I moved to Colorado, to a skunk works I had set up, and the focus of my work shifted to software for the Internet, specifically on ideas that became Java and Jini.

Then, last summer, Brosl Hasslacher told me that nanoscale molecular electron- 41 ics was now practical. This was *new* news, at least to me, and I think to many people— and it radically changed my opinion about nanotechnology. It sent me back to *Engines of Creation*. Rereading Drexler's work after more than 10 years, I was dismayed to realize how little I had remembered of its lengthy section called "Dangers and Hopes," including a discussion of how nanotechnologies can become "engines of destruction." Indeed, in my rereading of this cautionary material today, I am struck by how naive some of Drexler's safeguard proposals seem, and how much greater I judge the dangers to be now than even he seemed to then. (Having anticipated and described many technical and political problems with nanotechnology, Drexler started the Foresight Institute in the late 1980s "to help prepare society for anticipated advanced technologies"—most important, nanotechnology.)

The enabling breakthrough to assemblers seems quite likely within the next 20 42 years. Molecular electronics—the new subfield of nanotechnology where individual molecules are circuit elements—should mature quickly and become enormously lucrative within this decade, causing a large incremental investment in all nanotechnologies.

Unfortunately, as with nuclear technology, it is far easier to create destructive 43 uses for nanotechnology than constructive ones. Nanotechnology has clear military and terrorist uses, and you need not be suicidal to release a massively destructive nanotechnological device—such devices can be built to be selectively destructive, affecting, for example, only a certain geographical area or a group of people who are genetically distinct.

An immediate consequence of the Faustian bargain in obtaining the great power 44 of nanotechnology is that we run a grave risk—the risk that we might destroy the biosphere on which all life depends.

As Drexler explained: 45

"Plants" with "leaves" no more efficient than today's solar cells could out-compete real plants, crowding the biosphere with an inedible foliage. Tough omnivorous "bacteria" could out-compete real bacteria: They could spread like blowing pollen, replicate swiftly, and reduce the biosphere to dust in a matter of days. Dangerous replicators could easily be too tough, small, and rapidly spreading to stop—at least if we make no preparation. We have trouble enough controlling viruses and fruit flies.

Among the cognoscenti of nanotechnology, this threat has become known as the 46 "gray goo problem." Though masses of uncontrolled replicators need not be gray or gooey, the term "gray goo" emphasizes that replicators able to obliterate life might be less inspiring than a single species of crabgrass. They might be superior in an evolutionary sense, but this need not make them valuable.

The gray goo threat makes one thing perfectly clear: We cannot afford certain 47 kinds of accidents with replicating assemblers.

Gray goo would surely be a depressing ending to our human adventure on Earth, 48 far worse than mere fire or ice, and one that could stem from a simple laboratory accident.[4] Oops.

It is most of all the power of destructive self-replication in genetics, nanotechnol- 49 ogy, and robotics (GNR) that should give us pause. Self-replication is the modus operandi of genetic engineering, which uses the machinery of the cell to replicate its designs, and the prime danger underlying gray goo in nanotechnology. Stories of run-amok robots like the Borg, replicating or mutating to escape from the ethical constraints imposed on them by their creators, are well established in our science fiction books and movies. It is even possible that self-replication may be more fundamental than we thought, and hence harder—or even impossible—to control. A recent article by Stuart Kauffman in *Nature* titled "Self-Replication: Even Peptides Do It" discusses the discovery that a 32-amino-acid peptide can "autocatalyse its own synthesis." We don't know how widespread this ability is, but Kauffman notes that it may hint at "a route to self-reproducing molecular systems on a basis far wider than Watson-Crick base-pairing".[5]

In truth, we have had in hand for years clear warnings of the dangers inherent in 50 widespread knowledge of GNR technologies—of the possibility of knowledge alone enabling mass destruction. But these warnings haven't been widely publicized; the public discussions have been clearly inadequate. There is no profit in publicizing the dangers.

The nuclear, biological, and chemical (NBC) technologies used in 20th-century 51 weapons of mass destruction were and are largely military, developed in government laboratories. In sharp contrast, the 21st-century GNR technologies have clear commercial uses and are being developed almost exclusively by corporate enterprises. In this age of triumphant commercialism, technology—with science as its handmaiden—is delivering a series of almost magical inventions that are the most phenomenally lucrative ever seen. We are aggressively pursuing the promises of these new technologies within the now-unchallenged system of global capitalism and its manifold financial incentives and competitive pressures.

> This is the first moment in the history of our planet when any species, by its own volun- 52 tary actions, has become a danger to itself—as well as to vast numbers of others. . . . It might be a familiar progression, transpiring on many worlds—a planet, newly formed, placidly revolves around its star; life slowly forms; a kaleidoscopic procession of creatures evolves; intelligence emerges which, at least up to a point, confers enormous survival value; and then technology is invented. It dawns on them that there are such things as laws of Nature, that these laws can be revealed by experiment, and that knowledge of these laws can be made both to save and to take lives, both on unprecedented scales. Science, they recognize, grants immense powers. In a flash, they create world-altering contrivances. Some planetary civilizations see their way through, place limits on what may and what must not be done, and safely pass through the time of perils. Others, not so lucky or so prudent, perish.[6]

That is Carl Sagan, writing in 1994, in *Pale Blue Dot*, a book describing his vision 53 of the human future in space. I am only now realizing how deep his insight was, and how sorely I miss, and will miss, his voice. For all its eloquence, Sagan's contribution was not least that of simple common sense—an attribute that, along with humility, many of the leading advocates of the 21st-century technologies seem to lack.

Yes, I know, knowledge is good, as is the search for new truths. We have been 54 seeking knowledge since ancient times. Aristotle opened his Metaphysics with the simple statement. "All men by nature desire to know." We have, as a bedrock value in our society, long agreed on the value of open access to information, and recognize the problems that arise with attempts to restrict access to and development of knowledge. In recent times, we have come to revere scientific knowledge.

But despite the strong historical precedents, if open access to and unlimited 55 development of knowledge henceforth puts us all in clear danger of extinction, then common sense demands that we reexamine even these basic, long-held beliefs.

It was Nietzsche who warned us, at the end of the 19th century, not only that God 56 is dead but that "faith in science, which after all exists undeniably, cannot owe its origin to a calculus of utility; it must have originated *in spite of* the fact that the disutility and dangerousness of the "will to truth," of "truth at any price" is proved to it constantly." It is this further danger that we now fully face—the consequences of our truth-seeking. The truth that science seeks can certainly be considered a dangerous substitute for God if it is likely to lead to our extinction.

If we could agree, as a species, what we wanted, where we were headed, and why, 57 then we would make our future much less dangerous—then we might understand what we can and should relinquish. Otherwise, we can easily imagine an arms race developing over GNR technologies, as it did with the NBC technologies in the 20th century. This is perhaps the greatest risk, for once such a race begins, it's very hard to end it. This time—unlike during the Manhattan Project—we aren't in a war, facing an implacable enemy that is threatening our civilization; we are driven, instead, by our habits, our desires, our economic system, and our competitive need to know.

I believe that we all wish our course could be determined by our collective val- 58 ues, ethics, and morals. If we had gained more collective wisdom over the past few thousand years, then a dialogue to this end would be more practical, and the incredible powers we are about to unleash would not be nearly so troubling.

One would think we might be driven to such a dialogue by our instinct for self- 59 preservation. Individuals clearly have this desire, yet as a species our behavior seems to be not in our favor. In dealing with the nuclear threat, we often spoke dishonestly to ourselves and to each other, thereby greatly increasing the risks. Whether this was politically motivated, or because we chose not to think ahead, or because when faced with such grave threats we acted irrationally out of fear, I do not know, but it does not bode well.

The new Pandora's boxes of genetics, nanotechnology, and robotics are almost 60 open, yet we seem hardly to have noticed. Ideas can't be put back in a box; unlike uranium or plutonium, they don't need to be mined and refined, and they can be freely copied. Once they are out, they are out. Churchill remarked, in a famous left-handed compliment, that the American people and their leaders "invariably do the right thing, after they have examined every other alternative." In this case, however, we must act more presciently, as to do the right thing only at last may be to lose the chance to do it at all.

It is now more than a year since my first encounter with Ray Kurzweil and John 61 Searle. I see around me cause for hope in the voices for caution and relinquishment and in those people I have discovered who are as concerned as I am about our current predicament. I feel, too, a deepened sense of personal responsibility—not for the work I have already done, but for the work that I might yet do, at the confluence of the sciences.

But many other people who know about the dangers still seem strangely silent. 62 When pressed, they trot out the "this is nothing new" riposte—as if awareness of what could happen is response enough. They tell me, There are universities filled with bioethicists who study this stuff all day long. They say, All this has been written about before, and by experts. They complain, Your worries and your arguments are already old hat.

I don't know where these people hide their fear. As an architect of complex sys- 63 tems I enter this arena as a generalist. But should this diminish my concerns? I am aware of how much has been written about, talked about, and lectured about so author-itatively. But does this mean it has reached people? Does this mean we can discount the dangers before us?

Knowing is not a rationale for not acting. Can we doubt that knowledge has 64 become a weapon we wield against ourselves?

The experiences of the atomic scientists clearly show the need to take personal 65 responsibility, the danger that things will move too fast, and the way in which a process can take on a life of its own. We can, as they did, create insurmountable problems in almost no time flat. We must do more thinking up front if we are not to be similarly sur-prised and shocked by the consequences of our inventions.

My continuing professional work is on improving the reliability of software. Soft- 66 ware is a tool, and as a toolbuilder I must struggle with the uses to which the tools I make are put. I have always believed that making software more reliable, given its many uses, will make the world a safer and better place; if I were to come to believe the opposite, then I would be morally obligated to stop this work. I can now imagine such a day may come.

This all leaves me not angry but at least a bit melancholic. Henceforth, for me, 67 progress will be somewhat bittersweet.

Do you remember the beautiful penultimate scene in *Manhattan* where Woody 68 Allen is lying on his couch and talking into a tape recorder? He is writing a short story about people who are creating unnecessary, neurotic problems for themselves, because it keeps them from dealing with more unsolvable, terrifying problems about the universe.

He leads himself to the question, "Why is life worth living?" and to consider what 69 makes it worthwhile for him: Groucho Marx, Willie Mays, the second movement of the Jupiter Symphony, Louis Armstrong's recording of "Potato Head Blues," Swedish movies, Flaubert's *Sentimental Education*, Marlon Brando, Frank Sinatra, the apples and pears by Cézanne, the crabs at Sam Wo's, and, finally, the showstopper: his love Tracy's face.

Each of us has our precious things, and as we care for them we locate the essence 70 of our humanity. In the end, it is because of our great capacity for caring that I remain optimistic we will confront the dangerous issues now before us.

My immediate hope is to participate in a much larger discussion of the issues 71 raised here, with people from many different backgrounds, in settings not predisposed to fear or favor technology for its own sake.

As a start, I have twice raised many of these issues at events sponsored by the 72 Aspen Institute and have separately proposed that the American Academy of Arts and Sciences take them up as an extension of its work with the Pugwash Conferences. (These have been held since 1957 to discuss arms control, especially of nuclear weapons, and to formulate workable policies.)

It's unfortunate that the Pugwash meetings started only well after the nuclear 73 genie was out of the bottle—roughly 15 years too late. We are also getting a belated start on seriously addressing the issues around 21st-century technologies—the prevention of knowledge-enabled mass destruction—and further delay seems unacceptable.

So I'm still searching; there are many more things to learn. Whether we are to 74 succeed or fall, to survive or fall victim to these technologies, is not yet decided. I'm up late again—it's almost 6 am. I'm trying to imagine some better answers, to break the spell and free them from the stone.

## Notes

1. The passage Kurzwell quotes is from Kaczynski's Unabomber Manifesto, which was published jointly, under duress, by *The New York Times* and *The Washington Post* to attempt to bring his campaign of terror to an end. I agree with David Gelernter, who said about their decision:

   > "It was a tough call for the newspapers. To say yes would be giving in to terrorism, and for all they knew he was lying anyway. On the other hand, to say yes might stop the killing. There was also a chance that someone would read the tract and get a hunch about the author; and that is exactly what happened. The suspect's brother read it, and it rang a bell. "I would have told them not to publish. I'm glad they didn't ask me. I guess."
   > (*Drawing Life: Surviving the Unabomber*, Free Press, 1997: 120.)

2. Garrett, Laurie. *The Coming Plague: Newly Emerging Diseases in a World Out of Balance*. Penguin, 1994: 47–52, 414, 419, 452.
3. First Foresight Conference on Nanotechnology in October 1989, a talk titled "The Future of Computation." Published in Crandall, B. C. and James Lewis, editors. *Nanotechnology: Research and Perspectives*. MIT Press, 1992: 269. See also www.foresight.org/Conferences/MNT01/Nano1.html.
4. In his 1963 novel *Cat's Cradle*, Kurt Vonnegut imagined a gray-goo-like accident where a form of ice called ice-nine, which becomes solid at a much higher temperature, freezes the oceans.
5. Kauffman, Stuart, "Self-replication: Even Peptides Do It." *Nature*, 382, August 8, 1996: 496. See www.santafe.edu/sfi/People/kauffman/sak-peptides.html.
6. Sagan, Carl. *Pale Blue Dot: A Vision of the Human Future in Space* (New York: Random House, 1994), pp. 370–371 [Editor's note].

## READING FOR CONTENT

1. In paragraphs 15–20, what important differences does Joy note between the older technologies of computer networking in which he pioneered and the new technologies of genetics, nanosystems, and robotics which he warns about?
2. In paragraphs 57–60, what ethical conditions does Joy attach to the responsible development of the new technologies? Why does he urge us to relinquish this development?

## READING FOR GENRE, ORGANIZATION, AND STYLISTIC FEATURES

1. The genre of personal commentary relies upon anecdotes and narratives of experience to make an impact. How does Joy's anecdotal narrative in paragraphs 38–41 announce the decisive change in his point of view about the new technologies?
2. In paragraph 54, Joy writes, "Yes, I know, knowledge is good," and then counterpoints his claim in the next paragraph with "But despite the strong historical precedents. . . ." How does this pattern of concession and refutation organize his

argument? Underline other examples in the text where Joy uses the same pattern to advance his argument.

3. Reread the long quotation by Ray Kurzweil in paragraphs 6–8. What differences in tone mark Kurzweil's style as opposed to Joy's style? How close are the positions and points of view that they adopt?

## READING FOR RHETORICAL CONTEXT

1. What persuasive effects do Joy's personal testimonies convey in paragraphs 4, 21, 31, 38, and 61?

2. In paragraphs 61–66, how does Joy characterize members of the scientific profession who express no concerns about potential dangers of the research they are pursuing? Is he addressing his argument specifically to these colleagues? Or is he aiming at a wider audience by making these colleagues seem careless and irresponsible about the dangers?

## WRITING ASSIGNMENTS

1. Write a 750-word response to the editors of *Wired* magazine in which you develop your own commentary in support of Bill Joy's argument for relinquishing scientific developments in the new technologies.

2. Write a 750-word response to the editors of *Wired* magazine in which you develop your own commentary attacking Bill Joy's argument for relinquishing scientific developments in the new technologies.

## SYNTHESIS WRITING ASSIGNMENTS

1. Draw on at least four of the articles in this chapter to develop a 1,250-word essay that projects the future of human/machine interactions.

2. Draw on at least four of the articles in this chapter to develop a 1,250-word argument on what human rights should be accorded to robots and other forms of artificial intelligence that possess humanlike thought and emotions.

3. Some commentators have called virtual reality the "LSD of the 1990s." Use the articles in this chapter to write a 1,000-word response to that characterization of virtual reality.

4. Draw on the readings in this chapter to critique the portrayal of relationships between humans and machines in a work of science fiction you have read or seen (for example, a film such as *The Matrix*). What issues does the science fiction address? Are they the same issues that are raised in the nonfiction articles in this chapter?

5. Try to imagine a future in which humans and machines interact in the ways the articles in this chapter suggest they might. How would this future differ from the present? What would life be like for human beings? Would the human species have to change to live happily in that environment? Write a 1,000-word essay in response to these questions. You might organize your essay around a comparison between the present and the future.

# *Twelve*

# Crime-Fighting Technology:
## *Balancing Public Safety and Privacy*

Modern technology has created challenges to civil liberties that the framers of the Constitution did not envision. Audio and visual surveillance, monitoring of electronic communications, duplication of private or copyrighted computer files, DNA fingerprinting, and a host of other innovations make it much easier for government agencies, employers, and anyone else who takes an interest in our activities to find out what we are doing and thinking. When these technologies are employed to reduce crime, they usually receive support from the public. Since the attacks on the World Trade Center and the Pentagon on September 11, 2001, many Americans want the police and military to use any means available to reduce the risk of terrorism. On the other hand, Americans are quick to assert their personal rights, particularly their right to privacy. Although invasive technologies do assist police investigations, some commentators wonder if, by opting for technological quick fixes, we enter into a Faustian bargain that will eventually result in the loss of important constitutional rights.

The readings in this chapter focus on how our constitutional rights to privacy and to protection from illegal searches might be affected by technological innovations. The conversation recruits writers from the fields of newspaper reporting, forensic science, political activism, and legal affairs. Journalist Francis X. Clines describes Mosaic-2000, a computer program designed to identify students who might be prone to commit violent acts, and "Rooting Out the Bad Seeds?" by fellow-journalist Kelly Patricia O'Meara highlights the dangers to civil liberties posed by the Mosaic-2000 technology. Whereas Clines's article exemplifies science information reporting, O'Meara's exemplifies topical investigative reporting. In his study of "*Kyllo v. United States*: Technology v. Individual Privacy," FBI agent Thomas Colbridge analyzes the implications of a recent Supreme Court decision regarding the use of thermal imaging technology to detect indoor marijuana growing operations. Colbridge's detailed footnotes evoke a host of legal precedents as context for his argument about the limits of forensic science. In "DC's Virtual Panopticon," Christian Parenti describes the expansion of video surveillance in DC in the wake of the September 11 events. Its summary of developments in the field provides background for arguments about civil liberties that follow. Wendy Kaminer, the author of "Trading Liberty for Illusions," also focuses on the response to September 11 and argues that Americans should not surrender civil liberties in exchange for a false sense of security. Kaminer develops her legal perspective in a nontechnical style that complements her broad references to scientific technology as well. In "Invasion of Privacy," Joshua Quittner maintains that the benefits of modern technological advances are worth the reduction of individual privacy that comes with them. His reporting of conversations with scientists and government officials puts each of the parties on equal footing in the continuing debate. Finally, Richard A. Posner, a law professor and federal judge, applies his legal expertise to the debate and in "Wire Trap" he argues tendentiously that the government should have power to eavesdrop on private conversations. He constructs his argument by developing an imaginative hypothetical narrative about future terrorist attacks on the United States.

■ ■ ■ ■ ■ ■ ■ ■ ■ ■ ■ ■

# Computer Project Seeks to Avert Youth Violence

## Francis X. Clines

*Francis X. Clines, a prominent journalist, has been on the staff of* The New York Times *since 1958.*

## PREREADING

What do you know about the Columbine High School shootings that took place in Littleton, Colorado? If you are unfamiliar with that incident, ask a friend for information or do some quick online research. Write down the basic facts in the case.

Spurred by the deadly rampage at Columbine High School, the federal Bureau of  1
Alcohol, Tobacco and Firearms is working with a threat-evaluation company to develop a computer program to help school administrators spot troubled students who might be near the brink of violence.

When the national pilot program, known as Mosaic-2000, begins testing at more  2
than 20 schools in December, its technique of confidentially vetting and rating potentially violent students on a scale of 1 to 10 will come not a moment too soon for Steve Dackin, principal of Reynoldsburg High School.

"Columbine forever changed things for all of us," Dackin said of the school in  3
Littleton, Colorado, where two students shot thirteen people to death before killing themselves in April [1999].

Dackin knocked on wood in his office as he explained that his school, like most  4
in the nation, had been spared gun violence yet had suffered very real waves of post-Columbine panic and concern for safety that must now be dealt with through safeguard programs like Mosaic.

"I see this as being a useful tool," Dackin said of the program, which is based on 5 systems now variously employed by Yale University and federal courthouses to evaluate the potential for violence of individuals who make threats.

The Ohio chapter of the American Civil Liberties Union has criticized the pilot 6 program as a "technological Band-Aid" driven by profiteering in parental fears. "We are understandably hesitant about any program designed to classify students or anyone else in society as potentially dangerous based on supposedly credible data fed into a black box," said Raymond Vasvari, legislative director of the Ohio ACLU.

But the Ohio attorney general, Betty Montgomery, who favors the pilot project, 7 noted that school administrators must already maintain confidential files on troubled students who might veer toward violence. Mosaic, she said, will be a wonderful additional tool based on a wide range of objective experience. Far from Big Brother, she said, Mosaic is nothing more than highly useful software — a "three-ring notebook" to help worried school officials delve better into an existing area of responsibility.

"It brings together the shared experiences of many experts plus an evaluative 8 piece," Ms. Montgomery said. "It says, 'Look, we've gone back and spoken to X number of people who have committed these crimes, and these are the risk factors we feel are present in their lives. It collects these risk factors based on actual cases and organizes them in a way so we can have a consistent approach."

Mosaic programs, which are based on carefully worded questions about student 9 behavior based on case histories of people who have turned violent, are designed by Gavin de Becker, Inc., a private software company in California. They are intended to help officials discern a real threat amid the innocuous, if frightening, outbursts that regularly cause concern. For the last ten years, the company has tailored risk-assessment programs for special law-enforcement concerns like threats of domestic violence and threats to the safety of members of the Supreme Court and the governors of eleven states, according to the company.

"I think it's a wonderful tool that has a great deal of potential, and I hope it's prop- 10 erly used by the schools," said Andrew Vita, associate director for field operations of the Bureau of Alcohol, Tobacco and Firearms, who found the Mosaic approach useful in investigating bombings at abortion clinics.

"We are trying to get some of our focus and resources up front of violence, in vio- 11 lence prevention, violence avoidance," Vita said. He noted that his bureau was also developing a program with the Department of Education to train school officials to cope with another area of concern underlined at Columbine—homemade explosives in schools.

The Mosaic school program promises to provide questions carefully crafted from 12 case histories by two hundred experts in law enforcement, psychiatry and other areas. A variety of concerns beyond alarming talk or behavior will be included, from the availability of guns to a youngster's abuse of dogs and cats.

The questions allow a range of answers, from a student who has "no known gun 13 possession," for example, to one who has "friends with gun access." Not all the questions might be effectively answered by administrators who control the software, officials conceded. But they said the more that were, the greater the credibility of the rating would be in the hands of principals facing the responsibility of deciding when to step in and call for help from specialists.

Dackin . . . said Mosaic's immediate virtue would be in producing detailed docu- 14 mentation of its evaluation of a troubled student so that doubting parents could no longer challenge an administrator's judgment as too subjective. But Mosaic, he stressed, will at best be a useful instrument, with the school community's ultimate safeguard being in making sure that all students feel fully involved in school.

"It's easy to put up metal detectors," Dackin said, "but harder to create a system 15 where students feel connected."

The program, which is still being formulated, is to be tested from grades one 16 through twelve, with the main focus being in high schools. All the sites have not been determined. It will involve only students who give cause for special concern, school and law-enforcement officials emphasize. "We certainly wouldn't want to develop any kind of tool for labeling students in any way," Vita said.

Reynoldsburg school officials expressed confidence that the confidentiality of 17 student records required by law would not be breached by Mosaic. They emphasized that the software would not be connected to any central data program.

"It sounds okay, so long as you don't wind up labeling kids," said Shelly Darby, 18 who works at the Sun Tang Luck restaurant and is the mother of a second-grader. . . .

"There's kind of scary stuff out there," Ms. Darby said. "But there can be a real 19 fine line between a kid out to get attention and a really troubled kid."

She drew an empathetic nod from Aron Ross, the assistant superintendent of 20 schools in Reynoldsburg, a city of 35,000 just east of Columbus, Ohio.

"A few dramatic, sad incidents have spawned hysteria," he explained, describing a 21 nightmarish week of baseless rumors and countless alarms that caused midnight checks on school lockers after the Columbine killings. And through repeated meetings with anxious parents, Ross said, the question remains: What else can we do so it doesn't happen here?

"School people in my situation must respond to this new reality directly," he said. 22 "It used to be a platitude, but no longer, about creating an environment where students and teachers are safe and feel safe."

The de Becker company describes itself as a specialist in high-stakes assessments. 23 On its Internet site (www.gdbinc.com), the company has posted a detailed series of explanations and reassurances about the school software. "School administrators would use Mosaic-2000," the company asserts, "only in situations that reach a certain threshold (e.g., a student makes a threat, brings a weapon to school, teachers or students are concerned a student might act out violently)."

The system "merely brings organization and expert opinion to a process every 24 principal already has," the company says.

The company has not determined the overall cost of the program, but Ms. 25 Montgomery, the attorney general, described it as "very affordable" at less than $10,000 for the high school.

The Mosaic systems are "very well thought out and valuable tools," said James 26 Perrotti, chief of police at Yale University, which for five years has used the Mosaic-2000 program to assess threats received by professors and students.

Perrotti, one of the experts helping to shape the Mosaic-2000 questions, said the 27 system had offered effective warning about potentially violent situations that were nipped in the bud. "It's not a real predictor but it's the next best thing."

Vita, the federal firearms official, says school officials need Mosaic and other tools 28 to deal with an ever more complex threat in which relatively good students with access to guns may erupt because they feel victimized by bullies or by the school system.

"They're the hard ones for the school administrators to identify," Vita said. "It's 29 easy to pick out the gang members with tattoos. It's these other people that kind of surprise administrators, and these are the ones they really need to identify."

## READING FOR CONTENT

1. What is Mosaic-2000, and how does it function?
2. Give some examples of the questions that are included in the Mosaic-2000 database.
3. What age range is the Mosaic-2000 system designed for?
4. Who would have access to the data that Mosaic-2000 contains?
5. Summarize briefly the views of Ohio attorney general Betty Montgomery on the advantages of the Mosaic-2000 system over traditional methods of monitoring troubled students.
6. What criticisms of Mosaic-2000 are described in Clines's article?
7. What impact did the Columbine High School killings have on the way school officials, law enforcement authorities, and parents view issues of school safety?

## READING FOR GENRE, ORGANIZATION, AND STYLISTIC FEATURES

1. Describe the purpose of Clines's first paragraph.
2. In what ways is Clines's paragraph structure characteristic of journalistic writing rather than academic writing?
3. How does Clines's documentation of source material differ from what one would find in a piece of academic writing?

## READING FOR RHETORICAL CONTEXT

1. What is Clines's goal in writing?
2. Is there any indication in the article of what Clines thinks about the Mosaic-2000 system? Explain your answer.
3. Describe the expertise of the authorities Clines draws on. Did he draw on authorities that were appropriate for his topic? Explain your answer.

## WRITING ASSIGNMENTS

1. Write a 500-word summary of the viewpoints of Mosaic-2000 supporters, including Ohio attorney general Betty Montgomery; Bureau of Alcohol, Tobacco and Firearms agent Andrew Vita; Yale University chief of police James Perrotti; and high-school principal Steve Dackin.
2. Write a 750-word description of what you know from personal experience or the experience of your acquaintances about school safety in your hometown.
3. Using Clines's article and your own knowledge, explain in a 1,000-word essay how the Columbine High School killings affected American public education.

# Rooting Out the Bad Seeds?

## *Kelly Patricia O'Meara*

*Kelly Patricia O'Meara is an investigative reporter for* Insight on the News, *a conservative-based journal of opinion.*

## PREREADING

What does the term *criminal profiling* mean? Freewrite in response to this question for ten minutes. If you have never heard the term before, speculate on what you think it might mean.

To ensure that America's youth enjoy good mental health, psychologists have been   1
deployed to learning institutions to diagnose behavioral problems and distribute psychotropic drugs such as Ritalin. *Insight's* groundbreaking articles on this issue have excited commentary from *The New York Times* to *Time* and *Newsweek*. But, as with the gunmen at Columbine High School in Littleton, Colorado, or the six-year-old shooter in Flint, Michigan, crimes continue to occur in schools despite the growing network of prescription drugs and psychobabble. For parents who are becoming just a little crazed about all this psychological evaluation of their children, the newest initiative to weigh and record the state of mind of every student in the public schools may put them over the edge.

Mosaic-2000, a "method" designed to identify potentially violent children, is being   2
tested at random in high schools throughout the country. The problem for those wary of educators caught up in such psychological experiments is that parents will not have a clue about what soon could amount to criminal profiling of every child; nor will they know where, beyond the immediate school officials, the information obtained from their children is sent or how it might affect their future.

It is about as easy to contact Gavin de Becker, Inc., the California-based consulting   3
company specializing in personal security, as it has been to get White House officials to produce missing emails. The designer of the Mosaic-2000 system is in hiding and does not respond directly to questions. Its Web site, however, purports to provide a detailed explanation of its brainchild, and *Insight* has reviewed carefully its descriptions and claims.

This would-be electronic mind reader isn't the first of its kind. Mosaic computer-   4
profiling systems have been used for years by several federal law-enforcement agencies, including the Secret Service, the U.S. Marshals Service, and the Bureau of Alcohol, Tobacco and Firearms, or BATF. Contrary to media reports, the BATF is not "involved in Mosaic other than assisting de Becker in the preliminary screening," according to Jeff Roehm, chief of public information for that agency. Roehm explains: "We had a couple of folks who sat on the panel and shared their expertise in law enforcement. They helped in fleshing out the questions that may be asked, but de Becker is a private company offering it to schools."

BATF is just one of the law-enforcement agencies that played a major role in   5
developing criminal profiling of kids through Mosaic-2000. According to de Becker,
Gil Garcetti, the Los Angeles County district attorney; Richard Devine, the state's attorney for Cook County, Illinois; and Donald W. Ingwerson, superintendent of the Los
Angeles County Office of Education, are the "three leaders who partnered to facilitate
the development and testing of the new system for evaluating threats in schools."

So what did the best and brightest in law enforcement come up with to help their   6
partners seek out and identify the next Columbine shooter?

The Mosaic-2000 is described on the de Becker Web site as a "computer-assisted   7
method for helping evaluate situations involving students who make threats and might act
out violently." But it is not a test that students are asked to take. Children are questioned
by school or law-enforcement officials and the information fed into the Mosaic system
(the children are not told who will evaluate the information or how it will be analyzed).
The system then produces a report on the child being evaluated for criminal tendencies.

The computer-assisted system already has divined questions as well as possible   8
replies. After a subject's answers are run through the computer, they are rated on a scale
of one (low potential for violence) to ten (high potential for violence). School officials
or law officers then make a "threat assessment" of the student.

Critics say the worst potential problems with Mosaic-2000 are encapsulated in   9
what the company stresses never would occur. For instance, de Becker says, Mosaic-
2000 is "not a computer program. It will not share information about the students (at
least in the field tests), student names will be automatically deleted from the system after
the evaluation process is complete, and because Mosaic-2000 helps evaluate situations
and not students, it does not explore any demographic questions such as age, gender,
ethnicity, socioeconomic situations, et cetera." In other words, students are not being
evaluated—"situations" are evaluated. The information that is fed into the system about
the "situation" is not shared with anyone, and there is no record of the "assessment."

If that is the case, say critics, what is the purpose of all this? And why are parents who   10
become aware of the Mosaic system refused a list of the questions it poses? The most
important element of the system, the questions, are carefully guarded and simply unob-
tainable for independent evaluation. "We don't know if this thing is fish or fowl. We don't
know how the information is going to be used," Ted Deeds, chief operating officer of the
Law Enforcement Alliance of America, a Virginia-based coalition of law-enforcement officials, victims, and citizens united for justice, tells *Insight*. "First, if the data does work, what
the hell do you do with it? Will the schools segregate the potentially violent students, isolate them, carry out more locker checks, or send them into counseling? What's the review
mechanism? They all say it's not a profiling of the student, but we're not convinced."

Struggling to find a rationale for Mosaic-2000, Deeds comes up only with more   11
questions: "How do you train personnel for using such a system? How does one know
that the answer is truthful and whether the kid understands the questions being asked?
No one has addressed these questions. Remember, we're dealing with kids, not adults.
Parents would be insane to allow their children to be put into this kind of database—it
could show up for the next 20 years. Does anyone really believe that this information
won't be used by other law-enforcement agencies? Just look at the Social Security number, which we were promised would never be used for general identification. We've
seen these promises before. This isn't anything new; the spin is just a little different."

Officials participating in the trial program immediately are defensive and provide   12
conflicting views of Mosaic-2000. Aaron Ross, assistant superintendent of Reynoldsburg

School District in suburban Ohio, tells *Insight*, "We're trying to use the system, but we haven't found anyone to test. That's the good news." Questioned about Mosaic-2000 as a form of profiling for potentially violent students, Ross suddenly is emphatic. "Some people," Ross declares, "have said to me that Mosaic-2000 is profiling. That is just stupid. This system doesn't profile kids. It's just twenty questions. It's a piece of software that contains twenty questions that ask the investigating officer, principal, or counselor about a specific situation. What Mosaic-2000 permits that would not otherwise be available is [the gathering of] information that is organized into twenty categories that are relevant to risk assessment when the situation arises."

"The principal," Ross continues, "can make a decision with the additional infor-   13
mation that has been delivered by Mosaic-2000 with greater confidence in determination of the risk. It's a nice system. It takes the information from the answers provided by the student and organizes them into relevant categories. There is no rating of kids or situations. In fact, it can be completely anonymous. The point of the program is to help the investigator. When he's done, the notes will be thrown away."

Ross harbors doubts, nevertheless. "I have no idea if someone is keeping a record   14
of this information. The same can be said, however, of every other piece of information we keep on our students—grades, test scores, and disciplinary actions. The bottom line is that we have a situation around the country where kids are getting killed. We're always looking for tools to help in unusual situations—to make schools safe."

Although claiming to be more than willing to provide *Insight* with a copy of   15
Mosaic's twenty questions, Ross says he does not have them and is unaware of how they could be obtained short of requesting them directly from de Becker. (De Becker has not returned *Insight*'s calls or email requests.) Bob Benjamin, communications director for Devine, the Cook County, Illinois, state's attorney, one of the three leaders who partnered to come up with the system, says he is aware of Mosaic-2000 but, like Ross, does not have a copy of the profiling questions—even though Mosaic-2000 is being tested in three suburban Chicago high schools.

"This system," explains Benjamin, "is a consequence of what happened at   16
Columbine. What we're trying to find out is who is in such personal trouble that they might do something that may endanger another student or themselves. I don't think parental consent is necessary before the test is given. Everyone involved wants to see how this program will work. . . . The tests are ongoing and it will take time to assess the system."

Everyone concerned with this project agrees that Mosaic-2000 was born out of   17
the tragedy that occurred last year at Columbine High School and that its purpose is to identify the potential for violent behavior in schoolchildren. But according to data released by the Bureau of Justice Statistics, or BJS, and the National Center for Education Statistics, or NCES, schools are safer now than they have been in years. In fact, according to a recent BJS/NCES report, "a child is more likely to be a victim of a violent crime in their community or at home than at school."

In 1996 (the most recent data available), there were 255,000 incidents of nonfatal   18
but serious violent crime at school, but that figure nearly triples to 671,000 incidents concerning children away from school. The data further show a "decline in school crime and a reduction in the percentage of students carrying weapons to school." The data for the 1996–97 school year show that "10 percent of all public schools reported at least one serious violent crime to the police or a law-enforcement representative. Forty-seven percent of public schools reported less-serious violent or nonviolent crimes, and the remaining 43 percent of public schools reported none of these crimes."

It is precisely this kind of information that has critics questioning the need for 19 Mosaic-2000 as well as its methodology. "We've heard them say that they aren't going to use this information for anything," says Deeds. "So why are they taking it? The federal government likes to flush money away, but most of the time they do it with some purpose."

As a civil libertarian concerned about law enforcement, Deeds is both knowledge- 20 able and aware of the slippery slope. "Let's face it, the federal government has been profiling people for years," he says. "It's exactly like what happened with the National Instant Check System, or NICS. They said they weren't going to keep the records of the people who passed the firearms check, but they have. The people who cleared the system are not criminals, yet they remain in the system like they are. This administration keeps records on 99.9 percent of the people who aren't criminals. Remember Filegate? The administration was using secret or classified data on their Republican opponents. They've proved what they're about and they seem willing to do anything to push their political agendas."

It is unclear what Mosaic-2000 is about and whether the information it collects on 21 students will be shared with other agencies. But it isn't difficult for many in law enforcement to see it moving in that direction, especially because it is based on controversial profiling systems already in use by federal law-enforcement officials. Of such concerns de Becker writes in his Web site, "The first step toward understanding Mosaic-2000 is to recognize that it will not fit neatly into methods you may have encountered in the past. Though similar approaches are used in several sciences (most notably as part of medical diagnoses and decision-making), few people have encountered Artificial Intuition."

Apparently, de Becker is suggesting the computer-assisted system has a kind of 22 sixth sense. Of course, critics say that relying on this sort of "evaluation" amounts to kookery and increases the possibility of labeling innocent kids. Such worries may not be too big a leap, considering that some law-enforcement officials have been labeling as extremists motorists who display political or religious views on bumper stickers. For instance, according to a December 1999 article in the *FBI Law Enforcement Bulletin* titled "Vehicle Stops Involving Extremist Group Members," if motorists "sport bumper stickers with antigovernment or progun sentiments . . . and show other extremist signs such as presenting a copy of the Constitution, a Bible, or political literature," law enforcement is trained to handle the situation with caution.

The Constitution? A Bible? No wonder civil libertarians are complaining about 23 profiling.

## READING FOR CONTENT

1. Does O'Meara's description of how Mosaic-2000 functions differ in any respects from Clines's description? Explain your answer.
2. Working from paragraph 9, explain de Becker's rationale for claiming that Mosaic-2000 does not endanger students' privacy.
3. What is Ted Deeds's concern about how Mosaic-2000 data will be used?
4. What is the basis for O'Meara's claim that school officials provide conflicting information about Mosaic-2000?
5. How many questions are in the Mosaic-2000 database?
6. Why is O'Meara unable to get copies of the Mosaic-2000 questions?
7. What do data from the Bureau of Justice Statistics and the National Center for Educational Statistics indicate about the level of safety in schools?

8. What examples of criminal profiling are presented in O'Meara's article other than Mosaic-2000?

## READING FOR GENRE, ORGANIZATION, AND STYLISTIC FEATURES

1. Explain O'Meara's title.
2. Does O'Meara provide a thesis statement?
3. Describe the function of paragraph 6.
4. Describe and comment on O'Meara's closing strategy.

## READING FOR RHETORICAL CONTEXT

1. Based on the first paragraph, what is O'Meara's attitude toward efforts by public school officials to monitor and treat students' psychological problems?
2. Explain the tone and function of paragraph 3. What does the paragraph imply?
3. Who do you think is O'Meara's target audience? How does she intend to affect that audience?

## WRITING ASSIGNMENTS

1. Drawing on O'Meara, write a 500-word summary of the potential problems with the Mosaic-2000 system.
2. Imagine that you are the principal of the high school you attended and write a 500-word defense of using the Mosaic-2000 system.
3. Imagine that you are the student government president of the high school you attended and write a 500-word attack on using the Mosaic-2000 system.

■ ■ ■ ■ ■ ■ ■ ■ ■ ■ ■

# *Kyllo v. United States:* Technology v. Individual Privacy

## *Thomas D. Colbridge*

*Thomas Colbridge is an FBI agent and a legal instructor at the FBI Academy.*

## PREREADING

Do police officials need expanded powers to help them combat drug dealers? Freewrite for ten minutes in response to this question.

$F$ew issues evoke as much passionate debate as police use of new technologies to   1
combat crime. As noted in a previous article regarding thermal imaging,[1] the introduction

Colbridge, Thomas. "*Kyllo v. United States:* Technology v. Individual Privacy." *FBI Law Enforcement Bulletin* (October 2001): 25+.

of any advanced crime-fighting device into law enforcement's arsenal of weapons raises public concern about the erosion of constitutional rights. The specter of "Big Brother" looms large in the public mind. The debate is an honest one, raising basic issues regarding the proper balance between the personal privacy of individuals and the government's obligation to enforce the law and ensure public safety. Recently, the U.S. Supreme Court decided another skirmish in this ongoing philosophical battle in the case of *Kyllo v. United States,*[2] involving police use of thermal imaging.

This article discusses the Court's holding in the Kyllo case and its restrictions on police use of thermal-imaging devices.[3] The article also explores major themes developed by federal courts when assessing the impact of new police technologies on traditional Fourth Amendment search law.

## Fourth Amendment Search

The Fourth Amendment to the Constitution of the United States prohibits unreasonable searches.[4] The drafters of the Constitution never defined the concepts of "unreasonable" and "search" as used in the Fourth Amendment. The Supreme Court struggled with these constitutional definitions for many years. Finally, in 1967 in the famous case of *Katz v. United States,*[5] the Supreme Court formulated the modern definition of a search for purposes of the Constitution. The Court said that a Fourth Amendment search occurs whenever the government intrudes into an individual's reasonable expectation of privacy.[6] Supreme Court Justice Harlan, in a concurring opinion, established a useful two-prong test to determine if a reasonable expectation of privacy exists: (1) Do individuals have an actual (subjective) expectation that their activities will remain private? and (2) Is their subjective expectation of privacy one that society is willing to accept as reasonable (objectively reasonable)?[7] If the answer to both questions is yes, then a reasonable expectation of privacy exists, and any governmental invasion of that expectation is a search for Fourth Amendment purposes.

However, the Fourth Amendment does not prohibit all government searches, only unreasonable ones. Assuming the government does conduct a search as defined in *Katz,* is it reasonable or unreasonable? Unlike the question of whether a search has occurred, which can be difficult, the question of the reasonableness of the search is straightforward. If the search is conducted under the authority of a search warrant, or one of the recognized exceptions to the warrant requirement, the search is reasonable for Fourth Amendment purposes.[8]

## Thermal-Imaging Technology

Thermal imaging is not a new technology. It has been used by both the military and law enforcement for years. The public is accustomed to seeing thermal images of battlefields on the nightly news and thermal images of the streets on popular police reality television programs.

All objects with a temperature above absolute zero emit infrared radiation, which is invisible to the naked eye. The warmer an object is, the more infrared radiation it emits. The thermal imager detects this infrared radiation and converts it into a black-and-white picture. The hotter areas (i.e., those areas emitting more infrared radiation) appear lighter in the picture; the cooler areas appear darker. The device does not measure the actual temperature of objects, only the relative temperatures of the surfaces of objects scanned. It emits no rays or beams that penetrate the object viewed. Law enforcement has found several uses for the device, including locating bodies, tracking fleeing persons, and detecting possible indoor marijuana-growing operations. Using the thermal imager in the battle against indoor marijuana-growing operations brought Danny Kyllo and the thermal imager to the attention of the U.S. Supreme Court.

## The Kyllo Case

The facts of the Kyllo case are typical of these types of investigations. An agent of the   7
U.S. Bureau of Land Management developed information that Kyllo might be growing marijuana inside his home. Among the information he gathered were the facts that Kyllo's ex-wife, with whom he still was apparently living, was arrested the previous month for delivery and possession of a controlled substance; that Kyllo told a police informant that he could supply marijuana; and that other individuals suspected of drug trafficking lived in the same triplex occupied by Kyllo and his ex-wife. The agent subpoenaed Kyllo's utility records and concluded that his utility use was abnormally high. Finally, at the request of the investigator, a member of the Oregon National Guard scanned Kyllo's home using a thermal imager. The scan was made at approximately three o'clock in the morning from the streets in front of and behind the Kyllo residence. No search warrant authorizing the scan was sought. The scan revealed what investigators believed to be abnormally high amounts of heat coming from Kyllo's home. Investigators concluded that the facts of the case gave them probable cause to believe Kyllo was growing marijuana in his house. Investigators applied for and obtained a warrant to search Kyllo's home, using the results of the thermal scan as part of their probable cause. The search revealed marijuana plants, weapons, and drug paraphernalia.

After his indictment for manufacturing marijuana,[9] Kyllo moved to suppress the   8
evidence gathered in his home on several grounds, including the use of the thermal imager without a search warrant. Kyllo argued that targeting his home with a thermal imager was an unreasonable Fourth Amendment search because there was no warrant authorizing it, and the government could not justify the lack of a search warrant under one of the warrant exceptions. The trial court denied his motion and Kyllo was convicted. The case was appealed to the U.S. Court of Appeals for the Ninth Circuit.

## The Circuit Court's View

The U.S. Court of Appeals for the Ninth Circuit heard the Kyllo case three times before   9
it reached a final conclusion. The Ninth Circuit's struggle to decide this case is a reflection of the divergence of opinion that had developed in the courts regarding the warrantless thermal scanning of a home. It also is an interesting study of the difficulty that courts have in dealing with the impact of advancing technology on Fourth Amendment privacy issues.

The first time the Ninth Circuit considered Kyllo's appeal, it made no decision   10
regarding the constitutionality of a warrantless scan of a home with a thermal imager. Instead, it sent the case back to the trial court for additional hearings on the capabilities of the thermal imager.[10] The trial court found that the imager used by police in this case recorded no intimate details of life inside Kyllo's home; did not invade any personal privacy inside the home; could not penetrate walls or windows to reveal human activities or conversations; and recorded only heat escaping from the house.[11] On that basis, the trial court decided that the thermal scan did not invade a reasonable expectation

of privacy and therefore was not a search within the meaning of the Fourth Amendment. It again refused to suppress the evidence. The case went back to the Ninth Circuit for a second time.

This time, a three-judge panel of the Ninth Circuit decided that the warrantless 11 thermal scan of Kyllo's home was an unconstitutional search.[12] The court adopted the view that using a thermal imager to target a private home is a Fourth Amendment search, requiring probable cause and authorization of a search warrant or one of the exceptions to the warrant requirement.[13] Its decision was clearly a minority view among federal circuit courts at the time.[14] However, the Ninth Circuit's debate over the issue was not finished. In July 1999, the court withdrew this opinion[15] and decided to reconsider the issue.

On its third and final consideration of this case, the Ninth Circuit reversed 12 itself and held that a thermal scan of a residence is not a search under the Fourth Amendment.[16] It joined the majority of other federal circuit courts[17] in deciding that Kyllo had no actual (subjective) expectation of privacy in the "waste heat"[18] radiating from the surface of his home because he made no effort to conceal the emissions. Even if he could demonstrate an actual expectation of privacy in the escaping heat, the court reasoned that privacy expectation was not objectively reasonable. The court said that the crucial question to be answered in judging the impact of new technologies on privacy issues is whether the technology used to enhance the senses of the police officer is "so revealing of intimate details as to raise constitutional concerns."[19] This court decided thermal imaging was not so revealing. To resolve the conflicting views among federal circuit courts regarding the constitutionality of residential thermal scans, the U.S. Supreme Court agreed to hear the case.[20]

## The Supreme Court's View

The Supreme Court disagreed with the majority of the federal circuit courts. In a 5 to 13 4 decision, it ruled that targeting a home with a thermal imager by police officers is a search under the Fourth Amendment[21] and therefore requires probable cause and a search warrant unless the government can forego the warrant under one of the Court's recognized exceptions to the warrant requirement.[22]

The majority and dissenting opinions in this case reflect the difficulty courts in 14 general have resolving the tension between individual privacy and governmental use of technology to combat crime. Several themes emerged in the opinion that echoed arguments made in previous rulings involving police use of emerging technologies.

The first theme involves the area that actually was searched. The majority opin- 15 ion argued that the surveillance in this case was of the interior of a private home. The Court made it clear that the interior of a home indeed is still a castle. It said, "'[A]t the very core' of the Fourth Amendment 'stands the right of a man to retreat into his own home and there be free from unreasonable governmental intrusion.'"[23] While the Court often has held that naked-eye surveillance of the exterior of a home and its curtilage by the police is not objectionable as long as police have a lawful vantage point from which to see the home,[24] this case involved more. Using the thermal imager, the majority felt, police were able to explore details of the interior of Kyllo's house that they could not have gotten otherwise without going inside.[25]

The dissent disagreed. It distinguished between technology permitting "through-the- 16 wall surveillance," a search it admitted is presumptively unconstitutional,[26] and "off-the-wall surveillance," a search it assumed to be constitutional.[27] The thermal imager in this case, according to the dissent, passively measured heat emissions from the exterior surfaces of Kyllo's home. There was no penetration into the interior of the residence by the police or by rays or beams emitted by the imager. The dissent argued that police simply gathered information exposed to the public from the outside of Kyllo's home.

A second theme discussed by the Court is the public availability of the technol-    17
ogy used. This issue was raised in 1986 in the Dow Chemical Company[28] case. In that case, the Supreme Court noted in passing that "It may well be, . . . that surveillance of private property by using highly sophisticated surveillance equipment not generally available to the public . . . might be constitutionally proscribed absent a warrant."[29] It was significant to the majority in the Kyllo case that thermal-imaging technology is not widely available to the general public.[30]

While the dissent did not specifically disagree,[31] it criticized the majority for not    18
providing guidance regarding how much use constitutes general public use. It is diffi-cult to discern from the opinion why public availability is important or how important it actually is. It may be a recognition on the part of the Court that as technology makes its way into everyday life, it becomes more difficult for individuals to claim a reasonable expectation to be shielded from its impact.

A third theme that emerges in this case is the debate over the nature and quality    19
of the information supplied to the police by the thermal imager. The Court framed its discussion of this issue in terms of whether or not the technology enabled police to gather information regarding "intimate details"[32] of human activities in the home. This debate also arose in the Dow Chemical Company case. The issue there was the govern-ment's use of an aerial mapping camera to photograph a Dow Chemical plant to look for environmental violations. In its opinion, the Court said, ". . . but the photographs here are not so revealing of intimate details as to raise constitutional concerns."[33] The obvious corollary of that statement is that technology in the hands of the government that reveals intimate details of in-home activities does raise constitutional concerns.

The Kyllo majority rejected the government's contention that because the imager    20
used in this case did not provide exacting detail regarding activities inside Kyllo's home, it should not be of constitutional concern. As the majority opinion put it, "In the home, our cases show all details are intimate details because the entire area is held safe from prying government eyes."[34] The majority reasoned, for example, that the imager used in this case might reveal when a person inside the home regularly took a bath each night. Several previous Supreme Court cases were cited to support this view. In *United States v. Karo*,[35] where government agents simply detected the presence of a can of ether in a private residence by monitoring a beeper placed in the can, the Court found that the agents had conducted an unconstitutional search. In *Arizona v. Hicks*,[36] an officer lawfully inside a home moved a record player to see its serial number. The Court said that was an unlawful search because it went beyond what the officer could see in plain view. In both cases, the information gathered by the police was relatively insignificant, but because it was information about the inside of a home, the majority felt it was inti-mate enough to warrant protection from the government.

The dissent argued that the thermal scan here provided scant detail regarding the    21
exterior of Kyllo's home and certainly no information concerning its interior. In the dis-sent's view, the only information gathered by police was an indication that some areas of Kyllo's roof and outside walls were hotter than others. That kind of information, the dissent argued, is unworthy of Fourth Amendment protection because anyone can tell the warmth of a home's walls and roof by looking at evaporation or snowmelt patterns

on the roof, and because most people do not care if the amount of heat escaping from their homes is made public.[37]

These major themes are important for law enforcement for two reasons. The first 22 reason is practical—the Kyllo case will have an immediate impact on the use of thermal imaging in criminal investigations. The second reason is less immediate but more far-reaching. The Supreme Court has given law enforcement important clues regarding the government's future use of technology to gather criminal evidence.[38]

## Limitations on the Use of the Thermal Imager

The most immediate impact of the Kyllo case is the elimination of the thermal imager 23 as an investigative tool in residential indoor marijuana-growing cases. The majority opinion makes it clear that using a thermal imager to surveil a home is a search under the Fourth Amendment, requiring a search warrant supported by probable cause or justified by one of the search warrant exceptions. If officers have probable cause to believe marijuana is being grown inside a house (or any premises where there is a reasonable expectation of privacy), they will get the warrant and search, not get a warrant and conduct a thermal scan. Consequently, thermal imagers have been rendered superfluous in indoor residential marijuana-growing investigations.

However, the thermal imager still is a valuable tool for use where there is no 24 expectation of privacy or when police are excused from the warrant requirement. For example, using the device to search for fleeing fugitives in an open field, where there is no expectation of privacy, is permissible. In addition, using the thermal imager to target even a private residence still is arguably permissible in emergency situations where the search warrant requirement is excused.[39] For example, if faced with a dangerous barricaded subject or a hostage situation and officers decide an entry is necessary, no warrant would be necessary to thermally scan a premises as long as officers have reasonable suspicion to believe a threat to life exists.[40] Of course, if time permits, officers always should seek a warrant before entering a private area.

## Larger Implications of *Kyllo*

Law enforcement officers have sworn to uphold the Constitution of the United States 25 and of their respective states. The oath includes the obligation to assess their actions in light of ever-changing interpretations of the law by the courts. That assessment must include the increasing use of sophisticated technology to ferret out crime.

In *Kyllo*, the Supreme Court provided some guidance to law enforcement regard- 26 ing when its use of technology unreasonably infringes personal privacy. In light of *Kyllo*, law-enforcement officers should ask themselves certain questions before using sophisticated devices in their investigations.

## What is Being Targeted?

*Kyllo* confirms the familiar proposition that anytime police invade a reasonable expecta- 27 tion of privacy, it is a Fourth Amendment search requiring a warrant or an exception to the warrant requirement. That is true whether the invasion is physical or technological as in the Kyllo case. If the target of the technological surveillance is the interior of a home, the Supreme Court has made it clear that there is an expectation of privacy, and it is reasonable.[41] The same conclusion must be reached where the target of the surveillance is the interior of a commercial building inaccessible to the public. Where the target is the exterior of a premises, there likely is no expectation of privacy as long as police have a lawful vantage point from which to conduct their technological surveillance, and the results of the surveillance reveal nothing regarding the interior of the premises.

Similarly, if the thermal imager is used to search a person (as opposed to search   28 for a person in an area where there is no expectation of privacy), a reasonable expectation of privacy must be assumed. For example, using a thermal imager, it is theoretically possible to detect the presence of objects concealed under a person's clothing. Such a use of the thermal imager is a Fourth Amendment search and must comply with the constitutional requirements.

## What Information is Gathered?

It is clear from the *Kyllo* decision that the Supreme Court is concerned about the collec-   29 tion by the police of what it calls "intimate details" or "private activities occurring in private areas."[42] The Court did not define what details are intimate and private and what details are not, and wants to avoid deciding the issue on a case-by-case basis. Instead, the Court opted for a rule that within the confines of a home, "all details are intimate details"[43] and protected by the Fourth Amendment. Consequently, if officers are considering using a device that will enable them to gather any information regarding the interior of a home (or any area in which there is a reasonable expectation of privacy) from outside, they must comply with the provisions of the Fourth Amendment.

## Is the Device Generally Available to the Public?

As noted above, the Supreme Court often limits its reservations regarding police use of   30 technological devices to those devices not generally available to the public. It did so in its opinion in the Dow Chemical Company[44] case and in *Kyllo*.[45] It is unclear how important this consideration is to the Court. The implication seems to be that individuals cannot claim a reasonable expectation of privacy against technological intrusions that are widely known to occur and happen on a regular basis. The Court in *Kyllo* acknowledged that. It said, "It would be foolish to contend that the degree of privacy secured to citizens by the Fourth Amendment has been entirely unaffected by the advance of technology. For example . . . the technology enabling human flight has exposed to public view (and, hence, we have said, to official observation) uncovered portions of the house and its curtilage that once were private."[46]

Does that mean if thermal imagers become commonplace the Court will permit   31 police to routinely scan the interior of homes without warrants? Probably not, for two reasons. The Court has long distinguished between police surveillance of the exterior of homes and the interior of homes: "We have said that the Fourth Amendment draws a firm line at the entrance to the house, [citation omitted]. That line, we think, must be not only firm but also bright. . . ."[47] Given the strong language in the *Kyllo* opinion, it is unreasonable for police to assume that governmental intrusions into private areas are permissible simply because everyone is doing it. In addition, private (nongovernmental) and commercial use of new technologies does not raise constitutional concerns. The Constitution was written to limit the authority of the government, not private citizens.[48] Consequently, the Supreme Court will not question the use of a thermal imager by an insulation company to demonstrate homeowners' need to insulate their homes, but put the same thermal imager into the hands of the police investigating a crime, and a multitude of weighty legal issues will arise. When assessing the Fourth Amendment implications of using technological devices to gather information about the interior of premises, officers should not rely on the fact that the device is widely available.

## Why is the Device Being Used?

Using technology to gather evidence of criminal activity obviously raises Fourth 32 Amendment concerns. However, criminal investigation is not always the goal. Often, technology is employed by the government for the broader purpose of public safety. The most obvious example is the use of X-ray and magnetic screening devices at airports and government office buildings. Courts have long recognized that such warrantless searches are permissible because they are administrative in nature, not criminal, and are not very intrusive. They serve the valid governmental purpose of securing public safety rather than gathering evidence of criminal activity.[49] So long as the technological search is narrowly limited to serve only that public safety purpose, it will pass constitutional muster.

## Where and When is the Device Being Used?

Another factor courts consider when assessing police use of technology is where and 33 when the device is used. If the device is used in public areas, such as airports and public buildings, where people are aware of its presence, courts generally have fewer constitutional reservations regarding its use. Under those conditions, people can make a choice to enter the screening area or not. If they choose to enter, some courts have reasoned that they have consented to be searched by the device in use.[50] If the device is used in the dead of night, as happened in the Kyllo case, consent obviously is impossible.

## Conclusion

Historically, modern technology in the hands of the police has raised well-founded 34 fears in the public mind concerning the erosion of privacy rights. The police, however, have an obligation to protect the public safety through whatever constitutional means are available to them. Criminal elements are quick to adopt the latest technological gadgets in order to stay one step ahead of the police. Police quickly must respond in kind. The tension between these two legitimate interests has created some of the most difficult issues faced by U.S. courts.

In *Kyllo v. United States*, the U.S. Supreme Court drew a bright line around the 35 home and announced a rule that warrantless police use of technology stops at the front door. Simply put, the Court stated that if police use technology from outside the home to gather information they could not otherwise obtain without going inside, they have conducted a search within the meaning of the Constitution, which must be supported by a warrant or a recognized exception to the warrant requirement.

While the Kyllo case dealt specifically with thermal-imaging technology, it has 36 much larger implications. Law-enforcement officers have an obligation to assess all technological devices in their arsenal in light of the lessons delivered in this case.

## Notes

1. Thomas D. Colbridge, "Thermal Imaging: Much Heat but Little Light." *The FBI Law Enforcement Bulletin*, December 1997, 18–24.
2. 121 S. Ct. 2038 (2001).
3. While the Kyllo case dealt with a thermal imaging device, the legal principles discussed in this article apply equally to the Forward Looking Infrared Radar (FLIR) device, an adaptation of the thermal imager for use on aircraft.
4. U.S. Const. Amend IV: "The right of the people to be secure in their persons, houses, papers, and effects against unreasonable searches and seizures shall not be violated. . . ."
5. 389 U.S. 347 (1967).
6. Id.
7. Supra note 5 at 361 (J. Harlan, concurring).
8. Supra note 5 at 357. The exceptions to the search warrant requirement recognized by the Supreme Court are the consent search (*Schneckloth v. Bustamonte*, 412 U.S. 218 [1973]); the search incident to arrest (*U.S. v. Robinson*, 414 U.S. 218 [1973]); the emergency search or exigent circumstances search (*Warden v. Hayden*, 387 U.S. 394 [1967]); the motor vehicle search (*Carroll v. U.S.*, 267 U.S. 132 [1925]); the inventory search (*South Dakota v. Opperman*, 428 U.S. 364 [1976]); certain administrative searches of regulated businesses (*New York v. Berger*, 482 U.S. 691 [1987]); and "special needs" searches (*Veronia School District 47 J v. Acton*, 515 U.S. 646 [1995]).
9. 21 U.S.C. 841(a)(1).
10. *United States v. Kyllo*, 37 F.3d 526 (9th Cir. 1994).
11. *United States v. Kyllo*, No. CR 92-051-FR (D.Or. March 15, 1996).
12. *United States v. Kyllo*, 140 F.3d 1249 (9th Cir. 1998).
13. Id. at 1255.
14. The U.S. Court of Appeals for the Tenth Circuit held in 1995 that a thermal scan of a home was a search: *United States v. Cusumano*, 67 F.3d 1497 (10th Cir. 1995), vacated on other grounds, 83 F.3d 1247 (10th Cir. 1996). Two states also had adopted this minority view: *State v. Young*, 867 P.2d 593 (Wash. 1994) and *State v. Siegel*, 934 P.2d 176 (Mont. 1997).
15. *United States v. Kyllo*, 184 F.3d 1059 (9th Cir. July 29, 1999).
16. *United States v. Kyllo*, 190 F.3d 1041 (9th Cir. 1999).
17. See *United States v. Ishmael*, 48 F.3d 850 (5th Cir. 1995); *United States v. Myers*, 46 F.3d 668 (7th Cir. 1995); *United States v. Pinson*, 24 F.3d 1056 (8th Cir. 1994); *United States v. Robinson*, 62 F.3d 1325 (11th Cir. 1995).
18. Supra note 16 at 1046.
19. Supra note 16 at 1047 (quoting *Dow Chemical Co. v. United States*, 476 US 227 (1986) at 238).
20. *Kyllo v. United States*, 530 U.S. 1305 (2000).
21. *Kyllo v. United States*, 121 S. Ct. 2038 at 2043.
22. Supra note 8 lists the exceptions to the search warrant requirement.
23. *Kyllo*, 121 S. Ct. at 2043 quoting *Silverman v. United States*, 365 U.S. 505 (1961) at 511.
24. *California v. Ciraolo*, 476 U.S. 207 (1986); *Florida v. Riley*, 488 U.S. 445 (1989).
25. *Kyllo*, 121 S. Ct. at 2043.
26. *Kyllo*, 121 S. Ct. at 2048 (J. Stevens, dissenting), citing *Payton v. New York*, 445 U.S. 573 (1980).
27. *Kyllo*, 121 S. Ct. at 2048 (J. Stevens, dissenting), citing *California v. Ciraolo*, supra note 24; *Florida v. Riley*, supra note 24; *California v. Greenwood*, 486 U.S. 35 (1988); *Dow Chemical Co. v. United States*, supra note 19; and *Air Pollution Variance Board of Colorado v. Western Alfalfa Corporation*, 416 U.S. 861 (1974).
28. Supra note 19.
29. Dow Chemical Company, 476 U.S. at 238 (1986).
30. *Kyllo*, 121 S. Ct. at 2043.
31. The dissent did point out in a footnote that thousands of thermal imagers had been manufactured and are available for rental by anyone. See *Kyllo*, 121 S. Ct. at 2050, note 5. (J. Stevens, dissenting).
32. *Kyllo*, 121 S. Ct. at 2045.
33. Dow Chemical Company, 476 U.S. at 238 (1986).

34. Kyllo, 121 S. Ct. at 2045 (emphasis in original).
35. 468 U.S. 705 (1984).
36. 480 U.S. 321 (1987).
37. Kyllo, 121 S. Ct. at 2048 (J. Stevens, dissenting).
38. Regarding certain technology in development, the Court offered more than clues. In a foot-note, the majority specifically named surveillance devices under development and implied they would raise Fourth Amendment concerns. Those technologies are the Radar-Based Through-the-Wall Surveillance System, Handheld Through-the-Wall Surveillance, and a Radar Flashlight enabling officers to detect people through interior building walls. See Kyllo, 121 S.Ct. at 2044, footnote 3.
39. See *United States v. Johnson*, 9 F.3d 506 (6th Cir. 1993).
40. See *Terry v. Ohio*, 392 U.S. 1 (1968); *United States v. Menard*, 95 F.3d 9 (8th Cir. 1996).
41. Kyllo, 121 S. Ct. at 2043. Of course, even inside the home, there is no expectation of privacy regarding matters that individuals choose to expose to the public: *Katz v. United States*, 389 U.S. 347 at 351 (1967), and cases cited at supra note 27.
42. Kyllo, 121 S. Ct. at 2045.
43. Kyllo, 121 S. Ct. at 2045.
44. Supra note 29.
45. Supra note 30.
46. Kyllo, 121 S. Ct. at 2043.
47. Kyllo, 121 S. Ct. at 2046, citing *Payton v. New York*, 445 U.S. 573 (1980).
48. *United States v. Jacobson*, 466 U.S. 109 (1984); *United States v. Knoll*, 16 F. 3rd 1313 (2nd Cir.), cert. denied 115 S. Ct. 574 (1994).
49. *United States v. Bulalan*, 156 F. 3rd 963 (9th Cir. 1998); *United States v. John Doe, aka Geronimo Pizzaro-Calderon*, 61 F.3d 107 (1st Cir. 1995); *United States v. $124,570 U.S. Currency*, 873 U.S. 1240 (9th Cir. 1989).
50. *United States v. DeAngelo*, 584 F.2d 46 (4th Cir. 1978), cert. denied 440 U.S. 935 (1979); *United States v. Miner*, 484 F.2d 1075 (9th Cir. 1973).

## READING FOR CONTENT

1. Summarize the definition of privacy that emerged from *Katz v. United States*.
2. Summarize how thermal imagers function.
3. Summarize briefly the events that led up to Kyllo's arrest.
4. Explain briefly the basis for each of the three separate opinions on the Kyllo case that were issued by the U.S. Court of Appeals for the Ninth Circuit.
5. Summarize the basis for the majority opinion of the Supreme Court on the Kyllo case.
6. Summarize the basis for the dissenting opinions of the Supreme Court on the Kyllo case.
7. In the wake of the Kyllo decision, what options remain for police use of thermal imagers?
8. Summarize briefly what Colbridge believes are the implications of *Kyllo* for police searches that do not involve thermal imaging.

## READING FOR GENRE, ORGANIZATION, AND STYLISTIC FEATURES

1. Characterize Colbridge's use of language.
2. Comment on Colbridge's use of section headings to divide his article.

3. Explain Colbridge's extensive use of endnotes.
4. Does Colbridge's conclusion capture the essence of the Supreme Court's ruling in the Kyllo case? Explain your answer.

## READING FOR RHETORICAL CONTEXT

1. Who do you imagine is the target audience for *The FBI Law Enforcement Bulletin,* the publication in which Colbridge's article appears?
2. How does Colbridge establish his authority?
3. What is Colbridge's goal in writing?
4. How does Colbridge's job as an FBI agent complicate his role as author of an article on the Kyllo case?

## WRITING ASSIGNMENTS

1. Write a 500-word summary of the most important elements in the case against Kyllo and in the Supreme Court's ruling in *Kyllo v. United States.*
2. Write a 1,000-word essay that defends or attacks the Supreme Court's ruling in *Kyllo v. United States.*
3. In the movie *E.T.,* government agents use high-power listening devices to monitor conversations taking place within private homes in a neighborhood where they suspect children might be hiding an alien creature. Do you think the audio monitoring in *E.T.* would pass the standards for police searches set forth in *Kyllo?* Defend your answer in a 750-word essay.

■ ■ ■ ■ ■ ■ ■ ■ ■ ■ ■

# DC's Virtual Panopticon

### Christian Parenti

*Christian Parenti is the author of* Lockdown America: Police and Prisons in the Age of Crisis.

## PREREADING

In your everyday life, under what circumstances are you photographed by surveillance video cameras? Freewrite for ten minutes in response to that question.

The future is bearing down on Washington, DC. In recent weeks the District's police have begun constructing a centrally monitored, citywide closed-circuit television

(CCTV) surveillance system—the first of its kind in the nation. Eventually, the Metropolitan Police Department (MPD) plans to link 1,000 cameras to watch streets, public schools, the DC Metro transit system, federal facilities, and even part of a Georgetown business improvement district. The nucleus of this system, made up of thirteen $15,000-a-piece cameras, is already in place, mounted high on buildings, sending live wireless feed to the MPD's $7 million, NASA-style Joint Operations Command Center. In this room filled with video monitors, computers, and communications gear, surveillance images are recorded and logged by the police, Secret Service, FBI, and at times other agencies. Departmental brass say the Command Center and camera network are a response to the attacks of September 11, part of an effort to "enhance public safety" by fighting terrorism and crime. And they claim widespread public support for the project: recent opinion polls show 60 to 80 percent approval ratings for increased surveillance of streets and public space.

"We've started with important federal locations, but we've already had numerous   2 requests from nearby neighborhoods. People are like, 'Hey, we've got crime; we need some cameras over here,'" says Kevin Morison, communications director for the MPD. He predicts that "community extensions" will be the next phase of the surveillance system.

Once the full camera network is operative, police will be able to read license   3 plates and track cars as they move through the city, zoom in on individuals, read newsprint from hundreds of feet away, and send real-time images to the laptops of the department's 1,000 patrol cars. According to local press reports, engineers are even working to equip some of the cameras with night vision. They could also be outfitted with biometric facial-recognition software for comparing faces on the street against mug shots in the department's database. But so far, the police say they won't use biometrics, in part because facial recognition is still a very imperfect technology.

In preparation for the big linkup, both the school system and the Metro are retool-   4 ing and are connecting their surveillance systems. The school system started installing cameras at middle and high schools after the Columbine killings in 1999. The Metro has used cameras since the tunnels opened in the late 1970s, but the new Metro surveillance gear will include recorders and be linked by fiber optics into a centralized control station. Eventually the whole system will be connected to the Joint Operations Command Center. "It makes sense," explains Polly Hanson, deputy chief of the DC Metro Police. "When there are emergencies or demonstrations, we coordinate with the MPD anyway. This technical upgrade and connection seemed like a natural fit." Since September 11, the Metro has received $49 million in federal antiterrorist funding and has overhauled surveillance in fourteen key stations; completing the whole job will take several years.

As soon as news of the emerging DC surveillance network broke in late February   5 [2002], civil libertarians began raising questions. Particularly problematic in the eyes of many is the fact that the system was created without any written guidelines or community consultation. The outcry has forced DC Police Chief Charles Ramsey to promise a set of written parameters for the camera system's operation. But details of the surveillance plans remain a mystery.

"We still have a lot of unanswered questions," says Johnny Barnes, executive direc-   6 tor of the Washington American Civil Liberties Union. Despite meetings with the police brass, Barnes and the ACLU still want to know: Who will monitor the video? When will the system be complete? How long will the tapes be kept and by whom? What agencies will get access to the tapes? And what steps will be taken to prevent video voyeurism or racist and anti-homeless profiling? Nor are the ACLU's concerns merely hypothetical: Already, police in Detroit and DC have used CCTV to stalk personal foes, political opponents, and young women.

Other critics go even further, arguing that written regulations and police consul-    7
tations with the ACLU do little more than legitimize a dangerous and unnecessary surveillance network. "Police guidelines are very frequently violated and can always be
changed," says Mara Verheyden-Hilliard, a cofounder of, and attorney with, the Partnership for Civil Justice (PCJ). "Instead of signing off on this new system, we think it
needs to be abolished. We believe there's a very strong legal case for the elimination of
these cameras. People have the right to traverse the streets and parks of DC without
being under the scrutiny of Chief Ramsey and the FBI."

Though one does not have a total right to privacy while walking on the street —    8
we accept that being looked at is the price of being in public — people do have a Fourth
Amendment protection against unreasonable searches. And it could be argued by the
PCJ or others that when police watch a person with high-powered, interconnected, and
intelligent cameras that are linked to criminal-history databases, they are in effect conducting an unwarranted and possibly unconstitutional search. The PCJ also worries
that if allowed in DC, such camera networks will proliferate across the country.

Perhaps the most disturbing feature of the DC surveillance network is its past polit-    9
ical uses. District police first hooked up their camera surveillance and high-tech Joint
Ops Center in 1999 when thousands of activists protested at NATO's fiftieth-anniversary
summit. The gear was again deployed in April 2000 to monitor activists and control
crowds during mass protests against the joint World Bank and International Monetary
Fund meeting. And the same system spied on protesters during the contested inauguration of George W. Bush in 2001.

"Americans have the right to protest with some level of anonymity, but this system    10
and the other uses of surveillance are stripping people of that right," says Verheyden-
Hilliard. "After the inauguration we talked with numerous people who don't normally go
to demonstrations, but who went to protest Bush and the stolen election — many of them
were shocked and really intimidated by the police militarism and intense surveillance."
Many protesters agree that such intensive surveillance has a politically chilling effect.

Veteran activist and videographer Mark Liiv, of Whispered Media, says excessive    11
police surveillance is always "creepy" but that in DC it was particularly so. "At the IMF
protests, everyone in the convergence center felt really sketched out. There were lots of
cameras on the streets but also guys on rooftops. Some were filming, some were
snipers — a bullet backing every camera," says Liiv.

"There's definitely a performative aspect to police surveillance. If you shoot video    12
of the cops doing surveillance, they make a really big deal of getting up in your face and
letting you know that you're being filmed. If there are all these high-powered cameras
on buildings, why the guys in the street, if not to psych us out and breed paranoia?"

According to material handed over in court to the Partnership for Civil Justice,    13
the DC police even used their surveillance system to observe the superorderly, rather
mainstream Million Family March in October 2000. And along with powerful cameras
mounted on buildings, the DC police have equipped their helicopters with wireless
surveillance video that also feeds the screens monitored at the high-tech Command
Center. For a more close-up view from within the crowds of demonstrators, the MPD
contracts with a private "script to screen" video firm called SRB Productions. Advertised as "100 percent minority and woman-owned," SRB has worked for everyone from

the *Oprah Winfrey Show* to the Navy. As a hireling of the DC police, the firm conducts surveillance of demonstrations using its commercial television equipment, according to an SRB spokesperson. It also mixed a montage video of protest highlights for Chief Ramsey's viewing.

Neither the PCJ nor any other civil libertarians have yet filed a lawsuit demanding 14 that the new camera network be dismantled or that the surveillance of demonstrations be halted. PCJ is still waiting on Freedom of Information Act requests, and litigation may follow. Unfortunately, PCJ's legal argument that the DC surveillance actually constitutes an illegal search, however compelling, will probably not hold up in today's law-and-order courts.

The DC officialdom's interest in cameras closely parallels events from a decade 15 ago in Britain—the nation that now has the highest CCTV density in the world. In fact, Chief Ramsey is full of praise for the cameras of Britain. But recent history from across the Atlantic can also be read as a political warning.

During the early 1990s British media were gripped by a moral panic that fixated 16 on the double threat of crime and terrorism. When it was all over, Britain was covered with cameras. The cycle started in 1990 when the IRA resumed its "mainland campaign" with a bomb at the London Stock Exchange, followed by a mortar attack on a Cabinet meeting at No. 10 Downing Street in 1991. A bombing in April 1992 left London's financial district with three dead, ninety-one injured, and more than $1.2 billion in damages. The next year another massive "dump-truck bomb" in the same general area killed one and injured dozens. Later, the IRA bombed central Manchester and launched a mortar assault on Heathrow airport.

In response, the police erected a "Ring of Steel" security cordon around central 17 London, involving vehicle barriers, traffic bans, random armed checkpoints, and hundreds of new electronic eyes in the form of CCTV.

Amid this buildup, two 10-year-old boys abducted and killed a toddler named 18 Jamie Bulger. The kidnapping was caught on grainy surveillance film and endlessly looped on British television. All of this helped cast video surveillance as the public safety tool du jour. Now Britain has more than 2.5 million surveillance cameras; London alone is wired with 150,000.

But contrary to what the boosters say—here and in Britain—the record on 19 CCTV is mixed. In London cameras have indeed been correlated with declining crime rates, but now crime is on the rise again despite surveillance. And no terrorists were ever caught using CCTV. Leading British criminologists have found one clear trend: CCTV does lead to racial profiling. One large study by the well-known British criminologists Clive Norris and Gary Armstrong found that black people were twice as likely as whites to be watched for "no obvious reason."

Surveillance cameras are already spreading across the United States well beyond 20 DC. A survey done last year by the International Association of Chiefs of Police found that 80 percent of police departments use CCTV, while another 10 percent are planning to do so. A 1998 study by the New York Civil Liberties Union counted 2,397 surveillance cameras, many private but some controlled by the police, all "trained on public streets, sidewalks, buildings, and parks in Manhattan." When asked for an explanation, then-Mayor Rudy Giuliani waved the group away, saying. "They . . . raise questions about everything." Even more disturbing is the increased use of hidden or disguised CCTV cameras in Gotham.

In Oakland, California, more than seventy surveillance cameras watch the civic   21
center, and a private force of blazer-clad security personnel ushers away homeless sleep-
ers and skateboarding youth. A duplicate system exists around San Francisco's Yerba
Buena Center for the Arts, where the rules include everything from no lying down to
no kite flying to no bike riding. Santa Rosa, California, also has cameras watching its
Courthouse Square and "Transit Mail" with the explicit intent of discouraging the presence of homeless people and youth.

Scores of other towns have similar small-scale systems. Worcester, Massachusetts,   22
has CCTV around its parks. Virginia Beach uses CCTV to monitor the pedestrian
crowds of its boardwalk. Similar arrangements exist on Mobile, Alabama's Dauphin
Street, site of the local Mardi Gras. More cameras (paid for with money confiscated during drug busts) watch Mobile's Government Plaza, the park near its adjacent convention
center, and the traffic corridors that feed into downtown streets. In Los Angeles, police
are using motion-sensing cameras to combat graffiti around government buildings.

One thing is clear in most of these cases. Jeffrey Rosen of George Washington   23
School of Law sums it up well: "Surveillance cameras are technologies of classification
and exclusion." This can take the form of social prejudice, as when people of color, the
homeless, or youth are excessively monitored and driven from public space. Or, as in
the case with intensive surveillance of demonstrations in DC, the "exclusions" can be
more overtly political.

## READING FOR CONTENT

1. Describe the basic operational features of the video surveillance system that
   District of Columbia police are developing.
2. What areas in Washington will be under surveillance?
3. What are some of the examples Parenti gives to illustrate the quality of the video
   images that will be obtained with the new system?
4. Explain ACLU representative Johnny Barnes's concerns about the new video monitoring system.
5. Explain PCJ attorney Mara Verheyden-Hilliard's concerns about the new video
   monitoring system.
6. How has video surveillance been used in the past to monitor political protests in
   Washington?
7. Why does Parenti think that the courts will rule that the DC video surveillance
   system is constitutional?
8. What is the status of video surveillance in England?
9. What point does Parenti make in his final paragraph?

## READING FOR GENRE, ORGANIZATION, AND STYLISTIC FEATURES

1. What is the effect of Parenti's opening sentence?
2. Why does Parenti choose, for the most part, to quote authorities directly rather
   than to paraphrase their ideas?
3. Does Parenti have a thesis statement? Explain your answer.

## READING FOR RHETORICAL CONTEXT

1. Describe the authorities that Parenti cites in his article.
2. What is Parenti's viewpoint on the new DC video surveillance system? Where is that viewpoint indicated?
3. Does Parenti give a fair explanation of arguments both for and against the video surveillance system?

## WRITING ASSIGNMENTS

1. Imagine that you live in Washington, DC. Would you object to the new video surveillance system as an infringement on your privacy, or would you support it as an enhancement to your safety? Write a 750-word essay in response to this question.
2. Draw on Colbridge's and Parenti's articles to write a 1,000-word essay that compares and contrasts the level of privacy that you think people should have in their homes to the level of privacy you think they should have while driving cars and walking on the street.
3. Write a 1,000-word essay that compares and contrasts the video surveillance system that is being developed in DC with that described in George Orwell's *1984*.

■ ■ ■ ■ ■ ■ ■ ■ ■ ■ ■

# Trading Liberty for Illusions

## Wendy Kaminer

*Wendy Kaminer is a lawyer and has written several books, including* Sleeping with Extra-Terrestrials: The Rise of Irrationalism and the Perils of Piety.

## PREREADING

How have the events of September 11, 2001, affected your own views about crime detection efforts? Freewrite for ten minutes in response to that question.

Only a fool with no sense of history would have been sanguine about the prospects   1
for civil liberties after the September 11 attack. Whenever Americans have felt frightened or under siege, they have responded by persecuting immigrants, members of suspect ethnic groups, or others guilty only of real or apparent sympathy for unpopular ideologies. Our most revered, or at least respected, presidents have been among the

worst offenders: John Adams supported the Alien and Sedition Acts, which criminalized opposition to the government (and was used to imprison his political foes); Abraham Lincoln suspended habeas corpus and presided over the arrests of thousands of people for crimes like "disloyalty" (which sometimes consisted of criticizing the president); Woodrow Wilson imprisoned Eugene Debs for speaking out against America's entry into the First World War; Franklin Roosevelt famously and shamefully interned Japanese-Americans during World War II. Liberty was trampled by all of these measures, while security was enhanced by none of them.

But the cruelty and folly of imprisoning people for their political views or their   2 ethnicity is usually acknowledged only in hindsight. During World War II some people no doubt felt safer knowing that their Japanese-American neighbors were interned. The Supreme Court ruled at the time that the internment was justified on national security grounds. People felt safer last fall when the Bush administration swept up and detained over one thousand immigrants in the wake of the September 11 attack, even though the vast majority of them had no apparent connection to terrorism. History shows that frightened people tend to assume that restrictions on liberty make them safe. They support repressive measures instinctively in the expectation that other people will be targeted by them, and ask questions only decades later.

Consider the false promise of many electronic surveillance measures, like facial-   3 recognition systems. A recent report by the American Civil Liberties Union reveals that the widely publicized facial-recognition system used on the streets by police in Tampa, Florida, "never identified even a single individual contained in the department's data-base of photographs." Instead, "the system made many false positives, including such errors as confusing what were to a human easily identifiable male and female images." The ACLU report was based on a review of police logs obtained through Florida's open-records law.

Technological inaccuracies like these were coupled with human errors and abuses   4 of discretion. A facial-recognition system can only be as good as its database in identifying terrorists or other violent criminals, and in Tampa the photographic database was not limited to known criminals: It included people the police were interested in questioning in the belief that they might have "valuable intelligence." Under guidelines like this, ordi-nary law-abiding citizens who venture out in public might find themselves setting off alarms in facial-recognition systems (should they ever work properly).

Whether or not your photograph is in the database, your privacy is likely to be   5 invaded by a facial-recognition system. Cameras scan crowds and, as the ACLU observes, in Britain, where electronic surveillance is becoming routine, camera opera-tors are apt to focus disproportionately on racial minorities or while away the hours peering up women's skirts. In Michigan, according to a report by the *Detroit Free Press*, police used a database to stalk women and intimidate other citizens.

Considering the ways facial-recognition systems have been used and abused so far,   6 it's fair to say that they constitute a threat—to privacy, liberty and even physical safety—not a promise of security. But we are beginning to use them more, not less. Several cities have decided to deploy the kind of system that failed so miserably in Tampa, and of course, facial recognition is being touted as an important airport security tool. Airports in cities including Boston, Providence, and Palm Beach are installing facial-recognition systems. Meanwhile, precautions that might actually enhance security, like screening all checked bags and carry-ons, are as far from implementation as ever.

Why do a majority of Americans tolerate and support invasive or repressive faux 7
security measures? I suspect we're simply too frightened and uninformed to challenge
them. People who want or need to continue flying, for example, can't bear to devote
much thought to the continuing inadequacies of airport security; instead they take
comfort in whatever false promise of security they're offered. So, the problem for civil
libertarians isn't the tendency of people to trade liberty for security. It's their tendency
to trade liberty for mere illusions of security. Liberty would benefit greatly from a logical, pragmatic approach to safety. In our frightened, irrational world, freedom may be
threatened most by wishful thinking.

## READING FOR CONTENT

1. Paraphrase the first sentence of Kaminer's article.
2. According to Kaminer, how, in the past, have Americans responded when they felt threatened?
3. How does facial-recognition technology function?
4. According to Kaminer, how successful has facial recognition been in reducing crime?
5. What specific dangers of facial-recognition technology does Kaminer identify?
6. Why, according to Kaminer, do Americans accept "invasive or repressive faux security measures"?

## READING FOR GENRE, ORGANIZATION, AND STYLISTIC FEATURES

1. Describe Kaminer's opening strategy.
2. Describe Kaminer's organizational plan.
3. Comment on the length of Kaminer's piece.

## READING FOR RHETORICAL CONTEXT

1. Characterize Kaminer's attitude toward the government.
2. Who is Kaminer's intended audience? What assumptions does she make about her audience?
3. How do you think police officers would respond to Kaminer's article?

## WRITING ASSIGNMENTS

1. Write a 1,000-word essay that weighs the pros and cons of using facial-recognition technology to monitor the general public.
2. Write a 1,000-word essay of response to Kaminer's assertion that "freedom may be threatened most by wishful thinking."
3. Write a 1,000-word essay that compares and contrasts facial-recognition technol-ogy with one or more of the other infringements on personal freedom that are mentioned in Kaminer's first and second paragraphs.

■ ■ ■ ■ ■ ■ ■ ■ ■ ■ ■

# Invasion of Privacy

## *Joshua Quittner*

*Joshua Quittner, a journalist, is a frequent contributor to* Newsday *and* Wired. *Among the books he has coauthored with Michelle Slatalla are* Masters of Deception: The Gang That Ruled Cyberspace, Flame War, *and* Speeding the Net: The Inside Story of Netscape, How It Challenged Microsoft and Changed the World.

## PREREADING

Based on your own experience and that of your family and friends, are you confident in the safety of credit cards, ATM cards, phone cards, and other electronic records that control "private" business? Is the convenience of these computerized transactions worth any potential for loss or invasion of privacy?

For the longest time, I couldn't get worked up about privacy: my right to it; how it's 1 dying; how we're headed for an even more wired, underregulated, overintrusive, privacy-deprived planet.

I mean, I probably have more reason to think about this stuff than the average 2 John Q. All Too Public. A few years ago, for instance, after I applied for a credit card at a consumer-electronics store, somebody got hold of my name and vital numbers and used them to get a duplicate card. That somebody ran up a $3,000 bill, but the nice lady from the fraud division of the credit-card company took care of it with steely digital dispatch. (I filed a short report over the phone. I never lost a cent. The end.)

I also hang out online a lot, and now and then on the Net someone will imper- 3 sonate me, spoofing my email address or posting stupid stuff to bulletin boards or behaving in a frightfully un-Quittner-like manner in chat parlors from here to Bianca's Smut Shack. It's annoying, I suppose. But in the end, the faux Quittners get bored and disappear. My reputation, such as it is, survives.

I should also point out that as news director for Pathfinder, Time Inc.'s mega info 4 mall, and a guy who makes his living on the Web, I know better than most people that we're hurtling toward an even more intrusive world. We're all being watched by computers whenever we visit Web sites; by the mere act of "browsing" (it sounds so passive!) we're going public in a way that was unimaginable a decade ago. I know this because I'm a watcher too. When people come to my Web site, without ever knowing their names, I can peer over their shoulders, recording what they look at, timing how long they stay on a particular page, following them around Pathfinder's sprawling offerings.

None of this would bother me in the least, I suspect, if a few years ago, my phone, 5 like Marley's ghost, hadn't given me a glimpse of the nightmares to come. On Thanksgiving weekend in 1995, someone (presumably a critic of a book my wife and I had just written about computer hackers) forwarded my home telephone number to an out-of-state answering machine where unsuspecting callers trying to reach me heard a male voice identify himself as me and say some extremely rude things. Then, with typical hacker aplomb, the prankster asked people to leave their messages (which to my surprise many callers, including my mother, did). This went on for several days until my wife and I figured out that something was wrong ("Hey . . . why hasn't the phone rung since Wednesday?") and got our phone service restored.

It seemed funny at first, and it gave us a swell story to tell on our book tour. But the interloper who seized our telephone line continued to hit us even after the tour ended. And hit us again and again for the next six months. The phone company seemed powerless. Its security folks moved us to one unlisted number after another, half a dozen times. They put special PIN codes in place. They put traces on the line. But the troublemaker kept breaking through.     6

If our hacker had been truly evil and omnipotent, as only fictional movie hackers are, there would probably have been even worse ways he could have threatened my privacy. He could have sabotaged my credit rating. He could have eavesdropped on my telephone conversations or siphoned off my email. He could have called in my mortgage, discontinued my health insurance, or obliterated my Social Security number. Like Sandra Bullock in *The Net*, I could have been a digital untouchable, wandering the planet without a connection to the rest of humanity. (Although if I didn't have to pay back school loans, it might be worth it. Just a thought.)     7

Still, I remember feeling violated at the time and as powerless as a minnow in a flash flood. Someone was invading my private space—my family's private space—and there was nothing I or the authorities could do. It was as close to a technological epiphany as I have ever been. And as I watched my personal digital hell unfold, it struck me that our privacy—mine and yours—has already disappeared, not in one Big Brotherly blitzkrieg but in Little Brotherly moments, bit by bit.     8

Losing control of your telephone, of course, is the least of it. After all, most of us voluntarily give out our phone number and address when we allow ourselves to be listed in the *White Pages*. Most of us go a lot further than that. We register our whereabouts whenever we put a bank card in an ATM machine or drive through an E-Z Pass lane on the highway. We submit to being photographed every day—twenty times a day on average if you live or work in New York City—by surveillance cameras. We make public our interests and our purchasing habits every time we shop by mail order or visit a commercial Web site.     9

I don't know about you, but I do all this willingly because I appreciate what I get in return: the security of a safe parking lot, the convenience of cash when I need it, the improved service of mail-order houses that know me well enough to send me catalogs of stuff that interests me. And while I know we're supposed to feel just awful about giving up our vaunted privacy, I suspect (based on what the pollsters say) that you're as ambivalent about it as I am.     10

Popular culture shines its klieg lights on the most intimate corners of our lives, and most of us play right along. If all we really wanted was to be left alone, explain the lasting popularity of Oprah and Sally and Ricki tell-all TV. Memoirs top the best-seller lists, with books about incest and insanity and illness leading the way. Perfect strangers at cocktail parties tell me the most disturbing details of their abusive upbringings. Why?     11

"It's a very schizophrenic time," says Sherry Turkle, professor of sociology at the Massachusetts Institute of Technology, who writes books about how computers and online communication are transforming society. She believes our culture is undergoing     12 a kind of mass identity crisis, trying to hang on to a sense of privacy and intimacy in a global village of tens of millions. "We have very unstable notions about the boundaries of the individual," she says.

If things seem crazy now, think how much crazier they will be when everybody is   13 as wired as I am. We're in the midst of a global interconnection that is happening much faster than electrification did a century ago and is expected to have consequences at least as profound. What would happen if all the information stored on the world's computers were accessible via the Internet to anyone? Who would own it? Who would control it? Who would protect it from abuse?

Small-scale privacy atrocities take place every day. Ask Dr. Denise Nagel, execu-   14 tive director of the National Coalition for Patient Rights, about medical privacy, for example, and she rattles off a list of abuses that would make Big Brother blush. She talks about how two years ago, a convicted child rapist working as a technician in a Boston hospital riffled through 1,000 computerized records looking for potential victims (and was caught when the father of a nine-year-old girl used caller ID to trace the call back to the hospital). How a banker on Maryland's state health commission pulled up a list of cancer patients, cross-checked it against the names of his bank's customers, and revoked the loans of the matches. How Sara Lee bakeries planned to collaborate with Lovelace Health Systems, a subsidiary of Cigna, to match employee health records with work-performance reports to find workers who might benefit from antidepressants.

Not to pick on Sara Lee. At least a third of all Fortune 500 companies regularly   15 review health information before making hiring decisions. And that's nothing com-pared with what awaits us when employers and insurance companies start testing our DNA for possible imperfections. Farfetched? More than two hundred subjects in a case study published last January in the journal *Science and Engineering Ethics* reported that they had been discriminated against as a result of genetic testing. None of them were actually sick, but DNA analysis suggested that they might become sick someday. "The technology is getting ahead of our ethics," says Nagel, and the Clinton adminis-tration clearly agrees. It is about to propose a federal law that would protect medical and health-insurance records from such abuses.

But how did we arrive at this point, where so much about what we do and own   16 and think is an open book?

It all started in the 1950s, when, in order to administer Social Security funds, the   17 U.S. government began entering records on big mainframe computers, using nine-digit identification numbers as data points. Then, even more than today, the citizenry instinctively loathed the computer and its injunctions against folding, spindling, and mutilating. We were not numbers! We were human beings! These fears came to a head in the late 1960s, recalls Alan Westin, a retired Columbia University professor who publishes a quarterly report *Privacy and American Business*. "The techniques of intru-sion and data surveillance had overcome the weak law and social mores that we had built up in the pre–World War II era," says Westin.

The public rebelled, and Congress took up the question of how much the gov-   18 ernment and private companies should be permitted to know about us. A privacy bill of rights was drafted. "What we did," says Westin, "was to basically redefine what we meant by 'reasonable expectations of privacy'"—a guarantee, by the way, that comes from the Supreme Court and not from any constitutional "right to privacy."

The result was a flurry of new legislation that clarified and defined consumer and   19 citizen rights. The first Fair Credit Reporting Act, passed in 1970, overhauled what had once been a secret, unregulated industry with no provisions for due process. The new law gave consumers the right to know what was in their credit files and to demand corrections. Other financial and health privacy acts followed, although to this day no federal law protects the confidentiality of medical records.

As Westin sees it, the public and private sectors took two very different approaches. 20 Congress passed legislation requiring that the government tell citizens what records it keeps on them while insisting that the information itself not be released unless required by law. The private sector responded by letting each industry—credit-card companies, banking, insurance, marketing, advertising—create its own guidelines.

That approach worked—to a point. And that point came when mainframes 21 started giving way to desktop computers. In the old days, information stored in government databases was relatively inaccessible. Now, however, with PCs on every desktop linked to office networks and then to the Internet, data that were once carefully hidden may be only a few keystrokes away.

Suddenly someone could run motor-vehicle-registration records against voting 22 registrations to find six-feet-tall Republicans who were arrested during the past year for drunk driving—and who own a gun. The genie was not only out of the bottle, he was also peering into everyone's bedroom window. (Except the windows of the very rich, who can afford to screen themselves.)

"Most people would be astounded to know what's out there," says Carole Lane, 23 author of *Naked in Cyberspace: How to Find Personal Information Online.* "In a few hours, sitting at my computer, beginning with no more than your name and address, I can find out what you do for a living, the names and ages of your spouse and children, what kind of car you drive, the value of your house, and how much taxes you pay on it."

Lane is a member of a new trade: paid Internet searcher, which already has its 24 own professional group, the Association of Independent Information Professionals. Her career has given her a fresh appreciation for what's going on. "Real privacy as we've known it," she says, "is fleeting."

Now, there are plenty of things you could do to protect yourself. You could get an 25 unlisted telephone number, as I was forced to do. You could cut up your credit card and pay cash for everything. You could rip your E-Z Pass off the windshield and use quarters at tolls. You could refuse to divulge your Social Security number except for Social Security purposes, which is all that the law requires. You'd be surprised how often you're asked to provide it by people who have no right to see it.

That might make your life a bit less comfortable, of course. As in the case of Bob 26 Bruen, who went into a barbershop in Watertown, Massachusetts, recently. "When I was asked for my phone number, I refused to give them the last four digits," Bruen says. "I was also asked for my name, and I also refused. The girl at the counter called her supervisor, who told me I could not get a haircut in their shop." Why? The barbershop uses a computer to record all transactions. Bruen went elsewhere to get his locks shorn.

But can we do that all the time? Only the Unabomber would seriously suggest 27 that we cut all ties to the wired world. The computer and its spreading networks convey status and bring opportunity. They empower us. They allow an information economy to thrive and grow. They make life easier. Hence the dilemma.

The real problem, says Kevin Kelly, executive editor of *Wired* magazine, is that 28 although we say we value our privacy, what we really want is something very different: "We think that privacy is about information, but it's not—it's about relationships." The way Kelly sees it, there was no privacy in the traditional village or small town; everyone knew everyone else's secrets. And that was comfortable. I knew about you, and you knew about me. "There was a symmetry to the knowledge," he says. "What's gone out of whack is we don't know who knows about us anymore. Privacy has become asymmetrical."

The trick, says Kelly, is to restore that balance. And not surprisingly, he and others 29 point out that what technology has taken, technology can restore. Take the problem of "magic cookies"—those little bits of code most Web sites use to track visitors. We set up a system at Pathfinder in which, when you visit our site, we drop a cookie into the basket of your browser that tags you like a rare bird. We use that cookie in place of your name, which, needless to say, we never know. If you look up a weather report by keying in a zip code, we note that (it tells us where you live or maybe where you wish you lived). We'll mark down whether you look up stock quotes (though we draw the line at capturing the symbols of the specific stocks you follow). If you come to the *Netly News*, we'll record your interest in technology. Then, the next time you visit, we might serve up an ad for a modem or an online brokerage firm or a restaurant in Akron, Ohio, depending on what we've managed to glean about you.

Some people find the whole process offensive. "Cookies represent a way of 30 watching consumers without their consent, and that is a fairly frightening phenomenon," says Nick Grouf, CEO of Firefly, a Boston company that makes software offering an alternative approach to profiling, known as "intelligent agents."

Privacy advocates like Grouf—as well as the two companies that control the 31 online browser market, Microsoft and Netscape—say the answer to the cookie monster is something they call the Open Profiling Standard. The idea is to allow the computer user to create an electronic "passport" that identifies him to online marketers without revealing his name. The user tailors the passport to his own interests, so if he is passionate about fly-fishing and is cruising through L.L. Bean's Web site, the passport will steer the electronic-catalog copy toward fishing gear instead of, say, Rollerblades.

The advantage to computer users is that they can decide how much information 32 they want to reveal while limiting their exposure to intrusive marketing techniques. The advantage to Web site entrepreneurs is that they learn about their customers' tastes without intruding on their privacy.

Many online consumers, however, are skittish about leaving any footprints in 33 cyberspace. Susan Scott, executive director of TRUSTe, a firm based in Palo Alto, California, that rates Web sites according to the level of privacy they afford, says a survey her company sponsored found that 41 percent of respondents would quit a Web page rather than reveal any personal information about themselves. About 25 percent said when they do volunteer information, they lie. "The users want access, but they don't want to get correspondence back," she says.

But worse things may already be happening to their email. Many office electronic- 34 mail systems warn users that the employer reserves the right to monitor their email. In October software will be available to Wall Street firms that can automatically monitor correspondence between brokers and clients through an artificial-intelligence program that scans for evidence of securities violations.

"Technology has outpaced law," says Marc Rotenberg, director of the Washington- 35 based Electronic Privacy Information Center. Rotenberg advocates protecting the privacy of email by encrypting it with secret codes so powerful that even the National Security Agency's supercomputers would have a hard time cracking it. Such codes are legal within the United States but cannot be used abroad—where terrorists might use them to protect their secrets—without violating U.S. export laws. . . .

Rotenberg thinks we need a new government agency—a privacy agency—to sort 36 out the issues. "We need new legal protections," he says, "to enforce the privacy act, to keep federal agencies in line, to act as a spokesperson for the federal government and to act on behalf of privacy interests."

*Wired*'s Kelly disagrees. "A federal privacy agency would be disastrous! The 37 answer to the whole privacy question is more knowledge," he says. "More knowledge about who's watching you. More knowledge about the information that flows between us—particularly the meta information about who knows what and where it's going."

I'm with Kelly. The only guys who insist on perfect privacy are hermits like the 38 Unabomber. I don't want to be cut off from the world. I have nothing to hide. I just want some measure of control over what people know about me. I want to have my magic cookie and eat it too.

## READING FOR CONTENT

1. According to Quittner, what are some (name at least five) of the ways that we regularly surrender our privacy?
2. What examples does Quittner provide of potentially dangerous invasions of privacy?
3. What evidence does Quittner give to support his assertion that Americans don't really want to be left alone?
4. Why did some Americans react negatively to the introduction of the Social Security number in the 1950s?
5. How, according to Quittner, has the shift from large mainframe computers to desktop PCs affected privacy?
6. In response to the computer revolution, what steps did the federal government take to protect citizens' privacy? What steps did the private sector take?
7. According to Carole Lane, what information can you locate on the Web about a given individual, beginning with only a name and address?
8. What are "magic cookies"?
9. Explain the controversy over encryption technology.

## READING FOR GENRE, ORGANIZATION, AND STYLISTIC FEATURES

1. Quittner begins with a series of anecdotes. How do these anecdotes work together as an opening to his piece?
2. Based on the first ten paragraphs of the article, how would you characterize Quittner's writing style? Is this style appropriate, given the nature of the piece he is writing?
3. Describe Quittner's organizational plan.

## READING FOR RHETORICAL CONTEXT

1. What in the article indicates Quittner's intended audience?
2. Identify the two sections of the essay in which Quittner states his own opinion.

3. Paraphrase Quittner's proposal for balancing privacy concerns and access to technology.

4. In what way is Quittner's article confessional?

## WRITING ASSIGNMENTS

1. Write a 1,000-word essay that objectively describes how modern technology has eroded personal privacy. Draw on Quittner's article for examples.

2. In paragraph 10, Quittner asserts that "... I do all this [surrender privacy] willingly because I appreciate what I get in return: the security of a safe parking lot, the convenience of cash when I need it, the improved service of mail-order houses that know me well enough to send me catalogs of stuff that interests me ... while I know we're supposed to feel just awful about giving up our vaunted privacy, I suspect (based on what the pollsters say) that you're just as ambivalent about it as I am." In a 1,000-word essay, explain Quittner's assertion and respond to it based on your own views.

3. Do you think Quittner's views are consistent with constitutional guarantees of civil liberties? Defend your view in a 1,000-word essay.

■ ■ ■ ■ ■ ■ ■ ■ ■ ■ ■ ■

# Wire Trap

### Richard A. Posner

*Richard A. Posner is Professor of Law at the University of Chicago and was appointed by President Reagan as a judge of the U.S. Court of Appeals for the Seventh Circuit. He has written a number of books, including* Economic Analysis of Law *(1986);* Law and Literature *(1988);* The Federal Courts: Challenge and Reform *(1996);* The Problematics of Moral and Legal Theory *(1999);* Law, Pragmatism, and Democracy *(2003); and* Uncertain Shield: The U.S. Intelligence System in the Throes of Reform *(2006), as well as books on the Clinton* impeachment *and* Bush v. Gore.

## PREREADING

Is there a proper distinction between what is legal and what is right? Can you imagine pursuing a morally justified course of action even though it involves illegal activities? Freewrite about some possible examples. Do these examples concern the illegal activities of private individuals? Or do they concern illegal activities conducted by a powerful corporate or political body? Is there an ethical difference between such activities when they are performed by individuals as opposed to corporate or political bodies?

The revelation by *The New York Times* that the National Security Agency (NSA) is 1 conducting a secret program of electronic surveillance outside the framework of the Foreign Intelligence Surveillance Act (FISA) has sparked a hot debate in the press and in the blogosphere. But there is something odd about the debate: It is aridly legal. Civil libertarians contend that the program is illegal, even unconstitutional; some want President Bush impeached for breaking the law. The administration and its defenders have responded that the program is perfectly legal; if it does violate FISA (the administration denies that it does), then, to that extent, the law is unconstitutional. This legal debate is complex, even esoteric. But, apart from a handful of not very impressive anecdotes (did the NSA program really prevent the Brooklyn Bridge from being destroyed by *blowtorches?*), there has been little discussion of the program's concrete value as a counterterrorism measure or of the inroads it has or has not made on liberty or privacy.

Not only are these questions more important to most people than the legal questions; they are fundamental to those questions. Lawyers who are busily debating legality without first trying to assess the consequences of the program have put the cart before the horse. Law in the United States is not a Platonic abstraction but a flexible tool of social policy. In analyzing all but the simplest legal questions, one is well advised to begin by asking what social policies are at stake. Suppose the NSA program is vital to the nation's defense, and its impingements on civil liberties are slight. That would not prove the program's legality, because not every good thing is legal; law and policy are not perfectly aligned. But a conviction that the program had great merit would shape and hone the legal inquiry. We would search harder for grounds to affirm its legality, and, if our search were to fail, at least we would know how to change the law—or how to change the program to make it comply with the law—without destroying its effectiveness. Similarly, if the program's contribution to national security were negligible—as we learn, also from the *Times*, that some FBI personnel are indiscreetly whispering—and it is undermining our civil liberties, this would push the legal analysis in the opposite direction.

Ronald Dworkin, the distinguished legal philosopher and constitutional theorist, 3 wrote in *The New York Review of Books* in the aftermath of the September 11 attacks that "we cannot allow our Constitution and our shared sense of decency to become a suicide pact." He would doubtless have said the same thing about FISA. If you approach legal issues in that spirit rather than in the spirit of *ruat caelum fiat iusticia* (let the heavens fall so long as justice is done), you will want to know how close to suicide a particular legal interpretation will bring you before you decide whether to embrace it. The legal critics of the surveillance program have not done this, and the defenders have for the most part been content to play on the critics' turf.

Washington, D.C., which happens to be the home of *The New Republic*, could 4 be destroyed by an atomic bomb the size of a suitcase. Portions of the city could be rendered uninhabitable, perhaps for decades, merely by the explosion of a conventional bomb that had been coated with radioactive material. The smallpox virus—bioengineered to make it even more toxic and the vaccine against it ineffectual, then aerosolized and sprayed in a major airport—could kill millions of people. Our terrorist enemies have the will to do such things. They may soon have the means as well. Access to weapons of mass destruction is becoming ever easier. With the September 11 attacks now more than four years in the past, forgetfulness and complacency are the order of the day. Are we safer today, or do we just feel safer? The terrorist leaders, scattered by our invasion of Afghanistan and by our stepped-up efforts at counterterrorism (including the NSA program), may even now be regrouping and preparing an attack that will produce destruction on a scale to dwarf September 11. Osama bin Laden's latest audiotape claims that Al Qaeda is planning new attacks on the United States.

The next terrorist attack (if there is one) will likely be mounted, as the last one was, from within the United States but orchestrated by leaders safely ensconced abroad. So suppose the NSA learns the phone number of a suspected terrorist in a foreign country. If the NSA just wants to listen to his calls to others abroad, FISA doesn't require a warrant. But it does if either (A) one party to the call is in the United States and the interception takes place here or (B) the party on the U.S. side of the conversation is a "U.S person"— primarily either a citizen or a permanent resident. If both parties are in the United States, *no* warrant can be issued; interception is prohibited. The problem with FISA is that, in order to get a warrant, the government must have grounds to believe the "U.S. person" it wishes to monitor is a foreign spy or a terrorist. Even if a person is here on a student or tourist visa, or on no visa, the government can't get a warrant to find out whether he is a terrorist; it must already have a reason to believe he is one.

As far as an outsider can tell, the NSA program is designed to fill these gaps by conducting warrantless interceptions of communications in which one party is in the United States (whether or not he is a "U.S. person") and the other party is abroad and suspected of being a terrorist. But there may be more to the program. Once a phone number in the United States was discovered to have been called by a terrorist suspect abroad, the NSA would probably want to conduct a computer search of all international calls to and from that local number for suspicious patterns or content. A computer search does not invade privacy or violate FISA, because a computer program is not a sentient being. But, if the program picked out a conversation that seemed likely to have intelligence value and an intelligence officer wanted to scrutinize it, he would come up against FISA's limitations. One can imagine an even broader surveillance program, in which *all* electronic communications were scanned by computers for suspicious messages that would then be scrutinized by an intelligence officer, but, again, he would be operating outside the framework created by FISA.

The benefits of such programs are easy to see. At worst, they might cause terrorists to abandon or greatly curtail their use of telephone, e-mail, and other means of communicating electronically with people in the United States. That would be a boon to us, because it is far more difficult for terrorist leaders to orchestrate an attack when communicating by courier. At best, our enemies might continue communicating electronically in the mistaken belief that, through use of code words or electronic encryption, they could thwart the NSA.

So the problem with FISA is that the surveillance it authorizes is unusable to discover who is a terrorist, as distinct from eavesdropping on known terrorists—yet the former is the more urgent task. Even to conduct FISA-compliant surveillance of non-U.S. persons, you have to know beforehand whether they are agents of a terrorist group, when what you really want to know is who those agents are.

FISA's limitations are borrowed from law enforcement. When crimes are committed, there are usually suspects, and electronic surveillance can be used to nail them. In counterterrorist intelligence, you don't know whom to suspect—you need surveillance to find out. The recent leaks from within the FBI, expressing skepticism about the NSA program, reflect the FBI's continuing inability to internalize intelligence values. Criminal investigations are narrowly focused and usually fruitful. Intelligence is a search for the needle in the haystack. FBI agents don't like being asked to chase down clues gleaned from the NSA's interceptions, because 99 out of 100 (maybe even a higher percentage) turn out to lead nowhere. The agents think there are better uses of their time. Maybe so. But maybe we simply don't have enough intelligence officers working on domestic threats.

I have no way of knowing how successful the NSA program has been or will be, 10 though, in general, intelligence successes are underreported, while intelligence failures are fully reported. What seems clear is that FISA does not provide an adequate framework for counter-terrorist intelligence. The statute was enacted in 1978, when apocalyptic terrorists scrambling to obtain weapons of mass destruction were not on the horizon. From a national security standpoint, the statute might as well have been enacted in 1878 to regulate the interception of telegrams. In the words of General Michael Hayden, director of NSA on September 11 and now the principal deputy director of national intelligence, the NSA program is designed to "detect and prevent," whereas "FISA was built for long-term coverage against known agents of an enemy power."

In the immediate aftermath of the September 11 attacks, Hayden, on his own ini- 11 tiative, expanded electronic surveillance by NSA without seeking FISA warrants. The United States had been invaded. There was fear of follow-up attacks by terrorists who might already be in the country. Hayden's initiative was within his military authority. But, if a provision of FISA that allows electronic surveillance without a warrant for up to 15 days following a declaration of war is taken literally (and I am not opining on whether it should or shouldn't be; I am not offering any legal opinions), Hayden was supposed to wait at least until September 14 to begin warrantless surveillance. That was the date on which Congress promulgated the Authorization for Use of Military Force, which the administration considers a declaration of war against Al Qaeda. Yet the need for such surveillance was at its most acute on September 11. And, if a war is raging inside the United States on the sixteenth day after an invasion begins and it is a matter of military necessity to continue warrantless interceptions of enemy communications with people in the United States, would anyone think the 15-day rule prohibitive?

We must not ignore the costs to liberty and privacy of intercepting phone calls and 12 other electronic communications. No one wants strangers eavesdropping on his personal conversations. And wiretapping programs have been abused in the past. But, since the principal fear most people have of eavesdropping is what the government might do with the information, maybe we can have our cake and eat it, too: Permit surveillance intended to detect and prevent terrorist activity but flatly forbid the use of information gleaned by such surveillance for any purpose other than to protect national security. So, if the government discovered, in the course of surveillance, that an American was not a terrorist but was evading income tax, it could not use the discovery to prosecute him for tax evasion or sue him for back taxes. No such rule currently exists. But such a rule (if honored) would make more sense than requiring warrants for electronic surveillance.

Once you grant the legitimacy of surveillance aimed at detection rather than at 13 gathering evidence of guilt, requiring a warrant to conduct it would be like requiring a warrant to ask people questions or to install surveillance cameras on city streets. Warrants are for situations where the police should not be allowed to do something (like search one's home) without particularized grounds for believing that there is illegal activity going on. That is too high a standard for surveillance designed to learn rather than to prove.

## READING FOR CONTENT

1.  Paraphrase the distinction that Posner makes between legality and concrete, practical, and effective consequences in paragraph 2.
2.  Summarize the benefits of wiretapping that Posner postulates in paragraphs 6–7.
3.  State in your own words the difference between wiretapping for surveillance and wiretapping for prosecution that Posner describes in paragraph 12.

## READING FOR GENRE, ORGANIZATION, AND STYLISTIC FEATURES

1.  How do Posner's concessions that "I have no way of knowing" and "I am not offering any legal opinions" in paragraphs 10–11 exemplify the genre of personal commentary that he professes to be writing?
2.  In paragraph 12, how does the formula "We must not ignore . . . . But, since the principle fear. . . " help to organize Posner's argument? Underline in the text similar formulas that he uses throughout the essay.
3.  In paragraphs 5 and 11, Posner speculates about forms that the next terrorist attack on the United States and the FBI's attitudes toward counterterrorist intelligence might take. How do such imaginative exercises match the style of personal commentary?

## READING FOR RHETORICAL CONTEXT

1.  In paragraph 1, how does a newspaper report about the government's abuse of electronic surveillance provide a rhetorical context for Posner's argument?
2.  In paragraph 11, how does Posner's account of surveillance missteps on September 11, 2001, provide a rhetorical context for his argument?

## WRITING ASSIGNMENTS

1.  Write a 750-word response to the editors of *The New Republic* in which you develop your own commentary in support of Richard Posner's argument for relaxing the legal standards for wiretapping by the government.
2.  Write a 750-word response to the editors of *The New Republic* in which you develop your own commentary attacking Richard Posner's argument for relaxing the legal standards for wiretapping by the government.

## SYNTHESIS WRITING ASSIGNMENTS

1.  In a 1,000-word essay, compare and contrast Quittner's and Kaminer's attitudes toward the development of advanced surveillance technology and its effect on individual rights.
2.  Many private citizens and law-enforcement officers maintain that if you have done nothing wrong, then you have nothing to fear from surveillance of your activities or searches of your home or car. Respond to that belief in a 1,250-word essay that draws on at least three readings from this chapter.

3. Are the amendments to the Constitution sufficient to protect our individual rights, given recent advances in surveillance technology? Answer this question in a 1,250-word essay that draws on at least three of the articles in this chapter.

4. Under what circumstances, if any, do we have to give up our right to privacy? Answer this question in a 1,250-word essay that draws on at least three of the articles in this chapter.

5. Do the events of September 11, 2001, justify employing technology that may violate individual privacy? Answer this question in a 1,250-word essay that draws on at least three of the articles in this chapter.

6. Write a 1,250-word essay that distinguishes between types of high-tech evidence that should be admitted in court and types that should be excluded. Cover all the varieties of crime-fighting technology that are described in this chapter.

7. How far has technology taken us along the path Orwell predicted in *1984?* In response to this question, write a 1,250-word essay that draws on at least three of the articles in this chapter.

8. In the first paragraph of his article, Colbridge points out that it is difficult to maintain the "proper balance between the personal privacy of individuals and the government's obligation to enforce the law and ensure public safety." Draw on at least two other articles to write a 1,250-word response to Colbridge's statement.

# Social Sciences

■■ **SUBJECTS AND METHODS OF STUDY
IN THE SOCIAL SCIENCES**

Anthropology, economics, education, political science, psychology, sociology, and geography are called social sciences because they use the process of scientific inquiry to study various aspects of society, such as human behavior (psychology), human relationships (family studies), social conditions (sociology), political conduct (government), and cultural practices (anthropology). Social scientists begin their inquiry by **asking questions or identifying problems** related to particular phenomena. In Chapter 13, Pauline Irit Erera asks, "What Is a Family?" and Rebecca M. Blank asks, "Absent Fathers: Why Don't We Ever Talk About the Unmarried Men?"

Such questions reveal the sorts of conversation conducted by social scientists. The writers posing those questions identify possible causes of the phenomena they are studying and then form a **hypothesis** based on certain assumptions they have made. They next try to verify the hypothesis by making a series of **careful observations**, assembling and analyzing **data**, and determining a clear **pattern of response**. If the data verify their hypothesis, they will declare it confirmed. Many social scientists conduct investigations "**in the field**," testing their hypotheses in actual problem situations by making onsite observations, interviewing, conducting case studies and cross-sectional and longitudinal studies, collecting surveys and questionnaires, examining artifacts and material remains, and studying landscapes and ecology. Kathryn Edin and Maria Kefalas derive "Unmarried with Children" (Chapter 13) from a sociological case study they conducted. Other social scientists, such as experimental psychologists, work under carefully controlled conditions in laboratory settings.

## ◾ SPECIAL TYPES OF SOCIAL SCIENCE WRITING

When researchers complete their studies, they present their findings in official reports, organized in accordance with the scientific method (see the introductory section on the natural sciences). A format commonly found in research articles is introduction with background and problem statement; method; results; discussion; summary. An **abstract** (a brief summary of the article) may precede the study. Usually, the study begins with a **literature** review in which the writer recapitulates previous research. Social scientists regard this acknowledgment of their predecessors' work and of divided opinion about it to be crucial to the development of any new thesis or interpretation. Often, when they publish their work, they designate it as a "**proposal**" or a "**work in progress**" because they have not yet arrived at conclusions that they are willing to consider final. They view this kind of publication as a means of receiving feedback or peer review that will enable them to continue with new insights and perspectives. They believe that a community of scholars cooperating within a complex system of checks and balances will ultimately arrive at some statement of truth.

Advanced social science courses teach students how to evaluate these formal reports of research findings. Meanwhile, all students should be familiar with less specialized forms of writing in the social sciences, such as summaries of research; reviews of the literature; case studies; proposals; position papers; presentation of new theories and methods of analysis; commentaries, reviews, analyses, critiques, and interpretations of research.

For examples of various genres of social science writing, consult the following sources:

*Review of the literature*: Robert L. Barret and Bryan E. Robinson's "Children of Gay Fathers," Chapter 13; Wade F. Horn's "Promoting Marriage as a Means for Promoting Fatherhood," Chapter 13; Pauline Irit Erera's "What Is a Family?" Chapter 13.

*Case study*: Barret and Robinson's "Children of Gay Fathers," Chapter 13; Kathryn Edin and Maria Kefalas's "Unmarried with Children," Chapter 13.

*Theory*: James Q. Wilson's "Cohabitation Instead of Marriage," Chapter 13.

*Position paper*: Herbert Gans's "The War Against the Poor Instead of Programs to End Poverty," Chapter 14.

*Interpretation of research*: *The Economist*, "Middle of the Class," Chapter 14.

*Proposal*: Rebecca M. Blank, "Absent Fathers: Why Don't We Ever Talk About the Unmarried Men?" Chapter 13.

Regardless of the specialized genre, writers in the social sciences are expected to engage in a spirited conversation with other writers on the topic they address. Most of the articles mentioned offer footnotes and bibliographies that report on the parameters of their conversation with others.

Student papers in the social sciences are likewise expected to engage in this kind of conversation. Here are some typical writing assignments in the social sciences, as drawn from exercises in the following chapters:

Use Pauline Irit Erera's arguments in "What Is a Family?" to write a defense of the family arrangements described in Barret and Robinson's "Children of Gay Fathers" and Edin and Kefalas's "Unmarried with Children." (page 497)

How widespread are the class discrimination and prejudice that Gans discusses in "The War Against the Poor Instead of Programs to End Poverty"? Use the selections by Angela Locke, Charmion Browne, and Dirk Johnson to write an essay in response. (page 535)

Write an essay in which you agree or disagree with Rebecca Blank's view in "Absent Fathers: Why Don't We Ever Talk About the Unmarried Men?" that the problems of poor single men have not been fully investigated. (page 499)

Note that these assignments do not ask you to do original data research or draw statistical inferences from data already collected. They do, however, require you to join the conversation recorded in academic publications, field studies, personal narratives, and journalistic reports.

## ■ PERSPECTIVES ON SOCIAL SCIENCE WRITING

In this anthology, we present reading selections on social science topics by journalists and other popular writers as well as by social scientists. As with scientific writers of research reports and summary or speculative articles, these social science writers treat a common subject matter, but their approaches differ. Take, for example, Angela Locke, whose article in the feminist news-journal *off our backs*, "Born Poor and Smart," appears on pages 502–03, and Dirk Johnson, whose *New York Times* article, "Economic Pulse: Indian Country," appears on pages 532–34. These writers do not use special modes of social science writing, nor do they rely heavily on other sources or write for specialized readers. Still, their writing is very important for social scientists because it reflects the very stuff of everyday life that social scientists study. Likewise, consider Barbara Ehrenreich's "Serving in Florida" from her popular book, *Nickel and Dimed: On (Not) Getting By in America*. Ehrenreich treats an issue that social scientists find extremely important as a barometer of public feeling, and not surprisingly her book has generated extensive conversation among journalists and popular writers as well as among academic scholars in the social sciences.

## ■ SOCIAL SCIENCE WRITERS' ORGANIZATIONAL PLANS

Social science writers rely on a variety of organizational plans: time order, narration, process; antecedent-consequent, cause-effect; description; statement-response; comparison and contrast; analysis, classification; definition; problem-solution; question-answer. You will find that some plans appear more frequently than others. Given the nature of the inquiry process, social scientists use the **statement-response, problem-solution, question-answer** plans with some regularity. Notice that in Rebecca M. Blank's "Absent Fathers: Why Don't We Ever Talk About the Unmarried Men?" (Chapter 13), the title indicates a question that will be answered. Also popular is the **antecedent-consequent** plan, because it enables writers to analyze and explain the causes of behaviors and events. Notice how Wade F. Horn structures "Promoting Marriage as a Means of Promoting Fatherhood" (Chapter 13) according to this plan. When you are reading social science writing, look for overlapping organizational plans. Very few social science writers rely on only one; they use networks of different plans, often intermeshing them in a single piece.

# ◼ AUTHORS' LITERARY TECHNIQUES

Did you ever wonder why some writers are clear and easy to understand and others are pedantic and inaccessible? Clear writers process their information and ideas in an organized and modulated sequence, and they articulate their thinking in crisp, uncluttered prose. Pedantic and inaccessible writers often presume that their readers know a great deal of specialized terminology that allows them to dispense with explanations, examples, and illuminating details. Writers make themselves understood by defining new terms, concepts, and specialized vocabulary; providing examples, scenarios, and illustrations; and using figurative language.

You will find that many of the selections in this unit display a specialized vocabulary. In some cases, familiar terms are often given new, specialized meanings. Take, for example, the various definitions of "family" in Chapter 13. As you read, pay close attention to the different ways writers handle vocabulary. Some use specialized words with impunity, assuming that their readers have sufficient background knowledge for comprehension. Other writers provide helpful contexts that give clues to verbal meaning. Still others supply definitions of specialized vocabulary. Definitions may take the form of explanations of causes, effects, or functions; synonyms; negations; analogies; descriptions; and classifications. Some definitions are brief, like the following from Pauline Irit Erera's "What Is a Family?"

> Only half of American children live in families that the Census Bureau defines as the traditional nuclear family: a married couple living with their biological children and no one else (Vobejda, 1994). (p. 463)

Other definitions are long, extended ones, such as Herbert Gans's definition of "undeserving poor" in "The War Against the Poor Instead of Programs to End Poverty" (Chapter 14).

Another technique social science writers use to make specialized subjects more accessible to nonspecialized readers is to provide concrete examples and illustrations. Notice the effective examples found in the writing of Kathryn Edin and Maria Kefalas and Barbara Ehrenreich.

Writing in the social sciences, then, invites a wide variety of approaches, organizational plans, styles, authorial presences, and literary techniques. Although the selections in this chapter do not always exemplify wholly academic social science writing, they do suggest the range of types, modes, and styles in that discourse. Writers in the social sciences often vary their own range from the extreme impersonality of technical reports to the impassioned concern of urgent social issues. The social sciences, after all, study people and their interaction in society. The diversity of the social sciences, therefore, is as broad as the diversity of people and institutions they examine and as broad as the conversations that are swirling around in the public forum and in the academic ivory tower.

*Thirteen*

# The Changing
# American Family

Drawing on research in sociology, psychology, and social psychology, the six readings in this chapter focus on the dramatic challenges confronting American families. Our traditional views of families come into question as families are being transformed and redefined by forces such as single parenting, divorce, maternal employment, delayed child-bearing, adult independent living, and homosexual parenting couples. As the authors in this chapter point out, the American family is both vulnerable and resilient in the face of these forces.

In the opening selection, "Children of Gay Fathers," Robert L. Barret and Bryan E. Robinson discuss the ramifications of homosexual parents for children's development. Their essay is the product of a case study of attitudes toward homosexuality held by a young man raised by a gay father, which the authors analyze and interpret in the light of a specialized bibliography of twenty-six academic books and articles. Next, Pauline Irit Erera traces the rise and fall of the traditional family in "What Is a Family?" Central to Erera's discussion is a defense of diverse, nontraditional families. Her study presents data about such families gleaned from a specialized bibliography of thirty-seven academic books and articles.

Alarmed by the dissolution of the nuclear family, James Q. Wilson writes the next essay on the pros and cons of "Cohabitation Instead of Marriage." A distinguished professor of government and of management and public policy, Wilson weighs the costs and benefits of cohabitation as an alternative to marriage and concludes that living together is less socially advantageous than being married. His essay, an analysis of concepts and ideas rather than of data or statistics, provides an example of theoretical writing in the social sciences. In the next selection, "Promoting Marriage as a Means for Promoting Fatherhood," Wade F. Horn focuses on the problem of the increasing number of father-absent households. According to Horn, a revitalization of marriage is the chief means of strengthening father–child relationships. Horn's extensively documented footnotes lend authority to his recommendations, exemplifying a union of academic research and public-spirited advocacy for a better parenting environment.

Kathryn Edin and Maria Kefalas illustrate yet another form of academic competence united with public awareness in their essay, "Unmarried with Children." Their collaboration as professors of sociology has resulted less in statistical gathering or interpretation than in an in-depth field study of the opportunities and life choices available to one young single parent in a poor urban environment. Low in the number of its footnotes, charts, graphs, and other conventional tools of academic social science, but high in the intensity of its questions, observations, and interpretation of details, Edin and Kefalas's essay typifies a respected form of sociological analysis in today's universities. In "Absent Fathers: Why Don't We Ever Talk About the Unmarried Men?" Rebecca M. Blank deploys the conventional methodology of the social sciences, but she directs it toward a wholly unexpected question. While most academic studies of single parenting focus on unmarried mothers, Blank's study focuses on unmarried fathers and produces a surprising conclusion that many of them have contact with their children but provide low child support because employment opportunities have passed them by. Evolving methodologies and approaches in the social sciences have enriched academic conversations about the changing American family, and these conversations have in turn contributed to a renewed discussion of the topic in the public arena.

■ ■ ■ ■ ■ ■ ■ ■ ■ ■ ■

# Children of Gay Fathers

## *Robert L. Barret and Bryan E. Robinson*

*Bob Barret is a professor of counseling at the University of North Carolina at Charlotte, a psychologist, a gay father, and a grandfather of five. His current writings include* Gay Fathers: Encouraging the Hearts of Gay Dads and Their Families, *coauthored with Bryan E. Robinson;* Counseling Gay Men and Lesbians, *coauthored with Colleen Logan; and* Ethical Issues in HIV-Related Psychotherapy *with Jon Anderson.*

*Bryan E. Robinson, a professor of counseling, special education, and child development at the University of South Carolina, has authored over twenty-five books and more than one hundred articles. His most recent books include* Gay Fathers: Encouraging the Hearts of Gay Dads and Their Families, *coauthored with Bob Barret;* Don't Let Your Mind Stunt Your Growth, *and* A Guidebook for Workaholics, Their Partners and Children and the Clinicians Who Treat Them.

## PREREADING

Comment on your familiarity with the issue of homosexual parenting. Did the idea of a gay man choosing to be an active parent and visible father ever occur to you? Why, or why not? Freewrite your response.

The children of gay fathers are like children from all families. Some are academi-   1
cally talented, some struggle to get through school, some are model students, and some

are constantly in trouble. In thinking about the children of gay fathers, it is essential to recognize that many of them have experienced the divorce of their parents, others have grown up in single-parent homes, and still others have been caught in major crossfire between their parents, grandparents, and perhaps their community over the appropriateness of gay men serving in the father role. Much of any distress that one sees in a child living with a gay father may in fact be the result of the divorce or other family tensions. Legitimate concerns about the impact of living with a gay father include the developmental impact of the knowledge that one's father is gay, reasonable worries about the timing of coming out to children, and creating sensitivity to how the children will experience society's generally negative attitudes towards homosexuality.

Coming out to children is usually an emotion-laden event for gay fathers. The disclosure of one's homosexuality creates anxiety about rejection, fear of hurting or damaging the child's self-esteem, and grieving over the loss of innocence. Some gay fathers never accomplish this task and remain deeply closeted, citing legal and emotional reasons (Bozett, 1980, 1981; Humphreys, 1979; Spada, 1979). Recent publications report the intricacies of this question (Corley, 1990). Those who never disclose their homosexuality often lead deeply conflicted lives and present parenting styles that are characterized by psychological distance (Miller, 1979). Those who do come out to their children do so in the desire to be more of a whole person as a father. As they try to merge their gayness with the father role, they encounter a different kind of conflict: deciding how open to be about their sexual relationships and how much exposure to the gay community to offer their children (Robinson & Barret, 1986).

Fathers report that the first concern they have about coming out is the well-being and healthy adjustment of their children. Many gay fathers seek the help of counselors or specialists in child development as they decide when and how to tell their children about their homosexuality. Research studies indicate that fathers and children report that they are closer after self-disclosure about the father's sexual orientation (Bozett, 1980; Miller, 1979). Bigner and Bozett (1989) studied the reasons that gay fathers give for coming out to their children. Among the most cited were wanting their children to know them as they are, being aware that children will usually discover for themselves if there is frequent contact, and the presence of a male lover in the home.

Gay fathers may come out indirectly by showing affection to men in front of their children or by taking them to gay community events. Others choose to come out verbally or by correspondence (Maddox, 1982). Factors in disclosure are the degree of intimacy between the father and his children and the obtrusiveness of his gayness (Bozett, 1988). By and large, the research suggests that children who are told at an earlier age have fewer difficulties with the day-to-day issues that accompany their father's homosexuality (Bozett, 1989).

The parenting styles of gay fathers are not markedly different from those of other single fathers, but gay fathers try to create a more stable home environment and more positive relationships with their children than traditional heterosexual parents (Bigner & Jacobsen, 1989a; Bozett, 1989). One study found that homosexual fathers differed from their heterosexual counterparts in providing more nurturing and in having less traditional parenting attitudes (Scallen, 1981). Another study of gay fathers found no differences in paternal involvement and amount of intimacy (Bigner & Jacobsen, 1989b). In general, investigators have found that gay fathers feel an additional responsibility to provide effective fathering because they know their homosexuality causes others to examine their parenting styles more closely (Barret & Robinson, 1990). This is not to say that no risk is involved in gay fathering. Miller (1979) found that six daughters of the gay fathers in his study had significant life problems. Others have reported that the children of gay fathers must be prepared to face ridicule and harassment (Bozett, 1980; Epstein, 1979) or may be alienated from their agemates, may become confused about their sexual identity, and may express discomfort with their father's sexual orientation (Lewis, 1980). Most researchers have concluded that being homosexual is compatible with effective parenting and is not usually a major issue in parental relationships with children (Harris & Turner, 1986).

As Chip reveals (Figure 13–1), dealing with the outside world is a task that gay fathers and their children must master. Gay families live in a social system that is generally uncomfortable with homosexuality and that certainly does not overtly support gay

6

---

## CASE STUDY—CHIP SPEAKS

My name is Chip and I'm seventeen and in twelfth grade. When we first moved to Indianapolis, I learned my dad was gay. I was twelve. I didn't really think much about it. There was a birthday coming up and Dad said we were going to go out and buy a birthday card. He went out, drove around the block and then parked in front of our house. Then he took me to the park and told me the facts of life. He asked me if I knew what it meant to be gay. I told him, "Yeah, it means to be happy and enjoy yourself." Then he started to explain to me about being homosexual. I really didn't know what it was at that point, until he explained it to me.

It's an accepted part of my life now. I've been growing up with it almost five years. When he invites another guy into the house it's OK. I don't bring other kids home then. One of my friends is extremely homophobic and he lets that fact be known. I wouldn't dare risk anything or it would be like "goodbye" to my friend. My other two friends, I don't know how they would react. So I have to be careful about having certain friends over. To me it's blatantly obvious. Having been exposed to so many gay people, I know what to look for and what I'm seeing. Sometimes it's kind of hard because people make fun of gay people. And, if I stick up for their rights, then I get ridiculed. So I just don't say anything at school. It's kind of hard sometimes.

The good thing is that you get a more objective view of people in general, being raised by someone who's so persecuted by society. You begin to sympathize with anyone who is persecuted by society. You tend not to be as prejudiced. You need to appreciate people for what they are personally, not just in terms of color, religion, or sexual preference. That's the best thing. The hardest thing is hearing all those people making cracks or jokes on TV or at school and not being really able to do anything about it. Because he's my dad after all, it makes me kind of sad. I never feel ashamed or embarrassed, but I do feel a little pressured because of this. One time a friend of mine made a joke about gay people. I just played it off like I thought it was funny, but I didn't. You have to pretend you think the same thing they do when you don't. That makes me feel like a fraud.

When my dad puts his arm around another man, the first thing I think is, "I could never do that." It makes me a little bit uncomfortable, but I'm not repulsed by it. There are times I wish he wouldn't do it, but other times I'm glad he can have the freedom to do it. When he first came out to me, the only question I asked him was, "What are the chances of me being gay?" He couldn't answer it. But today, to the best of my knowledge, I'm not gay. I like chasing after girls.

Sometimes I feel like I'm keeping a big secret. My dad had a holy union with a man once. My friends had big plans and we were all going out on the day of the big event. And

---

**Figure 13–1**

**Figure 13–1   (cont'd.)**

I couldn't go and couldn't explain why. Things like that have happened a number of times. I can't go and I can't tell why. They start yelling at me and get mad. They'll get over it; it's none of their business.

As fathers go, mine tends to be a little nicer—almost a mother's temperament. A friend of mine's father doesn't spend much time with him. They just seem to have stricter parents than mine. I don't know if that's just because of his personality in general or if it's because he's gay. He's a very emotional person; he cries easily. I love him. He's a good dad. He's more open than other dads. He doesn't let me get away with a lot. He tends to be more worried about me and a girl together than some other fathers are about their sons—more worried about my having sex. Whenever I go out on a date, he always says something like, "Don't do anything I wouldn't do," only he doesn't say it jokingly. Sometimes he's just overly cautious.

If I could change my dad and make him straight, I wouldn't do it. It might make things easier for me in some ways, but I wouldn't have grown up the way I have. Being exposed to the straight world and gay world equally has balanced me out more than some of the other people I know. The only things I'd want to change is society's treatment of him. (Barret & Robinson, 1990, pp. 14–15)

(*Note:* Chip's dad died of AIDS two years after this interview took place.)

parenting. One reality for gay fathers is figuring out how to interact successfully with the world of schools, after-school activities, PTAs, churches, and their children's social networks. Many gay fathers see no choice other than to continue living relatively closeted lives (Bozett, 1988; Miller, 1979). Others, fearing the damage that exposure may bring to their children and/or possible custody battles involving their homosexuality, live rigidly controlled lives and may never develop a gay identity. Those who are more open about their gayness struggle to help their children develop a positive attitude toward homosexuality while simultaneously cautioning them about the dangers of disclosure to teachers and friends. Teaching their children to manage these two tasks is a major challenge for gay fathers (Morin & Schultz, 1978; Riddle, 1978). Accomplishing this task when there are virtually no visible role models frequently leaves these fathers and their children feeling extremely isolated.

Bozett (1988) identified several strategies that these children use as they experience both their own and the public's discomfort with their gay fathers. The children of gay fathers in his study used boundary control, nondisclosure, and disclosure as they interacted with their fathers and the outside world. For example, some children limited or attempted to control the content of their interactions with their father. One father we talked with (Barret & Robinson, 1990) reported that he had offered to introduce his teenaged daughter to some of his gay friends in the hope that she would see how normal they were. Her reply was a curt "Dad, that will never happen!" Another father told of trying to reconcile with his son but being rebuffed by the comment, "I don't want to hear anything about your personal life. I can't handle it." Such boundary control limits the ability of the relationship to grow. Other ways that children control boundaries are by not introducing their friends to their fathers or by carefully managing the amount of time they spend together, as Chip reveals in his interview.

Some children do learn to let their friends know carefully about their father's   8
homosexuality. These disclosures have a potential for both increased intimacy and
rejection. Helping children discriminate when and how to inform their friends is a critical challenge of gay parenting. As children grow up, these issues may become more
complex, as families struggle to involve gay fathers in events such as weddings, graduations, and birth celebrations, where the presence of the gay father and his partner may
raise questions.

Children of gay fathers do sometimes worry that their sexual orientation may   9
become contaminated by their father's homosexuality. Either they or their friends may
begin to question whether they are gay as well. Those children who do disclose their
father's homosexuality report being harassed by the use of such terms as *queer* and *fag*.
Naturally, this concern is greatest during their teenage years (Riddle & Arguelles,
1981). Obviously, the children of gay fathers need to consider carefully the consequences of disclosure. Keeping this aspect of their lives secret may have the same negative impact on their development as isolation, alienation, and compartmentalization
does on gay men.

This is not to say that the responses of social support networks are universally neg-   10
ative. Many children with gay fathers report that their friends are both curious and supportive. It is important to recognize that coming out is a process rather than a discrete
event. Fathers, children, and their friends need time to move into the process and to
examine their own feelings and attitudes so that acceptance and understanding replace
confusion and fear. One child of a gay father said:

> At first, I was really angry at my dad. I couldn't figure out how to tell my friends what
> was going on, so I said nothing. My dad and I had terrible fights as he put pressure on
> me to say it was OK. I thought what he was doing was sinful and embarrasing. But
> over time, I began to realize that he is the same dad he has always been, and now we
> are closer than ever. My friends have also got used to the idea and like to spend time
> with him, too.

## State of Research on Children of Gay Fathers

In reviewing the impact of gay fathering on children, it is important to acknowledge that   11
most children who live with gay fathers are also the products of divorce and may show
the psychological distress that typically accompanies the experience of marital dissolution. All too often, the emotional distress of children with gay parents is solely attributed
to the parents' sexual orientation and is not seen as a complex mixture of family dynamics, divorce adjustment, and the incorporation of the parents' sexual coming out.

Only two studies have directly addressed the children of gay fathers (Green, 1978;   12
Weeks, Derdeyn, & Langman, 1975). In both studies, the researchers gave psychological tests to the children. The findings from this testing have been used to support the
notion that a parent's homosexuality has little bearing on the child's sexual orientation.
Children showed clear heterosexual preferences or were developing them. Green concluded that "The children I interviewed were able to comprehend and verbalize the
atypical nature of their parents' lifestyles and to view their atypicality in the broader
perspective of the cultural norm" (p. 696). Our interviews with children have also supported this finding (Barret & Robinson, 1990). Still, the problem is that the observations of Weeks and his colleagues (1975) are based on the clinical assessment of only

two children, and the Green study (1978) observed only the children of lesbian mothers and the children of parents who had experienced sex-change surgery. None of the parents in that sample were classified as gay fathers. The findings of these two studies and others of lesbian mothers (e.g., Goodman, 1973; Hoeffer, 1981; Kirkpatrick, Smith, & Roy, 1981) are frequently generalized to include the gay father's children, even though important differences exist between transsexuals and gay men as well as between gay men and lesbians.

## Conclusions

The profile we use to understand and describe gay fathers and their children is far from conclusive. Clearly, the literature has improved, after 1982, in its use of comparison groups and a more diverse, nationwide sampling. Still, until researchers can obtain larger, more representative samples and use more sophisticated research designs, caution must be exercised in making sweeping generalizations about gay fathers and their families. Meanwhile, it is possible to speculate from some limited data that, although not fully developed, provides an emerging picture of the children of gay fathers: 13

1. They are like all kids. Some do well in just about all activities; some have problems; and some are well adjusted.
2. They live in family situations that are unique and must develop strategies to cope with these situations.
3. They need help sorting out their feelings about homosexuality and their anxieties about their own sexual orientation.
4. They may be isolated and angry and may have poor relationships with their fathers.
5. They are in little danger of sexual abuse and unlikely to "catch" homosexuality.
6. Many of them adjust quite well to their family situation and use the family as a means to develop greater tolerance of diversity.
7. Some of them become involved in the human rights movement as they promote gay rights.
8. Their relationships with their fathers have a potential for greater honesty and openness.

## References

Barret, R., & Robinson, B. (1990). *Gay fathers.* New York: Free Press.

Bigner, J., & Bozett, F. (1989). Parenting by gay fathers. *Marriage and Family Review, 14,* 155–175.

Bigner, J., & Jacobson, R. (1989a). Parenting behaviors of homosexual and heterosexual fathers. *Journal of Homosexuality, 18,* 173–186.

Bigner, J., & Jacobsen, R. (1989b). The value of children to gay and heterosexual fathers. *Journal of Homosexuality, 18,* 163–172.

Bozett, F. (1980). Gay fathers: How and why they disclose their homosexuality to their children. *Family Relations: Journal of Applied Family and Child Studies, 29,* 173–179.

Bozett, F. (1981). Gay fathers: Evolution of the gay father identity. *American Journal of Orthopsychiatry, 51,* 552–559.

Bozett, F. (1988). Social control of identity of gay fathers. *Western Journal of Nursing Research, 10,* 550–565.

Bozett, F. (1989). Gay fathers: A review of the literature. *Journal of Homosexuality, 18,* 137–162.

Corley, R. (1990). *The final closet: The gay parent's guide to coming out to their children.* Miami: Editech Press.

Epstein, R. (1979, June). Children of gays. *Christopher Street,* 43–50.

Goodman, B. (1973). The lesbian mother. *American Journal of Orthopsychiatry, 43,* 283–284.

Green, R. (1978). Sexual identity of 37 children raised by homosexual or transsexual parents. *American Journal of Psychiatry, 135,* 692–697.

Harris, M., & Turner, P. (1986). Gay and lesbian parents. *Journal of Homosexuality, 18,* 101–113.

Hoeffer, B. (1981). Children's acquisition of sex-role behavior in lesbian-mother families. *American Journal of Orthopsychiatry, 51,* 536–544.

Humphreys, L. (1979). *Tearoom trade.* Chicago: Aldine.

Kirkpatrick, M., Smith, C., & Roy, R. (1981). Lesbian mothers and their children. *American Journal of Orthopsychiatry, 51,* 545–551.

Lewis, K. (1980). Children of lesbians: Their point of view. *Social Work, 25,* 200.

Maddox, B. (1982, February). Homosexual parents. *Psychology Today,* 62–69.

Miller, B. (1979, October). Gay fathers and their children. *The Family Coordinator, 28,* 544–551.

Morin, S., & Schultz, S. (1978). The gay movement and the rights of children. *Journal of Social Issues, 34,* 137–148.

Riddle, D. (1978). Relating to children: Gays as role models. *Journal of Social Issues, 34,* 38–58.

Riddle, D., & Arguelles, M. (1981). Children of gay parents: Homophobia's victims. In I. Stuart & L. Abt (Eds.), *Children of separation and divorce.* New York: Van Nostrand Reinhold.

Robinson, B., & Barret, R. (1986). *The developing father.* New York: Guilford Press.

Scallen, R. (1981). *An investigation of paternal attitudes and behaviors in homosexual and hetero-sexual fathers.* Doctoral dissertation, California School of Professional Psychology, San Francisco, CA. (*Dissertation Abstracts International, 42,* 3809B).

Spada, J. (1979). *The Spada report.* New York: Signet Books.

Weeks, R. B., Derdeyn, A. P., & Langman, M. (1975). Two cases of children of homosexuals. *Child Psychiatry and Human Development, 6,* 26–32.

## READING FOR CONTENT

1. Why do Barret and Robinson mention repeatedly that most children of gay fathers have experienced their parents' divorce? Why is that an important consideration?

2. Why is it that some gay fathers never disclose their sexuality to their children?

3. List the three strategies that children of gay fathers use when they have to interact with the outside world.

4. Summarize what the research reveals about the effect of parents' homosexuality on their children.

5. According to Barret and Robinson, why must we exercise caution in making generalizations about gay fathers and their children?

## READING FOR GENRE, ORGANIZATION, AND STYLISTIC FEATURES

1. Underline and identify the various types of data, research findings, and authorities Barret and Robinson cite to support their view.

2. Which features of Barret and Robinson's writing are particularly scholarly or "academic"?

3. Compare Barret and Robinson's writing style with that of Chip in the case study. How are the two styles similar or different?

4. Notice how Barret and Robinson conclude the selection. Explain whether or not you think the ending is effective.

## READING FOR RHETORICAL CONTEXT

1. What is Barret and Robinson's rhetorical purpose? What is the central point they want to communicate to their readers?

2. Why do you think the authors include the case study of Chip? What is the effect on the reader? What would be gained or lost if the case study were left out?

3. Why do you think Barret and Robinson refer to Chip only once? Why don't they analyze or respond to Chip's story?

## WRITING ASSIGNMENTS

1. Write a brief summary of the barriers that gay parents and their children must overcome.

2. For an audience who has not read "Children of Gay Fathers," write an essay in which you discuss the problems that children of gay fathers face and explain how these children turn out.

3. Go to the library and research the topic of homosexual parenting. Write a three- to four-page paper answering questions like the following: How do gay men and lesbians become parents? Are the numbers of homosexual families increasing? What is the reaction of conservative groups to gay parenting? What are the views of the gay community?

■ ■ ■ ■ ■ ■ ■ ■ ■ ■ ■

# What Is a Family?

## *Pauline Irit Erera*

*Pauline Irit Erera, Associate Professor at the University of Washington School of Social Work, has written extensively about family diversity, focusing on step-, foster, and lesbian families, and on noncustodial fathers. This selection is from her recent book,* Family Diversity: Continuity and Change in the Contemporary Family.

## PREREADING

Respond to the title "What Is a Family?" by writing out your definition for family. Share your definition with the other students in your class.

$\mathrm{F}$amilies have always come in various forms, reflecting social and economic condi-   1
tions and the cultural norms of the times. However, since the 1960s, the increasing
diversity among families in the United States and most other Western nations has been
especially striking. At a dizzying pace, the traditional, two-parent, heterosexual family
has given way to a variety of family arrangements. Today, most adults no longer live in a
coresident nuclear family (Hill, 1995). The first-married, heterosexual family we have
cherished since at least Victorian times is but one of numerous alternative family structures (Csikszentmihalyi, 1997).

In 1998, just 26 percent of American households were composed of married   2
couples with children. This was down from 45 percent in the early 1970s (University of
Chicago National Opinion Research Center, 1999). Only half of American children
live in families that the Census Bureau defines as the traditional nuclear family: a married couple living with their biological children and no one else (Vobejda, 1994). Furthermore, family arrangements differ considerably according to race and ethnicity.
Although about 56 percent of white American children live in a traditional nuclear
family, only about 26 percent of African American children and 38 percent of Hispanic
children do (Vobejda, 1994).

In this [reading] I examine alternative constructions of what a family is. I trace the   3
rise and decline of the traditional family, outline the subsequent increase in family
diversity, and examine reactions to family diversity as expressed in the debate about
"family values." I also discuss the continuing influence of the traditional family model.
Finally, I consider the strengths and promise of family diversity, and set forth the perspectives that inform the analysis of the families in this book.

## DEFINING FAMILIES

The family is not simply a social institution. It is an ideological construct laden with   4
symbolism and with a history and politics of its own. As Jagger and Wright (1999) put it,
"The groupings that are called families are socially constructed rather than naturally or
biologically given" (p. 3). In studying families, we need to keep clear the distinctions
between the institutionalized family, the ideology of the family, and the lives of actual
families. Although social and economic forces shape family life, our understanding of
family is shaped by the evolving patterns of the actual families around us. Furthermore,
conceptions of what constitutes a family are necessarily rooted in time and place.
White, Western, two-parent families have generally been regarded, explicitly or implicitly, as the model or template against which we compare all families, regardless of culture, ethnicity, race, or class. This parochial view distorts our understanding of diverse
families by considering them deviations from the norm (Smith, 1995; Thorne, 1982).

One early definition of the family was that offered by the anthropologist George   5
Peter Murdock (1949), based on his survey of 250 ethnographic reports:

> The family is a social group characterized by common residence, economic coopera-
> tion, and reproduction. It includes adults of both sexes, at least two of whom maintain
> a socially approved sexual relationship, and one or more children, own or adopted, of
> the sexually cohabiting adults. (p. 1)

Murdock identified the basic family unit found in about one quarter of the societies he
surveyed as "a married man and woman with their offspring" (p. 1), which he termed

a nuclear family. Another quarter of the societies were predominantly polygamous, with families based on plural marriages of a spouse, hence, in his view, constituting two or more nuclear families. In the remaining half surveyed, the families were extended in that the nuclear family resided with the bride's or the groom's parents and/or other relatives. Murdock, reflecting the prevailing orthodoxy of the times, concluded that the nuclear family was universal and inevitable, the basis for more complex family forms.

Given the diversity of families and the political debates about them, a single, all-    6
encompassing definition of "family" is impossible to achieve. Families are defined in a variety of ways depending on the purposes and circumstances (Smith, 1995; Sprey, 1988). Although traditionalists have held blood ties or consanguinity to be a defining characteristic of the family, others argue that we should define families according to the attachments and intimacy that individuals have toward significant people in their lives. This latter definition shifts the focus from the family's structure or legal status to the nature and meaning of relationships (Dowd, 1997).

Diverse families challenge our definition and perceptions of what a family is.    7
These families also "challenge gender roles and influence gender typing by what they say and what they do" (Dowd, 1997, p. 110). They force us to reconsider our conceptions of what a mother, father, parent, and sibling are. Is a family defined by genes and blood relationships? Shared residence? Is it a group of people who provide one another social, emotional, and physical support, caring, and love? Does a family necessarily involve two adults? Are these adults necessarily of the opposite sex? Must families be based on marriage? Can a child have two or more mothers or fathers? Is a parent more "real" by virtue of biological or legal status? Does a family have to share a common residence, economic cooperation, and reproduction to be a family? Such questions are the subject of heated debates about the family and "family values."

## The Rise and Decline of the Traditional Family:

### The Heyday of the Traditional Family

The 1950s saw a surge in family formation associated with the end of the depression    8
and World War II. Although few Americans ever enjoyed family lives as harmonious, wholesome, or predictable as the ones portrayed in those beloved fifties television sitcoms, such programs symbolized a definition of ideal family life that was widely shared in that decade. Three fifths of U.S. households in that period fit the model of the nuclear family structure, with its breadwinner-husband and homemaker-wife, of their pop culture icons. The economy was booming and even many working-class men earned enough to support such families. Yet this upsurge in marriage and childbearing proved to be a short-lived experiment. Starting in the 1960s, fertility rates began to decline, and the trend to early marriage was reversed (Silverstein & Auerbach, 1999).

Family life in the 1950s was hardly ideal. Families were not as well off economi-    9
cally as they would become by the end of the 1960s; African Americans in particular had higher rates of poverty than they do now. Women, minorities, lesbians, gays, and nonconforming groups were subject to discrimination, and family problems got little attention or social assistance (Coontz, 1997).

In some ways, the decline of the 1950s family grew out of the trends and contra-    10
dictions of the fifties themselves. The main reason for family change was the breakdown of the postwar social compact between government, corporations, and workers.

The 1950s were years of active government assistance to families. Government-backed home mortgages financed many of the new family homes, and the minimum wage was set high enough to support a family of three above the poverty level. Large numbers of workers joined unions, received pensions and health benefits, and worked a relatively short workweek. Corporations and the wealthy were taxed at high rates to support high levels of spending on veterans benefits and public works (Coontz, 1997).

## Family Diversity in the 1960s and 1970s

The affluence and optimism that explains the family behavior of the postwar generation 11 were challenged by America's new economic problems, whose impact was felt at the family level in the form of inflation and lower real earnings. Public policies aggravated these problems by cutting taxes for corporations and the wealthy while cutting spending for services, public works, and investments in human capital (Coontz, 1997). This meant that families had to modify the socially valued form of the family to try to protect their socially valued lifestyle: the standard of living to which they had become accustomed. Economic pressures made women's employment more a matter of necessity than of choice (Coontz, 1997). Today's politicians are being disingenuous when they advocate a return to the 1950s family while opposing the kinds of social and political supports that helped make it possible (Coontz, 1997).

Along with the economic shifts in the late 1950s and early 1960s came techno- 12 logical developments and social movements that also contributed to the stunning increase in family diversity. The example of African Americans' struggle to secure civil rights inspired other minorities and marginalized groups—women, gay men and lesbians, the disabled—to fight for their rights. The 1960s and 1970s became an era of diversity and identity politics as a host of "others" sought recognition and liberation from the constraints of discriminatory laws, social policies, and negative stereotypes. Foremost among those claiming their rights were women.

The struggle for women's liberation was advanced by the availability of the birth 13 control pill and other methods that gave women control over reproduction. These changes generated an increased acceptance of sexual behavior not necessarily linked with marriage, for women as well as for men (Riley, 1997). While white feminists began to claim the right to control and limit their fertility through the use of contraception and abortion, women of color started claiming the right to have their fertility not be controlled by forced contraception and sterilization (Hargaden & Llewellin, 1996). By 1973, many women in the United States and other industrialized countries were able to prevent pregnancies, had access to legal abortion, and could end unwanted pregnancies before birth (Riley, 1997).

The movement for gender equality led to increased employment opportunities 14 for women, while at the same time declining wage rates for unskilled male workers made them less desirable marriage partners. Although paid far less than their male counterparts, an increasing number of women were now employed and financially independent. Consequently, more women who were unhappy in their marriages were able to divorce (Coontz, 1997; Riley, 1997). The changing roles of women, their increasing participation in the labor force, and their economic independence had undercut the economic basis of marriage (Lichter & McLaughlin, 1997). With divorce becoming more available, community norms regarding divorce, single parenthood, and nonmarital childbearing began to change. More people were themselves the product of diverse families, and were more accepting of divorce, single parenthood, and women's right to live independently.

Single-parent families were in many respects the pioneers of family diversity, 15 paving the way for the recognition of other families. The growing acceptance of divorced, single-parent families facilitated the emergence of yet another form of single parenthood: that resulting not from divorce but from women electing to give birth while remaining single. Women increasingly saw motherhood without marriage as offering greater satisfaction and security than a marriage of questionable stability (Mann & Roseneil, 1999). Increasingly, women chose to cohabit rather than formally marry, to postpone marriage and childbearing, and to live alone. Still others chose to give birth, adopt, or foster children as single parents. Many women, defying the stigma attached to childless women, elected not to have children at all, thus creating a new family configuration: childless families by choice.

With fewer unwanted pregnancies and fewer unwanted births, and with more 16 white, single mothers keeping their babies as had African American mothers in the past, fewer white babies were available for adoption (Riley, 1997). The decline in the number of babies placed for adoption precipitated an increased interest in international adoptions as an alternative. Because these adoptions often involved children who were racially and/or ethnically different from their adoptive parents, the adoption could not be kept secret as had been the practice in the past. The growing acceptance of adoptive families, in turn, facilitated a greater acceptance of stepfamilies and other families not related by blood.

With the increasing numbers and visibility of single-parent, step-, and adoptive 17 families, the gay liberation movement opened the way for the emergence of gay and lesbian families. Some gay men and lesbians were divorced and had custody of the children, becoming in the process single-parent families. Others chose to give birth to a child within the lesbian/gay relationship.

Another factor contributing to family diversity since the 1970s, and especially to 18 foster families and grandmother-headed families, has been a dramatic increase in the imprisonment of women and mothers, a legacy of the war on drugs with its harsh sentencing policies. Most of the women in prison are there for drug-related offenses, often because of the activities of a male partner. This, together with the growing number of women, especially women of color, infected by HIV (the human immunodeficiency virus) has contributed to an increasing number of children whose mothers are not able to parent them. In addition, many children, and especially African American children, are removed from homes considered unfit and placed in foster care, sometimes with relatives. Increasingly, grandmothers are assuming responsibility for raising their grandchildren.

Finally, innovations in reproductive technology have vastly opened up the possi- 19 bilities for people to create new kinds of families, further challenging conventional definitions of family. New reproductive technologies (NRTs) include donor insemination, embryo freezing and transfer, ovum extraction, and *in vitro* fertilization (IVF). The first test-tube baby, conceived through *in vitro* fertilization, was born in England in 1978, and the first surrogate birth, in which an embryo was transferred to a woman with no genetic connection to it, took place in 1986. In 1992, a postmenopausal grandmother gave birth to her own granddaughter in South Africa, having served as a surrogate for her daughter's embryo.

To protect marriages, the law in most jurisdictions recognizes husbands of insem- 20 inated women as the "real" fathers (Benkov, 1997) while denying parental rights to donors (Bartholet, 1993). Although NRTs reflect a preference for biological reproduction over social parenting through adoption, fostering, or informal care of relatives (McDaniel, 1988), social parenting has become a powerful force in family diversity. NRTs were originally administered to support traditional nuclear families, and were denied to unmarried women. However, as they became increasingly available through for-profit laboratories seeking to expand their markets, they were offered to single women, including lesbians. To date, about one million children have been conceived in laboratories in the United States (Benkov, 1997). The NRTs have undermined the cultural norm that blood relations are the *sine qua non* of families, and that nonbiological members are not "real" family members. Families created through reproductive technologies, similar to adoptive-foster families, and to some extent like stepfamilies, defy the notion that biological conception has to be the basis for family formation. This disjunction between reproduction and parenting, between the biological and social aspects of parenting, alters the meaning of parenthood, kinship, and family (Benkov, 1997; Gross, 1997; Stacey, 1996).

## Families in the 1980s and 1990s: The Backlash Against Family Diversity

The 1980s and 1990s were, in many respects, a period of regression in the United 21 States with respect to civil rights and policies supporting diversity. The family became, and continues to be, a battleground over contending visions of what a family ought to be. Voices on the right blame changes in the family for a wide range of social problems, while voices on the left look to the family to provide the basis for a more communitarian society. At one extreme, we hear claims that the family is obsolete, a reactionary institution destined to disappear. At the other, conservatives strive to uphold "family values," advocating a return to the conventional family arrangements enshrined in mid-century television sitcoms (Csikszentmihalyi, 1997). Across the political spectrum, invoking "family values" is a way of idealizing the traditional nuclear family to the exclusion of other family forms (Jagger & Wright, 1999).

Family values proponents offer a simple and dangerous misdiagnosis of what they 22 consider wrong in America—the "family breakdown" thesis (Stacey, 1998). Family breakdown—namely the high divorce rates, the decline of the two-parent married family, and the increase in family diversity—has been blamed for everything from child poverty, declining educational standards, substance abuse, high homicide rates, AIDS (acquired immune deficiency syndrome), infertility, and teen pregnancy to narcissism and the Los Angeles riots (Coontz, 1997; Jagger & Wright, 1999; Wright & Jagger, 1999). Family breakdown is in turn attributed to a generalized decline in family values, which is often blamed on a lack of commitment to marriage, an acceptance of female-headed families as a way of life, feminism, the sexual revolution, and gay liberation (Beca Zinn, 1997; Coontz, 1997). Hence women's desire for personal fulfillment is described by conservatives as an egotistic abandonment of parental obligations that sacrifices the well-being of children (Council on Families in America, 1996). Ironically, the current emphasis on family self-sufficiency and the pressure on single mothers to be self-supporting are in direct conflict with conservatives' traditional preference for full-time mothers (Wright & Jagger, 1999).

In keeping with the family breakdown thesis, political discourse in the 1990s 23 blamed single motherhood for the perpetuation of an "underclass" in British and

American society. Although there is little consensus among scholars about the under-class, or whether it exists at all, under the label of the underclass debate, researchers returned to old questions about the relationship between family structure, race, and poverty. In the 1960s and early 1970s, the discussion focused on how poor families adapted to poverty; current discussions, in contrast, are primarily concerned with the failure of women-headed families to lift themselves and their children out of poverty (Jarrett, 1994). For example, American conservative Charles Murray, who played a prominent role in blaming single motherhood for poverty and violence, argued (in Wright & Jagger, 1999) that more young women were choosing unwed motherhood because the sexual revolution had destigmatized it and the welfare system was reward-ing it. Though welfare costs have always been a very small portion of the federal budget, single-parent families were also held responsible for a "crisis" of the welfare state (Beca Zinn, 1997; Mann & Roseneil, 1999; Wright & Jagger, 1999).

24    Although single mothers were being attacked, they suffered high rates of poverty, a legacy of social policies that especially disadvantages women and children. Welfare ben-efits to impoverished single mothers and their children in the United States declined markedly from the 1970s to the 1990s, and in 1996, the federal welfare entitlement was abolished in favor of a drastically limited employment-based program. The attacks on welfare were, in effect, attacks against struggling and vulnerable families (Stacey, 1996).

25    The attack on single mothers is partly a backlash against feminism, an attempt to restore fathers to their "rightful role." It is also motivated by concerns over how women are exercising their agency and their freedom of choice to become mothers or not. Instead of viewing disadvantaged women as committed, responsible mothers who assume custody and care of their children, the rhetoric portrays them as oppressors of the fathers. The fathers, on the other hand, who are at least as responsible for the cre-ation of poor single-parent families, are often viewed as the victims. If they pay child support, they are heralded as responsible fathers, even though the child support is usu-ally insufficient to meet the expense of raising the children, and even though they gen-erally forgo the daily responsibilities of caring for the children. This rhetoric justifies reductions in government assistance to single mothers and their children, making their situations even worse (Mann & Roseneil, 1999).

## The Family Values Agenda

26    Family values proponents define the family as an institution comprising people related by blood and marriage that performs specific social functions. The majority of family values advocates use "the family" to mean a heterosexual, conjugal, nuclear, domestic unit, ide-ally one with a male breadwinner, female homemaker, and their dependent offspring—a version of the 1950s television Ozzie-and-Harriet family, sometimes updated to include employed wives and mothers (Stacey, 1998). This prescriptive definition of what consti-tutes a proper family obscures racial, class, and sexual diversity in domestic arrangements, as well as masking the inequities within the traditional family (Stacey, 1998). Pluralism, so commonly recognized in other aspects of American society, has yet to be fully accepted when it comes to the family (Klee, Schmidt, & Johnson, 1989).

27    A striking feature of our contemporary family politics is the chasm between behavior and ideology. Most family values enthusiasts still judge our "brave new fami-lies" by a fifties standard to which only a minority of citizens would wish to return

(Stacey, 1998). In a 1999 national survey, for example, only a third of the respondents thought that parents should stay together just because they have children (University of Chicago National Opinion Research Center, 1999).

Support for "traditional family values" serves political purposes. It provides a 28 rationale for family surveillance and intervention, focuses attention on individual moral solutions to social problems rather than costly public solutions, and offers a simple alternative to dealing with the real complexities of social change. The new call for family values represents an effort to reduce collective responsibility and increase the dependency of family members on one another (Wright & Jagger, 1999).

Pro-family values stories are appearing in the press, in popular magazines, on 29 radio and television talk shows, and in scholarly journals. During the late 1980s, a network of research and policy institutes, think tanks and commissions, began mobilizing to forge a national consensus on family values and to shape the family politics of the "new" Democratic Party. Central players were the Institute for American Values and the Council on Families in America, whose goal is to restore the privileged status of lifelong, heterosexual marriage.

The Council on Families in America (1996) urges marriage counselors, family 30 therapists, and family life educators to approach their work "with a bias in favor of marriage" and to "link advocacy for children to advocacy for marriage" (p. 311). It advocates a revision of the federal tax code "to provide more favorable treatment for married couples with children" (p. 313), and advocates a "bias in favor of marriage-with-children in the allocation of subsidized housing loans and public housing" (p. 314).

Marriage has become increasingly fragile with the increase in women's employ- 31 ment and their reduced economic dependency on men. It has also become less obligatory, particularly for women. In all cultures and eras, stable marriage systems have rested upon coercion—overt or veiled—and on inequality. Proposals to restrict access to divorce and parenting implicitly recognize this. Without coercion, divorce and single motherhood will remain commonplace. It seems a poignant commentary on the benefits to women of modern marriage that even when women retain chief responsibility for supporting children, raising them and caring for them, when they earn much less than men with similar "cultural capital," and when they and their children suffer major economic loss after divorce, so many regard divorce as the lesser evil.

Rather than examining and solving the problems of traditional marriages that so 32 often end up in divorce, advocates of family values aim to coerce women to stay in marriages by erecting barriers to divorce. They wish to restore fault criteria to divorce proceedings and impose new restrictions, like mandatory waiting periods and compulsory counseling. Claiming that divorce and unwed motherhood inflict devastating harm on children, they seek to revive the social stigma that once marked these "selfish" practices. They advocate restricting adoption to married couples, and they oppose welfare payments to unmarried mothers. However, in their staunch advocacy of marriage, they avoid examining what might be lacking in a traditional marriage, especially for women, or questioning why so many women choose to divorce or not to marry.

What is primarily at stake in the debate over the family is the relationship 33 between the sexes. Advocates of family values assign responsibilities to families without explicitly acknowledging the burdens that family life places on women or the gender conflicts resulting from unequal roles. At the same time, they place most of the blame for family problems on "deviant" women, especially those who raise children alone.

## The Significance of Family Structure

Contrary to the claims of family values advocates, there is no empirical basis for granting 34 privileged status to the heterosexual, nuclear, two-parent family (Acock & Demo, 1994; Dowd, 1997; Silverstein & Auerbach, 1999). Few social scientists would agree that a family's structure is more important than the quality of the relationships between parents and children. Revisionists employ academic sleights of hand to evade this consensus. For example, they rest claims on misleading comparison groups and on studies that do not use any comparison groups at all. In fact, most children from both divorced or non-divorced families turn out reasonably well; and when other parental resources—like income, education, self-esteem, and a supportive social environment—are roughly similar, signs of two-parent privilege largely disappear. Most research indicates that a stable, intimate relationship with one responsible, nurturing adult is a child's surest path to becoming a nurturing adult as well (Furstenberg & Cherlin, 1991). As Dowd (1997) points out, "Dysfunctional families come in all shapes and sizes; so do healthy families" (p. xv). There is no question that two responsible, loving parents generally can offer children more than one parent can. However, three or four might prove even better. Putting the case against the essential significance of structure, Dowd (1997) concludes,

> Children need love, care, and parenting. Structure neither produces nor insures that those things will be present. We need to put children first, structure second. It makes no sense to punish children or separate them from their families as the consequence of structure that they had no hand in creating and that are unconnected to their well-being. (p. xix)

## The "Essential Father"

With many mothers no longer at home full time, and in the absence of universal child 35 care and policies to help families integrate work and caregiving, the conservative stance taps into widespread anxiety about "who will raise the children" (Silverstein & Auerbach, 1999). Attacks on single-parent families are also based on claims that families without fathers cannot socialize sons into civilized manhood (Charles Murray, in Wright & Jagger, 1997). These concerns about the well-being of children, and especially boys, represent a reaction against the women's movement, the perceived loss of male privilege, and the gay liberation movement (Silverstein & Auerbach, 1999). As expressed by the Council on Families in America (1996), "The explosion of never-married motherhood in our society means that fathers are increasingly viewed as superfluous, unnecessary, and irrelevant" (pp. 302–303). Men have lost their position at the center of family life. With marriage losing its normative force and with increasing numbers of women working, men have seen their economic ascendancy over the family being eroded, and most are expected to share at least some of the domestic tasks. The conservative concern about the necessity of the "essential father" can be seen as an effort to reestablish male dominance by rescuing the traditional family based on traditional gender roles (Silverstein & Auerbach, 1999).

Conservatives have it backward when they argue that the collapse of traditional fam- 36 ily values is at the heart of our social decay. The losses in real earnings and in breadwinner jobs, the persistence of low-wage work for women, global economic restructuring, and corporate greed have wreaked far more havoc on Ozzie-and-Harriet land than have the combined effects of feminism, the sexual revolution, gay liberation, the counterculture, narcissism, and every other value flip of the past half-century. There is no going back to the "good old 1950s," when breadwinner-husbands had unpaid homemaker wives who tended dependent children and the household full time. The modern family has been decisively replaced by the postmodern family of working mothers, high divorce rates, and diverse family arrangements (Coontz, 1997; Stacey, 1998). Nevertheless, the traditional family continues to cast its shadow over other family forms.

## The Hegemony of the Traditional Family

The overpowering strength of the paradigm of the first-married, heterosexual family  37 lingers even though this family style has long since lost its place as the most prevalent (Glick, 1989). Despite the diversity, society's institutions continue to support a single family structure that is no longer applicable to the majority of families. As Dowd (1997) states,

> We as a society, through law, support nuclear marital families in significant material and ideological ways. We provide resources including financial support, fringe benefits, tax breaks, and housing. We facilitate the use of reproductive technology or adoption for favored families. We define our vision of family, ideologically and practically . . . by limiting recognition of non-marital families. (p. 4)

The supremacy and the idealization of the traditional family model are expressed  38 in laws, policies, and institutional practices, attitudes, and behaviors. Nuclear families have historically provided a model of normalcy for which family specialists, such as psychologists, social workers, family researchers and theorists, have based their ideals (Adams & Steinmetz, 1993). Increased social tolerance for diversity has, to some extent, modified the notion that nuclear families offer an exemplary family structure. Nevertheless, social policies and attitudes still favor the traditional family. This puts enormous pressures on diverse families to play down their uniqueness and to act like the traditional family, as if this is the only "right" kind of family, irrespective of the differences in structure and style. Despite its demographic decline, "The image of this idealized form [of the traditional nuclear family] persists in the social consciousness and remains the standard against which all other configurations are compared" (Allen & Baber, 1992, p. 379).

Viewed against a template of the first-married, heterosexual family, other family  39 structures tend to fall into two broad stereotypical categories: the deviant and the variant. A deviant stereotype is assigned to families that seem much too different to be regarded as a variation of the first-married, heterosexual family. In the past, this included the single-parent family, and now includes lesbian and gay families, teenage single-parent families, and childless families, among others. Deviant implies not only that these families are different, but that they are bad or wrong in some way. Therefore, "deviant" families need somehow to prove their legitimacy.

The variant family stereotype views diverse families more positively, considering  40 them more or less like first-married, heterosexual families, but with a difference. Families considered variant usually have two parents of the opposite sex who reside with children in the same household; notable examples are adoptive and stepfamilies. Although lacking the negative connotation of deviance, this positive stereotype is also problematic. It establishes unrealistic expectations based on the model of the traditional nuclear family. Because such families are not quite the same when measured against the template, they may be left feeling that they are falling short in some respects. The stereotypes exert pressures on families to try to function in the same mold as the traditional family, or to "pass" in order to gain the legitimacy and resources reserved for traditional families. The appeal of assimilation is especially attractive for those families that most resemble a traditional family. "Passing," however, creates tensions between the actual and idealized lifestyles of family members. As Eheart and Power (1995) found in their study of adoptive families, "failure occurs when families live stories that differ in acceptable ways from their expectations of what their family life should be like" (p. 211). It engenders a falsehood that may lead family members to experience a sense of failure, shame, and identity confusion. At the same time, it restricts their creativity, flexibility, and uniqueness (Biddle, Kaplan, & Silverstein, 1998). In contrast, when families manage to let go of myths of the ideal family life, their lives are experienced as appropriate and fitting.

It is therefore not surprising that with the exception of stepfamilies and single-parent families, families . . . have rarely been examined as family structures in their own right. To the extent that they have been considered at all, it has been from a particular academic or practice perspective. Foster families, viewed as nuclear families temporarily hosting an additional child, are examined from the standpoint of child welfare; gay and lesbian families, under gender or women's studies; and grandmother-headed families, within gerontology or race and gender studies. Furthermore, these families are often characterized as lacking something. Single-parent families are deemed deficient for lack of a father. Grandparents raising grandchildren are discounted because they are old, are not the parents, and are frequently people of color and poor. Gay and lesbian families are not considered as families at all because the partners are of the same sex and because they are not married. The refusal to acknowledge them as families is a denial that their relationships count, regardless of their stability, duration, or quality.

Family theories do not sufficiently account for families in their diversity. New perspectives are needed that value family plurality and resilience (Demo & Allen, 1996; McAdoo, 1998). As Weitzman (1975) noted a quarter of a century ago, in a diverse society, a single family form cannot fit the needs of all. Rather than shaping concepts of the family from a single mold, we must recognize the diversity and fluidity of family and household arrangements, and acknowledge change in families as a sign of strength.

## References

Acock, A. C., & Demo, D. H. (1994). *Family diversity and well-being.* Thousand Oaks, CA; Sage.

Adams, B. N., & Steinmetz, S. K. (1993). Family theory and methods in the classics. In P. G. Boss & W. J. Doherty (Eds.), *Sourcebook of family theories and methods: A contextual approach* (pp. 71–94). New York: Plenum.

Allen, K. R., & Baber, K. M. (1992). Starting the revolution in family life education: A feminist vision. *Family Relations, 41,* 378–384.

Bartholet, E. (1993). *Family bonds: Adoption and the politics of parenting.* Boston: Houghton Mifflin.

Beca Zinn, M. B. (1997). Family, race, and poverty. In A. S. Skolnick & J. H. Skolnick (Eds.), *Family in transition* (9th ed., pp. 316–329). New York: HarperCollins.

Benkov, L. (1997). Reinventing the family. In A. S. Skolnick & J. H. Skolnick (Eds.), *Family in transition* (9th ed., pp. 354–379). New York: HarperCollins.

Biddle, C., Kaplan, S. R., & Silverstein, D. (1998). *Kinship: Ties that bind.* Available at: http://www.adopting.org/silveroze/html/kinship.html.

Coontz, S. (1997). *The way we really are: Coming to terms with America's changing families.* New York: Basic Books.

Council on Families in America. (1996). Marriage in America: A report to the nation. In D. Popenoe, J. Bethke-Elshtain, & D. Blankenhorn (Eds.), *Promises to keep: Decline and renewal of marriage in America* (pp. 293–317). Lanham, MD: Rowman & Littlefield.

Csikszentmihalyi, M. (1997). *Finding flow: The psychology of engagement with everyday life.* New York: Basic Books.

Demo, D. H., & Allen, K. R. (1996). Diversity within lesbian and gay families: Challenges and implications for family theory and research. *Journal of Social and Personal Relationships, 13*(3), 415–434.

Dowd, N. E. (1997). *In defense of single-parent families.* New York: New York University Press.

Eheart, B. K., & Power, M. B. (1995). Adoption: Understanding the past, present, and future through stories. *Sociological Quarterly, 36*(1), 197–216.

Furstenberg, F. F., Jr., & Cherlin, A. J. (1991). *Divided families: What happens to children when parents part.* Cambridge, MA: Harvard University Press.

Glick, P. C. (1989). Remarried families, stepfamilies, and stepchildren: A brief demographic analysis. *Family Relations, 38,* 24–27.

Gross, H. E. (1997). Variants of open adoptions: The early years. *Marriage and Family Review, 25*(1–2), 19–42.

Hargaden, H., & Llewellin, S. (1996). Lesbian and gay parenting issues. In D. Davies & C. Neal (Eds.), *Pink therapy: A guide for counselors and therapists working with lesbian, gay and bisexual clients* (pp. 116–130). Buckingham, England: Open University Press.

Hill, M. S. (1995). When is a family a family? Evidence from survey data and implications for family policy. *Journal of Family and Economic Issues, 16*(1), 35–64.

Jagger, G., & Wright, C. (1999). Introduction: Changing family values. In G. Jagger & C. Wright (Eds.), *Changing family values* (pp. 1–16). London: Routledge.

Jarrett, R. L. (1994). Living poor: Family life among single parent, African-American women. *Social Problems, 41*(1), 30–49.

Klee, L., Schmidt, C., & Johnson, C. (1989). Children's definitions of family following divorce of their parents. In C. A. Everett (Ed.), *Children of divorce: Developmental and clinical issues* (pp. 109–127). New York: Haworth.

Lichter, D. T., & McLaughlin, D. K. (1997). Poverty and marital behavior of young women. *Journal of Marriage and the Family, 59*(3), 582–595.

Mann, K., & Roseneil, S. (1999). Poor choices? Gender, agency and the underclass debate. In G. Jagger & C. Wright (Eds.), *Changing family values* (pp. 98–118). London: Routledge.

McAdoo, H. P. (1998). African-American families: Strengths and realities. In H. I. McCubbin, E. A. Thompson, A. I. Thompson, & J. A. Futrell (Eds.), *Resiliency in African-American families* (pp. 17–30). Thousand Oaks, CA: Sage.

McDaniel, S. A. (1988). Women's roles, reproduction, and the new reproductive technologies: A new stork rising. In N. Mandell & A. Duffy (Eds.), *Reconstructing the Canadian family: Feminist perspectives* (pp. 175–206). Toronto, Ontario: Butterworths.

Murdock, G. P. (1949). *Social structure.* New York: Free Press.

Riley, N. (1997). American adoptions of Chinese girls: The socio-political matrices of individual decisions. *Women's Studies International Forum, 20*(1), 87–102.

Silverstein, L. B., & Auerbach, C. F. (1999). Deconstructing the essential father. *American Psychologist, 54*(6), 397–407.

Smith, T. E. (1995). What a difference a measure makes: Parental-separation effect on school grades, not academic achievement. *Journal of Divorce and Remarriage, 23*(3–4), 151–164.

Sprey, J. (1988). Current theorizing on the family: An appraisal. *Journal of Marriage and the Family, 50*(4), 875–890.

Stacey, J. (1996). *In the name of the family: Rethinking family values in the postmodern age.* Boston: Beacon.

Stacey, J. (1998). *Brave new families: Stories of domestic upheaval in late twentieth century America* (Rev. ed.). New York: Basic Books.

Thorne, B. (1982). Feminist rethinking of the family: An overview. In B. Thorne & M. Yalom (Eds.), *Rethinking the family: Some feminist questions* (pp. 1–24). New York: Longman.

University of Chicago National Opinion Research Center. (1999, November 24). *The emerging 21st century American family.* Available at: http://www.norc.uchicago.edu/new/homepage. htm.

Vobejda, B. (1994). Study alters image of "typical" family. *Seattle Times.* Available at: http://seattle times.nwsource.com.

Weitzman, L. J. (1975). To love, honor, and obey? Traditional legal marriage and alternative family forms. *Family Coordinator,* 24(4), 531–547.

Wright, C., & Jagger, G. (1999). End of century, end of family? Shifting discourses of family "crisis." In G. Jagger & C. Wright (Eds.), *Changing family values* (pp. 17–37). London: Routledge.

## READING FOR CONTENT

1. Explain what Erera means when she says, "The main reason for family change was the breakdown of the postwar social compact between government, corporations, and workers" (paragraph 10).

2. Make a list of the various complaints about single mothers. Explain how Erera defends single moms against each attack.

3. Summarize Erera's argument against proponents of family values.

4. Does Erera view fathers as "essential" to the well-being of children? Why, or why not?

5. Explain the distinction Erera makes between deviant and variant families.

## READING FOR GENRE, ORGANIZATION, AND STYLISTIC FEATURES

1. Use the section of Chapter 8 devoted to argument to explain how Erera has fashioned an argument in which she accounts for both sides of the problem.

2. What devices or aids help the reader follow Erera's argument?

3. What types of sources does Erera draw upon, and what functions do those sources serve?

## READING FOR RHETORICAL CONTEXT

1. Toward the beginning of the selection, Erera provides a number of alarming statistics. What purpose do they serve?

2. What is the function of the questions in paragraph 7?

3. How do you think readers will be affected by Erera's argument? After reading the selection, would you support her position? Why, or why not?

## WRITING ASSIGNMENTS

1. After reading the selection, respond to the question, "What is a family?" Compare your postreading response to the definition you wrote for your prereading. Write a brief essay comparing and/or contrasting the two definitions.

2. How do the statistics in paragraph 2 compare to your experience? Is your family included in the 26 percent of American households with married couples and children? Write an essay that describes your family.

3. Interview an individual or couple who are representative of one of the nontraditional structures or lifestyles—single-parent families, lesbian and gay families, teenage single-parent families, childless families, grandmother-headed families, foster families—that Erera discusses. Ask the interviewee(s) to explain what he or she sees as the advantages and disadvantages of the particular lifestyle. Then write an essay in which you compare your interviewee's explanations with those presented by Erera. Draw your own conclusions.

4. Using Erera's explanation of the family breakdown thesis and her description of the attack on single mothers as a base, conduct some research on separated, divorced, never married, and widowed single-parent families. Drawing on the guidelines for synthesis essays in Chapter 7, write an essay addressed to your classmates explaining the rewards and difficulties of single parenting today.

■ ■ ■ ■ ■ ■ ■ ■ ■ ■ ■

# Cohabitation Instead of Marriage

## James Q. Wilson

*James Q. Wilson served as the Shattuck Professor of Government at Harvard University and the James Collins Professor of Management and Public Policy at UCLA. He is the author or coauthor of fourteen books, including* Moral Judgement, Moral Sense, American Government, Bureaucracy, Thinking About Crime, Varieties of Police Behavior, Political Organizations, *and* Crime and Human Nature *(coauthored with Richard J. Herrnstein). This selection is from his 2002 book,* The Marriage Problem: How Our Culture Has Weakened Families.

## PREREADING

In your view, is marriage a prerequisite to living with a partner? Why do you think increasing numbers of people are deciding to live together rather than marry? Respond to these questions in your writer's notebook.

If marriage is designed to help solve a society's need to maintain family, and if modern societies such as ours have created ways of raising children that are independent of family life, then family life ought not to be very important. If a child can be raised by a nanny or a day-care center, if its education can be left in the hands of public and private schools, if its physical well-being can be entrusted to police officers and social workers,    1 then marriage does not offer much to the father and mother. And if the couple has no wish for children, then marriage offers nothing at all. Perhaps men and women can simply decide to live together—to cohabit—without any formalities that define a "legal" marriage.

But cohabitation creates a problem that most people will find hard to solve. If people are free to leave cohabitation (and they must be, or it would be called a marriage instead), then in many cases, neither the man nor the woman has any strong incentive to invest heavily in the union. Marriage is a way of making such investments plausible by telling each party that they are united forever, and if they wish to dissolve this union that they will have to go through an elaborate and possibly costly legal ritual called divorce. Marriage is a way of restricting the freedom of people so that investing emotionally and financially in the union makes sense. I can join my money with yours because, should we ever wish to separate, we would have to go through a difficult process of settling our accounts. That process, divorce, makes merged accounts less risky. If a cohabiting couple has a child, its custody can be decided by one parent taking it. If we marry, however, the custody of the child will be determined by a judge, and so each of our interests in its custody will get official recognition. This fact makes it easier for us to have a child.

And love itself is helped by marriage. If we cohabit and I stop loving you, I walk away. This means that you have less of an incentive to love me, since your affection may not be returned by me for as long as you would like and hence your love might be wasted. But if we promise to live together forevermore (even though we know that we can get a divorce if we are willing to put up with its costs), each of us is saying that since you have promised to love me, I can afford to love you.

Cohabiting couples in the United States tend to keep separate bank accounts and divide up the expenses of their life together. And this financial practice signals a potential social burden. While married couples with unequal incomes are less likely to get a divorce than those with more equal ones, cohabiting ones with unequal incomes are likely to split apart. If our money is kept in separate accounts, then your having more (or less) money than I makes a difference. If it is kept in merged accounts, then nobody observes differences in income.

Cohabitation ordinarily does not last very long; most such unions in America break up (sometimes with a split, sometimes with a marriage) within two years. Scholars increasingly regard cohabitation as a substitute to being single, not an alternative to marriage. And a good thing, since people seem to bring different expectations to the former than to the latter. When high-school seniors were followed into their early thirties, women who highly valued having a career and men who greatly valued leisure were more likely to cohabit than were people with the opposite views. Women seemed to think that cohabitation helps their careers, men to think it helps them spend more time with "the boys." Neither view makes much sense, since cohabitation not only does not last very long, most people think cohabiting couples are doing something odd. Like it or not, the couple living together will discover in countless ways that society thinks they should either get married or split apart. And society's opinion makes sense. As Linda Waite and Maggie Gallagher put it,

> . . . marriage makes you better off, because marriage makes you very important to someone. When you are married you know that someone else not only loves you, but needs you and depends on you. This makes marriage a contract like no other.

Until recently, cultures set rules for marriage that were not only designed to protect  6
the child but to achieve a variety of other goals as well. A family was a political, economic,
and educational unit as well as a child-rearing one. It participated in deciding who would
rule the community and (except in wandering hunter-gatherer groups) control or have
privileged access to land that supplied food and cattle. Until the modern advent of
schools, families educated their children, not with books, but by demonstrating how to
care for other children, perform certain crafts, and mind cattle and agricultural fields.
These demonstrations sometimes took the form of games and sometimes depended
simply on show-and-tell, but a child's life in either event was governed by the need to
demonstrate, year by year, that it had learned how to watch, carry, feed, hunt, fish, and
build. These tutorial, educational, and economic families were linked together in kinship
groupings that constituted the whole of the small society—often no more than two hundred people, and sometimes even fewer—that lived together in a settlement.

These social functions did not prevent married men and women from caring for  7
each other, even in arranged marriages. Affection existed, though of course it was
sometimes interrupted by quarrels and beatings. This affection and the companionship
it entailed were valuable supports to family life, but they were not until recently the
chief, much less the sole, grounds for maintaining the union.

Today, the family has lost many of these functions. Politically, the family has been  8
replaced by the voting booth and the interest group, economically by the office and the
factory, and educationally by the school and the Internet. Modernity did not simply
produce these changes: Capitalism did not change the family (the family first changed
in ways that made capitalism possible), and schools did not make families less relevant
(families changed in ways that made schools more valuable). In later chapters we shall
see how these complex alterations occurred.

But for now it is important to observe that the family now rests almost entirely on  9
affection and child care. These are powerful forces, but the history of the family suggests
that almost every culture has found them to be inadequate to producing child support. If
we ask why the family is, for many people, a weaker institution today than it once was, it is
pointless to look for the answer in recent events. Our desire for sexual unions and romantic attachments is as old as humankind, and they will continue forever. But our ability to
fashion a marriage that will make the union last even longer than the romance that
inspired it depends on cultural, religious, and legal doctrines that have slowly changed.
Today people may be facing a challenge for which they are utterly unprepared: a vast,
urban world of personal freedom, bureaucratized services, cheap sex, and easy divorce.

Marriage is a socially arranged solution for the problem of getting people to stay  10
together and care for children that the mere desire for children, and the sex that makes
children possible, does not solve. The problem of marriage today is that we imagine
that its benefits have been offset by social arrangements, such as welfare payments,
community tolerance, and professional help for children, that make marriage unnecessary. But as we have already seen, the advantages of marriage—personal health, longer
lives, and better children—remain great. The advantages of cohabitation are mostly
illusory, but it is an illusion that is growing in its appeal.

## READING FOR CONTENT

1. What does Wilson say about the longevity of cohabitation?
2. Do women and men cohabit for the same reasons?

3. According to Wilson, the family has lost many of its traditional functions. What has been lost?

4. Summarize Wilson's explanation of the problem of marriage today.

## READING FOR GENRE, ORGANIZATION, AND STYLISTIC FEATURES

1. What effect does Wilson achieve with the sequence of "If . . . then" constructions in the first paragraph?

2. How would you describe the overall organizational structure of the selection? What other organizational patterns do you notice in the various paragraphs?

## READING FOR RHETORICAL CONTEXT

1. Explain Wilson's rhetorical purpose. What is the main point he is trying to get across?

2. Notice that Wilson draws heavily on one particular source. How strong would his argument be if he did not use that source to bolster his case?

## WRITING ASSIGNMENTS

1. Write an essay in which you compare and contrast a marriage contract and a cohabitation arrangement.

2. Write an essay in response to Wilson's definition of marriage as "a socially arranged solution for the problem of getting people to stay together and care for children" (paragraph 10). If you wish, you may draw upon other sources in this chapter.

■ ■ ■ ■ ■ ■ ■ ■ ■ ■ ■ ■

# Promoting Marriage as a Means for Promoting Fatherhood

## Wade F. Horn

*Wade F. Horn served as the assistant secretary for Children and Families for the U.S. Department of Health and Human Services during the Bush II administration. He also served as president of the National Fatherhood Initiative and as the U.S. Commissioner for Children, Youth, and Families. He has coauthored several books on parenting, including* The Better Homes and Gardens New Father Book *and* The Better Homes and Gardens New Teen Book.

## PREREADING

Read the first two paragraphs of the selection and speculate on the reasons for the dramatic increase in father-absent households. Record your response in your writer's notebook.

## Introduction

The most disturbing and consequential social trend of our time is the dramatic increase over the past four decades in the number of children living in father-absent households. In 1960, the total number of children living absent their biological fathers was less than 10 million. Today, that number stands at nearly 25 million, more than one-third of all children in the United States.[1]

The situation is getting worse, not better. By some estimates, 60 percent of children born in the 1990s will spend a significant portion of their childhoods in a father-absent home.[2] For the first time in our nation's history, the average expectable experience of childhood now includes time spent living without one's own father.

This is not good news, especially for children. Almost 75 percent of American children living in single-parent families will experience poverty before they turn eleven years old, compared to only 20 percent of children in two-parent families.[3] Moreover, violent criminals are overwhelmingly males who grew up without fathers, including up to 60 percent of rapists,[4] 75 percent of adolescents charged with murder,[5] and 70 percent of juveniles in state reform institutions.[6]

Children living in a father-absent home are also more likely to be suspended or expelled from school,[7] or to drop out,[8] develop an emotional or behavioral problem requiring psychiatric treatment,[9] engage in early and promiscuous sexual activity,[10] develop drug and alcohol problems,[11] commit suicide as an adolescent,[12] and be a victim of child abuse or neglect.[13] On almost any measure one can imagine, children who grow up absent their fathers do worse compared to those who live with their two, married parents.[14] In the realm of social science, there are few statements one can make with certitude, but here is one: When fatherhood falters, children suffer.

Fortunately, America seems to be awakening from its three-decade denial about the importance of fathers to families and children. A recent Gallup poll indicates that nearly 80 percent of Americans agree, "The most significant family or social problem facing America is the physical absence of the father from the home."[15] The question is no longer whether fatherlessness matters. The new question is, what can be done about it?

## Child Support Enforcement

The historic answer to the problem of fatherlessness has been child support enforcement. This, of course, is not without merit. Any man who fathers a child ought to be held financially responsible for that child. But as important as child support enforcement may be, it is unlikely by itself to substantially improve the well-being of children for several reasons.

First, having a child support order in place is no guarantee that child support will actually be paid. Some men—the true "deadbeat dads"—can pay, but don't. Others, however, are undereducated and underemployed and have little ability to pay child support. Indeed, 20 percent of all nonresident fathers earn less than $6,000 annually.[16] These fathers are not so much "deadbeat" as "dead broke." Trying to extract child support from such men has been likened to the proverbial attempt to get blood from a turnip.

Second, while receipt of child support has consistently been found to be associ-  8
ated with improvements in child outcomes, the magnitude of the effects tend to be
small. That's because the average level of child support paid to custodial mothers is
quite modest, only about $2,500 per year.[17] Such a modest amount of additional
income, although certainly helpful, is unlikely to substantially improve the life trajec-
tory of most children.

Third, an exclusive emphasis on child support enforcement may drive many low-  9
income, nonresident fathers farther away from their children. As word circulates within
low-income communities that cooperating with paternity establishment, but failing to
comply with subsequent child support orders, may result in imprisonment or revocation
of one's driver's license, many marginally employed fathers may choose to disappear
rather than face the possibility of such harsh consequences. Hence, the unintended
consequence of tough child support enforcement policies may be to decrease, not
increase, the number of children growing up with an actively involved father, proving
once again that no good deed goes unpunished.

Finally, an exclusive focus on child support enforcement ignores the many  10
noneconomic contributions that fathers make to the well-being of their children. If,
however, we want fathers to be more than cash machines for their children, we will need
to encourage their work as nurturers, disciplinarians, mentors, moral instructors, and
skill coaches, and not just as economic providers. To do otherwise is to effectively downgrade fathers to, in the words of social historian Barbara Dafoe Whitehead, "paper dads."

## Visitation

Some people, dissatisfied with the results of using child support enforcement as the pri-  11
mary strategy for dealing with today's crisis of fatherlessness, advocate enhanced visitation
as the mechanism for improving the well-being of children. Indeed, there is evidence that
positive involvement by non-custodial fathers enhances child well-being. For example, a
recent meta-analysis of sixty-three studies by Paul Amato and Joan Gilbreth found that
children who reported feeling close to their noncustodial fathers and had fathers who
engaged in authoritative parenting—that is, they listened to their children's problems,
gave them advice, provided explanations for rules, monitored their academic performance, helped with their homework, engaged in mutual projects, and disciplined
them—were significantly more likely to do well at school and show greater psychological
health compared to children whose noncustodial fathers mostly engaged them in recreational activities, such as going out to dinner, taking them on vacations, and buying them
things.[18] Hence, positive father involvement by nonresident fathers does count.

Unfortunately, other research has found that nonresident fathers are far less likely  12
than in-the-home dads either to have a close relationship with their children or to
engage in authoritative parenting.[19] One reason for this, as Amato and Gilbreth point
out, is the constraints inherent in traditional visitation arrangements. Because their
time with their children is often severely limited, many nonresident fathers strive to
make sure their children enjoy themselves when they are with them. As a result, nonresident fathers tend to spend less time than in-the-home fathers helping their children
with their homework, monitoring their activities, and setting appropriate limits, and
more time taking them to restaurants or the movies, activities that are not associated
with enhanced child outcomes. In essence, many nonresident, but visiting, fathers
transform into "treat dads." As such, while visitation by nonresident fathers is certainly

to be encouraged, the context of visitation reduces the likelihood that nonresident fathers will engage in behavior most associated with enhanced child well-being.

## Cohabitation

If, some argue, enhanced visitation is not the answer, perhaps cohabitation is. In fact, 13 cohabitation is one of the fastest growing family forms in the United States today. In 1997, 4.13 million couples were cohabiting outside of wedlock, compared to fewer than a half million in 1960.[20] Of these cohabiting couples, 1.47 million, or about 36 percent, have children younger than eighteen residing with them, up from 21 percent in 1987. For unmarried couples in the twenty-five to thirty-four age group, almost half have children living with them.[21] Indeed, it is estimated that nearly half of all children today will spend some time in a cohabiting family before the age of sixteen.[22]

Strengthening cohabitation as a means of strengthening fatherhood has found new 14 impetus in recent research by Sara McLanahan and Irwin Garfinkel, who studied "fragile families"—low-income, nonmarried couples who have had a child out-of-wedlock. Preliminary analysis of data from two cities, Oakland, California, and Austin, Texas, suggests that at the time a child is born out-of-wedlock, more than half of these couples are cohabiting.[23] Consequently, the argument goes, interventions should be aimed at strengthening this "fragile family" (so named to emphasize that these families are at greater risk of breaking up and living in poverty compared to more traditional families) and encouraging "team parenting."

Other research, however, suggests that cohabitation is unlikely to produce life- 15 time dads for children. First of all, cohabitation is a weak family form. Cohabiting couples break up at much higher rates than married couples.[24] Furthermore, only four out of ten couples who have a child while cohabiting ever go on to get married, and those that do are more likely to divorce than couples who wait until after marriage to have children.[25] Overall, three-quarters of children born to cohabiting parents will see their parents split up before they reach age sixteen, compared to only about one-third of children born to married parents.[26]

The fact that children born to cohabiting couples are likely to see their dads 16 eventually transform into occasional visitors is worrisome for several reasons. First, research on disruptions in early attachment figures suggests children may fare worse when their father is involved early in their life only to disappear than they would fare if they never established a relationship with their father in the first place. If so, encouraging cohabitation may actually be making a bad situation worse.

Second, many men in cohabiting relationships are not the biological father of 17 the children in the household, or at least are not the biological father of all the children in the household. By one estimate, 63 percent of children in cohabiting households are born not to the cohabiting couple, but to a previous union of one of the adult partners, most often the mother.[27] This is problematic in that cohabitation involving biologically unrelated children substantially increases the risk of physical and sexual child abuse.[28] Thus, not only is cohabitation unlikely to deliver a lifetime father to a child, it also brings with it an increased risk for child abuse.

Neither child support enforcement, increased visitation, nor cohabitation is the 18 answer—but that doesn't mean there is no answer.

While it is becoming increasingly popular to speak of the importance of fathers 19 to the well-being of children, it is still out of fashion to speak of the importance of marriage to the well-being of fatherhood. Yet research has consistently found that, over time, nonmarried fathers tend to become disconnected, both financially and psychologically, from their children.[29] Robert Lerman and Theodora Ooms, for example, found that whereas six of ten unwed fathers were visiting their children at least once a week during the first two years of their children's lives, by the time the children were 7.5 years old, that number dropped to only two of ten.[30] Overall, 40 percent of children living absent their fathers have not seen their fathers in more than a year. Of the remaining 60 percent, only one in five sleeps even one night per month in the father's home. Remarriage, or, in cases of unwed fatherhood, marriage to someone other than the child's mother, makes it especially unlikely that a noncustodial father will remain in contact with his children.[31]

Marriage, on the other hand, is a much more effective glue for binding fathers to 20 their children. Indeed, an analysis of a national probability sample of over thirteen thousand households found the most important determinant of whether a father lived with his children was marital status at the time of the child's birth. Fully 80 percent of fathers who were married to the mother at the time of the child's birth were living with all their biological children, compared to only 23 percent of unwed fathers.[32] Given that about 40 percent of all first marriages end in divorce, marriage is not a certain route to a lifetime father. It is, however, a more certain route than any other.

Nevertheless, discussing marriage as the ideal or even preferred family structure 21 is difficult for several reasons. First, marriage is a deeply personal issue. One can safely assume that at least 40 percent of adults in any given audience are divorced. Many others will either have parents who are divorced, a spouse who is from a divorced family, or children who are divorced. When adults touched by divorce hear others suggest that marriage is the "best" or "ideal" situation, they often interpret this as a personal rebuke. No one likes to be told that his or her situation is somehow "second best."

Second, some have bought into the notion of "family relativism"; the idea that all 22 family structures are inherently equal, with no differential consequences for children (or adults) except for the greater propensity of single parent families to be poor. Indeed, this argument goes, if we solve the economic disadvantage of single-parent households, there will be no ill effects of growing up in a home without two married parents.

Third, some simply don't like marriage. They either see marriage promotion as a 23 thinly veiled strategy for withdrawing support from single mothers or as a means for reasserting male privilege and dominance over women. To such folks, marriage promotion is not just foolish, but downright dangerous.

The empirical literature is quite clear, however, that children do best when they 24 grow up in an intact, two-parent, married household. We know, for example, that children who grow up in a continuously married household do better at school, have fewer emotional problems, are more likely to attend college, and are less likely to commit crime or develop alcohol or illicit drug problems.[33] That these results are not simply due to differences in income is attested to by the fact that children reared in stepfamilies, which have household incomes nearly equivalent to continuously married households, do not fare any better than children reared in single-parent households. On some measures they may even do worse.[34]

The empirical evidence also is quite clear that adults—women as well as men— 25 are happier, healthier, and wealthier than their single counterparts. Moreover, married adults report having more satisfying sex than nonmarried adults, and married men show an earnings boost that is not evident in cohabiting relationships.[35] In regards to fatherhood, married fathers are, on average, more likely to be actively engaged in their children's lives and, perhaps just as important, are more accessible to them.

Of course, some married households, especially those in which domestic vio- 26 lence and child abuse are present, are horrible places for both children and adults. But contrary to the stereotypes perpetuated by the media and some advocacy groups, the reality is that domestic violence and child abuse are substantially less likely to occur in intact, married households than in any other family arrangement. The truth is the most dangerous place for women and children is a household in which mom is cohabiting with a man who isn't biologically related to the children.[36]

Given that marriage is so important to the well-being of children, adults, and 27 communities, how do we overcome our reluctance to talk about it? Syndicated colum- nist William Raspberry suggests the answer: Put children back at the center of things.

Adults have spent far too much time arguing among themselves about the virtues 28 of marriage and far too little time helping our children understand why marriage is important and how to form and sustain healthy marriages. Yet national surveys consis- tently show that young people, far from rejecting marriage as an ideal, desperately want to avoid the serial marriages and high divorce rates of their elders.[37] It is time for us to give our children what they want.

Accomplishing this is not as simple as pointing young couples to the altar and 29 insisting they marry. We do not need more bad marriages. What we need is more healthy, mutually satisfying, equal-regard marriages. To attain that, young couples will need help in acquiring the knowledge and skills necessary to form and sustain healthy marriages. That requires a new commitment of both public and private resources aimed at providing meaningful premarital education to couples contemplating mar- riage, marital enrichment to those couples who are already married, and outreach to couples in troubled marriages.

It is not, however, just children and young adults in the middle class who want 30 stable marriages. Data from the Fragile Families Initiative suggests that at the time of the child's birth, two-thirds of low-income, unwed couples want—and expect—to get married.[38] The problem is that many, if not most, of these low-income couples do not go on to get married. That, however, may be as much our fault as theirs, for our reluc- tance even to bring up the topic sends the not-so-subtle message that marriage is nei- ther expected nor valued. When we are afraid even to say the "m"-word, the wonder is not that so few ever get married, but that some actually do.

## Conclusion

Marriage cannot be the only answer to strengthening father–child relationships. Not all 31 marriages are made in heaven. Some nonresident fathers are terrific dads. Some male cohabiting partners provide children with valuable economic and social resources. And when nonresident fathers are capable of providing financial support for their children but do not, laws and policies should seek to right this wrong. Nevertheless, if what we really care about is the well-being of children, rather than the desires of adults, the inescapable conclusion is this: Children want and need their fathers as well as their mothers, and fathers are most likely to be positively involved in their children's lives if they are married to the mother. Saying so may not give much comfort to those adults who worship at the altar of self-fulfillment, but it surely gives a greater measure of hope to children who hunger for their dads.

The views expressed in this chapter do not necessarily represent the views of the [32] Administration for Children and Families, the United States Department of Health and Human Services, or the United States government.

## Notes

1. Wade F. Horn, *Father Facts*, 3rd ed. (Gaithersburg, Md.: The National Fatherhood Initiative, 1998).
2. Frank F. Furstenberg, Jr., and Andrew J. Cherlin, *Divided Families: What Happens to Children When Parents Part* (Cambridge: Harvard University Press, 1991).
3. National Commission on Children, *Just the Facts: A Summary of Recent Information on America's Children and Their Families* (Washington, D.C., 1993).
4. Karl Zinsmeister, "Crime Is Terrorizing Our Nation's Kids," *Citizen* (August 20, 1990): 2.
5. Dewey Cornell et al., "Characteristics of Adolescents Charged with Homicide," *Behavioral Sciences and the Law* 5 (1987): 11–23.
6. M. Eileen Matlock et al., "Family Correlates of Social Skills Deficits in Incarcerated and Nonincarcerated Adolescents," *Adolescence* 29 (1994): 119 130.
7. Deborah Dawson, "Family Structure and Children's Well-Being: Data from the 1988 National Health Survey," *Journal of Marriage and Family* 53 (August 1991): 573–584.
8. Sara McLanahan and Gary Sandefur, *Growing Up with a Single Parent: What Hurts, What Helps* (Cambridge: Harvard University Press, 1994), 58–59.
9. Ronald J. Angel and Jacqueline L. Angel, "Physical Comorbidity and Medical Care Use in Children with Emotional Problems," *Public Health Reports* 111 (1996): 140–145.
10. Christina Lammers et al., "Influences on Adolescents' Decision to Postpone Onset of Sexual Intercourse: A Survival Analysis of Virginity Among Youths Aged 13 to 18 Years," *Journal of Adolescent Health* 26 (2000): 42–48.
11. John P. Hoffman and Robert A. Johnson, "A National Portrait of Family Structure and Adolescent Drug Use," *Journal of Marriage and the Family* 60 (August 1998): 633–645.
12. Judith Rubenstein et al., "Suicidal Behavior in Adolescents: Stress and Protection in Different Family Contexts," *American Journal of Orthopsychiatry* 68 (1998): 274–284.
13. Catherine M. Malkin and Michael E. Lamb, "Child Maltreatment: A Test of Sociobiological Theory," *Journal of Comparative Family Studies* 25 (1994): 121–130.
14. For a complete review of this literature see Horn, *Father Facts*.
15. George Gallup, "Report on Status of Fatherhood in the United States," *Emerging Trends* 20 (September 1998): 3–5.
16. Irwin Garfinkel, Sara S. McLanahan, Daniel R. Meyer, and Judith A. Seltzer, *Fathers Under Fire: The Revolution in Child Support Enforcement* (New York: Russell Sage Foundation, 1998).
17. U.S. Bureau of the Census, *Child Support for Custodial Mothers and Fathers: 1997* (Washington, D.C., 2000).
18. Paul R. Amato and Joan G. Gilbreth, "Nonresident Fathers and Children's Well-Being: A Meta-Analysis," *Journal of Marriage and the Family* 61 (August 1999): 557–573.
19. Susan D. Steward, "Disneyland Dads, Disneyland Moms? How Nonresident Parents Spend Time with Absent Children," *Journal of Family Issues* 20 (July 1999): 539–556.
20. Lynne Casper and Ken Bryson, *Household and Family Characteristics: March 1997* (Washington, D.C.: U.S. Bureau of the Census).
21. Wendy Manning and Daniel T. Lichter, "Parental Cohabitation and Children's Economic Well-Being," *Journal of Marriage and the Family* 58 (November 1996): 998–1010.
22. Larry Bumpass and Hsien-Hen Lu, *Trends in Cohabitation and Implications for Children's Family Contexts in the U.S.*, CDE Working Paper No. 98-15 (Center for Demography Ecology, University of Wisconsin-Madison, 1999).
23. *Dispelling Myths About Unmarried Fathers*, Fragile Families Research Brief, Number 1 (Bendhelm-Thoman Center For Research and Child Well-Being Princeton University and Social Indicators Survey Center, Columbia University, May 2000).
24. Bumpass and Lu, *Trends in Cohabitation*.
25. Kristin A. Moore, "Nonmarital Childbearing in the United States," in *Report to Congress on Out-of-Wedlock Childbearing* (Washington, D.C.: U.S. Department of Health and Human Services, September, 1995), vii.

26. David Popenoe and Barbara Dafoe Whitehead, *Should We Live Together? What Young Adults Need to Know About Cohabitation Before Marriage* (New Brunswick, NJ: The National Marriage Project, 1999), 7.

27. Deborah R. Graefe and Daniel T. Lichter, "Life Course Transitions of American Children: Parental Cohabitation, Marriage, and Single Motherhood," *Demography* 36 (May 1999).

28. Robert Whelan, *Broken Homes and Battered Children: A Study of the Relationship Between Child Abuse and Family Type* (London, England: Family Education Trust, 1993), 29, table 12; see also Martin Daly and Margo Wilson, "Evolutionary Psychology and Marital Conflict: The Relevance of Stepchildren," in David M. Buss and Neil Malamuth, ed., *Sex, Power, Conflict: Evolutionary and Feminist Perspectives* (New York: Oxford University Press, 1996), 9–28; Leslie Margolin, "Child Abuse by Mothers' Boyfriends: Why the Over-Representation?" *Child Abuse and Neglect* 16 (1992): 541–551.

29. E. G. Cooksey and P. H. Craig, "Parenting From a Distance: The Effects of Paternal Characteristics on Contact Between Nonresidential Fathers and Their Children," *Demography* 35 (1998): 187–200.

30. Robert Lerman and Theodora Ooms, *Young Unwed Fathers: Changing Roles and Emerging Policies* (Philadelphia: Temple, 1993), 45.

31. Linda S. Stephens, "Will Johnny See Daddy This Week?" *Journal of Family Issues* 17 (July 1996): 466–494.

32. L. Clarke, E. C. Cooksey, and G. Verropoulou, "Fathers and Absent Fathers: Sociodemographic Similarities in Britain and the United States," *Demography* 35 (1998): 217–228.

33. Linda J. Waite and Maggie Gallagher, *The Case for Marriage: Why Married People Are Happier, Healthier and Better Off Financially* (New York: Doubleday, 2000).

34. Nicholas Zill, Donna Ruane Morrison, and Mary Jo Coiro, "Long-Term Effects of Parental Divorce on Parent–Child Relationships, Adjustment, and Achievement in Young Adulthood," *Journal of Family Psychology* 7 (1993): 91–103.

35. Steven Stack and J. Ross Eshleman, "Marital Status and Happiness: A 17-Nation Study," *Journal of Marriage and the Family* 60 (May 1998): 527–536; see also Maggie Gallagher, *The Abolition of Marriage* (Washington, D.C.: Regnery, 1996); Linda J. Waite, "Does Marriage Matter?" *Demography* 32 (1995): 483–501.

36. Waite and Gallagher, *The Case for Marriage*, 150–160.

37. David Popenoe and Barbara Dafoe Whitehead, *The State of Our Unions, 1999* (New Brunswick, NJ: National Marriage Project, 1999).

38. *Dispelling Myths About Unmarried Fathers.*

## READING FOR CONTENT

1. Why does an exclusive focus on child support enforcement downgrade fathers to the position of "cash machines"?

2. Explain why enhanced visitation will not necessarily encourage nonresident dads to become further involved with their children.

3. Why is cohabitation unlikely to result in more positive father involvement?

4. Summarize Horn's claims as to why marriage is the most "effective glue for binding fathers to their children."

## READING FOR GENRE, ORGANIZATION, AND STYLISTIC FEATURES

1. In the first section of the article, Horn draws heavily on scholarship, incorporating information from fifteen different sources. What effect does this strategy have on the reader?

2. Construct an outline that depicts the organization of Horn's argument. You may wish to consult the arrangements for argument essays in Chapter 8.

3. Cite the paragraphs in which Horn anticipates conflicting views, acknowledges them, and directly addresses them.

## READING FOR RHETORICAL CONTEXT

1. How does Horn's background prepare you for his argument?
2. Consider where the material was originally published. How does that information contribute to your understanding of the selection? Explain.

## WRITING ASSIGNMENTS

1. Write an essay in which you agree or disagree with Horn's claim that when it comes to the topic of absentee fathers, people are reluctant to talk about marriage.
2. Collaborative assignment: Break into three groups, each of which is responsible for researching one of the solutions to the problem of fatherlessness—child support enforcement, enhanced visitation rights, and cohabitation—and determining whether or not the particular solution will be more effective than Horn's recommendations with regard to stable marriages. After evaluating the arguments and evidence offered for each solution, each group will write an essay and report its findings to the class.

■ ■ ■ ■ ■ ■ ■ ■ ■ ■ ■ ■

# Unmarried with Children

### Kathryn Edin and Maria Kefalas

*Kathryn Edin is Professor of Sociology at the University of Pennsylvania. As part of this project, she moved with her family into a poor community in East Camden, N.J. With Maria Kefalas she has coauthored* Promises I Can Keep: Why Poor Women Put Motherhood Before Marriage *(2006). Maria Kefalas is Professor of Sociology at St. Joseph's College, Philadelphia. She is the author of* Working-Class Heroes: Protecting Home, Community, and Nation in a Chicago Neighborhood *(2003).*

## PREREADING

Review your notes on other essays in this section of the anthology. What might you conclude about the relationship of marriage to absentee fathers? Do fathers seem more likely to leave women who have borne their children if they are not married to each other? Does marriage help to reduce the numbers of absentee fathers? Or is the relationship between

From: *Contexts*, vol 4, issue 2, 2005, pp. 16–22.

marriage and absentee fatherhood more tenuous than we might imagine? Have poor unmarried mothers given up on marriage? Or are they waiting for the right partner and situation to commit themselves? Freewrite your responses to these questions on the basis of what you have read in the preceding essays.

Jen Burke, a white tenth-grade dropout who is 17 years old, lives with her step-  1 mother, her sister, and her 16-month-old son in a cramped but tidy row home in Philadelphia's beleaguered Kensington neighborhood. She is broke, on welfare, and struggling to complete her GED. Wouldn't she and her son have been better off if she had finished high school, found a job, and married her son's father first?

In 1950, when Jen's grandmother came of age, only 1 in 20 American children  2 was born to an unmarried mother. Today, that rate is 1 in 3—and they are usually born to those least likely to be able to support a child on their own. In our book, *Promises I Can Keep: Why Poor Women Put Motherhood Before Marriage*, we discuss the lives of 162 white, African American, and Puerto Rican low-income single mothers living in eight destitute neighborhoods across Philadelphia and its poorest industrial suburb, Camden. We spent five years chatting over kitchen tables and on front stoops, giving mothers like Jen the opportunity to speak to the question so many affluent Americans ask about them: Why do they have children while still young and unmarried when they will face such an uphill struggle to support them?

## Romance at Lightning Speed

Jen started having sex with her 20-year-old boyfriend Rick just before her 15th birthday.  3 A month and a half later, she was pregnant. "I didn't want to get pregnant," she claims. "*He* wanted me to get pregnant." "As soon as he met me, he wanted to have a kid with me," she explains. Though Jen's college-bound suburban peers would be appalled by such a declaration, on the streets of Jen's neighborhood, it is something of a badge of honor. "All those other girls he was with, he didn't want to have a baby with any of them," Jen boasts. "I asked him, 'Why did you choose me to have a kid when you could have a kid with any one of them?' He was like, 'I want to have a kid with *you*.'" Looking back, Jen says she now believes that the reason "he wanted me to have a kid that early is so that I didn't leave him."

In inner-city neighborhoods like Kensington, where child-bearing within mar-  4 riage has become rare, romantic relationships like Jen and Rick's proceed at lightning speed. A young man's avowal, "I want to have a baby by you," is often part of the courtship ritual from the beginning. This is more than idle talk, as their first child is typically conceived within a year from the time a couple begins "kicking it." Yet while poor couples' pillow talk often revolves around dreams of shared children, the news of a pregnancy—the first indelible sign of the huge changes to come—puts these still-new relationships into overdrive. Suddenly, the would-be mother begins to scrutinize her mate as never before, wondering whether he can "get himself together"—find a job, settle down, and become a family man—in time. Jen began pestering Rick to get a real job instead of picking up day-labor jobs at nearby construction sites. She also wanted him to stop hanging out with his ne'er-do-well friends, who had been getting him into serious trouble for more than a decade. Most of all, she wanted Rick to shed what she calls his "kiddie mentality"—his habit of spending money on alcohol and drugs rather than recognizing his growing financial obligations at home.

Rick did not try to deny paternity, as many would-be fathers do. Nor did he aban- 5 don or mistreat Jen, at least intentionally. But Rick, who had been in and out of juvenile detention since he was 8 years old for everything from stealing cars to selling drugs, proved unable to stay away from his unsavory friends. At the beginning of her seventh month of pregnancy, an escapade that began as a drunken lark landed Rick in jail on a carjacking charge. Jen moved back home with her stepmother, applied for welfare, and spent the last two-and-a-half months of her pregnancy without Rick.

Rick sent penitent letters from jail. "I thought he changed by the letters he wrote 6 me. I thought he changed a lot," she says. "He used to tell me that he loved me when he was in jail. . . . It was always gonna be me and him and the baby when he got out." Thus, when Rick's alleged victim failed to appear to testify and he was released just days before Colin's birth, the couple's reunion was a happy one. Often, the magic moment of childbirth calms the troubled waters of such relationships. New parents typically make amends and resolve to stay together for the sake of their child. When surveyed just after a child's birth, eight in ten unmarried parents say they are still together, and most plan to stay together and raise the child.

Promoting marriage among the poor has become the new war on poverty, Bush 7 style. And it is true that the correlation between marital status and child poverty is strong. But poor single mothers already believe in marriage. Jen insists that she will walk down the aisle one day, though she admits it might not be with Rick. And demographers still project that more than seven in ten women who had a child outside of marriage will eventually wed someone. First, though, Jen wants to get a good job, finish school, and get her son out of Kensington.

Most poor, unmarried mothers and fathers readily admit that bearing children 8 while poor and unmarried is not the ideal way to do things. Jen believes the best time to become a mother is "after you're out of school and you got a job, at least, when you're like 21. . . . When you're ready to have kids, you should have everything ready, have your house, have a job, so when that baby comes, the baby can have its own room." Yet given their already limited economic prospects, the poor have little motivation to time their births as precisely as their middle-class counterparts do. The dreams of young people like Jen and Rick center on children at a time of life when their more affluent peers plan for college and careers. Poor girls coming of age in the inner city value children highly, anticipate them eagerly, and believe strongly that they are up to the job of mothering—even in difficult circumstances. Jen, for example, tells us, "People outside the neighborhood, they're like, 'You're 15! You're pregnant?' I'm like, it's not none of their business. I'm gonna be able to take care of my kid. They have nothing to worry about." Jen says she has concluded that "some people . . . are better at having kids at a younger age. . . . I think it's better for some people to have kids younger."

## When I Became a Mom

When we asked mothers like Jen what their lives would be like if they had not had chil- 9 dren, we expected them to express regret over foregone opportunities for school and careers. Instead, most believe their children "saved" them. They describe their lives as spinning out of control before becoming pregnant—struggles with parents and peers, "wild," risky behavior, depression, and school failure. Jen speaks to this poignantly. "I was just real bad. I hung with a real bad crowd. I was doing pills. I was really depressed. . . . I was drinking. That was before I was pregnant." "I think," she reflects, "if I never had a baby or anything, . . . I would still be doing the things I was doing. I would probably still be doing drugs. I'd probably still be drinking." Jen admits that when she first became pregnant, she was angry that she "couldn't be out no more. Couldn't be out with my friends. Couldn't do nothing." Now, though, she says, "I'm glad I have a son . . . because I would still be doing all that stuff."

Children offer poor youth like Jen a compelling sense of purpose. Jen paints a 10 before-and-after picture of her life that was common among the mothers we interviewed. "Before, I didn't have nobody to take care of. I didn't have nothing left to go home for. . . . Now I have my son to take care of. I have him to go home for. . . . I don't have to go buy weed or drugs with my money. I could buy my son stuff with my money! . . . I have something to look up to now." Children also are a crucial source of relational intimacy, a self-made community of care. After a nasty fight with Rick, Jen recalls, "I was crying. My son came in the room. He was hugging me. He's 16 months and he was hugging me with his little arms. He was really cute and happy, so I got happy. That's one of the good things. When you're sad, the baby's always gonna be there for you no matter what." Lately she has been thinking a lot about what her life was like back then, before the baby. "I thought about the stuff before I became a mom, what my life was like back then. I used to see pictures of me, and I would hide in every picture. This baby did so much for me. My son did a lot for me. He helped me a lot. I'm thankful that I had my baby."

Around the time of the birth, most unmarried parents claim they plan to get mar- 11 ried eventually. Rick did not propose marriage when Jen's first child was born, but when she conceived a second time, at 17, Rick informed his dad, "It's time for me to get married. It's time for me to straighten up. This is the one I wanna be with. I had a baby with her, I'm gonna have another baby with her." Yet despite their intentions, few of these couples actually marry. Indeed, most break up well before their child enters preschool.

## I'd Like to Get Married, but . . .

The sharp decline in marriage in impoverished urban areas has led some to charge that 12 the poor have abandoned the marriage norm. Yet we found few who had given up on the idea of marriage. But like their elite counterparts, disadvantaged women set a high financial bar for marriage. For the poor, marriage has become an elusive goal—one they feel ought to be reserved for those who can support a "white picket fence" lifestyle: a mortgage on a modest row home, a car and some furniture, some savings in the bank, and enough money left over to pay for a "decent" wedding. Jen's views on marriage provide a perfect case in point. "If I was gonna get married, I would want to be married like my Aunt Nancy and my Uncle Pat. They live in the mountains. She has a job. My Uncle Pat is a state trooper; he has lots of money. They live in the [Poconos]. It's real nice out there. Her kids go to Catholic school. . . . That's the kind of life I would want to have. If I get married, I would have a life like [theirs]." She adds, "And I would wanna have a big wedding, a real nice wedding."

Unlike the women of their mothers' and grandmothers' generations, young 13 women like Jen are not merely content to rely on a man's earnings. Instead, they insist on being economically "set" in their own right before taking marriage vows. This is partly because they want a partnership of equals, and they believe money buys say-so in a relationship. Jen explains, "I'm not gonna just get into marrying him and not have my own house! Not have a job! I still wanna do a lot of things before I get married. He [already] tells me I can't do nothing. I can't go out. What's gonna happen when I marry him? He's gonna say he owns me!"

Economic independence is also insurance against a marriage gone bad. Jen 14 explains, "I want to have everything ready, in case something goes wrong. . . . If we got a divorce, that would be my house. I bought that house, he can't kick me out or he can't take my kids from me." "That's what I want in case that ever happens. I know a lot of people that happened to. I don't want it to happen to me." These statements reveal that despite her desire to marry, Rick's role in the family's future is provisional at best. "We get along, but we fight a lot. If he's there, he's there, but if he's not, that's why I want a job . . . a job with computers . . . so I could afford my kids, could afford the house. . . . I don't want to be living off him. I want my kids to be living off me."

Why is Jen, who describes Rick as "the love of my life," so insistent on planning 15 an exit strategy before she is willing to take the vows she firmly believes ought to last "forever?" If love is so sure, why does mistrust seem so palpable and strong? In relationships among poor couples like Jen and Rick, mistrust is often spawned by chronic violence and infidelity, drug and alcohol abuse, criminal activity, and the threat of imprisonment. In these tarnished corners of urban America, the stigma of a failed marriage is far worse than an out-of-wedlock birth. New mothers like Jen feel they must test the relationship over three, four, even five years' time. This is the only way, they believe, to insure that their marriages will last.

Trust has been an enormous issue in Jen's relationship with Rick. "My son was 16 born December 23rd, and [Rick] started cheating on me again . . . in March. He started cheating on me with some girl—Amanda. . . . Then it was another girl, another girl, another girl after. I didn't wanna believe it. My friends would come up to me and be like, 'Oh yeah, your boyfriend's cheating on you with this person.' I wouldn't believe it. . . . I would see him with them. He used to have hickies. He used to make up some excuse that he was drunk—that was always his excuse for everything." Things finally came to a head when Rick got another girl pregnant. "For a while, I forgave him for everything. Now, I don't forgive him for nothing." Now we begin to understand the source of Jen's hesitancy. "He wants me to marry him, [but] I'm not really sure. . . . If I can't trust him, I can't marry him, 'cause we would get a divorce. If you're gonna get married, you're supposed to be faithful!" she insists. To Jen and her peers, the worst thing that could happen is "to get married just to get divorced."

Given the economic challenges and often perilously low quality of the romantic 17 relationships among unmarried parents, poor women may be right to be cautious about marriage. Five years after we first spoke with her, we met with Jen again. We learned that Jen's second pregnancy ended in a miscarriage. We also learned that Rick was out of the picture—apparently for good. "You know that bar [down the street?] It happened in that bar. . . . They were in the bar, and this guy was like badmouthing [Rick's friend] Mikey, talking stuff to him or whatever. So Rick had to go get involved in it and start with this guy. . . . Then he goes outside and fights the guy [and] the guy dies of head trauma. They were all on drugs, they were all drinking, and things just got out of control, and that's what happened. He got fourteen to thirty years."

## These are Cards I Dealt Myself

Jen stuck with Rick for the first two and a half years of his prison sentence, but when 18 another girl's name replaced her own on the visitors' list, Jen decided she was finished with him once and for all. Readers might be asking what Jen ever saw in a man like Rick. But Jen and Rick operate in a partner market where the better-off men go to the better-off women. The only way for someone like Jen to forge a satisfying relationship with a man is to find a diamond in the rough or improve her own economic position so that she can realistically compete for more upwardly mobile partners, which is what Jen is trying to do now. "There's this kid, Donny, he works at my job. He works on C shift. He's a supervisor! He's funny, three years older, and he's not a geek or anything, but he's not a real preppy good boy either. But he's not [a player like Rick] and them. He has a job, you know, so that's good. He doesn't do drugs or anything. And he asked my dad if he could take me out!"

These days, there is a new air of determination, even pride, about Jen. The aim- 19 less high school dropout pulls ten-hour shifts entering data at a warehouse distribution center Monday through Thursday. She has held the job for three years, and her aptitude and hard work have earned her a series of raises. Her current salary is higher than anyone in her household commands—$10.25 per hour, and she now gets two weeks of paid vacation, four personal days, 60 hours of sick time, and medical benefits. She has saved up the necessary $400 in tuition for a high school completion program that offers evening and weekend classes. Now all that stands between her and a diploma is a passing grade in mathematics, her least favorite subject. "My plan is to start college in January. [This month] I take my math test . . . so I can get my diploma," she confides.

Jen clearly sees how her life has improved since Rick's dramatic exit from the 20 scene. "That's when I really started [to get better] because I didn't have to worry about what *he* was doing, didn't have to worry about him cheating on me, all this stuff. [It was] then I realized that I had to do what I had to do to take care of my son. . . . When he was there, I think that my whole life revolved around him, you know, so I always messed up somehow because I was so busy worrying about what *he* was doing. Like I would leave the [GED] programs I was in just to go home and see what he was doing. My mind was never concentrating." Now, she says, "a lot of people in my family look up to me now, because all my sisters dropped out from school, you know, nobody went back to school. I went back to school, you know? . . . I went back to school, and I plan to go to college, and a lot of people look up to me for that, you know? So that makes me happy . . . because five years ago nobody looked up to me. I was just like everybody else."

Yet the journey has not been easy. "Being a young mom, being 15, it's hard, hard, 21 hard, you know." She says, "I have no life. . . . I work from 6:30 in the morning until 5:00 at night. I leave here at 5:30 in the morning. I don't get home until about 6:00 at night." Yet she measures her worth as a mother by the fact that she has managed to provide for her son largely on her own. "I don't depend on nobody. I might live with my dad and them, but I don't depend on them, you know." She continues, "There [used to] be days when I'd be so stressed out, like, 'I can't do this!' And I would just cry and cry and cry. . . . Then I look at Colin, and he'll be sleeping, and I'll just look at him and think I don't have no [reason to feel sorry for myself]. The cards I have I've dealt myself so I have to deal with it now. I'm older. I can't change anything. He's my responsibility—he's nobody else's but mine—so I have to deal with that."

Becoming a mother transformed Jen's point of view on just about everything. She 22 says, "I thought hanging on the corner drinking, getting high—I thought that was a good life, and I thought I could live that way for eternity, like sitting out with my friends. But it's not as fun once you have your own kid. . . . I think it changes [you]. I think, "Would I want Colin to do that? Would I want my son to be like that . . . ?' It was fun to me but it's not fun anymore. Half the people I hung with are either . . . Some have died from drug overdoses, some are in jail, and some people are just out there living the same life that they always lived, and they don't look really good. They look really bad." In the end, Jen believes, Colin's birth has brought far more good into her life than bad. "I know I could have waited [to have a child], but in a way I think Colin's the best thing that could have happened to me. . . . So I think I had my son for a purpose because I think Colin changed my life. He *saved* my life, really. My whole life revolves around Colin!"

## Promises I can Keep

There are unique themes in Jen's story—most fathers are only one or two, not five years 23 older than the mothers of their children, and few fathers have as many glaring problems as Rick—but we heard most of these themes repeatedly in the stories of the 161 other poor, single mothers we came to know. Notably, poor women do not reject marriage; they revere it. Indeed, it is the conviction that marriage is forever that makes them think that divorce is worse than having a baby outside of marriage. Their children, far from being liabilities, provide crucial social-psychological resources—a strong sense of purpose and a profound source of intimacy. Jen and the other mothers we came to know are coming of age in an America that is profoundly unequal—where the gap between rich and poor continues to grow. This economic reality has convinced them that they have little to lose and, perhaps, something to gain by a seemingly "ill-timed" birth.

The lesson one draws from stories like Jen's is quite simple: Until poor young 24 women have more access to jobs that lead to financial independence—until there is reason to hope for the rewarding life pathways that their privileged peers pursue—the poor will continue to have children far sooner than most Americans think they should, while still deferring marriage. Marital standards have risen for all Americans, and the poor want the same things that everyone now wants out of marriage. The poor want to marry too, but they insist on marrying well. This, in their view, is the only way to avoid an almost certain divorce. Like Jen, they are simply not willing to make promises they are not sure they can keep.

## Recommended Resources

Kathryn Edin and Maria Kefalas. *Promises I Can Keep: Why Poor Women Put Motherhood Before Marriage* (University of California Press, 2005). An account of how low-income women make sense of their choices about marriage and motherhood.

Christina Gibson, Kathryn Edin, and Sara McLanahan. "High Hopes but Even Higher Expectations: A Qualitative and Quantitative Analysis of the Marriage Plans of Unmarried Couples Who Are New Parents." Working Paper 03-06-FF, Center for Research on Child Wellbeing, Princeton University, 2004. Online at http://crcw. princeton.edu/workingpapers/WP03-06-FF-Gibson.pdf. The authors examine the rising expectations for marriage among unmarried parents.

Sharon Hays. *Flat Broke with Children: Women in the Age of Welfare Reform* (Oxford University Press, 2003). How welfare reform has affected the lives of poor moms.

Annette Lareau. *Unequal Childhoods: Class, Race, and Family Life* (University of California Press, 2003). A fascinating discussion of different childrearing strategies among low-income, working-class, and middle-class parents.

Timothy J. Nelson, Susan Clampet-Lundquist, and Kathryn Edin. "Fragile Fatherhood: How Low-income, Non-Custodial Fathers in Philadelphia Talk About Their Families." In *The Handbook of Father Involvement: Multidisciplinary Perspectives*, ed. Catherine Tamis-LeMonda and Natasha Cabrera (Lawrence Earlbaum Associates, 2002). What poor, single men think about fatherhood.

## READING FOR CONTENT

1. In your own words, recount the reasons in paragraph 10 for why parenthood offers poor youth a compelling sense of purpose.

## READING FOR GENRE, ORGANIZATION, AND STYLISTIC FEATURES

1. The genre of sociological case study relies upon close observation of the behavior of its subject participants. How does the narrative about Jen and Rick in paragraphs 3–6, 9–11, and 13–20 lead to the conclusions that the authors draw in paragraph 24? Underline the important features of the narrative in your text.
2. Paragraphs 2, 9, and 12 move outside the focus of Jen and Rick's narrative to frame it within a wider focus. What general observations does this organization enable the authors to make in these paragraphs?
3. The authors present much of Jen's narrative in her own words. Do the stylistic features of her account add to or detract from the scientific perspective of this study?

## READING FOR RHETORICAL CONTEXT

1. In paragraph 7, how does the Bush II administration's promotion of marriage among the poor as a weapon in the war on poverty generate the argument of this essay? How do the authors argue that, contrary to the administration's sloganeering, poor women have always valued marriage?
2. How do the authors' concessions in paragraph 23 about the "unique" and atypical features of Jen's story contribute to the conclusions that they draw from it? Do their concessions strengthen rather than weaken their argument?

## WRITING ASSIGNMENTS

1. Using the narrative about Jen and Rick in this article, write a short analytical essay of 600 words in which you draw your own conclusions about whether poor single mothers value or reject marriage.
2. Using the narrative about Jen and Rick in this article, write a long analytical essay of 1,000 words in which you draw your own conclusions about whether poor single mothers value or reject marriage. If your interpretations modify or contradict

those drawn by the authors, address the differences directly in your analysis. If they support the authors' interpretations, mention that too and explain how your own arguments strengthen theirs.

■ ■ ▓ ■ ■ ■ ■ ■ ■ ▓ ▓ ▓

# Absent Fathers: Why Don't We Ever Talk about the Unmarried Men?

## *Rebecca M. Blank*

*Rebecca M. Blank is Professor of Economics at Northwestern University, where she has directed the Joint Center for Poverty Research. During the Clinton administration, she served on the Council of Economic Advisors. Her publications include* Why Were Poverty Rates So High in the 1980s? *(1991),* It Takes a Nation: A New Agenda for Fighting Poverty *(1997),* The Clinton Legacy for America's Poor *(2001), and* The New World of Welfare *(2001).*

## PREREADING

Turn to the table on page 496. What might the statistics imply about Rebecca Blank's topic and argument? Her title focuses on "Absent Fathers" and "Unmarried Men," but the graph focuses on "Child Support Awards among Women with Children Whose Father Is Not Present in the Household." Despite its focus on mothers, what might the graph tell us about absent fathers and unmarried men? Freewrite your response.

SUMMARY. *The lives of poor single men are much less well understood, since these men typically have less contact with the public and private organizations that serve the poor. By most accounts, poor unmarried men exhibit far more behavioral problems than single mothers, despite the fact that much of the policy discussion focuses on the mothers. A high share of younger men are under the supervision of the judicial system in this country. Child support payments from absent fathers to their children are extremely low, and this lack of parental support is a major factor contributing to the poverty of single mothers and their children. These problems are correlated with the larger economic trends that have affected these men's lives: lessskilled men have faced declines in wages, the changing location of jobs in cities, and high and persistent unemployment rates.*

For every single mother, there is a father who is not living with his children. For every unwed mother, there is a father who did not marry her. The public discussion about    [1]

From: Rebecca M. Blank, *It Takes a Nation: A New Agenda for Fighting Poverty* (Princeton: Princeton University Press, 1997), pp. 42–47. Copyright 1997 Russell Sage Foundation, published by Princeton University Press. Reprinted by permission of Princeton University Press.

growing numbers of divorced and never-married mothers too rarely mentions the missing men in these families. Here we will focus on the absent fathers and their behavior.

We know surprisingly little about the lives of the low-income single men who father the children in low-income single-mother families. This is true for at least two reasons. First, because these men are much less publicly visible than the mothers of their children, they are often ignored in the policy discussion. Because we provide little public assistance to single men, they have less contact with the public and private organizations that serve low-income families. Disproportionately, it is the mothers who show up at schools, who bring their children in for health care, or who apply for public assistance. Thus, these men appear to cost society nothing; it is mothers and children whom we support. Of course, as any economist will tell you, this is a false notion. To the extent that *both* the men and the women choose to divorce or not marry, the resulting social costs are due to the men's behavior as much as the women's.

Second, because none of the data the government collects links absent fathers with their children, they are often ignored in the research literature. The data collected on family and child poverty are based on information about all family members who *live together,* thus we know little about the absent fathers. As noted below, a substantial number of fathers in out-of-wedlock births are not identified on birth certificates. Some of these fathers may not even know they have children. Among those who are known, the fathers typically do not live in the household. It is not possible to study absent fathers without collecting new data that will help identify and contact men who are not living with their children. This is an expensive undertaking.

As a result, we know very little about how absent fathers behave, or even about who they are. At best, we can talk about less-skilled and low-income unmarried men, assuming that many of them are part of the absent-fathers population. In general, this group exhibits more behavioral problems than single mothers.

These men are at greater risk of homelessness, and they are more likely to be involved in crime or illegal drug-related activities. By the mid-1990s, the number of men under the supervision of the judicial system (either in jail or on probation or parole) relative to the male workforce was 7 percent, that is, there was one man under court supervision for every twelve men working; this is higher than the unemployment rate for this group. Among young men between the ages of 18 and 34, 11 percent are under the supervision of the judicial system; among black men between these ages, the share under judicial supervision is an amazing 37 percent.[1] Why are these numbers so high? There is evidence of increasing criminal involvement among younger men, and this interacts with stronger sentencing laws and a growing willingness to incarcerate those involved with drug dealing.

All of this has led to soaring prison populations and large increases in the number of men on probation or parole. These numbers are disturbing not just because of what they signal about current behavioral problems, but also because of the long-term problems they create for these men in finding employment as ex-offenders.[2]

Without excusing these behavioral problems, it is important to recognize that the world has changed for the worse for many less-skilled, low-income men. As discussed in the next chapter, less-skilled men have faced major declines in their earning ability, and high rates of unemployment. These economic changes are strongly correlated with both declines in work effort in the mainstream labor market and increases in criminal activity.

Among African American and Latino men, these problems are greatest and overlap with ongoing problems of discrimination and job access. A number of authors have described the many ways in which young black men are treated hostilely by white society, learn distrust and anger, and develop a responding culture of hostility and violence.[3] The result is a downward cycle, in which problematic behavior and economic and social constraints interact with and reinforce each other.

It is also worth emphasizing that these problems are concentrated among a minority of the poor men. Most poor men are employed at least part-time or part-year or are actively searching for work. Most are not in jail or on probation. Many are married to the mothers of their children. We should not let the real problems of some low-income men shape our image of all low-income men.     9

## Child Support and Absent Fathers

Many less-skilled single mothers find it difficult to escape poverty through their own earnings. One obvious way for these families to obtain more income is through support from absent fathers. Whether divorced or never married, fathers should bear their fair share of the financial responsibility for raising their children.     10

The growth in never-married mothers has exacerbated the problems of non-support from fathers, although many divorced women also receive little support. Of all children born to unmarried women, less than one-third have paternity established at time of birth.[4] That means that if support from the father is sought at a later stage, he first must be found and identified, not always an easy process.     11

The level of child support collected among single women in this country is extremely low. Table 13.1 presents the data, showing child support receipt among poor and nonpoor women in 1989.[5] Only 43 percent of poor mothers with children whose father lives outside the household have ever received a child support award by the courts, ordering the father to pay ongoing support. Among never-married women, less than one quarter have such an award. Among women who are divorced or married to     12

**TABLE 13–1   Child Support Awards among Women with Children Whose Father Is Not Present in the Household, 1989**

| | *Current Marital Status* | | | |
| | *All* | *Divorced* | *Never Married* | *Married** |
| --- | --- | --- | --- | --- |
| *Poor Mothers* | | | | |
| Percent with child support award | 43.3 | 70.4 | 24.5 | 72.2 |
| Percent with child support award and receiving payments | 25.4 | 42.4 | 14.4 | 40.4 |
| Average payments among recipients | $1,889 | $2,112 | $1,553 | $2,275 |
| *Nonpoor Mothers* | | | | |
| Percent with child support award | 64.5 | 79.1 | 23.2 | 79.5 |
| Percent with child support award and receiving payments | 43.1 | 57.5 | 14.5 | 48.6 |
| Average payments among recipients | $3,304 | $3,649 | $2,276 | $2,972 |

*Source:* U.S. Bureau of the Census (1991).
*The "Married" column shows women who are currently married to a man who is not the father of their children.

a man who is not the father of their children, about 70 percent have an award. While nonpoor women do slightly better, table 13.1 indicates that substantial numbers of nonpoor women are also without child support assistance.

Simply having an award does not guarantee that the father will make regular pay- 13 ments, however. Only 25 percent of poor women actually receive child support payments, and only 14 percent of never-married poor women receive payments. Many women who receive payments do not receive the full amount of their support order, but get only partial amounts. This is reflected in the fact that the amounts of money received are quite low. Among those poor single parents who do receive child support payments, the average payment received for all children is under $2,000 per year.

Teenage men who father children are particularly unlikely to live with the mother 14 of their children, unlikely to pay child support, and have low earnings and employment levels. Thus, the problems of teen fatherhood are closely related to the problems of teen motherhood. Many teen fathers, however, receive higher earnings as they move into their twenties. While they may be able to pay little child support initially, if teen fathers are followed by the child support system, they may be able to contribute more as their children grow older.[6]

The rise in single parenting has not simply led to an increase in the number of 15 children who physically live with and are primarily raised by their mothers. It has also meant massive financial desertion of these children by their fathers. This is a major reason why the women who raise children on their own are so likely to be poor.

One caveat on this statement needs to be noted: at least some financial support 16 from absent fathers to their children goes unreported. For men whose children receive public assistance, the incentives to provide much in the way of financial support are minimal. The first fifty dollars that a man pays in child support each month increases the income of the mother and her children. After that, any additional money goes to offset the cost of public assistance. The result is that child support payments above fifty dollars per month result in absolutely no additional income to the mother and children. This provides a strong incentive for under-the-table payments by men to their girlfriends and children. In-depth interviews with women on welfare in a few selected cities indicate that about one-quarter of welfare recipients in poor urban neighborhoods receive unreported contributions from absent fathers. The average amount of unreported income from children's fathers was relatively small, however, averaging thirty dollars per month.[7]

Of course, many less-skilled women with limited earning ability have children 17 with men of similar economic backgrounds. Thus, the absent fathers of many poor children are themselves poor, suggesting that these men would not be able to pay substantial amounts of child support. Researchers have tried to simulate the effect on poverty among single-parent families of substantially increased enforcement of child support orders, assuming that the absent fathers have the same educational background as the mothers. The results indicate that this would help lessen the depth of poverty among single-mother families but, by itself, would move only some families out of poverty entirely. The amounts that the noncustodial fathers could afford to pay are limited, because many of these fathers are not employed or because they have very low earnings. But these studies also conclude that better child support enforcement would make many single-mother families less poor, raising their income closer to the poverty line. For mothers living on $6,000 per year with their children, an additional $1,000 per year in child support payments provides a substantial increase in income.[8]

Finally, it is worth underscoring the fact that nonpayment of child support awards [18] and nonidentification of fathers among unwed mothers are not problems solely among poor women. A substantial number of single mothers who are well above the poverty line receive little ongoing support from the fathers of their children. Most of the billions of dollars in unpaid child support is owed to nonpoor single women from men who have steady jobs with good incomes. Demanding that fathers accept financial responsibility for their children is not just an antipoverty agenda, but a move that will benefit working women and their children at all income levels.

Lack of financial involvement does not necessarily mean lack of parental involve- [19] ment. While few men provide much financial support, particularly to low-income mothers, many of them remain in contact with their children. Sociologists Sara McLanahan and Gary Sandefur indicate that two-thirds of all children who live apart from their fathers have contact with them.[9] Surprisingly, this number is only slightly lower among children of unmarried versus divorced women. About one-third of the children who do not live with their father report seeing him once per week.

This information suggests that a substantial number of "absent fathers" are not [20] entirely absent. They are present in their children's lives, even if they do little of the primary parenting and provide only minimal or irregular child support payments. Clearly, many fathers do feel ongoing responsibility and love for their children.

It is worth putting all of this into the context of the larger economic changes that [21] chapter 2 will discuss in more depth. The decline in marriage and the decreased support for children by their fathers are both intimately linked to the economic changes of the last two decades. Less-skilled men—exactly the group most likely to father the children in poor single-mother families—are the group most affected by the changing economy. They have experienced big declines in wages, high and persistent unemployment rates, and (particularly among African American men) a loss of jobs from the changing location of employment in urban areas. Judging their changing parental behavior without these economic trends in mind is to miss an important component of the picture. Demanding that men be more responsible with regard to their children— particularly asking them to provide more financial support—is a harder demand to make when these men are more and more pressed by limited economic opportunities. Though their behavior may not be excusable, ordering them to get a job and/or pay more in child support may not be as easily accomplished as in years past.

Finally, it is important to keep in mind that there is a great deal of variability in the [22] behavior of fathers of poor children. As discussed in the first section of this chapter, in almost 40 percent of all poor families with children *both* parents are present. Many fathers do *not* desert their children. And of those children whose parents are divorced or never married, there are a substantial minority of fathers who stay in their children's lives, spend time with them, and contribute regularly to their financial well-being. While worrying about the missing fathers, we should not forget to appreciate those who are present.

## Notes

1. These numbers are from Freeman (1995). Similar data are in Mauer and Huling (1995).
2. For a review of the problem relating criminal involvement to labor market earnings and participation, see Freeman (1992, 1995). Wilson and Petersilia (1995) provide a range of evidence on recent changes in criminal behavior, its causes and implications.
3. For instance, see Mincy (1994).
4. U.S. House of Representatives (1994), page 470.

5. Data in Table 13.1 and the textual discussion from U.S. Bureau of the Census (1991).
6. See Pirog-Good and Good (1995).
7. Edin and Lein (forthcoming).
8. For a discussion of the estimated impact of child support enforcement on poverty status, see Robins (1986) or U.S. House of Representatives (1994), pp. 500–502. More extensive child support assurance systems would do more to reduce poverty, as Meyer et al. (1992) indicate.
9. McLanahan and Sandefur (1994), fig. 12.

## Works Cited

Edin, Kathryn, and Laura Lein. 1997. *Making Ends Meet: How Single Mothers Survive Welfare and Low-Wage Work.* New York: Russell Sage Foundation.

Freeman, Richard B. 1992. "Crime and the Employment of Disadvantaged Youths." In *Urban Labor Markets and Job Opportunity*, George E. Peterson and Wayne Vroman, editors. Washington, D.C.: The Urban Institute Press.

Freeman, Richard B. 1995. "The Labor Market." In *Crime*, James Q. Wilson and Joan Petersilia, editors. San Francisco: ICS Press.

Mauer, Marc, and Tracy Huling. 1995. *Young Black Americans and the Criminal Justice System: Five Years Later.* Washington, D.C.: The Sentencing Project.

McLanahan, Sara, and Gary Sandeful. 1994. *Growing Up with a Single Parent: What Hurts, What Helps.* Cambridge, Mass.: Harvard University Press.

Meyer, Daniel R., et al. 1992. "Who Should Be Eligible for an Assured Child Support Benefit?" In *Child Support Assurance*, Irwin Garfinkel, et al., editors. Washington D.C.: The Urban Institute Press.

Mincy, Ronald B. 1994. *Nuturing Young Black Males.* Washington, D.C.: The Urban Institute Press.

Pirog-Good, Maureen A., and David H. Good. 1995. "Child Support Enforcement for Teenage Fathers: Problems and Prospects." *Journal of Policy Analysis and Management* 14 (1, Winter): 25–42.

Robins, Philip K. 1986. "Child Support, Welfare Dependency, and Poverty." *American Economic Review* 76 (4, September): 768–88.

U.S. Bureau of the Census. 1991. *Child Support and Alimony, 1989.* Current Population Reports, Series P60–173. Washington, D.C.: U.S. Government Printing Office.

U.S. House of Representatives. 1994. *1994 Green Book: Overview of Entitlement Programs.* Washington, D.C.: U.S. Government Printing Office.

Wilson, James Q., and Joan Petersilia, editors. 1995. *Crime.* San Francisco: ICS Press.

## READING FOR CONTENT

1. In paragraph 7, how does the comment on declining economic opportunities among low-income men contribute to the author's argument?

2. In paragraphs 19–20, how do the comments that differentiate financial uninvolvement from parental uninvolvement contribute to the author's argument?

## READING FOR GENRE, ORGANIZATION, AND STYLISTIC FEATURES

1. In paragraph 21, how does the focus on the context of larger economic changes reinforce the author's claim to write an economic essay about absent fathers rather than a sociocultural or moral essay?

2. In paragraphs 5, 12, 13, 16, and 17, underline the statistics that Blank uses to organize her argument about economic motivations for absent fatherhood.
3. In paragraphs 7, 9, 16, 18, 21, and 22, how do such stylistic markers as "it is important to recognize" and "one caveat needs to be noted" accentuate Blank's argument?

## READING FOR RHETORICAL CONTEXT

1. What social conditions do paragraphs 2 and 3 evoke as a rhetorical context for Blank's argument?
2. What cultural conditions does paragraph 22 evoke as a rhetorical context for Blank's argument?

## SYNTHESIS WRITING ASSIGNMENTS

1. Use Erera's arguments in "What Is a Family?" to write a defense of the family arrangements described in Barret and Robinson's "Children of Gay Fathers" and Edin and Kefalas's "Unmarried with Children."
2. In "What Is a Family?" Erera explains how new reproductive technologies have enabled people to create various forms of alternative, nontraditional families. How do you think cloning might affect marriage and the family? After reading the selections in Chapters 10 and 13, write an essay explaining your position.
3. In your view, is cohabitation a true testing ground for marriage, or is it simply "playing house"? Write an essay in response to this question and support your position by drawing on the selections in this chapter.
4. Write an essay in which you compare and contrast Wilson's and Horn's arguments as to why marriage is the preferred family arrangement.
5. Drawing upon the selections in this chapter, write an argument essay in which you defend your position with regard to the future of the American family.

# *Fourteen*

# Social Class and Inequality

The selections in Chapter 14 examine ideas about social class from different perspectives and offer explanatory principles for the unequal distribution of income, power, and prestige. The authors discuss class conflict, examine factors that profoundly affect the existence and continuance of poverty, and offer solutions for dealing with these persistent problems. The evidence these authors supply has political, psychological, cultural, and moral ramifications as well as social consequences.

In the first selection, "Born Poor and Smart," Angela Locke interprets the unexamined assumption that poor people aren't smart and smart people aren't poor from her own experience of being both smart and poor. Her account initiates our conversation on poverty by challenging stereotypes that limit our full understanding of its reality, its causes, and its consequences. Next, the distinguished sociologist Herbert J. Gans debunks the concept of "underclass" and similar stereotypes in his essay on "The War Against the Poor Instead of Programs to End Poverty," and he offers a cultural and intellectual defense of poor people. Drawing upon a spectrum of theoretical tenets which are themselves derived from different sorts of statistical study, Gans formulates an argument on behalf of job-centered economic growth that creates better public and private employment.

The third selection is "Serving in Florida," Barbara Ehrenreich's riveting account of her experiences as a low-wage worker trying to survive on six to seven dollars an hour as a server in restaurants in Key West, Florida. Recording personal observations and linking them in a narrative of her day-to-day hardships and frustrations, Ehrenreich provides abundant evidence of worker exploitation in some of America's largest and most well-known service industries. A magazine article from *The Economist* entitled "Middle of the Class" frames Ehrenreich's experiences in a larger context as it argues that equality of opportunity is increasingly diminishing in the United States. Gathering and interpreting a vast amount of statistic evidence, this article exemplifies the technical precision of academic writing in the social sciences while nonetheless addressing a general readership of intelligent, concerned, and educated citizens.

Charmion Browne brings the conversation to a striking academic level in her personal account of living in homeless shelters, "When Shelter Feels Like a Prison." Browne, herself a young college student, draws upon her teen-age experiences as the child of a homeless single parent, and she contrasts these experiences with her current campus activities in a large university. Finally, Dirk Johnson gives us a glimpse of two faces of poverty in the Native American population in his essay on "Economic Pulse: Indian Country." As a newspaper reporter, Johnson is weaving together diverse facts, statistics, references to authorities, and personal experiences to warn against imposing white standards of poverty on Navajo populations. The approaches to poverty illustrated in this chapter by factual reports, narrative accounts, statistical gathering, statistical interpretations, and theoretical speculations represent different aspects of source study in the social sciences. Each of them contributes to the academic conversation about poverty in an important way.

■ ■ ■ ■ ■ ■ ■ ■ ■ ■ ■ ■ ■

# Born Poor and Smart

## Angela Locke

*Angela Locke is a writer for the feminist news journal* off our backs.

## PREREADING

Preview the article by reading paragraph 2. What does the author mean when she writes, "Oppression can't perpetuate itself without the cooperation of the oppressed"? Explain the sentence in your own words and elaborate it with examples from your own experience.

M y mother was smart, and she was poor. She did things that poor people aren't     1
supposed to do. Between working at the E-Z Bargain Center and cleaning up the messes that my father made around town and her four children made around the house, she read. She read to me when I was young. Later, she always wanted to know what I was reading, and she taught me how to talk about what I was reading. She didn't read romances or crime novels from the Five and Dime. Just a glance at one of her bookshelves shows Martin Buber, Carl Jung, John Gardner, John Barth, Margaret Atwood, Germaine Greer. She bought most of her books at yard sales and library sales, and she actually read them. She didn't just put them on her shelf for show.

Oppression can't perpetuate itself without the cooperation of the oppressed. One     2
way that cooperation works with class is that intelligence is scorned within the ranks of the poor. I still hear the voices in my head—"Don't show off." "She thinks she's better than the rest of us." "Let me slap that superior look right off your face." "Don't get it into your head that you're going to college." "Learn something practical, so you can take care of yourself."

My mother would have been lucky to find a friend at her dead-end nonunion job ₃ to talk to about books, but she didn't. She worked her ass off all her life, eventually leaving the E-Z Bargain Center for the halls of the Nestle factory. At least it had a union and some procedures for raises. She worked for years on the assembly line, finally landing a position in the lab, where she made coffee for her male coworkers just to get along with them well enough to work without conflict. Even if one of those guys had been interested in discussing what Carl Jung said about dream imagery, he wouldn't have been interested in discussing it with the woman who made his coffee.

But her intelligence paid off with her kids. Two out of four got college degrees, ₄ and I was one of them. Class accompanied me all the way.

It took me years longer to finish college than it took others whose parents and ₅ social class supported them. I paid my own way in between having children and working low-end jobs. I only finished when a wealthier partner of mine helped with the finances.

Attending college put me in the company of women with class advantages. But ₆ rather than finding a home there, I felt like an outsider in two worlds. What I had heard and feared was true. The price I paid for trying to break the class pattern I was raised with was that I belonged nowhere.

Something I struggle with to this day is that I never developed the sense of entitle- ₇ ment that distinguishes the rich from the poor. Success is a given in upper-class families, a habit as nonnegotiable as brushing one's teeth. I have never been able to convince myself that I am "worthy" of success, whereas my wealthier friends have never questioned that they are. And that feeling can make the difference between accomplishment and failure.

So my relationship to class isn't only about a relationship to money. It's about a ₈ relationship to success. My definition of success has something to do with money, but everything to do with class.

Success is not only living by the values that you believe in, but being in some way ₉ recognized in the world for those values. Success is not only discovering your talents and your interests, but being able to make a living using them.

In my extended working-class family, there are no models of success. My mother ₁₀ fulfilled the first terms of my definition, but she couldn't fulfill the second. It remains to be seen if I can.

## READING FOR CONTENT

1. Paraphrase in your own words and then elaborate upon what Locke means when she writes "intelligence is scorned within the ranks of the poor" in paragraph 2.
2. Paraphrase in your own words and then elaborate upon Locke's definition of success in paragraph 9. How does her definition relate to her argument about social class?

## READING FOR GENRE, ORGANIZATION, AND STYLISTIC FEATURES

1. How does Locke use her personal experience to strengthen her argument about entitlement in paragraph 7?
2. How does Locke organize her definition of success in paragraph 9 around her personal experience in the rest of the essay?

## READING FOR RHETORICAL CONTEXT

1. In paragraph 2, Locke writes that oppressed people cooperate in their own oppression. To what audience does she direct this comment? How might a nonoppressed person understand this comment? How might an oppressed person understand it?

2. In paragraph 6, Locke writes that she felt like an outsider both among her college classmates and among her family. To what audience does she direct this comment? How might a person who has experienced only one social class understand it? How might a person who has experienced class differences understand it?

## WRITING ASSIGNMENTS

1. Write a 500-word personal essay recounting your experience of class difference.

2. Write a 500-word commentary on Locke's essay arguing that, besides class, other factors such as gender or ethnic identity have some bearing upon attitudes toward intelligence and success.

■ ■ ■ ■ ■ ■ ■ ■ ■ ■ ■ ■

# The War Against the Poor Instead of Programs to End Poverty

### Herbert J. Gans

*Herbert J. Gans is a professor of sociology at Columbia University. He has written numerous articles and books on the subject of poverty, including* The Urban Villagers, The Levittowners, People and Plans, Popular Culture and High Culture, Deciding What's News, The War against the Poor, *and* Making Sense of America.

## PREREADING

Before you read the article, take a few minutes to write a response to the title. Do you think we are making a serious effort to end poverty in the United States? Can you think of why we might be accused of engaging in a war against the poor instead of a battle to improve their condition?

While liberals have been talking about resuming the War on Poverty, elected officials are doing something very different: waging a war on the poor. Even the riot that took place in Los Angeles in early May [1992] did not interrupt that war, perhaps because the riot was a mixture of protest, looting, and destruction.

Reprinted by permission of *Dissent* Magazine and Herbert J. Gans from the Fall, 1992 issue of *Dissent* Magazine.

The war on the poor was initiated by dramatic shifts in the domestic and world　2
economy, which have turned more and more unskilled and semiskilled workers into
surplus labor. Private enterprise participated actively by shipping jobs overseas and by
treating workers as expendable. Government has done its part as well, increasingly
restricting the welfare state safety net to the middle class. Effective job-creation
schemes, housing programs, educational and social services that serve the poor—and
some of the working classes—are vanishing. Once people become poor, it becomes
ever harder for them to escape poverty.

Despite the willingness to help the poor expressed in public opinion polls, other,　3
more covert, attitudes have created a political climate that makes the war on the poor
possible. Politicians compete with each other over who can capture the most headlines
with new ways to punish the poor. However, too many of their constituents see the poor
not as people without jobs but as miscreants who behave badly because they do not
abide by middle-class or mainstream moral values. Those judged "guilty" are dismissed
as the "undeserving poor"—or the underclass in today's language—people who do not
deserve to escape poverty.

True, *some* people are indeed guilty of immoral behavior—that is, murderers,　4
street criminals, drug sellers, child abusers.

Then there are poor people whose anger at their condition expresses itself in the　5
kind of nihilism that cannot be defined as political protest. Even so, most of those
labeled "undeserving" are simply poor people who for a variety of reasons cannot live
up to mainstream behavioral standards, like remaining childless in adolescence, finding and holding a job, and staying off welfare. This does not make them immoral.
Because poor adolescents do not have jobs does not mean they are lazy. Because their
ghetto "cool" may deter employers does not mean they are unwilling to work. Still, the
concept of an underclass lumps them with those who are criminal or violent.

Why do Americans accept so many untruths about the poor and remain unwilling　6
to accept the truth when it is available? The obvious answer is that some of the
poor frighten or anger those who are better off. But they also serve as a lightning rod—
scapegoats—for some problems among the better off. Street criminals rightly evoke fears
about personal safety, but they and the decidedly innocent poor also generate widespread anger about the failure of government to reduce "urban" and other problems.

Among whites, the anger is intertwined with fears about blacks and "Hispanics,"　7
or the newest immigrants, reflecting the fear of the stranger and newcomer from which
their own ancestors suffered when they arrived here. (Few remember that at the start of
the twentieth century, the "Hebrews" then arriving were sometimes described as a
"criminal race"—as the Irish had been earlier in the nineteenth century.)

The hostility toward today's welfare recipients is a subtler but equally revealing　8
index to the fears of the more fortunate. This fear reflects a historic belief that people
who are not economically self-sufficient can hurt the economy, although actual expen-
ditures for welfare have always been small. Welfare recipients are also assumed to be
getting something for nothing, often by people who are not overly upset about corrupt
governmental or corporate officials who get a great deal of money for nothing or
very little.

Welfare recipients possibly provoke anger among those concerned about their　9
own economic security, especially in a declining economy. Welfare recipients are seen
as living the easy life while everyone else is working harder than ever—and thus become
easy scapegoats, which does not happen to the successful, who often live easier lives.

The concern with poor unmarried mothers, especially adolescents, whose number 10 and family size have in fact long been declining, epitomizes adult fears about the high levels of sexual activity and the constant possibility of pregnancy among *all* adolescent girls. In addition, the notion of the "undeserving poor" has become a symbol for the general decline of mainstream moral standards, especially those celebrated as "traditional" in American society.

Ironically, however, the "undeserving poor" can be forced to uphold some of these 11 very standards in exchange for welfare, much as some Skid Row homeless still get a night's dinner and housing in exchange for sitting through a religious service. The missionaries in this case are secular: social workers and bureaucrats. But the basic moralistic expectations remain the same, including the demand that the poor live up to values that their socioeconomic superiors preach but do not always practice. Thus, social workers can have live-in lovers without being married, but their clients on welfare cannot. Members of the more fortunate classes are generally free from moral judgments altogether; no one talks about an undeserving middle class or the undeserving rich.

The war on the poor is probably best ended by job-centered economic growth 12 that creates decent public and private jobs. Once poor people have such jobs, they are almost automatically considered deserving, eligible for a variety of other programs to help them or their children escape poverty.

The most constructive way to supply such jobs would be an updated New Deal 13 that repairs failing infrastructures, creates new public facilities (including new databases), and allows the old ones to function better—for example, by drastically reducing class size in public schools. Equally important are ways of reviving private enterprise and finding new niches for it in the global economy. Without them, there will not be enough well-paying jobs in factories, laboratories, and offices—or taxes to pay for public programs. Such programs are already being proposed these days, by Bill Clinton and in the Congress, but mainly for working-class people who have been made jobless and are now joining the welfare rolls.

Last but not least is a new approach to income grants for those who cannot work 14 or find work. The latest fashion is to put welfare recipients to work, which would be a good idea if even decent entry-level jobs for them could be found or created. (Alas, when taxpayers discover how much cheaper it is to pay welfare than to create jobs, that remedy may end as it has before.)

Also needed is a non-punitive, universal income grant program, which goes to all 15 people who still end up as part of the labor surplus. If such a program copied the European principle of not letting the incomes of the poor fall below 60 to 70 percent of the median income—in the United States, welfare recipients get a fifth of the median on average—the recipients would remain integral members of society, who could be required to make sure their children would not become poor. (Such a solution would also cut down the crime rate.)

However, even minimal conventional antipoverty programs are politically 16 unpopular at the moment. The 1992 Democratic presidential candidates paid little attention to the poor during the primaries, except, in passing, in New York City and, then again, after Los Angeles. The future of antipoverty programs looks no brighter than before.

The time may be ripe to look more closely at how nonpoor Americans feel about 17 poverty, and try to reduce their unwarranted fear and anger toward the poor—with the hope that they would then be more positive about reviving antipoverty efforts.

The first priority for reducing that anger is effective policies against drugs and 18 street crime, though they alone cannot stem all the negative feelings. Probably the only truly effective solution is a prosperous economy in which the anger between all groups is lessened; and a more egalitarian society in which the displacement of such anger on the poor is no longer necessary, and the remaining class conflicts can be fought fairly.

This ideal is today more utopian than ever, but it ought to be kept in mind. Every 19 step toward it will help a little. Meanwhile, in order to bring back antipoverty programs, liberals, along with the poor and others who speak for the poor, could also try something else: initiating an intellectual and cultural defense of the poor. In a "sound bite": to fight *class* bigotry along with the racial kind.

Anti-bigotry programs work slowly and not always effectively, but they are as 20 American as apple pie. Class bigotry is itself still a novel idea, but nothing would be lost by mounting a defense of the poor and putting it on the public agenda. Ten such defenses strike me as especially urgent:

1. *Poverty is not equivalent to moral failure.* That moral undesirables exist among 21 the poor cannot be denied, but there is no evidence that their proportion is greater than among the more fortunate. "Bums" can be found at all economic levels. However, more prosperous miscreants tend to be less visible; the alcoholic co-worker can doze off at his desk, but the poor drunk is apt to be found in the gutter. Abusive middle class parents may remain invisible for years, until their children are badly hurt, but violent poor parents soon draw the attention of child-welfare workers and may lose their children to foster care.

Troubled middle-class people have access to experts who can demonstrate that 22 moral diagnoses are not enough. The abusive mother was herself abused; the school dropout has a learning disability; the young person who will not work suffers from depression. Poor people, on the other hand, rarely have access to such experts or to clinical treatment. For the poor, the explanations are usually moral, and the treatment is punitive.

2. *"Undeservingness" is an effect of poverty.* Whatever else can be said about unmar- 23 ried mothers on welfare, school dropouts, and people unwilling to take minimum-wage dead-end jobs, their behavior is almost always *poverty-related.*

This is, of course, also true of many street criminals and drug sellers. Middle-class 24 people, after all, do not turn into muggers and street drug dealers any more than they become fifteen-year-old unmarried mothers.

People who have not been poor themselves do not understand how much of what 25 the poor do is poverty-related. Poor young women often do not want to marry the fathers of their children because such men cannot perform as breadwinners and might cope with their economic failures by battering their wives. Although a great deal of publicity is given to school dropouts, not enough has been said about the peer pressure in poor, and even working-class, neighborhoods that discourages doing well in school.

3. *The responsibilities of the poor.* Conservatives, often mute about the responsi- 26 bilities of the rich, stress the responsibilities of the poor. However, poor people sometimes feel no need to be responsible to society until society treats them responsibly. Acting irresponsibly becomes an angry reaction to, even a form of power, over that society. Those whose irresponsibility is criminal deserve punishment and the clearly lazy deserve to lose their benefits. But who would punish an unmarried mother who goes on welfare to obtain medical benefits that a job cannot supply? Is she not acting responsibly toward her child? And how well can we judge anyone's responsibility without first knowing that choices, responsible and irresponsible, were actually open? Being poor often means having little choice to begin with.

4. *The drastic scarcity of work for the poor.* Many Americans, including too many 27 economists, have long assumed that there are always more jobs than workers, that the properly eager can always find them, hence the jobless are at fault. This is, however, a myth—one of many Ronald Reagan liked to promote when he was president. The facts are just the opposite. Decent jobs that are open to the poor, especially to blacks, were the first to disappear when our deindustrialization began. This helps to explain why so many poor men have dropped out of the labor force, and are no longer even counted as jobless.

Incidentally, the myth that the unemployed are unwilling to work is never 28 attached to the rising number of working- and middle-class jobless. But, then, they are not yet poor enough to be considered undeserving.

5. *Black troubles and misbehavior are caused more by poverty than by race.* 29 Because the proportion of blacks who are criminals, school dropouts, heads of single-parent families, or unmarried mothers is higher than among whites, blacks increasingly have to face the outrageous indignity of being considered genetically or culturally undesirable. The plain fact is that the higher rates of nearly all social problems among blacks are the effects of being poor—including poverty brought about by discrimination. When poor whites are compared with poor blacks, those with social problems are not so different, although black proportions remain higher. Even this difference can be attributed to income disparity. Black poverty has been worse in all respects and by all indicators ever since blacks were brought here as slaves.

6. *Blacks should not be treated like recent immigrants.* Black job-seekers some- 30 times face the additional burden of being expected, both by employers and the general public, to compete for jobs with recently arrived immigrants. This expectation calls on people who have been in America for generations to accept the subminimum wages, long hours, poor working conditions, and employer intimidation that are the lot of many immigrants. Actually, employers prefer immigrants because they are more easily exploited or more deferential than native-born Americans. To make matters worse, blacks are then blamed for lacking an "immigrant work ethic."

7. *Debunking the metaphors of undeservingness.* Society's word-smiths—academics, 31 journalists, and pundits—like to find, and their audiences like to hear, buzzwords that caricature moral failings among the poor; but it should not be forgotten that these terms were invented by the fortunate. *Not only is there no identifiable underclass, but a class "under" society is a social impossibility.* Welfare "dependents" are in that condition mainly because the economy has declared them surplus labor and because they must rely on politicians and officials who determine their welfare eligibility.

Such metaphors are never applied to the more affluent. There are no hard-core 32 millionaires, and troubled middle-class people will never be labeled an under-middle class. Women who choose to be financially dependent on their husbands are not described as spouse-dependent, while professors who rely on university trustees for their income are not called tenure-dependent.

8. *The dangers of class stereotypes.* Underclass and other terms for the undeserv- 33 ing poor are class stereotypes, which reinforce class discrimination much as racial stereotypes support racial discrimination. The many similarities between class and racial stereotypes still need to be identified.

Stereotypes sometimes turn into everyday labels that are so taken for granted that 34 they turn into self-fulfilling prophecies—and then cause particular havoc among the more vulnerable poor. For example, boys from poor single-parent families are apt to be punished harder for minor delinquencies simply because of the stereotype that they are growing up without paternal or other male supervision. Once they, and other poor people, are labeled as undeserving, public officials who are supposed to supply them with services feel justified in not being as helpful as before—though depriving poor people of an emergency rent payment or food grant may be enough to push them closer to homelessness or street crime.

The recent display of interest in and appeals for affirmative action along class 35 lines—even by conservatives like Dinesh D'Souza—suggests that the time may be ripe to recognize, and begin to fight, the widespread existence of class discrimination and prejudice. The confrontation has to take place not only in everyday life but also in the country's major institutions, politics, and courts. The Constitution that is now interpreted as barring racial discrimination can perhaps be interpreted to bar class discrimination as well.

9. *Blaming the poor reduces neither poverty nor poverty-related behavior.* Labeling 36 the poor as undeserving does not attack the causes of street crime, improve the schools of poor children, or reduce adult joblessness. Such labels are only a way of expressing anger toward the poor. Blaming the victim solves nothing except to make blamers feel better temporarily. Such labeling justifies political ideologies and interests that oppose solutions, and thus increases the likelihood that nothing will be done about poverty—or crime.

10. *Improving reporting and scholarship about the poor.* Most poverty news is 37 about crime, not poverty. How many reporters ever ask whether economic hardship is part of the crime story? The government's monthly jobless rate is reported, but not the shortage of jobs open to the poor. Likewise, the percentage of people below the poverty rate is an annual news story, but the actual income of the poor, often less than half the poverty line, or about $6,000 a year, is not mentioned.

The "spins," both in government statistics and in journalism, carry over into 38 scholarship. Millions were spent to find and measure an underclass, but there is little ethnographic research to discover why the poor must live as they do. Researchers on homelessness look at mental illness as a cause of homelessness; they do not study it as a possible *effect!*

There are also innumerable other studies of the homeless, but too few about the 39 labor markets and employers, housing industry and landlords, and other factors that create homelessness in the first place.

The Americans who feel most threatened by the poor are people from the work- 40 ing class, whom journalists currently call the middle class. They are apt to live nearest the poor. They will suffer most, other than the poor themselves, from street crime, as well as from the fear that the poor could take over their neighborhoods and jobs. Indeed, as inexpensive housing and secure jobs requiring little education become more scarce, the people only slightly above the poor in income and economic security fear that their superior status will shrink drastically. Viewing the poor as undeserving helps to maintain and even widen that status gap.

No wonder, then, that in the current economic crisis, the journalists' middle 41 class and its job problems are the big story, and the poor appear mainly as the underclass, with candidates ignoring poverty. The political climate being what it is, this may even be unavoidable. Indeed, if the winner's margin in the coming elections comes from that middle class, the candidate must initiate enough economic programs to put *its* jobless back to work and to solve its health care, housing, and other problems.

That winner should be bold enough to make room in the program for the poor as 42 well. Poverty, racial polarization, crime, and related problems cannot be allowed to rise higher without further reducing morale, quality of life, and economic competitiveness. Otherwise, America will not be a decent, safe, or pleasant place to live, even for the affluent.

## READING FOR CONTENT

1. Summarize how the economy, the government, and the political climate have participated in the war against the poor.
2. Paraphrase Gans's objections to the concept of "underclass" (paragraphs 33 and 34).
3. Discuss why people who are better off are frightened and angered by the poor. Do you agree with Gans's explanation?
4. List Gans's solutions for ending the war on the poor. Do you think they are workable?
5. What is the ideal way of reducing the anger directed against the poor?
6. In your own words, explain which of Gans's ten defenses against class bigotry are the most workable.
7. React to Gans's forecast for the future.

## READING FOR GENRE, ORGANIZATION, AND STYLISTIC FEATURES

1. Explain Gans's overall organizational plan. What other organizational patterns does he use?
2. What is the function of paragraphs 11, 21, 22, and 32?
3. Describe the features of the article that help the reader to follow Gans's train of thought.
4. Why do you think Gans concludes the article as he does? What effect did the conclusion have on you as a reader?

## READING FOR RHETORICAL CONTEXT

1. What do you think prompted Gans to write this article?
2. Do you think Gans provides his readers with enough background to support his premise about the war against the poor? What additional information would be useful?
3. What impact does Gans want to have on his audience? Do you think he is successful?

## WRITING ASSIGNMENTS

1. Write a two- to three-page essay explaining why you agree or disagree with Gans's observation that "the Americans who feel most threatened by the poor are people from the working class" (paragraph 40).
2. Write an essay in which you argue for or against Gans's claim that Americans need to fight against class bigotry as well as racial discrimination and prejudice.

3.  For a two-week period, keep a written record of how poor people are treated in a daily newspaper or a daily news broadcast. Then, use your notes to write an essay explaining whether or not the media stereotype poor people as undeserving.

# Serving in Florida

## *Barbara Ehrenreich*

*Barbara Ehrenreich has contributed articles to many magazines and written twelve books, including* The Worst Years of Our Lives, Blood Fires, Fear of Falling, *and* Nickel and Dimed: On (Not) Getting By in America, *from which this selection was taken.*

## PREREADING

This selection is a chapter in Barbara Ehrenreich's book, *Nickel and Dimed: On (Not) Getting By in America*. From 1998 to 2000, Ehrenreich went undercover and became a low-wage worker in order to experience firsthand what it is like to survive on six to seven dollars an hour. Before Ehrenreich embarked on the project, she set three rules for herself: that in her search for jobs she would not rely on her education or former occupation; that she would accept the highest paying job she was given; and that she would lower her expenses by taking the cheapest housing she could find. Over the course of the project, Ehrenreich took jobs in Key West, Florida; Portland, Maine; and Minneapolis, Minnesota.

In this selection Ehrenreich relates her experiences as a server, first at the Hearthside Restaurant where she worked from 2:00 p.m. to 10:00 p.m. for $2.43 per hour plus tips, and then at Johnny's Restaurant. She also worked briefly as a housekeeper in the hotel attached to Johnny's.

What is the lowest paid job you ever held? Take 10 to 15 minutes to write a journal entry explaining what it entailed. In small groups, share your experience with your classmates.

I still flinch to think that I spent all those weeks under the surveillance of men (and later women) whose job it was to monitor my behavior for signs of sloth, theft, drug abuse, or worse. Not that managers and especially "assistant managers" in low-wage settings like this are exactly the class enemy. Mostly, in the restaurant business, they are former cooks still capable of pinch-hitting in the kitchen, just as in hotels they are likely to be former clerks, and paid a salary of only about $400 a week. But everyone knows they have crossed over to the other side, which is, crudely put, corporate as opposed to human. Cooks want to prepare tasty meals, servers want to serve them graciously, but managers are there for only one reason—to make sure that money is made for some theoretical entity, the corporation, which exists far away in Chicago or New York, if a corporation can be said to have a physical existence at all. Reflecting on her career,

Gail tells me ruefully that she swore, years ago, never to work for a corporation again. "They don't cut you no slack. You give and you give and they take."

Managers can sit—for hours at a time if they want—but it's their job to see that no one else ever does, even when there's nothing to do, and this is why, for servers, slow times can be as exhausting as rushes. You start dragging out each little chore because if the manager on duty catches you in an idle moment he will give you something far nastier to do. So I wipe, I clean, I consolidate catsup bottles and recheck the cheesecake supply, even tour the tables to make sure the customer evaluation forms are all standing perkily in their places—wondering all the time how many calories I burn in these strictly theatrical exercises. In desperation, I even take the desserts out of their glass display case and freshen them up with whipped cream and bright new maraschino cherries; anything to look busy. When, on a particularly dead afternoon, Stu finds me glancing at a *USA Today* a customer has left behind, he assigns me to vacuum the entire floor with the broken vacuum cleaner, which has a handle only two feet long, and the only way to do that without incurring orthopedic damage is to proceed from spot to spot on your knees.

On my first Friday at Hearthside there is a "mandatory meeting for all restaurant employees," which I attend, eager for insight into our overall marketing strategy and the niche (your basic Ohio cuisine with a tropical twist?) we aim to inhabit. But there is no "we" at this meeting. Phillip, our top manager except for an occasional "consultant" sent out by corporate headquarters, opens it with a sneer: "The break room—it's disgusting. Butts in the ashtrays, newspapers lying around, crumbs." This windowless little room, which also houses the time clock for the entire hotel, is where we stash our bags and civilian clothes and take our half-hour meal breaks. But a break room is not a right, he tells us, it can be taken away. We should also know that the lockers in the break room and whatever is in them can be searched at any time. Then comes gossip; there has been gossip; gossip (which seems to mean employees talking among themselves) must stop. Off-duty employees are henceforth barred from eating at the restaurant, because "other servers gather around them and gossip." When Phillip has exhausted his agenda of rebukes, Joan complains about the condition of the ladies' room and I throw in my two bits about the vacuum cleaner. But I don't see any backup coming from my fellow servers, each of whom has slipped into her own personal funk; Gail, my role model, stares sorrowfully at a point six inches from her nose. The meeting ends when Andy, one of the cooks, gets up, muttering about breaking up his day off for this almighty bullshit.

Just four days later we are suddenly summoned into the kitchen at 3:30 P.M., even though there are live tables on the floor. We all—about ten of us—stand around Phillip, who announces grimly that there has been a report of some "drug activity" on the night shift and that, as a result, we are now to be a "drug-free" workplace, meaning that all new hires will be tested and possibly also current employees on a random basis. I am glad that this part of the kitchen is so dark because I find myself blushing as hard as if I had been caught toking up in the ladies' room myself: I haven't been treated this way—lined up in the corridor, threatened with locker searches, peppered with carelessly aimed accusations—since at least junior high school. Back on the floor, Joan cracks, "Next they'll be telling us we can't have *sex* on the job." When I ask Stu what happened to inspire the crackdown, he just mutters about "management decisions" and takes the opportunity to upbraid Gail and me for being too generous with the rolls. From now on there's to be only one per customer and it goes out with the dinner, not with the salad. He's also been riding the cooks, prompting Andy to come out of the kitchen and observe—with the serenity of a man whose customary implement is a butcher knife—that "Stu has a death wish today."

Later in the evening, the gossip crystallizes around the theory that Stu is himself the drug culprit, that he uses the restaurant phone to order up marijuana and sends one of the late servers out to fetch it for him. The server was caught and she may have ratted out Stu, at least enough to cast some suspicion on him, thus accounting for his pissy behavior. Who knows? Personally, I'm ready to believe anything bad about Stu, who serves no evident function and presumes too much on our common ethnicity, sidling up to me one night to engage in a little nativism directed at the Haitian immigrants: "I feel like I'm the foreigner here. They're taking over the country." Still later that evening, the drug in question escalates to crack. Lionel, the busboy, entertains us for the rest of the shift by standing just behind Stu's back and sucking deliriously on an imaginary joint or maybe a pipe.

The other problem, in addition to the less-than-nurturing management style, is that this job shows no sign of being financially viable. You might imagine, from a comfortable distance, that people who live, year in and year out, on $6 to $10 an hour have discovered some survival stratagems unknown to the middle class. But no. It's not hard to get my coworkers talking about their living situations, because housing, in almost every case, is the principal source of disruption in their lives, the first thing they fill you in on when they arrive for their shifts. After a week, I have compiled the following survey:

Gail is sharing a room in a well-known downtown flophouse for $250 a week. Her roommate, a male friend, has begun hitting on her, driving her nuts, but the rent would be impossible alone.

Claude, the Haitian cook, is desperate to get out of the two-room apartment he shares with his girlfriend and two other, unrelated people. As far as I can determine, the other Haitian men live in similarly crowded situations.

Annette, a twenty-year-old server who is six months pregnant and abandoned by her boyfriend, lives with her mother, a postal clerk.

Marianne, who is a breakfast server, and her boyfriend are paying $170 a week for a one-person trailer.

Billy, who at $10 an hour is the wealthiest of us, lives in the trailer he owns, paying only the $400-a-month lot fee.

The other white cook, Andy, lives on his dry-docked boat, which, as far as I can tell from his loving descriptions, can't be more than twenty feet long. He offers to take me out on it once it's repaired, but the offer comes with inquiries as to my marital status, so I do not follow up on it.

Tina, another server, and her husband are paying $60 a night for a room in the Days Inn. This is because they have no car and the Days Inn is in walking distance of the Hearthside. When Marianne is tossed out of her trailer for subletting (which is against trailer park rules), she leaves her boyfriend and moves in with Tina and her husband.

Joan, who had fooled me with her numerous and tasteful outfits (hostesses wear their own clothes), lives in a van parked behind a shopping center at night and showers in Tina's motel room. The clothes are from thrift shops.[1]

It strikes me, in my middle-class solipsism, that there is gross improvidence in some of these arrangements. When Gail and I are wrapping silverware in napkins—the only task for which we are permitted to sit—she tells me she is thinking of escaping from her roommate by moving into the Days Inn herself. I am astounded: how she can even think of paying $40 to $60 a day? But if I was afraid of sounding like a social worker, I have come out just sounding like a fool. She squints at me in disbelief: "And where am I supposed to get a month's rent and a month's deposit for an apartment?" I'd been feeling pretty smug about my $500 efficiency, but of course it was made possible only by the $1,300 I had allotted myself for start-up costs when I began my low-wage life: $1,000 for the first month's rent and deposit, $100 for initial groceries and cash in my pocket, $200 stuffed away for emergencies. In poverty, as in certain propositions in physics, starting conditions are everything.

There are no secret economies that nourish the poor; on the contrary, there are a host of special costs. If you can't put up the two months' rent you need to secure an apartment, you end up paying through the nose for a room by the week. If you have only a room, with a hot plate at best, you can't save by cooking up huge lentil stews that can be frozen for the week ahead. You eat fast food or the hot dogs and Styrofoam cups of soup that can be microwaved in a convenience store. If you have no money for health insurance—and the Hearthside's niggardly plan kicks in only after three months—you go without routine care or prescription drugs and end up paying the price. Gail, for example, was doing fine, healthwise anyway, until she ran out of money for estrogen pills. She is supposed to be on the company health plan by now, but they claim to have lost her application form and to be beginning the paperwork all over again. So she spends $9 a pop for pills to control the migraines she wouldn't have, she insists, if her estrogen supplements were covered. Similarly, Marianne's boyfriend lost his job as a roofer because he missed so much time after getting a cut on his foot for which he couldn't afford the prescribed antibiotic. 8

My own situation, when I sit down to assess it after two weeks of work, would not be much better if this were my actual life. The seductive thing about waitressing is that you don't have to wait for payday to feel a few bills in your pocket, and my tips usually cover meals and gas, plus something left over to stuff into the kitchen drawer I use as a bank. But as the tourist business slows in the summer heat, I sometimes leave work with only $20 in tips (the gross is higher, but servers share about 15 percent of their tips with the busboys and bartenders). With wages included, this amounts to about the minimum wage of $5.15 an hour. The sum in the drawer is piling up but at the present rate of accumulation will be more than $100 short of my rent when the end of the month comes around. Nor can I see any expenses to cut. True, I haven't gone the lentil stew route yet, but that's because I don't have a large cooking pot, potholders, or a ladle to stir with (which would cost a total of about $30 at Kmart, somewhat less at a thrift store), not to mention onions, carrots, and the indispensable bay leaf. I do make my lunch almost every day—usually some slow-burning, high-protein combo like frozen chicken patties with melted cheese on top and canned pinto beans on the side. Dinner is at the Hearthside, which offers its employees a choice of BLT, fish sandwich, or hamburger for only $2. The burger lasts longest, especially if it's heaped with gut-puckering jalapeños, but by midnight my stomach is growling again. 9

So unless I want to start using my car as a residence, I have to find a second or an alternative job. I call all the hotels I'd filled out housekeeping applications at weeks ago—the Hyatt, Holiday Inn, Econo Lodge, HoJo's, Best Western, plus a half dozen locally run guest houses. Nothing. Then I start making the rounds again, wasting whole mornings waiting for some assistant manager to show up, even dipping into places so 10 creepy that the front-desk clerk greets you from behind bullet-proof glass and sells pints of liquor over the counter. But either someone has exposed my real-life housekeeping habits—which are, shall we say, mellow—or I am at the wrong end of some infallible ethnic equation: Most, but by no means all, of the working housekeepers I see on my job searches are African Americans, Spanish-speaking, or refugees from the Central European post-Communist world, while servers are almost invariably white and mono-lingually English-speaking. When I finally get a positive response, I have been identi-fied once again as server material. Jerry's—again, not the real name—which is part of a well-known national chain and physically attached here to another budget hotel, is ready to use me at once. The prospect is both exciting and terrifying because, with about the same number of tables and counter seats, Jerry's attracts three or four times the volume of customers as the gloomy old Hearthside.

Picture a fat person's hell, and I don't mean a place with no food. Instead there is  11 everything you might eat if eating had no bodily consequences—the cheese fries, the chicken-fried steaks, the fudge-laden desserts—only here every bite must be paid for, one way or another, in human discomfort. The kitchen is a cavern, a stomach leading to the lower intestine that is the garbage and dishwashing area, from which issue bizarre smells combining the edible and the offal: creamy carrion, pizza barf, and that unique and enigmatic Jerry's scent, citrus fart. The floor is slick with spills, forcing us to walk through the kitchen with tiny steps, like Susan McDougal in leg irons. Sinks everywhere are clogged with scraps of lettuce, decomposing lemon wedges, water-logged toast crusts. Put your hand down on any counter and you risk being stuck to it by the film of ancient syrup spills, and this is unfortunate because hands are utensils here, used for scooping up lettuce onto the salad plates, lifting out pie slices, and even mov-ing hash browns from one plate to another. The regulation poster in the single unisex rest room admonishes us to wash our hands thoroughly, and even offers instructions for doing so, but there is always some vital substance missing—soap, paper towels, toilet paper—and I never found all three at once. You learn to stuff your pockets with napkins before going in there, and too bad about the customers, who must eat, although they don't realize it, almost literally out of our hands.

The break room summarizes the whole situation: There is none, because there  12 are no breaks at Jerry's. For six to eight hours in a row, you never sit except to pee. Actu-ally, there are three folding chairs at a table immediately adjacent to the bathroom, but hardly anyone ever sits in this, the very rectum of the gastroarchitectural system. Rather, the function of the peri-toilet area is to house the ashtrays in which servers and dishwash-ers leave their cigarettes burning at all times, like votive candles, so they don't have to waste time lighting up again when they dash back here for a puff. Almost everyone smokes as if their pulmonary well-being depended on it—the multinational mélange of cooks; the dishwashers, who are all Czechs here; the servers, who are American natives—creating an atmosphere in which oxygen is only an occasional pollutant. My first morning at Jerry's, when the hypoglycemic shakes set in, I complain to one of my fellow servers that I don't understand how she can go so long without food. "Well, I don't understand how *you* can go so long without a cigarette," she responds in a tone of reproach. Because work is what you do for others; smoking is what you do for yourself. I don't know why the antismoking crusaders have never grasped the element of defiant self-nurturance that makes the habit so endearing to its victims—as if, in the American workplace, the only thing people have to call their own is the tumors they are nourishing and the spare moments they devote to feeding them.

Now, the Industrial Revolution is not an easy transition, especially, in my experi-   13
ence, when you have to zip through it in just a couple of days. I have gone from craft
work straight into the factory, from the air-conditioned morgue of the Hearthside
directly into the flames. Customers arrive in human waves, sometimes disgorged fifty at
a time from their tour buses, peckish and whiny. Instead of two "girls" on the floor at
once, there can be as many as six of us running around in our brilliant pink-and-orange
Hawaiian shirts. Conversations, either with customers or with fellow employees, seldom last more than twenty seconds at a time. On my first day, in fact, I am hurt by my
sister servers' coldness. My mentor for the day is a supremely competent, emotionally
uninflected twenty-three-year-old, and the others, who gossip a little among themselves
about the real reason someone is out sick today and the size of the bail bond someone
else has had to pay, ignore me completely. On my second day, I find out why. "Well, it's
good to see *you* again," one of them says in greeting. "Hardly anyone comes back after
the first day." I feel powerfully vindicated—a survivor—but it would take a long time,
probably months, before I could hope to be accepted into this sorority.

I start out with the beautiful, heroic idea of handling the two jobs at once, and for   14
two days I almost do it: working the breakfast/lunch shift at Jerry's from 8:00 till 2:00,
arriving at the Hearthside a few minutes late, at 2:10, and attempting to hold out until
10:00. In the few minutes I have between jobs, I pick up a spicy chicken sandwich at
the Wendy's drive-through window, gobble it down in the car, and change from khaki
slacks to black, from Hawaiian to rust-colored polo. There is a problem, though. When,
during the 3:00–4:00 o'clock dead time, I finally sit down to wrap silver, my flesh seems
to bond to the seat. I try to refuel with a purloined cup of clam chowder, as I've seen
Gail and Joan do dozens of time, but Stu catches me and hisses "No *eating!*" although
there's not a customer around to be offended by the sight of food making contact with a
server's lips. So I tell Gail I'm going to quit, and she hugs me and says she might just follow me to Jerry's herself.

But the chances of this are minuscule. She has left the flop-house and her annoy-   15
ing roommate and is back to living in her truck. But, guess what, she reports to me
excitedly later that evening, Phillip has given her permission to park overnight in the
hotel parking lot, as long as she keeps out of sight, and the parking lot should be totally
safe since it's patrolled by a hotel security guard! With the Hearthside offering benefits
like that, how could anyone think of leaving? This must be Phillip's theory, anyway. He
accepts my resignation with a shrug, his main concern being that I return my two polo
shirts and aprons.

Gail would have triumphed at Jerry's, I'm sure, but for me it's a crash course in   16
exhaustion management. Years ago, the kindly fry cook who trained me to waitress at a
Los Angeles truck stop used to say: Never make an unnecessary trip; if you don't have to
walk fast, walk slow; if you don't have to walk, stand. But at Jerry's the effort of distinguishing necessary from unnecessary and urgent from whenever would itself be too
much of an energy drain. The only thing to do is to treat each shift as a one-time-only
emergency: You've got fifty starving people out there, lying scattered on the battlefield,
so get out there and feed them! Forget that you will have to do this again tomorrow, forget that you will have to be alert enough to dodge the drunks on the drive home
tonight—just burn, burn, burn! Ideally, at some point you enter what servers call a
"rhythm" and psychologists term a "flow state," where signals pass from the sense
organs directly to the muscles, bypassing the cerebral cortex, and a Zen-like emptiness
sets in. I'm on a 2:00–10:00 P.M. shift now, and a male server from the morning shift

tells me about the time he "pulled a triple"—three shifts in a row, all the way around the clock—and then got off and had a drink and met this girl, and maybe he shouldn't tell me this, but they had sex right then and there and it was like *beautiful*.

But there's another capacity of the neuromuscular system, which is pain. I start 17 tossing back drugstore-brand ibuprofens as if they were vitamin C, four before each shift, because an old mouse-related repetitive-stress injury in my upper back has come back to full-spasm strength, thanks to the tray carrying. In my ordinary life, this level of disability might justify a day of ice packs and stretching. Here I comfort myself with the Aleve commercial where the cute blue-collar guy asks: If you quit after working four hours, what would your boss say? And the not-so-cute blue-collar guy, who's lugging a metal beam on his back, answers: He'd fire me, that's what. But fortunately, the commercial tells us, we workers can exert the same kind of authority over our painkillers that our bosses exert over us. If Tylenol doesn't want to work for more than four hours, you just fire its ass and switch to Aleve.

True, I take occasional breaks from this life, going home now and then to catch 18 up on email and for conjugal visits (though I am careful to "pay" for everything I eat here, at $5 for a dinner, which I put in a jar), seeing *The Truman Show* with friends and letting them buy my ticket. And I still have those what-am-I-doing-here moments at work, when I get so homesick for the printed word that I obsessively reread the six-page menu. But as the days go by, my old life is beginning to look exceedingly strange. The emails and phone messages addressed to my former self come from a distant race of people with exotic concerns and far too much time on their hands. The neighborly market I used to cruise for produce now looks forbiddingly like a Manhattan yuppie emporium. And when I sit down one morning in my real home to pay bills from my past life, I am dazzled by the two- and three-figure sums owed to outfits like Club Body Tech and Amazon.com.

Management at Jerry's is generally calmer and more "professional" than at the 19 Hearthside, with two exceptions. One is Joy, a plump, blowsy woman in her early thirties who once kindly devoted several minutes of her time to instructing me in the correct one-handed method of tray carrying but whose moods change disconcertingly from shift to shift and even within one. The other is B.J., aka B.J. the Bitch, whose contribution is to stand by the kitchen counter and yell, "Nita, your order's up, move it!" or "Barbara, didn't you see you've got another table out there? Come *on*, girl!" Among other things, she is hated for having replaced the whipped cream squirt cans with big plastic whipped-cream-filled baggies that have to be squeezed with both hands—because, reportedly, she saw or thought she saw employees trying to inhale the propellant gas from the squirt cans, in the hope that it might be nitrous oxide. On my third night, she pulls me aside abruptly and brings her face so close that it looks like she's planning to butt me with her forehead. But instead of saying "You're fired," she says, "You're doing fine." The only trouble is I'm spending time chatting with customers: "That's how they're getting you." Furthermore I am letting them "run me," which means harassment by sequential demands: You bring the catsup and they decide they want extra Thousand Island; you bring that and they announce they now need a side of fries, and so on into distraction. Finally she tells me not to take her wrong. She tries to say things in a nice way, but "you get into a mode, you know, because everything has to move so fast."[2]

I mumble thanks for the advice, feeling like I've just been stripped naked by the 20 crazed enforcer of some ancient sumptuary law: No chatting for *you*, girl. No fancy service ethic allowed for the serfs. Chatting with customers is for the good-looking young college-educated servers in the downtown carpaccio and ceviche joints, the kids who can make $70–$100 a night. What had I been thinking? My job is to move orders from tables to kitchen and then trays from kitchen to tables. Customers are in fact the major obstacle to the smooth transformation of information into food and food into money—they are, in short, the enemy. And the painful thing is that I'm beginning to see it this way myself. There are the traditional asshole types—frat boys who down multiple Buds and then make a fuss because the steaks are so emaciated and the fries so sparse—as well as the variously impaired—due to age, diabetes, or literacy issues—who require patient nutritional counseling. The worst, for some reason, are the Visible Christians—like the ten-person table, all jolly and sanctified after Sunday night service, who run me mercilessly and then leave me $1 on a $92 bill. Or the guy with the crucifixion T-shirt (SOMEONE TO LOOK UP TO) who complains that his baked potato is too hard and his iced tea too icy (I cheerfully fix both) and leaves no tip at all. As a general rule, people wearing crosses or WWJD? ("What Would Jesus Do?") buttons look at us disapprovingly no matter what we do, as if they were confusing waitressing with Mary Magdalene's original profession.

I make friends, over time, with the other "girls" who work my shift: Nita, the tattooed twenty-something who taunts us by going around saying brightly, "Have we started making money yet?" Ellen, whose teenage son cooks on the graveyard shift and who once managed a restaurant in Massachusetts but won't try out for management here because she prefers being a "common worker" and not "ordering people around." Easy-going fiftyish Lucy, with the raucous laugh, who limps toward the end of the shift because of something that has gone wrong with her leg, the exact nature of which cannot be determined without health insurance. We talk about the usual girl things— men, children, and the sinister allure of Jerry's chocolate peanut-butter cream pie—though no one, I notice, ever brings up anything potentially expensive, like shopping or movies. As at the Hearthside, the only recreation ever referred to is partying, which requires little more than some beer, a joint, and a few close friends. Still, no one is homeless, or cops to it anyway, thanks usually to a working husband or boyfriend. All in all, we form a reliable mutual-support group: If one of us is feeling sick or overwhelmed, another one will "bev" a table or even carry trays for her. If one of us is off sneaking a cigarette or a pee, the others will do their best to conceal her absence from the enforcers of corporate rationality.[3]

But my saving human connection—my oxytocin receptor, as it were—is George, 22 the nineteen-year-old Czech dishwasher who has been in this country exactly one week. We get talking when he asks me, tortuously, how much cigarettes cost at Jerry's. I do my best to explain that they cost over a dollar more here than at a regular store and suggest that he just take one from the half-filled packs that are always lying around on the break table. But that would be unthinkable. Except for the one tiny earring signaling his allegiance to some vaguely alternative point of view, George is a perfect straight arrow—crew-cut, hardworking, and hungry for eye contact. "Czech Republic," I ask, "or Slovakia?" and he seems delighted that I know the difference. "Vaclav Havel," I try, "Velvet Revolution, Frank Zappa?" "Yes, yes, 1989," he says, and I realize that for him this is already history.

My project is to teach George English. "How are you today, George?" I say at the 23 start of each shift. "I am good, and how are you today, Barbara?" I learn that he is not paid by Jerry's but by the "agent" who shipped him over—$5 an hour, with the agent getting the dollar or so difference between that and what Jerry's pays dishwashers. I learn also that he shares an apartment with a crowd of other Czech "dishers," as he calls them, and that he cannot sleep until one of them goes off for his shift, leaving a vacant bed. We are having one of our ESL sessions late one afternoon when B.J. catches us at it and orders "Joseph" to take up the rubber mats on the floor near the dishwashing sinks and mop underneath. "I thought your name was George," I say loud enough for B.J. to hear as she strides off back to the counter. Is she embarrassed? Maybe a little, because she greets me back at the counter with "George, Joseph—there are so many of them!" I say nothing, neither nodding nor smiling, and for this I am punished later, when I think I am ready to go and she announces that I need to roll fifty more sets of silverware, and isn't it time I mixed up a fresh four-gallon batch of blue-cheese dressing? May you grow old in this place, B.J., is the curse I beam out at her when I am finally permitted to leave. May the syrup spills glue your feet to the floor.

I make the decision to move closer to Key West. First, because of the drive. Second and third, also because of the drive: Gas is eating up $4–$5 a day, and although Jerry's is as high-volume as you can get, the tips average only 10 percent, and not just for a newbie like me. Between the base pay of $2.15 an hour and the obligation to share tips with the busboys and dishwashers, we're averaging only about $7.50 an hour. Then there is the $30 I had to spend on the regulation tan slacks worn by Jerry's servers—a setback it could take weeks to absorb. (I had combed the town's two downscale department stores hoping for something cheaper but decided in the end that these marked-down Dockers, originally $49, were more likely to survive a daily washing.) Of my fellow servers, everyone who lacks a working husband or boyfriend seems to have a second job: Nita does something at a computer eight hours a day; another welds. Without the forty-five-minute commute, I can picture myself working two jobs and still having the time to shower between them.

So I take the $500 deposit I have coming from my landlord, the $400 I have earned toward the next month's rent, plus the $200 reserved for emergencies, and use the $1,100 to pay the rent and deposit on trailer number 46 in the Overseas Trailer Park, a mile from the cluster of budget hotels that constitute Key West's version of an industrial park. Number 46 is about eight feet in width and shaped like a barbell inside, with a narrow region—because of the sink and the stove—separating the bedroom from what might optimistically be called the "living" area, with its two-person table and half-sized couch. The bathroom is so small my knees rub against the shower stall when I sit on the toilet, and you can't just leap out of the bed, you have to climb down to the foot of it in order to find a patch of floor space to stand on. Outside, I am within a few yards of a liquor store, a bar that advertises "free beer tomorrow," a convenience store, and a Burger King—but no supermarket or, alas, Laundromat. By reputation, the Overseas park is a nest of crime and crack, and I am hoping at least for some vibrant multicultural street life. But desolation rules night and day, except for a thin stream of pedestrians heading for their jobs at the Sheraton or the 7-Eleven. There are not exactly people here but what amounts to canned labor, being preserved between shifts from the heat.

In line with my reduced living conditions, a new form of ugliness arises at Jerry's. First we are confronted—via an announcement on the computers through which we input orders—with the new rule that the hotel bar, the Driftwood, is henceforth off-limits to restaurant employees. The culprit, I learn through the grapevine, is the ultra-efficient twenty-three-year-old who trained me—another trailer home dweller and a mother of three. Something had set her off one morning, so she slipped out for a nip and returned to the floor impaired. The restriction mostly hurts Ellen, whose habit it is to free her hair from its rubber band and drop by the Driftwood for a couple of Zins before heading home at the end of her shift, but all of us feel the chill. Then the next day, when I go for straws, I find the dry-storage room locked. It's never been locked before; we go in and out of it all day—for napkins, jelly containers, Styrofoam cups for takeout. Vic, the portly assistant manager who opens it for me, explains that he caught one of the dishwashers attempting to steal something and, unfortunately, the miscreant will be with us until a replacement can be found—hence the locked door. I neglect to ask what he had been trying to steal but Vic tells me who he is—the kid with the buzz cut and the earring, you know, he's back there right now.

I wish I could say I rushed back and confronted George to get his side of the story. 27 I wish I could say I stood up to Vic and insisted that George be given a translator and allowed to defend himself or announced that I'd find a lawyer who'd handle the case pro bono. At the very least I should have testified as to the kid's honesty. The mystery to me is that there's not much worth stealing in the dry-storage room, at least not in any fenceable quantity: "Is Gyorgi here, and am having 200—maybe 250—catsup packets. What do you say?" My guess is that he had taken—if he had taken anything at all— some Saltines or a can of cherry pie mix and that the motive for taking it was hunger.

So why didn't I intervene? Certainly not because I was held back by the kind of 28 moral paralysis that can mask as journalistic objectivity. On the contrary, something new—something loathsome and servile—had infected me, along with the kitchen odors that I could still sniff on my bra when I finally undressed at night. In real life I am moderately brave, but plenty of brave people shed their courage in POW camps, and maybe something similar goes on in the infinitely more congenial milieu of the low-wage American workplace. Maybe, in a month or two more at Jerry's, I might have regained my crusading spirit. Then again, in a month or two I might have turned into a different person altogether—say, the kind of person who would have turned George in.

But this is not something I was slated to find out. When my monthlong plunge 29 into poverty was almost over, I finally landed my dream job—housekeeping. I did this by walking into the personnel office of the only place I figured I might have some credibility, the hotel attached to Jerry's, and confiding urgently that I had to have a second job if I was to pay my rent and, no, it couldn't be front-desk clerk. "All *right*," the personnel lady fairly spits, "so it's *housekeeping*," and marches me back to meet Millie, the housekeeping manager, a tiny, frenetic Hispanic woman who greets me as "babe" and hands me a pamphlet emphasizing the need for a positive attitude. The pay is $6.10 an hour, and the hours are nine in the morning till "whenever," which I am hoping can be defined as a little before two. I don't have to ask about health insurance once I meet Carlotta, the middle-aged African American woman who will be training me. Carlie, as she tells me to call her, is missing all of her top front teeth.

On that first day of housekeeping and last day—although I don't yet know it's 30 the last—of my life as a low-wage worker in Key West, Carlie is in a foul mood. We have been given nineteen rooms to clean, most of them "checkouts," as opposed to "stay-overs," and requiring the whole enchilada of bed stripping, vacuuming, and bathroom scrubbing. When one of the rooms that had been listed as a stay-over turns out to be a checkout, she calls Millie to complain, but of course to no avail. "So make up the motherfucker," she orders me, and I do the beds while she sloshes around the bathroom. For four hours without a break I strip and remake beds, taking about four and a half minutes per queen-sized bed, which I could get down to three if there were any reason to. We try to avoid vacuuming by picking up the larger specks by hand, but often there is nothing to do but drag the monstrous vacuum cleaner—it weighs about thirty pounds—off our cart and try to wrestle it around the floor. Sometimes Carlie hands me the squirt bottle of "Bam" (an acronym for something that begins, ominously, with "butyric"—the rest of it has been worn off the label) and lets me do the bathrooms. No service ethic challenges me here to new heights of performance. I just concentrate on removing the pubic hairs from the bathtubs, or at least the dark ones that I can see.

I had looked forward to the breaking-and-entering aspect of cleaning the stay- 31 overs, the chance to examine the secret physical existence of strangers. But the contents of the rooms are always banal and surprisingly neat—zipped-up shaving kits, shoes lined up against the wall (there are no closets), flyers for snorkeling trips, maybe an empty wine bottle or two. It is the TV that keeps us going, from Jerry to Sally to *Hawaii Five-0* and then on to the soaps. If there's something especially arresting, like "Won't Take No for an Answer" on Jerry, we sit down on the edge of a bed and giggle for a moment, as if this were a pajama party instead of a terminally dead-end job. The soaps are the best, and Carlie turns the volume up full blast so she won't miss anything from the bathroom or while the vacuum is on. In Room 503, Marcia confronts Jeff about Lauren. In 505, Lauren taunts poor cheated-on Marcia. In 511, Helen offers Amanda $10,000 to stop seeing Eric, prompting Carlie to emerge from the bathroom to study Amanda's troubled face. "You take it, girl," she advises. "I would for sure."

The tourists' rooms that we clean and, beyond them, the far more expensively 32 appointed interiors in the soaps begin after a while to merge. We have entered a better world—a world of comfort where every day is a day off, waiting to be filled with sexual intrigue. We are only gate-crashers in this fantasy, however, forced to pay for our presence with backaches and perpetual thirst. The mirrors, and there are far too many of them in hotel rooms, contain the kind of person you would normally find pushing a shopping cart down a city street—bedraggled, dressed in a damp hotel polo shirt two sizes too large, and with sweat dribbling down her chin like drool. I am enormously relieved when Carlie announces a half-hour meal break, but my appetite fades when I see that the bag of hot dog rolls she has been carrying around on our cart is not trash salvaged from a checkout but what she has brought for her lunch.

Between the TV and the fact that I'm in no position, as a first dayer, to launch new 33 topics of conversation, I don't learn much about Carlie except that she hurts, and in more than one way. She moves slowly about her work, muttering something about joint pain, and this is probably going to doom her, since the young immigrant housekeepers—Polish and Salvadoran—like to polish off their rooms by two in the afternoon, while she drags the work out till six. It doesn't make any sense to hurry, she observes, when you're being paid by the hour. Already, management has brought in a woman to do what sounds like time-motion studies, and there's talk about switching to paying by the room.[4] She broods, too, about all the little evidences of disrespect that come her way, and not only from management. "They don't care about us," she tells me of the hotel guests; in fact, they don't notice us at all unless something gets stolen from a room—"then they're all over you." We're eating our lunch side by side in the break room when a white guy in a maintenance uniform walks by and Carlie calls out, "Hey you," in a friendly way, "what's your name?"

"Peter Pan," he says, his back already to us.                                    34

"That wasn't funny," Carlie says, turning to me. "That was no kind of answer. 35 Why did he have to be funny like that?" I venture that he has an attitude, and she nods as if that were an acute diagnosis. "Yeah, he got a attitude all right."

"Maybe he's a having a bad day," I elaborate, not because I feel any obligation to 36 defend the white race but because her face is so twisted with hurt.

When I request permission to leave at about 3:30, another housekeeper warns me 37 that no one has so far succeeded in combining housekeeping with serving at Jerry's: "Some kid did it once for five days, and you're no kid." With that helpful information in mind, I rush back to number 46, down four Advils (the name brand this time), shower, stooping to fit into the stall, and attempt to compose myself for the oncoming shift. So much for what Marx termed the "reproduction of labor power," meaning the things a worker has to do just so she'll be ready to labor again. The only unforeseen obstacle to the smooth transition from job to job is that my tan Jerry's slacks, which had looked reasonably clean by 40-watt bulb last night when I hand washed my Hawaiian shirt, prove by daylight to be mottled with catsup and ranch-dressing stains. I spend most of my hour-long break between jobs attempting to remove the edible portions of the slacks with a sponge and then drying them over the hood of my car in the sun.

I can do this two-job thing, is my theory, if I can drink enough caffeine and avoid 38 getting distracted by George's ever more obvious suffering.[5] The first few days after the alleged theft, he seemed not to understand the trouble he was in, and our chirpy little conversations had continued. But the last couple of shifts he's been listless and unshaven, and tonight he looks like the ghost we all know him to be, with dark half-moons hanging from his eyes. At one point, when I am briefly immobilized by the task of filling little paper cups with sour cream for baked potatoes, he comes over and looks as if he'd like to explore the limits of our shared vocabulary, but I am called to the floor for a table. I resolve to give him all my tips that night, and to hell with the experiment in low-wage money management. At eight, Ellen and I grab a snack together standing at the mephitic end of the kitchen counter, but I can only manage two or three mozzarella sticks, and lunch had been a mere handful of McNuggets. I am not tired at all, I assure myself, though it may be that there is simply no more "I" left to do the tiredness monitoring. What I would see if I were more alert to the situation is that the forces of destruction are already massing against me. There is only one cook on duty, a young man named Jesus ("Hay-Sue," that is), and he is new to the job. And there is Joy, who shows up to take over in the middle of the shift dressed in high heels and a long, clingy white dress and fuming as if she'd just been stood up in some cocktail bar.

Then it comes, the perfect storm. Four of my tables fill up at once. Four tables is 39 nothing for me now, but only so long as they are obligingly staggered. As I bev table 27, tables 25, 28, and 24 are watching enviously. As I bev 25, 24 glowers because their bevs haven't even been ordered. Twenty-eight is four yuppyish types, meaning everything on the side and agonizing instructions as to the chicken Caesars. Twenty-five is a middle-aged black couple who complain, with some justice, that the iced tea isn't fresh and the tabletop is sticky. But table 24 is the meteorological event of the century: ten British tourists who seem to have made the decision to absorb the American experience entirely by mouth. Here everyone has at least two drinks—iced tea *and* milk shake, Michelob *and* water (with lemon slice in the water, please)—and a huge, promiscuous orgy of breakfast specials, mozz sticks, chicken strips, quesadillas, burgers with cheese and without, sides of hash browns with cheddar, with onions, with gravy, seasoned fries, plain fries, banana splits. Poor Jesus! Poor me! Because when I arrive with their first tray of food—after three prior trips just to refill bevs—Princess Di refuses to eat her chicken strips with her pancake and sausage special since, as she now reveals, the strips were meant to be an appetizer. Maybe the others would have accepted their meals, but Di, who is deep into her third Michelob, insists that everything else go back while they work on their starters. Meanwhile, the yuppies are waving me down for more decaf and the black couple looks ready to summon the NAACP.

Much of what happens next is lost in the fog of war. Jesus starts going under. The little printer in front of him is spewing out orders faster than he can rip them off, much less produce the meals. A menacing restlessness rises from the tables, all of which are full. Even the invincible Ellen is ashen from stress. I take table 24 their reheated main courses, which they immediately reject as either too cold or fossilized by the microwave. When I return to the kitchen with their trays (three trays in three trips) Joy confronts me with arms akimbo: "What *is* this?" She means the food—the plates of rejected pancakes, hash browns in assorted flavors, toasts, burgers, sausages, eggs. "Uh, scrambled with cheddar," I try, "and that's—" "No," she screams in my face, "is it a traditional, a super-scramble, an eye-opener?" I pretend to study my check for a clue, but entropy has been up to its tricks, not only on the plates but in my head, and I have to admit that the original order is beyond reconstruction. "You don't know an eye-opener from a traditional?" she demands in outrage. All I know, in fact, is that my legs have lost interest in the current venture and have announced their intention to fold. I am saved by a yuppie (mercifully not one of mine) who chooses this moment to charge into the kitchen to bellow that his food is twenty-five minutes late. Joy screams at him to get the hell out of her kitchen, *please*, and then turns on Jesus in a fury, hurling an empty tray across the room for emphasis.

I leave. I don't walk out, I just leave. I don't finish my side work or pick up my credit card tips, if any, at the cash register or, of course, ask Joy's permission to go. And the surprising thing is that you *can* walk out without permission, that the door opens, that the thick tropical night air parts to let me pass, that my car is still parked where I left it. There is no vindication in this exit, no fuck-you surge of relief, just an overwhelming dank sense of failure pressing down on me and the entire parking lot. I had gone into this venture in the spirit of science, to test a mathematical proposition, but somewhere along the line, in the tunnel vision imposed by long shifts and relentless concentration, it became a test of myself, and clearly I have failed. Not only had I flamed out as a housekeeper/server, I had forgotten to give George my tips, and, for reasons perhaps best known to hardworking, generous people like Gail and Ellen, this hurts. I don't cry, but I am in a position to realize, for the first time in many years, that the tear ducts are still there and still capable of doing their job.

When I moved out of the trailer park, I gave the key to number 46 to Gail and arranged for my deposit to be transferred to her. She told me that Joan was still living in her van and that Stu had been fired from the Hearthside. According to the most up-to-date rumors, the drug he ordered from the restaurant was crack and he was caught dipping into the cash register to pay for it. I never found out what happened to George.

## Notes

1. I could find no statistics on the number of employed people living in cars or vans, but according to a 1997 report of the National Coalition for the Homeless, "Myths and Facts about Homelessness," nearly one-fifth of all homeless people (in twenty-nine cities across the nation) are employed in full- or part-time jobs.

2. In *Workers in a Lean World: Unions in the International Economy* (Verso, 1997), Kim Moody cites studies finding an increase in stress-related workplace injuries and illness between the mid-1980s and the early 1990s. He argues that rising stress levels reflect a new system of "management by stress" in which workers in a variety of industries are being squeezed to extract maximum productivity, to the detriment of their health.

3. Until April 1998, there was no federally mandated right to bathroom breaks. According to Marc Linder and Ingrid Nygaard, authors of *Void Where Prohibited: Rest Breaks and the Right to Urinate on Company Time* (Cornell University Press, 1997), "The right to rest and void at work is not high on the list of social or political causes supported by professional or executive employees, who enjoy personal workplace liberties that millions of factory workers can only dream about. . . . While we were dismayed to discover that workers lacked an acknowledged right to void at work, [the workers] were amazed by outsiders' naïve belief that their employers would permit them to perform this basic bodily function when necessary. . . . A factory worker, not allowed a break for six-hour stretches, voided into pads worn inside her uniform; and a kindergarten teacher in a school without aides had to take all twenty children with her to the bathroom and line them up outside the stall door while she voided."

4. A few weeks after I left, I heard ads on the radio for housekeeping jobs at this hotel at the amazing rate of "up to $9 an hour." When I inquired, I found out that the hotel had indeed started paying by the room, and I suspect that Carlie, if she lasted, was still making the equivalent of $6 an hour or quite a bit less.

5. In 1996 the number of persons holding two or more jobs averaged 7.8 million, or 6.2 percent of the workforce. It was about the same rate for men and for women (6.1 versus 6.2). About two-thirds of multiple jobholders work one job full-time and the other part-time. Only a heroic minority—4 percent of men and 2 percent of women—work two full-time jobs simultaneously (John F. Stinson Jr., "New Data on Multiple Jobholding Available from the CPS," *Monthly Labor Review*, March 1997).

## READING FOR CONTENT

1. Explain why affordable housing is the principal problem for low-wage workers.

2. Paraphrase the passage (paragraph 18) in which Ehrenreich contrasts her life as a low-wage worker with her middle-class life.

3. Did any of the working conditions Ehrenreich describes shock you? Give some examples.

4. In your own words, explain why Ehrenreich did not intervene on behalf of the dishwasher, George.

5. Ehrenreich describes a number of humiliations she was subjected to as a low-wage worker. Cite some examples.

## READING FOR GENRE, ORGANIZATION, AND STYLISTIC FEATURES

1. Ehrenreich breathes life into her story by including rich, vivid detail. Divide the class into small groups, each of which is responsible for a certain number of pages of the text. Identify details and explain why they are effective.

2. Reread paragraph 11 and comment on the effectiveness of the imagery Ehrenreich uses to describe Jerry's Restaurant.

3. What function do Ehrenreich's footnotes serve?

4. Throughout the selection, Ehrenreich uses humor to convey some serious thoughts to the reader. Cite five to ten examples.

## READING FOR RHETORICAL CONTEXT

1. Whom do you think Ehrenreich visualizes as her audience? What role does she assume in relation to these readers?
2. How would you describe Ehrenreich's tone: complacency? moral outrage? or something in between? Explain.

## WRITING ASSIGNMENTS

1. Write an essay in which you compare and contrast your work experiences with those of Ehrenreich and her coworkers. Consider questions such as the following:

   What types of obstacles did you have to overcome?
   How were you treated by your boss?
   Did you get along with your coworkers?
   Was your workplace environment satisfactory and safe?
   Did you experience any type of class bigotry or discrimination?
   Were your working conditions reasonable?

2. Ehrenreich's experiences take place from 1998 to 2000, years of unprecedented prosperity in the United States. What does this say about the growing economic chasm between the rich and the poor that the following article from *The Economist* discusses in this chapter? Respond in essay form.

3. In "The War Against the Poor Instead of Programs to End Poverty," Herbert Gans writes, "People who have not been poor themselves do not understand how much of what the poor do is poverty-related" (paragraph 25). What insights did you gain from Ehrenreich's experiences? Write an essay in response.

■ ■ ■ ■ ■ ■ ■ ■ ■ ■ ■

# Middle of the Class

## *The Economist*

*The Economist* is a weekly magazine published in England by The Economist Group. Begun in 1843 and employing many famous editors throughout the years, the magazine is known for its international perspective on links between economic issues, current affairs, business, finance, science, technology and the arts. Most articles are published with no authorial byline.

## PREREADING

Scan the article for its topical subdivisions. What do the headings "Equality of Opportunity Is Under Threat," "A Harder Climb," and "The Trouble with Being Poor" lead you to expect about its argument? Because the magazine originates as a British publication, what might

From: *The Economist* vol. 376, issue 8435, July 16, 2005, p. 12.

you expect about its attitude toward society in the United States—which professes to be class-free? Freewrite your responses to these questions.

## Equality of Opportunity is Under Threat

For the past three years, the most successful shows on American television have been    1
*American Idol* and *The Apprentice*. This spring, millions tuned in to watch Carrie Underwood, a 21-year-old country-and-western singer from small-town Oklahoma, win the entertainment contest and to see Bill Rancic, who put himself through university by cleaning boats, land a six-figure salary as Donald Trump's chosen sidekick. The success of these shows in America testifies to the endurance and popularity of the American Dream—the idea that anything is possible if you work at it hard enough.

America's founding document declares all men to be created equal. From Benjamin    2
Franklin, the 15th child of a candlemaker, to Bill Clinton, whose mother was widowed before he was born, the American creed proclaims that the ladder of success can be climbed by all. A decline in social mobility would run counter to American's deepest beliefs about their country. Unfortunately, that is what seems to be happening. Class is reappearing in a new form.

For the quarter-century after the second world war, income growth in America was    3
fairly evenly spread. According to a study by the Economic Policy Institute (EPI), the poorest fifth of the population saw its income increase by as much as the next-poorest fifth, and so on in equal steps to the top. But in the past quarter-century, the rich have been doing dramatically better than the less well off. Since 1979, median family incomes have risen by 18% but the incomes of the top 1% have gone up by 200%. In 1970, according to the Census Bureau, the bottom fifth received 5.4% of America's total national income and the richest fifth got 40.9%. Twenty-five years later, the share of the bottom fifth had fallen to 4.4% but that of the top fifth had risen to 46.5%.

## A Harder Climb

This makes America unusual. Thomas Piketty and Emmanuel Saez examined the    4
incomes of the top 0.1% of people in America, France and Britain from 1913 to 1998. The fortunes of the three countries' super-rich kept fairly closely in step for most of the 20th century, until America began to diverge in the late 1970s. Now the top 0.1% of Americans earn two or three times as much as their peers in Britain and France. If America is a ladder, the rungs have been moved further apart.

Perhaps Americans think the rich deserve their success. They certainly work    5
more than they used to. In the 1970s, the top 10% worked fewer hours than the bottom 10%; now the reverse is true. Back in 1929, 70% of the income of the extremely rich (the top 0.01%) came from capital (dividends, rent and interest). Now, 80% comes from wages and stock options, which is earned income of a sort.

Or perhaps what really matters is how the poor are doing in absolute terms rather    6
than in relation to the wealthy. Americans' average salaries have risen over the past 30 years, though admittedly not by much. A far smaller share of the population lives in poverty now than in the supposedly golden age of equality in the 1950s (12% compared with 22%). Moreover, a surge of immigrants on minimum wages tends to bring down the average: home-grown Americans are probably better off than the figures suggest.

The rich have not got richer at the expense of the poor. The rising tide has lifted dinghies as well as yachts.

Anyway, what Americans seem to mind about most is equality of opportunity—and people do not feel there is any less of it now than there used to be. Some 80% (a higher proportion than in the 1980s) think it is possible to start out poor, work hard and become rich. A poll for the *New York Times* found that twice as many Americans reckon that their chances of moving up a notch have improved over the past 30 years than think their chances have gone down. Most Americans say their standard of living is higher than that of their parents, and that their children will do better than they are doing. 7

So, on the face of it, rising inequality is not affecting the optimism and ambition of average Americans, and these are what matter to the country's entrepreneurial spirit and social cohesion. But there are three big problems with this rosy view. The first is that America has never been as socially mobile as Americans like to believe. According to a long-term research project carried out at the University of Michigan, led by Gary Solon, America's score on social mobility is not particularly high or low, but middling. 8

That does not sound too bad. But it means that, if you are among the poorest 5% of the population, your chances of achieving an average income are only one in six. If you are among the poorest 1%, they become very dim indeed. Moreover—and this was the most surprising thing about the study—despite America's more flexible labour markets, social mobility there is no longer greater than in supposedly class-ridden Europe, and if anything it seems to be declining. 9

A study by Katharine Bradbury and Jane Katz for the Federal Reserve Bank of Boston found that in the 1970s, 65% of people changed their social position (that is, moved out of the income bracket in which they had started the decade). In the 1990s, only 60% did. Not a huge change, but consistent with Mr Solon's study showing that the correlation between parents' and children's income is even closer now than it was in the 1980s. The authors also found decreasing amounts of social mobility at the top and the bottom. This is squeezing the middle class. Americans may be sorting themselves into two more stable groups, haves and have-nots. This is the same trend that geographical mobility has been encouraging. Decreasing mobility may one day come to erode Americans' faith in the fairness of their economy. 10

The second reason for pessimism is that mobility may continue to decline because it is rooted in fundamental changes to the economy. These explain both the big rise in income inequality and the smaller shift in social mobility. Over the past 25 years, globalisation has increased rewards for intellectual skills, pushing up the value of a degree. The income gap between college graduates and those without university degrees doubled between 1979 and 1997. 11

This has gone hand in hand with changes in the nature of work. It used to be possible to start at the bottom of a big firm and work your way up. But America's corporate giants have got rid of their old hierarchies. Lifetime employment is at an end, and managers hop from job to job. That makes a degree essential. In the 1930s and 1940s, only half of all American chief executives had a college degree. Now almost all of them do, and 70% also have a higher degree, such as an MBA. People with a university degree are now more likely to move up an income bracket than those without. This is a big change since the 1970s, when income rises were distributed equally across all educational levels. America is becoming a stratified society based on education: a meritocracy. 12

But what if education itself becomes stratified? Historically, America's education 13 system has been the main avenue for upward mobility. Mass secondary education supplied the workforce of the world's most successful industrial economy in the late 19th century; mass university education did the same for the period of American economic dominance after the second world war. But now, worries Lawrence Summers, the president of Harvard University, what had been engines of social mobility risk becoming brakes.

At secondary-school level, American education is financed largely by local prop- 14 erty taxes. Naturally, places with big houses paying larger property taxes have schools with more resources. At university level, the rise in the cost of education has taken Ivy League universities out of the reach of most middle-class and poor families. The median income of families with children at Harvard is $150,000. The wealthy have always dominated elite schools, but their representation is rising. Between 1976 and 1995, according to one study, students from the richest quarter of the population increased their share of places at America's elite universities from 39% to 50%.

Even outside elite schools, students from poor backgrounds are becoming rarer. 15 The budget squeeze on states in 2001–04 forced them to increase fees at state colleges, traditionally the places where the children of less wealthy parents went. Those children also face increasing competition from richer kids squeezed out of the Ivy League. As a result, a student from the top income quarter is six times more likely to get a BA than someone from the bottom quarter. American schools seem to be reinforcing educational differences rather than reducing them.

The third reason for gloom is perhaps the most worrying. It is the possibility that, 16 as Isabel Sawhill of the Brookings Institution argues, your chances of a good education, good job and good prospects—in other words, of moving upwards—are partly determined by family behaviour. On this view, the rich really are different, and not just because they have more money; moreover, these differences are becoming embedded in the structure of the family itself. Class stratification, in other words, is more than a matter of income or inherited wealth.

College graduates tend to marry college graduates. Both go out to work, so in the 17 households of the most educated the returns to a university education are doubled. College-educated women are also postponing children for the sake of their careers. On average, they have their first child at 30, five years later than in the 1970s and eight years later than their contemporaries who have not been to college.

## The Trouble with Being Poor

At the bottom of the heap, you see the opposite: women have children younger, often 18 out of wedlock and without a job. True, out-of-wedlock births are falling and welfare reform has increased the chances of mothers holding down jobs, but the gap is still vast. If, as Ms Sawhill argues, the key to upward mobility is finishing your education, having a job and getting and staying married, then the rich start with advantages beyond money.

This does not mean that America's meritocracy is a fake, or that nothing can be 19 done. The country faced a similar rise in inequality in the early 20th century and rallied against it. President Roosevelt sought to save American capitalism from its own excesses so that "malefactors of great wealth" would not become a hereditary aristocracy.

Today, policy changes, such as reforming the way schools are financed, or giving 20 federal help to poorer college students, would lessen social inequality. But for that to happen, American politicians and the public must first acknowledge that there is a problem. At the moment, they do not.

## READING FOR CONTENT

1. The article points out that average Americans do not seem alarmed by rising levels of inequality in the United States. What three problems does the article expose about this attitude in paragraphs 8, 11, and 16? Summarize these problems in your own words.

2. Summarize the threat to social mobility presented by changes in university and secondary-school education discussed in paragraphs 11–15.

## READING FOR GENRE, ORGANIZATION, AND STYLISTIC FEATURES

1. The genre of economic analysis relies upon statistics and their interpretation. How does the article interpret its statistics in paragraphs 3, 6, 9, 12, and 15?

2. How do the headings before paragraphs 1, 4, and 18 organize the argument?

3. How do the statistics in paragraphs 4, 5, 7, 10, 11, and 14 explain features of American society for an international audience? Do these statistics surprise you?

## READING FOR RHETORICAL CONTEXT

1. *The Economist* is a British publication, but it addresses its articles to an international readership. How does paragraph 3 use an elementary lesson in American history to prepare readers for its argument that in the United States class is reappearing in a new form?

2. How does paragraph 20 use an appeal to American politicians and the public to conclude its argument about the threat to equality of opportunity in recent U.S. history?

## WRITING ASSIGNMENTS

1. Write a letter to the editor of *The Economist* explaining that, as a North American college student, you agree or disagree with the article's assessment of the role that class differences play in American education. Use statistics given in the article to defend your argument even if you arrive at conclusions that may differ from the ones presented in the article.

2. Write a letter to the administration of your college about the problems raised by this article. Draw upon your own experience at the college to illustrate these problems and formulate some provisional advice about what the college can do to resolve some of them before they get out of hand.

# When Shelter Feels Like a Prison

*Charmion Browne*

*When Charmion Browne wrote this article, she was a senior at Cornell University.*

## PREREADING

In an article published in *The New York Times* on March 24, 2002, Jennifer Egan writes, "Today, families make up 75 percent of New York's homeless-shelter population, with more than 13,000 children having slept in city shelters and temporary apartments most nights this winter" (Jennifer, Egan. "Be Young and Homeless." *The New York Times*. Sunday Magazine, March 24, 2002. Pp. E 32–35, 58–59, 34). Egan goes on to say, "In an era regarded as generally prosperous, the numbers are staggering: Between 900,000 and 1.4 million children in America are homeless for a time in a given year" (34–35). Were you aware that children make up a large percentage (up to 40 percent) of the nation's homeless population? Respond in your writer's notebook.

During my early childhood I lived in four or five different homeless shelters in New York City. It's a good thing my mother found employment when she did; otherwise I, too, might have been like one of the homeless children in the city today, left without even a shelter to live in because of overcrowding. Last week some of these children were sent to an unused jail in the Bronx—and then removed when lead paint was found there—because the city could find nowhere else for them to live.

From a house to a shelter to a former jail—not the most desirable pathway to take in life. I only had to deal with having to write down an address in school that was never going to be my own, living in a "house" where I had an extended family of one-hundred strangers, being cramped in a room as small as a bathroom with three other families besides my own, with no sense of privacy—ever. Some homeless children in New York can now add to their childhood memories the time they had no place else to live but a former jail.

My mother had financial difficulties as a single mother taking care of my brother and me on her own. She worked very hard to move us from a small one-bedroom apartment to a two-bedroom apartment. We finally did move into that bigger apartment when I was around 8, but after living there a week we discovered that the place was infested with centipedes and we had to move out before my mother could find us another apartment. So we ended up in a shelter. I think my mother thought it was only going to be a temporary situation until she could find someplace else to go.

On that first night without a home, I fell asleep as we waited in line at the department of homeless services to find out which shelter would take us. There were no more seats available and we were there for over five hours before my mother even got to talk to someone. We then had to wait another two hours before a van came to pick us up and take us to the shelter in downtown Manhattan where we would be spending the next two months.

It still puzzles me how so many beds could fit in the room we stayed in. There were four bunk beds crammed into one tiny room. I shared a top bunk with my brother, with my mother sleeping below. Every time we wanted to get to our bed, we had to jump across someone else's bed. Since we had been the last to arrive at the shelter, we had no choice; we got the bed farthest back in the room.

My brother and I learned quickly that there were unspoken rules for living in these places. In a way, living there was like living in a kind of prison. You had to fit in fast or someone would take advantage of you. There weren't any curtains in the bathrooms and everyone on the floor—100 or more people—had to use the same facility. My mother quickly picked up the habit of waking us at 4 a.m. to make sure we took a shower before anyone else awakened. Later, we learned that if you didn't start lining up for meals at least two hours before the kitchen was open, you might as well forget about eating. We had to watch our things at all times, because if you weren't careful someone might take your things and you'd never see them again.

I was in high school when I finally accepted the fact that I was homeless. Until that point I was in complete denial. During those miserable times, my brother and I learned how to become expert liars. We never let our friends in school know where we were living. In some cases we were lucky enough not to be going to the local school, so no one ever walked home with us. If the shelter was near our school or one of our friends caught us coming out of the "bums" building, as the kids in the neighborhood used to call it, then we would tell them our mother worked there and we had to meet her there after school. It is difficult enough to fit in when you are a kid, and worse yet when you can never invite anyone home to visit because you don't have a home.

Being in those shelters, though, helped me to see that the biggest cause of homelessness is not lack of money to pay rent. There were a lot of broken families in these shelters: broken by drugs, alcohol abuse, divorce, AIDS, early pregnancy, lack of education and, most important, lack of information about how to get out of these troubles. Many of the kids I knew at the shelter really wanted to change their circumstances, but few of them did—few of them knew how. There weren't many social workers around, and even when they were around and noticed a problem, they rarely followed up. The children in these situations need a listening ear, someone to turn to consistently.

Sure, having a bed to sleep on is better than having no bed at all. But sleeping on a bed in a shelter that was once a jail doesn't help ease the psychological burden of being homeless in the first place. I understand that Mayor Michael Bloomberg's administration is trying to make sure that the new shelter in the Bronx is safe, but is it working to make it seem less prison-like? A line for food, cramped space, no privacy—sounds a lot like a prison to me. The only difference now is that the city is calling a homeless shelter what it really is.

## READING FOR CONTENT

1. What event prompted Browne to write this piece?
2. In your own words, explain why living in a homeless shelter is like living in a prison.

## READING FOR GENRE, ORGANIZATION, AND STYLISTIC FEATURES

1. Explain how the opening paragraph informs the reader of the direction Browne will take in the remainder of the selection.
2. Describe the type of evidence Browne uses to support her position. Is the evidence effective?

## READING FOR RHETORICAL CONTEXT

1. Describe Browne's purpose. What is she trying to get across to the readers of *The New York Times*?
2. How would you characterize Browne's tone of voice? Is it appropriate for her rhetorical purpose?

## WRITING ASSIGNMENTS

1. In response to Charmion Browne's article, write a letter to the editor of *The New York Times*.
2. In "Serving in Florida," Barbara Ehrenreich provides insights into the problem of homelessness when she discusses the acute shortage of affordable housing for extremely low-income families. Write an essay in which you draw upon Barbara Ehrenreich as well as other authors in Chapter 14 to explain Charmion Browne's childhood of homelessness.

■ ▓ ■ ▓ ■ ■ ■ ▓ ■ ▓ ▓ ▒

# Economic Pulse: Indian Country

## *Dirk Johnson*

*Dirk Johnson is a journalist who has written for* Newsweek *and* The New York Times. *He is a five-time winner of* The New York Times Publisher's Award *and author of* Biting the Dust: The Wild Ride *and* Dark Romance of the Rodeo.

## PREREADING

Before reading this short selection, comment on the economic conditions of Native Americans. Answer the following questions in your writer's notebook: To which social class do many Native Americans belong? Do you think there is much poverty on Indian reservations? Do you think white people's standard of poverty is different from that of Indians? Freewrite your response.

The rough dirt path to the Navajo sheep camp meanders between ancient dunes   1
and slabs of sandstone rising in huge, shattered plates. A few rare trees, planted next to
a hogan, or *cha ha'oh*—a summer shade house made of branches—stick up from an
ocean of low greasewood. In some places, the skin of the earth has been peeled away by
scouring sandstorms and washed clean by pummeling summer rain.

This is some of the rawest land on the Navajo reservation, a place where water must   2
be hauled in barrels by pick-up from Tuba City, some 40 miles away, and where two elderly women, Dorothy Reed and Jeanette Lewis, survive by raising sheep and cows.

By most measures, American Indians are the poorest ethnic group in the country.   3
On some reservations, unemployment exceeds 80 percent. Of the ten poorest United
States counties in the last census, four were Indian lands in South Dakota. On the
Navajo lands, unemployment ranges from 30 percent to 40 percent, and shacks are
more common than houses.

Income among Indians has not grown for the past decade. Some experts say those   4
figures mask real progress, however, since a baby boom among Indians in the last generation has sharply increased the number of young people. Nearly 20 percent of Indians
are younger than ten, twice the national rate.

To be sure, welfare payments account for a great share of the money on some   5
reservations. And yet, tribal leaders say, there are two faces of poverty in Indian Country.

Rates of Indian suicide and alcoholism far exceed the national averages. Some   6
reservations now have street gangs, a new phenomenon. And domestic violence continues to be a serious problem.

And yet, many Indian people are poor, but hardly broken. "It's important not to   7
impose the non-Indian values of poverty on Indians," said David Lester of the Council
of Energy Resource Tribes. "There are worse things than being poor. Don't get me
wrong—nobody likes suffering. But money is just not the measure of success."

Many of them value the traditional ways more than modern contrivances, and no   8
federal program could persuade them to follow a new way, even if it seemed easier.

"In the beginning, the earth was made for us by Changing Woman," said Mrs.   9
Reed, referring to a Navajo deity. "My grandfather used to tell me that you were supposed to make a living from the earth and the sheep."

This is part of the Indian Country economy largely missing from government   10
charts and graphs on employment and production: traditional Navajos who raise their
own food, or wait by the roadside to sell herbs they have picked from the hills or wood
they have gathered or rugs they have woven by hand.

Many of them barter goods and services: a coat in exchange for a car battery,   11
babysitting in exchange for repair work.

Some have never seen the inside of a bank. In some areas, the Indian economy   12
has stagnated because banks are unwilling to count reservation homes as collateral,
since the land is held in a trust. They will, however, lend money for trailers, since they
can be repossessed and hauled away.

When Navajos run low on money, they sometimes drive or hitch-hike to the   13
pawnshops in the dusty town of Gallup, New Mexico, where they plop saddles and
blankets and pieces of jewelry on the counter as collateral for high-interest loans. Often
they are later unable to come up with the cash required to retrieve their belongings,
which are then declared "dead pawn," and sold, frequently to prosperous tourists stopping off Interstate 40 in search of an Indian souvenir.

The Navajo women had been up since dawn, in a one-room house with bare 14
sheetrock walls, with the front facing, to greet the sunrise, as tradition decrees it. There
was fry bread for breakfast. Both wore the traditional attire for elderly Navajo women:
velveteen blouse closed at the neck with a turquoise clasp, long tiered satin dresses,
socks and inexpensive running shoes known by the young ones as "sani sneakers" —
grandma sneakers.

On this morning, some of their children and grandchildren had arrived to help 15
round up some stray cows. As in many Navajo families, their children had become educated and moved to town, living in houses with plumbing and electricity. But they
come back often and help out with some money when they can.

Mrs. Reed's son, Willie, won a scholarship to attend an Eastern prep school, and 16
then earned bachelor's and master's degrees from Stanford University. With his education,
he could have landed a high-paying job and taken a home in the city, with air-conditioning
and cable television and home-delivered pizza. Instead, he returned to a tiny house on the
reservation and now teaches science at a Navajo high school.

## READING FOR CONTENT

1. What do you think David Lester means when he says, "It's important not to
   impose the non-Indian values of poverty on Indians" (paragraph 7)?
2. Describe in your own words the "hidden" or unpublished side of the Indian
   economy.
3. What types of wealth do Dorothy Reed and Jeanette Lewis possess? Do you think
   white Americans value those types of wealth?

## READING FOR GENRE, ORGANIZATION, AND STYLISTIC FEATURES

1. What characteristics of Johnson's piece reveal that it was written for a newspaper?
   Explain how it differs from other selections in this chapter.
2. Underline examples of the types of evidence (facts, statistics, references to
   authorities, personal experiences) Johnson uses. Do you think that evidence is
   effective? Explain.

## READING FOR RHETORICAL CONTEXT

1. How did you react to this article? Explain the effect it will have on the readers of
   *The New York Times*.
2. How would you describe Johnson's tone? How does it differ from Barbara Ehrenreich's tone in "Serving in Florida"?

## WRITING ASSIGNMENTS

1. Drawing on Johnson's article, your own experience, and other selections you
   have read, write an essay in which you explain why some people prefer modest
   traditional ways to modern technology and contrivances. Write for classmates
   who have not read Johnson's article.

2. Some sociologists and economists report that although most Native Americans are still very poor, in recent years some have improved their economic standing. Visit the library and search for recent magazine and newspaper articles dealing with the economy of Native Americans. How do your findings compare with Johnson's? Write an essay in which you synthesize the information you locate.

## SYNTHESIS WRITING ASSIGNMENTS

1. Conduct research on the Personal Responsibility and Work Opportunity and Reconciliation Act (PRWORA) that Congress enacted as part of welfare reform in 1996. Your objective is to determine whether or not Herbert Gans's forecast, written in 1992, was accurate:

   The latest fashion is to put welfare recipients to work, which would be a good idea if even decent entry-level jobs for them could be found or created. (Alas, when taxpayers discover how much cheaper it is to pay welfare than to create jobs, that remedy may end as it has before.) (paragraph 14)

   Write an essay in which you assess the extent to which the reform has made a long-term difference in lifting poor people, especially women, out of poverty.

2. At the end of her book, *Nickel and Dimed*, Barbara Ehrenreich writes:

   When someone works for less pay than she can live on—when, for example, she goes hungry so that you can eat more cheaply and conveniently—then she has made a great sacrifice for you, she has made you a gift of some part of her abilities, her health, and her life. The "working poor," as they are approvingly termed, are in fact the major philanthropists of our society. They neglect their own children so that the children of others will be cared for; they live in substandard housing so that other homes will be shiny and perfect; they endure privation so that inflation will be low and stock prices high. To be a member of the working poor is to be an anonymous donor, a nameless benefactor, to everyone else. (221)

   Drawing on *The Economist*'s "Middle of the Class" and other selections in this chapter, write an essay in response to Ehrenreich's statement.

3. Drawing on the selections in this chapter, write an essay explaining why poverty and class divisions exist in the United States today. Write for an audience who has not read this chapter.

4. How widespread are the class discrimination and prejudice that Gans discusses in "The War Against the Poor Instead of Programs to End Poverty"? Use the selections by Angela Locke, Charmion Browne, and Dirk Johnson to write an essay in response.

5. Show how Ehrenreich's "Serving in Florida" communicates the exploitation, prejudice, discrimination, and injustice that are discussed by the other writers in this chapter. Write an essay addressed to your classmates.

# *Humanities*

## ■ SUBJECTS OF STUDY IN THE HUMANITIES

The subjects that humanists study have cultural, historical, critical, and theoretical orientations. There is a great deal of overlap among these subjects as, for example, music or the visual arts can be studied from a performance or creative practitioner's perspective, or from a cultural perspective in terms of their impact upon social life, or from an historical perspective in terms of their development over time, or from a critical perspective in terms of their formal structures, or from a theoretical perspective in terms of their relationship to other discourse.

- The **historical** subjects are history; various area studies, such as ancient classical civilization, Latin American studies, and Asian studies; and historical studies of particular disciplines, such as the history of science, the history of art, and historical linguistics. Humanists approach these subjects by studying the causes, effects, development, and interaction of peoples, nations, institutions, ideas, fashions, styles, and the like.
- The **critical** subjects are literature, drama, music, the visual arts, and other expressive arts. Humanists approach them by analyzing, interpreting, and evaluating "texts," understood in the broadest sense of the term as novels, poems, plays, films, paintings, sculpture, dance, musical scores, musical performances, and so forth.
- The **theoretical** subjects are philosophy, linguistics, and semiotics. Humanists approach them from a broad perspective and at close range by examining thought, language, structures of meaning and expression, and other significant evidence of human rationality.

The conversation among students and scholars in these subjects can be intense. An array of approaches defines this conversation through cultural studies, gender studies, media studies, and critical theory in its various historical, philosophical, linguistic, social, and psychoanalytical forms.

## ◼ METHODS OF STUDY IN THE HUMANITIES

The cultural, historical, critical, and theoretical orientations of the humanities also describe the methods that humanists use. The study of history, for example, requires a **critical reading** of documents from the past as well as a theoretical probing of their importance. The study of literature and the arts usually emphasizes **critical interpretation**, but it also calls for some cultural study of how styles, forms, and themes developed, and for a theoretical study of how we understand them. When you are reading in the humanities, therefore, you need to recognize how the various theoretical, historical, and critical approaches work in the various disciplines. The chapters on the humanities in this anthology provide examples from the cultural, historical, critical, and sociological study of music (Chapter 15); a literary study of some short stories about ethnic diversity in the United States (Chapter 16); and examples from the cultural, historical, critical, and analytic study of photographic images (Chapter 17).

## ◼ WRITING IN THE HUMANITIES

Assignments for writing in the humanities require you to exercise your analytical judgment. In this anthology, for example, writing assignments in the humanities run the gamut from critical summary to theoretical speculation. Shorter assignments may call for various types of writing: a summary or **précis** of an article, chapter, or book; a critical report on an article, chapter, or book; or a review of research in several publications. Each of these assignments requires you to select important issues from the content of your source text, to focus upon the author's treatment of them, and to analyze the author's argument as it is shaped by stylistic and rhetorical turns of phrase and idea.

Here, for example, is a writing assignment in music criticism. It requires you to analyze and evaluate a professional music critic's argument about generic rock. Note that it requires you to develop your own argument about the value of such music.

> Write a 750-word critical response to Bayles's article in which you sharpen her defense of rock by elaborating upon its positive features. Extend the "conversation" that her article initiates by referring to other champions of the music and musicians in the form. (p. 595)

In selecting issues to write about, you would want them to amount to something more than random observations drawn from the text. You would aim to trace a **pattern of thought** that conveys the author's dominant argument. As you explore relationships among these ideas, you would be constructing your own argument about the author's contribution to the conversation that engages music critics. When you organize your treatment of these issues, you would decide whether to write about them in the order in which the source text presents them, or in the order of importance that you attribute to them, or in a logical or sequential order that advances your own argument about them. Longer assignments may require a close analysis of several texts. Here's an example from Chapter 16 of this anthology:

> Drawing on short stories by Mukherjee, Jen, Viramontes, and Saunders, write a five- to six-page essay in which you compare and contrast the experiences of different ethnic

groups as they interact with one another in North America. What conditions drive members of these groups to different forms of economic survival? Address your essay to an audience of students who have not read these texts. (page 645)

Note that, because this assignment asks you to "address your essay to an audience of students who have not read these texts," it implicitly requires you to summarize and paraphrase portions of the authors' stories, indicating their thematic concerns and stylistic features. It also implicitly requires you to speculate on the stories' common engagement with representations of economic survival. For this purpose, you will have to think about how Mukherjee, Jen, Viramontes, and Saunders might contribute to a conversation about such survival if they were brought together to discuss the topic.

## ■ PERSPECTIVES ON WRITING IN THE HUMANITIES

Most writing assignments in the humanities will call upon you to use critical skills in one way or another, but some higher-level writing assignments may also require you to use historical and theoretical skills as well. You may be asked to examine a certain problem in its historical context or to discuss the theoretical implications of another problem on a broad scale. Other writing assignments in the humanities will call upon you to analyze a creative text such as a work of music, visual art, or literature. In such assignments, you will focus your critical skills directly upon the musical or visual or literary text in order to analyze, interpret, and evaluate it as deeply as you can. In Chapters 5 and 6, we presented models for approaching such texts and writing papers about them.

### ■ Organizational Patterns of Writing in the Humanities

Organizational patterns for writing in the humanities follow models similar to those in the natural and social sciences. In the most common pattern, the writer explains each proposition, event, or detail in its order of occurrence from his or her perspective. The good writer, however, will vary this basic pattern in many subtle ways. Sometimes he or she may take a number of points from the same source and classify them under general headings—for example, all the negative arguments against a certain moral or ethical position; or all the long-term and short-term implications of an argument based on analyzing current political conditions. Or the writer may endorse and appropriate some conclusions from a given source but contest and refute others from the same source. In "Toward an Aesthetic of Popular Music" (Chapter 15), Simon Frith organizes his argument by introducing a seemingly unlikely sociological approach that avoids aesthetic value judgment and then by aligning his aesthetic theory directly with this approach so that one illuminates the other:

> My particular concern is to suggest that the sociological approach to popular music does not rule out an aesthetic theory but, on the contrary, makes one possible. At first sight this proposition is unlikely. There is no doubt that sociologists have tended to explain away pop music. . . . And yet for ten years or more I have also been a working rock critic, making such judgments as a matter of course, assuming, like all rock fans, that our musical choices matter. (p. 544)

Other organizational patterns may contrast statement with response or question with answer, each time penetrating deeper into the problem being investigated. The same writer, Simon Frith, examines popular music by posing questions that require sustained analysis:

> Are such judgments spurious—a way of concealing from myself and other consumers the ways in which our tastes are manipulated? Can it really be the case that my pleasure in a song by the group Abba carries the same aesthetic weight as someone else's pleasure in Mozart?. . . The question facing sociologists and aestheticians in both cases is the same: how do we make musical value judgments? How do such value judgments articulate the listening experiences involved? (p. 544)

The rest of Frith's essay pursues answers to these questions.

Still other organizational patterns may establish cause-and-effect relationships in their critical assessment of diverse sources. In Chapter 16, Ronald Takaki reviews several sources and finds that "by 1900, 60 percent of Japan's industrial laborers were women" (p. 604). He therefore speculates that "while it is not known how many of the women who emigrated had been wage-earners, this proletarianization of women already well underway in Japan paved the way for such laborers to consider working in America" (pp. 604–05). Takaki then considers the impact of such research upon his own argument.

## ■ Styles of Writing in the Humanities

Some styles of writing in the humanities suggest—within limits—the tone of the author's personal and idiosyncratic voice. This quality distinguishes it radically from impersonal styles of writing in the natural and social sciences. The major evidence for critical assessments of texts in the humanities is direct observation of details in the texts themselves, close reference to them, and pointed quotation from them. How the author of an article projects an attitude toward these texts often counts as much as what he or she directly says about them.

In "Studying Heavy Metal: The Bricolage of Culture" (Chapter 15), Deena Weinstein examines a musical genre that has attracted contentious criticism, but she distances her voice from contention by acknowledging the genre's merits as well as its shortcomings. Referring to the book in which it appears, she writes that it

> is not meant to be another voice in the controversy, but an effort to step back and reveal the elusive subject that is at the center of the controversy. In light of public debates over the advisability of censoring heavy metal music, this study is meant to show how heavy metal music is made, used, and transmitted by social groups. (p. 584)

Later in her argument, Weinstein interjects that neither its conservative nor progressive adversaries has quite understood heavy metal's cultural value:

> Thus the two opponents of metal distort it in their own ways, according to how they can fit into the categories of their ideologies. Their policy stances toward the "social problem" of heavy metal reflect their ideological construction of heavy metal rather than what heavy metal is to its fans, the artists who create it, its mediators, or an ethnographer. (p. 589)

Conversely, the author implies that she has overcome such distortion and has now positioned herself to understand its positive contributions.

## ■ Personal Voice

Writing in the humanities not only tolerates the development of a personal voice but also encourages it. Listen to Camille Paglia's voice as she projects an enthusiasm for rock music when she argues in "Rock as Art" (Chapter 15) for public resources to support it:

> This natively American art form deserves national support. Foundations, corporations and Federal and state agencies that award grants in the arts should take rock musicians as seriously as composers and sculptors. Colleges and universities should designate special fellowships for talented rock musicians. (p. 556)

In the same chapter, Theodore A. Gracyk expresses similar enthusiasm for it when he argues in "Romanticizing Rock Music" against Paglia's proposal on grounds that such support would stifle the creativity of rock:

> But the select few who will be singled out for support will face the same problems that already occur in a patronage system. While there is intense competition for scarce resources, very little of the money is risked on artists whose work is genuinely avant-garde, and less still on those whose work is highly political in content. (p. 568)

Paglia and Gracyk stand on opposing sides of the question about public support for rock music, and their differing voices reinforce their differing perspectives.

Because the humanities propose to exercise and develop critical thinking, the issue of "what you think and why" becomes crucial. The "what" and "why" seldom generate straightforward, unequivocal answers. To the casual observer, some answers may seem curious, whimsical, arbitrary, entirely subjective. To others more deeply acquainted with the humanistic disciplines, open-endedness confers its own rewards. Among them is the light it casts upon our processes of thought, our understanding of complex issues, and the wide-ranging and often contradictory interpretations of them. In "A Different Mirror" (Chapter 16), Ronald Takaki begins his essay on American multiculturalism with a personal account of how his Asian facial features led a taxi driver in Virginia to mistake him for a foreign visitor:

> He glanced at me in the mirror. Somehow I did not look "American" to him; my eyes and complexion looked foreign. (p. 599)

Takaki's anecdote proves as germane to his historical argument as statistical data would to a scientific argument.

A writer in the humanities measures the success of an argument by how it accommodates divergent explanations and shows their relationships. Significantly, most writers in the humanities do not agree on the universal applicability of any single formula, method, or approach for solving problems. The best solutions usually entail a combination of formulas, methods, and approaches.

Reading and writing in the humanities, therefore, requires a tolerance for ambiguity and contradiction. Oddly enough, however, most writers in the humanities defend their assertions with a strong and aggressive rhetoric. At best, this rhetoric scrupulously avoids bloat, pomposity, and roundabout ways of saying things. Instead of "It was decided that they would utilize the sharp instrument for perforating and unsealing aluminum receptacles," it prefers "They decided to use the can opener." It uses technical vocabulary when necessary, but it usually prefers clear, precise, intelligible diction to stilted, awkward jargon. It uses figurative language and analogy, but not for their own sake; it uses them to express meanings and relationships that literal language sometimes obscures.

In Chapter 16, Ronald Takaki concludes his study of Japanese immigration with a poem that expresses the emotions of young women leaving their place of birth for the uncertainties of a marriage in America. As their ships sailed from the harbor, many women gazed at the diminishing shore:

> With tears in my eyes
> I turn back to my homeland
> Taking one last look. (p. 606)

Writing in the humanities strives for a richness of texture and implication but at the same time it highlights important threads in that texture and designates them as central to the unraveling. Readers, however, should not allow assertiveness to fool them. Few examples of good writing in the humanities are completely intolerant of opposing views. There's always room for another perspective.

*Fifteen*

# Rock Music and Cultural Values

In the mid-1950s when rock and roll was born, much of it was considered countercultural and most of it found a hostile reception. A half-century later, it is consumed by the masses and solidly established as a major component of popular culture. As the essays in this chapter suggest, however, even though rock has been integrated into the mainstream culture and become respectable, it is still a subject of controversy. These essays exemplify some of the arguments in the controversy. Though the conversation unfolds with civility and academic decorum, the old antagonisms still haunt the boundaries of the discourse. An academic footnote or two mutes but does not tame the combatants.

The selections in this chapter begin with a discussion of aesthetics. Simon Frith's "Toward an Aesthetic of Popular Music" asks, "How do we make value judgments about popular music?" Frith explains that we value music when it fulfills such social functions as giving us an identity, enabling us to manage our feelings, and offering us a sense of time and place. The next three articles present a modern version of the old debate for or against the respectability of rock music. Their conversation records the academic voices of, respectively, a professor of English, a professor of philosophy, and a professor of journalism, and each enters the debate from the perspective of his or her discipline. In "Rock as Art," Camille Paglia argues that rock is a legitimate and valuable cultural form and that as such its artists deserve the same respect and national funding that we give to serious composers and sculptors. She claims that its integration into college and university education and continued financial support systems will enable rock musicians to immerse themselves in their art, to experiment, and thereby to resist the temptation of self-defeating market forces and crass commercialism. Theodore A. Gracyk challenges this position. In "Romanticizing Rock Music," he cautions against associating rock music with Romanticism and he challenges the proposal to train rock musicians as we train other artists. Gracyk concludes that rock does not possess the virtues of Romantic art, nor is it firmly rooted in the values of folk music. It is an artistic expression of the masses, and it would be a great mistake to encourage it to take an elitist and academic turn. In "Redeeming the

Rap Music Experience," Venise Berry examines the sex, violence, and racism of its lyrics in the context of urban Afro-American youth. She contends that the genre "serves as a bridge from favorite songs and artists to personal and social realities" and in so doing empowers low-income black youth.

The final two articles include voices from still other academic disciplines. In "Studying Heavy Metal: The Bricolage of Culture," Deena Weinstein, a professor of sociology, assesses opposition to newer forms of music through the lens of social group formation. Refusing to evaluate heavy metal from an aesthetic perspective, she instead examines the ways in which its critics misinterpret the text of its lyrics and the intentions of its performers. In "Music, Philosophy, and Generation Y," Martha Bayles, a teacher and cultural commentator, discusses the value of having every type of music at our fingertips. Referring to philosophers such as Plato, academic critics such as Allan Bloom, and performers such as Nine Inch Nails, she concludes that each audience will have to evaluate the merits of different musical genres by comparing good with better and bad with worse. Even as the conversation about the cultural value of rock music continues outside the walls of academe, it develops with robust energy inside these walls.

■ ■ ■ ■ ■ ■ ■ ■ ■ ■ ■

# Toward an Aesthetic of Popular Music

## Simon Frith

*Simon Frith holds the Tovey Chair of Music at Edinburgh University, Scotland. He has published numerous articles on the sociology of music and major studies of popular music institutions and aesthetics, including* Sound Effects *and* Performing Rites.

## PREREADING

What is your preferred style of music? Who are your favorite musicians, singers, or groups? Why does their sound appeal to you more than the sound of others? Do you think some types of music are better than others? Why or why not?

## Introduction: The "Value" of Popular Music

Underlying all the other distinctions critics draw between "serious" and "popular" music is an assumption about the source of musical value. Serious music matters    1 because it transcends social forces; popular music is aesthetically worthless because it is determined by them (because it is "useful" or "utilitarian"). This argument, common

Frith, Simon. *Toward an Aesthetic of Popular Music.* In Music *and Society: The Politics of Composition, Performance, and Reception.* Ed. Richard Leppert and Susan McClary. New York: Cambridge UP, 1987. 113–49. Reprinted with the permission of Cambridge University Press.

enough among academic musicologists, puts sociologists in an odd position. If we venture to suggest that the value of, say, Beethoven's music can be explained by the social conditions determining its production and subsequent consumption we are dismissed as philistines—aesthetic theories of classical music remain determinedly non-sociological. Popular music, by contrast, is taken to be good only for sociological theory. Our very success in explaining the rise of rock 'n' roll or the appearance of disco proves their lack of aesthetic interest. To relate music and society becomes, then, a different task according to the music we are treating. In analyzing serious music, we have to uncover the social forces concealed in the talk of "transcendent" values; in analyzing pop, we have to take seriously the values scoffed at in the talk of social functions.

In this paper I will concentrate on the second issue; my particular concern is to   2
suggest that the sociological approach to popular music does not rule out an aesthetic theory but, on the contrary, makes one possible. At first sight this proposition is unlikely. There is no doubt that sociologists have tended to explain away pop music. In my own academic work I have examined how rock is produced and consumed, and have tried to place it ideologically, but there is no way that a reading of my books (or those of other sociologists) could be used to explain why some pop songs are good and others bad, why Elvis Presley is a better singer than John Denver, or why disco is a much richer musical genre than progressive rock. And yet for ten years or more I have also been a working rock critic, making such judgments as a matter of course, assuming, like all pop fans, that our musical choices matter.

Are such judgments spurious—a way of concealing from myself and other con-   3
sumers the ways in which our tastes are manipulated? Can it really be the case that my pleasure in a song by the group Abba carries the same aesthetic weight as someone else's pleasure in Mozart? Even to pose such a question is to invite ridicule—either I seek to reduce the "transcendent" Mozart to Abba's commercially determined level, or else I elevate Abba's music beyond any significance it can carry. But even if the pleasures of serious and popular musics are different, it is not immediately obvious that the difference is that between artistic autonomy and social utility. Abba's value is no more (and no less) bound up with an experience of transcendence than Mozart's; the meaning of Mozart is no less (and no more) explicable in terms of social forces. The question facing sociologists and aestheticians in both cases is the same: how do we make musical value judgments? How do such value judgments articulate the listening experiences involved?

The sociologist of contemporary popular music is faced with a body of songs,   4
records, stars and styles which exists because of a series of decisions, made by both producers and consumers, about what is a successful sound. Musicians write tunes and play solos; producers choose from different sound mixes; record companies and radio programmers decide what should be released and played; consumers buy one record rather than another and concentrate their attention on particular genres. The result of all these apparently individual decisions is a pattern of success, taste and style which can be explained sociologically.

If the starting question is why does this hit sound this way, then sociological   5
answers can be arranged under two headings. First, there are answers in terms of technique and technology: people produce and consume the music they are capable of producing and consuming (an obvious point, but one which opens up issues of skill, background and education which in pop music are applied not to individual

composers but to social groups). Different groups possess different sorts of cultural capital, share different cultural expectations and so make music differently—pop tastes are shown to correlate with class cultures and subcultures; musical styles are linked to specific age groups; we take for granted the connections of ethnicity and sound. This is the sociological common sense of rock criticism, which equally acknowledges the determining role of technology. The history of twentieth-century popular music is impossible to write without reference to the changing forces of production, electronics, the use of recording, amplification and synthesizers, just as consumer choices cannot be separated from the possession of transistor radios, stereo hi-fis, ghetto blasters and Walkmen.

While we can thus point to general patterns of pop use, the precise link (or   6 homology) between sounds and social groups remains unclear. Why is rock 'n' roll youth music, whereas Dire Straits is the sound of Yuppie USA? To answer these questions there is a second sociological approach to popular music, expressed in terms of its functions. This approach is obvious in ethnomusicology, that is in anthropological studies of traditional and folk musics which are explained by reference to their use in dance, in rituals, for political mobilization, to solemnize ceremonies or to excite desires. Similar points are made about contemporary pop, but its most important function is assumed to be commercial—the starting analytical assumption is that the music is made to sell; thus research has focused on who makes marketing decisions and why, and on the construction of "taste publics." The bulk of the academic sociology of popular music (including my own) implicitly equates aesthetic and commercial judgments. The phenomenal 1985 successes of Madonna and Bruce Springsteen are explained, for example, in terms of sales strategies, the use of video, and the development of particular new audiences. The appeal of the music itself, the reason Madonna's and Springsteen's fans like them, somehow remains unexamined.

From the fans' perspective it is obvious that people play the music they do   7 because it "sounds good," and the interesting question is why they have formed that opinion. Even if pop tastes are the effects of social conditioning and commercial manipulation, people still explain them to themselves in terms of value judgment. Where, in pop and rock, do these values come from? When people explain their tastes, what terms do they use? They certainly know what they like (and dislike), what pleases them and what does not. Read the music press, listen to band rehearsals and recording sessions, overhear the chatter in record shops and discos, note the ways in which disc jockeys play records, and you will hear value judgments being made. The discriminations that matter in these settings occur *within* the general sociological framework. While this allows us at a certain level to "explain" rock or disco, it is not adequate for an understanding of why one rock record or one disco track is better than another. Turn to the explanations of the fans or musicians (or even of the record companies) and a familiar argument appears. Everyone in the pop world is aware of the social forces that determine "normal" pop music—a good record, song, or sound is precisely one that transcends those forces!

The music press is the place where pop value judgments are most clearly articu-   8 lated. A reading of British music magazines reveals that "good" popular music has always been heard to go beyond or break through commercial routine. This was as true for critics struggling to distinguish jazz from Tin Pan Alley pop in the 1920s and black jazz from white jazz in the 1930s as for critics asserting rock's superiority to teen pop in the late 1960s. In *Sound Effects*[1] I argued that rock's claim to a form of aesthetic auton-omy rests on a combination of folk and art arguments: as folk music rock is heard to rep-resent the community of youth, as art music rock is heard as the sound of individual, creative sensibility. The rock aesthetic depends, crucially, on an argument about authenticity. Good music is the authentic expression of something—a person, an idea, a feeling, a shared experience, a *Zeitgeist*. Bad music is inauthentic—it expresses noth-ing. The most common term of abuse in rock criticism is "bland"—bland music has nothing in it and is made only to be commercially pleasing.

"Authenticity" is, then, what guarantees that rock performances resist or subvert    9 commercial logic, just as rock-star quality (whether we are discussing Elvis Presley or David Bowie, the Rolling Stones or the Sex Pistols), describes the power that enables certain musicians to drive something individually obdurate through the system. At this point, rock criticism meets up with "serious" musicology. Wilfrid Mellers' scholarly books on the Beatles and Bob Dylan,[2] for example, describe in technical terms their subjects' transcendent qualities; but they read like fan mail and, in their lack of self-conscious hipness, point to the contradiction at the heart of this aesthetic approach. The suggestion is that pop music becomes more valuable the more independent it is of the social forces that organize the pop process in the first place; pop value is dependent on something outside pop, is rooted in the person, the *auteur*, the community or the subculture that lies behind it. If good music is authentic music, then critical judgment means measuring the performers' "truth" to the experiences or feelings they are describing.

Rock criticism depends on myth—the myth of the youth community, the myth of   10 the creative artist. The reality is that rock, like all twentieth-century pop musics, is a commercial form, music produced as a commodity, for a profit, distributed through mass media as mass culture. It is in practice very difficult to say exactly who or what it is that rock expresses or who, from the listener's point of view, are the authentically cre-ative performers. The myth of authenticity is, indeed, one of rock's own ideological effects, an aspect of its sales process: rock stars can be marketed as artists, and their par-ticular sounds marketed as a means of identity. Rock criticism is a means of legitimat-ing tastes, justifying value judgments, but it does not really explain how those judgments came to be made in the first place. If the music is not, in fact, made accord-ing to the "authentic" story, then the question becomes how we are able to judge some sounds as more authentic than others: what are we actually listening for in making our judgments? How do we know Bruce Springsteen is more authentic than Duran Duran, when both make records according to the rules of the same complex industry? And how do we recognize good sounds in non-rock genres, in pop forms like disco that are not described in authentic terms in the first place? The question of the value of pop music remains to be answered.

## An Alternative Approach to Music and Society

In an attempt to answer these questions I want to suggest an alternative approach to   11 musical value, to suggest different ways of defining "popular music" and "popular cul-ture." The question we should be asking is not what does popular music *reveal* about "the people" but how does it *construct* them. If we start with the assumption that pop is expressive, then we get bogged down in the search for the "real" artist or emotion or belief lying behind it. But popular music is popular not because it reflects something, or authentically articulates some sort of popular taste or experience, but because it creates our understanding of what popularity is. The most misleading term in cultural theory is, indeed, "authenticity." What we should be examining is not how true a piece of music is to something else, but how it sets up the idea of "truth" in the first place—successful pop music is music which defines its own aesthetic standard.

A simple way to illustrate the problems of defining musical popularity is to look at 12 its crudest measure, the weekly record sales charts in the British music press and the American *Billboard*. These are presented to us as market research: the charts measure something real—sales and radio plays—and represent them with all the trimmings of an objective, scientific apparatus. But, in fact, what the charts reveal is a specific definition of what can be counted as popular music in the first place—record sales (in the right shops), radio plays (on the right stations). The charts work not as the detached measure of some agreed notion of popularity, but as the most important determination of what the popularity of popular music means—that is, a particular pattern of market choice. The charts bring selected records together into the community of the market place; they define certain sorts of consumption as being collective in certain sorts of ways.

The sales charts are only one measure of popularity; and when we look at others, 13 it becomes clear that their use is always for the creation (rather than reflection) of taste communities. Readers' polls in the music press, for example, work to give communal shape to disparate readers; the Pazz 'n' Jop poll in *The Village Voice* creates a sense of collective commitment among the fragmented community of American rock critics. The Grammy awards in the United States and the BPI awards in Britain, present the industry's view of what pop music is about—nationalism and money. These annual awards, which for most pop fans seem to miss the point, reflect sales figures and "contributions to the recording industry" measures of popularity no less valid than readers' or critics' polls (which often deliberately honor "unpopular" acts). In comparing poll results, arguments are really not about who is more popular than whom empirically (see rock critics' outrage that Phil Collins rather than Bruce Springsteen dominated the 1986 Grammys) but about what popularity means. Each different measure measures something different or, to put it more accurately, each different measure constructs its own object of measurement. This is apparent in *Billboard*'s "specialist" charts, in the way in which "minority" musics are defined. "Women's music," for example, is interesting not as music which somehow expresses "women," but as music which seeks to define them, just as "black music" works to set up a very particular notion of what "blackness" is.

This approach to popular culture, as the creation rather than the expression of 14 the people, need not be particular to music. There are numerous ways in our everyday life in which accounts of "the people" are provided. Turn on the television news and notice the ways in which a particular mode of address works, how the word "we" is used, how the word "you." Advertisers in all media are clearly in the business of explaining to us who we are, how we fit in with other people in society, why we necessarily consume the way we do. Each mass medium has its own techniques for addressing its audience, for creating moments of recognition and exclusion, for giving us our sense of ourselves. Pop music does, though, seem to play a particularly important role in the way in which popular culture works. On the one hand, it works with particularly intense emotional experiences—pop songs and pop stars mean more to us emotionally than other media events or performers, and this is not just because the pop business sells music to us through individual market choices. On the other hand, these musical experiences always contain social meaning, are placed within a social context—we are not free to read anything we want into a song.

The experience of pop music is an experience of placing: in responding to a song, 15 we are drawn, haphazardly, into affective and emotional alliances with the performers and with the performers' other fans. Again this also happens in other areas of popular culture. Sport, for example, is clearly a setting in which people directly experience community, feel an immediate bond with other people, articulate a particular kind of collective pride (for a non-American, the most extraordinary aspect of the 1984 Olympics was the display/construction of the Reagan ideology of both the United States and patriotism). And fashion and style—both social constructions—remain the keys to the ways in which we, as individuals, present ourselves to the world: we use the public meanings of clothes to say "this is how I want to be perceived."

But music is especially important to this process of placement because of some- 16 thing specific to musical experience, namely, its direct emotional intensity. Because of its qualities of abstractness (which "serious" aestheticians have always stressed) music is an individualizing form. We absorb songs into our own lives and rhythms into our own bodies; they have a looseness of reference that makes them immediately accessible. Pop songs are open to appropriation for personal use in a way that other popular cultural forms (television soap operas, for example) are not—the latter are tied into meanings we may reject. At the same time, and equally significant, music is obviously rule-bound. We hear things as music because their sounds obey a particular, familiar logic, and for most pop fans (who are, technically, non-musical) this logic is out of our control. There is a mystery to our musical tastes. Some records and performers work for us, others do not—we know this without being able to explain it. Somebody else has set up the conventions; they are clearly social and clearly apart from us.

This interplay between personal absorption into music and the sense that it is, 17 nevertheless, something out there, something public, is what makes music so important in the cultural placing of the individual in the social. To give a mundane example, it is obviously true that in the last thirty years the idea of being a "fan," with its oddly public account of private obsessions, has been much more significant to pop music than to other forms of popular culture. This role of music is usually related to youth and youth culture, but it seems equally important to the ways in which ethnic groups in both Britain and the United States have forged particular cultural identities and is also reflected in the ways in which "classical" music originally became significant for the nineteenth-century European bourgeoisie. In all these cases music can stand for, symbolize *and* offer the immediate experience of collective identity. Other cultural forms—painting, literature, design—can articulate and show off shared values and pride, but only music can make you *feel* them.

## The Social Functions of Music

It is now possible to move back to the starting point of this essay—the social functions of 18 music and their implications for aesthetics. I will begin by outlining the four most significant ways in which pop is used and then suggest how these uses help us to understand how pop value judgments are made.

The first reason, then, we enjoy popular music is because of its use in answer- 19 ing questions of identity: we use pop songs to create for ourselves a particular sort of self-definition, a particular place in society. The pleasure that pop music produces is a pleasure of identification—with the music we like, with the performers of that music, with the other people who like it. And it is important to note that the production of identity is also a production of nonidentity—it is a process of inclusion and exclusion. This is one of the most striking aspects of musical taste. People not only know what they like, they also have very clear ideas about what they don't like and often have very aggressive ways of stating their dislikes. As all sociological studies of pop consumers have shown, pop fans define themselves quite precisely according to their musical preferences. Whether they identify with genres or stars, it seems of greater importance to people what they like musically than whether or not they enjoyed a film or a television program.

The pleasure of pop music, unlike the pleasures to be had from other mass cultural forms, does not derive in any clear way from fantasy: it is not mediated through daydreams or romancing, but is experienced directly. For example, at a heavy metal concert you can certainly see the audience absorbed in the music; yet for all the air-guitar playing they are not fantasizing being up on stage. To experience heavy metal is to experience the power of the concert as a whole—the musicians are one aspect of this, the amplification system another, the audience a third. The individual fans get their kicks from being a necessary part of the overall process—which is why heavy metal videos always have to contain moments of live performance (whatever the surrounding story line) in order to capture and acknowledge the kind of empowerment that is involved in the concert itself. [20]

Once we start looking at different pop genres we can begin to document the different ways in which music works to give people an identity, to place them in different social groups. And this is not just a feature of commercial pop music. It is the way in which all popular music works. For example, in putting together an audience, contemporary black-influenced pop clearly (and often cynically) employs musical devices originally used in religious music to define men's and women's identity before God. Folk musics, similarly, continue to be used to mark the boundaries of ethnic identity, even amidst the complications of migration and cultural change. In London's Irish pubs, for example, "traditional" Irish folk songs are still the most powerful way to make people feel Irish and consider what their "Irishness" means. (This music, this identity, is now being further explored by post-punk London Irish bands, like the Pogues.) It is not surprising, then, that popular music has always had important nationalist functions. In Abel Gance's "silent" film, *Napoleon*, there is a scene in which we see the *Marseillaise* being composed, and then watch the song make its way through the Assembly and among the crowds until everyone is singing it. When the film was first shown in France, the cinema audience rose from their seats and joined in singing their national anthem. Only music seems capable of creating this sort of spontaneous collective identity, this kind of personally felt patriotism. [21]

Music's second social function is to give us a way of managing the relationship between our public and private emotional lives. It is often noted but rarely discussed that the bulk of popular songs are love songs. This is certainly true of twentieth-century popular music in the West; but most non-Western popular musics also feature romantic, usually heterosexual, love lyrics. This is more than an interesting statistic; it is a centrally important aspect of how pop music is used. Why are love songs so important? Because people need them to give shape and voice to emotions that otherwise cannot be expressed without embarrassment or incoherence. Love songs are a way of giving emotional intensity to the sorts of intimate things we say to each other (and to ourselves) [22] in words that are, in themselves, quite flat. It is a peculiarity of everyday language that our most fraught and revealing declarations of feeling have to use phrases—"I love/hate you," "Help me!," "I'm angry/scared"—which are boring and banal; and so our culture has a supply of a million pop songs, which say these things for us in numerous interesting and involving ways. These songs do not replace our conversations—pop singers do not do our courting for us—but they make our feelings seem richer and more convincing than we can make them appear in our own words, even to ourselves.

23    The only interesting sociological account of lyrics in the long tradition of American content analysis was Donald Horton's late 1950s study[3] of how teenagers used the words of popular songs in their dating rituals. His high school sample learned from pop songs (public forms of private expression) how to make sense of and shape their own inchoate feelings. This use of pop illuminates one quality of the star/fan relationship: people do not idolize singers because they wish to be them but because these singers seem able, somehow, to make available their own feelings—it is as if we get to know ourselves via the music.

24    The third function of popular music is to shape popular memory, to organize our sense of time. Clearly one of the effects of all music, not just pop, is to intensify our experience of the present. One measure of good music, to put it another way, is, precisely, its "presence," its ability to "stop" time, to make us feel we are living within a moment, with no memory or anxiety about what has come before, what will come after. This is where the physical impact of music comes in—the use of beat, pulse and rhythm to compel our immediate bodily involvement in an organization of time that the music itself controls. Hence the pleasures of dance and disco; clubs and parties provide a setting, a society, which seems to be defined only by the time-scale of the music (the beats per minute), which escapes the real time passing outside.

25    One of the most obvious consequences of music's organization of our sense of time is that songs and tunes are often the key to our remembrance of things past. I do not mean simply that sounds—like sights and smells—trigger associated memories, but, rather, that music in itself provides our most vivid experience of time passing. Music focuses our attention on the feeling of time; songs are organized (it is part of their pleasure) around anticipation and echo, around endings to which we look forward, choruses that build regret into their fading. Twentieth-century popular music has, on the whole, been a nostalgic form. The Beatles, for example, made nostalgic music from the start, which is why they were so popular. Even on hearing a Beatles song for the first time there was a sense of the memories to come, a feeling that this could not last but that it was surely going to be pleasant to remember.

26    It is this use of time that makes popular music so important in the social organization of youth. It is a sociological truism that people's heaviest personal investment in popular music is when they are teenagers and young adults—music then ties into a particular kind of emotional turbulence, when issues of individual identity and social place, the control of public and private feelings, are at a premium. People do use music less, and less intently, as they grow up; the most significant pop songs for all generations (not just for rock generations) are those they heard as adolescents. What this suggests, though, is not just that young people need music, but that "youth" itself is defined by music. Youth is experienced, that is, as an intense presence, through an impatience for time to pass and a regret that it is doing so, in a series of speeding, physically insistent moments that have nostalgia coded into them. This is to reiterate my general point about popular music: youth music is socially important not because it reflects youth

experience (authentically or not), but because it defines for us what "youthfulness" is. I remember concluding, in my original sociological research in the early 1970s, that those young people who, for whatever reasons, took no interest in pop music were not really "young."

The final function of popular music I want to mention here is something more 27 abstract than the issues discussed so far, but a consequence of all of them: popular music is something possessed. One of the first things I learned as a rock critic—from abusive mail—was that rock fans "owned" their favorite music in ways that were intense and important to them. To be sure, the notion of musical ownership is not peculiar to rock— Hollywood cinema has long used the clichéd line, "they're playing our song"—and this reflects something that is recognizable to all music lovers and is an important aspect of the way in which everyone thinks and talks about "their" music. (British radio has programs of all sorts built around people's explanations of why certain records "belong" to them.) Obviously it is the commodity form of music which makes this sense of musical possession possible, but it is not just the record that people think they own: we feel that we also possess the song itself, the particular performance, and its performer.

In "possessing" music, we make it part of our own identity and build it into our 28 sense of ourselves. To write pop criticism is, as I have mentioned, to attract hate mail; mail not so much defending the performer or performance criticized as defending the letter writer: criticize a star and the fans respond as if you have criticized them. The biggest mail bag I ever received was after I had been critical of Phil Collins. Hundreds of letters arrived (not from teenyboppers or gauche adolescents, but from young professionals) typed neatly on headed notepaper, all based on the assumption that in describing Collins as ugly, Genesis as dull, I was deriding their way of life, undermining their identity. The intensity of this relationship between taste and self-definition seems peculiar to popular music—it is "possessable" in ways that other cultural forms (except, perhaps, sports teams) are not.

To summarize the argument so far: the social functions of popular music are in the 29 creation of identity, in the management of feelings, in the organization of time. Each of these functions depends, in turn, on our experience of music as something which can be possessed. From this sociological base it is now possible to get at aesthetic questions, to understand listeners' judgments, to say something about the value of pop music. My starting question was how is it that people (myself included) can say, quite confidently, that some popular music is better than others? The answer can now be related to how well (or badly), for specific listeners, songs and performances fulfill the suggested functions. But there is a final point to make about this. It should be apparent by now that people do hear the music they like as something special: not, as orthodox rock criticism would have it, because this music is more "authentic" (though that may be how it is described), but because, more directly, it seems to provide an experience that transcends the mundane, that takes us "out of ourselves." It is special, that is, not necessarily with reference to other music, but to the rest of life. This sense of specialness, the way in which music seems to make possible a new kind of self-recognition, frees us from the everyday routines and expectations that encumber our social identities, is a key part of the way in which people experience and thus value music: if we believe we possess our music, we also often feel that we are possessed by it. Transcendence is, then, as much a part of the popular music aesthetic as it is of the serious music aesthetic; but, as I hope I have indicated, in pop, transcendence marks not music's freedom from social forces but its patterning by them. (Of course, in the end the same is true of serious music, too.)

## The Aesthetics of Popular Music

I want to conclude with another sort of question: what are the factors in popular music   30
that enable it to fulfill these social functions, which determine whether it does so well
or badly? Again, I will divide my answer into four points; my purpose is less to develop
them in depth than to suggest important issues for future critical work.

My first point is brief, because it raises musicological issues which I am not com-   31
petent to develop. The most important (and remarkable) feature of Western popular
music in the twentieth century has been its absorption of and into Afro-American forms
and conventions. In analytical terms, to follow the distinction developed by Andrew
Chester at the end of the 1960s, this means that pop is complex "intentionally" rather
than, like European art music, "extensionally." In the extensional form of musical construction, argues Chester, "theme and variations, counter-point, tonality (as used in
classical composition) are all devices that build diachronically and synchronically out-
wards from basic musical atoms. The complex is created by combination of the simple,
which remains discrete and unchanged in the complex unity." In the intentional
mode, "the basic musical units (played/sung notes) are not combined through space
and time as simple elements into complex structures. The simple entity is that constituted by the parameters of melody, harmony and beat, while the complex is built up by
modulation of the basic notes, and by inflexion of the basic beat.[4] Whatever the problems of Chester's simple dichotomy between a tradition of linear musical development
and a tradition of piled-up rhythmic interplay, he does pose the most important musicological question for popular music: how can we explain the *intensity* of musical experience that Afro-American forms have made possible? We still do not know nearly
enough about the musical language of pop and rock: rock critics still avoid technical
analysis, while sympathetic musicologists, like Wilfrid Mellers, use tools that can only
cope with pop's non-intentional (and thus least significant) qualities.

My second point is that the development of popular music in this century has   32
increasingly focused on the use of the voice. It is through the singing voice that people
are most able to make a connection with their records, to feel that performances are
theirs in certain ways. It is through the voice that star personalities are constructed (and
since World War II, at least, the biggest pop stars have been singers). The tone of voice is
more important in this context than the actual articulation of particular lyrics—which
means, for example, that groups, like the Beatles, can take on a group voice. We can thus
identify with a song whether we understand the words or not, whether we already know
the singer or not, because it is the voice—not the lyrics—to which we immediately
respond. This raises questions about popular non-vocal music, which can be answered
by defining a voice as a sign of individual personality rather than as something necessarily mouthing words. The voice, for example, was and is central to the appeal of jazz, not
through vocalists as such but through the way jazz people played and heard musical
instruments—Louis Armstrong's or Charlie Parker's instrumental voices were every bit
as individual and personal as a pop star's singing voice.

Today's commercial pop musics are, though, song forms, constructing vocal   33
personalities, using voices to speak directly to us. From this perspective it becomes possible to look at pop songs as narratives, to use literary critical and film critical terms to
analyze them. It would be fairly straightforward, for example, to make some immediate
genre distinctions, to look at the different ways in which rock, country, reggae, etc. work
as narratives, the different ways they set up star personalities, situate the listener, and

put in play patterns of identity and opposition. Of course, popular music is not simply analogous to film or literature. In discussing the narrative devices of contemporary pop in particular, we are not just talking about music but also about the whole process of packaging. The image of pop performers is constructed by press and television advertisements, by the routines of photo-calls and journalists' interviews, and through gesture and performance. These things all feed into the way we hear a voice; pop singers are rarely heard "plain" (without mediation). Their vocals already contain physical connotations, associated images, echoes of other sounds. All this needs to be analyzed if we are going to treat songs as narrative structures; the general point, to return to a traditional musicological concern, is that while music may not represent anything, it nevertheless clearly communicates.

The third point is an elaboration of the suggestion I have just made: popular music  34 is wide open for the development of a proper genre analysis, for the classification of how different popular musical forms use different narrative structures, set up different patterns of identity, and articulate different emotions. Take, for example, the much discussed issue of music and sexuality. In the original article on rock and sexuality I wrote with Angela McRobbie at the end of the 1970s,[5] we set up a distinction between "cock" rock and teenybop narratives, each working to define masculinity and femininity but for different audiences and along different contours of feeling. Our distinctions are still valid but we were looking only at a subdivision of one pop genre. Other musical forms articulate sexuality in far more complicated ways; thus it would be impossible to analyze the sexuality of either Frank Sinatra or Billie Holiday, and their place in the history of crooning and torch singing, in the terms of the "cock" rock/teenybop contrast. Even Elvis Presley does not fit easily into these 1970s accounts of male and female sexuality.

The question these examples raise is how popular musical genres should be  35 defined. The obvious approach is to follow the distinctions made by the music industry which, in turn, reflect both musical history and marketing categories. We can thus divide pop into country music, soul music, rock 'n' roll, punk, MOR, show songs, etc. But an equally interesting way of approaching genres is to classify them according to their ideological effects, the way they sell themselves as art, community or emotion. There is at present, for example, clearly a form of rock we can call "authentic." It is represented by Bruce Springsteen and defines itself according to the rock aesthetic of authenticity which I have already discussed. The whole point of this genre is to develop musical conventions which are, in themselves, measures of "truth." As listeners we are drawn into a certain sort of reality: this is what it is like to live in America, this is what it is like to love or hurt. The resulting music is the pop equivalent of film theorists' "classic realist text." It has the same effect of persuading us that this is how things really are—realism inevitably means a non-romantic account of social life, and a highly romantic account of human nature.

What is interesting, though, is how this sort of truth is constructed, what it rests  36 on musically; and for an instant semiotic guide I recommend the video of *We Are the World*. Watch how the singers compete to register the most sincerity; watch Bruce Springsteen win as he gets his brief line, veins pop up on his head and the sweat flows down. Here authenticity is guaranteed by visible physical effort.

To approach pop genres this way is to look at the pop world in terms rather differ-  37 ent from those of the music industry. Against the authentic genre, for instance, we can pitch a tradition of artifice: some pop stars, following up on David Bowie's and Roxy Music's early 1970s work, have sought to create a sense of themselves (and their listeners) as artists in cool control. There is clearly also an avant-garde within popular music, offering musicians and listeners the pleasures of rule breaking, and a sentimental genre, celebrating codes of emotion which everyone knows are not real but carry nostalgic weight—if only they were! What I am arguing here is that it is possible to look at pop genres according to the effects they pursue. Clearly we can then judge performers within genres (is John Cougar Mellencamp's music as truthful as Springsteen's?), as well as use different genres for different purposes (the sentimental genre is a better source of adult love songs than the avant-garde or the artificers). To really make sense of pop genres, though, I think we need to place this grid of ideologies over the industry's grid of taste publics. To understand punk, for example, we need to trace within it the interplay of authenticity and artifice; to understand country we need to follow the interplay of authenticity and sentiment.

In everyday life we actually have a rather good knowledge of such conventional confusions. To know how to listen to pop music is to know how to classify it. One thing all pop listeners do, whether as casual fans or professional critics, is to compare sounds—to say that A is like B. Indeed, most pop criticism works via the implicit recognition of genre rules, and this brings me to my final point. Our experience of music in everyday life is not just through the organized pop forms I have been discussing. We live in a much more noisy soundscape; music of all sorts is in a constant play of association with images, places, people, products, moods, and so on. These associations, in commercial and film soundtracks, for example, are so familiar that for much of the time we forget that they are "accidental." We unthinkingly associate particular sounds with particular feelings and landscapes and times. To give a crude example, in Britain it is impossible now for a ballet company to perform the *Nutcracker Suite* for an audience of children without them all, at the key moment, breaking into song: "Everyone's a fruit and nut case," has been instilled into them as a Cadbury's jingle long before the children hear of Tchaikovsky. Classical or "serious" music, in short, is not exempt from social use. It is impossible for me, brought up in post-war popular culture, to hear Chopin without immediately feeling a vaguely romantic yearning, the fruit of many years of Chopinesque film soundtracks.

There is no way to escape these associations. Accordions played a certain way mean France, bamboo flutes China, just as steel guitars mean country, drum machines the urban dance. No sort of popular musician can make music from scratch—what we have these days instead are scratch mixers, fragmenting, unpicking, reassembling music from the signs that already exist, pilfering public forms for new sorts of private vision. We need to understand the lumber-room of musical references we carry about with us, if only to account for the moment that lies at the heart of the pop experience, when, from amidst all those sounds out there, resonating whether we like them or not, one particular combination suddenly, for no apparent reason, takes up residence in our own lives.

## Conclusion

In this paper I have tried to suggest a way in which we can use a sociology of popular music as the basis of an aesthetic theory, to move, that is, from a description of music's social functions to an understanding of how we can and do value it (and I should perhaps stress that my definition of popular music includes popular uses of "serious" music). One of my working assumptions has been that people's individual tastes—the ways they experience and describe music for themselves—are a necessary part of academic analysis. Does this mean that the value of popular music is simply a matter of personal preference?

The usual sociological answer to this question is that "personal" preferences are 41 themselves socially determined. Individual tastes are, in fact, examples of collective taste and reflect consumers' gender, class and ethnic backgrounds; the "popularity" of popular music can then be taken as one measure of a balance of social power. I do not want to argue against this approach. Our cultural needs and expectations are, indeed, materially based; all the terms I have been using (identity, emotion, memory) are socially formed, whether we are examining "private" or public lives. But I do believe that this derivation of pop meaning from collective experience is not sufficient. Even if we focus all our attention on the collective reception of pop, we still need to explain why some music is better able than others to have such collective effects, why these effects are different, anyway, for different genres, different audiences and different circumstances. Pop tastes do not just derive from our socially constructed identities; they also help to shape them.

For the last fifty years at least, pop music has been an important way in which we 42 have learned to understand ourselves as historical, ethnic, class-bound, gendered subjects. This has had conservative effects (primarily through pop nostalgia) and liberating ones. Rock criticism has usually taken the latter as a necessary mark of good music but this has meant, in practice, a specious notion of "liberation." We need to approach this political question differently, by taking seriously pop's individualizing effects. What pop can do is put into play a sense of identity that may or may not fit the way we are placed by other social forces. Music certainly puts us in our place, but it can also suggest that our social circumstances are not immutable (and that other people—performers, fans—share our dissatisfaction). Pop music is not in itself revolutionary or reactionary. It is a source of strong feelings that because they are also socially coded can come up against "common sense." For the last thirty years, for example, at least for young people, pop has been a form in which everyday accounts of race and sex have been both confirmed and confused. It may be that, in the end, we want to value most highly that music, popular and serious, which has some sort of collective, disruptive cultural effect. My point is that music only does so through its impact on individuals. That impact is what we first need to understand.

## Notes

1. Simon Frith, *Sound Effects: Youth, Leisure and the Politics of Rock 'n' Roll* (New York, 1981).
2. Wilfrid Mellers, *Twilight of the Gods: The Beatles in Retrospect* (London, 1973), and *A Darker Shade of Pale: A Backdrop to Bob Dylan* (London, 1984).
3. Donald Horton, "The Dialogue of Courtship in Popular Songs," *American Journal of Sociology*, 62 (1957), pp. 569–78.
4. Andrew Chester, "Second Thoughts on a Rock Aesthetic: The Band," *New Left Review*, 62 (1970), pp. 78–9.
5. Simon Frith and Angela McRobbie, "Rock and Sexuality," *Screen Education* 29 (1978/9), pp. 3–19.

## READING FOR CONTENT

1. What are Frith's views on the "authenticity" of rock music? What should we be examining instead of authenticity?
2. List the four social functions of popular music cited in the essay.
3. Frith says that four factors determine whether music will fulfill its social functions. What are these factors?
4. Summarize Frith's conclusion in paragraphs 40 to 42.

# READING FOR GENRE, ORGANIZATION AND STYLISTIC FEATURES

1. Describe the contrasts Frith sets up in the first paragraph.
2. Frith divides the article into five parts. How does each part contribute to his argument?
3. Do you think that Frith is addressing his article to a wide general audience or to specialized scholarly readers? How did you come to that conclusion?

# READING FOR RHETORICAL CONTEXT

1. Explain Frith's purpose for writing the article. What does he want to achieve?
2. Find the places in the article where Frith refers to his previous work. What function do these references serve?
3. In a number of paragraphs (3, 6, 7, 10, 22, 29, 30, 31, 40), Frith poses questions. What function do the questions serve? How do they affect the reader?

# WRITING ASSIGNMENTS

1. Frith says that for all people the most significant pop songs "are those they heard as adolescents" (paragraph 26). Which songs are most memorable to you? What memories do these songs trigger? Write an essay in which you recall songs and experiences and reflect upon the meaning they hold for you.
2. As a prereading question, we asked you to explain why some types of music are better than others. Reread your response. Rewrite your response in light of Frith's argument, explaining how well specific songs and performances fulfill various social functions for you.
3. Write an essay in which you agree or disagree with Frith's statement, "Pop tastes do not just derive from our socially constructed identities; they also help shape them" (paragraph 41).

# Rock as Art

## Camille Paglia

*Camille Paglia teaches humanities at the University of the Arts in Philadelphia and is the author of* Sexual Personae *(1990),* Sex, Art, and American Culture *(1991), and* Vamps and Tramps: New Essays *(1994).*

# PREREADING

Write a reaction to Paglia's two opening sentences. Do you agree that rock musicians are the country's "most wasted natural resource"? Why or why not?

Rock is eating its young. Rock musicians are America's most wasted natural resource. 1

Popular music and film are the two great art forms of the twentieth century. In 2 the past twenty-five years, cinema has gained academic prestige. Film courses are now a standard part of the college curriculum and grants are routinely available to noncommercial directors.

But rock music has yet to win the respect it deserves as the authentic voice of our 3 time. Where rock goes, democracy follows. The dark poetry and surging Dionysian rhythms of rock have transformed the consciousness and permanently altered the sensoriums of two generations of Americans born after World War Two.

Rock music should not be left to the Darwinian laws of the marketplace. This 4 natively American art form deserves national support. Foundations, corporations and Federal and state agencies that award grants in the arts should take rock musicians as seriously as composers and sculptors. Colleges and universities should designate special scholarships for talented rock musicians. Performers who have made fortunes out of rock are ethically obligated to finance such scholarships or to underwrite independent agencies to support needy musicians.

In rock, Romanticism still flourishes. All the Romantic archetypes of energy, 5 passion, rebellion and demonism are still evident in the brawling, boozing bad boys of rock, storming from city to city on their lusty, groupie-dogged trail.

But the Romantic outlaw must have something to rebel against. The pioneers 6 of rock were freaks, dreamers and malcontents who drew their lyricism and emotional power from the gritty rural traditions of white folk music and African-American blues.

Rock is a victim of its own success. What once signified rebellion is now only a 7 high-school affectation. White suburban youth, rock's main audience, is trapped in creature comforts. Everything comes to them secondhand, through TV. And they no longer have direct contact with folk music and blues, the oral repository of centuries of love, hate, suffering and redemption.

In the Sixties, rock became the dominant musical form in America. And with the 8 shift from singles to albums, which allowed for the marketing of personalities, it also became big business. The gilded formula froze into place. Today, scouts beat the bushes for young talent, squeeze a quick album out of the band, and put them on the road. "New" material is stressed. Albums featuring cover tunes of classics, as in the early Rolling Stones records, are discouraged.

From the moment the Beatles could not hear themselves sing over the shrieking 9 at Shea Stadium in the mid-Sixties, the rock concert format has become progressively less conducive to music-making. The enormous expense of huge sound systems and grandiose special effects has left no room for individualism and improvisation, no opportunity for the performers to respond to a particular audience or to their own moods. The show, with its army of technicians, is as fixed and rehearsed as the Ziegfeld Follies. Furthermore, the concert experience has degenerated. The focus has switched from the performance to raucous partying in the audience.

These days, rock musicians are set upon by vulture managers, who sanitize and 10 repackage them and strip them of their unruly free will. Like sports stars, musicians are milked to the max, then dropped and cast aside when their first album doesn't sell.

Managers offer all the temptations of Mammon to young rock bands: wealth, 11 fame, and easy sex. There is not a single public voice in the culture to say to the musician: You are an artist, not a money machine. Don't sign the contract. Don't tour. Record only when you are ready. Go off on your own, like Jimi Hendrix, and live with your guitar until it becomes part of your body.

How should an artist be trained? Many English rock musicians in the Sixties and 12 early Seventies, including John Lennon and Keith Richards, emerged from art schools. We must tell the young musician: Your peers are other artists, past and future. Don't become a slave to the audience, with its smug hedonism, short attention span and hunger for hits.

Artists should immerse themselves in art. Two decades ago, rock musicians read 13 poetry, studied Hinduism, and drew psychedelic visions in watercolors. For rock to move forward as an art form, our musicians must be given the opportunity for spiritual development. They should be encouraged to read, to look at paintings and foreign films, to listen to jazz and classical music.

Artists with a strong sense of vocation can survive life's disasters and triumphs 14 with their inner lives intact. Our musicians need to be rescued from the carpetbaggers and gold-diggers who attack them when they are young and naïve. Long, productive careers don't happen by chance.

## READING FOR CONTENT

1. According to Paglia, what type of support does rock music deserve?
2. Explain why, according to Paglia, rock is an art in the Romantic tradition.
3. How has rock changed since the 1960s?
4. How has it become "big business"?
5. How should rock musicians be educated?

## READING FOR GENRE, ORGANIZATION, AND STYLISTIC FEATURES

1. What is the effect on the reader of the two opening sentences? Why do you think Paglia begins the piece in this way?
2. How does Paglia structure her argument? Construct a graphic overview (see pp. 50–52) of the selection.
3. How does Paglia conclude the piece?

## READING FOR RHETORICAL CONTEXT

1. Whom do you think Paglia visualizes as her audience? How does she expect her readers to view rock musicians after they have read this piece?
2. How would you characterize Paglia's voice? What does it suggest about the author?

# WRITING ASSIGNMENTS

1. Write an essay in which you agree or disagree with Paglia's statement that today rock is "only a high-school affectation," whereas in the past it was the music of rebellion.

2. Write a brief essay evaluating Paglia's argument. Mention its strengths and weaknesses and explain how well Paglia supports her points.

3. Compare Paglia's comments about the commercialization of rock music with those of Frith in "Toward an Aesthetic of Popular Music."

# Romanticizing Rock Music

## *Theodore A. Gracyk*

*Theodore A. Gracyk is an associate professor of philosophy at Moorhead State University. He has published* Rhythm and Noise: An Aesthetics of Rock *and articles in the* Musical Quarterly, *the* International Philosophical Quarterly, *and the* British Journal of Aesthetics.

## PREREADING

Before you read this article, take a few minutes to respond to the title. Do you recall reading Romantic poetry by such writers as Byron, Shelley, Wordsworth, Coleridge, and Keats in high school and college literature classes? How would you characterize that poetry? Would you say that rock music has some of the same characteristics?

If now we reflect that music at its greatest intensity must seek to attain also to its highest symbolization, we must deem it possible that it also knows how to find the symbolic expression for its unique Dionysian wisdom.

— Nietzsche, *The Birth of Tragedy*

$\text{T}$o the extent that theorists are willing to treat rock music as art, most of them con- 1 sider it popular art rather than fine art. But several recent writers contend that rock music is a manifestation of the aesthetics of Romanticism and as such can be understood in terms of the same categories that are applied to artists who produce fine art. We are invited to conclude that rock musicians deserve the same respect as such poets as Wordsworth and Byron and such musicians as Chopin and Liszt, because the accomplishment of the Rolling Stones is of the same type as that of these nineteenth-century precursors. The major obstacle to admitting that rock musicians are important artists is supposedly the common confusion of a commercial product ("pop" music) with rock music.

Another manifestation of the aesthetics of Romanticism is the idea that rock    2
music is not fine art, but rather modern urban folk music.[1] As one rock critic put it, "It
is just because they didn't worry about art that many of the people who ground out the
rock-and-roll of the fifties—not only the performers, but all the background people—
were engaged (unconsciously, of course) in making still another kind of art, folk art."[2]
Again, a distinction is to be made between popular art, an inauthentic exploitation of
the masses, and this modern folk art. Yet another position, to be considered at length in
this essay, brings the two strands together in the claim that rock possesses the virtues of
Romantic art while drawing much of its power from its folk music roots.

Tied to each of these positions is an attempt to bring rock music into the domains    3
of art and aesthetic education. (At present, academic attention on rock is almost
entirely sociological in perspective.) While I sympathize with attempts to locate an aesthetic of rock music, I do not believe that Romanticism is the right model. And it is an
even greater mistake to believe that rock musicians should be trained according to the
model for educating other artists.

# I

The boldest and most uncompromising of those who would romanticize rock is    4
Camille Paglia. She contends that it is time to accept rock musicians as legitimate
artists and to treat rock as we treat other arts, supporting it directly with government subsidies and private grants and indirectly through special college scholarships. Paglia calls
for a return to rock's past glories, when the music was rebellious, vital, and pulsating
with "surging Dionysian rhythms."[3] It turns out that, like Nietzsche, she does not
regard the masses as capable of appreciating true art when they encounter it. But unlike
Nietzsche, she does not give us any sense that the highest art will be a fusion of the
Dionysian and Apollonian strains.

Paglia's argument is worth considering because it adopts, without criticism, the    5
prevailing story of rock music. Except for her proposal that we treat rock musicians as
full-fledged artists, she depends on common assumptions, so common that most rock
fans would probably applaud her endorsement and ignore the distortions, half-truths,
and stereotypes. The story is this: "The pioneers of rock were freaks, dreamers and malcontents" who drew on an authentic tradition of "white folk music and African-American
blues." The sixties were rock's golden age, when rock musicians drew their inspiration
from poetry and Eastern religions. (She doesn't point out that groups like Steppenwolf,
Mott the Hoople, and Steely Dan got their names from literary works, but I assume that
that's the sort of thing she has in mind.) Above all, rock musicians were the inheritors of
Romanticism. They were outlaws, "storming from city to city on their lusty, groupie-
dogged trail." Because she regards them as sensitive artists, Paglia here brushes over the
fact that she's really talking about their sexual exploitation of women, many of them
underage.

But rock soon fell victim to capitalism. Market forces corrupted rock. Paglia    6
offers three pieces of evidence. First, the authentic source is lost; neither fans nor musicians have direct knowledge of folk music and blues, "the oral repository of centuries of
love, hate, suffering and redemption." Second, live performance has atrophied, leaving
no room for spontaneous musical expression or artist-audience interaction. Once it was
a performing art, with the focus on the performance. Now it is a mere show—fully
rehearsed and with no room for artistic spontaneity—and an excuse for partying. Third,

greedy and manipulative managers exploit innocent young artists, turning them from self-expression to pandering to crass commercial interests, "milking" them for profit in exchange for "wealth, fame and easy sex." Knowingly or not, Paglia is paraphrasing Bob Geldof's remark that people join rock bands for "three very simple rock and roll reasons: to get laid, to get fame, and to get rich."[4]

Her remedy? Divorce rock from the commercial marketplace. We should provide an escape from the commercial interests that divert rock artists from serious music making. Like classical musicians, rock musicians must relocate to colleges and universities. (Was Bob Dylan ahead of his time when, on his debut, he introduced a traditional song as having been acquired among the fair fields of Harvard?) Supported by government and private grants, prestige and artistic freedom will follow, compensating the musicians for the lost wealth, fame, and sex. After all, Paglia notes, both Keith Richards and John Lennon attended English "art schools." Never mind that they were barely able to obtain passing grades and that the schools were as much trade schools as art institutes; perhaps we should instead be satisfied that Mick Jagger went to the London School of Economics and Lou Reed studied with poet Delmore Schwarz. Complementing their musical studies with art history and literature, a liberal arts education will guide rock musicians' spiritual development, and rock will recover as the "authentic voice of our times." 7

Charming as this is, it disintegrates when we go through it one claim at a time. Let us start with the pioneers of rock as Romantic archetypes. Paglia offers no examples, but obvious cases would have to include Bill Haley, Elvis Presley, Chuck Berry, Little Richard, Bo Diddley, Carl Perkins, Buddy Holly, Jerry Lee Lewis, Fats Domino, and Ray Charles.[5] While this may be a list of freaks and dreamers, their dreams were mostly about making hit records and a lot of money. They were hardly malcontents, unless being an African American or poor Southern white in the nineteen-fifties automatically qualified one. If anything, they represent the American underclass of the period, seeking respectability in money and fame. Perhaps Paglia is thinking of the sixties and its political posturing, but at that point we are already far from the folk and blues roots that she identifies as the source of their authenticity and expressive power. 8

The rebellion of rock's pioneers was of the James Dean variety, strictly adolescent. If we are to believe any of the prevailing *sociological* analysis of rock, it tells us this: 9

> What mattered about rock 'n' roll in the 1950s was its youth; its expression of a community of interest between performer and audience; and its account of a generation bound by age and taste in a gesture of self-celebration, in defiance against the nagging, adult routines of home and work and school. . . . rock 'n' roll stardom soon became a matter of the youth voice and the youth song, so that Elvis Presley became rock 'n' roll's superstar because he so clearly *represented* his listeners and Chuck Berry became the most successful R & B performer to adapt its loose limbed lyrics to the interests of the white, teenaged record-buyer.[6]

It was also rooted in a very American desire for material comforts like a sharp wardrobe (blue suede shoes immediately come to mind) and a pink Cadillac. Paglia complains that rock's original rebellion has been reduced to "high-school affectation." Yet search as we might through early rock, the only *social* protest comes mainly from Chuck Berry, and it was *very* high school: "School Days," "Too Much Monkey Business," and "No Particular

Place to Go." The Coasters' "Yakety Yak" and Eddie Cochran's "Summertime Blues" likewise gave voice to teens' railing against parental authority. There is occasional social commentary, but it is fairly mild, as in the undercurrent of black pride in Chuck Berry's "Brown-Eyed Handsome Man" or the Coaster's "Shopping for Clothes" and "Framed" (both written by the white production team of Leiber and Stoller).

Her complaint is also odd in light of analyses given by Nik Cohn and Carl Belz. 10 Writing in the late sixties, Cohn reflected the prevalent British enthusiasm for rock and American "pop" *as* reflections of America. He praised rock because it voiced teen concerns; the best popular music, he wrote, "is all teenage property and it mirrors everything that happens to teenagers in this time, in this American 20th century. It is about clothes and cars and dancing, it's about parents and high school."[7] Carl Belz, defending a view of rock as modern folk music, praised Chuck Berry for "unconsciously" expressing the "ordinary realities of their world: . . . cars, girls, growing up, school, or music."[8] Rock's decline started, on these analyses, when the Beatles and others turned to self-expression and musical experimentation for its own sake. The point is not whether Cohn and Belz are right and Paglia is wrong; both seem rather simplistic. The point is that to many at the time, rock and roll had always been the music of teenagers, and only later did it develop affectations toward art. So Paglia's alternative story of rock's decline, as a shift from genuine rebellion to high school values, sounds like selective memory that focuses on the late 1960s rather than rock's first decade as the point for all comparisons. As such, it is too hopelessly slanted to form the basis for any argument that appeals to rock's special strengths.

It is also hard to believe that only *subsequent* rock musicians were corrupted by 11 money, fame, and sex. If rock's pioneers had any consistent message, it was a desire for sex. As critic Dave Marsh says of Buddy Holly's 1957 hit "Oh Boy," "Edgy and excited, he sings the opening way too fast. . . . But as he jitters along, the cause of Buddy's nervousness becomes clear: He's about to get laid. Probably for the very first time."[9] There is Hank Ballard's widely banned "Work with Me, Annie," Elvis Presley's cover of "Good Rockin' Tonight," Chuck Berry's less overt "Carol," and hundreds of others that relied on innuendo to make their point. Anyone who has seen Martin Scorsese's *The Last Waltz* knows that easy sex could be a powerful incentive to becoming a rock musician. In one of the interview sequences, Robbie Robertson and the others who were to become The Band confess that they hit the road with Canadian rockabilly singer Ronnie Hawkins because he promised them more groupies than Frank Sinatra had.

As for fame, when the musicians who became three-fourths of the Beatles were 12 depressed and ready to throw in the towel, John Lennon rallied them with a chant. He would say, "Where are we going, fellows?" and they answered, "To the top, Johnny" in American accents, followed by, "Where is that, fellows?" and, "To the toppermost of the poppermost."[10] In other words, they were going to the top of the record (pop) charts. Why the faked American accents? Because, as Lennon said, "Elvis was the biggest. We wanted to be the biggest, doesn't everybody? . . . Elvis was the thing. Whatever people say, he was it."[11] Paglia's complaints about managers who take advantage of innocent young musicians date from this same period; Britain's *Daily Worker* made precisely the same criticisms in 1963.[12] Keith Richards and Mick Jagger have made no secret about the degree to which their manager, Andrew Oldham, manipulated the press to achieve notoriety and fame for the Rolling Stones.

Finally, even the sixties musicians that Paglia specifically singles out as purer and 13 artistically truer than those of today, the Beatles and the Rolling Stones, were infiltrated by Philistines who worried as much about their bank accounts as they did about their spiritual development. The Stones had difficulty recruiting drummer Charlie Watts because he refused to quit his day job and its steady paycheck, and bass player Bill Wyman was chosen as much for his having a good amplifier as for his artistic potential. They were unwilling to fulfill the Romantic stereotype of the starving artist. Stu Sutcliffe served as the Beatles' bass player before Paul McCartney; Lennon convinced his art school friend to buy a bass and join because he *looked* the part. A wretched musician, he played his first audition with his back to the promoter in an effort to hide his ineptitude. Ringo Starr later joined as drummer with the expectation of salting away enough money to open a hairdressing parlor when the group lost its popular appeal. Of course, Paglia might dismiss such anecdotes because they involve nonwriting members of rhythm sections, whereas her focus is squarely on the singers and songwriters. But she thereby neglects the very players who give rock its Dionysian rhythms.

The greatest distortion in Paglia's argument is probably the idea that early rockers 14 had some "direct" connection with an authentic oral tradition which accounts for their expressive power. To begin with, there were few "white folk music" sources for rock. Rock's pioneers knew hill-billy and country in a commercial form. Chuck Berry's first record, "Maybellene" (1955), was a simple rewrite of a country standard, "Ida Red." And most of what the early rockers knew of music—black or white—was obtained secondhand, from records. For the white rock and rollers in particular, the primary noncommercial source was gospel music. When Elvis Presley walked into Sun Records in 1953 and taped two songs (purportedly as a birthday gift to his mother, although her birthday was months away), he covered the Ink Spots. When producer Sam Phillips invited Elvis to audition in January of 1954, Elvis chose two country tunes, also learned from records. At their next meeting, Elvis ran through a broader repertoire, "heavy on the Dean Martin stuff. Apparently he'd decided, if he was going to sound like anybody, it was gonna be Dean Martin."[13] So much for "direct contact" with rural traditions on the part of rock's first great popularizer.

The recordings of Buddy Holly are another good case in point. Holly was immor- 15 talized by his death in an airplane crash. (Touring the Midwest in January and February of 1959, he and Ritchie Valens and the Big Bopper [J. P. Richardson] chartered a light plane and flew ahead after a gig in Clear Lake, Iowa, so that they could get some laundry done before the next night's show in Minnesota.) Virtually everything that Holly ever put on tape has been released, most of it in a box set *The Complete Buddy Holly* (MCA Records, 1979). Holly was one of the first rockers to have some control over production and, like Chuck Berry but unlike Elvis Presley, founded his career on his own songs. Nonetheless, much of Holly's recorded legacy consists of cover versions of earlier songs. Many were rock and roll hits that had just been released by *other* rock pioneers: the Robins' (later the Coasters) "Smokey Joe's Cafe," Carl Perkins's "Blue Suede Shoes," Chuck Berry's "Brown-Eyed Handsome Man," Little Richards's "Slippin' and Slidin'," Fats Domino's "Blue Monday." He continued this practice right to the end. One of the very last things he recorded, on a tape recorder in his New York apartment, was a haunting version of Mickey and Sylvia's 1955 hit "Love Is Strange." His other sources were country; his first business card advertised "Western and Bop," and his early radio performances in Lubbock covered the music of Hank Williams, Flatt and Scruggs, and the Louvin Brothers.

Finally, consider Paglia's complaint that live performance has lost its spontaneity 16 and communication and has become a rehearsed and meaningless show. She points to the Beatles' stadium performances as the point of decline. How so? When the Beatles earlier played the cellars of Hamburg's red-light district, singing American hits in Liverpool accents to drunk Germans, was the setting really all that conducive to genuine artistic expression? By all accounts, including the one tape recording made in Hamburg, they played brutal rock and roll for up to six hours a night. And the mix of beer and amphetamines that kept them going hardly made them sensitive to the audience or to their own development as "artists." Paul McCartney had it right when he described it as "noise and beat all the way."[14]

Where Paglia claims that the audience-artist bond was severed by the complexity     17
and expense of ever larger sound systems, coupled with increasingly elaborate special effects, it was certainly these very things that first made rock concerts into something more than party music. The elaborate improvisations of Cream, the Grateful Dead, and the rest of the San Francisco scene, Led Zeppelin and Jimi Hendrix, all came in the five years *after* the Beatles abandoned the stage for the studio. And their achievements depended on superior sound systems; improvisational rock was hardly possible when the musicians had no stage monitors and the cheap amplification system distorted the music into a dull roar, with a sound mix that put the tinny vocals far out in front. Concerts as we understand them today, as extended performances by one or more artists, were rare events before the advent of the modern sound system. In rock's early days, the audience usually saw a specific singer or act as part of a "package" show featuring a half dozen acts, each performing two or three songs and then making way for the next group and its performance of selected hits.

Rather than modern counterparts of Wordsworth, Coleridge, Shelley, Keats, and     18
Byron, rock musicians have always had crass commercial motives, playing dance music to mostly teen audiences. Their direct musical sources were commercial recordings by earlier musicians, and their lyrics featured heavy doses of innuendo but little in the way of overt rebellion and, prior to 1965, almost nothing in the way of personal expression. None of this is offered with the intention of denigrating rock musicians. But if we are considering the claim that rock is either folk or fine art, the available facts count heavily against such status.

## II

I have outlined the historical distortions of Paglia's story in order to clear the stage for     19
the main thrust of her proposal: "Rock music should not be left to the Darwinian laws of the marketplace. . . . For rock to move forward as an art form, our musicians must be given an opportunity for spiritual development." Having constructed a selective history that postulates an "authentic" tradition with a subsequent commercial distortion, she thinks that rock has a legitimate claim to being a true art form. But even if successful rock musicians have actually been those who could adapt to the commercial demands of entertainment, Paglia is advocating that rock can be fine art if the musicians can be freed from these commercial constraints. Paglia might have quoted composer Roger Sessions for support: "The artist's values are not, and cannot be, those of the market. If one must think of him as writing *for* anyone, the answer is . . . he is writing for all who love music."[15] If modern composers have lost out to popular music, Sessions argues, it is mainly the fault of audiences who have become too lazy to listen with sympathy and understanding. In the same vein, Paglia recommends that rock artists write for posterity, not the commercial audience.

Paglia believes that rock, purged of its economic dependence on a fickle and 20 immature audience, will be recognized as the equal (or better) of current painting, sculpture, and serious composed music. She never explicitly says so, but her only standard of artistic achievement is rooted in her own acceptance of the aesthetics of Romanticism and its assumptions about the goals and value of art. I will argue that this line of argument is of no use if one wants to bring rock music and musicians into academia.

In the story she tells of rock's decline, Paglia singles out the following features as 21 having been lost: individualism, spontaneity, energy, passion, and rebellion. Paglia has accepted Josiah Royce's "creed" of the Romantic artist: "Trust your genius; follow your noble heart; change your doctrine whenever your heart changes, and change your heart often."[16] It is also clear that she does not regard the artist's role as one of reflecting society. Disdaining the trivial concerns of the "white suburban youth" who are rock's primary audience, she believes that serious rock focuses on "dark" emotions, demonism, and spirituality. In Paglia's controversial book *Sexual Personae*, she contends that despite its commercialism, American radio proves that we "still live in the age of Romanticism." The Rolling Stones "are heirs of stormy Coleridge."[17] Other writers have analyzed rock in the same terms:

> In part because of its contradictions, the best way to understand rock and roll is to see it as a twentieth-century popular expression of Western romanticism. In fact, rock may even by the last gasp of romanticism in this anxious materialistic and scientific age. More than any other contemporary cultural form, rock captures the central elements of the romantic spirit: its individuality, freedom, and rebellion, . . . its exultation of emotion, physicality, and imagination, and its relish of contradictions, extremes, and paradoxes.[18]

The most detailed attempt to link rock and Romanticism is Robert Pattison's *The* 22 *Triumph of Vulgarity*, subtitled "Rock Music in the Mirror of Romanticism." Pattison contends that rock "is a unique integration of Romantic mythology and American blues."[19] Like Paglia, he identifies the Rolling Stones as the greatest rock band ever. (The Beatles, we are left to presume, are just not demonic enough.)

Unlike Paglia, Pattison does not endorse Romanticism, and he is sometimes condescending toward his subjects. While he is aware that the Romantic myths are espoused by rock musicians, he does not regard them as anything but myths. With particular attention to the idea of rock's "primitive" sources, he believes that rock artists themselves have adopted the doctrines of nineteenth-century Romanticism. He contends that the "vulgar mode" of Romanticism is the cultural force behind rock, "and the Sex Pistols come to fulfill the prophecies of Shelley."[20] His argumentation amounts to quoting extensively but selectively from rock lyrics, putting rather too much weight on rock's supposed pantheism as the primary evidence of romanticist influences. A more serious weakness is a tendency to equate rock's mythology, as expressed in its lyrics, with the forces actually driving it; he likes to quote obscure groups like the Fall and then to assure us that in "describing themselves, they describe all rockers."[21] Yet there is every reason to believe that the attitudes of most rock lyrics are posturing and image-making for commercial purposes and that many of the musicians are themselves perfectly aware of this.

There is also a tendency toward circularity. Anything that does not reflect Romanti- 24 cism is written off as nonrock, so Pattison does not recognize soul and other black popular music as rock. Black music "has supplied the raw materials, but there is no reason to suppose that blacks share the Romantic preoccupations necessary for rock."[22] But it is absurd to think that such preoccupations are *necessary* for rock. When the Beatles covered black musicians like Chuck Berry and Little Richard, and when the Rolling Stones covered Chuck Berry and Otis Redding, they were not taking "raw materials" from black musicians and transforming them. They were taking songs from musicians whom they admired as models of rock musicianship. On Pattison's thesis, what are we to make of Aretha Franklin's late-sixties work with producer Jerry Wexler (backed by several white musicians), or of Sly and the Family Stone, Little Feat, the Allman Brothers, the Doobie Brothers, Bruce Springsteen's E Street Band, and other racially integrated groups? Do the white members supply the requisite romanticist mythology to transform the black musicians' contributions into rock?

I do not deny that as an aesthetic program Romanticism enshrined many of the values that are popularly attributed to rock. As a reaction against Enlightenment classicism and its emphasis on "intellectual" values of order, structure, precision, and technical polish, Romanticism first surfaced in serious music with the *Sturm und Drang*, flowered with program music and tone poems, and peaked with Wagner's music drama and chromactic explorations. The new values were "emotional" and were manifested overtly in change, excess, personal meanings, ambiguity, and idiosyncratic structures. But even if we can construct a case that the same conflict of values is present in any contrast of serious music with rock, parallels do not show causality. **25**

The problem with the whole line of analysis is that *most* opinions about music sound like *some* aspect of Romanticism, if only because of the general presumption that music is preeminently concerned with the expression of emotion. These characteristics all fit jazz as easily as rock. In fact, with writers like Paglia and Pattison we may have a case of critical history repeating itself. Those who link Romanticism and rock sound like earlier writers on jazz who found in jazz the same characteristics that are now attributed to rock, particularly the uncompromised and spontaneous nature of the performance and the freedom and instinctive self-expression of the performer.[23] And these values were often espoused by jazz performers themselves. **26**

Consider Billie Holiday. Not exactly known for her art school background or reading of Byron and Shelley, she denied having any influences except the records of Bessie Smith and Louis Armstrong: **27**

> If you find a tune and it's got something to do with you, you don't have to evolve anything. You just feel it, and when you sing it other people can feel something too. With me, it's got nothing to do with working or arranging or rehearsing. . . . But singing songs like "The Man I Love" or "Porgy". . . . When I sing them I live them again and I love them.[24]

However much this sounds like Wordsworth's formula that poetry is a spontaneous overflow of emotions "recollected in tranquility," we have no reason to regard Lady Day as influenced by Wordsworth. Likewise, we have no reason to regard rock as an expression of Western Romanticism. As Peter Kivy has so carefully documented, most of these ideas about music were first advanced in the seventeenth and eighteenth centuries.[25] It might be better to regard romanticist aesthetics as a generalization to all the arts of assumptions that had long been held of music, in which case rock has no special connection to Romanticism.

Furthermore, Paglia's account of rock music is fraught with the same internal ten-  28
sions that characterize Romanticism, particularly in relation to the folk tradition that she
praises as a source of power in early rock. To the extent that such traditions have survived
in Western culture in our century, oral folk traditions are communal rather than individual artistic creations, and they reflect the community rather than the personal self-
expression of the Romantic genius. Yet Paglia criticizes rock musicians who cater to or
reflect the values of the audience. The idea of a "folk" dimension in rock is also present
in her ideal of an authentic and spontaneous interaction between performer and audience, but this conflicts with the reality that rock fans are self-consciously aware that they
are members of a distinct subculture, and of distinct subcultures within rock.[26]

It is no surprise that Paglia tries to find a link between rock and folk music. One  29
of Romanticism's several themes was a glorification of the rural "folk" and of their collective art as a less intellectual, more spontaneous, and thus purer mode of expression.
When the Rolling Stones imitated black American singers in a self-conscious blues
purism, they were indeed behaving like many Romantic composers. Chopin and
Dvořák borrowed musical materials from their native folk traditions, and Wagner and
Mahler adopted folk poems and myths as texts. But the aesthetics of Romanticism are
fraught with internal contradictions, among them the fact the very process of appropri-
ating these sources contradicts the desired spontaneity and authenticity of expression,
no less for rock musicians than for nineteenth-century composers.[27]

According to Peter Wicke, the aesthetic values imparted to British rockers who  30
attended art schools led to a calculated bohemianism and intellectual snobbery. Among
those who articulated their aesthetic principles, pop art and then situationism appear to
be the most prominent influences. Their preoccupation with the authenticity of their
self-expression precluded their participation in any sort of community with their audience, and in fact they were often aware of the distance between their own privileged status and the working-class lives of most of their audience.[28] These attitudes may even
have worked against direct political activism on the part of British rockers. Prior to the
Beatles' single "Revolution" (1968), British rock lyrics stayed away from anything overtly
political, whereas the American charts had featured political material since 1965.

Rock recreates Romantic contradictions in another way when the ideology of artis-  31
tic freedom comes up against the reality that the musicians are engaged in a commercial
enterprise. Within the actual context of the nineteenth century, Romanticism glorified
the sensitivity and sensibility of the individual artist/genius; but the requisite artistic freedom had its price in the commercialization of music. We might even say that when
Romanticism valued both individuality and folk traditions, it did so in conscious opposition to the standardization and industrialization of the emerging bourgeois capitalism.
Thus Paglia has nothing but disdain for those who get their rock from MTV. A parallel is
present within the rock audience; fans of hardcore express contempt for mainstream audiences who imitate their slam-dancing and thus strip it of its "underground" status.

Yet it was bourgeois capitalism and the opportunity for self-promotion that pro-  32
vided the composer's freedom. When earlier composers like Bach or Handel supported
themselves with pupils and commissioned works, their music was largely utilitarian,
written for specific occasions: Bach's masses and chorales, Handel's oratorios with their
religious texts and his *Water Music* and *Royal Fireworks Music*. Beethoven solidified the
shift from the composer-for-hire to the composer-as-entrepreneur, with works sold to
publishers rather than commissioned by royal patrons. Concerts became money-making
ventures, designed to please the bourgeois crowd who can afford the fee. Beethoven was

attuned to the need to please the audience, repeating movements of symphonies when the concert audience called for it and showing off with piano improvisations when challenged. He could also be sensitive to criticism, withdrawing and replacing the final movement (the *Grosse Fugue*) of the String Quartet in B-flat Minor when the audience at its premiere reacted negatively.

At the other end of the spectrum, Wagner scraped together funding for his music 33 dramas by a combination of self-promotion and spectacle. Wagner was keen to wrap himself in Beethoven's mantle, conducting the latter's Ninth Symphony at the 1872 dedication of Bayreuth. But Beethoven's willingness to meet the audience half-way had given way to Wagner's self-conscious Romanticism. Stubborn and uncompromising, his vision required absolute control of his creations, and he was vicious to anyone who criticized him. The result was precisely the opposite of Paglia's ideal performance as an audience-artist interaction that features improvisation and spontaneity. Ideally, the audience comes to the Bayreuth festival theater and listens to the *Ring* cycle in a hushed silence, broken only by the turning of pages as devoted Wagnerites follow the score. In short, there is no spontaneity of any kind; the Bach mass had found its secular parallel.

Which of these artists represents Paglia's ideal? Her advice to rock musicians, 34 "Don't become a slave to the audience" and "Don't tour" (study art instead), points to Wagner and not to Beethoven or to Romantics like Berlioz, Chopin, and Liszt, who more or less invented the modern promotional tour. More pointedly, she expects rock to combine two artistic goals that have been at odds ever since Romanticism cobbled them together. On the one hand there is the development of the individual artist, cushioned from and thus impervious to commercial demands. But this sort of autonomy is unlikely to foster energy, rebellion, and the emotional power of rock's pioneers. On the other hand there is the emotional power of the folk tradition, where the music emerges from the community in a way that blurs the line between creator and audience. But the communal nature of the folk process fits uncomfortably with the self-conscious artistry of the trained professional; training rock musicians at colleges and universities is not likely to connect rock with centuries of folk music.

Finally, Paglia is recommending that rock musicians trade the vicissitudes of 35 commerce for a system of artistic patronage. But are commercial demands always an artistic kiss of death? Paglia links popular music and film as the two great art forms of our time, but film has fared quite well without much institutional support. Paglia is really recommending that rock shouldn't remain popular music any longer, that is, a commodity designed for consumption by masses of listeners of varying degrees of musical knowledge. Rock musicians are to regard themselves as fine artists and to train accordingly. Putting aside the conflict with folk ideology, such ideas fail to address how rock music would retain its identity apart from its popular base. Romanticism has a healthy strain of artistic elitism that is antithetical to rock, and patronage is likely to reinforce that strain in rock. While I would not go as far as Nietzsche did, he captures the problem involved when he attacks Romanticism: "The artist who began to understand himself would misunderstand himself: he ought not to look back, he ought not to look at all, he ought to give."[29] Can rock deliver on its own terms if its artists are successful at the transformations that Paglia recommends?

We should also consider the likely consequences of treating rock like the other arts. 36 Funding through grants, scholarships, and the like is increasingly limited, so the proposal could cover only a fraction of the ten thousand or more artists who release rock recordings each year (many of these being groups of several members). In practical terms, freeing artists from traditional commercial concerns means that *most* rock music will remain exactly what it is anyway: product for popular consumption. So the scheme is likely to split rock into two camps. One will carry on as before, and the other will consist of artists with grants, afforded the freedom to follow their own muse. (This would reverse the current process, where *mature* successful artists like Dire Straits, George Harrison, the Grateful Dead, Bruce Springsteen, and the Rolling Stones can wait five years between records and tours, producing what they like when they choose to do so.) But the select few who would be singled out for support will face the same problems that already occur in a patronage system. While there is intense competition for scarce resources, very little of the money is risked on artists whose work is genuinely avant-garde, and less still on those whose work is highly political in content. One has difficulty imagining the Clash or rappers N.W.A. and Ice-T getting a grant under Paglia's scheme. Training rock musicians at colleges and universities is likely to result in music that parallels the output of similarly trained jazz and classical musicians: highly accomplished, technically excellent, and intellectually challenging music that values extreme polish, individuality, experimentation, and novelty for their own sake as well as continuous progressive change. But there is little reason to think that the music produced by these musicians is going to connect with the general public and conquer the top ten. (If we were talking about music with commercial potential, Paglia would lose her basic premise that commercial demands corrupt the music.)

Although those involved with the fine arts do not like to say so, there is also a fun- 37 damental unfairness to this system, particularly if we are funding artists who are not interested in producing music that the general public wants to hear. As Jeremy Bentham argued, the arts "are useful only to those who take pleasure in them," and to the extent that public patronage is set up to further arts which lack widespread appeal, we are instituting a regressive tax, "laying burdens on the comparatively indigent many, for the amusement of the comparatively opulent few."[30] We do this with other arts in the United States, with mixed success. Consider the National Endowment for the Arts (NEA). In recent years we have seen an overt politicization of the patronage system as politicians on the right have demanded that public funding be restricted to art that expresses mainstream values. Yet by operating within the sphere of mass entertainment, rock music has gradually loosened the bonds of censorship. The Rolling Stones had to sing "Let's Spend the Night Together" as "Let's Spend Some Time Together" on the Ed Sullivan Show in 1967, a form of self-censorship difficult to imagine in the 1990s. Stephen Sondheim recently rejected an NEA grant because of the restrictions involved, preferring the freedom of artistic free enterprise. Why advocate a patronage system that is just as likely to control and censor artistic expression as to encourage it?[31]

As Ezra Pound said, "Music rots when it gets *too far* from the dance. Poetry atro- 38 phies when it gets too far from music."[32] While teachers and literature professors like to think that schools and colleges have some special ability to bring poetry and literature to the masses, there is plenty of evidence that "good" literature is not what the masses want. It is not even what most college students and graduates want, as junk fiction and "Calvin and Hobbes" collections repeatedly top the sales lists of college bookstores. I do not mean to put down junk fiction and comics, but there is little reason to think that poetry has much meaning for the majority of people. It has gotten too far from music, and most of the "serious" music composed in our century has gotten too far from the dance. In my more cynical moments I believe that both are mainly produced by college professors for other college professors (they seem to make up most of the audience when I attend local "new music" concerts). Academics, however well meaning, are the last group to keep rock rooted in the syncopated and danceable rhythms that have made it one of America's most successful exports. If the lyrics to rap have vitality, it may be because they aren't composed by college students who have immersed themselves in great literature.

If there is any element of Romanticism that we ought to keep out of art educa- [39] tion, it is the notion of the artistic genius as a superior soul requiring special nourishment, for this is probably one of the great obstacles to full enjoyment and participation in the arts by large numbers of our students. Why inject elitism into popular culture, where students engage at least one form of art without anxiety or feelings of inferiority? Romanticism is a poor model for understanding the achievements of rock music, and it is worse yet as a justification for treating rock music as we now treat the fine arts.

## Notes

1. An interesting variation of this thesis is defended in Richard Shusterman, "The Fine Art of Rap," in his *Pragmatist Aesthetics* (Oxford: Blackwell, 1992), pp. 201–35. Shusterman's argument focuses on showing that rap is the form of popular music which best exemplifies a postmodern aesthetic; for this reason, his version avoids endorsing rap as folk music.
2. Robert Christgau, "Rock Lyrics Are Poetry (Maybe)," in *The Age of Rock*, ed. Jonathan Eisen (New York: Random House, 1969), p. 232.
3. Camille Paglia, "Endangered Rock," *The New York Times*, Thursday, 16 April 1992, p. A23. Reprinted in Camille Paglia, *Sex, Art, and American Culture* (New York: Vintage Books, 1992), pp. 19–21. Unless otherwise credited, all further quotations from Paglia are from this editorial, which was widely reprinted.
4. Quoted in *Melody Maker*, 27 August 1977; quotation disseminated in Tony Angarde, *The Oxford Dictionary of Modern Quotations* (New York: Oxford University Press, 1991), p. 89.
5. In *Sexual Personae* (New York: Vintage Books, 1990), Camille Paglia does offer parallels between Elvis Presley and Lord Byron; most of them are physical similarities such as their early deaths and enlarged hearts.
6. Simon Frith, "Popular Music 1950–1980," in *Making Music*, ed. George Martin (New York: William Morrow, 1983), p. 24.
7. Nik Cohn, *Pop from the Beginning* (United Kingdom: Weidenfeld and Nicholson, 1969), p. 133.
8. Carl Belz, *The Story of Rock*, 2d ed. (New York: Oxford University Press, 1972), p. 64.
9. Dave Marsh, *The Heart of Rock and Soul* (New York: Plume, 1989), pp. 474–75.
10. John Lennon, quoted in David Sheff and G. Barry Golson, *The Playboy Interviews with John Lennon and Yoko Ono* (New York: Berkley Books, 1981), pp. 170–71.
11. John Lennon quoted in Jann Wenner, *Lennon Remembers* (San Francisco: Straight Arrow Books, 1971), p. 70; interview conducted in December 1970.
12. "Working Class?" *Daily Worker*, 7 September 1963, p. 5.
13. Quotation of Marion Keisker, who was present at the sessions; Ed Ward, in *Rock of Ages* (New York: Rolling Stone Press/Summit Books, 1986), pp. 78–79.
14. Quoted in Geoffrey Stokes, *The Beatles* (New York: Rolling Stone Press/Times Books, 1980), p. 45.
15. Roger Sessions, *Questions about Music* (New York: W. W. Norton, 1970), p. 11.
16. Quoted in Frederick B. Artz, *From Renaissance to Romanticism: Trends in Art, Literature, and Music, 1300–1930* (Chicago: University of Chicago Press, 1962), p. 227.
17. Paglia, *Sexual Personae*, p. 358.
18. Quentin J. Schultze, et al., *Dancing in the Dark* (Grand Rapids, Mich.: William B. Eerdmans, 1991), p. 164.
19. Robert Pattison, *The Triumph of Vulgarity* (Oxford: Oxford University Press, 1987), p. 63.
20. Ibid., p. xi.
21. Ibid., p. 10.
22. Ibid., p. 64.
23. See Andy Hamilton, "The Aesthetics of Imperfection," *Philosophy* 65, no. 253 (1990), pp. 323–40; and Ted Gioia, *The Imperfect Art* (New York: Oxford University Press, 1988), pp. 19–49.

24. Billie Holiday with William Dufty, *Lady Sings the Blues* (New York: Penguin, 1984), p. 39. There is a certain irony here for anyone who wants to fit Holiday into the Romantic archetype, since she is talking about commercial songs by white composers.

25. See chaps. 3–5 of Peter Kivy, *Sound Sentiment*, (Philadelphia: Temple University Press, 1989); this incorporates his earlier book *The Corded Shell*.

26. See Simon Frith, *Sound Effects* (New York: Pantheon, 1981), pp. 202–34.

27. Attempts to legitimize rock by association with folk music first arose among rock critics; see Simon Frith, "'The Magic That Can Set You Free': The Ideology of Folk and the Myth of the Rock Community," in *Popular Music*, vol. 1, ed. Richard Middleton and David Horn (Cambridge: Cambridge University Press, 1981), pp. 159–68.

28. Peter Wicke, *Rock Music: Culture, Aesthetics and Sociology*, trans. Rachel Fogg (Cambridge: Cambridge: Cambridge University Press, 1990), chaps. 5 and 7.

29. Friedrich Nietzsche, *Will to Power*, trans. Walter Kaufmann and R. J. Hollingdale (New York: Vintage/Random House, 1968), p. 429 (section 811).

30. Jeremy Bentham, "Reward Applied to Art and Science," *The Works of Jeremy Bentham*, vol. 2, ed. John Bowring (New York: Russell & Russell, 1962), p. 253.

31. See Edward C. Banfield, *The Democratic Muse* (New York: Basic Books, 1984).

32. Ezra Pound, *ABC of Reading* (Norfolk, Conn.: New Directions, n.d.), p. 61.

## READING FOR CONTENT

1. Explain why the pioneers of rock were neither Romantic archetypes nor rebels.

2. To what extent were early rockers influenced by an authentic oral tradition?

3. According to Gracyk, why is it that rock "has no special connections to Romanticism"?

4. Does Gracyk find links between rock and folk music? What are they?

5. What are the consequences of treating rock like the fine arts?

## READING FOR GENRE, ORGANIZATION, AND STYLISTIC FEATURES

1. Gracyk has written an essay of analysis and evaluation. Which genres of analysis described in Chapters 4 and 5—cause and effect, comparison and contrast, structure of the reading source, or argument—does he use?

2. What types of sources does Gracyk draw upon, and what function do the sources serve?

3. Give examples of the various types of evidence—facts, statistics, references to authorities—that Gracyk uses to support his position.

## READING FOR RHETORICAL CONTEXT

1. Describe the organizational features that make Gracyk's article easy to follow.

2. Is Gracyk's argument one-sided, or does he concede alternative viewpoints? Underline passages pertaining to alternate views.

3. Underline words that reveal Gracyk's tone. How would you characterize the tone?

## WRITING ASSIGNMENTS

1. After reading Gracyk's article, what do you think of Camille Paglia's idea about training rock musicians in colleges and universities? Write a brief essay expressing your views.

2. Write an essay in which you argue point A or point B.

   a. Grants and scholarships should fund artists and musicians who take risks, those whose work is genuinely avant-garde or political in nature.

   b. Grants and scholarships should fund artists and musicians who express mainstream values and produce art music that appeals to the general public.

3. Write an essay in which you agree or disagree with Gracyk's statement: "If there is any element of Romanticism that we ought to keep out of art education, it is the notion of the artistic genius as a superior soul requiring special nourishment, for this is probably one of the great obstacles to full enjoyment and participation in the arts by large numbers of our students" (paragraph 39).

■ ■ ■ ■ ■ ■ ■ ■ ■ ■ ■ ■

# Redeeming the Rap Music Experience

## Venise Berry

*Venise Berry is an assistant professor in the School of Journalism and Mass Communication at the University of Iowa. She is the co-editor of* Mediated Messages and African-American Culture: Contemporary Issues. *She has published book chapters in* Adolescents and Their Music, Cecilia Reclaimed: Feminist Perspectives on Gender and Music, Viewing War: How the Media Handled the Persian Gulf, *and* Men, Masculinity, and the Media, *and she is the author of the novel,* So Good *(1996).*

## PREREADING

React to the title of the article. What is your opinion of rap music? Do you think it needs to be redeemed? Freewrite your reactions.

You know—parents are the same no matter time nor place.
They don't understand that us kids are gonna make some mistakes.
So to you other kids all across the land, there's no need to argue—
           PARENTS JUST DON'T UNDERSTAND!

(DJ Jazzy Jeff and The Fresh Prince 1988)

## Introduction

When rap music first appeared on the scene, music critics said it wouldn't last, record   1
companies felt it was too harsh and black-oriented to cross over, and parents dismissed it as the latest fad. Ten years later, rap has become a powerful and controversial force in American popular culture. Rap music has grown significantly from its humble street beginnings in Harlem and the South Bronx. It now encompasses a dominant media paradigm through traditional music vehicles like cassettes and CDs, as well as televi-

Berry, Venise. "Redeeming the Rap Music Experience." *Adolescents and Their Music.* Ed. Jonathan S. Epstein. New York: Garland, 1994. 165–87. Reprinted by permission of the publisher.

sion coverage in videos and talk shows, rappers as actors, film themes, concerts, adver-  2
tising, and other promotional components.

On *Billboard*'s top 200 album list on January 18, 1992, rappers were found as high
as #3 and as low as #184. Despite, or maybe because of, the controversies, groups such as
Hammer, Public Enemy, Ice Cube, Ghetto Boyz, Salt N' Pepa, 2 Live Crew, NWA,
Tone Loc, and Queen Latifah have reached mainstream popularity, and each success
pushes the rap genre into new directions. Rap music is constantly testing the boundaries
of commercialism, sexism, radicalism, feminism, and realism, and a growing concern  3
over the music's disrespect for traditional boundaries keeps it on the cutting edge.

Current literature on rap music has taken varied approaches, from content analyses which analyze and critique images and messages, to trade articles which offer promotional information on the artists and their music. One of the most important, yet
least explored, areas in this discourse is the relationship between the music and its fans;  4
particularly those whom it represents: black urban youths.

This chapter will explore three controversial issues in rap music: sex, violence, and
racism, in relation to the social, cultural, and historical reality of urban black American
youth. My analysis will draw on both secondary and primary sources. It will incorporate
related articles and previous literature, as well as worksheet responses collected from
black high school participants in the Upward Bound Program at Huston-Tillotson College in Austin, Texas, between 1987 and 1989 and personal comments from an October  5
17, 1990, discussion group with twenty-four of the Upward Bound juniors and seniors.

In developing a conceptual framework for this examination of rap music experience, it is necessary to distinguish between the pop-cultural and pop-crossover
domains. The pop-cultural domain involves rap music, which, despite its popularity,
maintains a black cultural focus in its message and style. For example, rap groups like
NWA, Ice T, KRS One, Public Enemy, Ice Cube, and Queen Latifah are popular rap-  6
pers with messages and styles that reflect an overt black consciousness.

In contrast, the pop-crossover domain involves rap music which follows a more com-
mercialized format. The message and style of these rap songs are more generalizable and
acceptable to mainstream audiences. Hammer, Salt N' Pepa, DJ Jazzy Jeff and the Fresh
Prince, Tone Loc, and Kid and Play are examples of pop-crossover rap artists. The distinction between these two rap domains is important in recognition of their place in the American popular culture movement. The popularity of one helps to fuel the popularity of the
other, just as the acceptable nature of one limits the acceptable nature of the other.  7

This research evolves from a broad sociocultural ideology, focusing on the wish to
understand the meaning and place assigned to popular culture in the experience of a particular group in society—the young, black, urban minority. It supports the pluralist
approach, which considers rap music an example of how media systems, despite their
attempt to control, are basically nondominant and open to change, and can be used effectively to present alternative views. Gurevitch (1982) has examined pluralism as a component of democracy and emancipatory media. Their work advocates the idea of media as
public vehicles used for enhancing and encouraging self-expression and self-conscious-
ness by a culture. As this chapter will highlight, cultural rap is just such a vehicle.

## Black Music as Cultural Communication

In the work of Standifer (1980), the musical behaviors of black society are explained as  8
"movement with existence." From spirituals to rap, black music style is a communicative

process interwoven deep within the black American experience. For example, the spiritual served as an underground form of communication and a mechanism for emotional release. Natural words and phrases had secret meanings for slave communities. According to Cone (1972), words and phrases which seemed harmless were filled with latent meanings, such as, "De promise land on the other side of Jordan," which meant: "freedom north" and later "Canada," rather than "heaven" as slave owners were led to believe.

B. B. King has told the story of how blues evolved from the unanswered prayers of   9
slaves. He explained that slaves sang to God, but remained oppressed. As a result they began to lose at least part of their faith, and started to sing what was on their minds: the blues. Walton (1972) agrees, defining the blues as a composition grounded in individual experience and one with which the audience tends to identify.

When avant-garde jazz emerged, it was in protest to mainstream-appropriated   10
music styles such as ragtime and boogie-woogie. Kofsky (1970) explains that the revolutionary jazz style used the piano as a distraction, abandoning the traditional diatonic scale, and incorporating an atonal key structure in direct opposition to Western music form. He says the harsh and abrasive music represented the dissatisfaction of Black Americans with what they had been promised, but ultimately denied: a chance to have the American dream.

Soul music in the 1960s and 1970s presented itself as a blatantly rebellious black   11
musical genre. It created for black American culture a sense of heightened black consciousness, unity and pride. Soul music, ultimately, served as a powerful catalyst for protest and social change during the civil rights and black power movements (Maultsby, 1983).

Finally, today's rap music style reflects the distinct experience of urban black   12
culture. Black slang, street attitude, and fashion are reflected in powerful spoken song. Name-brand tennis shoes, sweatsuits, and an exorbitant display of gold chains and rings create a sense of appropriated success. The heavy beat, incessant scratching, aggressive delivery, and lyrical storyline present a message of anger and frustration from urban existence.

Just as socially, culturally, and historically music has always been essential to the   13
evolution of the black American experience, an essential part of contemporary black culture is the urban environment which manifests itself within the context of rap music. Several scholars have discussed the power of rap music as a mechanism of communication involving the struggle for a recognized black cultural empowerment.

Dyson (1991) examines performance, protest, and prophecy in the culture of hip   14
hop. He suggests that it is difficult for a society that maintains social arrangements, economic conditions, and political choices so that it can create and reproduce poverty, racism, sexism, classism, and violence to appreciate a music that contests and scandalizes such problems. He fears that the pop success of rap artists often means mainstream dilution; the sanitizing of rap's expression of urban realities, resulting in sterile hip hop devoid of its original fire and offensive to no one.

The communicative power of rap music is traced back to an African tradition   15
called "nommo" by Stephens (1991). Nommo refers to the supernatural power of the spoken word. The rhyme and rhythm which are part of African-American speech, literature, music, and dance are essential elements of nommo. He says it is believed in Africa that nommo can create changes in attitude. It can evoke unity, identity, and an atmosphere where everyone can relate.

Perkins (1991) explains how the ideology of the Nation of Islam has become an   16
important element of rap music's message. Perkins feels that rap artists such as Public

Enemy and KRS One are social revolutionaries and their role is to carry the black nationalist tradition forward by heightening awareness, stimulating thought, and provoking the true knowledge of self.

The messages in rap music have also been compared to the messages in blues by [17] Nelson (1991). She contrasts themes such as poverty and despair that appear in both and discusses how both musical forms are based on truth and reality. Dixon (1989) speaks about the context of rap music as truth. He feels rap music " . . . unites the listeners of the music into a common group with clear and readily identifiable racial, cultural, economic, and political/sexual shared concerns and emerges as the voice of its adherents."

Finally, the issue of rap as historical account is raised by Shusterman (1991). He [18] says, "Many rappers have taken their place as insightful inquirers into reality and teachers of truth, particularly those aspects of reality and truth which get neglected or distorted by establishment history books and contemporary media coverage." Shusterman attributes the audible voice of rap music in popular culture to its commercial success in the mass media, which has enabled renewed artistic investment as an undeniable source of black cultural pride.

## Rap Music, Urban Reality, and Popular Culture

Popular culture is made by subordinated peoples in their own interests out of resources [19] that also, contradictorily, serve the economic interests of the dominant. Popular culture is made from within and below, not imposed from without and above as mass cultural theorists would have it. There is always an element of popular culture that lies outside of social control, that escapes or opposes hegemonic forces.

The power and promise of rap music rests in the bosom of urban America; an [20] environment where one out of twenty-two black males will be killed by violent crimes, where the black high-school dropout rate is as high as 72 percent and where 86 percent of black children grow up in poverty. Years of degradation, welfare handouts, institutional racism, and discrimination have created a community where little hope, low self-esteem and frequent failure translate into drugs, teen pregnancy, and gang violence. These are the social, cultural, and economic conditions which have spurred rap's paradoxical position within American popular culture.

The relationship between low socioeconomic status and the negative self-evaluation [21] of black urban youth results in problems of low self-esteem. These feelings are prominent because of limited opportunities, unsatisfied needs, instability, estrangement, racial prejudice, and discrimination (Hulbary, 1975). As these youth struggle with questions of independence and control in their environment, they embrace a sense of powerlessness. Mainstream society tends to view the lifestyles of low-income communities as deviant. The poor are believed to be perpetuating their own poverty because of their nonconforming attitudes and unconventional behavior (Gladwin, 1967). Poussaint and Atkinson (1972) suggest that the stereotypes of deviance, a lack of motivation, and limited educational achievements ultimately become a part of their identity.

The youth movement which is evident in popular culture has, therefore, brought [22] about only illusions for many urban American youth. The term "youth," which came to mean a specific attitude including pleasure, excitement, hope, power, and invincibility, was not experienced by these kids. Their future was mangled by racism, prejudice, discrimination, and economic and educational stagnation. As Bernard (1991) suggests, they found themselves in a gloomy darkness without friendship, trust, or hope; backed into a corner where life is all about self.

As a product of the black urban community, rap music is indisputably entangled with 23 the struggle for black identity and legitimacy within mainstream society. Although rap music is undergoing significant changes, much of it remains true to its aesthetic purpose of bringing to the forefront the problematic nature of urban American experience.

Cultural rap music is, therefore, often seen in a negative light. The "culture of 24 rap music" has been chracterized as a "culture of attitude" by Adler (1990), who suggests that attitude is something civilized society abhors and likes to keep under control. He concludes that the end of attitude is nihilism, which by definition leads nowhere, and that the culture of attitude is repulsive, mostly empty of political content.

Costello and Wallace (1990), in *Signifying Rappers*, say that vitalists have argued 25 for forty years that postwar art's ultimate expression will be a kind of enormous psychosocial excrement and the real aesthetic (conscious or otherwise) of today's best serious rap may be nothing but the first wave of this great peristalsis.

Negative images of rap are dominant in the news. The 2 Live Crew controversy 26 in Florida concerning sexually explicit lyrics made big headlines, along with the charity basketball game by rap artists in New York which resulted in nine kids being trampled to death. Violence has also been reported at movies where rap themes are prominent. And, the music of defiant rap groups like NWA (Niggas with Attitude) have been considered radical and extremist. They made history as the first musical group to receive a warning from the FBI about the negative content of their song, "Fuck the Police," which encourages a lack of respect for the system.

Urban black American culture exists within a large infrastructure, segmented by 27 various negative individual and situational environments. The relationship between the rap fan and his or her music, therefore, involves the larger contextual environment of the urban street. At the same time, it is important to recognize how the mainstream success of the rap genre has made urban language, style, dance, and attitude viable components of popular cultural form.

## The Issue of Sex

The 2 Live Crew appeared in the public eye in 1986 with their first album, *The 2 Live* 28 *Crew Is What We Are*. Their most successful hit, which is now considered tame, was entitled, "Hey, We Want Some Pussy." It sold a half-million copies without the backing of a major record company. The Crew's next album took sexual rap to a new level. *Move Something* sold more than a million copies and included songs like, "Head," "Booty and Cock," and "Me so Horny."

It was their third album, *As Nasty as We Wanna Be*, which made the group a 29 household name. On June 6, 1990, U.S. District Judge Jose Gonzales, Jr., said the album was "utterly without any redeeming social value." The obscenity issue created a media bonanza for 2 Live Crew and boosted the sale of their album to more than two million copies.

Luther Campbell, leader of the group, has been on a number of talk shows and in 30 many articles defending his right to produce sexually explicit rap music. In an interview in *Black Beat* magazine, he called the lyrics funny. "The stuff on our X-rated albums is meant to be funny. We sit down and laugh about our lyrics. We don't talk about raping women or committing violence against them or anything like that" (Henderson, February 1990).

An analysis by Peterson-Lewis (1991) presents a different perspective: ". . . their 31 lyrics lack the wit and strategic use of subtle social commentary necessary for effective satire; thus they do not so much debunk myths as create new ones, the major one being that in interacting with black women 'anything goes.' Their lyrics not only fail to satirize the myth of the hypersexual black, they also commit the moral blunder of sexualizing the victimization of women, black women in particular."

Campbell adds that the group's lyrics are a reflection of life in America's black 32 neighborhoods. Yet he admits he won't let his seven-year-old daughter listen to such music. While 2 Live Crew served as the thrust of the controversy, the negative images of women in this society have been a concern of feminists for many years, through various media forms.

Peterson-Lewis goes on to question the extent of the ethical and moral responsi- 33 bilities of artists to their audiences and the larger public. She focuses her argument on the constitutionality and racially motivated persecution and prosecution of 2 Live Crew, which she feels overshadowed the real criticism—the sexually explicit nature of their lyrics and their portrayal of women as objects for sexual assault.

Frankel (1990) agrees that the 2 Live Crew situation took away the real focus. She 34 says the attack on the 2 Live Crew group made it an issue of censorship, racism, and free speech, rather than an issue of disgust at how women are portrayed, especially since an act like Andrew Dice Clay, who also promotes women and sex from a negative perspective, has not been sanctioned by the law.

Even though the controversy about sexually explicit lyrics in rap music has 35 become a heated issue, out of a list of the top fifty rap groups, only about 10 percent can actually be identified as using truly obscene and violent lyrics in relation to women. An analysis of the number of more generally negative images of females as loose and whorish would probably double that percentage.

In a discussion on the subject of sex in rap with a group of Upward Bound high 36 school juniors and seniors, there was a split on the 2 Live Crew issue. Bené said their records contain too much profanity and are obscene, so maybe they should be sold in X-rated stores. Steve felt that fifteen- and sixteen-year-olds are able to drive, and if they can be trusted with their lives in a car, why not be trusted to select their own music? Tamara compared the group's lyrics to the Playboy channel or magazine, and wondered why access to 2 Live Crew's music is not limited as well. Marty said that teenagers are still going to get the album if they want it, despite warning labels. Finally, Dewan explained that the warning labels can't stop the sexual things teens think in their minds.

When asked about record censorship, most of them felt that some kind of censor- 37 ship was acceptable for kids ages twelve and under. But they also cited television, movies, and magazines as the places where they usually receive new sexual information, rather than music.

Female rappers like Salt N' Pepa, Queen Latifah, Yo Yo, and MC Lyte have 38 stepped forward to dispel many of the negative images of women with their own lyrical rhetoric and aggressive performance style. Yo Yo, a popular nineteen-year-old female rapper, says that she got into rap to help improve women's self-esteem because a lot of black women don't believe in themselves. She has created an organization for teenage women called the Intelligent Black Women's Coalition (IBWC), which speaks on issues of social concern.

In direct opposition to positive female rappers are the controversial groups, 39 Bytches wit' Problems and Hoes wit' Attitude. According to Lyndah and Michelle of

Bytches wit' Problems, "There's a little bitch in all women, and even some men . . . and we're just the bitches to say it" (October 1991). Lyndah and Michelle's new album, B.Y.T.C.H.E.S., reflects another side of black urban reality. They feel they can say what they want just like men do, which is evident from their songs "Two Minute Brother," "Fuck a Man," and "Is the Pussy still Good." Their definition of a bitch is "a powerful woman in control of her life, going after what she wants and saying what's on her mind" (October 1991).

The female trio, Hoes wit' Attitude, has been called the raunchiest all-girl rap  40 group. With hit songs like "Eat This," "Little Dick," and "Livin' in a Hoe House," they constantly test their motto, "If men can do it we can too." The girls, 2 Jazzy, Baby Girl, and D. Diva, argue that "hoein' is the oldest profession, whether you're sellin' your body or something else. A hoe is a business woman. We're in business, the business of selling records."

When asked about their perceptions of such aggressive female images, the discus-  41 sion group of Upward Bound students again split. Lanietra said, "All women are not like that and the words they use to describe themselves are not necessary." Louis felt rappers don't actually use the lyrics they sing about as a personal thing with another person, they are using the lyrics to warn people about the females and males of today. Tonje added concern that such rap music makes females seem like sex objects that can only be used to satisfy a man's needs.

These youth easily identified specific popular songs which had messages that  42 were positive and negative in relation to sex. The top three songs named as "good for moral thinking" were "Let's Wait Awhile" by Janet Jackson; "Growing Up" by Whodini; and "I Need Love" by L L Cool J. The top three songs listed as "bad for moral thinking about sex" were "Hey, We Want some Pussy" by the 2 Live Crew; "I Want Your Sex" by George Michael; and "Kanday" by L L Cool J.

## The Issue of Violence

Another prominent issue which seems to follow the rap music phenomenon is vio-  43 lence. On December 28, 1991, nine youths were trampled to death at a charity basket-ball game with rap artists at City College in New York. On July 12, 1991, Alejandra Phillips, a supermarket clerk, was shot outside a theater showing of *Boyz N' the Hood*. Cultural rap is often connected with such negative images of the black underclass. Pic-tures of pimps, drug dealers, and gang members riding around with rap music blasting loudly are prevalent in the media. Scholars like Jon Spencer have questioned the link between rap and rape made by Tipper Gore's editorial in *The Washington Post*, "Hate, Rape, and Rap" and the juxtapositioning of the 2 Live Crew's lyrics with the rape of a New York jogger in Central Park. Spencer suggests that when people see the word "rap" they read the word "rape," and they often view "rappists" as rapists.

One of the groups most publicized when exploring violence are NWA (Niggas  44 with Attitude). NWA consists of five L.A. rappers whose controversial lyrics include top-ics like gang banging, drive-by shootings, and police confrontations. MTV refused to air their video, "Straight Outta Compton," because they said it "glorified violence." The ex-leader of the group, Ice Cube, says the group's lyrics deal with reality and vio-lence is their reality. "Our goals are to show the audience the raw reality of life. When they come out the other end they gonna say, 'damn, it's like that for real?' And, we're gonna make money" (Hochman 1989).

Williams (1990) disagrees that rap images and music are representative of the 45 beliefs and ethics of black communities. He says when women are treated like sex slaves and ideas like "materialism is God" are put forth, they are not true visions of black America or black culture, but a slice of the worst of a small element of black culture that is not emblematic of the black community at large.

The positive efforts of black rappers to eliminate violence in their music and 46 neighborhoods have not received as much publicity as the negative. For example, various popular rap stars from the West Coast such as NWA, Hammer, Young MC, and Digital Underground came together to record a single entitled "We're All in the Same Gang." It was a rap song that spoke out against the senseless violence of gangs.

The East Coast's "Stop the Violence" campaign raised more than $300,000 for 47 youth-oriented community programs in New York. More than a dozen rappers, like Ice T, Tone Loc, and King Tee participated in the "Self Destruction" record and video which addressed the need to end black-on-black crime. The powerful lyrics and images of the song brought a new positive black urban consciousness into focus. As the song points out:

> Back in the sixties our brothers and sisters were hanged, how could you gangbang?
> I never ran from the Ku Klux Klan, and I shouldn't have to run from a black man.
> 'Cause that's self-destruction, self-destruction, you're headed for self-destruction.

Kids are forced to learn from the rhythm of life around them. Rap songs often 48 include graphic images of drug dealers. The drug dealer is a very real personality in low-income neighborhoods. When asked to write down three questions they would include on a drug survey, Tamara asked, "Why do they (adults, authorities) allow the pushers to sell drugs on the corner by my school?" She later told me that it was very obvious what happens on that corner, but nobody bothers to do anything about it, so kids come to accept it too.

There is an obvious struggle going on in these kids' lives that links them to the 49 conflict-oriented nature of cultural rap. The violent urban environment which is a prominent theme in rap music is also a prominent reality. One example of that reality came from a worksheet concerning a rap tune called "Wild Wild West" by Kool Moe Dee. In the song, Kool Moe Dee raps about how he and his buddies stop others (including gangs) from coming into their neighborhoods and terrorizing people. He talks about taking control of his environment in a fashion appropriate to the Old West. In response to the song, Mary said she could relate to it because in her neighborhood, people are always getting into other people's personal business. Tim also knew what Kool Moe Dee was talking about because he and his homeboys (friends) were always scuffling (fighting) with somebody for respect. Michael said the song means that kids are growing up too hard in the streets. He added, "My school and neighborhood are a lot like that." Finally, James said he had a friend who got shot at a party "because of the way he looked at a guy and that's just how it is."

On a more positive side, several of the kids have come to understand and change 50 these negatives through their own raps. The Get It Girl Crew, four young ladies who love to rap, wrote the rap below as a testimony of their spirit and hope for the future.

> Tricky B, Lady J, Lady Love and Kiddy B from up above,
> we're the Get It Girl Crew and we're doing the do.
> And, yes when we're on the mic we're talking to you,

homeboys and homegirls, with your jheri curls,
we'll blow you away, knock out those curls.
This is a rap for World Wide peace,
listen to my rhyme while my beat's released.
White and black, we're not the same color,
but in this world we're sisters and brothers.
I'll say this rhyme till my dying day,
I'd rather be dead, dead in my grave.
You talk about me and put my name down,
but when I take revenge I put your face in the ground.
This is Baby Rock in the place to be,
throwing a def rap on the M.I.C.
The Get It Girl Crew, there is none finer,
'cause we're the freshest and we're on fire.
We're the Get It Girl Crew with strength from above
We need peace, unity and love!

## The Issue of Racism

The issue of race in America is not a silent one today. Separate ideologies of black 51
power and white supremacy are prominent and dividing the nation even further as
indicated by an ex-KKK leader, David Duke, running for public office, the travesty of
Rodney King's beating and trial in Los Angeles that ignited riots, and the powerful
slogan of Malcolm X, "By any means necessary," as reemerging popular black ideology.

According to Pareles (1992), rap often sounds like a young black man shouting 52
about how angry he is and how he's going to hurt people. Pareles says, "Rap's internal
troubles reflect the poverty, violence, lack of education, frustration and rage of the
ghetto. . . . Hating rap can be a synonym for hating and fearing young black men who
are also the stars of rap."

Samuels (1991) voices concern about the acceptance of racism in this country 53
through rap. He writes, "Gangster and racist raps foster a voyeurism and tolerance of
racism in which black and white are both complicit, particularly when whites treat
gangster raps as a window into ghetto life."

Until recently, Public Enemy was the rap group who seemed to be in the middle 54
of the racist controversy. In response to the negative environment in the United States
concerning race relations, rapper Chuck D (1990) of Public Enemy makes statements
such as "a black person is better off dealing with a Klansman than a liberal." He goes on
to quote Neely Fuller, Jr.'s, definition of a white liberal: "a white person who speaks
and/or acts to maintain, expand and/or refine the practice of white supremacy (racism)
by very skillfully pretending not to do so." Public Enemy has also called for the reorganization of the Black Panther party, a group considered radical in the 1960s that
advocated violence and racism.

Public Enemy emerged into the headlines as racist when an ex-member, Professor 55
Griff, made several statements that were considered anti-Semitic in a speech. Griff's
comment involved his belief that Jews financed the slave trade and are responsible for
apartheid in South Africa. He went on to ask, "Is it a coincidence that Jews run the jew-
elry business and it's named jew-elry?" (Dougherty, 1990.)

After firing Professor Griff, Chuck D responded to his comments in *Billboard* 56 magazine. "We aren't anti-Jewish. We're pro-black," he said. "We're pro-culture, we're pro-human race. You can't talk about attacking racism and be racist" (Newman, 1989). According to Chuck D, the group is not here to offend anyone, but to fight the system which works against blacks twenty-four hours a day, 365 days a year. He adds, "We're not racists, we're nationalists, people who have pride and want to build a sense of unity amongst our own" (Newman, 1989).

Ice Cube is the second most prominent rapper to be labelled racist because 57 of several controversial songs on his hit album, *Death Certificate*. He calls Koreans "Oriental one-penny motherfuckers" and lambasts members of his old group, NWA, about their Jewish manager. He raps, "Get rid of that Devil, real simple, put a bullet in his temple, 'cause you can't be the nigger for life crew, with a white Jew telling you what to do." In response to the criticism, Ice Cube says people need to pay heed to the frustration as they [black men] demand respect.

Ideology from the Nation of Islam, which is often called racist, is a major part of 58 the controversy. Many rappers are reviving the words of black leaders like Elijah Muhammad and Louis Farrakhan, calling the white society devils and snakes, and advocating a new black solidarity. Several popular rappers are actually emerging from the Nation of Islam calling themselves "The 5 Percenters." These artists base their raps on the Islamic belief that only about 5 percent of the black nation knows that the black man *is* God and it's their duty to teach others.

Finally, racism is sometimes attributed to the Afrocentric voice; the pro-black atti- 59 tude. The controversial KRS-One (Knowledge Reigns Supreme over Nearly Everyone) condemns gang violence, poor educational systems, and drug use, but his attack on the "white system" has been called racially motivated. At fourteen, KRS One was a homeless runaway sleeping on steaming New York City sidewalk grates. At twenty-four, he has become a popular, positive rap star and educator. Queen Latifah is one of the most positive and powerful black female rappers. Her albums are rich in African cultural ideology and images as she dresses in African garb and tells kids that all black men and women are kings and queens. Queen Latifah believes that the only way to fight bigotry is to teach black children their history.

Cultural rap is so direct and angry that it can be frightening to those who don't 60 understand the frustration of these storytellers. For example, the decision not to honor the birthday of Martin Luther King, Jr., as a holiday in Arizona brought forth a rap from NWA with the theme "Gonna find a way to make the state pay" and the video portrayed the violent murders of several Arizona officials. Militant rapper Paris, on his album debut, *The Devil Made Me Do It*, presents a powerful, hard-edged commentary on the murder of Yousuf Hawkins in Bensonhurst called "The Hate that Hate Made." And the logo of Public Enemy shows the black male youth as a hunted animal with the motto "Kill or Be Killed." The image of a black silhouette is chilling within the crosshairs of a gun.

When Upward Bound students were asked to respond to the work-sheet question, 61 "How has growing up black, in your opinion, made a difference in your life?" a theme ran through the responses: the need to struggle or fight. Carlos, for instance, said being black causes him to struggle more for what he wants. He said, "At school, on TV, every-where, other people get the things they want, but not me." Titus and Karon felt they had to fight a lot because of the color of their skin. "Fighting," according to Titus, "not only with people of other races." Damon explained, "Color really doesn't matter, but just because I'm black people expect me to be able to play sports and fight." When

Damon went on to list the things which he felt might hinder him in his future success, his list included skin color, money, and friends.

As a whole, the group split on the issue of whether or not they felt their skin color 62 would affect their future. About half agreed with the statement "In the past, my skin color would have hindered my success, but that is not true today," and the other half disagreed.

When asked if they see Public Enemy, NWA, and other black-conscious rappers 63 as role models and heroes, the group said yes unanimously. As William explained, "They say what's going on in their hearts and that's what needs to be said." John added, "When brothers keep the pain inside they explode and that happens a lot around here." Nichole says she owns all of Public Enemy's tapes and she feels their music is important to help white people understand how black people feel about what's happening in black communities.

## Conclusion

The history of black music is a history of adaptation, rebellion, acculturation, and 64 assimilation. An essential part of black music rests inherently in black experience. As we look closely, we realize that black music has always been a communicative response to the pressures and challenges within black American society.

The cultural rap music experience exists within the realm of specific environmen- 65 tal contexts. For the black urban adolescent, the environment manifests itself through their most popular music choice: rap. As they listen, they construct both shared and personal realities. Rappers rising from this context are empowering storytellers. Their oral wit and unique street style create a purposeful presence for inner-city ideology. Rap music has become the champion of an otherwise ignored and forgotten reality. Through critical spoken song, rappers are forcing cultural realities into the public arena. Rap music, therefore, serves not only as a mirror to this problematic community, but as a catalyst for it, providing legitimacy and hope.

Within popular culture, rap music has increased the sense of awareness outside 66 urban black America and interrupted normal flow of the commercialization process with a large dose of substance. Cultural musics, such as rap, often get caught in a repetitive cycle of acculturation, and are gradually absorbed into the pop mode. But, in opposition to pop-crossover rap, cultural rap has somehow managed to maintain elements which lie outside of social control, and escape the oppressive hegemonic forces.

Fiske's (1989) observations about such resistance and popular culture can be 67 applied to the rap phenomenon. "The resistances of popular culture are not just evasive or semiotic; they do have a social dimension at the micro-level. And at this micro-level, they may well act as a constant erosive force upon the macro, weakening the system from within so that it is more amenable to change at the structural level." This is the power and promise of cultural rap.

The negative climate toward rap has been challenged by various scholars as inac- 68 curate and inadequate. Spencer (1991) believes that the current emergence of rap is a by-product of the "emergency of black." He connects rap ideology to the racial concerns of scholar Manning Marable, saying, "This emergency still involves the dilemma of the racial colorline, but it is complicated by the threat of racial genocide, the obliteration of all black institutions, the political separation of the black elite from the black working class, and the benign decimation of the 'ghetto poor,' who are perceived as nonproduction and therefore dispensable."

Dyson (1991) views rap music as a form of profound musical, cultural, and social creativity. He says, "It expresses the desire of young black people to reclaim their history, reactivate forms of black radicalism, and contest the powers of despair, hopelessness, and genocide that presently besiege the black community. . . . It should be promoted as a worthy form of artistic expression and cultural projection, and as an enabling source of community solidarity." 69

Finally, Stephens (1991) sees rap music as a "crossroad to a new transnational culture." He believes that "by conceptualizing rap as an intercultural communication crossroads located on a racial frontier, we can conceive how rap's non-black constituents use this artform as an interracial bridge, even as many blacks by defining it as 'only black' attempt to use it as a source of power and exclusive identify formation." 70

In considering such a transnational culture, the source of rap's popularity for white youth is then, less difficult to ascertain. It is obvious, however, that the rebellious nature of rap in many way parallels the rebellious nature of original rock and roll. Grossberg (1987), in discussing rock and roll today, says that the practice of critical encapsulation divides the cultural world into Us and Them. "While being a rock and roll fan," he goes on to explain, "sometimes does entail having a visible and self-conscious identity (such as punks, hippies, or mods), it more often does not appear visibly, on the surface of a fan's life, or even as a primary way in which most fans would define themselves." 71

Rap is also seen as an icon of resentment to the white status quo. According to Spencer, as in any situation where an icon such as rap is attacked, there is always the potential that the attention will grant the music even further symbolic potency and, as a result, increase the population of listeners who subscribe to its newly broadened symbolism of protest. 72

As rock music sinks deeper into the mainstream, cultural rap music has risen as a new rebellious youth movement. Self-understanding and practice are important elements in the cultural mirror of rap music style and it has fostered a liberating transcultural understanding. This rap experience becomes an all-encompassing one, which includes the outward projection and acceptance of rebellious identity and beliefs for all who listen. 73

I believe that through rap music, low-income black youth are able to develop empowering values and ideologies, strengthen cultural interaction and establish positive identities. Rap music acts as a distinguishing mechanism as well as an informative cultural force for the mainstream system, similar to other cultural musics such as heavy metal and punk. As an integral part of the urban experience, the rap genre serves as a bridge from favorite songs and artists to personal and social realities. It is easy to see why mainstream society would feel uncomfortable with the sudden popularity of traditionally negative images like dope dealers, pimps, and prostitutes in rap music. Yet these are very real images and messages in the everyday world of the rapper and his original fan: the black urban youth. 74

Rap music offers itself up as a unique and cohesive component of urban black culture and is a positive struggle for black signification within popular culture. While there remain conflicts between negative and positive, right and wrong, good and bad, the rap dynamic is an explicit means of cultural communication fostering a crucial awareness of a reawakening urban reality. 75

# REFERENCES

Adler, Jerry, "The Rap Attitude," *Newsweek*, March 19, 1990, p. 59.

Bernard, James, "Bitches and Money," *The Source*, November 1991, p. 8.

Berry, Venise, "The Complex Relationship between Pop Music and Low-Income Black Adolescents: A Qualitative Approach," Dissertation, The University of Texas at Austin, May 1989.

Chuck D, "Black II Black," *SPIN*, 6, October 1990, pp. 67–68.

Cocks, Jay, "A Nasty Jolt for the Top Pops," *Time*, July 1, 1991, p. 78.

Cone, James, *The Spirituals and the Blues*. New York: Seabury Press, 1972.

Costello, Mark, and David Foster Wallace, *Signifying Rappers: Rap and Race in the Urban Present*, New York: The Ecco Press, 1990.

Dixon, Wheeler, "Urban Black American Music in the Late 1980s: The 'Word' as Cultural Signifier," *The Midwest Quarterly*, 30, Winter 1989, pp. 229–241.

Dougherty, Steve, "Charges of Anti-Semitism Give Public Enemy a Rep That's Tough to Rap Away," *People Weekly*, 33, March 5, 1990, pp. 40–41.

Dyson, Michael, "Performance, Protest and Prophecy in the Culture of Hip Hop," *Black Sacred Music: A Journal of Theomusicology*, 5, Spring 1991, p. 24.

Fiske, John, *Reading the Popular*, Boston: Unwin Hyman, 1989.

Frankel, Martha, "2 Live Doo Doo," *SPIN*, 6, October 1990, p. 62.

Garland, Phyl, *The Sound and Soul: Story of Black Music*, New York: Simon and Schuster, 1971.

Gates, David, "Decoding Rap Music," *Newsweek*, March 19, 1990, pp. 60–63.

Gladwin, Thomas, *Poverty U.S.A.*, Boston: Little, Brown, 1967.

Green, Kim, "Sisters Stompin' in the Tradition," *Young Sisters and Brothers*, November 1991, pp. 51–53.

———, "The Naked Truth," *The Source*, November 1991, pp. 33–36.

Grossberg, Lawrence, "Rock and Roll in Search of an Audience," in *Popular Music and Communication*. Ed. James Lull, Beverly Hills: Sage Publishing, 1987, pp. 175–198.

Gurevitch, Michael, *Culture, Society and the Media*, London: Methuen, 1982.

Haring, Bruce, "Lyric Concerns Escalate," *Billboard*, 101, November 11, 1989, p. 1.

Henderson, Alex, "New Rap Pack: Public Enemy," *Black Beat*, 20, January 1989, p. 44.

———, "2 Live Crew," *Black Beat*, 21, February 1990, pp. 15–16.

———, "LA Rap All Stars: We're All in the Same Gang," *Black Beat*, 21, December 1990, p. 16.

Hochman, Steve, "NWA Cops an Attitude," *Rolling Stone*, 555, June 29, 1989, p. 24.

Hulbary, William, "Race, Deprivation and Adolescent Self-Images," *Social Science Quarterly*, 56, June 1975, pp. 105–114.

Kofsky, Frank, *Black Nationalism and the Revolution in Music*. New York: Pathfinder Press, 1970.

Kot, Greg, "Rap Offers a Soundtrack of Afro-American Experience," *Chicago Sunday Times*, February 16, 1992, Section 13, pp. 5, 24–25.

Leland, John, "Cube on Thin Ice," *Newsweek*, December 2, 1991, pp. 69.

Levine, David, "Good Business, Bad Messages," *American Health*, May 1991, p. 16.

Logan, Andy, "Around City Hall," *The New Yorker*, January 27, 1992, pp. 64–65.

Lyndah and Michelle (Bytches wit' Problems), "A Bitch Is a Badge of Honor for Us," *Rappages*, 1, October 1991, p. 46.

Maultsby, Portia, "Soul Music: Its Sociological and Political Significance in American Popular Culture," *Journal of Popular Culture*, 17, Fall 1983, pp. 51–60.

Miller, Trudy, " '91 Holiday-Week Biz 3.7% Jollier than '90," *Billboard*, February 1, 1992, p. 46.

Mills, David, "The Obscenity Case: Criminalizing Black Culture," *Washington Post*, June 17, 1990, pp. G1, G8–G9.

——, "Five Percent Revolution," *Washington Post*, January 6, 1991, pp. G-1, G-6.

Nelson, Angela, "Theology in the Hip Hop of Public Enemy and Kool Moe Dee," *Black Sacred Music: A Journal of Theomusicology*, 5, Spring 1991, pp. 51–60.

Newman, Melinda, "Public Enemy Ousts Member over Remarks," *Billboard*, 101, July 1, 1989, pp. 1, 87.

"Paralyzed Man Files Suit over Boyz N' the Hood," *Jet*, 18, April 20, 1992, p. 61.

Pareles, Jon, "Fear and Loathing Along Pop's Outlaw Trail," *New York Times*, February 2, 1992, pp. 1, 23.

Perkins, William, "Nation of Islam Ideology in the Rap of Public Enemy," *Black Sacred Music: A Journal of Theomusicology*, 5, Spring, 1991, pp. 41–51.

Peterson-Lewis, Sonja, "A Feminist Analysis of the Defenses of Obscene Rap Lyrics," *Black Sacred Music: A Journal of Theomusicology*, 5, Spring 1991, pp. 68–80.

Poussaint, Alvin, and Carolyn Atkinson, "Black Youth and Motivation," in *Black Self Concept*, Ed. James Banks and Jean Grambs, New York, McGraw-Hill, 1972, pp. 55–69.

Riley, Norman, "Footnotes of a Culture at Risk," *The Crisis*, 93, March 1986, p. 24.

Roberts-Thomas, K., "Say It Loud I'm Proud," *Eight Rock*, 1, Summer 1990, pp. 28–31.

Rogers, Charles, "New Age Rappers with a Conscience," *Black Beat*, 20, April 1989, pp. 41, 75.

Royster, Phillip, "The Rapper as Shaman for a Band of Dancers of the Spirit: 'U Can't Touch This,' " *Black Sacred Music: A Journal of Theomusicology*, 5, Spring 1991, pp. 60–68.

Samuels, David, "The Rap on Rap," *The New Republic*, 205, November 11, 1991, pp. 24–26.

Shusterman, Richard, "The Fine Art of Rap," *New Literary History*, 22, Summer 1991, pp. 613–632.

Singletary, Sharon, "Livin' in a Hoe House?" *Rappages*, 1, October 1991, p. 60.

Spencer, Jon Michael, "The Emergency of Black and the Emergence of Rap: Preface," *Black Sacred Music: A Journal of Theomusicology*, 5, Spring 1991, pp. v–vii.

Standifer, James, "Music Behavior of Blacks in American Society," *Black Music Research Journal*, 1, 1980, pp. 51–62.

Stephens, Gregory, "Rap Music's Double Voiced Discourse: A Crossroads for Interracial Communication," *Journal of Communication Inquiry*, 15, Summer 1991, p. 72.

Stephens, Ronald, "Three Waves of Contemporary Rap Music," in *Black Sacred Music: A Journal of Theomusicology*, 5, Spring 1991, pp. 25–41.

"Top 200 Albums," *Billboard*, January 18, 1992, p. 86.

Walton, Ortiz, *Music Black, White and Blue*, New York: William Morrow and Co., 1972.

Williams, Juan, "The Real Crime: Making Heroes of Hate Mongers," *Washington Post*, June 17, 1990, pp. G-1, G-8.

## READING FOR CONTENT

1. Underline Berry's statement of intent. What will she explore in the essay?
2. Differentiate between pop-cultural and pop-crossover domains.
3. Explain how spirituals, the blues, jazz, soul, and rap are forms of cultural communication.
4. Why is "cultural rap" viewed negatively?
5. How did the Upward Bound students view 2 Live Crew (paragraph 36), record censorship (paragraph 37), and aggressive female images in rap (paragraph 41)?
6. Explain how black rappers have tried to eliminate violence in their music and neighborhoods.
7. Has anyone challenged the negative climate toward rap?

# READING FOR GENRE, ORGANIZATION, AND STYLISTIC FEATURES

1. Comment on Berry's opening paragraphs. Are they effective? Why or why not?
2. What types of evidence (facts, statistics, references to authorities, and so forth) does Berry use to develop and support her argument?
3. Describe the features of the article that help the reader follow Berry's train of thought.

# READING FOR RHETORICAL CONTEXT

1. Describe Berry's rhetorical goal. Do you think she achieves it?
2. Do you think Berry gives sufficient weight to opposing views? Why or why not?
3. Compare Berry's intended audience to Grayck's.

# WRITING ASSIGNMENTS

1. Write an essay in which you agree or disagree with Berry's views on popular culture:

   > Popular culture is made by subordinated peoples in their own interests out of resources that also, contradictorily, serve the economic interests of the dominant. Popular culture is made from within and below, not imposed from without and above as mass cultural theorists would have it. There is always an element of popular culture that lies outside of social control, that escapes or opposes hegemonic forces. (paragraph 19)

2. Write a short evaluative essay about whether or not Berry's assessment of the subject of sex in rap is accurate.
3. Write a brief essay describing the cultural conditions out of which rap emerges.
4. Write a critical response to Berry's claim that rap music is not only the mirror to black urban adolescents, it also provides them with "legitimacy and hope" (paragraph 65).

---

# Studying Heavy Metal: The Bricolage of Culture

## Deena Weinstein

*Deena Weinstein is Professor of Sociology at De Paul University. She is the author of* Bureaucratic Opposition: Challenging Abuses at the Workplace *(1979),* Serious Rock *(1985), and* Postmodern(ized) Simmel *(1993).*

# PREREADING

Review the publishing credentials of Deena Weinstein listed above. What do its range and extent tell you about her professional interests? Is her account of the cultural sociology of

From: *Heavy Metal: A Cultural Sociology* (New York: Lexington Books-Macmillan Inc., 1991), pp. 1–3, 237–49.

heavy metal likely to incorporate a good deal of specialized musical analysis? of partisan advocacy? of negative debunking? What expectations do you have about its genre, style, and rhetorical context?

*Sonorous metal blowing martial sounds;*
*At which the universal host upsent*
*A shout that tore Hell's concave, and beyond*
*Frighted the reign of Chaos and old Night.*

—*Milton*, Paradise Lost[1]

"Heavy metal: pimply, prole, putrid, unchic, unsophisticated, anti-intellectual [1] (but impossibly pretentious), dismal, abysmal, terrible, horrible, and stupid music, barely music at all; death music, dead music, the beaten boogie, the dance of defeat and decay; the *huh?* sound, the *duh* sound, . . . music made *by* slack-jawed, alpaca-haired, bulbous-inseamed imbeciles in jackboots and leather and chrome *for* slack-jawed, alpaca-haired, downy-mustachioed imbeciles in cheap, too-large T-shirts with pictures of comic-book Armageddon ironed on the front."[2] So heavy metal music is described by Robert Duncan, a rock critic.

Baptist minister Jeff R. Steele is known for his lectures on the adverse effects of [2] rock and roll. Certainly, few of his values are the same as those of Duncan or other rock journalists. But he shares a disgust for heavy metal, judging that it "is sick and repulsive and horrible and dangerous."[3]

Dr. Joe Stuessy, a professor of music at the University of Texas at San Antonio, testi- [3] fied about heavy metal before a United States Senate Committee. "Today's heavy metal music is categorically different from previous forms of popular music. It contains the element of hatred, a meanness of spirit. Its principal themes are . . . extreme violence, extreme rebellion, substance abuse, sexual promiscuity, and perversion and Satanism. I know personally of no form of popular music before which has had as one of its central elements the element of hatred."[4] Professor Stuessy served as a consultant to the religiously oriented Parents Music Resource Center (PMRC). His testimony to the Senate Committee also included this observation: "Martin Luther said, 'Music is one of the greatest gifts that God has given us; it is divine and therefore Satan is its enemy. For with its aid, many dire temptations are overcome; the devil does not stay where music is.' We can probably assume that Martin Luther was not familiar with Heavy Metal!"[5]

In the early 1970s a rock critic characterized the quintessential heavy metal band [4] Black Sabbath as having the "sophistication of four Cro-Magnon hunters who've stumbled upon a rock band's equipment."[6]

A journalist in the *Musician* noted that most people see heavy metal as "a musical [5] moron joke, fodder for frustrated teens and dominion of dim-witted devil-worshippers."[7]

A *Rolling Stone* review of a recent heavy metal album claims that the singer's [6] "voice rarely drops below a banshee soprano, and the content of the lyrics is a hoot."[8] Eighteen years earlier a *Los Angeles Times* reviewer described another heavy metal group as having "a complete lack of subtlety, intelligence and originality."[9]

Lester Bangs, the only noted rock critic who had anything favorable to say about [7] heavy metal at its inception, writes some years later: "As its detractors have always claimed, heavy-metal rock is nothing more than a bunch of noise; it is not music, it's distortion—and that is precisely why its adherents find it appealing. Of all contemporary rock, it is the genre most closely identified with violence and aggression, rapine and carnage. Heavy metal orchestrates technological nihilism."[10]

An academic scholar who specializes in the history of the devil concluded that [8] "Overt Satanism faded rapidly after the 1970s, but elements of cultural Satanism continued into the 1980s in 'heavy metal' rock music with its occasional invocation of the Devil's name and considerable respect for the Satanic values of cruelty, drugs, ugliness, depression, self-indulgence, violence, noise and confusion, and joylessness."[11]

In his social history of rock music, Loyd Grossman referred to the genre of heavy [9] metal as "Downer Rock," commenting that its "chief exponents were Black Sabbath, a thuggy, atavistic, and philosophically lugubrious British quartet who became quite successful performing songs about paranoia, World War III, and other whistle-a-happy-tune subjects."[12]

Politicians have also passed judgment on the genre. Senator Albert Gore, during [10] Senate hearings on record labeling, asked a witness "Do you agree that there does seem to be a growing trend, at least in the heavy metal area, that emphasizes explicit violence and sex and sado-masochism and the rest?"[13]

The mass media has joined the chorus of contempt. *Newsweek*, in 1990, ran the [11] following advertisement for its upcoming issue on youth: "Is being a teenager still something to look forward to? Little kids think teenagers are really cool. But how cool is it to come of age in the age of AIDS, crack and heavy metal?"[14]

Heavy metal music is a controversial subject that stimulates visceral rather than [12] intellectual reactions in both its partisans and its detractors. Many people hold that heavy metal music, along with drugs and promiscuous sex, proves that some parts of youth culture have gone beyond acceptable limits. To many of its detractors heavy metal embodies a shameless attack on the central values of Western civilization. But to its fans it is the greatest music ever made.

The severity of the denunciations directed at heavy metal and the disagreement [13] exhibited by its two major opponents, the liberal-left rock critics and the religious right, concerning what to denounce are enough to pique a sociologist's interest. Why should a style of music have occasioned such extravagant rhetoric, not only from members of the lunatic fringe, but also from responsible elements on both sides of the political spectrum? Can a form of music that has attracted millions of fans for more than twenty years be all that dangerous? Does a form of music warrant being placed along with a dread disease (AIDS) and drug abuse? Are the critics of heavy metal really talking about music? If not, what is it that they are talking about?

The broadest purpose of this book is to show how sociology can inform public dis- [14] cussion of heavy metal. This book is not meant to be another voice in the controversy, but an effort to step back and reveal the elusive subject that is at the center of the controversy. In light of public debates over the advisability of censoring heavy metal music, this study is meant to show how heavy metal music is made, used, and transmitted by social groups. Only an objective inquiry can permit rational judgment about the merits of the proposals to limit the freedom of heavy metal's artists, audiences, and media.

The focus here is on the social dimension of heavy metal, not on the individual [15] bands and personalities that are the usual concerns of almost everyone who writes about the genre. You do not have to be a fan or a detractor of heavy metal to read this book and gain an understanding of how this genre of popular culture is put together. If you have little or no acquaintance with the music, you can listen to some of the "suggested hearings" I list in Appendix A. If you are familiar with heavy metal, you will find that the specific examples that appear in the discussion reinforce and deepen the general analysis. You will also be able to think of other examples that substantiate or perhaps challenge the claims made in the text.

*"Am I Evil?"*
*— Metallica*

Perhaps Newton's Second Law of Motion, which states that for every action there is 16 an equal and opposite reaction, also applies to some sociocultural phenomena. It certainly seems to hold for heavy metal. The intense loyalty and devotion of its fans is matched by the contempt and loathing for the genre expressed by those who presume to pass judgment on cultural phenomena. Indeed, it is hard to think of other human phenomena, outside child torture and cannibalism, that evoke such intense abhorrence. Heavy metal polarizes people. Those who are aware of it either love it or hate it.

The cultured and no-so-cultured despisers of heavy metal form an unfamiliar, if 17 not unholy, alliance. Heavy metal is one of the few sociocultural phenomena in the United States that evokes the same response from those normally bitter opponents, the politically correct progressive critics and the religious and populist right wing. What is so special about heavy metal that has made it one of the few things that unite Left and Right in a common cause?

The maligners of metal come to their positions for superficially different reasons. 18 To summarize what will be presented in detail below, the progressives repudiate heavy metal because it substitutes hedonic ecstasy for the political commitment and social concern that they would like to see in popular music. They find it difficult to criticize heavy metal on any intellectual basis because their system of criticism is framed by a dichotomy between serious and politically committed rock music and mass popular music, which takes the edge off life and pacifies the subjects of a disciplinary/ consumer society. Heavy metal, as has been shown in the preceding chapters, is not commercial pop, but neither is it politically progressive. Its spirit is that of Dionysian rebellion that challenges static order in the name of the freedom to exercise vital power. The progressive critics have no place in their ideology for something like metal, which is not pop, but which also does not meet their criteria for good music.[15] Thus, they try to reduce metal to nonsense, making no effort to grasp it as a cultural form, and dismissing it as a revolt against form, "noise," and "drivel."[16]

The cultural conservatives, in contrast, do not play on the binary opposition of 19 hedonism-commitment, but instead focus on what they see as the anti-Christian symbolism of metal. For them, heavy metal, with its themes of evil and use of symbols associated with Christian religiosity, is a systematic temptation whose aim is to lead youth into the paths of sin. Whereas for the progressives metal is a competitor for the rebellious energies of youth, for the conservatives it is a competitor for their souls. The root of the complaint, however, is the same. In metal Dionysian rebellion often takes the form of transvaluing—changing the value signs—of the objects of the Judeo-Christian tradition. Heavy metal stresses the power of the world as a positive dynamism, whereas the religious right condemns "the world," along with "the flesh and the devil." When heavy metal appropriates Christian symbolism, it absorbs it into its Dionysian sensibility, giving "the world, the flesh, and the devil" new meaning as rebellious play, as in AC/DC's thought that "Hell Ain't a Bad Place to Be." Metal's reinterpretation of these symbols is lost on the cultural conservatives, who stick to their own "literal" reading of those symbols. Their dichotomy is between faith and sin. Lacking any conception of a positive affirmation of rebellious vitality, they must judge heavy metal to be sinful and a direct competitor to them.

Heavy metal, then, is the common enemy because it is the proud pariah. It sins 20 by excess of ecstasy and of play with symbols that some segments of the society hold sacred. The left is repelled by its focus on present pleasure rather than the need for future change, and the right is offended by its substitution of symbolic play for belief in their code. Of course, neither of metal's adversaries appreciates metal for what it is, since neither values Dionysian experience. Metal's ecstasy is seen as mindless and gross sensation by the progressives. Its play is viewed as a malign will to corrupt by the conservatives. Thus, the two opponents of metal distort it in their own ways, according to how they can fit it into the categories of their ideologies. Their policy stances toward the "social problem" of heavy metal reflect their ideological constructions of heavy metal rather than what heavy metal is to its fans, the artists who create it, its mediators, or an ethnographer. The public criticism of metal is as clear a case as can be presented of the tendency of the discussion of public policy to mischaracterize its objects through the projection of ideological constructions.

## Notes

1. John Milton, *"Paradise Lost" and Other Poems*, p. 52, lines 540–43.
2. Robert Duncan, *The Noise*, 36–37.
3. Cited in Linda Martin and Kerry Segrave, *Anti-Rock*, 233.
4. Testimony of Dr. Joe Stuessy, U.S. Congress, *Record Labeling (Senate Hearing 99–529)*, 117.
5. Ibid., 119.
6. Paul Battiste (*Creem*; 1972), cited in Philip Bashe, *Heavy Metal Thunder*, 24.
7. J. D. Considine, "Purity and Power," 46.
8. David Fricke, "The Year in Records," 218.
9. Cited by Mike Clifford, *The Harmony Illustrated Encyclopedia of Rock*, 57.
10. Lester Bangs, "Heavy Metal," 332.
11. Jeffrey Burton Russell, *Mephistopheles*, 256.
12. Loyd Grossman, *Social History of Rock Music*, 93–94.
13. His question was directed, incongruously, to John Denver; U.S. Congress, *Record Labeling (Senate Hearing 99–529)*, 70.
14. Advertisement for *Newsweek* special issue on youth, *Newsweek*, 14 May 1990, 71.
15. There are alternative theories for why heavy metal is so despised by the rock critics. In an analysis of the genre for *Musician*, Charles Young suggests that the critics heap scorn on the music in order to show their supposed superiority to its audience ("Heavy Metal," 43).
16. Cited in Joseph A. Kotarba, "Adolescent Use of Heavy Metal Rock Music as a Resource for Meaning," 9.

## Works Cited

Bangs, Lester. "Heavy Metal." In *The Rolling Stone Illustrated History of Rock and Roll*, edited by Jim Miller, 332–35. New York: Rolling Stone Press/Random House, 1976.

Bashe, Philip. *Heavy Metal Thunder: The Music, Its History, Its Heroes*. Garden City, N.Y.: Dolphin, 1985.

Clifford, Mike. *The Harmony Illustrated Encyclopedia of Rock*. New York: Salamander/ Harmony/ Crown, 1983.

Considine, J. D. "Purity and Power." *Musician*, September 1984, 46–50.

Duncan, Robert. *The Noise: Notes from a Rock 'n' Roll Era*. New York: Ticknor and Fields, 1984.

Fricke, David. "The Year in Records." *Rolling Stone*, 13–27 December 1990, 201–26.

Grossman, Loyd. *A Social History of Rock Music: From the Greasers to Glitter Rock*. New York: David McKay, 1976.

Kotarba, Joseph A. "Adolescent Use of Heavy Metal Rock Music as a Resource for Meaning." Paper presented at the annual meeting of the American Sociological Association, Washington, D.C., August 1990.

Martin, Linda, and Kerry Segrave. *Anti-Rock: The Opposition to Rock 'n' Roll*. Cambridge, Mass.: DaCapo Press, 2000.

Milton, John. *Paradise Lost and Other Poems*. New York: New American Library, 1981.

Russell, Jeffrey Burton. *Mephistopheles: The Devil in the Modern World*. Ithaca, N.Y.: Cornell University Press, 1984.

U.S. Congress. Senate. *Record Labeling (Senate Hearing 99–529): Hearing before the Committee of Commerce, Science, and Transportation*. United States Senate, Ninety-Ninth Congress, First Session on Contents of Music and the Lyrics of Records. Washington, D.C.: U.S. Government Printing Office, 1985.

Young, Charles M. "Heavy Metal: In Defense of Dirtbags and Worthless Puds." *Musician*, September 1984, 41–44.

## READING FOR CONTENT

1. Summarize in your own words the reasons for opposing heavy metal articulated by critics on both the liberal left and the religious right in paragraphs 18–19.

2. Summarize in your own words the conclusions in paragraph 20.

## READING FOR GENRE, ORGANIZATION, AND STYLISTIC FEATURES

1. List the diverse opponents of heavy metal cited in paragraphs 1–10. What range of the political spectrum do they represent? Why does the author include criticism from the liberal left as well as from the religious right?

2. Paraphrase in your own words the questions that the author asks in paragraph 13. How might her attention to heavy metal's opponents from both the liberal-left and the religious right organize her efforts to explain the form?

3. How might the author's style suggest that her account of opposition to heavy metal is written from a neutral if not pro-metal point of view? To what extent does her account suggest that metal-bashing represents an age-old problem of sociological group-formation?

## READING FOR RHETORICAL CONTEXT

1. Summarize in your own words the author's purposes announced in paragraphs 14–15. What audience does she anticipate for her writing?

2. Review your list of the diverse opponents cited in paragraphs 1–10. Do you think any of them might be likely to read Weinstein's sociological study? Why or why not?

## WRITING ASSIGNMENTS

1. Use the Internet to retrieve the lyrics of a heavy metal song and then write a literary analysis of it. Call particular attention to whether or not the nihilist morality alleged by metal's critics dominates the song. If you wish, draw upon more than one song to argue your thesis.

2. Write a 1,000-word critical supplement to Weinstein's account of heavy metal's cultural sociology by extending her argument and approach to more recent forms of popular music such as punk rock or gangsta rap. Use your knowledge of these forms and their evolution to develop your argument.

■ ■ ■ ■ ■ ■ ■ ■ ■ ■ ■ ■

# Music, Philosophy, and Generation Y

## Martha Bayles

*Martha Bayles has taught in public schools in Boston and Philadelphia and at Claremont College. She has written critical columns on music, television, and the arts for the* Wall Street Journal *and the* Weekly Standard. *She is the author of* Hole in Our Soul: The Loss of Beauty and Meaning in American Popular Music *(1994) and* Off-White: A Personal Memoir about Race *(2006).*

## PREREADING

Return to Simon Frith's "Toward an Aesthetic of Popular Music." on pages 542–56. From that article, reread paragraphs 18–29 about the public outcry against the emotional turbulence of 1950s rock music. Can you imagine anyone criticizing rock on these grounds today? Does this outcry echo opposition to newer forms of music such as heavy metal? Freewrite your response.

"Is there such thing as an evil sound?"                                      1

That question, one of the most interesting I've been asked, was posed by a young    2
musician named Kevin Max Smith at a lecture I gave in Nashville to a group of rock
musicians who were also evangelical Christians. Smith was with a band called dc Talk,
which started out as a rap group then switched to a mixture of styles. But many genres
were represented in the room, including heavy metal, which is usually not associated
with Christianity.

Smith's question cut to the heart of the ancient view of music, older than Chris-    3
tianity, that I call didactic. The ancients ranked musical sounds in a hierarchy understood to be causally related to the hierarchy of human virtues and vices, in the soul and
in the polity. Says Socrates in Plato's *Republic*: "Never are the ways of music moved

without the greatest political laws being moved." Confucius, incidentally, said something similar: "If you would know whether a people are well governed, and if its laws are good or bad, examine the music it practices."

I respect this didactic view because it respects the powers of music. These powers  4
range widely. At one end of the spectrum, music has the power to soothe, to calm, to "sing the savageness out of a bear," in Shakespeare's words. At the other end, music can also drum the savageness back into the bear. Flaubert had this in mind when he wrote sarcastically, "Music makes a people's disposition more gentle: for example 'The Marseillaise.'"

This is why the ancients sought to control the effects of music. Allan Bloom sum-  5
marizes Socrates' teaching with his customary eloquence. "The taming or domestication of the soul's raw passions," he writes, must not mean "suppressing or excising them, which would deprive the soul of its energy" but rather "forming and informing them." The trouble comes when we try to apply this wise abstraction to actual music. To do so is to shoot at a moving target, because Western music has long been violating Plato's specific prescriptions.

For example, Plato taught that too much music confuses the mind and distracts  6
from logos. The Hebrew prophets took the same view, which is why early Christians spurned the rich instrumental homophony of pagan music in favor of a spare vocal monophony, a single melodic line song without accompaniment. But during the late Middle Ages, the monks in Notre Dame began to interpolate new sections of chant containing more than one melodic line. This switch to polyphony, or harmonic counterpoint, gave birth to the glories of Western music.

To put my point in a nutshell: we may believe that Bach and Mozart are good for  7
the soul and good for the polity, but we should also keep in mind that they violate quite promiscuously the specific rules set down by Plato.

Where does that leave us? Disinclined, probably, to issue any specific decrees about  8
musical sounds. To the question posed above, "Is there such a thing as an evil sound?" my initial response is "no." No sound by itself is evil. Sounds that are harsh, ugly, or disturbing can be used in aesthetically and morally admirable ways. And the sweetest, most pleasing sounds can be put to evil uses. So it's a matter of how the sound is employed.

If we look at contemporary music in Socratic terms, and ask how well it is form-  9
ing and informing the raw passions of individual souls and of the polity, what do we see?

To judge by the opinion of many experts, we see a stratified musical landscape in  10
which some people listen to "serious" music, others to "popular."

For some critics of our democratic culture (Allan Bloom again), the mere exis-  11
tence of vulgar music exerts a fatal and irreversible downward pressure on the soul, the culture, and the polity. It's a persuasive argument, if all we look at is Mozart on the one hand, and the grossest and most offensive popular music on the other.

Which is pretty much what Bloom did in his famous chapter on music in *The*  12
*Closing of the American Mind*. He focused on the stuff that Tipper Gore went after in those famous Senate hearings of the mid-'80s: rapaciously violent heavy metal, hardcore and punk bands out to shock what was left of the bourgeoisie; Madonna in her underwear phase; Prince at his most priapic.

I, too, have criticized this vulgarity. But I also contend that the vilest strain of pop-  13
ular music, and of popular culture in general, arises less from ordinary vulgarity than from cultivated perversity.

American popular music has not always been vile. On the contrary, certain strains  14
of it, notably popular song and jazz, have achieved worldwide distinction in a century

when so-called serious music embraced rationalism, mathematics, noise, and games of chance to the point of cutting itself off from the educated as well as the popular audience.

If you look closely, you see that the most troubling impulses in popular music 15 came from the artistic elite. The process began in the late 1960s, when the countercul-ture went sour, and rock'n'roll began to attract the sort of people who were less inter-ested in music than in using such a popular medium for their own culturally radical purposes.

Prior to that, rock'n'roll was vulgar, but not culturally radical. It was inferior in some 16 ways to the musical culture that had produced Louis Armstrong, Benny Goodman, and Frank Sinatra. But rock also shared many positive traits with the older musical culture, such as a stance of old-fashioned courtesy toward the audience. That persisted into the mid-1960s in soul music, Motown, and the early Beatles.

Then came the transformation. Concerning Mick Jagger, Bloom's instincts are 17 right on target. Jagger's stage persona does express a kind of pop-Nietzschean erotic lib-erationism. The Rolling Stones relished the blues, especially the rough-edged Chicago blues. But coming from the hothouse atmosphere of British art colleges, they also turned the blues into a vehicle for shocking the bourgeoisie.

More drastic was the transformation wrought by groups marginal at the time but 18 since lionized. Inspired by cutting-edge visual artists and avant-garde theater, Frank Zappa, Iggy Pop, Alice Cooper, and the New York Dolls put on stage shows that resem-bled "happenings" more than concerts. In turn, they helped to inspire punk, the 1970s phenomenon that was, and is, a form of performance art, not music. The pure legacy of punk, which pervades gangsta rap as well as much alternative rock, is a cult of in-your-face attitude and (in punk, at least) musical incompetence.

Does this stuff have an unhealthy effect on our souls and our polity? It's hard to 19 argue otherwise. There may be no such thing as an evil sound, but we live in a culture very skilled at using all sorts of sounds to create evil effects.

The film soundtrack is a good example. Consider how directors like Quentin 20 Tarantino combine cheerful upbeat music with grisly violence. In *Pulp Fiction* he used Al Green, Kool & the Gang, surf music, Dusty Springfield, and the Statler Brothers to accompany the happy hit men's splattering of blood and guts over everything—a gimmick that creates instant irony, a feeling of detachment from mayhem that is ever so 20th-century.

Quite different is the soundtrack for *Natural Born Killers*. For that film about two 21 young slackers who go around blowing people's heads off, director Oliver Stone asked the industrial rock band Nine Inch Nails to create an accompaniment that, in my judg-ment, comes close to being evil. Younger readers will recognize it as neck-breaking mosh pit noise. Older readers will imagine a Stealth Bomber forcing its attentions on a threshing machine.

But even so, I can think of good uses for this sound. Scenes of black despair and 22 chaotic passion have their place in great art. Remember Oedipus gouging out his eyes? Or Medea butchering her children? Nine Inch Nails could handle those moments.

Thus I am not issuing any decrees. I do not wish to live in a didactic culture, one 23 that believes and acts on the notion of a one-to-one correspondence between auditory stimuli and characterological effects. That has been tried, and somehow the guys in charge are never philosopher kings.

The worst stuff is still out there, attracting the vulnerable and being defended by 24 pundits and academics who ought to know better. But for people coming of age today—Generation Y, if you will—there is also incredible ferment, as technology brings all kinds of music to all kinds of ears.

This situation of having every variety of music at our fingertips is part of what is 25 meant by postmodernism. The received wisdom, on the right as well as the left, is that this puts everything on the same debased level. I disagree. I think it gives the audience a chance to compare the good with the better, the bad with the worse.

To say this is, I realize, to express far more optimism about democratic culture 26 than the ancients might regard as wise. But consider the positive aspects of the case. Taking the long view of American culture, music included, what do we see?

We see a systematic rejection of snobbery, because snobbery says that to be 27 knowledgeable and cultivated you must be to the manor born, and most of us are not. But at the same time we see a lot of people who acquire knowledge and cultivation by hook or by crook—and then play it down—because they know that the best way to learn about others is to surprise them by not fulfilling their expectations.

We see the widespread belief, against expert opinion, that there do exist fairly 28 objective standards of excellence in the arts: a stubborn tendency to stand in awe of Rembrandt, and to tell the kids that if they don't practice, they won't be able to play like Itzhak Perlman or Artie Shaw.

Finally, we see the conviction that there is such a thing as morality and decency 29 in the arts, and that to be shocked and offended by their blatant violation doesn't make someone a prude or a philistine.

Every kind of audience has its vices. Personally, I find the vices of the democratic 30 audience preferable to those of the elite. Tocqueville, who wrote about the arts in America but sadly failed to mention music, observed that "In democracies, the springs of poetry are fine but few." I'm inclined to turn that around and say that while the springs of great music in America have been few, they have also been very fine.

## READING FOR CONTENT

1. In the context of the philosophy summarized in paragraph 7, how does Bayles answer her opening question in paragraph 8?

2. In paragraph 25, how does Bayles use her definition of "postmodernism" to mount both a criticism and a defense of rock music? How does her defense use the claim of paragraph 8 that "it's a matter of how the sound is employed"?

## READING FOR GENRE, ORGANIZATION, AND STYLISTIC FEATURES

1. The genre of critical commentary tries to articulate careful distinctions in terminology that defines the topic. Paraphrase in your own words and elaborate upon the distinction that Bayles makes in paragraph 16 when she writes, "rock 'n' roll was vulgar, but not culturally radical."

2. Bayles organizes her argument as a response to an imagined conversation with such writers on music as Plato and Allan Bloom, referred to in paragraphs 3, 5, 6, 7, 11, and 12. Summarize her specific responses to these writers.

3. In paragraph 13, Bayles coins the phrase "cultivated perversity" as a stylistic criticism of rock. What does she mean by this phrase?

## READING FOR RHETORICAL CONTEXT

1. In paragraphs 6, 7, 16, 17, 18, 20, and 21, Bayles refers to a wide range of music and musical styles from medieval chant through Bach and Mozart, to Frank Sinatra and Nine Inch Nails. Underline such references and speculate about what they presume about the reader's knowledge of such diverse styles and forms.

2. Summarize Bayles's "long view of American culture" in paragraphs 27–29. What does this view imply about the standard of values that she uses to criticize rock music?

## WRITING ASSIGNMENTS

1. Write a 750-word critical response to Bayles's article in which you sharpen her criticism of rock by elaborating upon its negative features. Extend the "conversation" that her article initiates by referring to still other detractors of the music and musicians in the form.

2. Write a 750-word critical response to Bayles's article in which you sharpen her defense of rock by elaborating upon its positive features. Extend the "conversation" that her article initiates by referring to other champions of the music and musicians in the form.

## SYNTHESIS WRITING ASSIGNMENTS

1. Drawing on selections by Frith, Gracyk, and Berry, write a five-page essay in which you synthesize the three critics' ideas about the value of rock music. Address your essay to an audience of students who have read the texts.

2. Drawing on selections by Frith and Berry, write a five-page essay in which you demonstrate how rap music serves social functions for urban African-American youth. Address your essay to an audience of students who have not read the texts.

3. Write a five-page essay explaining how Bayles might qualify Paglia's, Gracyk's, and Berry's views on rock music. Address your essay to an audience of students who have not read the texts.

4. Drawing on selections by Paglia, Gracyk, and Berry, either challenge or support Frith's argument about the social functions of music. Address your essay to an audience of students who have read the texts.

5. Draw upon selections by Frith, Paglia, Gracyk, and Berry to write a critical response to the selection by Weinstein.

6. Gracyk claims that Paglia, like Nietzsche, "does not regard the masses as capable of appreciating true art when they encounter it" (paragraph 4). Would the same criticism apply to Frith, Berry, and Weinstein? Write an essay in response. Address your essay to an audience of students who have read the texts.

7. Drawing on upon selections by Berry, Weinstein, and Bayles, write a five-page essay on whether their arguments apply to more recent forms such as metal, rap, and gangsta music. Are such forms of music "authentic" expression, or are they created only for the mainstream and compromised for profit?

# Stories of Ethnic Difference

Within the humanities, the various disciplines of literary criticism, theater arts, history of art, and musicology attempt to assess the cultural products of human civilization. Courses in literature, drama, art, and music train students to analyze, interpret, and evaluate meaningful "texts." We use the word "text" in a broad sense to refer to any composition, whether of words, as in poetry, drama, and prose fiction or nonfiction; of color, line, and texture, as in painting, sculpture, and architecture; or of sound and movement, as in music and dance, film, and television. The questions one might ask about one sort of text resemble those one might ask about other sorts. They concern the selection and arrangement of appropriate materials; the tone, attitude, and point of view that govern their selection and arrangement; similarities to and comparisons and contrasts with other texts; and further questions about relationships between texts and the sociocultural contexts of their production and reception.

One aim of literary criticism, art history, and music theory is to make the meaning of such "texts" more accessible to us. This aim is especially visible when the text displays a social, historical, or cultural otherness whose assumptions differ from ours. Shakespeare's plays, for example, profit from a critical and historical analysis that illuminates differences between early modern attitudes and our own. Sometimes the technical jargon of an analysis may have the opposite effect: It may make the object of study appear more impenetrable than ever. A musicological study of flats and sharps, harmonies and counterpoints, arpeggios and staccatos in one of Mozart's string quarters may distance us entirely from the sound of the music. If we reflect upon its purpose, however, we may find that it evokes complexity only because the process of understanding any worthwhile text is correspondingly complex. It does not seek to replace an experience of the work of art. It seeks, rather, to explore the ramifications of that experience as it connects with social, historical, moral, political, philosophical, ideological, psychological, aesthetic, and other experiences.

The outcome of good criticism shows us that what we take for granted in a text may be not so simple after all.

If academic approaches to expressive forms demonstrate the otherness, difference, and complexity of those forms, many of the texts that they study deal with otherness, difference, and complexity in a primary way. Fiction, nonfiction, poetry, drama, painting, sculpture, photography, film, television, song, dance, and instrumental music all provide us with glimpses into other worlds. They can represent customs, conventions, ways of life, and human experiences that different audiences might not otherwise have. Or, if they represent a world accessible to their audience, they do so best when they afford a new perspective on that world.

The selections in this chapter deal with otherness, difference, and accessibility by focusing on a range of texts that reflect a heterogeneous world culture. The theme that draws them together is the diversity of ethnic backgrounds that compose ethnic identity in the Western hemisphere. The first selection, "A Different Mirror," is an historical meditation by Ronald Takaki on patterns of Japanese immigration to America. Takaki, a professional historian, uses techniques of personal narrative, dramatic story-telling, factual reporting, and broad historical perspective to compare distinctive qualities of immigrant groups to the United States at the end of the nineteenth century.

The remaining selections offer contemporary short stories that depict the experiences of individuals who are reminded of their ethnic identities in particularly striking ways. "Jasmine" by Bharati Mukherjee recounts the assimilation of an illegal immigrant from the West Indies into the academic community of Ann Arbor, Michigan. Its style abounds in unexpected and good-natured humor as its title character encounters a lifestyle that she had never imagined in her native Trinidad. "Snapshots" by Helena Maria Viramontes presents a poignant account of a middle-aged woman's struggle to adjust to a life without her husband after their divorce and without her daughter after she has left home as an adult. The woman's origins in an extended, warm, embracing Mexican family contrast with her present loneliness long after her immigration to the United States. "Between the Pool and the Gardenias" by Edwige Danticat narrates the harrowing tragedy of a woman's life in the poverty and political factionalism of Haiti. Childless and deserted by her husband, she represents the plight of a cast-away in the poorest nation in the Western hemisphere.

The remaining stories depict the variety of multicultural, multiethnic America with funny, ironic, and hauntingly reflective insight. "Birthmates" by Gish Jen pits a middle-aged American-born man of Chinese descent against a kind-spirited African-American woman who reaches out to him and various professional acquaintances of different ethnic descent who compete against him. The man's belated recognition of the fine line between altruism and egotism heightens his melancholy assessment of his own strengths and weaknesses. Finally, "Bohemians" by George Saunders presents a boy's unexpected awakening to the diversity of immigrant experience in his community as he encounters the differences between two obscurely foreign-born neighbors. Their outlandish departures from conventional behavior seem both strange and yet predictable in a nation where we all share immigrant backgrounds.

# A Different Mirror

## *Ronald Takaki*

*Ronald Takaki is a professor and Chair of the Department of Ethnic Studies at the University of California, Berkeley. He is the author of* Iron Cages: Race and Culture in Nineteenth-Century America (1979), Strangers from a Different Shore: A History of Asian Americans (1989), A Different Mirror (1993), From Different Shores: Perspectives on Race and Ethnicity in America, *and other historical studies.*

## PREREADING

In paragraph 5 of the following essay, Takaki cites an article in *Time* magazine that reports that "white Americans will become a minority group" within the next century. How might our knowledge of past history illuminate this future? What kinds of attention should historians pay to accounts about the multicultural foundation, growth, and development of the United States? How might personal narratives contribute to this history? Freewrite some responses to these questions.

## A Different Mirror

I had flown from San Francisco to Norfolk and was riding in a taxi to my hotel to attend   1
a conference on multiculturalism. Hundreds of educators from across the country were meeting to discuss the need for greater cultural diversity in the curriculum. My driver and I chatted about the weather and the tourists. The sky was cloudy, and Virginia Beach was twenty minutes away. The rearview mirror reflected a white man in his forties. "How long have you been in this country?" he asked. "All my life," I replied, wincing. "I was born in the United States." With a strong southern drawl, he remarked: "I was wondering because your English is excellent!" Then, as I had many times before, I explained: "My grandfather came here from Japan in the 1880s. My family has been here, in America, for over a hundred years." He glanced at me in the mirror. Somehow I did not look "American" to him; my eyes and complexion looked foreign.

Suddenly, we both became uncomfortably conscious of a racial divide separating   2
us. An awkward silence turned my gaze from the mirror to the passing landscape, the shore where the English and the Powhatan Indians first encountered each other. Our highway was on land that Sir Walter Raleigh had renamed "Virginia" in honor of Elizabeth I, the Virgin Queen. In the English cultural appropriation of America, the indigenous peoples themselves would become outsiders in their native land. Here, at the eastern edge of the continent, I mused, was the site of the beginning of multicultural America. Jamestown, the English settlement founded in 1607, was nearby: the first twenty Africans were brought here a year before the Pilgrims arrived at Plymouth Rock.

Several hundred miles offshore was Bermuda, the "Bermoothes" where William Shakespeare's Prospero had landed and met the native Caliban in *The Tempest*. Earlier, another voyager had made an Atlantic crossing and unexpectedly bumped into some islands to the south. Thinking he had reached Asia, Christopher Columbus mistakenly identified one of the islands as "Cipango" (Japan). In the wake of the admiral, many peoples would come to America from different shores, not only from Europe but also Africa and Asia. One of them would be my grandfather. My mental wandering across terrain and time ended abruptly as we arrived at my destination. I said goodbye to my driver and went into the hotel, carrying a vivid reminder of why I was attending this conference.

Questions like the one my taxi driver asked me are always jarring, but I can    3 understand why he could not see me as American. He had a narrow but widely shared sense of the past—a history that has viewed American as European in ancestry. "Race," Toni Morrison explained, has functioned as a "metaphor" necessary to the "construction of Americanness": in the creation of our national identity, "American" has been defined as "white."[1]

But America has been racially diverse since our very beginning on the Virginia    4 shore, and this reality is increasingly becoming visible and ubiquitous. Currently, one-third of the American people do not trace their origins to Europe; in California, minorities are fast becoming a majority. They already predominate in major cities across the country—New York, Chicago, Atlanta, Detroit, Philadelphia, San Francisco, and Los Angeles.

This emerging demographic diversity has raised fundamental questions about    5 America's identity and culture. In 1990, *Time* published a cover story on "America's Changing Colors." "Someday soon," the magazine announced, "white Americans will become a minority group." How soon? By 2056, most Americans will trace their descent to "Africa, Asia, the Hispanic world, the Pacific Islands, Arabia—almost anywhere but white Europe." This dramatic change in our nation's ethnic composition is altering the way we think about ourselves. "The deeper significance of America's becoming a majority nonwhite society is what it means to the national psyche, to individuals' sense of themselves and their nation—their idea of what it is to be American."[2]

. . . Our diversity was tied to America's most serious crisis: the Civil War was    6 fought over a racial issue—slavery. In his "First Inaugural Address," presented on March 4, 1861, President Abraham Lincoln declared: "One section of our country believes slavery is *right* and ought to be extended, while the other believes it is *wrong* and ought not to be extended." Southern secession, he argued, would be anarchy. Lincoln sternly warned the South that he had a solemn oath to defend and preserve the Union. Americans were one people, he explained, bound together by "the mystic chords of memory, stretching from every battlefield and patriot grave to every living heart and hearthstone all over this broad land." The struggle and sacrifices of the War for Independence had enabled Americans to create a new nation out of thirteen separate colonies. But Lincoln's appeal for unity fell on deaf ears in the South. And the war came. Two and a half years later, at Gettysburg, President Lincoln declared that "brave men" had fought and "consecrated" the ground of this battlefield in order to preserve the Union. Among the brave were black men. Shortly after this bloody battle, Lincoln acknowledged the military contributions of blacks. "There will be some black men," he wrote in a letter to an old friend, James C. Conkling, "who can remember that with silent tongue, and clenched teeth, and steady eye, and well-poised bayonet, they have helped mankind on to this great consummation. . . ." Indeed, 186,000 blacks served in the Union Army, and one-third of them were listed as missing or dead. Black men in blue, Frederick Douglass pointed out, were "on the battlefield mingling their blood with that of white men in one common effort to save the country." Now the mystic chords of memory stretched across the new battlefields of the Civil War, and black soldiers were buried in "patriot graves." They, too, had given their lives to ensure that the "government of the people, by the people, for the people shall not perish from the earth."[3]

Like these black soldiers, the people in our study have been actors in history, not merely victims of discrimination and exploitation. They are entitled to be viewed as subjects — as men and women with minds, wills, and voices.   7

> In the telling and retelling of their stories,
> They create communities of memory.

They also re-vision history. "It is very natural that the history written by the victim," said a Mexican in 1874, "does not altogether chime with the story of the victor." Sometimes they are hesitant to speak, thinking they are only "little people." "I don't know why anybody wants to hear my history," an Irish maid said apologetically in 1900. "Nothing ever happened to me worth the tellin'."[4]

But their stories are worthy. Through their stories, the people who have lived America's history can help all of us, including my taxi driver, understand that Americans originated from many shores, and that all of us are entitled to dignity. "I hope this survey do a lot of good for Chinese people," an immigrant told an interviewer from Stanford University in the 1920s. "Make American people realize that Chinese people are humans. I think very few American people really know anything about Chinese." But the remembering is also for the sake of the children. "This story is dedicated to the descendants of Lazar and Goldie Glauberman," Jewish immigrant Minnie Miller wrote in her autobiography. "My history is bound up in their history and the generations that follow should know where they came from to know better who they are." Similarly, Tomo Shoji, an elderly Nisei woman, urged Asian Americans to learn more about their roots: "We got such good, fantastic stories to tell. All our stories are different." Seeking to know how they fit into America, many young people have become listeners; they are eager to learn about the hardships and humiliations experienced by their parents and grandparents. They want to hear their stories, unwilling to remain ignorant or ashamed of their identity and past.[5]   8

The telling of stories liberates. By writing about the people on Mango Street, Sandra Cisneros explained, "the ghost does not ache so much." The place no longer holds her with "both arms. She sets me free." Indeed, stories may not be as innocent or simple as they seem to be. Native-American novelist Leslie Marmon Silko cautioned:   9

> I will tell you something about stories . . .
> They aren't just entertainment.
> Don't be fooled.

Indeed, the accounts given by the people in this study vibrantly recreate moments, capturing the complexities of human emotions and thoughts. They also provide the authenticity of experience. After she escaped from slavery, Harriet Jacobs wrote in her autobiography: "[My purpose] is not to tell you what I have heard but what I have seen—and what I have suffered." In their sharing of memory, the people in this study offer us an opportunity to see ourselves reflected in a mirror called history.[6]

In his recent study of Spain and the New World, *The Buried Mirror,* Carlos 10 Fuentes points out that mirrors have been found in the tombs of ancient Mexico, placed there to guide the dead through the underworld. He also tells us about the legend of Quetzalcoatl, the Plumed Serpent: when this god was given a mirror by the Toltec deity Tezcatlipoca, he saw a man's face in the mirror and realized his own humanity. For us, the "mirror" of history can guide the living and also help us recognize who we have been and hence are. In *A Distant Mirror,* Barbara W. Tuchman finds "phenomenal parallels" between the "calamitous 14th century" of European society and our own era. We can, she observes, have "greater fellow-feeling for a distraught age" as we painfully recognize the "similar disarray," "collapsing assumptions," and "unusual discomfort."[7]

But what is needed in our own perplexing times is not so much a "distant" mirror, 11 as one that is "different." While the study of the past can provide collective self-knowledge, it often reflects the scholar's particular perspective or view of the world. What happens when historians leave out many of America's peoples? What happens, to borrow the words of Adrienne Rich, "when someone with the authority of a teacher" describes our society, and "you are not in it"? Such an experience can be disorienting—"a moment of psychic disequilibrium, as if you looked into a mirror and saw nothing."[8]

Through their narratives about their lives and circumstances, the people of 12 America's diverse groups are able to see themselves and each other in our common past. They celebrate what Ishmael Reed has described as a society "unique" in the world because "the world is here"—a place "where the cultures of the world crisscross." Much of America's past, they point out, has been riddled with racism. At the same time, these people offer hope, affirming the struggle for equality as a central theme in our country's history. At its conception, our nation was dedicated to the proposition of equality. What has given concreteness to this powerful national principle has been our coming together in the creation of a new society. "Stuck here" together, workers of different backgrounds have attempted to get along with each other

> People harvesting
> Work together unaware
> Of racial problems,

wrote a Japanese immigrant describing a lesson learned by Mexican and Asian farm laborers in California.[9]

Finally, how do we see our prospects for "working out" America's racial crisis? Do 13 we see it as through a glass darkly? Do the televised images of racial hatred and violence that riveted us in 1992 during the days of rage in Los Angeles frame a future of divisive race relations—what Arthur Schlesinger, Jr., has fearfully denounced as the "disuniting of America"? Or will Americans of diverse races and ethnicities be able to connect themselves to a larger narrative? Whatever happens, we can be certain that much of our society's future will be influenced by which "mirror" we choose to see ourselves. America does not belong to one race or one group, the people in this study remind us, and Americans have been constantly redefining their national identity from the moment of first contact on the Virginia shore. By sharing their stories, they invite us to see ourselves in a different mirror.[10]

## Pacific Crossings: Seeking the Land of Money Trees

During the 1890s, American society witnessed not only the Wounded Knee massacre and    14
the end of the frontier, but also the arrival of a new group of immigrants. Unlike the Irish, the Japanese went east to America. But they, too, were pushed here by external influences. During the nineteenth century, America's expansionist thrust reached all the way across the Pacific Ocean. In 1853, Commodore Matthew C. Perry had sailed his armed naval ships into Tokyo Bay and forcefully opened Japan's doors to the West. As Japanese leaders watched Western powers colonizing China, they worried that their country would be the next victim. Thus, in 1868, they restored the Meiji emperor and established a strong centralized government. To defend Japan, they pursued a twin strategy of industrialization and militarization and levied heavy taxes to finance their program.

Bearing the burden of this taxation, farmers suffered severe economic hardships    15
during the 1880s. "The distress among the agricultural class has reached a point never before attained," the *Japan Weekly Mail* reported. "Most of the farmers have been unable to pay their taxes, and hundreds of families in one village alone have been compelled to sell their property in order to liquidate their debts." Thousands of farmers lost their lands, and hunger stalked many parts of the country. "What strikes me most is the hardships paupers are having in surviving," reported a journalist. "Their regular fare consists of rice husk or buckwheat chaff ground into powder and the dregs of bean curd mixed with leaves and grass."[11]

Searching for a way out of this terrible plight, impoverished farmers were seized    16
by an emigration *netsu*, or "fever." Fabulous stories of high wages stirred their imaginations. A plantation laborer in the Kingdom of Hawaii could earn six times more than in Japan; in three years, a worker might save four hundred yen—an amount equal to ten years of earnings in Japan. When the Japanese government first announced it would be filling six hundred emigrant slots for the first shipment of laborers to Hawaii, it received 28,000 applications. Stories about wages in the United States seemed even more fantastic—about a dollar a day, or more than two yen. This meant that in one year a worker could save about eight hundred yen—an amount almost equal to the income of a governor in Japan. No wonder a young man begged his parents: "By all means let me go to America." Between 1885 and 1924, 200,000 left for Hawaii and 180,000 for the United States mainland. In haiku, one Japanese migrant captured the feeling of expectation and excitement:

> Huge dreams of fortune
> Go with me to foreign lands,
> Across the ocean.

To prospective Japanese migrants, "money grew on trees" in America.[12]

## Picture Brides in America

Initially, most of the migrants from Japan were men, but what became striking about    17
the Japanese immigration was its eventual inclusion of a significant number of women.

By 1920, women represented 46 percent of the Japanese population in Hawaii and 35 percent in California. Clearly, in terms of gender, the Japanese resembled the Irish and Jews rather than the Chinese. This difference had consequences for the two Asian groups in terms of the formation of families. In 1900, fifty years after the beginning of Chinese immigration, only 5 percent were women. In this community composed mostly of "bachelors," only 4 percent were American-born. "The greatest impression I have of my childhood in those days was that there were very few families in China-town," a resident recalled. "Babies were looked on with a kind of wonder." On the other hand, in 1930, 52 percent of the Japanese population had been born in America. But why did proportionately more women emigrate from Japan than China?[13]

Unlike China, Japan was ruled by a strong central government that was able to regulate emigration. Prospective immigrants were required to apply to the government for permission to leave for the United States and were screened by review boards to certify that they were healthy and literate and would creditably "maintain Japan's national honor." Japan had received reports about the Chinese in America and was determined to monitor the quality of its emigrants. Seeking to avoid the problems of prostitution, gambling, and drunkenness that reportedly plagued the predominantly male Chinese community in the United States, the Japanese government promoted female emigration. The 1882 Chinese Exclusion Act prohibited the entry of "laborers," both men and women, but militarily strong Japan was able to negotiate the 1908 Gentlemen's Agreement. While this treaty prohibited the entry of Japanese "laborers," it allowed Japanese women to emigrate to the United States as family members.[14]

Through this opening in immigration policy came over sixty thousand women, many as "picture brides." The picture bride system was based on the established custom of arranged marriage. In Japanese society, marriage was not an individual matter but rather a family concern, and parents consulted go-betweens to help them select partners for their sons and daughters. In situations involving families located far away, the prospective bride and groom would exchange photographs before the initial meeting. This traditional practice lent itself readily to the needs of Japanese migrants. "When I told my parents about my desire to go to a foreign land, the story spread throughout the town," picture bride Ai Miyasaki later recalled. "From here and there requests for marriage came pouring in just like rain!" Similarly, Riyo Orite had a "picture marriage." Her marriage to a Japanese man in America had been arranged through a relative. "All agreed to our marriage, but I didn't get married immediately," she recalled. "I was engaged at the age of sixteen and didn't meet Orite until I was almost eighteen. I had seen him only in a picture at first. . . . Being young, I was unromantic. I just believed that girls should get married. I felt he was a little old, about thirty, but the people around me praised the match. His brother in Tokyo sent me a lot of beautiful pictures [taken in the United States]. . . . My name was entered in the Orites' *koseki* [family register]. Thus we were married."[15]

The emigration of Japanese women occurred within the context of internal economic developments. While women in China were restricted to farm and home, Japanese women were increasingly entering the wage-earning work force. Thousands of them were employed in construction work as well as in the coal mines where they carried heavy loads on their backs out of the tunnels. Young women were leaving their family farms for employment in textile mills where they worked sixteen-hour shifts and lived in dormitories. By 1900, 60 percent of Japan's industrial laborers were women. While it is not known how many of the women who emigrated had been wage-earners, this proletarianization of women already well under way in Japan paved the way for such laborers to consider working in America.[16]

Japanese women were also more receptive to the idea of traveling overseas than 21 Chinese women. The Meiji government required the education of female children, stipulating that "girls should be educated . . . alongside boys." Emperor Meiji himself promoted female education. Japanese boys as well as girls, he declared, should learn about foreign countries and become enlightened about the world. Female education included reading and writing skills as well as general knowledge. Japanese women, unlike their Chinese counterparts, were more likely to be literate. "We studied English and Japanese, mathematics, literature, writing, and religion," recalled Michiko Tanaka. Under the reorganization of the school system in 1876, English was adopted as a major subject in middle school. This education exposed Japanese women to the outside world. They also heard stories describing America as "heavenly," and some of the picture brides were more eager to see the new land than to meet their husbands. "I wanted to see foreign countries and besides I had consented to marriage with Papa because I had the dream of seeing America," Michiko Tanaka revealed to her daughter years later. "I wanted to see America and Papa was a way to get there." "I was bubbling over with great expectations," said another picture bride. "My young heart, 19 years and 8 months old, burned, not so much with the prospects of reuniting with my new husband, but with the thought of the New World."[17]

The emigration of women was also influenced by Japanese views on gender. 22 A folk saying popular among farmers recommended that a family should have three children: "One to sell, one to follow, and one in reserve." The "one to sell" was the daughter. Of course, this was meant only figuratively: she was expected to marry and enter her husband's family. "Once you become someone's wife you belong to his family," explained Tsuru Yamauchi. "My parents said once I went over to be married, I should treat his parents as my own and be good to them." One day, Yamauchi was told that she would be going to Hawaii to join her future husband: "I learned about the marriage proposal when we had to exchange pictures." Emigration for her was not a choice but an obligation to her husband.[18]

Whether a Japanese woman went to America depended on which son she 23 married—the son "to follow" or the son "in reserve." Unlike the Chinese, Japanese farmers had an inheritance system based on impartible inheritance and primogeniture. Only one of the sons in the family, usually the eldest, inherited the family's holdings: he was the son who was expected "to follow" his father. In the mountainous island nation of Japan, arable land was limited, and most of the farm holdings were small, less than two and a half acres. Division of a tiny family holding would mean disaster for the family. As the possessor of the family farm, the eldest son had the responsibility of caring for his aged parents and hence had to stay home. The second or noninheriting son—the one held "in reserve" in case something happened to the first son—had to leave the family farm and find employment in town. This practice of relocating within Japan could easily be applied to movement abroad. Thus, although the migrants included first sons, they tended to be the younger sons. Unlike Chinese sons who had to share responsibility for their parents, these Japanese men were not as tightly bound to their parents and were allowed to take their wives and children with them to distant lands.[19]

But whether or not women migrated was also influenced by the needs in the 24 receiving countries. In Hawaii, the government initially stipulated that 40 percent of the Japanese contract labor emigrants—laborers under contract to work for three years—were to be women. During the government-sponsored contract labor period from 1885 to 1894, women constituted 20 percent of the emigrants. During the period from 1894 to 1908, thousands of additional women sailed to Hawaii as private contract laborers. Planters viewed Japanese women as workers and assigned 72 percent of them to field labor. Furthermore, they promoted the Japanese family as a mechanism of labor control. In 1886, Hawaii's inspector-general of immigration reported that Japanese men were better workers on plantations where they had their wives: "Several of the planters are desirous that each man should have his wife." After 1900, when Hawaii became a territory of the United States, planters became even more anxious to bring Japanese women to Hawaii. Since the American law prohibiting contract labor now applied to the islands, planters had to find ways to stabilize their labor force. Realizing that men with families were more likely to stay on the plantations, managers asked their business agents in Honolulu to send "men with families."[20]

Meanwhile, Japanese women were pulled to the United States mainland where 25 they were needed as workers by their husbands. Shopkeepers and farmers sent for their wives, thinking they could assist as unpaid family labor. Wives were particularly useful on farms where production was labor intensive. "Nearly all of these tenant farmers are married and have their families with them," a researcher noted in 1915. "The wives do much work in the fields."[21]

As they prepared to leave their villages for Hawaii and America, many of these 26 women felt separation anxieties. One woman remembered her husband's brother saying farewell: "Don't stay in the [United] States too long. Come back in five years and farm with us." But her father quickly remarked: "Are you kidding? They can't learn anything in five years. They'll even have a baby over there. . . . Be patient for twenty years." Her father's words shocked her so much that she could not control her tears: suddenly she realized how long the separation could be. Another woman recalled the painful moment she experienced when her parents came to see her off: "They did not join the crowd, but quietly stood in front of the wall. They didn't say 'good luck,' or 'take care,' or anything. . . . They couldn't say anything because they knew, as I did, that I would never return." As their ships sailed from the harbor many women gazed at the diminishing shore:

> With tears in my eyes
> I turn back to my homeland,
> Taking one last look.[22]

## Notes

1. Toni Morrison, *Playing in the Dark: Whiteness in the Literary Imagination* (Cambridge, Mass., 1992), p. 47.
2. William A. Henry III, "Beyond the Melting Pot," in "America's Changing Colors," *Time*, vol. 135, no. 15 (April 9, 1990), pp. 28–31.
3. Abraham Lincoln, "First Inaugural Address," in *The Annals of America*, vol. 9, 1863–1865; *The Crisis of the Union* (Chicago, 1968), p. 255; Lincoln, "The Gettysburg Address," pp. 462–463; Abraham Lincoln, letter to James C. Conkling, August 26, 1863, in *Annals of America*, p. 439; Frederick Douglass, in Herbert Aptheker (ed.), *A Documentary History of the Negro People in the United States* (New York, 1951), vol. 1, p. 496.
4. Weber (ed.), *Foreigners in Their Native Land*, p. vi; Hamilton Holt (ed.), *The Life Stories of Undistinguished Americans as Told by Themselves* (New York, 1906), p. 143.

5. "Social Document of Pany Lowe, interviewed by C. H. Burnett, Seattle, July 5, 1924," p. 6, Survey of Race Relations, Stanford University, Hoover Institution Archives; Minnie Miller, "Autobiography," private manuscript, copy from Richard Balkin; Tomo Shoji, presentation, Ohana Cultural Center, Oakland, California, March 4, 1988.

6. Sandra Cisneros, *The House on Mango Street* (New York, 1991), pp. 109–110; Leslie Marmon Silko, *Ceremony* (New York, 1978), p. 2; Harriet A. Jacobs, *Incidents in the Life of a Slave Girl, written by herself* (Cambridge, Mass., 1987; originally published in 1857), p. xiii.

7. Carlos Fuentes, *The Buried Mirror; Reflections on Spain and the New World* (Boston, 1992), pp. 10, 11, 109; Barbara W. Tuchman, *A Distant Mirror: The Calamitous 14th Century* (New York, 1978), p. xiii, xiv.

8. Adrienne Rich, *Blood, Bread, and Poetry: Selected Prose, 1979–1985* (New York, 1986), p. 199.

9. Ishmael Reed, "America: The Multinational Society," in Rick Simonson and Scott Walker (Eds.), *Multi-cultural Literacy* (St. Paul, 1988), p. 160; Ito, *Issei*, p. 497.

10. Arthur M. Schlesinger, Jr., *The Disuniting of America: Reflections on a Multicultural Society* (Knoxville, Tenn., 1991); Carlos Bulosan, *America Is in the Heart: A Personal History* (Seattle, 1981), pp. 188–189.

11. *Japan Weekly Mail*, December 20, 1884, reprinted in Nippu Jiji, *Golden Jubilee of the Japanese in Hawaii, 1885–1935* (Honolulu, 1935), n.p.; Yuji Ichioka, *The Issei: The World of the First Generation Japanese Immigrants, 1885–1924* (New York, 1988), p. 45. Ichioka's is the best book on the subject.

12. Kazuo Ito, *Issei: A History of the Japanese Immigrants in North America* (Seattle, 1973), pp. 27, 38, 29. Ito's study is a massive and wonderful compilation of stories, oral histories, and poems. It is indispensable.

13. Victor and Brett de Bary Nee, *Longtime Californ': A Documentary Study of an American Chinatown* (New York, 1972), p. 148.

14. Robert Wilson and Bill Hosokawa, *East to America: A History of the Japanese in the United States* (New York, 1980), pp. 47, 113–114.

15. Eileen Sunada Sarasohn (ed.), *The Issei: Portrait of a Pioneer, An Oral History* (Palo Alto, Calif., 1983), pp. 44, 31–32.

16. Thomas C. Smith, *Nakahara: Family Farming and Population in a Japanese Village, 1717–1830* (Stanford, Calif., 1977), pp. 134, 152, 153; Sheila Matsumoto, "Women in Factories," in Joyce Lebra et al. (eds.), *Women in Changing Japan* (Boulder, Colo., 1976), pp. 51–53; Sharon L. Sievers, *Flowers in Salt: The Beginnings of Feminist Consciousness in Modern Japan* (Stanford, Calif., 1983), pp. 55, 62, 66, 84; Yukiko Hanawa, "The Several Worlds of Issei Women," unpublished M.A. thesis, California State University, Long Beach, 1982, pp. 31–34; Yasuo Wakatsuki, "Japanese Emigration to the United States, 1866–1924," *Perspectives in American History*, vol. 12 (1979), pp. 401, 404; Wilson and Hosokawa, *East to America*, p. 42.

17. Hanawa, "Several Worlds," pp. 13–16; Susan McCoin Kataoka, "Issei Women: A Study in Subordinate Status," unpublished Ph.D. thesis, University of California, Los Angeles, 1977, p. 6; Akemi Kikumura, *Through Harsh Winters: The Life of a Japanese Immigrant Woman* (Novato, Calif., 1981), pp. 18, 25; Emma Gee, "Issei: The First Women," in Emma Gee (ed.), *Asian Women* (Berkeley, Calif., 1971), p. 11.

18. Tsuru Yamauchi is quoted in Ethnic Studies Oral History Project (ed.), *Uchinanchu: A History of Okinawans in Hawaii* (Honolulu, 1981), pp. 490, 491; the folk saying can be found in Tadashi Fukutake, *Japanese Rural Society* (Ithaca, N.Y., 1967), p. 47.

19. Fukutake, *Japanese Rural Society*, pp. 6, 7, 39, 40, 42; Victor Nee and Herbert Y. Wong, "Asian American Socioeconomic Achievement: The Strength of the Family Bond," *Sociological Perspectives*, vol. 28, no. 3 (July 1985), p. 292.

20. Katherine Coman, *The History of Contract Labor in the Hawaiian Islands* (New York, 1903), p. 42; Allan Moriyama, "Causes of Emigration: The Background of Japanese Emigration to Hawaii, 1885–1894," in Edna Bonacich and Lucie Cheng (eds.), *Labor Immigration under Capitalism: Asian Workers in the United States before World War II* (Berkeley, Calif., 1984), p. 273; Republic of Hawaii, Bureau of Immigration, *Report* (Honolulu, 1886), p. 256; manager of the Hutchinson Sugar Company to W. G. Irwin and Company, February 5, 1902, and January 25, 1905, Hutchinson Plantation Records; for terms of the Gentlemen's Agreement, see Frank Chuman, *The Bamboo People: The Law and Japanese-Americans* (Del Mar, Calif., 1976), pp. 35–36.

21. H. A. Millis, *The Japanese Problem in the United States* (New York, 1915), p. 86.
22. Sarasohn (ed.), *Issei*, p. 34; Yuriko Sato, "Emigration of Issei Women" (Berkeley, 1982), in the Asian American Studies Library, University of California, Berkeley; Ito, *Issei*, p. 34.

## READING FOR CONTENT

1. In paragraph 6, Takaki refers to the American Civil War as a struggle "to defend and preserve the Union." Summarize the ideas about "union" that motivate his discussion. What use does Takaki make of Lincoln's phrase "the mystic chords of memory"?

2. List features of Japanese history in paragraphs 14 and 15 that Takaki regards as important for understanding patterns of Japanese emigration to America.

3. Summarize Japanese views on gender that Takaki discusses in paragraphs 22 and 23 as they bear upon the history of Japanese emigration. How do Takaki's stories about "picture brides" relate to those views?

## READING FOR GENRE, ORGANIZATION, AND STYLISTIC FEATURES

1. List the immigrant groups that Takaki mentions in paragraphs 6–8. Could you add other groups to this list? Why does Takaki propose that their stories are worth telling?

2. Describe the use that Takaki makes of statistics in paragraph 17. How does he interpret them to fashion an account of distinctive features about Japanese immigration?

3. Summarize the contrasts between Chinese and Japanese patterns of immigration that Takaki develops in paragraphs 18 and 20. Describe the major features of this contrast.

## READING FOR RHETORICAL CONTEXT

1. Explain why Takaki begins his essay in paragraphs 1 and 2 with a personal account of his conversation with a taxicab driver. How does that account color his scholarly presentation of historical materials in the rest of the essay?

2. In paragraphs 10 and 11, Takaki cites two recent books with *Mirror* in their titles and suggests that his use of the word will differ from theirs. Explain how it differs. What role does he attribute to the idea of "mirroring" in the study of history?

3. Paraphrase Takaki's discussion of the family as a "mechanism of labor control" in paragraph 24. Describe Takaki's attitude toward that development.

## WRITING ASSIGNMENTS

1. Write an argumentative essay about how American history should record patterns of racial diversity since the beginning of our nation. Reflect upon your own racial roots and comment upon how they are represented in American history.

2. Write a comparison and contrast essay drawing points of similarity and difference between Takaki's case history of Japanese picture brides and the case history of women in some other immigrant group who arrived in America with expectations of marrying and raising a family.

# Jasmine

## *Bharati Mukherjee*

*Bharati Mukherjee was born in Calcutta and currently teaches English at the University of California, Berkeley. She has published many short stories, four novels, including* The Tiger's Daughter *(1972),* Darkness *(1985),* Jasmine *(1989), and* The Holder of the World *(1993); and two works of nonfiction written with her husband, Clark Blaise,* Days and Nights in Calcutta *(1977) and* The Sorrow and Terror *(1987).*

## PREREADING

Inquire at the reference desk of your college library to obtain a copy of the latest legislation on Immigration Reform and Control. Designed to restrict the flow of illegal immigrants into the United States, it imposes harsh penalties on employers who knowingly hire undocumented aliens. Read its provisions, and freewrite on some of the likely consequences of this act, including subtle and sometimes blatant racism, economic hardships, and class tensions.

Jasmine came to Detroit from Port-of-Spain, Trinidad, by way of Canada. She 1 crossed the border at Windsor in the back of a gray van loaded with mattresses and box springs. The plan was for her to hide in an empty mattress box if she heard the driver say, "All bad weather seems to come down from Canada, doesn't it?" to the customs man. But she didn't have to crawl into a box and hold her breath. The customs man didn't ask to look in.

The driver let her off at a scary intersection on Woodward Avenue and gave her 2 instructions on how to get to the Plantations Motel in Southfield. The trick was to keep changing vehicles, he said. That threw off the immigration guys real quick.

Jasmine took money for cab fare out of the pocket of the great big raincoat that 3 the van driver had given her. The raincoat looked like something that nuns in Port-of-Spain sold in church bazaars. Jasmine was glad to have a coat with wool lining, though; and anyway, who would know in Detroit that she was Dr. Vassanji's daughter?

All the bills in her hand looked the same. She would have to be careful when she 4 paid the cabdriver. Money in Detroit wasn't pretty the way it was back home, or even in Canada, but she liked this money better. Why should money be pretty, like a picture? Pretty money is only good for putting on your walls maybe. The dollar bills felt businesslike, serious. Back home at work, she used to count out thousands of Trinidad dollars every day and not even think of them as real. Real money was worn and green, American dollars. Holding the bills in her fist on a street corner meant she had made it in okay. She'd outsmarted the guys at the border. Now it was up to her to use her wits to do something with her life. As her Daddy kept saying, "Girl, is opportunity come only once." The girls she'd worked with at the bank in Port-of-Spain had gone green as bananas when she'd walked in with her ticket on Air Canada. Trinidad was too tiny. That was the trouble. Trinidad was an island stuck in the middle of nowhere. What kind of place was that for a girl with ambition?

The Plantations Motel was run by a family of Trinidad Indians who had come    5
from the tuppenny-ha'penny country town, Chaguanas. The Daboos were nobodies back home. They were lucky, that's all. They'd gotten here before the rush and bought up a motel and an ice cream parlor. Jasmine felt very superior when she saw Mr. Daboo in the motel's reception area. He was a pumpkin-shaped man with very black skin and Elvis Presley sideburns turning white. They looked like earmuffs. Mrs. Daboo was a bumpkin, too; short, fat, flapping around in house slippers. The Daboo daughters seemed very American, though. They didn't seem to know that they were nobodies, and kept looking at her and giggling.

She knew she would be short of cash for a great long while. Besides, she wasn't    6
sure she wanted to wear bright leather boots and leotards like Viola and Loretta. The smartest move she could make would be to put a down payment on a husband. Her Daddy had told her to talk to the Daboos first chance. The Daboos ran a service fixing up illegals with islanders who had made it in legally. Daddy had paid three thousand back in Trinidad, with the Daboos and the mattress man getting part of it. They should throw in a good-earning husband for that kind of money.

The Daboos asked her to keep books for them and to clean the rooms in the new    7
wing, and she could stay in 16B as long as she liked. They showed her 16B. They said she could cook her own roti; Mr. Daboo would bring in a stove, two gas rings that you could fold up in a metal box. The room was quite grand, Jasmine thought. It had a double bed, a TV, a pink sink and matching bathtub. Mrs. Daboo said Jasmine wasn't the big-city Port-of-Spain type she'd expected. Mr. Daboo said that he wanted her to stay because it was nice to have a neat, cheerful person around. It wasn't a bad deal, better than stories she'd heard about Trinidad girls in the States.

All day every day except Sundays Jasmine worked. There wasn't just the book-    8
keeping and the cleaning up. Mr. Daboo had her working on the match-up marriage service. Jasmine's job was to check up on social security cards, call clients' bosses for references, and make sure credit information wasn't false. Dermatologists and engineers living in Bloomfield Hills, store owners on Canfield and Woodward: she treated them all as potential liars. One of the first things she learned was that Ann Arbor was a magic word. A boy goes to Ann Arbor and gets an education, and all the barriers come crashing down. So Ann Arbor was the place to be.

She didn't mind the work. She was learning about Detroit, every side of it.    9
Sunday mornings she helped unload packing crates of Caribbean spices in a shop on the next block. For the first time in her life, she was working for a black man, an African. So what if the boss was black? This was a new life, and she wanted to learn everything. Her Sunday boss, Mr. Anthony, was a courtly, Christian, church-going man, and paid her the only wages she had in her pocket. Viola and Loretta, for all their fancy American ways, wouldn't go out with blacks.

One Friday afternoon she was writing up the credit info on a Guyanese Muslim    10
who worked in an assembly plant when Loretta said that enough was enough and that there was no need for Jasmine to be her father's drudge.

"Is time to have fun," Viola said. "We're going to Ann Arbor."

Jasmine filed the sheet on the Guyanese man who probably now would never get    11
a wife and got her raincoat. Loretta's boyfriend had a Cadillac parked out front. It was

the longest car Jasmine had ever been in and louder than a country bus. Viola's boyfriend got out of the front seat. "Oh, oh, sweet things," he said to Jasmine. "Get in front." He was a talker. She'd learned that much from working on the matrimonial match-ups. She didn't believe him for a second when he said that there were dudes out there dying to ask her out.

Loretta's boyfriend said, "You have eyes I could leap into, girl." 12

Jasmine knew he was just talking. They sounded like Port-of-Spain boys of three 13 years ago. It didn't surprise her that these Trinidad country boys in Detroit were still behind the times, even of Port-of-Spain. She sat very stiff between the two men, hands on her purse. The Daboo girls laughed in the back seat.

On the highway the girls told her about the reggae night in Ann Arbor. Kevin and 14 the Krazee Islanders. Malcolm's Lovers. All the big reggae groups in the Midwest were converging for the West Indian Students Association fall bash. The ticket didn't come cheap but Jasmine wouldn't let the fellows pay. She wasn't that kind of girl.

The reggae and steel drums brought out the old Jasmine. The rum punch, the 15 dancing, the dreadlocks, the whole combination. She hadn't heard real music since she got to Detroit, where music was supposed to be so famous. The Daboos girls kept turning on rock stuff in the motel lobby whenever their father left the area. She hadn't danced, really *danced*, since she'd left home. It felt so good to dance. She felt hot and sweaty and sexy. The boys at the dance were more than sweet talkers; they moved with assurance and spoke of their futures in America. The bartender gave her two free drinks and said, "Is ready when you are, girl." She ignored him but she felt all hot and good deep inside. She knew Ann Arbor was a special place.

When it was time to pile back into Loretta's boyfriend's Cadillac, she just couldn't 16 face going back to the Plantations Motel and to the Daboos with their accounting books and messy files. "I don't know what happen, girl," she said to Loretta. "I feel all crazy inside. Maybe is time for me to pursue higher studies in this town."

"This Ann Arbor, girl, they don't just take you off the street. It *cost* like hell."

She spent the night on a bashed-up sofa in the Student Union. She was a well- 17 dressed, respectable girl, and she didn't expect anyone to question her right to sleep on the furniture. Many others were doing the same thing. In the morning, a boy in an army parka showed her the way to the Placement Office. He was a big, blond, clumsy boy, not bad-looking except for the blond eyelashes. He didn't scare her, as did most Americans. She let him buy her a Coke and a hotdog. That evening she had a job with the Moffits.

Bill Moffitt taught molecular biology and Lara Hatch-Moffitt, his wife, was a per- 18 formance artist. A performance artist, said Lara, was very different from being an actress, though Jasmine still didn't understand what the difference might be. The Moffitts had a little girl, Muffie, whom Jasmine was to look after, though for the first few months she might have to help out with the housework and the cooking because Lara said she was deep into performance rehearsals. That was all right with her, Jasmine said, maybe a little too quickly. She explained she came from a big family and was used to heavy-duty cooking and cleaning. This wasn't the time to say anything about Ram, the family ser-vant. Americans like the Moffitts wouldn't understand about keeping servants. Ram and she weren't in similar situations. Here mother's helpers, which is what Lara called her — Americans were good with words to cover their shame — seemed to be as good as anyone.

Lara showed her the room she would have all to herself in the finished basement. 19 There was a big, old TV, not in color like the motel's, and a portable typewriter on a desk which Lara said she would find handy when it came time to turn in her term papers. Jasmine didn't say anything about not being a student. She was a student of life, wasn't she? There was a scary moment after they'd discussed what she would expect as salary, which was three times more than anything Mr. Daboo was supposed to pay her but hadn't. She thought Bill Moffitt was going to ask her about her visa or her green card number and social security. But all Bill did was smile and smile at her—he had a wide, pink, baby face—and play with a button on his corduroy jacket. The button would need sewing back on, firmly.

Lara said, "I think I'm going to like you, Jasmine. You have a something about 20 you. A something real special. I'll just bet you've acted, haven't you?" The idea amused her, but she merely smiled and accepted Lara's hug. The interview was over.

Then Bill opened a bottle of Soave and told stories about camping in northern 21 Michigan. He'd been raised there. Jasmine didn't see the point in sleeping in tents; the woods sounded cold and wild and creepy. But she said, "Is exactly what I want to try out come summer, man. Campin and huntin."

Lara asked about Port-of-Spain. There was nothing to tell about her hometown 22 that wouldn't shame her in front of nice white American folk like the Moffitts. The place was shabby, the people were grasping and cheating and lying and life was full of despair and drink and wanting. But by the time she finished, the island sounded romantic. Lara said, "It wouldn't surprise me one bit if you were a writer, Jasmine."

Ann Arbor was a huge small town. She couldn't imagine any kind of school the 23 size of the University of Michigan. She meant to sign up for courses in the spring. Bill brought home a catalogue bigger than the phonebook for all of Trinidad. The university had courses in everything. It would be hard to choose; she'd have to get help from Bill. He wasn't like a professor, not the ones back home where even high school teachers called themselves professors and acted like little potentates. He wore blue jeans and thick sweaters with holes in the elbows and used phrases like "in vitro" as he watched her curry up fish. Dr. Parveen back home—he called himself "doctor" when everybody knew he didn't have even a Master's degree—was never seen without his cotton jacket which had gotten really ratty at the cuffs and lapel edges. She hadn't learned anything in the two years she'd put into college. She'd learned more from working in the bank for two months than she had at college. It was the assistant manager, Personal Loans Department, Mr. Singh, who had turned her on to the Daboos and to smooth, bargain-priced emigration.

Jasmine liked Lara. Lara was easygoing. She didn't spend the time she had 24 between rehearsals telling Jasmine how to cook and clean American-style. Mrs. Daboo did that in 16B. Mrs. Daboo would barge in with a plate of stale samosas and snoop around giving free advice on how mainstream Americans did things. As if she were dumb or something! As if she couldn't keep her own eyes open and make her mind up for herself. Sunday mornings she had to share the butcher-block workspace in the kitchen with Bill. He made the Sunday brunch from new recipes in *Gourmet* and *Cuisine*. Jasmine hadn't seen a man cook who didn't have to or wasn't getting paid to do it. Things were topsy-turvy in the Moffitt house. Lara went on two- and three-day road trips and Bill stayed home. But even her Daddy, who'd never poured himself a cup of tea, wouldn't put Bill down as a woman. The mornings Bill tried out something complicated, a Cajun shrimp, sausage, and beans dish, for instance, Jasmine skipped church services. The Moffitts didn't go to church, though they seemed to be good Christians. They just didn't talk church talk, which suited her fine.

Two months passed. Jasmine knew she was lucky to have found a small, clean, 25 friendly family like the Moffitts to build her new life around. "Man!" she'd exclaim as she vacuumed the wide-plank wood floors or ironed (Lara wore pure silk or pure cotton). "In this country Jesus givin out good luck only!" By this time they knew she wasn't a student, but they didn't care and said they wouldn't report her. They never asked if she was illegal on top of it.

To savor her new sense of being a happy, lucky person, she would put herself 26 through a series of "what ifs": what if Mr. Singh in Port-of-Spain hadn't turned her on to the Daboos and loaned her two thousand! What if she'd been ugly like the Mintoo girl and the manager hadn't even offered! What if the customs man had unlocked the door of the van! Her Daddy liked to say, "You is a helluva girl, Jasmine."

"Thank you, Jesus," Jasmine said, as she carried on.

Christmas Day the Moffitts treated her just like family. They gave her a red cash- 27 mere sweater with a V neck so deep it made her blush. If Lara had worn it, her bosom wouldn't hang out like melons. For the holiday weekend Bill drove her to the Daboos in Detroit. "You work too hard," Bill said to her. "Learn to be more selfish. Come on, throw your weight around." She'd rather not have spent time with the Daboos, but that first afternoon of the interview she'd told Bill and Lara that Mr. Daboo was her mother's first cousin. She had thought it shameful in those days to have no papers, no family, no roots. Now Loretta and Viola in tight, bright pants seemed trashy like girls at Two-Johnny Bissoondath's Bar back home. She was stuck with the story of the Daboos being family. Village bumpkins, ha! She would break out. Soon.

Jasmine had Bill drop her off at the RenCen. The Plantations Motel, in fact, the 28 whole Riverfront area, was too seamy. She'd managed to cut herself off mentally from anything too islandy. She loved her Daddy and Mummy, but she didn't think of them that often anymore. Mummy had expected her to be homesick and come flying right back home. "Is blowin sweat-of-brow money is what you doing, Pa," Mummy had scolded. She loved them, but she'd become her own person. That was something that Lara said: "I am my own person."

The Daboos acted thrilled to see her back. "What you drinkin, Jasmine girl?" 29 Mr. Daboo kept asking. "You drinkin sherry or what?" Pouring her little glasses of sherry instead of rum was a sure sign he thought she had become whitefolk-fancy. The Daboo sisters were very friendly, but Jasmine considered them too wild. Both Loretta and Viola had changed boyfriends. Both were seeing black men they'd danced with in Ann Arbor. Each night at bedtime, Mr. Daboo cried. "In Trinidad we stayin we side, they stayin they side. Here, everything mixed up. Is helluva confusion, no?"

On New Year's Eve the Daboo girls and their black friends went to a dance. 30 Mr. and Mrs. Daboo and Jasmine watched TV for a while. Then Mr. Daboo got out a brooch from his pocket and pinned it on Jasmine's red sweater. It was a Christmasy brooch, a miniature sleigh loaded down with snowed-on mistletoe. Before she could pull away, he kissed her on the lips. "Good luck for the New Year!" he said. She lifted her head and saw tears. "Is year for dreams comin true."

Jasmine started to cry, too. There was nothing wrong, but Mr. Daboo, Mrs. Daboo, 31 she, everybody was crying.

What for? This is where she wanted to be. She'd spent some damned uncomfort- 32 able times with the assistant manager to get approval for her loan. She thought of Daddy. He would be playing poker and fanning himself with a magazine. Her married sisters would be rolling out the dough for stacks and stacks of roti, and Mummy would be steamed purple from stirring the big pot of goat curry on the stove. She missed them. But. It felt strange to think of anyone celebrating New Year's Eve in summery clothes.

In March Lara and her performing group went on the road. Jasmine knew that 33 the group didn't work from scripts. The group didn't use a stage, either; instead, it took over supermarkets, senior citizens' centers, and school halls, without notice. Jasmine didn't understand the performance world. But she was glad that Lara said, "I'm not going to lay a guilt trip on myself. Muffie's in super hands," before she left.

Muffie didn't need much looking after. She played Trivial Pursuit all day, usually 34 pretending to be two persons, sometimes Jasmine, whose accent she could imitate. Since Jasmine didn't know any of the answers, she couldn't help. Muffie was a quiet, precocious child with see-through blue eyes like her dad's, and red braids. In the early evenings Jasmine cooked supper, something special she hadn't forgotten from her island days. After supper she and Muffie watched some TV, and Bill read. When Muffie went to bed, Bill and she sat together for a bit with their glasses of Soave. Bill, Muffie, and she were a family, almost.

Down in her basement room that late, dark winter, she had trouble sleeping. She 35 wanted to stay awake and think of Bill. Even when she fell asleep it didn't feel like sleep because Bill came barging into her dreams in his funny, loose-jointed, clumsy way. It was mad to think of him all the time, and stupid and sinful; but she couldn't help it. Whenever she put back a book he'd taken off the shelf to read or whenever she put his clothes through the washer and dryer, she felt sick in a giddy, wonderful way. When Lara came back things would get back to normal. Meantime she wanted the performance group miles away.

Lara called in at least twice a week. She said things like, "We've finally obliter- 36 ated the margin between realspace and performancespace." Jasmine filled her in on Muffie's doings and the mail. Bill always closed with, "I love you. We miss you, hon."

One night after Lara had called—she was in Lincoln, Nebraska—Bill said to 37 Jasmine, "Let's dance."

She hadn't danced since the reggae night she'd had too many rum punches. Her 38 toes began to throb and clench. She untied her apron and the fraying, knotted-up laces of her running shoes.

Bill went around the downstairs rooms turning down lights. "We need atmo- 39 sphere," he said. He got a small, tidy fire going in the living room grate and pulled the Turkish scatter rug closer to it. Lara didn't like anybody walking on the Turkish rug, but Bill meant to have his way. The hissing logs, the plants in the dimmed light, the thick patterned rug: everything was changed. This wasn't the room she cleaned every day.

He stood close to her. She smoothed her skirt down with both hands.                    40

"I want you to choose the record," he said.

"I don't know your music."

She brought her hand high to his face. His skin was baby smooth.

"I want *you* to pick," he said. "You are your own person now."

"You got island music?"

He laughed, "What do you think?" The stereo was in a cabinet with albums 41 packed tight alphabetically into the bottom three shelves. "Calypso has not been a force in my life."

She couldn't help laughing. "Calypso? Oh, man." She pulled dust jackets out at 42 random. Lara's records. The Flying Lizards. The Violent Femmes. There was so much still to pick up on! "This one," she said finally.

He took the record out of her hand. "God!" he laughed. "Lara must have found 43 this in a garage sale!" He laid the old record on the turntable. It was "Music for Lovers," something the nuns had taught her to fox-trot to way back in Port-of-Spain.

They danced so close that she could feel his heart heaving and crashing against 44 her head. She liked it, she liked it very much. She didn't care what happened.

"Come on," Bill whispered. "If it feels right, do it." He began to take her clothes off.

"Don't Bill," she pleaded.

"Come on, baby," he whispered again. "You're a blossom, a flower."

He took off his fisherman's knit pullover, the corduroy pants, the blue shorts. She 45 kept pace. She'd never had such an effect on a man. He nearly flung his socks and Adidas into the fire. "You feel so good," he said. "You smell so good. You're really something, flower of Trinidad." "Flower of Ann Arbor," she said, "not Trinidad."

She felt so good she was dizzy. She'd never felt this good on the island where men 46 did this all the time, and girls went along with it always for favors. You couldn't feel really good in a nothing place. She was thinking this as they made love on the Turkish carpet in front of the fire: she was a bright, pretty girl with no visa, no papers, and no birth certificate. No nothing other than what she wanted to invent and tell. She was a girl rushing wildly into the future.

His hand moved up her throat and forced her lips apart and it felt so good, so 47 right; that she forgot all the dreariness of her new life and gave herself up to it.

## READING FOR CONTENT

1. List the business and commercial enterprises of the Daboo family in paragraphs 5, 6, and 8. What attitude does the narrator project toward those activities?
2. List the various racial and ethnic groups with which Jasmine has contact in paragraphs 5, 9, 10, 17, and 18.
3. Paraphrase and compare the story's representations of Christmastime with the Hatch-Moffitts, the Daboos, and Jasmine's parents in paragraphs 27, 30, and 32.

## READING FOR GENRE, ORGANIZATION, AND STYLISTIC FEATURES

1. Summarize the features of Lara's first meeting with Jasmine in paragraphs 18, 19, 20, and 22. Why does Lara assume that Jasmine is a student, actress, and writer?
2. Explain why in paragraph 24 Jasmine thinks that the Hatch-Moffitt household is "topsy-turvy."
3. Explain the significance of Bill's "Learn to be more selfish" in paragraph 27, of Jasmine's "But" in paragraph 32, and of Lara's "guilt trip" in paragraph 33.

## READING FOR RHETORICAL CONTEXT

1. Describe Jasmine's attitude toward the Daboo family in paragraph 5. Why does she feel superior to them?
2. Summarize the account of Jasmine's upbringing in Jamaica as related in paragraphs 3, 4, 6, and 18.
3. Explain the significance of Bill's "If it feels right, do it" in paragraph 44.

## WRITING ASSIGNMENTS

1. Write a critical analysis of the story's action from the points of view of the Daboos, the Hatch-Moffitts, and Jasmine. Comment upon the narrator's implied attitude toward each of these points of view.

2. Write a critical evaluation of Jasmine's character. Is she an outright opportunist? Or does she acquiesce to her crises, accepting the provisional good that comes to her? To what extent does she control what's happening to her? In the final scene, who seduces whom?

■ ■ ■ ■ ■ ■ ■ ■ ■ ■ ■ ■

# Snapshots

### *Helena Maria Viramontes*

*Helena Maria Viramontes was born in East Los Angeles and now teaches at Cornell University. Her books include* The Moths and Other Stories *(1985) and* Chicana Creativity and Criticism: Charting New Frontiers in American Literature *(1988).*

## PREREADING

Recall the photographs that have been taken of you and your family. Is there a particular snapshot that stands out among all the rest? For ten minutes, freewrite about the memories the photo evokes in you.

It was the small things in life, I admit, that made me happy; ironing straight arrow    1
creases on Dave's work khakis, cashing in enough coupons to actually save some money, or having my bus halt just right, so that I don't have to jump off the curb and crack my knee cap like that poor shoe salesman I read about in Utah. Now, it's no wonder that I wake mornings and try my damndest not to mimic the movements of ironing or cutting those stupid, dotted lines or slipping into my house shoes, groping for my robe, going to Marge's room to check if she's sufficiently covered, scruffling to the kitchen, dumping out the soggy coffee grounds, refilling the pot and only later realizing that the breakfast nook has been set for three, the iron is plugged in, the bargain page is open in front of me and I don't remember, I mean I really don't remember doing any of it because I've done it for thirty years now and Marge is already married. It kills me, the small things.

Like those balls of wool on the couch. They're small and senseless and yet, every    2
time I see them, I want to scream. Since the divorce, Marge brings me balls and balls and balls of wool thread because she insists that I "take up a hobby," "keep as busy as a bee," or "make the best of things" and all that other good-natured advice she probably hears from

"Snapshots" by Helena Maria Viramontes is reprinted with permission from the publisher of *The Moths and Other Stories* (Houston: Arte Público Press-University of Houston, 1985).

old folks who answer in such a way when asked how they've managed to live so long. Honestly, I wouldn't be surprised if she walked in one day with bushels of straw for me to weave baskets. My only response to her endeavors is to give her the hardest stares I know how when she enters the living room, opens up her plastic shopping bag and brings out another ball of bright colored wool thread. I never move. Just sit and stare.

"Mother."                                                                                                    3

She pronounces the words not as a truth but as an accusation.

"Please, Mother. Knit. Do something." And then she places the new ball on top of the others on the couch, turns toward the kitchen and leaves. I give her a minute before I look out the window to see her standing on the sidewalk. I stick out my tongue, even make a face, but all she does is stand there with that horrible yellow and black plastic bag against her fat leg, and wave good-bye.

Do something, she says. If I had a penny for all the things I have done, all the   4
little details I was responsible for but which amounted to nonsense, I would be rich. But I haven't a thing to show for it. The human spider gets on prime time television for climbing a building because it's there. Me? How can people believe that I've fought against motes of dust for years or dirt attracting floors or perfected bleached white sheets when a few hours later the motes, the dirt, the stains return to remind me of the useless-ness of it all? I missed the sound of swans slicing the lake water or the fluttering wings of wild geese flying south for a warm winter or the heartbeat I could have heard if I had just held Marge a little closer.

I realize all that time is lost now, and I find myself searching for it frantically under   5
the bed where the balls of dust collect undisturbed and untouched, as it should be.

To be quite frank, the fact of the matter is I wish to do nothing, but allow indul-   6
gence to rush through my veins with frightening speed. I do so because I have never been able to tolerate it in anyone, including myself.

I watch television to my heart's content now, a thing I rarely did in my younger   7
days. While I was growing up, television had not been invented. Once it was and became a must for every home, Dave saved and saved until we were able to get one. But who had the time? Most of mine was spent working part time as a clerk for Grants, then returning to create a happy home for Dave. This is the way I pictured it:

> His wife in the kitchen wearing a freshly ironed apron, stirring a pot of soup, whistling a whistle-while-you-work tune, and preparing frosting for some cupcakes so that when he drove home from work, tired and sweaty, he would enter his castle to find his cherub baby in a pink day suit with newly starched ribbons crawling to him and his wife looking at him with pleasing eyes and offering him a cupcake.

It was a good image I wanted him to have and every day I almost expected him to   8
stop, put down his lunch pail and cry at the whole scene. If it wasn't for the burnt cup-cakes, my damn varicose veins, and Marge blubbering all over her day suit, it would have made a perfect snapshot.

Snapshots are ghosts. I am told that shortly after women are married, they   9
become addicted to one thing or another. In *Reader's Digest* I read stories of closet alco-holic wives who gambled away grocery money or broke into their children's piggy banks in order to quench their thirst and fill their souls. Unfortunately I did not become addicted to alcohol because my only encounter with it had left me senseless and with my face in the toilet bowl. After that, I never had the desire to repeat the performance of

a senior in high school whose prom date never showed. I did consider my addiction a lot more incurable. I had acquired a habit much more deadly: nostalgia.

I acquired the habit after Marge was born, and I had to stay in bed for months 10 because of my varicose veins. I began flipping through my family's photo albums (my father threw them away after mom's death) to pass the time and pain away. However I soon became haunted by the frozen moments and the meaning of memories. Looking at the old photos, I'd get real depressed over my second grade teacher's smile or my father's can of beer or the butt naked smile of me as a young teen, because every detail, as minute as it may seem, made me feel that so much had passed unnoticed. As a result, I began to convince myself that my best years were up and that I had nothing to look forward to in the future. I was too young and too ignorant to realize that that section of my life relied wholly on those crumbling photographs and my memory and I probably wasted more time longing for a past that never really existed. Dave eventually packed them up in a wooden crate to keep me from hurting myself. He was good in that way. Like when he clipped roses for me. He made sure the thorns were cut off so I didn't have to prick myself while putting them in a vase. And it was the same thing with the albums. They stood in the attic for years until I brought them down a day after he remarried.

The photo albums are unraveling and stained with spills and fingerprints and 11 filled with crinkled faded gray snapshots of people I can't remember anymore, and I turn the pages over and over again to see if somehow, some old dream will come into my blank mind. Like the black and white television box does when I turn it on. It warms up then flashes instant pictures, instant lives, instant people.

Parents. That I know for sure. The woman is tall and long, her plain, black dress 12 is over her knees, and she wears thick spongelike shoes. She's over to the right of the photo, looks straight ahead at the camera. The man wears white, baggy pants that go past his waist, thick suspenders. He smiles while holding a dull-faced baby. He points to the camera. His sleeves pulled up, his tie undone, his hair is messy, as if some wild woman has driven his head between her breasts and run her fingers into his perfect greased ducktail.

My mother always smelled of smoke and vanilla and that is why I stayed away from 13 her. I suppose that is why my father stayed away from her as well. I don't even remember a time when I saw them show any sign of affection. Not like today. No sooner do I turn off the soaps when I turn around and catch two youngsters on a porch swing, their mouths open, their lips chewing and chewing as if they were sharing a piece of three day old liver. My mom was always one to believe that such passion be restricted to the privacy of one's house and then, there too, be demonstrated with efficiency and not this urgency I witness almost every day. Dave and I were good about that.

Whenever I saw the vaseline jar on top of Dave's bedstand, I made sure the door 14 was locked and the blinds down. This anticipation was more exciting to me than him lifting up my flannel gown over my head, pressing against me, slipping off my underwear then slipping in me. The vaseline came next, then he came right afterwards. In the morning, Dave looked into my eyes and I could never figure out what he expected to find. Eventually, there came a point in our relationship when passion passed to Marge's generation, and I was somewhat relieved. And yet, I could never imagine Marge doing those types of things that these youngsters do today, though I'm sure she did them on those Sunday afternoons when she carried a blanket and a book, and told me she was going to the park to do some reading and returned hours later with the bookmark in the same place. She must have done them, or else how could she have gotten engaged, married, had three children all under my nose, and me still going to check if she's sufficiently covered?

"Mother?" Marge's voice from the kitchen. It must be evening. Every morning it's 15 the ball of wool, every evening it's dinner. Honestly, she treats me as if I have an incurable heart ailment. She stands under the doorway.

"Mother?" Picture it: She stands under the doorway looking befuddled, as if a 16 movie director instructs her to stand there and look confused and upset; stand there as if you have seen you mother sitting in the same position for the last nine hours.

"What are you doing to yourself?" Marge is definitely not one for originality and 17 she repeats the same lines every day. I'm beginning to think our conversation is coming from discarded scripts. I know the lines by heart, too. She'll say: "Why do you continue to do this to us?" and I'll answer: "Do what?" and she'll say: "This"—waving her plump, coarse hands over the albums scattered at my feet—and I'll say: "Why don't you go home and leave me alone?" This is the extent of our conversation and usually there is an optional line like: "I brought you something to eat," or "Let's have dinner," or "Come look what I have for you," or even "I brought you your favorite dish."

I think of the times, so many times, so many Mother's Days that passed without so 18 much as a thank you or how sweet you are for giving us thirty years of your life. I know I am to blame. When Marge first started school, she had made a ceramic handprint for me to hang in the kitchen. My hands were so greasy from cutting the fat off some porkchops, I dropped it before I could even unwrap my first Mother's Day gift. I tried gluing it back together again with flour and water paste, but she never forgave me and I never received another gift until after the divorce. I wonder what happened to the ceramic handprint I gave to my mother?

In the kitchen I see that today my favorite dish is Chinese food getting cold in 19 those little coffin-like containers. Yesterday my favorite dish was a salami sandwich, and before that a half eaten rib, no doubt left over from Marge's half hour lunch. Last week she brought me some Sunday soup that had fish heads floating around in some greenish broth. When I threw it down the sink, all she could think of to say was: "Oh, Mother."

We eat in silence. Or rather, she eats. I don't understand how she can take my 20 indifference. I wish that she would break out of her frozen look, jump out of any snapshot and slap me in the face. Do something. Do something. I began to cry.

"Oh, Mother," she says, picking up the plates and putting them in the sink.

"Mother, please."

There's fingerprints all over this one, my favorite. Both woman and child are 21 clones: same bathing suit, same ponytails, same ribbons. The woman is looking directly at the camera, but the man is busy making a sand castle for his daughter. He doesn't see the camera or the woman. On the back of this one, in vague pencil scratching, it says: San Juan Capistrano.

This is a bad night. On good nights I avoid familiar spots. On bad nights I am 22 pulled towards them so much so that if I sit on the chair next to Dave's I begin to cry. On bad nights I can't sleep and on bad nights I don't know who the couples in the snapshots are. My mother and me? Me and Marge? I don't remember San Juan Capistrano and I don't remember the woman. She faded into thirty years of trivia. I don't even remember what I had for dinner, or rather, what Marge had for dinner, just a few hours before. I wrap a blanket around myself and go into the kitchen to search for some evidence, but except for a few crumbs on the table, there is no indication that Marge was here. Suddenly, I am relieved when I see the box containers in the trash under the sink.

I can't sleep the rest of the night wondering what happened to my ceramic handprint, or what was in the boxes. Why can't I remember? My mind thinks of nothing but those boxes in all shapes and sizes. I wash my face with warm water, put cold cream on, go back to bed, get up and wash my face again. Finally, I decide to call Marge at 3:30 in the morning. The voice is faint and there is static in the distance.

"Yes?" Marge asks automatically.                                                        23

"Hello," Marge says. I almost expected her to answer her usual "Dave's Hardware."

"Who is this?" Marge is fully awake now.

"What did we . . ." I ask, wondering why it was suddenly so important for me to know what we had for dinner. "What did you have for dinner?" I am confident that she'll remember every movement I made or how much salt I put on whatever we ate, or rather, she ate. Marge is good about details.

"Mother?"

"Are you angry that I woke you up?"

"Mother. No. Of course not."

I could hear some muffled sounds, vague voices, static. I can tell she is covering 24 the mouthpiece with her hand. Finally George's voice.

"Mrs. Ruiz," he says, restraining his words so that they almost come out 25 slurred, "Mrs. Ruiz, why don't you leave us alone?" and then there is a long, buzzing sound. Right next to the vaseline jar are Dave's cigarettes. I light one though I don't smoke. I unscrew the jar and use the lid for an ashtray. I wait, staring at the phone until it rings.

"Dave's Hardware," I answer. "Don't you know what time it is?"

"Yes." It isn't Marge's voice. "Why don't you leave the kids alone?" Dave's voice is not angry. Groggy, but not angry. After a pause I say:

"I don't know if I should be hungry or not."

"You're a sad case." Dave says it as coolly as a doctor would say, you have terminal cancer. He says it to convince me that it is totally out of his hands. I panic. I picture him sitting on his side of the bed in his shorts, smoking under a dull circle of light. I know his bifocals are down to the tip of his nose.

"Oh, Dave," I say. "Oh, Dave." The static gets worse.

"Let me call you tomorrow."

"No. It's just a bad night."

"Olga," Dave says so softly that I can almost feel his warm breath on my face.

"Olga, why don't you get some sleep?"

The first camera I ever saw belonged to my grandfather. He won it in a cock fight. 26 Unfortunately he didn't know two bits about it, but he somehow managed to load the film. Then he brought it over to our house. He sat me on the lawn. I was only five or six years old, but I remember the excitement of everybody coming around to get into the picture. I can see my grandfather clearly now. I can picture him handling the camera slowly, touching the knobs and buttons to find out how the camera worked while the men began milling around him expressing their limited knowledge of the invention. I remember it all so clearly. Finally he was able to manage the camera, and he took pictures of me standing near my mother with the wives behind us.

My grandmother was very upset. She kept pulling me out of the picture, yelling 27 to my grandfather that he should know better, that snapshots steal the souls of the people and that she would not allow my soul to be taken. He pushed her aside and clicked the picture.

The picture, of course, never came out. My grandfather, not knowing better, 28 thought that all he had to do to develop the film was unroll it and expose it to the sun. After we all waited for an hour, we realized it didn't work. My grandmother was very upset and cut a piece of my hair, probably to save me from a bad omen.

It scares me to think that my grandmother may have been right. It scares me even 29 more to think I don't have a snapshot of her. If I find one, I'll tear it up for sure.

## READING FOR CONTENT

1. What clues does the opening paragraph give you about the type of family life Mrs. Ruiz has led?
2. Even though Marge is intent on getting her mother interested in a hobby, Mrs. Ruiz wishes to do nothing. Explain why she feels that way.
3. Explain what Mrs. Ruiz means when she says that after her daughter was born, she became addicted to nostalgia.
4. How do you think Mrs. Ruiz views Marge's daily visits? What does she mean when she says, "I wish that she would break out of her frozen look, jump out of any snapshot and slam me in the face" (paragraph 20)?
5. Why does Mrs. Ruiz think that her grandmother's remark that "snapshots steal the souls of the people" (paragraph 27) may be correct?

## READING FOR GENRE, ORGANIZATION, AND STYLISTIC FEATURES

1. How does Viramontes establish the conflict between Mrs. Ruiz and her daughter? Point out specific details.
2. Explain what the references to snapshots, photo album, television, movie script, and cameras contribute to the story.
3. How do you react to Mrs. Ruiz's image of the "happy home"? How did that image control her life?
4. Underline passages that contain humor. How would the story's impact be different if the humor were left out?
5. What is the function of Mrs. Ruiz's recollection of her grandfather's camera? What does this scene add to the story?

## READING FOR RHETORICAL CONTEXT

1. How do you think Viramontes wants you to view Mrs. Ruiz?
2. What point do you think Viramontes is making about living in the past rather than dealing with present realities?
3. How would the story have been different if it had been narrated by Marge instead of her mother?

## WRITING ASSIGNMENTS

1. Write a short critical analysis of the story's point of view.
2. Write an essay discussing Mrs. Ruiz's image of the perfect family in paragraph 7. Is that image borne out in reality? In Mrs. Ruiz's life? In your own family experience?

■ ■ ▓ ■ ■ ■ ■ ■ ■ ■ ▓ ▒

# Between the Pool and the Gardenias

## Edwidge Danticat

*Edwidge Danticat (b. 1969) emigrated at the age of twelve from Haiti to the United States and received a B.A. from Barnard College and an M.F.A. from Brown University. Her novels about Haitians and Haitian immigrants include* Breath, Eyes, Memory *(1994),* The Farming of Bones *(1999), and* The Dew Breaker *(2004). Her early short stories are collected in* Krik? Krak! *(1996). She lives and writes in Brooklyn, New York.*

## PREREADING

The poorest nation in the Western hemisphere, the Republic of Haiti has suffered a tumultuous political history for more than fifty years, first under the dictatorial Duvalier father-and-son rulers, and then since 1991 under a series of military and rebel terrorist coups that twice ousted the democratically elected president, Jean-Bertrand Aristide, and paralyzed the government of his successor, René Préval. With a dismal record of human rights violations, violence against women, drug and arms smuggling, and deplorable health issues, Haiti has lost great numbers of its population to disease, torture, death, and stealth emigration. Browse the Internet for sites about the nation's social, political, economic, and health problems, and compile a list of issues that recur on various Web sites.

$S$he was very pretty. Bright shiny hair and dark brown skin like mahogany cocoa.  1
Her lips were wide and purple, like those African dolls you see in tourist store windows but could never afford to buy.

I thought she was a gift from Heaven when I saw her on the dusty curb, wrapped  2
in a small pink blanket, a few inches away from a sewer as open as a hungry child's yawn. She was like Baby Moses in the Bible stories they read to us at the Baptist Literary Class. Or Baby Jesus, who was born in a barn and died on a cross, with nobody's lips to kiss before he went. She was just like that. Her still round face. Her eyes closed as though she was dreaming of a far other place.

Her hands were bony, and there were veins so close to the surface that it looked  3
like you could rupture her skin if you touched her too hard. She probably belonged to someone, but the street had no one in it. There was no one there to claim her.

From: *Krik? Krak!* (New York: Soho Press, 1996), pp. 89–100.

At first I was afraid to touch her. Lest I might disturb the early-morning sun rays   4
streaming across her forehead. She might have been some kind of *wanga*, a charm sent
to trap me. My enemies were many and crafty. The girls who slept with my husband
while I was still grieving over my miscarriages. They might have sent that vision of love-
liness to blind me so that I would never find my way back to the place that I yanked out
my head when I got on that broken down minibus and left my village months ago.

The child was wearing an embroidered little blue dress with the letters R-O-S-E   5
on a butterfly collar. She looked the way that I had imagined all my little girls would
look. The ones my body could never hold. The ones that somehow got suffocated
inside me and made my husband wonder if I was killing them on purpose.

I called out all the names I wanted to give them: Eveline, Josephine, Jacqueline,   6
Hermine, Marie Magdalène, Célianne. I could give her all the clothes that I had sewn
for them. All these little dresses that went unused.

At night, I could rock her alone in the hush of my room, rest her on my belly, and   7
wish she were inside.

When I had just come to the city, I saw on Madame's television that a lot of poor   8
city women throw out their babies because they can't afford to feed them. Back in Ville
Rose you cannot even throw out the bloody clumps that shoot out of your body after
your child is born. It is a crime, they say, and your whole family would consider you
wicked if you did it. You have to save every piece of flesh and give it a name and bury it
near the roots of a tree so that the world won't fall apart around you.

In the city, I hear they throw out whole entire children. They throw them out   9
anywhere: on doorsteps, in garbage cans, at gas pumps, sidewalks. In the time that I had
been in Port-au-Prince, I had never seen such a child until now.

But Rose. My, she was so clean and warm. Like a tiny angel, a little cherub, sleep-   10
ing after the wind had blown a lullaby into her little ears.

I picked her up and pressed her cheek against mine.   11

I whispered to her, "Little Rose, my child," as though that name was a secret.   12

She was like the palatable little dolls we played with as children—mango seeds   13
that we drew faces on and then called by our nicknames. We christened them with
prayers and invited all our little boy and girl friends for colas and cassavas and—when
we could get them—some nice butter cookies.

Rose didn't stir or cry. She was like something that was thrown aside after she   14
became useless to someone cruel. When I pressed her face against my heart, she
smelled like the scented powders in Madame's cabinet, the mixed scent of gardenias
and fish that Madame always had on her when she stepped out of her pool.

I have always said my mother's prayers at dawn. I welcomed the years that were   15
slowing bringing me closer to her. For no matter how much distance death tried to put
between us, my mother would often come to visit me. Sometimes in the short sighs and
whispers of somebody else's voice. Sometimes in somebody else's face. Other times in
brief moments in my dreams.

There were many nights when I saw some old women leaning over my bed.   16

"That there is Marie," my mother would say. "She is now the last one of us left."   17

Mama had to introduce me to them, because they had all died before I was born.   18
There was my great grandmother Eveline who was killed by Dominican soldiers at the
Massacre River. My grandmother Défilé who died with a bald head in a prison, because
God had given her wings. My godmother Lili who killed herself in old age because her
husband had jumped out of a flying balloon and her grown son left her to go to Miami.

*We all salute you Mary, Mother of God. Pray for us poor sinners, from now until* 19
*the hour of our death. Amen.*

I always knew they would come back and claim me to do some good for some- 20
body. Maybe I was to do some good for this child.

I carried Rose with me to the outdoor market in Croix-Bossale. I swayed her in 21
my arms like she was and had always been mine.

In the city, even people who come from your own village don't know you or care 22
about you. They didn't notice that I had come the day before with no child. Suddenly,
I had one, and nobody asked a thing.

In the maid's room, at the house in Pétion-Ville, I laid Rose on my mat and 23
rushed to prepare lunch. Monsieur and Madame sat on their terrace and welcomed the
coming afternoon by sipping the sweet out of my sour-sop juice.

They liked that I went all the way to the market every day before dawn to get them 24
a taste of the outside country, away from their protected bourgeois life.

"She is probably one of those *manbos*," they say when my back is turned. "She's 25
probably one of those stupid people who think that they have a spell to make themselves invisible and hurt other people. Why can't none of them get a spell to make
themselves rich? It's that voodoo nonsense that's holding us Haitians back."

I lay Rose down on the kitchen table as I dried the dishes. I had a sudden desire to 26
explain to her my life.

"You see, young one, I loved that man at one point. He was very nice to me. He 27
made me feel proper. The next thing I know, it's ten years with him. I'm old like a piece
of dirty paper people used to wipe their behinds, and he's got ten different babies with
ten different women. I just had to run."

I pretended that it was all mine. The terrace with that sight of the private pool and 28
the holiday ships cruising in the distance. The large television system and all those
French love songs and *rara* records, with the talking drums and conch shell sounds in
them. The bright paintings with white winged horses and snakes as long and wide as
lakes. The pool that the sweaty Dominican man cleaned three times a week. I pretended that it belonged to us: him, Rose, and me.

The Dominican and I made love on the grass once, but he never spoke to me 29
again. Rose listened with her eyes closed even though I was telling her things that were
much too strong for a child's ears.

I wrapped her around me with my apron as I fried some plantains for the evening 30
meal. It's so easy to love somebody, I tell you, when there's nothing else around.

Her head fell back like any other infant's. I held out my hand and let her three 31
matted braids tickle the lifelines in my hand.

"I am glad you are not one of those babies that cry all day long," I told her. "All 32
little children should be like you. I am glad that you don't cry and make a lot of noise.
You're just a perfect child, aren't you?"

I put her back in my room when Monsieur and Madame came home for their sup- 33
per. As soon as they went to sleep, I took her out by the pool so we could talk some more.

You don't just join a family not knowing what you're getting into. You have to 34
know some of the history. You have to know that they pray to Erzulie, who loves men
like men love her, because she's mulatto and some Haitian men seem to love her kind.
You have to look into your looking glass on the day of the dead because you might see
faces there that knew you even before you ever came into this world.

I fell asleep rocking her in a chair that wasn't mine. I knew she was real when 35 I woke up the next day and she was still in my arms. She looked the same as she did when I found her. She continued to look like that for three days. After that, I had to bathe her constantly to keep down the smell.

I once had an uncle who bought pigs' intestines in Ville Rose to sell at the market 36 in the city. Rose began to smell like the intestines after they hadn't sold for a few days.

I bathed her more and more often, sometimes three or four times a day in the 37 pool. I used some of Madame's perfume, but it was not helping. I wanted to take her back to the street where I had found her, but I'd already disturbed her rest and had taken on her soul as my own personal responsibility.

I left her in a shack behind the house, where the Dominican kept his tools. Three 38 times a day, I visited her with my hand over my nose. I watched her skin grow moist, cracked, and sunken in some places, then ashy and dry in others. It seemed like she had aged in four days as many years as there were between me and my dead aunts and grandmothers.

I knew I had to act with her because she was attracting flies and I was keeping her 39 spirit from moving on.

I gave her one last bath and slipped on a little yellow dress that I had sewn while 40 praying that one of my little girls would come along further than three months.

I took Rose down to a spot in the sun behind the big house. I dug a hole in the 41 garden among all the gardenias. I wrapped her in the little pink blanket that I had found her in, covering everything but her face. She smelled so bad that I couldn't even bring myself to kiss her without choking on my breath.

I felt a grip on my shoulder as I lowered her into the small hole in the ground. At 42 first I thought it was Monsieur or Madame, and I was real afraid that Madame would be angry with me for having used a whole bottle of her perfume without asking.

Rose slipped and fell out of my hands as my body was forced to turn around. 43

"What are you doing?" the Dominican asked. 44

His face was a deep Indian brown but his hands were bleached and wrinkled 45 from the chemicals in the pool. He looked down at the baby lying in the dust. She was already sprinkled with some of the soil that I had dug up.

"You see, I saw these faces standing over me in my dreams—" 46 I could have started my explanation in a million of ways.

"Where did you take this child from?" he asked me in his Spanish Creole. 47 He did not give me a chance to give an answer.

"I go already." I thought I heard a little *méringue* in the sway of his voice. "I call 48 the gendarmes. They are coming. I smell that rotten flesh. I know you kill the child and keep it with you for evil."

"You acted too soon," I said.

"You kill the child and keep it in your room."

"You know me," I said. "We've been together."

"I don't know you from the fly on a pile of cow manure," he said. "You eat little 49 children who haven't even had time to earn their souls."

He only kept his hands on me because he was afraid that I would run away and 50 escape.

I looked down at Rose. In my mind I saw what I had seen for all my other girls. 51 I imagined her teething, crawling, crying, fussing, and just misbehaving herself.

Over her little corpse, we stood, a country maid and a Spaniard grounds man. 52
I should have asked his name before I offered him my body.

We made a pretty picture standing there. Rose, me, and him. Between the pool 53
and the gardenias, waiting for the law.

## READING FOR CONTENT

1. Describe in your own words the dramatic situation implied in paragraph 2. What kind of relationship does the narrator appear to have with her mother and other female members of her family in paragraphs 15 and 18?

2. Describe in your own words the narrator's relationship with her husband in paragraph 27? What impact does her inability to bear a child have on the situation implied in paragraph 2?

3. How clear is the story about the death of baby Rose? Did she die in paragraph 35? Or was she already dead in paragraph 14? What is her probable history? Why does the Dominican man conclude in paragraph 48 that the narrator killed her? Did she? How do the ambiguities allow the narrator to stand-in for many different women who share her plight?

## READING FOR GENRE, ORGANIZATION, AND STYLISTIC FEATURES

1. The genre of the short story often draws great power from deliberate vagueness and crushing irony. List important features that you find vague about this story and speculate on the irony of the childless woman being accused of the child's death in its final paragraphs.

2. How do the interruptions in the story before paragraphs 15 and 23 help to organize the narrative? What do paragraphs 15–22 contribute to the characterization of the narrator and the atmosphere of the setting?

3. What stylistic effects heighten the attention called to the differences between country and city in paragraph 22? What stylistic effects heighten the attention called to casual sexual practices in paragraphs 29 and 34?

## READING FOR RHETORICAL CONTEXT

1. What cultural practices do the comparisons in paragraphs 13–14 evoke?

2. What cultural differences between the narrator and the rich people who have hired her as a maid do paragraphs 23–25 suggest?

## WRITING ASSIGNMENTS

1. Write a literary analysis of 1,000 words on the character of the narrator. What is her background? What has brought her into contact with baby Rose? What is she doing with the baby? What psychological factors might explain the action?

2. Write a literary analysis of 1,000 words on the relationship between the story and its social context. What is the setting? What social classes do the narrator and the other characters come from? What factors cause the events and their likely outcome?

# Birthmates

## *Gish Jen*

*Gish Jen (b. 1956) is a second-generation Chinese-American who grew up in Scarsdale, New York, and received a B.A. from Harvard University. Her novels include* Typical American *(1992),* Mona in the Promised Land *(1997), and* The Love Wife *(2004). Her early short stories are collected in* Who's Irish *(1999). She lives and writes in Cambridge, Massachusetts.*

## PREREADING

Scan through paragraphs 1, 4, 14, 31, and 42 to retrieve the names of the story's characters. What do these names tell you (or not tell you) about the characters' ethnic identities? Speculate about possible situations that might bring together a divorced middle-aged Chinese-American male, a young African-American single mother, and a not-too-bright Caucasian male businessman. As you read the complete story, check your speculations against the humorous ways the narrative manages to surprise you.

$T$his was what responsibility meant in a dinosaur industry, toward the end of yet  1
another quarter of bad-to-worse news: that you called the travel agent back, and even though there was indeed an economy room in the hotel where the conference was being held, a room overlooking the cooling towers, you asked if there wasn't something still cheaper. And when Marie-the-new-girl came back with something amazingly cheap, you took it—only to discover, as Art Woo was discovering now, that the doors were locked after nine o'clock. The neighborhood had looked not great but not bad, and the building itself, regular enough. Brick, four stories, a rolled-up awning. A bright-lit hotel logo, with a raised-plastic, smiling sun. But there was a kind of crossbar rigged across the inside of the glass door, and that was not at all regular. A two-by-four, it appeared, wrapped in rust-colored carpet. Above this, inside the glass, hung a small gray sign. If the taxi had not left, Art might not have rung the buzzer, as per the instructions.

But the taxi had indeed left, and the longer Art huddled on the stoop in the  2
clumpy December snow, the emptier and more poorly lit the street appeared. His buzz was answered by an enormous black man wearing a neck brace. The shoulder seams of the man's blue waffle-weave jacket were visibly straining; around the brace was tied a necktie, which reached only a third of the way down his chest. All the same, it was neatly fastened together with a hotel-logo tie tack about two inches from the bottom. The tie tack was smiling; the man was not. He held his smooth, round face perfectly expressionless, and he lowered his gaze at every opportunity—not so that it was rude, but so that it was clear he wasn't selling anything to anybody. Regulation tie, thought Art. Regulation jacket. He wondered if the man would turn surly soon enough.

For Art had come to few conclusions about life in his forty-nine years, but this was  3
one of them: that men turned surly when their clothes didn't fit them. This man, though,

From: *Who's Irish* (New York: Knopf, 1999), pp. 17–36.

belied the rule. He was courteous, almost formal in demeanor; and if the lobby seemed not only too small for him, like his jacket, but also too much like a bus station, what with its smoked mirror wall, and its linoleum, and its fake wood, and its vending machines, what did that matter to Art? The sitting area looked as though it was in the process of being cleaned; the sixties Scandinavian chairs and couch and coffee table had been pulled every which way, as if by someone hell-bent on the dust balls. Still Art proceeded with his check-in. He was going with his gut, here as in any business situation. Here as in any business situation, he was looking foremost at the personnel, and the man with the neck brace had put him at some ease. It wasn't until after Art had taken his credit card back that he noticed, above the checkout desk, a wooden plaque from a neighborhood association. He squinted at its brass faceplate: FEWEST CUSTOMER INJURIES, 1972–73.

What about the years since '73? Had the hotel gotten more dangerous, or had other hotels gotten safer? Maybe neither. For all he knew, the neighborhood association had dissolved and was no longer distributing plaques. Art reminded himself that in life, some signs were no signs. It's what he used to tell his ex-wife, Lisa. Lisa, who loved to read everything into everything; Lisa, who was attuned. She left him on a day when she saw a tree get split by lightning. Of course, that was an extraordinary thing to see. An event of a lifetime. Lisa said the tree had sizzled. He wished he had seen it, too. But what did it mean, except that the tree had been the tallest in the neighborhood, and was no longer? It meant nothing; ditto for the plaque. Art made his decision, which perhaps was not the right decision. Perhaps he should have looked for another hotel. 4

But it was late—on the way out, his plane had sat on the runway, just sat and sat, as if it were never going to take off—and God only knew what he would have ended up paying if he had relied on a cabbie simply to take him somewhere else. Forget twice—it could have been three, four times what he would have paid for that room with the view of the cooling towers, easy. At this hour, after all, and that was a conference rate. 5

So he double-locked his door instead. He checked behind the hollow-core doors of the closet, and under the steel-frame bed, and also in the swirly-green shower stall unit. He checked behind the seascapes to be sure there weren't any peepholes. The window opened onto a fire escape; not much he could do about that except check the window locks. Big help that those were—a sure deterrent for the subset of all burglars that was burglars too skittish to break glass. Which was what percent of intruders, probably? Ten percent? Fifteen? He closed the drapes, then decided he would be more comfortable with the drapes open. He wanted to be able to see what approached, if anything did. He unplugged the handset of his phone from the base, a calculated risk. On the one hand, he wouldn't be able to call the police if there was an intruder. On the other, he would be armed. He had read somewhere a story about a woman who threw the handset of her phone at an attacker, and killed him. Needless to say, there had been some luck involved in that eventuality. Still, Art thought that (a) surely he could throw as hard as that woman, and (b) even without the luck, his throw would most likely be hard enough to slow up an intruder at least. Especially since this was an old handset, the hefty kind that made you feel the seriousness of human communication. In a newer hotel, he probably would have had a lighter phone, with lots of buttons he would never use but which would make him feel he had many resources at his disposal. In the conference hotel, there were probably buttons for the health club, and for the concierge, and for the three restaurants, and for room service. He tried not to think about this as he went to sleep, clutching the handset. 6

He did not sleep well. 7

In the morning, he debated whether to take the handset with him into the eleva- 8
tor. It wasn't like a knife, say, that could be whipped out of nowhere. Even a pistol at
least fit in a guy's pocket. A telephone handset did not. All the same, he took it with
him. He tried to carry it casually, as if he was going out for a run and using it for a hand
weight, or as if he was in the telephone business.

He strode down the hall. Victims shuffled; that's what everybody said. A lot of 9
mugging had to do with nonverbal cues, which is why Lisa used to walk tall after dark,
sending vibes. For this, he used to tease her. If she was so worried, she should lift
weights and run, the way he did. That, he maintained, was the substantive way of helping oneself. She had agreed. For a while they had met after work at the gym. Then she
dropped a weight on her toe and decided she preferred to sip pina coladas and watch.
Naturally, he grunted on. But to what avail? Who could appreciate his pectorals
through his suit and overcoat? Pectorals had no deterrent value, that was what he was
thinking now. And he was, though not short, not tall. He continued striding. Sending
vibes. He was definitely going to eat in the dining room of the hotel where the conference was being held, he decided. What's more, he was going to have a full American
breakfast with bacon and eggs, none of this continental bullshit.

In truth, he had always considered the sight of men eating croissants slightly 10
ridiculous, especially at the beginning, when for the first bite they had to maneuver the
point of the crescent into their mouths. No matter what a person did, he ended up with
an asymmetrical mouthful of pastry, which he then had to relocate with his tongue to a
more central location. This made him look less purposive than he might. Also, croissants were more apt than other breakfast foods to spray little flakes all over one's clean
dark suit. Art himself had accordingly never ordered a croissant in any working situation, and he believed that attention to this sort of detail was how it was that he had not
lost his job like so many of his colleagues.

This was, in other words, how it happened that he was still working in a dying 11
industry, and was now carrying a telephone handset with him into the elevator. Art
braced himself as the elevator doors opened slowly, jerkily, in the low-gear manner of
elevator doors in the Third World. He strode in, and was surrounded by, of all things,
children. Down in the lobby, too, there were children and, here and there, women he
knew to be mothers by their looks of dogged exasperation. A welfare hotel! He laughed
out loud. Almost everyone was black; the white children stood out like little missed
opportunities of the type that made Art's boss throw his tennis racket across the room.
Of course, the racket was always in its padded protective cover and not in much danger
of getting injured, though the person in whose vicinity it was aimed sometimes was. Art
once suffered what he rather hoped would turn out to be a broken nose, but was only a
bone bruise. There was so little skin discoloration that people had a hard time believing
the incident had actually taken place. Yet it had. *Don't talk to me about fault. Bottom
line, it's you Japs who are responsible for this whole fucking mess,* his boss had said. Never
mind that what was the matter with minicomputers, really, was personal computers, a
wholly American phenomenon. And never mind that Art could have sued over this
incident if he could have proved that it had happened. Some people, most notably
Lisa, thought he at least ought to have quit.

But he didn't sue and he didn't quit. He took his tennis racket on the nose, so to 12
speak, and when his boss apologized the next day for losing control, Art said he understood. And when his boss said that Art shouldn't take what he said personally—that he
knew Art was not a Jap, but a Chink, plus he had called someone else a lazy Wop that

very morning, it was just his style—Art said again that he understood, and also that he hoped his boss would remember Art's great understanding come promotion time. Which his boss did, to Art's satisfaction. In Art's view, this was a victory. In Art's view, he had made a deal out of the incident. He had perceived leverage where others would only have perceived affront. He had maintained a certain perspective.

But this certain perspective was, in addition to the tree, why Lisa had left him. He 13 thought of that now, the children underfoot, his handset in hand. So many children. It was as if he were seeing before him all the children he would never have. His heart lost muscle. A child in a red running suit ran by, almost grabbed the handset out of Art's grasp. Then another, in a brown jacket with a hood. Art looked up. A group of grade-school boys was arrayed about the seating area, watching. Art had become the object of a dare, apparently; realizing this, he felt renewed enough to want to laugh again. When a particularly small child swung by in his turn—a child of maybe five or six, small enough to be wearing snow pants—Art almost tossed the handset to him. But who wanted to be charged for a missing phone?

As it was, Art wondered if he shouldn't put the handset back in his room rather than 14 carry it around all day. For what was he going to do at the hotel where the conference was, check it? He imagined himself running into Billy Shore—that was his counterpart at Info-Edge, and his competitor in the insurance market. A man with no management ability, and no technical background, either, but he could offer customers a personal computer option, which Art could not. What's more, Billy had been a quarterback in college. This meant he strutted around as though it still mattered that he had connected with his tight end in the final minutes of what Art could not help but think of as the Wilde-Beastie game. And it meant that Billy was sure to ask him, *What are you doing with a phone in your hand? Talking to yourself again?* Making everyone around them laugh.

Billy was that kind of guy. He had come up through sales, and was always crack- 15 ing a certain type of joke—about drinking, or sex, or how much the wife shopped. Of course, he never used those words. He never called things by their plain names. He always talked in terms of *knocking back some brewskis,* or *running the triple option,* or *doing some damage.* He made assumptions as though it were a basic bodily function. Of course his knowledge was the common knowledge. Of course people understood what it was that he was referring to so delicately. *Listen, champ,* he said, putting his arm around you. If he was smug, it was in an affable kind of way. *So what do you think the poor people are doing tonight?* Billy not only spoke what Art called Mainstreamese, he spoke such a pure dialect of it that Art once asked him if he realized he was a pollster's delight. He spoke the thoughts of thousands, Art told him; he breathed their very words. Naturally, Billy did not respond, except to say, *What's that?* and turn away. He rubbed his torso as he turned, as if ruffling his chest hairs through the long-staple cotton. Primate behavior, Lisa used to call this. It was her belief that neckties evolved in order to check this very motion, uncivilized as it was. She also believed that this was the sort of thing you never saw Asian men do—at least not if they were brought up properly.

Was that true? Art wasn't so sure. Lisa had grown up on the West Coast. She was 16 full of Asian consciousness, whereas all he knew was that no one had so much as smiled politely at his pollster remark. On the other hand, the first time Art was introduced to Billy, and Billy said, *Art Woo, how's that for a nice Pole-ack name,* everyone broke right up in great rolling guffaws. Of course, they laughed the way people laughed at conferences, which was not because something was really funny, but because it was part of being a good guy, and because they didn't want to appear to have missed their cue.

The phone, the phone. If only Art could fit it in his briefcase! But his briefcase 17 was overstuffed; it was always overstuffed; really, it was too bad he had the slim silhouette type, and hard-side besides. Italian. That was Lisa's doing; she thought the fatter kind made him look like a salesman. Not that there was anything the matter with that, in his view. Billy Shore notwithstanding, sales were important. But she was the liberal arts type, Lisa was, the type who did not like to think about money, but only about her feelings. Money was money to her, but support, and then a means of support much inferior to hand-holding or other forms of fingerplay. She did not believe in a modern-day economy, in which everyone played a part in a large and complex whole that introduced efficiencies that at least theoretically raised everyone's standard of living. She believed in expressing herself. Also in taking classes, and in knitting. There was nothing, she believed, like taking a walk in the autumn woods wearing a hand-knit sweater. Of course, she did look beautiful in them, especially the violet ones. That was her color—Asians are winters, she always said—and sometimes she liked to wear the smallest smidgen of matching violet eyeliner.

Little Snowpants ran at Art again, going for the knees. A tackle, thought Art as he 18 went down. Red Running Suit snatched away the handset and went sprinting off, triumphant. Teamwork! The children chortled together. How could Art not smile, even if they had gotten his overcoat dirty? He brushed himself off, ambled over.

"Hey, guys," he said. "That was some move back there." 19

"Ching chong polly wolly wing wong," said Little Snowpants.

"Now, now, that's no way to talk," said Art.

"Go to hell!" said Brown Jacket, pulling at the corners of his eyes to make them slanty.

"Listen up," said Art. "I'll make you a deal." Really he only meant to get the handset back, so as to avoid getting charged for it.

But the next thing he knew, something had hit his head with a crack, and he was out. 20

Lisa had left in a more or less amicable way. She had not called a lawyer, or a 21 mover. She had simply pressed his hands with both of hers and, in her most California voice, said, *Let's be nice.* Then she had asked him if he wouldn't help her move her boxes, at least the heavy ones. He had helped. He had carried the heavy boxes, and also the less heavy ones. Being a weight lifter, after all. He had sorted books and rolled glasses into pieces of newspaper, feeling all the while like a statistic. A member of the modern age, a story for their friends to rake over, and all because he had not gone with Lisa to her grieving group. Or at least that was the official beginning of the trouble. Probably the real beginning had been when Lisa—no, *they*—had trouble getting pregnant. When they decided to, as the saying went, do infertility. Or had he done the deciding, as Lisa later maintained? He had thought it was a joint decision, though it was true that he had done the analysis that led to the joint decision. He had been the one to figure the odds, to do the projections. He had drawn the decision tree according to whose branches they had nothing to lose by going ahead.

Neither one of them had realized how much would be involved—the tests, the 22 procedures, the drugs, the ultrasounds. Lisa's arms were black and blue from having her blood drawn every day, and before long he was giving practice shots to an orange, that he might prick her some more. Then he was telling her to take a breath so that on the exhale he could poke her in the bullocks. This was nothing like poking an orange. The first time, he broke out in such a sweat that his vision blurred; he pulled the needle out slowly and crookedly, occasioning a most unorangelike cry. The second time, he wore a sweatband. Her ovaries swelled to the point where he could feel them through her jeans.

Art still had the used syringes—snapped in half and stored, as per their doctor's  23
recommendation, in plastic soda bottles. Lisa had left him those. Bottles of medical waste, to be disposed of responsibly, meaning that he was probably stuck with them, ha-ha, for the rest of his life. This was his souvenir of their ordeal. Hers was sweeter—a little pile of knit goods. For through it all, she had knit, as if to demonstrate an alternative use of needles. Sweaters, sweaters, but also baby blankets, mostly to give away, only one or two to keep. She couldn't help herself. There was anesthesia, and egg harvesting, and anesthesia and implanting, until she finally did get pregnant, twice. The third time, she went to four and a half months before the doctors found a problem. On the amnio, it showed up, brittle-bone disease—a genetic abnormality such as could happen to anyone.

He steeled himself for another attempt; she grieved. And this was the difference  24
between them, that he saw hope, still, some feeble, skeletal hope, where she saw loss. She called the fetus her baby, though it was not a baby, just a baby-to-be, as he tried to say; as even the grieving-group facilitator tried to say. Lisa said Art didn't understand, couldn't possibly understand. She said it was something you understood with your body, and that it was not his body, but hers, which knew the baby, loved the baby, lost the baby. In the grieving class, the women agreed. They commiserated. They bonded, subtly affirming their common biology by doing 85 percent of the talking. The room was painted mauve—a feminine color that seemed to support them in their process. At times, it seemed that the potted palms were female, too, nodding, nodding, though really their sympathy was just rising air from the heating vents. Other husbands started missing sessions—they never talked anyway, you hardly noticed their absence—and finally he missed some also. One, maybe two, for real reasons, nothing cooked up. But the truth was, as Lisa sensed, that he thought she had lost perspective. They could try again, after all. What did it help to despair? Look, they knew they could get pregnant and, what's more, sustain the pregnancy. That was progress. But she was like an island in her grief—a retreating island, if there was such a thing, receding toward the horizon of their marriage, and then to its vanishing point.

Of course, he had missed her terribly at first. Now he missed her still, but more  25
sporadically, at odd moments—for example, now, waking up in a strange room with ice on his head. He was lying on an unmade bed just like the bed in his room, except that everywhere around it were heaps of what looked to be blankets and clothes. The only clothes on a hanger were his jacket and overcoat; these hung neatly, side by side, in the otherwise-empty closet. There was also an extra table in this room, with a two-burner hot plate, a pan on top of that, and a pile of dishes. A brown cube refrigerator. The drapes were closed. A chair had been pulled up close to him; the bedside light was on. A woman was leaning into its circle, mopping his brow.

"Don't you move, now," she said.  26

She was the shade of black Lisa used to call mochaccino, and she was wearing a  27
blue flowered apron. Kind eyes; a long face—the kind of face where you could see the muscles of the jaw working alongside the cheekbone. An upper lip like an archery bow; a graying Afro, shortish. She smelled of smoke. Nothing unusual except that she was so very thin, about the thinnest person he had ever seen, and yet she was cooking something—burning something, it seemed, though maybe the smell was just a hair fallen onto the

heating element. She stood up to tend the pan. The acrid smell faded. He saw powder on the table. White; there was a plastic bag full of it. His eyes widened. He sank back, trying to figure out what to do. His head pulsed. Tylenol, he needed, two. Lisa always took one because she was convinced the dosages recommended were based on large male specimens, and though she had never said that she thought he ought to keep it to one also, not being so tall, he was adamant about taking two. Two, two, two. He wanted his drugs; he wanted them now. And his own drugs, that was, not somebody else's.

"Those kids kind of rough," said the woman. "They getting to that age. I told 28 them one of these days somebody gonna get hurt, and sure enough, they knocked you right out. You might as well been hit with a bowling ball. I never saw anything like it. We called the Man, but they got other things on their mind besides to come see about trouble here. Nobody shot, so they went on down to the Dunkin' Donuts. They know they can count on a ruckus there." She winked. "How you feelin? That egg hurt?"

He felt his head. A lump sat right on top of it, incongruous as something left by a 29 glacier. What were those called, those stray boulders you saw perched in hair-raising positions? On cliffs? He thought.

"I feel like I died and came back to life headfirst," he said.                    30

"I gonna make you something nice. Make you feel a whole lot better."

"Uh," said Art. "If you don't mind, I'd rather just have a Tylenol. You got any Tylenol? I had some in my briefcase. If I still have my briefcase."

"Your what?"

"My briefcase," said Art again, with a panicky feeling. "Do you know what happened to my briefcase?"

"Oh, it's right by the door. I'll get it, don't move."

Then there it was, his briefcase, its familiar hard-sided Italian slenderness resting right on his stomach. He clutched it. "Thank you," he whispered.

"You need help with that thing?"

"No," said Art. But when he opened the case, it slid, and everything spilled out— his notes, his files, his papers. All that figuring. How strange his concerns looked on this brown shag carpet.

"Here," said the woman. And again—"I'll get it, don't move"—as gently, beautifully, she gathered up all the folders and put them in the case. There was an odd, almost practiced finesse to her movements; the files could have been cards in a card dealer's hands. "I used to be a nurse," she explained, as if reading his mind. "I picked up a few folders in my time. Here's the Tylenol."

"I'll have two."

"Course you will," she said. "Two Tylenol and some hot milk with honey. Hope you don't mind the powdered. We just got moved here, we don't have no supplies. I used to be a nurse, but I don't got no milk and I don't got no Tylenol, my guests got to bring their own. How you like that."

Art laughed as much as he could. "You got honey, though. How's that?"

"I don't know, it got left here by somebody," said the nurse. "Hope there's nothing growing in it."

Art laughed again, then let her help him sit up to take his pills. The nurse—her 31 name was Cindy—plumped his pillows. She administered his milk. Then she sat—very close to him, it seemed—and chatted amiably about this and that. How she wasn't going to be staying at the hotel for too long, how her kids had had to switch schools, how she wasn't afraid to take in a strange, injured man. After all, she grew up in the projects; she could take care of herself. She showed him her switchblade, which had somebody's initials carved on it, she didn't know whose. She had never used it, she said, somebody gave it to her. And that somebody didn't know whose initials those were, either, she said, at least so far as she knew. Then she lit a cigarette and smoked while he told her first about his conference and then about how he had ended up at this hotel by mistake. He told her the latter with some hesitation, hoping he wasn't offending her. She laughed with a cough, emitting a series of smoke puffs.

"Sure musta been a shock," she said. "End up in a place like this. This ain't no 32 place for a nice boy like you."

That stung a little, being called *boy*. But more than the stinging, he felt some- 33 thing else. "What about you? It's no place for you, either, you and your kids."

"Maybe so," she said. "But that's how the Almighty planned it, right? You folk rise 34 up while we set and watch." She said this with so little rancor, with something so like intimacy, that it almost seemed an invitation of sorts.

Maybe he was kidding himself. Maybe he was assuming things, just like Billy 35 Shore, just like men throughout the ages. Projecting desire where there was none, assigning and imagining, and in juicy detail. Being Asian didn't exempt him from that. *You folk.*

Art was late, but it didn't much matter. His conference was being held in conjunc- 36 tion with a much larger conference, the real draw; the idea being that maybe between workshops and on breaks, the conferees would drift down and see what minicomputers could do for them. That mostly meant lunch, which probably would be slow at best. In the meantime, things were totally dead, allowing Art to appreciate just how much the trade-show floor had shrunk—down to a fraction of what it had been in previous years, and the booths were not what they had been, either. It used to be that the floor was crammed with the fanciest booths on the market. Art's was twenty by twenty; it took days to put together. Now you saw blank spots on the floor where exhibitors didn't even bother to show up, and those weren't even as demoralizing as some of the makeshift jobbies—exhibit booths that looked like high school science-fair projects. They might as well have been made out of cardboard and Magic Marker. Art himself had a booth you could buy from an airplane catalog, the kind that rolled up into Cordura bags. And people were stingy with brochures now, too. Gone were the twelve-page, four-color affairs. Now the pamphlets were four-page, two-color, with extrabold graphics for attempted pizzazz, and not everybody got one, only people who were serious.

Art set up. Then, even though he should have been manning his spot, he drifted 37 from booth to booth, saying hello to people he should have seen at breakfast. They were happy to see him, to talk shop, to pop some grapes off the old grapevine. Really, if he hadn't been staying in a welfare hotel, he would have felt downright respected. *You folk.* What folk did Cindy mean? Maybe she was just being matter-of-fact, keeping her perspective. Although how could anyone be so matter-of-fact about something so bitter? He wondered this even as he imagined taking liberties with her. These began with a knock on her door and coursed through some hot times but finished (what a good boy he was) with him rescuing her and her children (he wondered how many there were) from their dead-end life. What was the matter with him, that he could not imagine mating without legal sanction? His libido was not what it should be, clearly, or at least it was not what Billy Shore's was. Art tried to think *game plan*, but in truth he could not even identify what a triple option would be in this case. All he knew was that, assuming, to begin with, that she was willing, he couldn't sleep with a woman like Cindy and then leave her flat. She could *you folk* him, he could never *us folk* her.

He played with some software at a neighboring booth. It appeared interesting 38 enough but kept crashing, so he couldn't tell much. Then he dutifully returned to his own booth, where he was visited by a number of people he knew, people with whom he was friendly—the sort of people to whom he might have shown pictures of his children. He considered telling one or two of them about the events of the morning. Not about the invitation that might not have been an invitation, but about finding himself in a welfare hotel and being beaned with his own telephone. Phrases drifted through his head. *Not as bad as you'd think. You'd be surprised how friendly. And how unpretentious. Though, of course, no health club.* But in the end, the subject simply did not come up and did not come up, until he realized that he was keeping it to himself, and that he was committing more resources to this task than he had readily available. He felt invaded—as if he had been infected by a self-replicating bug. Something that was iterating and iterating, crowding the cpu. The secret was intolerable; it was bound to spill out of him sooner or later. He just hoped it wouldn't be sooner.

He just hoped it wouldn't be to Billy Shore, for whom Art had begun to search, so 39 as to be certain to avoid him.

Art had asked about Billy at the various booths, but no one had seen him; his 40 absence spooked Art. When finally some real live conferees stopped by to see his wares, Art had trouble concentrating. Everywhere in the conversation he was missing opportunities, he knew it. And all because his cpu was full of iterating nonsense. Not too long ago, in looking over some database software in which were loaded certain fun facts about people in the industry, Art had looked up Billy, and discovered that he had been born the same day Art was, only four years later. It just figured that Billy would be younger. That was irritating. But Art was happy for the information, too. He had made a note of it, so that when he ran into Billy at this conference, he could kid him about their birthdays. Now, he rehearsed. *Have I got a surprise for you. I always knew you were a Leo. I believe this makes us birthmates.* Anything not to mention the welfare hotel and all that had happened there.

In the end, Art did not run into Billy at all. In the end, Art wondered about Billy 41 all day, only to learn, finally, that Billy had moved on to a new job in the Valley, with a start-up. In personal computers, naturally. A good move, no matter what kind of beating he took on his house.

"Life is about the long term," said Ernie Ford, the informant. "And let's face it, 42 there is no long term here."

Art agreed as warmly as he could. In one way, he was delighted that his competi- 43 tor had left. If nothing else, that would mean a certain amount of disarray at Info-Edge, which was good news for Art. The insurance market was, unfortunately, some 40 percent of his business, and he could use any advantage he could get. Another bonus was that Art was never going to have to see Billy again. Billy his birthmate, with his jokes and his Mainstreamese. Still, Art felt depressed.

"We should all have gotten out way before this," he said. 44

"Truer words were never spoke," said Ernie. Ernie had never been a particular 45 friend of Art's, but talking about Billy was somehow making him chummier. "I'd have packed my bags by now if it weren't for the wife, the kids—they don't want to leave their friends, you know? Plus, the oldest is a junior in high school. We can't afford for him to move now. He's got to stay put and make those nice grades so he can make a nice college. That means I've got to stay, if it means pushing McMuffins for Ronald McDonald. But now you . . . "                                                                                46

"Maybe I should go," said Art.

"Definitely, you should go," said Ernie. "What's keeping you?"

"Nothing," said Art. "I'm divorced now. And that's that, right? Sometimes people get undivorced, but you can't exactly count on it."

"Go," said Ernie. "Take my advice. If I hear of anything, I'll send it your way."

"Thanks," said Art.

But of course he did not expect that Ernie would likely turn anything up soon. It 47 had been a long time since anyone had called Art or anybody else he knew of. Too many people had gotten stranded, and they were too desperate, everybody knew it. Also, the survivors were looked upon with suspicion. Anybody who was any good had jumped ship early, that was the conventional wisdom. There was Art, struggling to hold on to his job, only to discover that there were times you didn't want to hold on to your job—times you ought to maneuver for the golden parachute and jump. Times the goal was to get yourself fired. Who would have figured that?

A few warm-blooded conferees at the end of the day—at least they were polite. 48 Then, as he was packing up to return to the hotel, a surprise. A headhunter approached him, a friend of Ernest's, he said.

"Ernest?" said Art. "Oh, Ernie! Ford! Of course!"

The headhunter was a round, ruddy man with a ring of hair like St. Francis of 49 Assisi, and, sure enough, a handful of bread crumbs. A great opportunity, he said. Right now he had to run, but he knew just the guy Art had to meet, a guy who was coming in that evening. For something else, it happened, but he also needed someone like Art. Needed him yesterday, really. Should've been a priority. Might just be a match. Maybe a quick breakfast in the a.m.? Could he call in an hour or so? Art said, Of course. And when Saint Francis asked his room number, Art hesitated, but then gave the name of the welfare hotel. How would Saint Francis know what kind of hotel it was? Art gave the name out confidently, making his manner count. He almost hadn't made it to the conference at all, he said. Being so busy. It was only at the last minute that he realized he could do it. Things moved around, he found an opening and figured what the hell. But it was too late to book the conference hotel. Hence he was staying elsewhere.

Success. All day Art's mind had been churning; suddenly it seemed to empty. He 50 might as well have been Billy, born on the same day as Art was, but in another year, under different stars. How much simpler things seemed. He did not labor on two, three, six tasks at once, multiprocessing. He knew one thing at a time, and that thing just now was that the day was a victory. He walked briskly back to the hotel. He crossed the lobby in a no-nonsense manner. An impervious man. He did not knock on Cindy's door. He was moving on, moving west. There would be a good job there, and a new life. Perhaps he would take up tennis. Perhaps he would own a Jacuzzi. Perhaps he would learn to like all those peculiar foods people ate out there, like jicama, and seaweed. Perhaps he would go macrobiotic.

It wasn't until he got to his room that he remembered that his telephone had no 51 handset.

He sat on his bed. There was a noise at his window, followed, sure enough, by 52 someone's shadow. He wasn't even surprised. Anyway, the fellow wasn't stopping at Art's room, at least not on this trip. That was luck. *You folk*, Cindy had said, taking back the ice bag. Art could see her perspective; he was luckier than she, by far. But just now, as the shadow crossed his window again, he thought mostly about how unarmed he was. If he had a telephone, he would probably call Lisa—that was how big a pool seemed to be forming around him, all of a sudden; an ocean, it seemed. Also, he would call the police. But first he would call Lisa, and see how she felt about his possibly moving west. *Quite possibly*, he would say, not wanting to make it sound as though he was calling her for nothing—not wanting to make it sound as though he was awash, at sea, perhaps drowning. He would not want to sound like a haunted man; he would not want to sound as though he was calling from a welfare hotel, years too late, to say *Yes, that was a baby we had together, it would have been a baby*. For he could not help now but recall the doctor explaining about that child, a boy, who had appeared so mysteriously perfect in the ultrasound. Transparent, he had looked, and gelatinous, all soft head and quick heart; but he would have, in being born, broken every bone in his body.

## READING FOR CONTENT

1. In paragraph 14, how does the story introduce Billy Shore as Art's "birthmate," similar to him in many ways, yet different in others?
2. As the story tends toward buoyant humor and even some slapstick comedy, how does it incorporate poignant feeling in the discussion of Art and Lisa's childlessness in paragraphs 21–24? Does the title "Birthmates" carry any special meaning in this context?
3. What does Cindy's phrase "you folk" mean in paragraph 34? How does Art interpret it in paragraphs 35 and 37?
4. In paragraph 45, how does the story represent Ernie Ford as similar to Art and Billy in some ways, yet different in others?

## READING FOR GENRE, ORGANIZATION, AND STYLISTIC FEATURES

1. The genre of the short story frequently draws great power from the surprising effects of a sudden but well-prepared ironic reversal. How does paragraph 51 amount to such a reversal? Is it funny, sad, or some combination of both?
2. How do the interruptions in the story before paragraphs 21, 25, 35, and 41 help to organize the narrative? What purposes do the italicized words serve in paragraphs 33, 35, 37, 38, 40, and 52?
3. Read through the story and annotate in the margin specific instances of humor, such as the clumsiness of the telephone handset in paragraph 8, the croissant crumbs in paragraph 10, the contradiction in paragraph 39, and the appearance of the title in paragraph 40?

## READING FOR RHETORICAL CONTEXT

1. What does Art mean by "Mainstreamese" in paragraph 15? Does the story offer examples of this kind of speech spoken by characters other than Billy?
2. What cultural stereotypes does Art's fantasy in paragraph 37 evoke?
3. What is the effect of the repetition of "Mainstreamese" in paragraph 43? Does Art himself attempt to speak in any of its forms?

## WRITING ASSIGNMENTS

1. Write a literary analysis of 1,000 words on the character of the narrator. What is his background? What choices, accidents, surprises, and coincidences bring him into contact with people from other ethnic backgrounds? How funny and sad are the features of his predicament that overlap with those of the other characters?

2. Write a literary analysis of 1,000 words on the relationship between the story and its social context. What is the setting? What social classes do the narrator and the other characters come from? How do the ethnic identities of the narrator and the other characters clarify or complicate their responses to the situation?

■ ■ ■ ■ ■ ■ ■ ■ ■ ■ ■ ■

# Bohemians

## *George Saunders*

*George Saunders (b. 1958) grew up in Chicago, Illinois, received a B.S. from the Colorado School of Mines, and pursued a career as (among other things) a geophysical engineer before turning to writing. He has published three collections of short stories, including* Civilwarland in Bad Decline *(1996),* Pastoralia *(1999), and* In Persuasion Nation *(2006); a novella,* The Brief and Frightening Reign of Phil *(2005); an all-ages book,* The Very Persistent Gappers of Frip *(2006); and nonfiction articles in* The New Yorker *and* Gentleman's Quarterly. *He is a Professor of English at Syracuse University.*

## PREREADING

Scan through paragraphs 1–3 to retrieve the profiles of important characters in the story. What do these profiles tell you (or not tell you) about them? What does Dad's greeting them so incongruously with the Czech word for "door" tell you about him? about them? about the narrator's family? about the humor of the story that will follow? Speculate about possible situations that might bring together the narrator and the two "Bohemians." As you read the complete story, check your speculations against unforeseen ways in which the story manages to surprise you.

In a lovely urban coincidence, the last two houses on our block were both occupied 1 by widows who had lost their husbands in Eastern European pogroms. Dad called them the Bohemians. He called anyone white with an accent a Bohemian. Whenever he saw one of the Bohemians, he greeted her by mispronouncing the Czech word for "door." Neither Bohemian was Czech, but both were polite, so when Dad said "door" to them they answered cordially, as if he weren't perennially schlockered.

Mrs. Poltoi, the stouter Bohemian, had spent the war in a crawl space, splitting a   2
daily potato with six cousins. Consequently she was bitter and claustrophobic and
loved food. If you ate something while standing near her, she stared at it going into your
mouth. She wore only black. She said the Catholic Church was a jeweled harlot drinking the blood of the poor. She said America was a spoiled child ignorant of grief. When
our ball rolled onto her property, she seized it and waddled into her backyard and
pitched it into the quarry.

Mrs. Hopanlitski, on the other hand, was thin, and joyfully made pipecleaner   3
animals. When I brought home one of her crude dogs in tophats, Mom said, "Take over
your Mold-A-Hero. To her, it will seem like the toy of a king." To Mom, the camps,
massacres, and railroad sidings of twenty years before were as unreal as covered wagons.
When Mrs. H. claimed her family had once owned serfs, Mom's attention wandered.
She had a tract house in mind. No way was she getting one. We were renting a remodeled
garage behind the Giancarlos. Dad was basically drinking up the sporting-goods store.
His NFL helmets were years out of date. I'd stop by after school and find the store closed
and Dad getting sloshed among the fake legs with Bennie Delmonico at Prosthetics
World.

Using the Mold-A-Hero, I cast Mrs. H. a plastic Lafayette, and she said she'd keep   4
it forever on her sill. Within a week, she'd given it to Elizabeth the Raccoon. I didn't
mind. Raccoon, an only child like me, had nothing. The Kletz brothers called her
Raccoon for the bags she had under her eyes from never sleeping. Her parents fought
nonstop. They fought over breakfast. They fought in the yard in their underwear. At
dusk they stood on their porch whacking each other with lengths of weather stripping.
Raccoon practically had spinal curvature from spending so much time slumped over
with misery. When the Kletz brothers called her Raccoon, she indulged them by rub-
bing her hands together ferally. The nickname was the most attention she'd ever had.
Sometimes she'd wish to be hit by a car so she could come back as a true Raccoon and
track down the Kletzes and give them rabies.

"Never wish harm on yourself or others," Mrs. H. said. "You are a lovely child."   5
Her English was flat and clear, almost like ours.

"Raccoon, you mean," Raccoon said. "A lovely Raccoon."

"A lovely child of God," Mrs. H. said.

"Yeah right," Raccoon said. "Tell again about the prince."

So Mrs. H. told again how she'd stood rapt in her yard watching an actual prince   6
powder his birthmark to invisibility. She remembered the smell of burning compost
from the fields, and men in colorful leggings dragging a gutted boar across a wooden
bridge. This was before she was forced to become a human pack animal in the
Carpathians, carrying the personal belongings of cruel officers. At night, they chained
her to a tree. Sometimes they burned her calves with a machine-gun barrel for fun.
Which was why she always wore kneesocks. After three years, she'd come home to find
her babies in tiny graves. They were, she would say, short-lived but wonderful gifts. She
did not now begrudge God for taking them. A falling star is brief, but isn't one nonetheless glad to have seen it? Her grace made us hate Mrs. Poltoi all the more. What was eating a sixth of a potato every day compared to being chained to a tree? What was being
crammed in with a bunch of your cousins compared to having your kids killed?

The summer I was ten, Raccoon and I, already borderline rejects due to our mutu-   7
ally unraveling households, were joined by Art Siminiak, who had recently made the
mistake of inviting the Kletzes in for lemonade. There was no lemonade. Instead, there

was Art's mom and a sailor from Great Lakes, passed out naked across the paper-drive stacks on the Siminiaks' sunporch.

This new, three-way friendship consisted of slumping in gangways, glovelessly 8 playing catch with a Wiffle, trailing hopefully behind kids whose homes could be entered without fear of fiasco.

Over on Mozart lived Eddie the Vacant. Eddie was seventeen, huge and simple. 9 He could crush a walnut in his bare hand, but first you had to put it there and tell him to do it. Once he'd pinned a "Vacant" sign to his shirt and walked around the neighborhood that way, and the name had stuck. Eddie claimed to see birds. Different birds appeared on different days of the week. Also, there was a Halloween bird and a Christmas bird.

One day, as Eddie hobbled by, we asked what kind of birds he was seeing. 10

"Party birds," he said. "They got big streamers coming out they butts."

"You having a party?" said Art. "You having a homo party?"

"I gone have a birthday party," said Eddie, blinking shyly.

"Your dad know?" Raccoon said.

"No, he don't yet," said Eddie.

His plans for the party were private and illogical. We peppered him with questions, 11 hoping to get him to further embarrass himself. The party would be held in his garage. As far as the junk car in there, he would push it out by hand. As far as the oil on the floor, he would soak it up using Handi Wipes. As far as music, he would play a trumpet.

"What are you going to play the trumpet with?" said Art. "Your asshole?"

"No, I not gone play it with that," Eddie said. "I just gone use my lips, okay?"

As far as girls, there would be girls; he knew many girls, from his job managing 12 the Drake Hotel. As far as food, there would be food, including pudding dumplings.

"You're the manager of the Drake Hotel," Raccoon said.

"Hey, I know how to get the money for pudding dumplings!" Eddie said.

Then he rang Poltoi's bell and asked for a contribution. She said for what. He said 13 for him. She said to what end. He looked at her blankly and asked for a contribution. She asked him to leave the porch. He asked for a contribution. Somewhere he'd got the idea that, when asking for a contribution, one angled to sit on the couch. He started in, and she pushed him back with a thick forearm. Down the front steps he went, ringing the iron banister with his massive head.

He got up and staggered away, a little blood on his scalp.

"Learn to leave people be!" Poltoi shouted after him.

Ten minutes later, Eddie Sr. stood on Poltoi's porch, a hulking effeminate tailor 14 too cowed to use his bulk for anything but butting open the jamming door at his shop.

"Since when has it become the sport to knock unfortunates down stairs?" he asked.

"He was not listen," she said. "I tell him no. He try to come inside."

"With all respect," he said, "it is in my son's nature to perhaps be not so respon-sive."

"Someone so unresponse, keep him indoors," she said. "He is big as a man. And I am old lady."

"Never has Eddie presented a danger to anyone," Eddie Sr. said.

"I know my rights," she said. "Next time, I call police."

But, having been pushed down the stairs, Eddie the Vacant couldn't seem to stay 15 away.

"Off this porch," Poltoi said through the screen when he showed up the next day, offering her an empty cold-cream jar for three dollars.

"We gone have so many snacks," he said. "And if I drink a alcohol drink, then watch out. Because I ain't allowed. I dance too fast."

He was trying the doorknob now, showing how fast he would dance if alcohol was served.

"Please, off this porch!" she shouted.

"Please, off this porch!" he shouted back, doubling at the waist in wacky laughter.

Poltoi called the cops. Normally, Lieutenant Brusci would have asked Eddie 16 what bird was in effect that day and given him a ride home in his squad. But this was during the OneCity fiasco. To cut graft, cops were being yanked off their regular beats and replaced by cops from other parts of town. A couple Armenians from South Shore showed up and dragged Eddie off the porch in a club-lock so tight he claimed the birds he was seeing were beakless.

"I'll give you a beak, Frankenstein," said one of the Armenians, tightening the choke hold.

Eddie entered the squad with all the fluidity of a hat rack. Art and Raccoon and 17 I ran over to Eddie Sr.'s tailor shop above the Marquee, which had sunk to porn. When Eddie Sr. saw us, he stopped his Singer by kicking out the plug. From downstairs came a series of erotic moans.

Eddie Sr. rushed to the hospital with his Purple Heart and some photos of Eddie 18 as a grinning wet-chinned kid on a pony. He found Eddie handcuffed to a bed, with an IV drip and a smashed face. Apparently, he'd bitten one of the Armenians. Bail was set at three hundred. The tailor shop made zilch. Eddie Sr.'s fabrics were a lexicon of yesteryear. Dust coated a bright-yellow sign that read "Zippers Repaired in Jiffy."

"Jail for that kid, I admit, don't make total sense," the judge said. "Three months in the Anston. Best I can do."

The Anston Center for Youth was a red-brick former forge now yarded in barbed 19 wire. After their shifts, the guards held loud hooting orgies kitty-corner at Zem's Lamplighter. Skinny immigrant women arrived at Zem's in station wagons and emerged hours later adjusting their stockings. From all over Chicago kids were sent to the Anston, kids who'd only ever been praised for the level of beatings they gave and received and their willingness to carve themselves up. One Anston kid had famously hired another kid to run over his foot. Another had killed his mother's lover with a can opener. A third had sliced open his own eyelid with a poptop on a dare.

Eddie the Vacant disappeared into the Anston in January and came out in March. 20

To welcome him home, Eddie Sr. had the neighborhood kids over. Eddie the 21 Vacant looked so bad even the Kletzes didn't joke about how bad he looked. His nose was off center and a scald mark ran from ear to chin. When you got too close, his hands shot up. When the cake was served, he dropped his plate, shouting, "Leave a guy alone!"

Our natural meanness now found a purpose. Led by the Kletzes, we cut through 22 Poltoi's hose, bashed out her basement windows with ball-peens, pushed her little shopping cart over the edge of the quarry and watched it end-over-end into the former Slag Ravine.

Then it was spring and the quarry got busy. When the noon blast went off, our 23 windows rattled. The three-o'clock blast was even bigger. Raccoon and Art and I made a fort from the cardboard shipping containers the Cline frames came in. One day, while pretending the three-o'clock blast was atomic, we saw Eddie the Vacant bounding toward our fort through the weeds, like some lover in a commercial, only fatter and falling occasionally.

His trauma had made us kinder toward him. 24

"Eddie," Art said. "You tell your dad where you're at?"

"It no big problem," Eddie said. "I was gone leave my dad a note."

"But did you?" said Art.

"I'll leave him a note when I get back," said Eddie. "I gone come in with you now."

"No room," said Raccoon. "You're too huge."

"That a good one!" said Eddie, crowding in.

Down in the quarry were the sad Cats, the slumping watchman's shack, the piles 25 of reddish discarded dynamite wrappings that occasionally rose erratically up the hillside like startled birds.

Along the quarryside trail came Mrs. Poltoi, dragging a new shopping cart.

"Look at that pig," said Raccoon. "Eddie, that's the pig that put you away."

"What did they do to you in there, Ed?" said Art. "Did they mess with you?"

"No, they didn't," said Eddie. "I just a say to them, 'Leave a guy alone!' I mean, sometime they did, okay? Sometime that one guy say, 'Hey Eddie, pull your thing! We gone watch you.' "

"Okay, okay," said Art.

At dusk, the three of us would go to Mrs. H.'s porch. She'd bring out cookies and 26 urge forgiveness. It wasn't Poltoi's fault her heart was small, she told us. She, Mrs. H., had seen a great number of things, and seeing so many things had enlarged her heart. Once, she had seen Göring. Once, she had seen Einstein. Once, during the war, she had seen a whole city block, formerly thick with furriers, bombed black overnight. In the morning, charred bodies had crawled along the street, begging for mercy. One such body had grabbed her by the ankle, and she recognized it as Bergen, a friend of her father's.

"What did you do?" said Raccoon. 27

"Not important now," said Mrs. H., gulping back tears, looking off into the quarry.

Then disaster. Dad got a check for shoulder pads for all six district football teams 28 and, trying to work things out with Mom, decided to take her on a cruise to Jamaica. Nobody in our neighborhood had ever been on a cruise. Nobody had even been to Wisconsin. The disaster was, I was staying with Poltoi. Ours was a liquor household, where you could ask a question over and over in utter sincerity and never get a straight answer. I asked and asked, "Why her?" And was told and told, "It will be a adventure."

I asked, "Why not Grammy?" 29

I was told, "Grammy don't feel well."

I asked, "Why not Hopanlitski?"

Dad did this like snort.

"Like that's gonna happen," said Mom.

"Why not, why not?" I kept asking.

"Because shut up," they kept answering.

Just after Easter, over I went, with my little green suitcase.

I was a night panicker and occasional bed-wetter. I'd wake drenched and panting. 30 Had they told her? I doubted it. Then I knew they hadn't, from the look on her face the first night, when I peed myself and woke up screaming.

"What's this?" she said.

"Pee," I said, humiliated beyond any ability to lie.

"Ach, well," she said. "Who don't? This also used to be me. Pee pee pee. I used to dream of a fish who cursed me."

She changed the sheets gently, with no petulance—a new one on me. Often Ma, 31 still half asleep, popped me with the wet sheet, saying when at last I had a wife, she herself could finally get some freaking sleep.

Then the bed was ready, and Poltoi made a sweeping gesture, like, Please.

I got in.

She stayed standing there.

"You know," she said, "I know they say things. About me, what I done to that boy. But I had a bad time in the past with a big stupid boy. You don't gotta know. But I did like I did that day for good reason. I was scared at him, due to something what happened for real to me."

She stood in the half-light, looking down at her feet.

"Do you get?" she said. "Do you? Can you get it, what I am saying?"

"I think so," I said.

"Tell to him," she said. "Tell to him sorry, explain about it, tell your friends also. If you please. You have a good brain. That is why I am saying to you."

Something in me rose to this. I'd never heard it before but I believed it: I had a good brain. I could be trusted to effect a change.

Next day was Saturday. She made soup. We played a game using three slivers of 32 soap. We made placemats out of colored strips of paper, and she let me teach her my spelling words.

Around noon the doorbell rang. At the door stood Mrs. H.  33

"Everything okay?" she said, poking her head in.

"Yes, fine," said Poltoi. "I did not eat him yet."

"Is everything really fine?" Mrs. H. said to me. "You can say."

"It's fine," I said.

"You can say," she said fiercely.

Then she gave Poltoi a look that seemed to say, Hurt him and you will deal with me.

"You silly woman," said Poltoi. "You are going now."

Mrs. H. went.

We resumed our spelling. It was tense in a quiet-house way. Things ticked. When 34 Poltoi missed a word, she pinched her own hand, but not hard. It was like symbolic pinching. Once when she pinched, she looked at me looking at her, and we laughed.

Then we were quiet again.

"That lady?" she finally said. "She like to lie. Maybe you don't know. She say she 35 is come from where I come from?"

"Yes," I said.

"She is lie," she said. "She act so sweet and everything but she lie. She been born in Skokie. Live here all her life, in America. Why you think she talk so good?"

All week Poltoi made sausage, noodles, potato pancakes; we ate like pigs. She had 36 tea and cakes ready when I came home from school. At night, if necessary, she dried me off, moved me to her bed, changed the sheets, put me back, with never an unkind word.

"Will pass, will pass," she'd hum.

Mom and Dad came home tanned, with a sailor cap for me, and in a burst of 37 post-vacation honesty, confirmed it: Mrs. H. was a liar. A liar and a kook. Nothing she said was true. She'd been a cashier at Goldblatt's but had been caught stealing. When caught stealing, she'd claimed to be with the Main Office. When a guy from the Main Office came down, she claimed to be with the FBI. Then she'd produced a letter from Lady Bird Johnson, but in her own handwriting, with "Johnson" spelled "Jonsen."

I told the other kids what I knew, and in time they came to believe it, even the 38 Kletzes.

And, once we believed it, we couldn't imagine we hadn't seen it all along.          39

Another spring came, once again birds nested in bushes on the sides of the 40 quarry. A thrown rock excited a thrilling upwards explosion. Thin rivers originated in our swampy backyards, and we sailed boats made of flattened shoeboxes, Twinkie wrappers, crimped tinfoil. Raccoon glued together three balsawood planes and placed on this boat a turd from her dog Svengooli, and, as Svengooli's turd went over a little waterfall and disappeared into the quarry, we cheered.

## READING FOR CONTENT

1. In paragraphs 4, 7, and 9, how does the narrator introduce his friends Racoon, Art, and Eddie as characters in many ways similar to him, yet also different from him?
2. In paragraphs 13 and 26, how does the narrator depict Mrs. Poltoi and Mrs. Hopanlitski as characters so different from each other, yet also similar in some ways?
3. How do paragraphs 30 and 31 prepare for the story's reversal?

## READING FOR GENRE, ORGANIZATION, AND STYLISTIC FEATURES

1. How does the phrase "Then disaster" in paragraph 28 divide the story into two distinct parts? What occupies the focus of the first part? What occupies the focus of the second part? How do these parts contrast with and yet relate to each other?
2. How does the dialogue indicate contrasts between and among characters in paragraphs 10, 14, 15, 24, 25, 27, 29, 31, 33, and 35?
3. As we have seen with Gish Jen's "Birthmates," the genre of the short story frequently draws great power from a sudden ironic reversal. In "Bohemians," how does paragraph 37 amount to such a reversal? Is it funny, sad, surprising, bizarre, or some combination of each?

## READING FOR RHETORICAL CONTEXT

1. What social commentary does the story imply about a mixed ethnic neighborhood such as the one it depicts? Do its inhabitants cohere? fall apart? harbor impenetrable secrets? perform acts of redeeming grace?
2. What does the narrator mean by "our natural meanness" in paragraph 22? How does the story prove or disprove the implications of this phrase?

## WRITING ASSIGNMENTS

1. Write a literary analysis of 1,000 words on the predicament of the narrator. In his relationships with his neighborhood peers, is he a typical young person or is he a misfit? Does his relationship with his Mom and Dad suggest that theirs is a functional family? a dysfunctional one? Does he fully comprehend the behavior of the adults in the story?

2. Write a literary analysis of 1,000 words on the relationship between the narrator and his social context. What may be his implied ethnic background? How funny, sad, uplifting, or puzzling are the overlapping features of his contact with people of the same age? of an older generation? of other ethnic backgrounds?

## SYNTHESIS WRITING ASSIGNMENTS

1. Drawing on selections by Takaki, Mukherjee, and Viramontes, write a five-page essay in which you synthesize their representations of the immigrant experience in America. Address your essay to an audience of classmates from high school with whom you have not been in contact since starting college.

2. Drawing on selections by Takaki and Danticat, write a five-page essay in which you compare and contrast the experiences of different ethnic groups as conditions in their countries of origin give them cause to contemplate emigration to a less stressful environment. Comment on the blurred lines between fictional and nonfictional situations that these authors sustain. Address your essay to students who have already read these texts.

3. Drawing on the stories of Mukherjee and Saunders, write a five-page essay in which you respond to their characters' various efforts, both successful and unsuccessful, to preserve their ethnic identities. Address your essay to members of the academic community at large as a critical review in your college newspaper.

4. Drawing on the stories of Viramontes and Jen, write a five-page essay in which you evaluate their narrative representations of outsiders' efforts to succeed as insiders in multicultural societies. Address your essay to members of the academic community at large as a critical review in your college newspaper.

5. Drawing on the stories of Jen and Saunders, write a five-page essay in which you evaluate the authors' use of humor and irony to record the complexities of interacting with people of different ethnic origins in multicultural neighborhoods and workplaces. Address your essay to classmates with whom you have discussed the texts.

*Seventeen*

# Three Visual Portfolios

In this chapter we present three portfolios of photographs on topics related to other chapters in our anthology. The first consists of seven photographs depicting various images of family life in modern America, some of them alluding to issues discussed in the essays of Chapter 13 on the Changing American Family. The second consists of seven photographs depicting various images of wealth, poverty, and the social markers that distinguish between them, some of them alluding to issues discussed in the essays of Chapter 14 on Social Class and Inequality. The third consists of seven photographs depicting various images of immigrant experience in the United States, some of them alluding to issues represented in the selections of Chapter 16 on Stories of Ethnic Difference.

These portfolios combine studio-posed pictures with newsworthy action shots, pictures taken by amateurs and by professionals, photos capturing the pulse of the present and prints capturing scenes from the past. The first portfolio, Images of Families, opens with two idealized portraits, the first of a three-generational family, the second of young parents with identical twins. Juxtaposed against them is the enigmatic "Vengeful Sister, Chicago," taken in 1956 by the prominent social landscape photographer David Heath (1931–), and a newspaper photo from 2004 showing a lesbian couple and their adopted children being heckled by antigay demonstrators. The ideal and the real confront each other in these two pairs of images, as the composure of the initial pair gives way to the turmoil of its successor.

Two classic images follow. Beneath the surface tranquility of their compositions lies an unspoken agitation. The first of them, taken in 1912 by Lewis Wickes Hine (1874–1940), depicts a mother and her adolescent children sitting at a dining room table. On closer inspection, it appears that the family is working at menial tasks for inevitably small wages. This picture belongs to the photographer's collection, "Let Children Be Children: Lewis Wickes Hine's Crusade Against Child Labor." The second was taken in 1941 by Arthur Fellig (1899–1968), a newspaper photographer whose pseudonym "Weegee" evokes the Ouija Board because of his uncanny ability to arrive instantaneously at the scene of a photo-worthy event. His "Heat Spell, May 23, 1941" bears the subtitle "Tenement Penthouse," referring to the inauspicious location of five family members on a cramped fire-escape as they seek respite during a sweltering night.

The first portfolio concludes with "Portrait of a Boy Overlooking Ocean" by the Cuban-American photographer Antonio Fernandez (1941–). Taken in Miami in 1968, it is part of a series entitled "Vision and Expression" that captures ordinary events from startling perspectives, investing them with a sense of mystery that defies the apparent subject matter. The minimal amount of visual information seems to cut the boy off from his family and erase any links he might have to a broader social environment.

The second portfolio presents Images of Inequality, and it too juxtaposes two pairs of contrasting images against a trio of related photographs. It opens with the portrait of an elegant table set for a choice meal at one of New York City's most fashionable and expensive restaurants, and it then shifts to the picture of a volunteer server at a soup kitchen for the homeless near the site of the Republican Presidential Convention at New York in 2004. Next, it offers the image of a homeless man pushing a cart with his belongings against a backdrop of Denver's downtown skyscrapers, visual emblems of the city's prosperity. The disparity in this image leads to the following one in which a homeless person amid a sea of other homeless people views a television monitor of George W. Bush during a presidential debate in 2000. This image of a picture-within-a-picture conveys a striking difference between political rhetoric and social reality.

Images of Inequality concludes with a trio of photographs that weigh contemporary representations of civil rights action against their counterparts more than four decades ago. First, a life-like modern sculpture of Rosa Parks sits in the replica of a Montgomery, Alabama, city bus where Ms. Parks defied segregation policies in the 1950s. Located at the National Civil Rights Museum in Memphis, the sculpture attracts the attention of four schoolchildren who are visiting the museum upon its opening in 1998. Next, a famous photograph of Martin Luther King Jr. at his "I Have a Dream" speech captures the galvanizing energy of the historic March on Washington, DC, in 1963. Finally, a newspaper photograph of a riot at a rally to reverse a 2001 ban on affirmative action pits students supporting affirmative action against those who oppose it. People who lived through the earlier period would find it hard to believe that the gains of their political conscience could come under such attack in recent times.

The third portfolio serves up Images of Ethnic Difference with an accent on conflicting experiences of immigrant groups arriving in the United States over the past century. The initial image is another classic photograph by Lewis Wickes Hine, and it is drawn from his famous "Ellis Island" series. Taken in 1906 and titled "Climbing into America," it affirms the aspirations and the promise that coincided with an immigrant's arrival in America at the time. Balancing it is a fairly cynical snapshot of a recent sign warning motorists of illegal border crossings in the Southwest. Aspirations and promise are radically dashed in the next two photos, which depict the potentially tragic consequences of illegal immigration. The first shows a U.S. Border Patrol Officer searching illegal aliens on the Texas border, and the second illustrates a newspaper account of the deaths and injuries to several Chinese illegal aliens who attempted to reach shore from a grounded vessel off New York harbor in 1993.

The final three photographs represent diverse aspects of coping with life in America after immigration. In one, a recent immigrant mother from Haiti confers with a teacher or librarian over a book that interests her. Whether she is a student or an information-seeker, she seems keen on bettering her chances for a successful adaptation to her new society.

In another, three Arab-Americans assemble at their office for an antidiscrimination group that they have just formed. In the wake of the September 11 terrorist attacks, many Americans of Muslim descent have experienced prejudice, discrimination, and curtailment of their civil liberties, a condition that this picture directly addresses. In the third, demonstrators march in a rally against draconian immigration reforms slated for legislation in Spring, 2006. Proclaiming their valuable contributions to America, hundreds of thousands of illegal aliens and their supporters took to the streets to petition for citizenship for immigrants and to protest measures against citizenship proposed by a Republican Congress.

The images in these portfolios fold into one another even as they refer back to earlier chapters in this anthology. The struggle for immigrants' rights in the last three pictures of Portfolio 3, for example, joins the conversation about civil rights in the last three pictures of Portfolio 2, and both sets of pictures echo the conversations about Social Class and Inequality and the Stories of Ethnic Difference conducted in Chapters 14 and 16 above. The pictures that depict various families in Portfolio 1 display markers of social class and inequality as well as of ethnic difference, and they sustain as many possible links to the previously mentioned anthology chapters as they do to Chapter 3 on the Mommy Wars and Chapter 13 on the Changing American Family. Pictures may constitute an international language, and they serve an important purpose as they stimulate each of us to formulate our own arguments about the topics they represent, to articulate them in the language of written discourse, and to enter the conversation about issues of our time as it is conducted in academic disciplines across the college curriculum.

## PREVIEWING

Survey the pictures offered in each of the three following portfolios. Jot down relationships that might link them to one another, both within a single portfolio and across different portfolios. Do you think that these pictures offer plausible representations of the world as you know it? Or do they instead project biased, limited, or idealized representations? Freewrite your response to this question. Do you know or can you imagine other photos that would better represent these topics? Search an online photographic archive such as corbis.com, accuweather.ap.org, or photosearch.com for different possibilities and download your most important findings for future reference and comparison.

# PORTFOLIO 1

## IMAGES OF FAMILIES

**Photo 17–1    Aging, generation gap, summer.** Courtesy of
FOTOSEARCH.com.

**Photo 17–2    Parents sitting on a sofa with twin babies.** Courtesy of FOTOSEARCH.com.

**Photo 17–3    David Heath, "Vengeful Sister, Chicago" (1956).** Courtesy of the George Eastman House, Rochester, N.Y.

**Photo 17–4    Stacey and Jessie Harris, of New Jersey, walk with their children, Zion, 4, and Torin, 15 months, through Rawson Square in downtown Nassau past a demonstration held to oppose the gay cruise on which the Harris family traveled Friday, July 16, 2004, to the Bahamas.** Photo by Tim Aylen, courtesy of Associated Press/World Wide Photos.

**Photo 17–5    Lewis Wickes Hine, "Child Labor," from "Let Children Be Children: Lewis Wickes Hine's Crusade Against Child Labor" (1912).** Courtesy of the George Eastman House, Rochester, N.Y.

**Photo 17–6    Weegee (Arthur Fellig), "Heat Spell, May 23, 1941: Tenement Penthouse."** Courtesy of the George Eastman House, Rochester, N.Y.

**Photo 17–7    Antonio Fernandez, "Portrait of a Boy Overlooking Ocean" (1968).**
Courtesy of the George Eastman House, Rochester, N.Y.

# PORTFOLIO 2

## IMAGES OF INEQUALITY

**Photo 17–8    A dessert plate of Grilled Fruit en Papillote is shown on an elegantly set dining table at the exclusive Le Bernadin Restaurant, New York City.** Photo by Bebeto Matthews, courtesy of Associated Press/World Wide Photos.

**Photo 17–9** **A volunteer passes out meals to the homeless at the Holy Apostle Church soup kitchen Friday, July 30, 2004, in New York City, near Madison Square Garden where the Republican National Convention is meeting to nominate George W. Bush for president.** Photo by Chad Rachman, courtesy of Associated Press/World Wide Photos.

**Photo 17–10** **A homeless man pushes a shopping cart with his possessions across a downtown Denver street Monday, May 8, 2006. More than 9,000 people were homeless in the metro Denver area in January of 2006.** Photo by Ed Andrieski, courtesy of Associated Press/World Wide Photos.

**Photo 17–11** **A homeless registered voter joins a former homeless person and an estimated 200 other homeless persons to watch George W. Bush on one of the television monitors set up for the second presidential debate in New York's Union Square Park, Wednesday, October 11, 2004.** Photo by Tina Fineberg, courtesy of Associated Press/World Wide Photos.

**Photo 17–12   Visitors at the National Civil Rights Museum in Memphis listen as a recording of the bus driver "threatens" the figure of Rosa Parks seated in the front of the bus. The bus, a real Montgomery, Alabama, city bus of the 1950s is one of the displays at the museum.** Photo by John LeFlocht, courtesy of Associated Press/World Wide Photos.

**Photo 17–13   The Rev. Martin Luther King Jr. acknowledges the crowd at the Lincoln Memorial for his "I Have a Dream" speech during the March on Washington, DC, on August 28, 1963.**
Photo courtesy of Associated Press/World Wide Photos.

**Photo 17–14    Students against affirmative action, right, are confronted by another group for affirmative action during the Day of Action to Reverse the Ban on Affirmative Action rally held on the University of California-Berkeley campus Thursday, March 8, 2001.** Photo by Jakub Mosur, courtesy of Associated Press/World Wide Photos.

# PORTFOLIO 3

## IMAGES OF ETHNIC DIFFERENCE

**Photo 17–15    Lewis Wickes Hine, "Ellis Island: Climbing into America" (1906).** Courtesy of the George Eastman House, Rochester, N.Y.

**Photo 17–16 Sign Warning Drivers of Illegal Border Crossings.** Courtesy of FOTOSEARCH.com.

**Photo 17–17 A United States Border Patrol Officer Searching Illegal Aliens in Del Rio, Texas.** Courtesy of FOTOSEARCH.com.

**Photo 17–18 A rescuer holds a Chinese illegal immigrant by the pants as he tries to transfer to a small boat from the grounded freighter Golden Vent off New York City, June 6, 1993. The vessel was carrying at least 200 Chinese illegals trying to enter the United States. Six were reported dead and at least sixteen were injured while trying to reach the shore.** Photo by Michael Alexander, courtesy of Associated Press/World Wide Photos.

**Photo 17–19    Immigrant Mother from Haiti with daughter.** Courtesy of FOTOSEARCH.com.

**Photo 17–20    Three members of the American-Arab Anti-Discrimination Committee pose at their new office in Clifton, N.J., Sunday, January 8, 2006. With bias incidents against Arab-Americans and Muslims running high in New Jersey, this antidiscrimination group is strengthening its presence here, hoping to become a larger part of the fight to defend civil rights and project a positive image of the state's Muslim community.** Photo by Mike Derer, courtesy of Associated Press/World Wide Photos.

**Photo 17–21   Immigrants and other supporters march down Broadway to call attention to the valuable position of immigrants in American society, Monday, April 10, 2006, in New York City. Hundreds of thousands of people demanding U.S. citizenship for illegal immigrants took to the streets in dozens of cities across the nation in peaceful protests against impending Republican legislation to limit immigrants' rights.** Photo by Louis Lanzano, courtesy of Associated Press/World Wide Photos.

## VIEWING FOR CONTENT

1. What stories or dramas do individual pictures represent? What preceded the action in each picture? What will follow it? How probable is the scenario we might imagine?

2. What stories or drama do groups of pictures represent? What "conversations" do these pictures conduct among themselves?

3. Who or what are the participants in each picture, and how do they relate to one another? Which ones are visible in the picture? Which ones are omitted?

4. Why does some of the action seem familiar and understandable? Why does some of it seem strange or unusual? What elements are mirrored or repeated within the frame?

5. When and where does the action occur? Is the setting likely or unlikely? Is it near or far? Is it contemporary or remote in time?

## VIEWING FOR GENRE, ORGANIZATION, AND STYLISTIC FEATURES

1. What kinds of content dominate the picture? What purposes does the picture serve: to document what happened? to teach a lesson? to aid in instruction or installation? to inform, advise, or warn? to advertise? to entertain? to preserve personal or group memories?

2. Which sorts of image dominate the picture? Which details are emphasized? Which ones are intensified? Which ones are exaggerated?

3. Which cultural values heighten the composition? Which historical values determine it? Which positive and negative emotions emanate from the picture?

4. What evidence of manipulation through selection, arrangement, cropping, and editing does the picture display?

5. Which images appear in focus? Which ones appear out of focus?

6. Which images dominate the background? Which ones dominate the foreground? Which appear on top? Which on bottom?

7. Which parallelisms, duplications, or analogues appear in the picture? Which contrasts, oppositions, or inversions appear in it? What hierarchical relationships do they suggest?

8. Is the picture posed or spontaneous?

9. What is the distance of the camera from the object photographed? Is it placed above or below the object? Is it natural or is it instead achieved by using a special lens?

10. What is the source of the lighting? Is it natural or artificial? Is it placed in front, in back, or to the side? How do shadows heighten or diminish the shape of the object?

11. Are the stylistic effects planned before the picture is taken, or do they result from studio manipulation afterward?

12. What emotional effects do such stylistic features summon?

## VIEWING FOR RHETORICAL CONTEXT

1. Who photographed, sponsored, or otherwise produced the image? Who are the intended viewers? Does the picture seek to gratify them? to challenge their assumptions? to motivate them to some specific action? What might be controversial about its content?

2. What normalizing effects does the picture project? Do its images invite acceptance and imitation? Do they invite repulsion or attack?

3. What alienating effects does the picture project? Do its images invite consideration and appraisal? Do they invite resistance and criticism?

4. What advertising or promotional effects does the picture evoke? Do its images move us to buy a product or buy into a movement represented in them? Do they convey options or alternatives to the outcomes suggested by them?

## WRITING ASSIGNMENTS

1. In an essay of 1,000 words, analyze the form and content of photographs in one of the preceding visual portfolios. Discuss the relationships to one another of the persons or objects pictured and offer a plausible argument about the rhetorical context of the picture or pictures you've selected.

2. In an essay of 1,000 words, analyze the form and content of photographs that link up with one another across two or more of the preceding visual portfolios. Discuss the relationships and present a plausible argument about their rhetorical contexts.

3. Search an online photographic archive for images that complement or supplement those in one of the preceding portfolios. Download them into your own portfolio

and write an essay of 1,000 words explaining how they relate to the selection offered in this anthology.

4. Search an online photographic archive such as corbis.com, accuweather.ap.org, or photosearch.com for images that update, revise, or contrast with those in one of the preceding portfolios. Download them into your own portfolio and write an essay of 1,000 words explaining how they represent the theme or topic better than the selection offered in this anthology.

5. Search an online photographic archive for images on any topic of your choice, such as sports events, historical events, cultural fashions, human-interest stories, and the like. Download them into you own portfolio and write an essay of 1,000 words explaining the significance of what they represent and principles by which they cohere and relate to one another.

# Appendix: Documenting Sources

## ◼◼ MLA DOCUMENTATION STYLE

With the exception of the sample research paper in Chapter 9, all the sample student essays in this book are written according to the MLA (Modern Language Association) rules for page format (margins, page numbering, titles, and so forth) and source documentation. In addition to providing many sample pages that illustrate MLA style, we describe how to type papers in MLA format (pp. 178–81); follow MLA guidelines for using parenthetical documentation to cite sources that you summarize (p. 53), paraphrase (p. 49), or quote (pp. 60–67); and construct a works-cited list (p. 163).

The first section of the appendix is an MLA "quick guide" that includes examples of how to document the types of sources that students use most often in academic papers. The next section explains the principles and rules for MLA documentation. The third section is a list of MLA documentation examples that covers a wider range of situations than does the quick guide. For an exhaustive discussion of MLA documentation style, see the *MLA Handbook for Writers of Research Papers*, 6th edition.

## ◼◼ MLA QUICK GUIDE

The following examples illustrate how to document in MLA style. We begin with the most commonly cited source types. If the Quick Guide does not provide a model that works for the source you are citing, look through the more extensive list of examples on pages 666–77.

### *Magazine or journal article obtained through a library-based online subscription service*

Simpson, Michael D. "Supreme Court to Hear Student Drug Testing." <u>NEA Today</u> Mar. 2002: 20. <u>Expanded Academic ASAP</u>. Ithaca College Library, Ithaca, NY. 2 July 2002 <http://infotrac.galegroup.com>.

### *Article, essay, poem, or short story that is reprinted in a textbook anthology*

Vogel, Steven. "Grades and Money." <u>Dissent</u> Fall 1997: 102–4. Rpt. in <u>Reading and Writing in the Academic Community</u>. 2nd ed. Eds. Mary Lynch Kennedy and Hadley M. Smith. Upper Saddle River, NJ: Prentice Hall, 2001. 337–40.

### Document on a World Wide Web site

American Civil Liberties Union Freedom Network. "Security and Freedom." 19 Feb. 2002. American Civil Liberties Union. 26 Aug. 2002 <http://aclu.org/students/>.

### Article, essay, poem, or short story in a magazine

Dickinson, Amy. "Video Playgrounds: New Studies Link Violent Video Games to Violent Behavior. So Check Out These Cool Alternatives." Time 8 May 2000: 100.

### Article in a newspaper

Becker, Elizabeth. "A New Villain in Free Trade: The Farmer on the Dole." New York Times 25 Aug. 2002, sec. 4: 10.

### Article, essay, poem, or short story in an academic or professional journal

Mirskin, Jerald. "Writing as a Process of Valuing." College Composition and Communication 46 (1995): 387–410.

### Book

Hower, Edward. Shadows and Elephants. Wellfleet, MA: Leapfrog, 2002.

### Article, essay, poem, or short story that appears in print for the first time in an anthology

McPherson, Diane. "Adrienne Rich." Contemporary Lesbian Writers of the United States: A Bio-Bibliographical Critical Sourcebook. Eds. Sandra Pollack and Denise D. Knight. Westport, CT: Greenwood, 1993. 433–45.

### Section, chapter, article, essay, poem, short story, or play in a book with one author

Brown, Cory. "Drought." A Warm Trend. Wesley Chapel, FL: Swallow's Tale Press, 1989. 29.

## ◼ PRINCIPLES AND RULES FOR MLA DOCUMENTATION

### ◼ Books

When documenting books, arrange the documentary information in the following order, including as many items as are available:

1. Author's name
2. Title of the part of the book (if you are referring to a section or chapter)
3. Title of the book
4. Name of the editor or translator
5. Edition
6. Number of volumes
7. Name of the series if the book is part of a series

8. City of publication
9. Abbreviated name of the publisher
10. Date of publication
11. Page numbers (if you are referring to a section or chapter)

## ■ Books Without Complete Publication Information or Pagination

Supply as much of the missing information as you can, enclosing the information you supply in square brackets to show your reader that the source did not contain this information—for example, Metropolis: U of Bigcity P, [1971]. Enclosing the date in brackets shows your reader that you found the date elsewhere: another source that quotes your source, the card catalog, your professor's lecture, and so on. If you are not certain of the date, add a question mark—for example, [1971?]. If you only know an approximate date, put the date after a "c." (for *circa*, meaning "around"). However, when you cannot find the necessary information, use one of the following abbreviation models to show this to your reader: n.d. (no date); N. pag. (no pagination); N.p. (no place of publication); n.p. (no publisher). For example, the following works cited entry would be used if you knew only the title of the book that served as your source:

Photographic View Album of Cambridge. [England]: N.p., n.d. N. pag.

## ■ Book Cross-References

If you cite two or more articles from the same anthology, list the anthology itself with complete publication information, then cross-reference the individual articles. In the cross-reference, the anthology editor's last name and the page numbers follow the article author's name and the title of the article. In the example below, the first and third entries are for articles reprinted in the second entry, the anthology edited by Kennedy, Kennedy, and Smith.

Frude, Neil. "The Intimate Machine." Kennedy, Kennedy, and Smith 268–73.

Kennedy, Mary Lynch, William J. Kennedy, and Hadley M. Smith, eds. Writing in the Disciplines. 4th ed. Upper Saddle River, NJ: Prentice Hall, 2000.

Rifkin, Jeremy. "The Age of Simulation." Kennedy, Kennedy, and Smith 284–93.

## ■ Periodicals

When documenting articles in a periodical, arrange the documentary information in the following order:

1. Author's name
2. Title of the article
3. Name of the periodical
4. Series number or name
5. Volume number (followed by a period and the issue number, if needed)
6. Date of publication
7. Page numbers

## ■ Online Sources That Are Also Available in Print

The World Wide Web offers electronic versions of many publications that are available in print, ranging from newspaper articles to full-length books. Entries for sources that have electronic addresses (URLs) should include as many of the following items as are available:

1. Author
2. Title of the source (book, article, poem, or other source type)
3. Editor, compiler, or translator (if relevant)
4. Complete publication information for the print version
5. Title of the Web site (if no title is given, provide a label such as "Home page") or name of the database
6. Name of the Web site editor or compiler (if available)
7. Version, volume, or issue number of the source (if relevant)
8. Date of electronic publication (latest update)
9. For articles accessed through a subscription service (InfoTrac, ProQuest, and so forth), the name of the service and, if a library is the subscriber, the name of the library and the city (state, if necessary) in which it is located
10. Number of total pages, paragraphs, or sections (if available)
11. Organization or institution associated with the Web site
12. Date when the researcher collected the information from the Web site
13. Electronic address, or URL, of the source (enclosed in angle brackets)

Each element listed above should follow the format specifications on page 670. For example, article titles should be placed in quotation marks, while book titles should be underlined.

## ■ Sources That Are Available Only Online

Certain electronic sources are available only online. A myriad of organizations and individuals maintain Web sites that provide information that is not published in print form. For sources that do not appear in print, MLA works-cited entries should include as many of the following items as possible:

1. Author
2. Title of the source (essay, article, poem, short story, or other source type); or title of a posting to an online discussion, followed by the label "Online posting"
3. Editor, compiler, or translator (if relevant)
4. Title of the Web site (if no title is given, provide a label such as "Home page")
5. Name of the Web site editor or compiler (if available)
6. Version, volume, or issue number of the source (if relevant)
7. Date of electronic publication (latest update) or of posting
8. Name of discussion list or forum (for a posting only)
9. Number of total pages, paragraphs, or sections (if available)
10. Organization or institution associated with the Web site

11. Date when the researcher collected the information from the Web site
12. Electronic address, or URL, of the source (enclosed in angle brackets)

All elements within entries should follow the format guidelines presented on pages 670–71. For example, article titles should be placed in quotation marks, while book titles should be underlined.

Some electronic sources are "portable," as is a CD-ROM, for example, and may or may not have print versions. Other electronic sources do not have URLs. In each case, use the style that applies, listing the publication medium (CD-ROM, for example), publisher, and the computer network or service for an online source (for example, a computer database such as PsychINFO reached through CompuServe). Give the electronic publication information after the author, title, editor or compiler, and print publication information.

## ■ Content Endnotes

In addition to a works-cited list, MLA style provides for a list of comments, explanations, or facts that relate to the ideas discussed in the essay but do not fit into the actual text. You may occasionally need these content endnotes to provide information that is useful but must, for some reason, be separated from the rest of the essay. The most common uses of endnotes are listed below.

1. Providing additional references that go beyond the scope of the essay but could help the reader understand issues in more depth
2. Discussing a source of information in more detail than is possible in a works-cited list
3. Acknowledging help in preparing an essay
4. Giving an opinion that does not fit into the text smoothly
5. Explaining ideas more fully than is possible in the text
6. Mentioning concerns not directly related to the content of the essay
7. Providing additional necessary details that would clutter the text
8. Mentioning contradictory information that goes against the general point of view presented in the essay
9. Evaluating ideas explained in the essay

In MLA style, endnotes are listed on separate pages just before the works-cited list. The first page of the endnote list is titled _Notes_. Notes are numbered sequentially (1, 2, 3, . . . ), and a corresponding number is included in the text of the essay, typed halfway between the lines (in superscript), to show the material to which the endnote refers. Notice in the example below that the reference numeral (that is, the endnote number) is placed in the text of the essay immediately after the material to which it refers. Usually, the reference numeral will appear at the end of a sentence. No space is left between the reference numeral and the word or punctuation mark that it follows. However, in the notes list, one space is left between the numeral and the first letter of the note. Notes are numbered according to the order in which they occur in the essay.

Any source that you mention in an endnote must be fully documented in the works-cited list. Do not include this complete documentation in the endnote itself. Never use endnotes as a substitute for the works-cited list, and do not overuse endnotes. If possible, include all information in the text of your essay. For most essays you write, no endnotes will be necessary.

The following excerpts from the text of an essay and its list of endnotes illustrate MLA endnote format. For example, in your text you would type

> For hundreds of years, scientists thought that the sun's energy came from the combustion of a solid fuel such as coal.[1] However, work in the early twentieth century convinced researchers that the sun sustains a continuous nuclear fusion reaction.[2] The sun's nuclear furnace maintains a temperature . . .

The notes on the notes page would be formatted with the first line of each note indented five spaces.

> [1] Detailed accounts of pre-twentieth-century views of solar energy can be found in Banks and Rosen (141–55) and Burger (15–21).
>
> [2] In very recent years, some scientists have questioned whether or not the sun sustains a fusion reaction at all times. Experiments described by Salen (68–93) have failed to detect the neutrinos that should be the by-products of the sun's fusion. This raises the possibility that the sun's fusion reaction turns off and on periodically.

## ◼ MLA DOCUMENTATION MODELS

### ◼ Books

#### *Book with one author*

Kennedy, William J. <u>Rhetorical Norms in Renaissance Literature</u>. New Haven: Yale UP, 1978.

#### *Two or more books by the same author (alphabetize by title)*

Kennedy, William J. <u>Jacopo Sannazaro and the Uses of the Pastoral</u>. Hanover, NH: UP of New England, 1983.

——. <u>Rhetorical Norms in Renaissance Literature</u>. New Haven: Yale UP, 1978.

#### *Book with two authors*

Kramnick, Isaac, and R. Laurence Moore. <u>The Godless Constitution: The Case against Religious Correctness</u>. New York: Norton, 1996.

#### *Book with three authors*

Bulkin, Elly, Minnie Bruce Pratt, and Barbara Smith. <u>Yours in Struggle: Three Feminist Perspectives on Anti-Semitism and Racism</u>. Ithaca, NY: Firebrand, 1988.

#### *Book with more than three authors*

Glock, Marvin D., et al. <u>Probe: College Developmental Reading</u>. 2nd ed. Columbus, OH: Merrill, 1980.

#### *Book with a corporate author*

Boston Women's Health Collective Staff. <u>Our Bodies, Ourselves</u>. Magnolia, MA: Peter Smith, 1998.

## Book with an anonymous author

Writers' and Artists' Yearbook, 1980. London: Adam and Charles Black, 1980.

## Book with an editor instead of an author

DiRenzo, Anthony, ed. If I Were Boss: The Early Business Stories of Sinclair Lewis. Carbondale, IL: Southern Illinois UP, 1997.

## Book with two or three editors

Anderson, Charles M., and Marian M. MacCurdy, eds. Writing and Healing: Toward an Informed Practice. Urbana, IL: National Council of Teachers of English, 1999.

## Book with more than three editors

Kermode, Frank, et al., eds. The Oxford Anthology of English Literature. 2 vols. New York: Oxford UP, 1973.

## Book with a translator

Allende, Isabel. The Stories of Eva Luna. Trans. Margaret Sayers Peden. New York: Macmillan, 1991.

## Book with more than one edition

Kennedy, Mary Lynch, William J. Kennedy, and Hadley M. Smith. Writing in the Disciplines. 5th ed. Upper Saddle River, NJ: Prentice Hall, 2004.

## Book that has been republished

Conroy, Frank. Stop-time. 1967. New York: Penguin, 1977.

## ■ Parts of Books

### Section, chapter, article, essay, poem, short story, or play in a book with one author

Chomsky, Noam. "Psychology and Ideology." For Reasons of State. New York: Vintage, 1973. 318–69.

Walker, Alice. "Everyday Use." In Love and Trouble: Stories of Black Women. San Diego: Harcourt, 1973. 47–59.

### Introduction, preface, or foreword written by someone other than the book's author

Piccone, Paul. General Introduction. The Essential Frankfurt Reader. Eds. Andrew Arato and Eike Gebhardt. New York: Urizen, 1978. xi–xxiii.

### Article or essay reprinted in an anthology

Au, Kathryn H. "Literacy for All Students: Ten Steps Toward Making a Difference." The Reading Teacher 51.3 (1997): 186–94. Rpt. in Perspectives: Literacy. Ed. C. Denise Johnson. Madison, WI: Coursewise, 1999. 3–9.

### Article, essay, poem, or short story that appears in print for the first time in an anthology

Horn, Wade F. "Promoting Marriage as a Means for Promoting Fatherhood." <u>Revitalizing the Institution of Marriage for the Twenty-First Century: An Agenda for Strengthening Marriage</u>. Eds. Alan J. Hawkins, Lynn D. Wardle, and David Orgon Coolidge. Westport, CT: Praeger, 2002. 101–109.

### Novel or play in an anthology

Gay, John. <u>The Beggar's Opera. Twelve Famous Plays of the Restoration and Eighteenth Century</u>. Ed. Cecil A. Moore. New York: Random, 1960. 573–650.

### Signed article in a reference work

Tilling, Robert I. "Vocanology." <u>McGraw Hill Encyclopedia of Science and Technology</u>. 8th ed. 1997.

### Unsigned article in a reference work

"Tenancy by the Entirety." <u>West's Encyclopedia of American Law</u>. 1998.

## ▓ Periodicals

### Article in a scholarly/professional journal; each issue numbers its pages separately

McCarty, Roxanne. "Reading Therapy Project." <u>Research and Teaching in Developmental Education</u> 18.2 (2002): 51–56.

### Article in a scholarly/professional journal; the entire volume has continuous page numbering

Trainor, Jennifer Seibel, and Amanda Godley. "After Wyoming: Labor Practices in Two University Writing Programs." <u>College Composition and Communication</u> 50 (1998): 153–81.

### Signed article in a weekly or monthly magazine

Jenkins, Henry. "Cyberspace and Race." <u>Technology Review</u> April 2002: 89.

### Unsigned article in a weekly or monthly magazine

"Dip into the Future, Far as Cyborg Eye Can See: And Wince." <u>The Economist</u> 3 Jan. 1998: 81–83.

### Poem or short story in a magazine

Flanagan, David. "Pilgrimage." <u>Creations Magazine</u> June/July 2001: 8.

### Signed article in a newspaper (in an edition with lettered sections)

Miller, Marjorie. "Britain Urged to Legalize Cloning of Human Tissue." <u>Los Angeles Times</u> 9 Dec. 1998: A1.

## Unsigned article in a newspaper (in a daily without labeled sections)

"Justice Proposes Immigration Laws." <u>Ithaca Journal</u> [Ithaca, NY] 28 Aug. 2002: 2.

## Editorial or special feature (in an identified edition with numbered sections)

"The Limits of Technology." Editorial. <u>New York Times</u> 3 Jan. 1999, early ed., sec. 4: 8.

## Published letter to the editor of a newspaper

Plotnick, Mermine. Letter. <u>New York Times</u> 25 Aug. 2002, sec. 4: 8.

## Review

Hoberman, J. "The Informer: Elia Kazan Spills His Guts." Rev. of <u>Elia Kazan: A Life</u>, by Elia Kazan. <u>Village Voice</u> 17 May 1988: 58–60.

## Article whose title contains a quotation

Nitzsche, Jane Chance. "'As swete as is the roote of lycorys, or any cetewale': Herbal Imagery in Chaucer's Miller's Tale." <u>Chaucerian Newsletter</u> 2.1 (1980): 6–8.

## Article from Dissertation Abstracts International (DAI)

Webb, John Bryan. "Utopian Fantasy and Social Change, 1600–1660." Diss. SUNY Buffalo, 1982. <u>DAI</u> 43 (1982): 8214250A.

## ▄ Other Written Sources

## Government publication

U.S. Dept. of Energy. <u>Winter Survival: A Consumer's Guide to Winter Preparedness</u>. Washington: GPO, 1980.

## Congressional Record

<u>Cong. Rec</u>. 13 Apr. 1967: S505457.

## Pamphlet

<u>Bias-Related Incidents</u>. Ithaca, NY: Ithaca College Bias-Related Incidents Committee, 2001.

## Dissertation

Boredin, Henry Morton. "The Ripple Effect in Classroom Management." Diss. U of Michigan, 1970.

## Personal letter

Siegele, Nancy. Letter to the author. 13 Jan. 2002.

## Public document

U.S. Depart. of Agriculture. "Shipments and Unloads of Certain Fruits and Vegetables. 1918–1923." <u>Statistical Bulletin</u> 7 Apr. 1925: 10–13.

### Information service

Edmonds, Edward L., ed. <u>The Adult Student: University Challenge</u>. Charlottetown: Prince Edward
  Island U, 1980. ERIC ED 190 008.

### CD-ROM

Stucky, Nathan. "Performing Oral History: Storytelling and Pedagogy." <u>Communication Education</u>
  44.1 (1995): 1–14. <u>CommSearch</u> 2nd ed. CD-ROM. Electronic Book Technologies. 1995.

## ■ Online Sources That Are Also Available in Print

### Book originally available in print that was located online

Yeats, W.B. <u>The Celtic Twilight</u>. 1893. <u>Sacred Texts Archive</u>. 26 May 2006 <http://www.sacredtexts.
  com/neu/yeats/twi/twi00/htm>.

### Poem originally available in print that was located online

Carroll, Lewis. "Jabberwocky." 1872. 6 Mar. 1998 <http://www.jabberwocky.com/carroll/jabber/
  jabberwocky.html>.

### Magazine article originally available in print that was located online

Viagas, Robert, and David Lefkowitz. "Capeman Closing Mar. 28." <u>Playbill</u> 5 Mar. 1998. 6 Mar.
  1998 <http:www.playbill.com/cgi-bin/plb/news?cmd=show&code=30763>.

### Journal article originally available in print that was located through a library-based subscription service

Davidson, Margaret. "Do You Know Where Your Children Are?" <u>Reason</u> 31.6 (Nov. 1999): 39.
  <u>Expanded Academic ASAP</u>. Ithaca College Library, Ithaca, NY. 8 Feb. 2000 <http://infotrac.
  galegroup.com>.

### Photo originally available in museum or gallery that was located online

Adams, Ansel. <u>Water and Foam</u>. 1955. Fresno Metropolitan Museum, Fresno, CA. 9 February 2006
  *<http://www.fresnomet.org/collection/the_ansel_adams_photo_collection>.*

## ■ Sources That Are Available Only Online

### Online book

Bazerman, Charles, and David R. Russell, eds. <u>Writing Selves/Writing Societies: Research from
  Activity Perspectives.</u> Fort Collins, Colorado: The WAC Clearinghouse and Mind, Culture,
  and Activity. 1 February 2003. 9 February 2007 *http://wac.colostate.edu/books/selves_societies/.*

### Online article

Purdy, James P. and Joyce R. Walker. "Digital Breadcrumbs: Case Studies of Online Research."
  <u>Kairos</u> 11:2 (2007). 9 February 2007 *http://english.ttu.edu/Kairos/11.2/binder.html?topoi/
  purdy-walker/index.htm.*

### Online photo

lifestyle, generation-gap, family, togetherness, summer, schoolgirl, ageing. 30686abf. Fotosearch. 2 February 2007. 9 February 2007 *http://www.fotosearch.com/SBY159/30686abf/*.

### Posting to an online discussion list

Grumman, Bob. "Shakespeare's Literacy." Online posting. 6 Mar. 1998. Deja News. 13 Aug. 1998 <humanities. lit.author.>.

### Scholarly project available online

Voice of the Shuttle: Web Page for Humanities Research. Ed. Alan Liu. 3 March 1998. U. California, Santa Barbara. 8 Mar. 1998 <http://humanitas.ucsb.edu/>.

### Professional Web site

The Nobel Foundation Official Website. The Nobel Foundation. Dec. 1998. 28 Feb. 1999 <http://www.nobel.se/>.

### Personal Web site

Thiroux, Emily. Home page. 7 Mar. 1998. 12 Jan. 1999 <http://academic.csubak.edu/home/acadpro/ departments/english/engthrx.html>.

### Email

Stone, Stephen. "Re: Research on the Mommy Wars." Email to the author. 9 February 2007.

### Blog

Reid, Alex. "Promise of Podcasting." [Weblog entry.] Digital Digs. 16 January 2007 *http://alexreid. typepad.com/digital_digs/2007/01/promise_of_podc.html* 9 February 2007.

### Synchronous communication (chat, such as MOO, MUD, and IRC)

"Ghostly Presence." Group discussion. Telenet 16 Mar. 1997 <moo.du.org:8000/80anon/anonview/ 14036#focus>.

### Gopher site

Banks, Vickie, and Joe Byers. "EDTECH." 18 Mar. 1997 <gopher://ericyr.syr.edu:70/00/Listervi/ EDTECH/README>.

### FTP (File Transfer Protocol) site

U.S. Supreme Court directory. 6 Mar. 1998 <ftp://<ftp.cwru.edu/U.S.Supreme.Court/>.

## ■ Nonprint Sources

### Film

Rebel without a Cause. Dir. Nicholas Ray. Perf. James Dean, Sal Mineo, and Natalie Wood. Warner Brothers, 1955.

### Television or radio program

Comet Halley. Prod. John L. Wilhelm. PBS. WNET, New York. 26 Nov. 1986.

### Personal (face-to-face) interview

Hall, Donald. Personal interview. 19 Apr. 2001.

### Telephone interview

Grahn, Judy. Telephone interview. 23 Mar. 2000.

### Performance of music, dance, or drama

Corea, Chick, dir. Chick Corea Electrik Band. Cornell U., Ithaca, New York. 15 Oct. 1985.

### Lecture

Gebhard, Ann O. "New Developments in Young Adult Literature." New York State English Council. Buffalo, NY. 15 Nov. 1984.

### Recording: CD

Cohen, Leonard. Ten New Songs. Sony, 2001.

### Recording: Cassette

Tchaikovsky, Piotr Ilich. Violin Concerto in D, op. 35. Itzhak Perlman, violinist. Audiocassette. RCA, 1975.

### Recording: LP

Taylor, James. "You've Got a Friend." Mud Slide Slim and the Blue Horizon. LP. Warner, 1971.

### Videotape

The Nuclear Dilemma. BBC-TV. Videocassette. Time-Life Multimedia, 1974.

### Computer program

Corel WordPerfect 7. Academic Ed. CD-ROM. Ottawa: Corel Corp., 1996.

### Work of art

da Vinci, Leonardo. The Virgin, the Child and Saint Anne. Louvre, Paris.

### Photograph

Ray, Man. Joseph Stella and Marcel Duchamp. 1920. J. Paul Getty Museum. Los Angeles, CA.

### Map or chart

Ireland. Map. Chicago: Rand, 1984.
Adolescents and AIDS. Chart. New York: Earth Science Graphics, 1988.

### Cartoon

Addams, Charles. Cartoon. New Yorker 16 May 1988: 41.

# ■ APA Documentation Style

While MLA documentation style is an important standard in the humanities, APA (American Psychological Association) style is used widely in the social sciences. APA style differs from MLA style in many details, but both share the basic principles of including source names and page numbers (APA also adds the publication date) in parentheses within the text of the paper and of listing complete publication information for each source in an alphabetized list. Below are Quick Guide to APA style and a point-by-point comparison of APA and MLA styles. For a complete explanation of APA style, consult the *Publication Manual of the American Psychological Association*, 5th edition. Pages 176–89 of this book contain a sample student paper written in APA style.

# ■ APA Quick Guide

The following examples illustrate how to document in APA style the types of sources that most often appear in college students' essays. They are arranged beginning with the most commonly cited source types. It may be helpful to contrast them with the MLA quick guide on pages 661–62, since the same examples are used in both quick guides.

## Magazine or journal article obtained through a library-based online subscription service

Guendouzi, J. (2006). "The guilt thing:" Balancing domestic and professional roles. Journal of Marriage and Family, 68 (4), 901–909. Retrieved February 9, 2007, from psycINFO database.

Simpson, M. D. (2002, March). Supreme court to hear student drug testing. NEA Today, 20, 20. Retrieved July 2, 2002 from Expanded Academic ASAP database.

## Article obtained from online journal

Yan, Zheng (2006). What influences children's and adolescents' understanding of the complexity of the Internet? [Electronic version]. Developmental Psychology, 42 (3), 418–428.

## Article, essay, poem, or short story that is reprinted in a textbook anthology

Vogel, S. (2001). Grades and money. In M. L. Kennedy & H. M. Smith (Eds.), Reading and writing in the academic community (pp. 337–340). Upper Saddle River, NJ: Prentice Hall. (Reprinted from [1997, Fall] Dissent, 44.4, 102–104)

## Unsigned document on a World Wide Web site

American Civil Liberties Union. (2002, February 19). Security and freedom. Retrieved August 26, 2002 from American Civil Liberties Union Web site: http://aclu.org/students/

## Article, essay, poem, or short story in a magazine

Dickinson, A. (2000, May 8). Video playgrounds: New studies link violent video games to violent behavior. So check out these cool alternatives. Time, 155, 100.

## Signed article in a newspaper

Becker, E. (2002, August 25). A new villain in free trade: The farmer on the dole. New York Times, p. 4.10.

### *Article, essay, poem, or short story in an academic or professional journal*

Mirskin, J. (1995). Writing as a process of valuing. <u>College Composition and Communication, 46</u>, 387–410.

### *Book*

Hower, E. (2002). <u>Shadows and elephants</u>. Wellfleet, MA: Leapfrog.

### *Article, essay, poem, or short story that appears in print for the first time in an anthology*

McPherson, D. (1993). Adrienne Rich. In S. Pollack & D. D. Knight (Eds.), <u>Contemporary lesbian writers of the United States: A bio-bibliographical critical sourcebook</u> (pp. 433–445). Westport, CT: Greenwood.

### *Section, chapter, article, essay, poem, short story, or play in a book with one author*

Brown, C. (1989). Drought. <u>A warm trend</u>. (p. 39) Wesley Chapel, FL: Swallow's Tale Press.

## ◼️ COMPARISON OF MLA AND APA DOCUMENTATION STYLES

### ◼ Parenthetical Documentation

#### *MLA*

Give the last name of the author and the page number if you are quoting a specific part of the source.

The question has been answered before (O'Connor 140–43).

O'Connor has already answered the question (140–43).

#### *APA*

Give the last name of the author, the publication date, and the page number if you are quoting a specific part of the source.

The question has been answered before (O'Connor, 2002, pp. 140–143).

O'Connor (2002) has already answered the question (pp. 140–143).

#### *MLA*

Omit the abbreviation for page. Drop redundant hundreds digit in final page number.

Walsh discusses this "game theory" (212–47).

#### *APA*

Use the abbreviation "p." for page or "pp." for pages to show page citation. Retain redundant hundreds digit in final page number.

Walsh (1979) discusses this "game theory" (pp. 212–247).

## MLA

Omit commas in parenthetical references.

The question has been answered before (O'Connor 140–43).

## APA

Use commas within parentheses.

The question has been answered before (O'Connor, 2002, pp. 140–143).

## MLA

Use a shortened form of the title to distinguish between different works by the same author.

Jones originally supported the single-factor explanation (<u>Investigations</u>) but later realized that the phenomenon was more complex (<u>Theory</u>).

## APA

Use publication date to distinguish between different works by the same author.

Jones originally supported the single-factor explanation (1996) but later realized that the phenomenon was more complex (2001).

## ■ List of Sources

## MLA

The title of the page listing the sources is Works Cited.

## APA

The title of the page listing the sources is References.

## MLA

Use the author's full name.

O'Connor, Mary Beth.

## APA

Use the author's last name, but only the initials of the author's first and middle names.

O'Connor, M. B.

## MLA

When there are two or more authors, invert the first author's name, insert a comma and the word "and," and give the second author's first name and surname in the common order.

Kennedy, Mary Lynch, and Hadley M. Smith.

## *APA*

When there are two or more authors, invert all the names. After the first author's name, insert a comma and an ampersand (&).

Kennedy, M. L., & Smith, H. M.

## *MLA*

Capitalize major words in the titles of books and periodicals and underline all words in those titles.

Silicon Snake Oil: Second Thoughts about the Information Highway.

Reading Research Quarterly.

## *APA*

Capitalize only the first word and all proper nouns of the titles (and subtitles) of books. Capitalize all major words in the titles of periodicals. Do not underline book and periodical titles but rather use italics.

Silicon snake oil: Second thoughts about the information highway.

Reading Research Quarterly.

## *MLA*

List book data in the following sequence: author, title of book, city of publication, shortened form of the publisher's name, date of publication.

Ozeki, Ruth L. My Year of Meats. New York: Penguin, 1998.

## *APA*

List book data in the following sequence: author, date of publication, title of the book, place of publication, publisher.

Ozeki, R. L. (1998). My year of meats. New York: Penguin.

## *MLA*

List journal article data in the following sequence: author, title of the article, title of the journal, volume number, date of publication, inclusive pages.

Yagelski, Robert P. "The Ambivalence of Reflection." College Composition and Communication 51 (1999): 32–50.

## *APA*

List journal article data in the following sequence: author, date of publication, title of the article, title of the journal, volume number, inclusive pages.

Yagelski, R. P. (1999). The ambivalence of reflection. College Composition and Communication, 51, 32–50.

## MLA

List the data for an article in an edited book in the following sequence: author of the article, title of the article, title of the book, editor of the book, place of publication, publisher, date of publication, inclusive pages.

Donaldson, E. Talbot. "Briseis, Briseida, Criseyde, Cresseid, Cressid: Progress of a Heroine." <u>Chaucerian Problems and Perspectives: Essays Presented to Paul E. Beichner, C.S.C.</u> Eds. Edward Vasta and Zacharias P. Thundy. Notre Dame: Notre Dame UP, 1979. 3–12.

## APA

List the data for an article in an edited book in the following sequence: author of the article, date, title of the article, name of the editor, title of the book, inclusive pages, place of publication, and publisher.

Donaldson, E. T. (1979). Briseis, Briseida, Criseyde, Cresseid, Cressid: Progress of a heroine. In E. Vasta & Z. P. Thundy (Eds.), <u>Chaucerian problems and perspectives: Essays presented to Paul E. Beichner, C.S.C.</u> (pp. 3–12). Notre Dame: Notre Dame University Press.

Note: The proper names in the article title are capitalized, as is the word following the colon.

## ■ Content Endnotes

### MLA

Title the list of endnotes: Notes.

### APA

Title the list of endnotes: Footnotes.

### MLA

Place the endnote list immediately before the works-cited page.

### APA

Place the endnote list immediately after the references page.

### MLA

Skip one space between the reference numeral and the endnote.

[1] For more information, see Jones and Brown.

### APA

Do not skip any space between the reference numeral and the endnote.

[1]For more information, see Jones (1983) and Brown (1981).

# INDEX